The Prophecy on the Mount

International Theological Studies:
Contributions of Baptist Scholars

General Editor

Thorwald Lorenzen

Advisory Editorial Board

Bruce Rumbold
Glenn Hinson
Ray Hobbs
Günter Wagner

Vol. 2

PETER LANG
Bern · Berlin · Frankfurt a.M. · New York · Paris · Wien

Keith D. Dyer

The Prophecy on the Mount

Mark 13
and the Gathering of the New Community

PETER LANG
Bern · Berlin · Frankfurt a.M. · New York · Paris · Wien

Die Deutsche Bibliothek – CIP-Einheitsaufnahme

Dyer, Keith D.:
The prophecy on the mount : Mark 13 and the gathering of the new
community / Keith D. Dyer. – Bern ; Berlin ; Frankfurt a.M. ; New York ;
Paris ; Wien : Lang, 1998
(International theological studies ; Vol. 2)
ISBN 3-906759-71-7

Library of Congress Cataloging-in-Publication Data

Dyer, Keith D., 1951-
The prophecy on the mount : Mark 13 and the gathering of the new
community / Keith D. Dyer.
p. cm. – (International theological studies, ISSN 0946-1507 ;
vol. 2)
Includes bibliographical references and indexes.
ISBN 0-8204-3433-7
1. Bible. N.T. Mark XIII–Criticism, interpretation, etc.
I. Title. II. Series.
BS2585.2.D98 1998
226.3'06–dc21   97-51290

ISSN 0946-1507
ISBN 3-906759-71-7
US-ISBN 0-8204-3433-7

© Peter Lang AG, European Academic Publishers, Berne 1998

CONTENTS

Preface and Acknowledgements   7

Abbreviations   8

Tables and Diagrams   8

Text Sheets   8

Introduction: Through the looking glass—darkly   9

I   A Jewish Apocalypse   27
        [Source and Form Analysis]
        Review: Colani, Bultmann, Kümmel *et al*   27
        Analysis: Constituent forms in Mk 13
                     and their linguistic background   33
        Statement: Linguistic influences in the sayings of Mk 13   63

II   Jesus' Eschatological Discourse   67
        [NT Traditio-Historical Analysis]
        Review: Beasley-Murray, Wenham [Perrin]   67
        Analysis: Unique syntax in Mk 13   81
        Statement: Distinctive traditions in Mk 13   90

III   A Danielic 'Midrash'   93
        [OT Traditio-Historical Analysis]
        Review: Hartman   93
        Analysis: Allusions to the Old Testament in Mk 13   97
        Statement: Intertextual traditions in Mk 13   118

IV   A Markan Anti-Apocalyptic Discourse   123
        [Redaction Analysis (i) (Editorial Analysis)]
        Review: Marxsen, Lambrecht, Pesch (1968)   123
        Analysis: Recurrent vocabulary, phraseology
                     and syntax in Mk 13   131
        Statement: Redaction in Mk 13   150

V   A Christian Prophetic Oracle   153
        [Redaction Analysis (ii) (Composition Analysis)]
        Review: Hahn, Pesch (1977/1980)
                     [Gaston, Boring, Theissen]   153
        Analysis: Markan composition and theology   165
        Statement: The composition of Mk 13   182

VI   **A Markan Apocalypse**   185
        [Religio-Literary Analysis]
        Review: Brandenburger   185
        Analysis: Mk 13 in its religio-literary context   191
        Statement: The structure of Mk 13   198

VII **A Parenesis for the Markan Community**   201
        [Socio-Political Analysis]
        Review: Kee, Kelber, Belo, Myers, Waetjen   201
        Analysis: Mk 13 in its socio-political context   221
        Statement: The *Sitz im Leben* of Mk 13   231

VIII **The Teacher's Farewell Discourse**   233
        [Literary Analysis]
        Review: Petersen, Robbins, Vorster, Mack,
                   Tolbert, Geddert, Fowler   233
        Analysis: Mk 13 in the context of the Gospel of Mark   258
                   Mk 13 in the context of the NT Canon   260
                   Mk 13 in its Greco-Roman literary context   262
        Statement: The literary context of Mk 13   265

IX   **A Markan Discourse on Discipleship and Mission**   267
        [Synthesis]
        Review: The sum of the analyses   267
        Analysis: A reinterpretation of Mk 13   269
        Statement: An interpretive outline of Mk 13   272

Conclusion: **Back to the future—hopefully**   275

Select Bibliography   279

Appendix 1. *Three word syntactical sequences unique in the
        Gospel of Mark*   293

Appendix 2. *Recurrent 6-word syntactical sequences in the
        Gospel of Mark*   300

Appendix 3. *Redaction in Mk 13 according to some major
        commentators*   311

Appendix 4. *Indicators of Redaction in Mk 13*   317

Index of Authors   321

Index of Biblical and Ancient Texts   325

PREFACE AND ACKNOWLEDGEMENTS

It will become obvious from the number of tables, lengthy footnotes, summary statements and appendices that this is a dissertation only thinly disguised as a book. Attempts to make the text more 'reader friendly' were only partially successful, mainly because there were those who felt that the detailed tables of syntactical and linguistic features should remain and be made more widely available as a published resource. And so the text remains largely in its original form, a rather ponderous testimony to the eclectic exegetical methods of the past two decades and the continuing opacity of the Markan eschatological discourse. Its publication can only be justified on the grounds that the *process* of open and honest biblical interpretation is in itself a worthwhile part of the ongoing obligation of the faith community to reflect critically on its origins, its praxis and its hopes.

This project had its roots in experiences of renewal in the Solomon Islands in the seventies, blossomed in the context of more formal theological study at Whitley College, Melbourne, in the eighties, and continued to be pruned and grafted whilst teaching at Rüschlikon, Switzerland, in the nineties. The Markan discipleship motif (ἐν τῇ ὁδῷ = 'on the way') has thus come to mean more than just a literary device. It is appropriate, therefore, to dedicate this book with sincere thanks to my parents, Donald Reay Dyer† and Margaret Adams Dyer, who started me on the way; to my *Doktorvater,* Dr Athol Gill†, who not only taught the way but lived it to the end; and especially to Lynne, source of all encouragement, and our sons Ben, Daniel, Jesse and Reuben—constant companions on the way.

There are many others to thank also: The Principal, Dr Ken Manley, President and Council of Whitley College and my esteemed colleagues there: Dr Mark Brett, Colin Hunter, Merrill Kitchen, Ross Langmead, Marita Munro, Dr Geoff Pound, Dr Frank Rees, Dr Bruce Rumbold, John U'Ren, Dr Philip Mosely, our Librarian Ann Close and our Secretary Rosemary Dillon. The teachers and students of the Evangelical Theological Association and the Melbourne College of Divinity have provided the wider network of encouragement, and in particular Dr Greg Elsdon, Principal of CCTC, and my postgraduate students, past and present. Among the latter, Rainer Schack was especially helpful in checking the Indexes for me. I want to thank the examiners of the original thesis, Dr George Beasley-Murray, Dr Francis Moloney and Dr Michael Fitzpatrick; the Faculty and Students of the Baptist Theological Seminary, Rüschlikon, Switzerland; my Parents-in-Law, Mike and Betty Downes, whose holiday house at Daylesford was the setting for much of my writing; Stan Innes, who straightened my back many times, and Joseph

Jagerhofer, who helped so much with German translation. I must also express my deep gratitude to the Staff of Peter Lang, Bern, and to the editors of the *ITS* series, Dr Thorwald Lorenzen, Dr Günter Wagner, Dr Bruce Rumbold and Dr Glen Hinson, for their friendship, patience and encouragement.

'The one who endures to the end shall be saved' (Mk 13:13b)

Whitley College, Melbourne
Easter, 1997

ABBREVIATIONS

Abbreviations of all Biblical and related literature follow the 2-letter shortenings specified in *The New Jerusalem Bible,* ed Henry Wansbrough, London: Darton, Longman & Todd, 2nd ed, 1985.

Abbreviations of Journal names are according to the *Journal of Biblical Literature* 107 (1988), 588-596, with the addition of: *ABR* = Australian Biblical Review, *RTR* = Reformed Theological Review, *PacThR* = Pacific Theological Review, and *TSFBull* = TSF Bulletin.

TABLES AND DIAGRAMS

An outline of constituent forms within Mk 13	35
Possible Latinisms in Mk 13	47
Semitic interference in Mk 13	49
Features reclassified as normal Koine usage in Mk 13	60
Syntactical features unique to Mk 13	82
Percentage of unique syntax in each section of the Gospel of Mark	88
Allusions to the Old Testament in Mk 13	101
Summary of indications of pre-Markan traditions in Mk 13	119
Duality in Mk 13 (Neirynck)	140
Recurrent phraseology in Mk 13 (Peabody)	145
Recurrent syntax (6-word sequences) in Mk 13	148
Discourse-level duality in Mk 13 (Neirynck)	169
Mapping some literary interpretations of Mk 13	235
A map of the Gospel of Mark	259
Mk 13 in its wider literary context	266

TEXT SHEETS

Text Sheet 1: Linguistic influences in Mk 13	64
Text Sheet 2: Unique vocabulary in Mk 13	74
Text Sheet 3: Unique syntax in Mk 13	86
Text Sheet 4: Allusions to the Old Testament in Mk 13	116
Text Sheet 5: Summary of the indicators of redaction in Mk 13	149

INTRODUCTION

THROUGH THE LOOKING GLASS—DARKLY

When this project first began to take shape back in the mid-eighties as an attempt at a 'wholistic' understanding of Mark 13, it became increasingly apparent that the intended methodology—a range of traditional exegetical tools—was being challenged by a whole new set of interpretive approaches. The neat historical sequence of continuity and discontinuity formed by the so-called 'historical-critical' methods in Biblical analysis (textual-, source-, form-, tradition- and redaction-criticism, leading on to sociological- and composition-criticism), was being seen by many interpreters as a hermeneutical paradigm that not only focussed on the past but that now also belonged in the past. A New Criticism was promulgated, one that focussed on *the whole text as it now stands* (rather than on fragments of text and oral tradition as they once may have stood), and one that sought to interpret and bring meaning *into the present context* (rather than into some half-imagined world of the author, the authorial audience, or even of the original participants behind the narrative). With some misgivings, I attempted to engage these newer approaches, yet without jettisoning all that seemed to me to have been worthwhile in the older critical methods. Thus my original thesis began with the following words:[1]

> To undertake an extended exegetical analysis at a time when many have been speaking of a 'New Hermeneutic' and of 'paradigm-shifts in New Testament studies',[2] is the academic equivalent of yacht racing in variable winds. The range of possible approaches to achieving the goal can be quite exciting, but there is always the danger of being left behind the fleet on the wrong side of the course. Obviously, this comparison is appropriate only if the talk of paradigm-shifts has as much validity as the weather forecasts about wind-shifts, for both phenomena are often better assessed retrospectively. Indeed, the definitive study of the evolution of a science through paradigm-shifts gives many examples of extended

[1] The original thesis was titled "'Reader Note Well': Intertextuality and Interpretation in Mark 13", (unpublished dissertation for the Melbourne College of Divinity, 1991), this quotation taken from pages 1-2. In that unpublished form it was reviewed and critiqued by George Beasley-Murray, *Jesus and the Last Days* (Peabody 1993), 313-321.

[2] See, for example, James P. Martin, "Towards a Post-Critical Paradigm", *NTS* 33 (1987), 370, and Herbert N. Schneidau, "'Let the Reader Understand'", *Semeia* 30 (1987), 135. At this early stage of my work, Daniel Patte, *What is Structural Exegesis?* (Philadelphia 1976), provided some clarity on the new winds that were blowing in Biblical exegesis. See also footnotes 6 and 7 below for more recent literature.

periods of uncertainty between dominant paradigms.[3] Yet some scholars have already hastened to write an epitaph for the historical-critical era of Biblical analysis by referring to perceived epochs in the history of hermeneutical methodology. They use such terminology as: Pre-critical (Vitalist, or Symbolic) of the pre-enlightenment approaches; Critical (Mechanical, or Analytic) of the historical-critical era; and Post-critical (Holistic) of the present era.[4] Some also like to differentiate between a diachronic historical paradigm—which uses the text as a window into another time and place; and a synchronic linguistic paradigm—which sees the text as a mirror reflecting meaning into the reader's time and place.[5]

Since those words were written, the uncertainties surrounding the delineation of an appropriate exegetical methodology have become even more critical. The problem is no longer just one of being left behind the fleet on the wrong side of the course—the questions now are: Which course are we on? Is it possible to agree on a common starting line and goal? Is there sufficient coherence even to use the image of a 'yacht race'? To continue the mixed metaphors used above, the choice now is not just between text-as-window and text-as-mirror, but also text-as-prism or text-as-mirror-ball.[6] The intention of New Criticism to recover the whole text from the fragmentalising tendencies of form-, tradition- and redaction-criticism has itself disintegrated into the deconstructionist approaches of the post-structuralists and post-modernists.[7] The yacht race

[3] Thomas S. Kuhn, *The Structure of Scientific Revolutions* (Chicago 1970), 53-61, where the 'discovery' of oxygen and then X-rays and their respective implications are discussed, to give but two of Kuhn's examples. The theories about phlogiston, caloric, and the principle of acidity lingered on well into the next century after the 'discovery' of oxygen in the 1770's, and it took at least a decade before the 'discovery' of X-rays began to make an impact on scientific theory. Certainly Martin, "Post-Critical Paradigm", 373, concedes that paradigm-shifts do not "happen suddenly or totally all at once" and that their "boundaries are ambiguous."

[4] So Martin, "Post-Critical Paradigm", 372. His preferred terms are Symbolic, Analytic and Holistic.

[5] Patte, *Structural Exegesis,* 1, 5 and 9f.

[6] For something approaching the image 'text-as-prism', see Janice Capel Anderson and Stephen D. Moore (eds), *Mark and Method: New Approaches in Biblical Studies* (Minneapolis 1992), vii, where the description of recent methodologies as "a five-sided prism through which the Gospel is refracted" appears. Sometimes the linguistic fireworks of interpreters like Moore call to mind the image of a disco mirror-ball, or better, a laser light show, rather than a prism, since the process of interpretation is no longer understood passively—as being transparent and objective (looking through a window) or reflective (looking in a mirror)—but as a *creative* process (generating a new kind of light like a laser, or at least fragmenting it into brilliant flashes like a mirror-ball).

[7] A definitive treatment of the origins and implications of all the recent philosophical, socio-linguistic and literary influences on Biblical hermeneutics is beyond the scope of this study (and this author). In recent times, besides the very helpful collection of essays on Mark just cited above (Anderson and Moore, *Mark and Method*), the following books have all become essential guides through the maze: Anthony C. Thiselton, *New Horizons in Hermeneutics. The Theory and Practice of Transforming Biblical Reading* (Grand Rapids 1992); Stephen D. Moore, *Literary Criticism and the Gospels: The Theoretical Challenge* (New Haven 1989); Elizabeth Struthers Malbon and Edgar V. McKnight

has become a chaotic flotilla where it is no longer possible to distinguish clearly between participants, spectators and the racing officials who once set the rules.

The attempt to describe this situation in terms of hermeneutical paradigm-shifts has been only partially successful. Sharply drawn, mutually exclusive paradigms may help to clarify some fundamental perspectives, but they do not accurately reflect the exegetical and hermeneutical plurality of present Biblical scholarship. Nor is it yet possible to accurately describe the proliferation of newer literary methods as a 'paradigm', when there is little agreement between them in the use of terminology, let alone on the relationship between the different approaches.[8]

More significantly, before it is possible to claim that a new paradigm has been established the audience being addressed must generally concede that it answers more questions—or that it is more relevant to present realities—than the old paradigm(s). Whereas concessions such as this may be agreed upon fairly readily (but never painlessly) within a University literature department, the peculiar status of the Biblical documents within faith communities can lead to another set of problems altogether. Insofar as exegesis is understood to address initially those faith communities, and insofar as they see themselves as heirs of the *process* of Biblical interpretation,[9] Biblical hermeneutics can never totally dissociate itself from the history of interpretation of the text. In this respect, a *Wirkungsgeschichte* is a necessary part of all Biblical exegesis. It may well be, for example, that a 'reader-response' methodology and perspective is more relevant to the current situation in Western secular society, but such a methodology *alone* could not cope with—that is, could

---

(eds), *The New Literary Criticism and the New Testament* (Sheffield 1994); and A. K. M. Adam, *What is Postmodern Biblical Criticism?* (Minneapolis 1995).

[8] This process *is* taking place, but it will be a lengthy one before an overall perspective is gained on which new methods will yield results of lasting value. See, for example, the collections by Anderson and Moore, *Mark and Method,* and Malbon and McKnight, *The New Literary Criticism,* already cited above.

[9] That is, they locate the inspiration and authority of the text as occurring *within* the context of the ongoing interpretive community [cf. Paul J. Achtemeier, *The Inspiration of Scripture: Problems and Proposals* (Philadelphia 1980), especially 135f, where the locus of inspiration is seen in the interrelationship of "tradition, situation and respondent"]. Of course, if the faith community locates the meaning and authority of the text *only* in the text itself (an impossible, but often stated position in some fundamentalist circles, for example), then it is theoretically possible to do exegesis solely within a non-historical hermeneutical paradigm and to push all the messy historical questions to one side—or more probably, to blithely assume that they don't exist. Of course, many recent exegetical strategies rightly emphasise the role of the *reader* and not just the text in the creation of meaning, but unless this is understood to include *all readers* (including the very earliest)—thus also tackling historical questions—there is no way of discriminating between a proliferation of 'readings'. A 'fundamentalist reading' is just as valid as a 'feminist reading', or a 'post-structuralist' reading, if no attempt is made to interact with the history of interpretation of the text. Indeed, this may be the tragedy of the pluralism resulting from the dominance of reader-response hermeneutics in present American Biblical scholarship—namely, that it cannot defend itself against fundamentalism.

not answer *more* of the questions concerning—the inevitable historical and theological presuppositions that those in the faith community bring to the text. If exegesis were undertaken purely for apologetic purposes, it could operate solely within the parameters of the latest hermeneutical trend in order to communicate its findings at the cutting edge of scholarship. But given its obligations to the faith community, past and present, and to the ongoing process of interpretation within that context, responsible exegesis must also at least enter into some dialogue with previous interpretive traditions.

For these reasons the approach to Mark 13 used here will involve a conscious interaction with—and critique of—those exegetical methods utilised since the beginning of this century. The title of this introductory chapter, "Through the looking glass—darkly", is intended to convey the attempt to bridge the 'paradigms'—to see the text as *both* window ('Through...') and mirror ('...the looking glass...'), whilst conceding that any interpretation of the text is in itself a creation (hopefully not quite so fanciful as Alice's Wonderland), fraught with incompleteness and ambiguity ('—darkly', 1 Cor 13:12). Such an eclectic approach not only takes seriously the history of interpretation of the text but may also be seen as appropriate and even necessary when the eclectic nature of the text itself is considered. Mark 13 (and apocalyptic, prophetic and eschatological literature in general) is noted as much for its re-working over time as for its use of traditional motifs. An eclectic (or better, wholistic) methodology is arguably the most productive way to tackle such a diversely constructed text. Clearly the text is loaded with symbols and enigmatic sayings ('the beginning of birth-pains', 'the abomination of desolation', 'the sprouting fig-tree') which lend themselves to close readings and deconstructionist approaches. Yet just as clearly, these same phrases are inseparable from the older traditions of the Hebrew bible and the later (mis)interpretations of the Christian church. To take seriously all these dimensions requires a range of methods—literary, sociological and historical. But it is important to note that the nexus between these three areas, both logically and in recent exegetical history, is redaction-criticism—the *Hauptstrasse* that has become a *Querstrasse*.[10]

Yet it is this very methodology, *Redaktionsgeschichte,* that has been the focus of much of the criticism directed at historical-critical exegesis. For some there appears to be a frustration with the lack of clear results from redaction analysis, particularly in Markan studies. The methodological problems are so great that the intention of the author and influence of the 'third' *Sitz im Leben* have never been convincingly demonstrated, they

[10] This is John R. Donahue's phrase, used in "Redaction Criticism: Has the *Hauptstrasse* Become a *Sackgasse?*" in *The New Literary Criticism,* (eds) Malbon and McKnight, 27-57, specifically 48, which builds on Norman Perrin's previous title: "The *Wredestrasse* Becomes the *Hauptstrasse:* Reflections on the Reprinting of the Dodd Festschrift", *JR* 46 (1966), 296-300. Donahue's article is exemplary for its clarity and even-handedness in surveying recent exegetical developments. A less charitable treatment might well have asked: "Has the *Autobahn* Reached a Spagghetti-junction?"

claim, and therefore such concerns should no longer be the focus of exegetical methodology.[11] According to such a view as this, redaction analysis is seen as failing at the level of exegeting the text. However, the lack of a clear scholarly consensus about Markan redaction—particularly obvious in studies on Mk 13—may simply demonstrate the extraordinary complexity, rather than the unsuitability or impossibility of the task. Such a negative assessment of redaction analysis on these grounds is also premature, as the greater availability of resources and recent developments in computers and software have made a whole new range of analyses possible which promise to provide a quicker means of testing supposed divisions of tradition and redaction.[12] This criticism of redaction analysis also fails to appreciate fully the considerable contribution of such studies to our understanding of Matthew and Luke in particular, but also of other texts where redaction is more easily discernible than in Mark.[13] The difficulty in determining the redactional processes that formed the Gospel of Mark is not in itself an adequate reason for abandoning the methodology—and this is especially so since the irregular style of Mark betrays its eclectic origins.

Other critics argue that it is not at the level of exegeting the text that redaction analysis is lacking, but rather in failing to lead the reader into a relevant interpretation of the text. It is conceded that historical-critical exegesis works brilliantly in uncovering the world of the text and its author, but in the process the text is always seen as a window into this other historical world and never as something having meaning in its own right. In Werner Kelber's words, the priority has been 'meaning-as-reference' rather than 'meaning-as-narrative, consciousness or system'.[14]

---

[11] The basic position of C. Clifton Black, "The Quest of Mark the Redactor: Why has it been pursued, and what has it taught us?" *JSNT* 33 (1988), 19-39. See page 19, for example: "given the enormous theoretical and practical problems entailed by the practice of Markan redaction criticism, especially when predicated on the assumption of Markan priority, one wonders why this exegetical approach for so long has held so many interpreters in thrall." Black does concede that there have been some positive benefits resulting from the attempts to differentiate tradition from redaction, but basically he regards the "methodological quandaries involved in the enterprise ... as unamenable to resolution" (footnote 7, page 34).

[12] Such new developments partly form the basis on which the analysis proceeds in the chapters which follow. Extensive collections of machine-readable Biblical and related texts (in Hebrew and Greek and using various grammatical codes) are now available (even for personal computers), enabling rapid searches and classification of material, to name only a few of the possibilities. See further: David Mealand, "Computers in New Testament Research: An Interim Report", *JSNT* 33 (1988), 97-115.

[13] To be fair to Black, "Quest", 23, he at least is prepared to concede "the impressive exegetical results of *Redaktionsgeschichte* when applied by Günther Bornkamm and his pupils to Matthew and by Hans Conzelmann to Luke". Donahue, "Redaction Criticism", 38-9, also points to the continuing use of redaction criticism in recent studies on Q and on John's Gospel.

[14] Werner H. Kelber, "Gospel Narrative and Critical Theory", *BTB* 18 (1988), 130. Kelber uses the phrases 'meaning-as-reference' in connection with the historical-critical approach; 'meaning-as-narrative' of literary, formalist interpretations; 'meaning-as-

Daniel Patte has gone further and concluded that the nature of a text "as defined by historical exegesis appears to be *meaningless:* no hermeneutic takes place", because "the believer (layman, minister, or theologian) seems paralysed, unable to cross the threshold which separates historical exegesis from hermeneutic."[15] The focus of historical methodology on the more objective and conscious events, beliefs and motivations of the past is no longer of immediate relevance in our 'post-modern' world, Patte contends. Rather, there is a need for a more wholistic approach to interpreting texts, including some interaction with their unconscious and mythical dimensions. In moving in this direction, Biblical studies brings itself into line with trends that have already dominated the wider fields of literature, linguistics and anthropology, and which are also modifying attitudes within the natural sciences. For Patte, exegesis is illegitimate if it fails to lead to a hermeneutic that is relevant to the culture in which it is practised. So the historical paradigm, whilst it has served—and may continue to serve—a useful preliminary function, must ultimately give way to a linguistic paradigm, where the text is taken as it stands and 'revitalized' so that it is brought into discourse with the reader.[16]

As a response to trends in modern Western consciousness (and subconsciousness), these new literary approaches certainly have some relevant insights to offer. The growth of interest in alternative medicine, organic farming and inter-disciplinary studies, to name but a few diverse fields, is evidence of a widespread reaction against 'science' as it has been narrowly defined and practised, and of a growing concern for a more wholistic approach to life and self-understanding. Such changes should certainly affect the way the Bible is explained within Western culture.[17] But the key issue is the question of continuity or discontinuity between the older and newer approaches. Do such reactions against the abuse of 'scientific' methodologies necessitate—or are they evidence of—a major paradigm-shift away from critical analysis as we have known it, or should they be regarded as indicators of the need for an extra 'mini-paradigm' to be added within the existing field of paradigms comprising historical-

---

consciousness' of the reader-response approaches; 'meaning-as-system' of structuralist exegesis; and 'meaning-as-deferment' of postmodernist or deconstructionist approaches.

[15] *Structural Exegesis,* 10.

[16] *Structural Exegesis,* 5. The concession by some structuralist (and post-structuralist) exegetes that historical-critical methods may provide useful preliminary tools for exegesis may be adequate as far as their purposes are concerned, but we wish to argue here that these tools are a *necessary* part of the whole hermeneutical process in the context of a faith community.

[17] Though even if it could be demonstrated that 'post-modernism' (for example) is the *dominant* framework for discourse within the scholarly community (which is possibly true these days), within society (less likely) or within the church (even more unlikely), this would not in itself be grounds for using *only* a 'post-modern' approach to interpreting the Bible. Exegetes must be aware of their audience, but not to the extent that they take over the role of apologists or evangelists.

critical exegesis.[18] Such an accommodation of new approaches has been the way that the historical-critical model has developed in the past, through the successive 'mini-paradigm-shifts' of source, form, and redaction criticisms. Together they form a composite collection of analyses which, whilst related, may be applied quite separately to a text to counterbalance the excesses of each other. If the so-called synchronic methods can be incorporated in the same way then they may well help to correct the over-emphasis on the historical background to the text of which the diachronic approaches may sometimes have been guilty.

The distinction between diachronic and synchronic approaches which is often made is also being too sharply drawn. Redaction analysis correctly understood and practised should never leave the interpreter in the world of the text without a bridge to the present, but ought to lead naturally on into considering the composition and implications of the whole text as it stands. A thorough analysis of the editorial work of a writer may well commence with a detailed examination of vocabulary and the specifics of words and phrases omitted or included, but it must also include the wider processes of ordering and structuring the available material. Redaction analysis should thus be seen as including composition analysis, which in turn leads on to the literary appreciation of the work as a whole. This progression, from an analytical to a literary approach, has been evident in the writings of many scholars but is perhaps best illustrated in the area of Markan studies by the work of Norman Perrin.

Perrin's early detailed consideration of tradition and redaction in Mark led him inevitably to an examination of that Gospel's literary qualities and then on to the use of symbolic language in the New Testament as a whole, especially as used in eschatological formulations.[19] Such investigations have served not only to increase our knowledge of early Christian eschatology, but have also been an attempt to assist our understanding of what that kind of language might mean today. Whether Perrin's attempt was successful or not is another matter; the point here is that there ought not be such a gulf between the newer literary methods and redactional analysis that a whole new paradigm is proposed. It is only if redaction

[18] This ambiguous use of the term 'paradigm' is consistent with Kuhn's usage: "On the one hand, it (= paradigm) stands for the entire constellation of beliefs, values, techniques, and so on shared by the members of a given community. On the other hand it denotes one sort of element in that constellation..." (*Structure,* 175). As in Biblical studies, so in the sciences generally, it is *not* 'the entire constellation of beliefs...' that should be overthrown by the recent concerns for a more wholistic approach. No doubt there are those who have totally abandoned 'Western' medicine for the many recent and traditional alternatives, for example, but the most exciting developments appear to be taking place where some kind of synthesis is encouraged.

[19] This pilgrimage of Perrin's can be illustrated by such articles as: "The Creative Use of the Son of Man Traditions by Mark", *USQR* 23 (1968), 357-365; and "Eschatology and Hermeneutics: Reflections on Method in the Interpretation of the New Testament", *JBL* 93 (1974), 3-14; and by his book: *Jesus and the Language of the Kingdom. Symbol and Metaphor in New Testament Interpretation* (London 1976). See also Donahue's reflections on the Perrin legacy in "Redaction Criticism", 26f.

analysis is defined very narrowly as the author's specific written contributions rather than including the tasks of selecting, ordering, shaping and structuring the material as a whole, that such a gulf may appear to exist.[20] And if redaction analysis is understood in such a limited way as this and rejected, and these wider tasks regarded as the domain of a separate literary analysis, there is the danger that the overall literary structure and the author's intentions may be analysed without proper regard for their historical context, and without any reference to possible distinctions between tradition and redaction.[21] This can have profound implications for the interpretation of a passage. For example, to ignore the possibility of a reference external to the text behind even one small clause such as "let the reader understand" (Mk 13:14), can make all the difference between seeing it as drawing attention to the most urgent statement of the whole Gospel, or as being part of a pre-Markan source incorporated as a way of placing recent social upheavals into a wider narrative context.[22]

Of course the newer literary approaches can bring a refreshing perspective to exegesis that is obsessed with the minutiae of an author's preferred vocabulary and syntax. But to regard the task of tackling the

[20] Such narrow definitions of redaction analysis are not endorsed by those who practise it. See, for example, the way that John Donahue summarises Perrin's understanding of redaction analysis as "editorial criticism, the author over against the tradition he inherits, and composition criticism: the author as master of the material whose purpose is found in the composition of material and creation of new forms." John R. Donahue, "Introduction: From Passion Traditions to Passion Narrative", in *The Passion in Mark. Studies on Mark 14-16,* ed Werner H. Kelber (Philadelphia 1976), 16. The natural progression from redaction criticism to literary and sociological methods is admirably described in Donahue's "Redaction Criticism", 41-48.

[21] This is one of the criticisms made against some of the newer literary approaches to Mk 13 outlined in chapter 8 below. Timothy J. Geddert, [*Watchwords. Mark 13 in Markan Eschatology* (Sheffield 1989), 19], states his goal (*"to uncover the intentions of the author of Mark's Gospel"*) and method (*"as they can be known by studying Mark 13 in its Gospel context"* by utilising many different exegetical tools), but singles out redaction criticism as particularly inadequate "to reach the goal"? No *one* exegetical method is ever adequate on its own, so it is certainly correct to make use of the benefits of a full range of exegetical approaches and to examine Mk 13 in the context of the whole Gospel. But to avoid redaction criticism altogether is to over-react against a perceived over-emphasis in recent exegetical studies on Mark. Surely the hermeneutical process must include an attempt to wrestle with the way the author has reinterpreted the tradition—rather than just assume that the author has full and equal control over all parts of the text. If the suggested alternative to redaction criticism is to "listen to the author's perspective" from a literary standpoint *only,* then any awareness of the constraints of pre-Markan tradition is lost and the Gospel is reduced to just a novel—albeit a "literary masterpiece" (*Watchwords,* 255).

[22] From a purely *literary* perspective, it would appear that the only direct appeal to the reader in the Gospel of Mark must be an exhortation to reflect on the most significant message it contains. This has led some to the *historical* conclusion that Mark was written before the fall of Jerusalem at a time of political turmoil and uncertainty. However, if on historical-critical grounds it can be shown that Mk 13:14 belongs to a pre-Markan source which has been retrospectively endorsed as a true prophecy by the author, then an entirely different set of conclusions may be drawn. See further below in chapter 7.

issues of tradition and redaction in Mark as no longer appropriate because it is either too difficult or considered irrelevant, and to embark *solely* on one of the new literary approaches, is to be in danger of either:

(i)   losing the tension between 'tradition received' and 'tradition interpreted' in the Gospel, (the whole of the Gospel becomes, in effect, Markan redaction, as the author is assumed to be totally responsible for the text as it stands); or

(ii)   of assuming, rather like a *nouveau fundamentalist,* that all that is necessary for understanding is the text as it stands, and what we as readers bring to it.

The first of these approaches assumes that the author of the Gospel is not answerable to a community and its traditions but has full creative control over the text rather like a novelist or fiction writer. The second leads to the opposite conclusion that it is only the text which has significance, and the intentions of the author, real or implied, are irrelevant for hermeneutics. Such approaches may well bring fresh insights to our understanding of the text (for those with a knowledge of the terminology involved),[23] but they are incomplete if they are carried out and presented with a total disregard for the historical context of the text and the insights gained through past centuries of scholarship.[24] Rather they should be

---

[23] It is apparent that diverse interpretive communities are developing in Biblical Studies, each with their own technical vocabulary and hierarchy of important questions. This may be illustrated by two reviews of recent commentaries on Matthew. Daniel Patte attempted to put his structuralist methodology into practice by writing a commentary: *The Gospel According to Matthew: A Structural Commentary on Matthew's Faith* (Philadelphia 1987), and should be congratulated for his relatively jargon-free approach. But to turn his own challenge to historical-critical analysis back at him (see page 14 above), we may well ask whether the results are any more helpful for the hermeneutical paralysis afflicting the "layman, minister or theologian" than the other recent commentary on Matthew [W. D. Davies and D. C. Allison, *The Gospel According to St Matthew,* vol 1, (Edinburgh 1988)] which adopts a more traditional exegetical methodology. See, for example, the judgment of one major reviewer of Patte's work: "let me stress that I had high hopes that a jargon-free structuralist commentary would result in a stimulating reading of the text, for I share the author's concern to find ways of letting the text come alive for the modern reader. I can only report that I was disappointed. I now have a better understanding of structuralism, but not of Matthew's Gospel." [Graham Stanton, "A Structuralist Approach to Matthew", *Int* 43 (1989), 184-186]. By way of contrast, a loose paraphrase of the gist of J. D. Kingsbury's review of the Davies and Allison commentary should also be given [*JBL* 110 (1991), 344-346], words to the effect that: I learnt a lot about scholarly observations and the supposed 'theology' of Matthew extracted from the text, but *nothing* about "any sense of the narrative and dramatic movement of Matthew's Gospel-story." (346). It is not in any one approach that satisfactory exegesis will be found, but in the *dialogue* between them.

[24] A purely literary approach may well suffice if it could be demonstrated that Christian origins were of a purely literary nature—along the lines of Paul Tillich's hypothetical suggestion that: "Suppose the bearer of the Spirit had another name than Jesus and did not come from Nazareth, and the New Testament picture of Jesus is essentially a creation of Mark (as has been said), then 'Mark' was the bearer of the Spirit through whom God has created the church and transformed . . . many in all generations, somehow including myself. Then this 'Mark' has expressed the inner events he has experienced in the symbolic imagery of the Christ story." P. Tillich, "Rejoinder", *JR* 46

seen, along with the other types of analysis, as one more way of deepening and sharpening those insights for application to the present situation of the interpreter. To lose that sense of continuity with past scholarship as well as the possibility of being confronted by the startling 'otherness' of the text and its world, is to radically diminish our chances of entering into meaningful discourse with the text. The *Sitz im Leben* of the text and of the author are more than just background information—they are an essential part of the challenge of the text to our own cultural presuppositions and 'rules' of interpretation. The social, political, religious and economic framework of the text (both for the tradition and the redaction—and even if they cannot be finally determined), are part of the necessary shaking of our own framework which must occur before we can understand the text anew.

One proponent of the newer exegetical perspectives illustrates the recent literary approaches by giving the example of a game of chess, half-way completed. He suggests that it is not necessary to know—indeed it may even be an advantage not to know—the moves that have already occurred in the game if one is to give a good analysis of the situation.[25] On one level this is certainly true. The dispassionate appraisal of an outsider can provide many insights into a situation.[26] But on another level, if one is concerned to get involved with the game and to contribute to its outcome, then the more one understands about the game—its history, the opponent(s), their past responses under pressure, the time left

---

(1966), 192. If this were the case and the Gospel of Mark simply a work of fiction, then it *would* be appropriate to interpret the Gospel *purely* as literature, and even with total disregard for any supposed historical background or authorial intent. But we may suspect that Tillich, like some who adopt an exclusively non-historical approach to exegesis, is endeavouring to cut loose from untidy and perplexing historical issues. He goes on to say: "All this is an historically absurd but logically necessary consequence of the attempt to liberate Christian faith in its very centre from the bondage to scholarship." But such an escape from awkward historical questions may lead to a 'literary docetism' rather than true hermeneutical liberation, for it is not just the scholars who are bound to ask questions about the history of Christian origins in a faith which refers so much to a specific revelation of God in space and time.

[25] R. B. Crotty, "Changing Fashions in Biblical Interpretation", *ABR* 33 (1985), 16.

[26] Assuming, of course, that the 'outsider' is aware of the rules of chess. It is all very well for scholars who have been steeped in the 'rules' of historical-critical exegesis to try their hand at the new literary analysis, but any *purely* literary analysis of the Biblical text without any knowledge of its origins would surely need to be treated with caution. It would be the equivalent of an attempted modern-day analysis of a Greek/Hebrew game of which we do not know the rules. Some interesting observations might well be made, but the chances of misinterpretations are high. Even those post-modern interpreters who rightly reject the notion of a 'rule of fact' underpinning 'disinterested and objective' Biblical criticism (Anderson and Moore, *Mark and Method,* "Introduction", 15) depend nevertheless on an accepted body of 'rules' that they share with other exegetes in order to make their point—even if it is to feed off the very rules they break. For example, Moore's brilliant reference to Mark as a "cross-disciplinary text/book … which demands a cross-disciplinary reading" (*Mark and Method,* "Deconstructive Criticism", 96) alludes to the vast scholarly literature on the two major themes in Mark—the way of the cross and the way of discipleship. *Because* Moore has knowledge 'of the rules of chess' he is able to suggest some scintillating new moves.

on the clock, and so on—the better the chances are of successfully entering into the game and having a realistic understanding of the situation. Best of all, if one can do both at the same time—enter into *and* objectively assess the game—then the processes of analysis and understanding, exegesis and hermeneutics, will occur together and inform each other. It is with this intention—to use an eclectic methodology to tackle an eclectic text—that we turn specifically to the interpretation of Mk 13.

Although it has been one of the first chapters tackled by scholars with the development of each new method of exegesis, Mk 13 remains one of the least satisfactorily resolved areas of synoptic studies. In some cases the interpretations of the chapter have made their own significant contributions to the evolution of exegetical methodology,[27] yet the diversity of opinion that persists about Mk 13 is remarkable. So too has been the necessity for some interpreters to publish 'second thoughts' about their original work on the chapter.[28] The problem lies not in any lack of progress being made through the application of historical-critical analysis. On the contrary, each particular approach seems to have yielded such a wealth of information that the difficulty is to find any sort of constructive synthesis that takes into account everything of value that has been discovered amidst the extraordinary diversity of views.

[27] It may be claimed that the work of T. Colani [*Jésus Christ et les croyances messianiques de son Temps* (Strasbourg 1864)] anticipated the results, if not the methodology, of the form critics; that certainly W. Marxsen [*Der Evangelist Markus,* (Göttingen 1959), ET R. A. Harrisville, *Mark the Evangelist* (Nashville 1969)] initiated a wave of redaction-critical studies of Mark's Gospel; that the close analysis of the structure and language of Mk 13 by J. Lambrecht [*Die Redaktion der Markus-Apokalypse. Literarische Analyse und Strukturuntersuchung* (Rome 1967)] and F. Rousseau ["La structure de Marc 13", *Bib* 56 (1975), 157-172] were forerunners to the detailed structural analyses of recent years; that R. Pesch's attempt to gauge authorial intent from an analysis of the total structure of the Gospel [*Naherwartungen. Tradition und Redaktion in Mk 13* (Düsseldorf 1968)], though faulted in its mathematical inflexibility, was certainly influential in its description of Markan redaction, and that the attempt by E. Brandenburger [*Markus 13 und die Apokalyptik* (Göttingen 1984)] to re-examine Mk 13 from a perspective of a more positive appreciation of apocalyptic literature breaks new ground. Of the newer literary approaches, only Geddert's *Watchwords* is specifically focussed on Mk 13, and it might be best described in terms of composition criticism rather than a narrative or reader-response approach. The latter are represented by Tolbert and Fowler's books on the whole of Mark's Gospel in chapter 8 below.

[28] None so dramatic as Pesch's about-face. Compare *Naherwartungen* with his *Das Markus-evangelium* (Freiburg 1977) and see his explanation in "Markus 13", in *l'Apocalypse johannique et l'Apocalyptique dans le Nouveau Testament* (Leuven 1980), 355-368. See also G. R. Beasley-Murray, "Second Thoughts on the Composition of Mark 13", *NTS* 29 (1982), 414-420; *Jesus and the Kingdom of God* (Grand Rapids 1986), 322-337; "The Vision on the Mount: The Eschatological Discourse of Mark 13", *Ex Auditu* 6 (1990), 39-52; "The Kingdom of God in the Teaching of Jesus", *JETS* 35 (1992), 19-38; and now *Jesus and the Last Days. The Interpretation of the Olivet Discourse* (Peabody 1993). This latter work contains an invitation to the present author also to have "Second Thoughts on the Eschatological Discourse of Mark 13" (*Last Days,* 321), a process which begins with the publication of this revised dissertation.

This lack of consensus is due at least as much to the wider questions Mk 13 is assumed to address as to the complexity of the text itself. It has been a central passage in debates over:

(i)   the 'apocalyptic', the 'eschatological', and/or the 'sapiential' nature of the teaching of Jesus;

(ii)   the role of apocalyptic literature in the formation of early Christian theology (and thus the very definition of apocalyptic literature);

(iii)   the expectation of an imminent *parousia* in the early church;

(iv)   the 'Synoptic Problem';

(v)   the *Sitz im Leben* of the Markan community (and thus the place and date of the composition of the Gospel of Mark);

(vi)   the use of the Son of Man designation;

(vii)   the use of the Old Testament in the Gospel of Mark;

(viii) the mission to Gentiles, and

(ix)   the events surrounding the fall of Jerusalem and the fate of the Jerusalem church.

Clearly these are important questions, but too often they have been brought to the text for answers rather than allowed to arise, or remain unanswered, out of an exegesis of the text. Often the dominant question in an interpreter's mind has determined too narrowly the methodology used to tackle the passage. This is apparent in the traditio-historical approach of those seeking to establish the historicity of the discourse, just as it is evident that many wishing to dissociate Jesus from apocalyptic utterances found form criticism a useful tool. No doubt the newer exegetical disciplines bring a useful perspective of their own, but if used in isolation from historical-critical approaches, one might suspect their proponents of wishing to avoid some of the more difficult historical questions altogether.

Such a statement of course, reveals at least one presupposition that this study will bring to the text—not one relating to any of the areas of debate mentioned above, but a methodological presupposition. Namely: that despite the limitations and alternatives acknowledged above, there is still value in the historical-critical paradigm for exegesis, and in particular in the attempt to gauge authorial intent from an analysis of tradition and redaction.[29] Indeed, such a methodology represents the very essence of the challenge of interpreting Mk 13, because as Brandenburger has demonstrated,[30] apocalyptic writings are eclectic and redactional by nature. If we are to evaluate them in any positive way at all, some appreciation of the stages through which they have moved—the crises they have addressed—is necessary. To do this out of a deep awareness of apocalyptic thought patterns, as Brandenburger has attempted, is surely

---

[29] The difficulties of this concept are freely acknowledged, as is the value of being open to other more 'subjective' approaches. See Nigel Watson, "Authorial Intention— Suspect Concept for Biblical Scholars?" *ABR*, 35 (1987), 12.

[30] Brandenburger, *Markus 13*. See chapter 6 below.

beneficial. But because Mk 13 is situated in a document not otherwise noted for its apocalyptic content,[31] some attempt must be made to reconcile the chapter to its context. This is redaction criticism understood with regard to its full literary and sociological implications. Not merely a word-count of the author's favourite vocabulary (though that is at least a starting point), but an attempt to come to terms with the theological and sociological significance of the total composition for the evangelist's community.

Thus the attempt will be made here to interpret Mk 13 in a wholistic way, making use of the best insights of a range of analytical approaches from both the traditional historical-critical methodologies and some of the newer literary ones, whilst recognising the limitations of each method.[32] The starting point in each succeeding chapter will be an attempt to review the insights of scholars over the last forty years, grouped according to their dominant methodological approach to the discourse. These insights will be assessed and developed further on each occasion, and the chapter will conclude with a statement of the contribution which each methodology can make to our understanding of the text, its sources and its wider context. An important focus of these analyses will be the re-appraisal of the arguments for the classification of tradition and redaction—intertextuality and interpretation—in Mk 13.[33] As a safeguard against approaching the text with a pre-conceived theological agenda, those methods of analysis which promise to be more impartial by nature shall be used to set the parameters of the debate. Tracing the development

---

[31] Apart from the apocalyptic viewpoints of Marxsen, Kee, Kelber *et al* (see chapters 4 and 7 below), most commentators have argued that discipleship teaching and/or Christology are the dominant Markan concerns. It may be argued however, according to Brandenburger's definition of an apocalypse (*Markus 13*, 13), that indeed the Gospel of Mark "mediates guidelines for behaviour" (teaching on discipleship), "through secret revelations" (the secrecy *motif* in the Gospel), "for those in a crisis situation" (the Markan community facing persecution). Perhaps this only serves to illustrate the all-encompassing nature of Brandenburger's definition rather than the apocalyptic nature of the Gospel of Mark as a whole.

[32] 'Wholistic' is being used here simply to mean the involvement of the 'whole' range of approaches, rather than the 'holistic' approach (as opposed to the 'analytic') suggested by Martin, "Post-Critical Paradigm", 372. See footnote 4 above. I would be happy to use the word 'eclectic', but this seems to have negative overtones for some.

[33] The original title of this dissertation was: "'Reader Note Well': Intertextuality and Interpretation in Mark 13." However, because of the current technical use of 'intertextuality' to refer to a non-chronological relationship between texts—a network of texts selected more by the modern reader than the original author—it was decided not to continue to use the word in what might be a misleading way. Cf. Willem S. Vorster, "Intertextuality and Redaktionsgeschichte", in *Intertextuality in Biblical Writings* (Kampen 1989), 16-22, for a helpful clarification of the two different perspectives: "...there also seems to be a great difference between perceptions which focus on the growth of texts and those which attend to the making and reception of texts." ("Intertextuality", 16). I would simply point out here that the focus of *Redaktionsgeschichte* is also very much on the *making* of the text—not just on its growth—and that it also has some concern at least for the initial reception of the text (by the Markan community).

of a text which is eclectic and redactional by nature—in that it involves re-applied apocalyptic thought patterns and imagery—requires a concentration on the more easily quantifiable indicators of tradition and an author's interference, such as vocabulary and syntax. But rather than commencing with and giving more attention to the *recurrent* features of the text which are usually taken to indicate redaction,[34] a major focus in the initial stages will be to examine what the *unique* features of the text might reveal about any pre-Markan traditions.

Of course it is not possible to break the hermeneutical circle simply by reference to such supposedly 'objective data', for already assumptions have been made and conclusions drawn about the nature of the text and how it may be analysed even as we begin to count. Yet it *is* possible to obtain a range of *possible* classifications and divisions within a text by mechanical means, which can then be subjected to further refinement by correlation with the broader and more illuminating questions of the author's literary methods, structure and theology. If such a rigorous cross-checking is maintained then the hermeneutical circle becomes an upward spiral, always moving on to higher levels of interpretation—relating to the discoveries of previous efforts, yet without necessarily assuming them as a starting point.

Too often, for example, the determination of redaction within Mk 13 has been built predominantly on the prior findings of form analysis, findings which have often been coloured by preconceptions about the nature of apocalyptic literature and whether or not Jesus could have uttered such words. Certainly form analysis remains a valid discipline and one which leads naturally—as it did historically—into redaction analysis. But redaction analysis must also be undertaken as a separate field of endeavour so that its results can be tested *against* the findings of form analysis, rather than the dregs of a form critical analysis forming the starting point for determining an author's redaction.[35] The evidence collected below will no doubt retain a certain ambiguity and many of the conclusions may be tentatively expressed, but this is surely a safer route to the interpretation of Mk 13 than to attribute full creative control over all the material to the author.

By insisting that the complex web of intertextuality that makes up Mk 13 can in some way be partially unravelled, we are affirming that the

---

[34] An approach already explored thoroughly, although in different ways, by F. Neirynck, *Duality in Mark. Contributions to the Study of the Markan Redaction* (Leuven, 1988, revised from the 1972 edition); and David Barrett Peabody, "The Redactional Features of the Author of Mark: A Method Focussing on Recurrent Phraseology and its Application", Unpublished PhD thesis, Southern Methodist University (1983), later published as *Mark as Composer* (Macon 1987). The work of these authors will, of course, be taken into consideration when examining the indications of redaction in Mk 13 in chapters 4 and 5 below.

[35] This is clearly one problem with Marxsen's analysis—he commences rather uncritically with the conclusions of the form critics as the basis for his determination of redaction. See chapter 4 below.

author of Mark wrote amidst the tension of the constraints of the tradition received and the creative application of that tradition to the Markan community—just as we construct our texts today. To deny any specific and traceable links with the tradition is in effect to make the author of Mark totally responsible for the creation—not only of the Gospel *genre*— but its content as well. As we have noted, this is indeed the position taken by some scholars,[36] who regard it as more prudent to sweep such questions under the mat of 'intertextuality', conceding the likelihood of a diverse textual background without in any way trying to specifically delineate its nature. Such an approach is both the presupposition and the outcome of analysing the Gospel of Mark *purely* at a literary level.[37] The intention of this study is to re-open these questions of tradition and redaction, at a time when many are either despairing that such an approach is unresolvable or declaring it to be meaningless. By making use of recent computer developments to accumulate and analyse the data necessary to isolate unique and recurrent syntax, we aim to further attempts to trace textual traditions and specify linguistic influences— thereby revealing possible traditional units within the text—and to use

[36] We have noted the (theoretical) position of Paul Tillich in footnote 24 above, but the work of Burton L. Mack, *A Myth of Innocence: Mark and Christian Origins* (Philadelphia 1988), takes this hypothetical position seriously—that Mark was the *creator* of the Gospel's content as well as of its form. The process Mark was engaged in was not (according to Mack) one of "'collecting' and 'passing on' early traditions about Jesus" but "a highly conscious scholarly effort in fabricating a new text by taking up strands from textual patterns that belonged to the multifaceted cultural fabric of his times" (323, footnote 3). Since this view of the composition of Mark is not demonstrated in detail in any way by Mack, it seems to be used more as a smoke-screen to hide the need for closer scrutiny of Mark's relationship to the tradition. Mack specifically denies that the Passion narrative is pre-Markan, for example, but what if it can be demonstrated that large portions of tradition exist both there and elsewhere in Mark? See further the discussion of Mack's approach in chapter 8 below.

[37] This is also the tendency of the socio-literary approach of Ched Myers, *Binding the Strong Man. A Political Reading of Mark's Story of Jesus* (Maryknoll 1988). Whilst Myers concedes the likelihood of traditions behind Mk 13, he does not attempt to specifically delineate them or consider their possible impact on his interpretation: "A socio-literary reading is not interested in reconstructing the traditions 'behind' this text, but recognizing some of its sources helps us to appreciate the complex fabric of intertextuality that characterizes this sermon" (*Strong Man,* 325). Myers goes on to mention some of the possible sources behind the 'sermon', yet without making any attempt to specify the extent of the tradition received by the author of the Gospel. Therefore one could challenge Myers' assumption that the anti-Temple stance of the Gospel of Mark is primary evidence of the evangelist's position, requiring a pre-70 CE dating of the Gospel. Could it not reflect a tradition going back to the historical Jesus? Ironically, having read the whole text of the Gospel as a guide to the Markan community's *Sitz im Leben,* Myers *then* appears to identify the resultant Markan theology with that of the historical Jesus in his Jesus/Mark/Gandhi typology. It would be better not to make historical judgments like this on the basis of a literary method alone. The historical question as to whether Jesus was the source of the anti-temple sayings must be dealt with *first,* and therefore the possibility of other sources behind the text must also be considered. Nevertheless, Myers' socio-historical background to the text is most illuminating and will be examined more fully in chapter 7 below.

this information to find a way through the labyrinth of scholarly interpretations that have accumulated around the text of Mk 13.

It is because these scholarly interpretations are seen as an important part of the exegetical procedure that the collective first sections of each chapter comprise a survey of the most significant interpretations of Mk 13 published since the 1950's, including an examination of the major issues and problems raised by each of them. Although such surveys have appeared occasionally in English,[38] only Beasley-Murray has taken full account of the recent contributions by Geddert, Brandenburger, Wenham, his own 'second thoughts', and the influence of Hahn on the 'about-face' by Pesch.[39] For these reasons alone a further review of the literature would be worthwhile, but it becomes mandatory in any attempt to evaluate the variety of exegetical methods practised in the past in order to determine the most appropriate method to adopt for any further interpretation of the chapter. For this reason the review of past interpretations undertaken here shall be grouped primarily according to their dominant methodological approach, though otherwise following a chronological order. This means, for example, that the first traditio-historical response of Beasley-Murray (and the later work of Wenham)[40]

---

[38] See, for example, K. Grayston, "The Study of Mark 13", *BJRL* 56 (1973-4), 371-387; D. Wenham, "Recent Study of Mark 13", *TSFBul* (1975), LXXI: 6-15, LXXII: 1-9; G. Smith, "Mark 13:9-13: Mission in Apocalyptic, with Special Reference to Jesus' Gentile Mission in Mark", unpublished PhD Thesis, Southern Baptist Theological Seminary (1981), 1-120; and Timothy J. Geddert, "Mark 13 in its Markan Interpretive Context", unpublished dissertation, Aberdeen University (1986). Beasley-Murray's survey of the pre-1950 literature in *Jesus and the Future. An Examination of the Criticism of The Eschatological Discourse, Mark 13 with Special Reference to the Little Apocalypse Theory* (London 1954), 1-112, may be found summarised in "The Rise and Fall of the Little Apocalypse Theory", *ExpTim* 64 (1952-53), 346-349, and the whole reprinted in *Last Days,* 1-161, with a comprehensive up-date, 162-349.

[39] This literature has been cited already with the exception of D. Wenham, *The Rediscovery of Jesus' Eschatological Discourse* (Sheffield 1984), and F. Hahn, "Die Rede von der Parusie des Menschensohnes Markus 13", in *Jesus und der Menschensohn,* eds R. Pesch and R. Schnackenburg (Freiburg 1975), 240-266.

[40] It should be noted that this grouping does not meet with Beasley-Murray's approval, cf *Last Days,* 321: "I admit to feeling less enthusiastic about his evaluation of my own work on Mark 13. I fail to comprehend how he should group David Wenham's investigation of the discourse with mine, as though we shared essentially the same approach." My only criterion for grouping Beasley-Murray's early work and Wenham together is that they both use other NT traditions which they see as having some connection with Mk 13 in order to argue that Mk 13 includes more sayings of the historical Jesus than many other scholars have concluded. I would agree that there the similarities end—Wenham argues that Mk 13 is but one of the cut-down versions of an extended pre-synoptic eschatological discourse of Jesus, whereas Beasley-Murray (especially in his later work) takes the much more tenable position (in my view), that Mk 13 is a redactional compilation which makes use of many isolated *logia* of Jesus (from Q and elsewhere), which have been used in different ways in the teaching of the early church. It is interesting to note, however, that Beasley-Murray apparently intended to name his *Jesus and the Last Days* book *The Eschatological Discourse of Jesus* (cf Wenham's *The Rediscovery of Jesus' Eschatological Discourse*). See Beasley-Murray, "The Kingdom of God", 38, and chapter 2 below for more details.

to the conclusions of the form critics shall be grouped together and placed *after* a brief review of the form critical approaches. It may seem strange that the traditional view that Mk 13 is predominantly a discourse of the historical Jesus should follow *after* the findings of many form critics that it represents part of a Jewish apocalypse, but in the context of the debate since the 1950's, this is indeed what has happened.

The headings from chapter 1 onwards are not meant to be definitive statements of the position of the authors examined thereunder, but rather an indication of the main direction in which each exegetical method leads. Nor are they to be understood as mutually exclusive labels, as it can be argued for example, that Mk 13 consists primarily of a Jewish apocalypse (the heading of chapter 1), with Markan anti-apocalyptic editorial insertions (chapter 4). It is hoped, however, that the chapter headings *will* indicate something of the range and diversity of approaches to Mk 13 and the findings which have resulted from them, as well as give a convenient shorthand description of the basic positions outlined in the critical review which commences each chapter. The analyses which then follow each review are not intended to form a totally new approach to the exegesis of the chapter, so much as an attempt to evaluate in a more systematic and rigorous way that which has already been uncovered by previous studies. By applying a different strategy and technique within a certain exegetical method, it is possible at times to decide between the deadlocked positions of past interpretations and to move ahead on surer ground.

Some of the types of analysis which follow below necessitated a careful consideration of what might be the earliest text of the Markan eschatological discourse. Ideally, this should have involved a detailed analysis of the text-critical problems of the Gospel as a whole, and of the tendency for some manuscripts to 'Hellenise' or 'Semitise' Markan syntax. Such an undertaking would have constituted a research project in its own right. Yet a decision still had to be made on the evidence available about the more noteworthy variants in the chapter. For this reason, the variant readings listed in the Nestle-Aland[27th]/UBS[4th] text and to some extent Legg,[41] and the specific suggestions made by Kilpatrick regarding vv.9-11,[42] Gaston regarding the use of γάρ in vv.6,7b and 9b,[43] and Beasley-Murray regarding v.32,[44] were carefully evaluated. In the original

[41] *Novum Testamentum Graece* (27th revised edition), eds Barbara and Kurt Aland, Johannes Karavidopoulos, Carlo M. Martini, Bruce M. Metzger (Stuttgart 1993); *The Greek New Testament* (4th revised edition), eds Barbara and Kurt Aland, Johannes Karavidopoulos, Carlo M. Martini, Bruce M. Metzger (Stuttgart 1993); and Bruce M. Metzger, *A Textual Commentary on the Greek New Testament* (London 1975); S. C. E. Legg, *Nouum Testamentum Graece* (Oxford 1935). This last work is known to contain errors (even in its title), but has yet to be replaced by something of comparable scope.

[42] G. D. Kilpatrick, "The Gentile Mission in Mark and Mark 13:9-11", in *Studies in the Gospels,* ed D. E. Nineham (Oxford 1957), 145-158; and "Mark XIII. 9-10", *JTS* 9 (1958), 81-86.

[43] Gaston, *No Stone,* 14 and 50-53.

[44] Beasley-Murray, *A Commentary on Mark Thirteen* (London 1957), 107-8.

dissertation on which this current text is based, this evaluation occupied a full chapter. But the modest conclusions reached (differing from the Nestle-Aland²⁷ᵗʰ/UBS⁴ᵗʰ 'standard text' only in the removal of the brackets in vv.15 and 27, and in the different paragraph divisions used—see the 'Text Sheets' which follow in the chapters below), hardly justified the inclusion of that chapter here. Assuming therefore this slightly modified 'standard text' of Mk 13 as a basis, the wholistic method adopted here shall proceed as follows:

Chapter 1: Form analysis—isolating the smallest possible form critical units in the discourse and evaluating their linguistic backgrounds.

Chapter 2: NT tradition analysis—examining possible links between Mk 13 and other NT traditions and whether the unique vocabulary or unique syntax of Mk 13 sets it apart from other traditions.

Chapter 3: OT tradition analysis—examining the many OT allusions in Mk 13 and analysing their textual origins to see if they indicate a unity or diversity behind the text.

At this stage a statement on the nature of the possible traditions behind Mk 13 will be made as a basis for commencing an analysis of the indicators of redaction.

Chapter 4: Redaction analysis (i) ['editorial analysis']—re-evaluating the analyses of Markan syntax and vocabulary which have been used to indicate those words and phrases most likely to have come from the evangelist.

Chapter 5: Redaction analysis (ii) ['composition analysis']—re-examining the use of literary and theological indicators of the evangelist's work in order to indicate the 'macro-redaction' or compositional intentions of the evangelist.

Chapter 6: Religio-literary analysis—clarifying and outlining the organisational structure and intention of the discourse by a comparison with other literature of a similar genre and provenance.

Chapter 7: Socio-political analysis—using the text itself as the primary source for information about the Markan *Sitz im Leben* and for relevant background to any pre-Markan sources.

Chapter 8: Literary analysis—an investigation into the contribution of various literary approaches to the text and of what they indicate about the immediate and the wider literary contexts of Mk 13.

The sum of these analyses will then be explored in chapter 9, followed by some concluding reflections on the nature of Mark's eschatology and Christian hope. It will be noted that the sequence of exegetical methods follows the order, by and large, in which those methods were developed and applied to Mk 13, and since each one grew as a response to—and often a corrective of—its predecessor, there is great value for exegesis today in following and critically re-evaluating the same sequence.

I

A JEWISH APOCALYPSE

Major proponents: Colani (1864), Bultmann, Kümmel, and thereafter many
   scholars until Pesch (1968) and later.
Basic thesis: That Mk 13 contains part, or all, of a Jewish apocalypse rather than
   the words of the historical Jesus.
Dominant methods: Source and form criticism.
Critique: Evaluating the suggested form-critical units by a linguistic analysis of
   'Latinisms', 'Semitisms' and normal *Koine* usage.

The contribution of source and form critics to the debate about Mk 13
in the century up to 1950 has been well documented elsewhere,[1] so a brief
outline of the results and limitations of these particular approaches will
suffice in this context. The motivations behind the methods employed will
also be examined to develop an awareness of the broader theological
issues of this period, issues that inevitably shaped the reasons for the
specific work undertaken. With hindsight it may be easy for us to see the
incestuous relationships between aims and methods that call into question
many of the supposedly 'objective' findings of this era—motivations that
shaped approaches that determined results that suited the purposes of the
investigators—but this does not entirely negate the value of the work
undertaken. Every generation of interpreters has done the same. We all
'create our own texts' as we respond to the Bible in the context of our life
situations, as recent critical theory has demonstrated so forcefully.[2] The
task here is to interact with, and learn from, these interpretive creations.

---

[1] For a magisterial review and critique of the literature see Beasley-Murray, *Jesus and
the Future* (1954), 1-112, reprinted in *Last Days* (1993), 1-161, with the addition of a
review of contributions since the rise of redaction criticism, 162-349.

[2] "Criticism is an inescapably creative activity. Prior to the interpretive act, there is
nothing definitive in the text to be discovered." Janice Capel Anderson and Stephen D.
Moore, *Mark and Method*, "Introduction: The Lives of Mark", 15. Thus far has the
pendulum swung away from the idea of an objective, historically interpreted text. Not
that this is a totally new idea in itself—Bultmann always pointed out that there was no
such thing as objective, 'presuppositionless exegesis'—but as stated by Anderson and
Moore the inference is that there is *only* 'presupposition-ful exegesis'. The distinction
between text and reader is abolished because all readers are authors—we all create our
own meaning. Such a realisation, if followed absolutely, heralds the death of exegesis
and leads to hermeneutical nihilism—a pluralism without ethics—and ultimately
meaninglessness. But to operate only at the extremes of the pendulum swings and in
radical *discontinuity* with the past is to throw out the baby with the bath water, the text
with its context(s). What must be preserved is a critical interaction with the communal
context of the continuing creativity of interpretation. It is the task of each succeeding
generation of interpreters to purify/replace the bath water so that the baby can thrive.

The first detailed investigations into the origins of Mk 13 were undertaken in the wider context of the initial quest for the historical Jesus and then, after Schweitzer, the continuing debate as to whether Jesus was an apocalyptic figure or not.[3] So source- and form-critical inquiry into the origins of the eschatological discourse arose out of the problems it presented for a rational understanding of the identity and self-awareness of the historical Jesus. On the one hand, the seemingly fulfilled prophecy of Mk 13:1-2 *(ex eventu?)* and the possible implication that in Mk 13:24-27 Jesus was claiming for himself (or for a third person?) some kind of extra-terrestrial role did not sit well with those who were endeavouring to interpret Jesus within what they understood as historically verifiable categories. The use of source- and form-criticism made it possible to ask whether the most overtly apocalyptic sections of the discourse could be attributed to Jewish sources rather than to Jesus. On the other hand, conservative defenders of traditional christology were also challenged by the self-confessed ignorance of Jesus ("no-one knows the hour, not even the angels, not even the Son...", Mk 13:32), and his apparently mistaken expectation of an imminent end of some kind ("this generation shall not pass away before *all* these things happen", Mk 13:30). So again, if these sayings could be shown to be non-Jesuanic—or at least their awkward juxtaposition be attributed to the early church—then they would be less of a problem for traditional christology, at least for those who could cope with the resulting challenge to their view of Biblical inspiration.

Clearly therefore, whatever the value of any other supporting evidence that could be produced, there were compelling *theological* reasons for a broad spectrum of scholars to want to attribute certain sections of the discourse to a source other than the historical Jesus. One of the earliest and most persuasive of such attempts was made by Timothy Colani, who argued that Mk 13:5-31 consisted of a Jewish apocalypse taken over by the early church and put into the mouth of Jesus.[4] There followed many variations on this 'Little Apocalypse' theory throughout the following

Then a productive dialectic involving continuity *and* discontinuity between hermeneutical methods can be maintained.

[3] This issue still has not been satisfactorily resolved. Cf William R. Herzog, "Apocalypse Then and Now: Apocalyptic and the Historical Jesus Reconsidered", *PTR* 18 (1984), 17-25; and "The Quest for the Historical Jesus and the Discovery of the Apocalyptic Jesus", *PTR* 19 (1985), 25-39. It is interesting to note that Herzog's former neighbours in New Testament research on the West Coast of the USA (such 'Jesus Seminar' luminaries as Funk, Crossan and Mack, for example) do not share his interest in an 'apocalyptic Jesus', but prefer to locate the historical Jesus in wisdom circles—as a wandering cynic philosopher or peasant sage. Cf Robert W. Funk, Roy W. Hoover, and the Jesus Seminar, *The Five Gospels. The Search for the Authentic Words of Jesus* (New York 1993), 4: "The liberation of the non-eschatological Jesus of the aphorisms and parables from Schweitzer's eschatological Jesus is the fifth pillar of contemporary scholarship." Perhaps it is not 'Apocalyptic' but really Great Aunt Sophia that is the mother of Christian theology?

[4] T. Colani, *Jésus Christ et les croyances messianiques de son Temps,* (1864). See chapter 2 below for further comments on Colani's motivations for analysing Mk 13.

century, with the debate centering on exactly which verses could be attributed to it, and what its *Sitz im Leben* might be.

The many attempts to show that a pre-Markan apocalyptic source lay behind Mk 13 were largely unconvincing however, despite the various efforts of scholars to identify the 'mini-apocalypse' as a response to threats by Pilate or Caligula, or to locate within the chapter a Jewish apocalyptic pamphlet.[5] The inability to achieve any sort of lasting consensus on this issue was the major hindrance in the interpretation of the discourse during the first two-thirds of this century. Were Mk 13 more obviously based on a written source, then the work of source criticism could have proceeded with purpose. Alternatively, if the chapter could have been broken down and analysed entirely within the classifications of oral traditions by form-critical methods, then study could have continued at that level. But Mk 13 sits awkwardly astride the two methods of analysis, a fact that caused even more difficulties when it came to attempts to ascertain Markan redaction,[6] and which drove some scholars to seek a solution to the problem within the confines of traditio-historical analysis alone.[7]

The most convincing evidence adduced for a written source behind Mk 13 is the density of Old Testament allusions in vv.7-8,12,14-20 and 24-27, which include in v.14 the remarkable aside to the *reader*.[8] However, the classic argument of the source critics, refined by Bultmann and the form critics, that some combination of these verses constituted a Jewish apocalypse became no longer so compellingly self-evident. Bultmann was once able to claim that there was "complete unanimity among scholars that the discourse in Mk. 13:5-27 contains material from Jewish

---

[5] That Mk 13 contains a Jewish apocalypse, or part thereof, has long been the contention of form critics, but that the apocalypse takes the form of a self-contained pamphlet *(Flugblatt)*, is a particular variation of that theory. See especially the suggestions of Pesch *(Naherwartungen)* in chapter 4 below.

[6] See the summary of redactional underlining in Appendix 3, and the discussion in chapters 4 and 5 below.

[7] See chapters 2 and 3 below and the discussion of Beasley-Murray, Wenham and Hartman. The later work of Beasley-Murray looks increasingly towards a redaction-critical explanation for the particular arrangement of the traditions in Mk 13.

[8] Reference to a *reader* implies, of course, a text—either Daniel (so Matthew), the Gospel of Mark itself (so Marxsen, for example, in chapter 4 below), or a written 'tract' (so Pesch, for example, in chapter 4 below). According to M. Eugene Boring, *Sayings of the Risen Jesus. Christian Prophecy in the Synoptic Tradition* (Cambridge 1982), 191, "the only parallel in early Christian literature to the absolute ὁ ἀναγινώσκων is found in Christian prophecy, Rev 1.3, which refers to the lector who reads aloud in public worship a prophetic document written for that purpose." Whether this prophetic document read by the lector should be understood as the written source behind Mk 13 or the whole Gospel of Mark itself [as argues Ernest Best, "The Gospel of Mark: Who was the Reader?" *IBS* 11 (1989), 124-132], is another question. It is also possible that the reference could be understood at a non-literary level: "Let the one who 'reads' the sign (a situation, a pictorial representation, or a coin) note well". See my own tentative reconstruction in chapter 7 below.

apocalyptic under Christian editing",[9] and that vv.7f,12,14-22 and 24-27 are Jewish apocalyptic sayings "which comprised a context that had been preserved intact before it was worked into Mark".[10] That consensus no longer applies, and perhaps never did. Clearly there *are* Jewish apocalyptic themes and motifs present—the connection between v.14 and Daniel is such an obvious one that Matthew makes it specific (Mt 24:15)—but whether they existed *together* as an apocalypse in some pre-Markan form is not so clear. Certainly the original claim by Colani that the three terms αἱ ὠδῖνες (v.8), ἡ θλῖψις (v.19) and τὸ τέλος (vv.7,13)[11] indicate three phases of a brief Jewish apocalypse extending from vv.5-31 had to be discarded as a greater appreciation of the diversity and complexities of Jewish and Christian apocalyptic literature was gained.[12]

One of the main problems was seen to be the presence of parenetic material in the body of the 'apocalypse'—a feature not uncommon in Christian apocalypses but supposedly rare in Jewish ones.[13] There was also the difficulty of locating an appropriate conclusion to this material if, as was argued, it was grouped together before the author of Mark received it. Bultmann suggested that vv.30 and 32 (without the Christian addition οὐδὲ ὁ υἱός, εἰ μὴ ὁ πατήρ) might follow on from v.27 and form a conclusion to a Jewish apocalypse,[14] but the *triple* designation of οἱ ἄγγελοι, ὁ υἱός and ὁ πατήρ seems much more likely to have been an early Christian formulation and cannot be so easily pulled apart.[15] These

[9] R. Bultmann, *The History of the Synoptic Tradition,* ET J. Marsh from the 2nd German edition, 1931 (Oxford 1963), 400-401.

[10] Bultmann, *Synoptic Tradition,* 122.

[11] Colani, *Jésus Christ et les croyances messianiques,* 204.

[12] See, for example, Christopher Rowland, *The Open Heaven. A Study of Apocalyptic in Judaism and Early Christianity* (London 1982), particularly 9-72 and 351-357; Elisabeth Schüssler Fiorenza, "The Phenomenon of Early Christian Apocalyptic. Some Reflections on Method", in *Apocalypticism in the Mediterranean World and the Near East,* ed D. Hellholm (Tübingen 1983), 295-316; and the attempts to delineate the characteristics of Jewish and Christian apocalypses by A. Y. Collins, "The Early Christian Apocalypses" and and J. J. Collins, "The Jewish Apocalypses", *Semeia* 14 (1979), 21-121. Compared with the other apocalyptic writings, Mk 13 does not rank very high in the number of apocalyptic characteristics it contains, yet compared with the rest of Mark's Gospel it is undeniably 'more apocalyptic'. In any case, it is clearly not possible simply to isolate a number of apocalyptic features as proof of the presence of an apocalypse, Jewish or Christian. On the other hand, there are dangers in assuming that Mk 13 is in some way 'anti-apocalyptic' (see the comments of Brandenburger in chapter 6 below).

[13] J. J. Collins, "Jewish Apocalypses" and A. Y. Collins, "Early Christian Apocalypses", list 4 Ezra as the only Jewish apocalypse containing parenesis by the revealer, whereas Revelation, Hermas, Test Lord 1:1-14, and Quest Bart are listed as Christian apocalypses containing parenesis by the mediator (Mk 13 is omitted because it has no 'other worldly mediator', and is thus classed as a prophetic oracle rather than an apocalypse). But see Brandenburger's comments on parenesis in Jewish apocalypses in chapter 6 below.

[14] Bultmann, *Synoptic Tradition,* 123.

[15] Perhaps even an early trinitarian formula? Beasley-Murray (*Commentary,* 106-7) considered the suggestion (which he attributes to Lohmeyer, supported later by Fuller) that the 'angels, Son of Man, the Father' form an apocalyptic trinity, a grotesque one.

problems were compounded by the extensive debate over whether the titular and eschatological use of 'the Son of Man' originated in a Jewish or Christian milieu. Recent opinion would seem to be leaning towards regarding the 'coming and/or returning' Son of Man imagery as a *Christian* development of the Danielic motif.[16] So these difficulties, together with the absence of so many Jewish apocalyptic motifs in Mk 13, threw considerable doubt on the simple equation of parts of the chapter with a Jewish apocalypse.[17]

Not that the verdict was ever as unanimous as Bultmann claimed. Kümmel for one always argued the opposite case, claiming that the alleged apocalypse would have been "extremely short and colourless", and that therefore "the whole discourse is constructed out of detached sayings or small groups of sayings of different origin",[18] even including a frag-

But the context of early Christian revelatory experiences, visions and prophecy, might provide a more likely *Sitz im Leben* for such a formulation than has been thought. On the interchangeability of 'angel' and 'spirit' as agents of revelatory experiences in the Lukan writings and in Revelation, and on the replacement of 'angel' by 'spirit' in the writings of Paul and John, see M. Eugene Boring, *Sayings of the Risen Jesus,* 122-124; and "The Influence of Christian Prophecy on the Johannine Portrayal of the Paraclete and Jesus", *NTS* 25 (1978), 113-123.

[16] Beasley-Murray, *Jesus and the Kingdom,* 322-323: "The notion that the chapter was based on a *Jewish* document is particularly questionable, since no example of a parousia prior to Mark (still less to 1 Thessalonians 1:15ff.) has been found." By 'parousia' Beasley-Murray means here the description of the coming Son of Man in Mk 13:24-27, though it is not a Markan term. Of course the next question is whether the extension of the Danielic 'Son of Man' usage goes back to Jesus or is a later development. The argument that in the earliest Gospel traditions it stems from an Aramaic circumlocution for 'I/this man', and that it had no titular significance prior to the Gospels, seems to be gaining some credence. This would mean that the association of ὁ υἱὸς τοῦ ἀνθρώπου and the anarthrous usage in Dn 7:13 is a later Christian interpretation. See, for example, Geza Vermes, "The Present State of the 'Son of Man' Debate", in *Jesus and the World of Judaism* (Philadelphia 1984), 89-99. Note also the jubilation of Barnabas Lindars, *JTS* 37 (1986), 180, in his review of Brandenburger's *Markus 13*—"The Son of Man can thus be regarded as an internal feature of Christian apocalyptic, and there is no necessity to seek an explanation in the Jewish apocalypses. I am cheered that this is at least a possibility of the facts marshalled by Brandenburger." For some constructive responses to this position see F. J. Moloney, "The End of the Son of Man?" *DownR* 94 (1980), 280-290; and Adela Yarbro Collins, "The Origin of the Designation of Jesus as 'Son of Man'", *HTR* 80 (1987), 391-407. An excellent overview and guide to the massive amount of literature on the whole debate is given by John R. Donahue, "Recent Studies on the Origin of 'Son of Man' in the Gospels", *CBQ* 48 (1986), 484-498. Delbert Burkett, "The Nontitular Son of Man: A History and Critique", *NTS* 40 (1994), 504-521, gives a helpful overview of the proponents of the circumlocutional Son of Man, and then attempts to bury the theory once and for all. He succeeds only in reasserting that the NT usages are (almost) all titular—a conclusion which few would dispute. As he concedes (520-21), the question as to *how* the phrase became a title remains open.

[17] Many of the Jewish themes prominent in post 70 CE apocalypses are lacking, understated or arguably even inverted in Mk 13: the glorious renewal of the temple; elaborate ideas about the fate of the elect compared with the sinners; the triumph over blasphemers; and the dominant position of Israel over the Gentiles, to name a few.

[18] W. G. Kümmel, *Promise and Fulfilment* (London 1957), 98. Kümmel claimed support for his opinions from Lohmeyer and Dibelius. Later authors who pursue the fragmentary sources thesis, including Q *logia,* are Lambrecht and Beasley-Murray.

ment of Q in vv. 15f. However, Kümmel still affirmed the classification of vv.7-8,12,14-20 and 24-27 as Jewish apocalyptic ideas, which, because of the literary tradition assumed by v.14 and the contradiction of Jesus' refusal to give a 'sign' earlier in the Gospel (8:12), he attributed not to Jesus but to "primitive Jewish Christian elements of tradition".[19] By such an argument as this, Kümmel endeavoured to demonstrate that Jesus was engaged in *eschatological proclamation* rather than *apocalyptic speculation,* an exegetical conclusion which left him, along with many other interpreters of recent times, open to charges of 'anti-apocalyptic bias' according to Brandenburger.[20] In a somewhat similar manner to Kümmel, Taylor also rejected the idea of a unitary Jewish apocalyptic source behind Mk 13 in favour of a more fragmentary grouping of traditions.[21]

It is not surprising, therefore, that some scholars began to re-examine the possibility that part or parts of a Jewish *Christian* apocalypse existed within Mk 13.[22] This change of view usually implies a shift in the *Sitz im Leben* of the source from a Jewish apocalypse relating to the threat of Caligula to erect his statue in the Temple around 40 CE, to a Jewish Christian apocalypse or oracle referring to the Jewish war of 66-70 CE.[23] Such a shift in opinion is perhaps best represented by the about-face of Rudolph Pesch,[24] who was instrumental in keeping alive the theory of a Jewish apocalyptic pamphlet as a source until well into the era of redaction analysis, but who subsequently favoured the view that part of Mk 13 may be the oracle (χρησμός) mentioned by Eusebius as being the cause of the flight of the Jerusalem church to Pella during the Jewish war.[25] In such a view as this, Jewish apocalyptic elements within the discourse are still recognised, but any pre-Markan unity is generally

[19] Kümmel, *Promise and Fulfilment,* 61-62.

[20] Brandenburger, *Markus 13,* 11, footnote 5—specifically against Kümmel, amongst many others. Brandenburger's analysis is examined in chapter 6 below.

[21] See here the discussion in Beasley-Murray, *Jesus and the Future,* 106-112, where Lohmeyer is also listed as a proponent of a 'dismembered apocalypse'. Taylor suggests four sources: vv.5-8, 24-27; vv.9-13; vv.14-23; and vv.28-37. Beasley-Murray's comment on this theory has gained a wider circulation than the theory itself: "Acknowledging the interest and value of this treatment, we must yet confess that the net result is to dismember the original Little Apocalypse and put its head and legs together, minus its torso; how well it walks, we are not sure" (*Jesus and the Future,* 107-108).

[22] An example is the work of Hahn, see chapter 5 below, although such a view dates back at least in part to Timothy Colani (1864), and more specifically to E. Meyer (1921), (so Kümmel, *Promise and Fulfilment,* 96). The distinction being made here is between Christian editing of a Jewish apocalypse and an apocalypse or prophetic document originating amongst Jewish Christians.

[23] Although Boring, *Sayings,* 193, is one who argues that the discourse contains early Christian prophecy, but relates it to the threat of Caligula rather than the Jewish war.

[24] Evident in a comparison of *Naherwartungen* (1968) and *Das Markus-Evangelium* (1977). See details in the Introduction, footnote 28 above, and the discussion in chapters 4 and 5 below.

[25] See the more detailed discussion in chapter 5 below.

attributed to a Christian prophet addressing the communities in Judea just prior to, or during, the Jewish war.

Thus the results of form analysis undertaken on its own were productive, but inconclusive. The various hypothetical reconstructions of sources and their situations have been suggestive of what *might* lie behind the origin of the text, but further evidence derived by using other methodologies is required to limit the range of possibilities to a useful number. In order to provide a basis for this further evaluation and cross-checking with the results of other interpretive approaches, an attempt will be made here to state concisely the contribution of form criticism to the classification of material within Mk 13, and to the questions of the *Sitz im Leben* and 'authenticity' of each classified unit of material.

The discussion over the form of Mk 13 remains open, but now at three levels: the literary consideration of the whole chapter and its function in the Gospel; the pre-Markan form, whether written or oral, of what has often been presumed to be the major part of the chapter; and the pre-Markan form of other smaller units from the oral tradition within the chapter. Thus, whether Mk 13 as a discourse within the Gospel of Mark is best described as an apocalypse (Jewish or Christian), a teaching discourse, an exhortation or a farewell discourse, still continues to be debated. However, we will distinguish here between the literary function of the chapter as a whole (to be examined in chapter 8 below); any major pre-Markan traditions (to be explored in chapters 2 to 7); and those smaller oral forms evident within the discourse (to be examined further here). There has been widespread agreement that multiple forms of various types exist within this passage: parables, exhortations and prophetic utterances to name only a few. The disagreement has been over what is seen as the dominant pre-Markan form (if any)—the basic underlying shape—of the chapter, and the way that the author of Mark has incorporated it into the Gospel. However any judgments in this latter area should be delayed until after a closer examination of the smallest possible units within the discourse.

Constituent forms in Mk 13 and their linguistic background

There is a fair degree of unanimity about the possible classifications of smaller units within Mk 13 which follow in the table below, and which will now be described and analysed. Any groups of verses (such as vv.3-5a,24-27), which appear to defy all attempts to sub-divide into smaller form-critical units, will be placed in brackets and a decision on the difficult question of a major pre-Markan tradition deferred until after further analysis is undertaken in the following chapters. The listing of a particular saying here does not preclude its involvement in any larger pre-Markan unit. On the contrary, what is being described here are the smallest possible units that make sense in form critical terms.

For convenience and to enable comparison with the analyses in later chapters, Mk 13 shall be divided into nine major sections before being broken down into even smaller units where necessary.[26] The analyses which may help us to decide which of these sayings belonged together—and at what stage—will be commenced shortly in this chapter using a linguistic approach, but further evidence will be required from later analyses before final conclusions can be reached. Similarly, most judgments regarding the *Sitz im Leben* and historicity of these units of the discourse will be only tentative at this stage, so as not to pre-empt the results of the analyses which follow.[27] Nor will these divisions and descriptions of the text of Mk 13 be used as the assumed starting point for the division of tradition and redaction, but rather as provisional categories of text which can then be tested, amalgamated or dispensed with as required by the evidence which follows.

[26] Namely: vv.1-2,3-6,7-8,9-13,14-20,21-23,24-27,28-31,32-37. These divisions are not meant to be form critical categories, but merely a convenient way of talking more specifically about portions of the text. They form something of a compromise between the differing divisions of the Nestle-Aland and the UBS Greek Texts.

[27] In any case, it is questionable whether form analysis alone can address the question of the *Sitz im Leben* of a saying without the assistance of socio-political analysis. Oscar Cullmann was already making this very point in 1925: "the most serious defect in studies in the form-critical mode which have appeared thus far is the absence of any sociological basis." Translated and quoted by John Gager, *Kingdom and Community: The Social World of Early Christianity* (Englewood Cliffs 1975), 7. Nevertheless, an attempt will be made in the table below to summarise the classic criteria for evaluating the 'authenticity' of the Jesus tradition as they apply (or do not apply) to each saying in Mk 13. This will be done by using the code E, D, M, C, R after the text in the first column (E̶, D̶, M̶, C̶, R̶ when the criteria do not apply, and E?, D?, M?, C?, R?, when the application of the criteria is uncertain). The letters refer to the criteria as summarised conveniently by John P. Meier, *A Marginal Jew. Rethinking the Historical Jesus* (New York, 1991), 167-177; namely: 'Embarrassment' (sayings that are obviously difficult for the early church); 'Discontinuity' (sayings that can't be explained as originating within Judaism or the early church); 'Multiple attestation' (sayings that occur in a similar form in different early Christian sources); 'Coherence' (sayings that are consistent with those derived from the first three categories, E, D and M); and 'Rejection' (sayings that help to explain why Jesus might have been crucified). Meier lists a further five minor criteria (sayings including Aramaic influences, & c.), but these are even less certain as indicators. The limitations of this classic form critical approach and its tendency to a minimalist evaluation of the 'authentic' sayings of Jesus are freely acknowledged—but the information is still relevant as an indicator (though not final arbiter) of surer ground in the debate, and as an example of the exegetical results from the form-critical era. The minimalist approach is still represented in the 'Red letter Gospels' of the Jesus Seminar, who do not find any certain (red) or probable (pink) words of Jesus in Mk 13 at all, but only those in the 'Well, maybe' ('gray') category, in vv.2,21,28-29,32 and 34-36. Funk, Hoover, and the Jesus Seminar, *Five Gospels,* 108-114 (with explanations of the colour-coding, 36-37).

An outline of constituent forms within Mk 13

Verses in Mk 13	Form[28]	Comments
vv.1-2: 1 Καὶ ἐκπορευομένου αὐτοῦ ἐκ τοῦ ἱεροῦ λέγει αὐτῷ εἷς τῶν μαθητῶν αὐτοῦ, Διδάσκαλε, ἴδε ποταποὶ λίθοι καὶ ποταπαὶ οἰκοδομαί. 2 καὶ ὁ Ἰησοῦς εἶπεν αὐτῷ, Βλέπεις ταύτας τὰς μεγάλας οἰκοδομάς; οὐ μὴ ἀφεθῇ ὧδε λίθος ἐπὶ λίθον ὃς οὐ μὴ καταλυθῇ. [E,D,M,C,R (v.2b,c)] (See footnote 27) Funk/Hoover (108-9) state that over 50% of the Jesus Seminar Fellows regarded v.2 as authentic or probably authentic words of Jesus, but that the final average was less certain ('gray').	Biographical apophthegm (pronouncement story), including in vv.1-2a "a scene constructed for a prophecy handed down in the Church", Bultmann (36); and in v.2b an apocalyptic prediction. Although secondary, the scene, according to Bultmann (56), is "not just symbolic or imaginary" but uses "some moment in the life of Jesus simply as a fitting place to introduce a prophecy." Thus he concludes that the saying itself is probably from the Palestinian tradition, but the framework may be of Hellenistic origin (60). Taylor (500) thinks that v.1a may be Markan.	It is not necessary to refer to the hope of a new temple in the Messianic Age or myths based on Mandaean texts (Bultmann, 120-121) to explain the origins of the prophecy against the temple. As Bultmann eventually concludes— albeit tentatively (128, cf 125)—Mk 13:2b can be ascribed to Jesus. It is consistent with the actions of Jesus in the temple and the charges made against him at the trial, all of which seem to have caused some offence, even to the early church. It is also clear that the saying has not been modified retrospectively to make it predict more accurately the burning of the temple in 70 CE,[29] or the fall of Jerusalem (cf Lk 21:20). In terms of literary structure, vv.1-2 belong more with the events of the previous chapter forming the closing scene in the collection of temple stories. As Gill, II/47, comments: "11.1-13.2 is a geographical unit circumscribed by Jesus' initial entry into, and final exit from, the temple, while both 11.1-13.2 and 13.3-37 begin with the Mount of Olives (11.1; 13.3)."

---

[28] All references in this table to Bultmann followed by page numbers in brackets, are to *Synoptic Tradition.* Similarly, page numbers in brackets after Beasley-Murray, refer to *Last Days,* after Brandenburger to *Markus 13;* after Marxsen, to *Mark the Evangelist;* after Taylor, to *The Gospel According to Mark;* after Gill, to W. A. Gill, "The Cleansing of the Temple", vol I & II, unpublished Dr theol thesis, (Zürich 1971); after Pesch, to *Das Markus-Evangelium;* after Kelber, to Werner H. Kelber, *The Kingdom in Mark. A New Place and a New Time* (Philadelphia 1974); and after Funk/Hoover, to Funk, Hoover, and the Jesus Seminar, *The Five Gospels.*

[29] Kümmel, *Promise and Fulfilment,* 100, footnote 42, lists Schniewind, Klostermann, Lohmeyer and Taylor as some of those who have pointed out that Mk 13:2 does not need to be regarded as a *vaticinium ex eventu,* since the most obvious aspect of the temple's destruction—its burning—is not mentioned.

vv.3-6: 3 Καὶ καθημένου αὐτοῦ εἰς τὸ Ὄρος τῶν Ἐλαιῶν κατέναντι τοῦ ἱεροῦ ἐπηρώτα αὐτὸν κατ᾽ ἰδίαν Πέτρος καὶ Ἰάκωβος καὶ Ἰωάννης καὶ Ἀνδρέας. 4 Εἰπὸν ἡμῖν πότε ταῦτα ἔσται, καὶ τί τὸ σημεῖον ὅταν μέλλῃ ταῦτα συντελεῖσθαι πάντα. 5 ὁ δὲ Ἰησοῦς ἤρξατο λέγειν αὐτοῖς·

A section linking the apophthegm with the instructions to the disciples by means of a change in setting and questions put by the disciples (cf Mk 4:10-13; 7:17-23; 9:28f; 10:10-12), Bultmann (330). Taylor (501) also sees v.3f as not comprising "a self-contained narrative, but an introduction to 5-37, possibly originally to 14-20, composed by Mark himself on the basis of tradition." (cf 4:10-13; 7:17-23; 9:11-13, 28f; 10:10-12).

Not a part of the early oral tradition but a literary setting and introduction to a scholastic dialogue, possibly containing a high proportion of Markan composition in order to set up the scene (opposite and overlooking—even *over-against*—the temple), and to present the double question of the disciples. These verses are widely regarded as containing a high proportion of Markan redaction (see Appendix 3). The question itself seems to reflect a concern to understand the link between the destruction of the temple and The End—which would have been of extreme relevance around the late 60s and early 70s CE.[30]

5b Βλέπετε μή τις ὑμᾶς πλανήσῃ·

[E,Đ,M,C?,R]

Parenesis (exhortation). Bultmann (122) attributes this (together with v.6) to Christian editing of the Jewish apocalypse and the commencement of "a *vaticinium* of historical events".

The first parenetic insertion (vv.5b-6) according to Brandenburger (18). The special use of βλέπετε as a warning up to Mk 13:33—where it is replaced by γρηγορέω for the rest of the Gospel—would suggest at least some authorial responsibility for its repeated use in Mk 13.

6 πολλοὶ ἐλεύσονται ἐπὶ τῷ ὀνόματί μου λέγοντες ὅτι Ἐγώ εἰμι, καὶ πολλοὺς πλανήσουσιν.

[E,Đ,M?,C?,R?]

ἐπὶ τῷ ὀνόματί μου has long been regarded as a Christian (perhaps Markan) addition (see Taylor, 503), especially if the Ἐγώ εἰμι is understood as indicating false Messiahs in the original source.

The whole verse is regarded by Brandenburger (24, and see chapter 6 below) as redactional (cf the εἰ δυνατόν of v.22, where there is perhaps more respect for the faithfulness of the elect). But at any level there is a difficulty in explaining the parallel use of *both* Ἐγώ εἰμι and ἐπὶ τῷ ὀνόματί μου unless there are false prophets actually claiming to be Jesus, for which there is no known historical evidence (Taylor, 504).

---

[30] The listing of Andrew 'out of order' (cf Mk 1:29, the only other mention of just these four) is interesting, perhaps indicating the authority for the modification of an esoteric tradition previously associated in some circles only with the three—but more likely it is a reversion to the traditional order of the Twelve (cf Mk 3:16-18).

vv.7-8: 7 ὅταν δὲ ἀκούσητε πολέμους καὶ ἀκοὰς πολέμων, μὴ θροεῖσθε· δεῖ γενέσθαι, ἀλλ᾽ οὔπω τὸ τέλος. 8 ἐγερθήσεται γὰρ ἔθνος ἐπ᾽ ἔθνος καὶ βασιλεία ἐπὶ βασιλείαν, ἔσονται σεισμοὶ κατὰ τόπους, ἔσονται λιμοί· ἀρχὴ ὠδίνων ταῦτα.

[E,D,M?,C?,R]

A catalogue of apocalyptic woes. Regarded by many form critics as part of the original Jewish apocalypse (so Bultmann, 122; Brandenburger, 24). The ὅταν δέ link between vv.7 and 14 suggests a unity at some level since it is unlikely to be a redactional gloss in v.14 given the continued (and unusual!) use of δέ in vv.14f.

There is certainly a density of OT allusions in these verses matched only by vv.12-13,14,19,22 and 24-27 (see chapter 3 below). Since Marxsen (173) the phrases at the end of v.7 and v.8 have been widely attributed to Markan redaction. But as he has pointed out himself, v.8d at least has parallels in the Rabbinic literature where ὠδίνων is used of the 'woes of the Messiah'. Vv. 7a and 8b in particular are phrases widely used in prophetic and apocalyptic literature in general, though this in itself doesn't mean that Jesus could not have used such words.

vv.9-13: 9a βλέπετε δὲ ὑμεῖς ἑαυτούς·

[E,D,M,C?,R]

Parenesis (exhortation). Again Bultmann sees vv.9-11 and 13a as Christian additions, in this case consisting of "vaticinia from the Church's mission and persecution" (122).

The second parenetic insertion, according to Brandenburger (18). The βλέπετε theme seems to be a particular concern of the Gospel of Mark since Mt and Lk do not make use of it to anywhere near the same extent.

9b παραδώσουσιν ὑμᾶς εἰς συνέδρια καὶ εἰς συναγωγὰς δαρήσεσθε καὶ ἐπὶ ἡγεμόνων καὶ βασιλέων σταθήσεσθε ἕνεκεν ἐμοῦ εἰς μαρτύριον αὐτοῖς.

[E?,D?,M,C,R]

Brandenburger regards vv.9b-13 as oral traditions based on the sayings of Jesus and the traditions around them. Taylor (507) argues that although Markan interests will have shaped these sayings (especially v.13), there is no reason why they can't in essence be attributed to Jesus. The phrase εἰς μαρτύριον αὐτοῖς seems to be of special Markan interest (cf 1:44; 6:11) and is best translated 'as a witness *against* them'.[31]

A catalogue of missionary woes— from the Sanhedrin to the Procurator, from the Synagogue to the King. Arguably a tradition at least modified by the use of παραδίδωμι by the evangelist of John the Baptist, Jesus and the true disciple. The list of officials possibly indicates the perspective of the later Gentile mission (and especially Paul's—so Streeter, Bultmann, Lohmeyer; see Taylor, 506), but others see no compelling reason why "the historical horizon of the saying extends beyond Palestine" (so Wellhausen, Turner, and eventually Taylor himself, 506).

---

[31] So Edwin K. Broadhead, "Mk 1,44: The Witness of the Leper", *ZNW* 83 (1992), 257-265, especially 260f.

10 καὶ εἰς πάντα τὰ ἔθνη πρῶτον δεῖ κηρυχθῆναι τὸ εὐαγγέλιον.

[E,Đ,M,Ɛ,Ʀ]

Logion, rather awkwardly intruding into the flow of the text from v.9 to v.11. After some hesitation, Brandenburger (30f) regards it as having been inserted into the pre-Markan tradition.

Has been regarded as an example of a Markan parenthesis by many (so Taylor, Pryke, after C. H. Turner). Fits the mission theme of vv.9,11-13—but why is it inserted at this particular point? Kelber (118) argues strongly that "13:10 is both a redactional insertion and a redactional composition. Markan linguistic features are: the paratactic *kai,* the use of *eis* for *en,* Markan key terms *euangelion* and *keryssein,* and the use of *pas* followed by a noun."

11 καὶ ὅταν ἄγωσιν ὑμᾶς παραδιδόντες, μὴ προμεριμνᾶτε τί λαλήστε, ἀλλ᾽ ὃ ἐὰν δοθῇ ὑμῖν ἐν ἐκείνῃ τῇ ὥρᾳ τοῦτο λαλεῖτε, οὐ γάρ ἐστε ὑμεῖς οἱ λαλοῦντες ἀλλὰ τὸ πνεῦμα τὸ ἅγιον.

[E?,D?,M,C?,Ʀ]

Logion continuing the mission and 'handing over' theme of v.9. The word προμεριμνάω has not been found anywhere else except in later ecclesiastical writers, and "may be a Markan coinage" (Taylor, 508), as may the reference to ἐν ἐκείνῃ τῇ ὥρᾳ (cf 'the hour' of 13:32; 14:41 and throughout chapters 14 and 15).

Arguably reflects the situation of the very early mission of the church, but perhaps with a later—even Markan—introduction and elaboration: ἀλλ᾽ ὃ ἐὰν δοθῇ ὑμῖν ἐν ἐκείνῃ τῇ ὥρᾳ τοῦτο λαλεῖτε.

12 καὶ παραδώσει ἀδελφὸς ἀδελφὸν εἰς θάνατον καὶ πατὴρ τέκνον, καὶ ἐπανα- στήσονται τέκνα ἐπὶ γονεῖς καὶ θανατώσουσιν αὐτούς·

[E,Đ,M?,C,R?]

Logion. Claimed as part of the Jewish apocalypse by many (so Bultmann, 122).

Again, vv.12-13 contain strong allusions to the prophets. The description of family betrayal and reprisals certainly fits the period of the Jewish war (66-70 CE) in Galilee and Judea when both Romans and zealots actively persecuted the uncooperative and polarised the community (see Myers, 334). It could also reflect the challenge to patriarchal family structures of very early Christianity.

13a καὶ ἔσεσθε μισούμενοι ὑπὸ πάντων διὰ τὸ ὄνομά μου.

[E?,Đ,M,C,R?]

Seen by Bultmann (122) as a Christian addition because of the way the person of Jesus is introduced into the dialogue.

Suffering for the sake of 'the Name' would seem to reflect the persecutions suffered by Christians on mission in the generation after Jesus. Thus Taylor (510) concludes that "we are near the actual words of Jesus in 9,11, but a greater distance from them in 12f."

13b ὁ δὲ
ὑπομείνας εἰς
τέλος οὗτος
σωθήσεται.

[E,Đ,M,C,Ʀ]

Seen by Taylor (510) as a
re-casting of Lk 21:19 in the
light of contemporary
apocalyptic (cf 4 Ezr 6:25).

A better link can be made with Mic
7:7 (see chapter 3 below), and
therefore there is no need to suggest
that Mk 13:13b is later than Lk
21:19.

vv.14-20:

14 Ὅταν δὲ ἴδητε τὸ βδέλυγμα τῆς
ἐρημώσεως ἑστηκότα ὅπου οὐ δεῖ,
ὁ ἀναγινώσκων νοείτω, τότε οἱ ἐν
τῇ Ἰουδαίᾳ φευγέτωσαν εἰς τὰ ὄρη,
15 ὁ δὲ ἐπὶ τοῦ δώματος μὴ
καταβάτω μηδὲ εἰσελθάτω ἆραί τι
ἐκ τῆς οἰκίας αὐτοῦ, 16 καὶ ὁ εἰς
τὸν ἀγρὸν μὴ ἐπιστρεψάτω εἰς τὰ
ὀπίσω ἆραι τὸ ἱμάτιον αὐτοῦ. 17
οὐαὶ δὲ ταῖς ἐν γαστρὶ ἐχούσαις
καὶ ταῖς θηλαζούσαις ἐν ἐκείναις
ταῖς ἡμέραις. 18 προσεύχεσθε δὲ
ἵνα μὴ γένηται χειμῶνος· 19
ἔσονται γὰρ αἱ ἡμέραι ἐκεῖναι
θλῖψις οἵα οὐ γέγονεν τοιαύτη ἀπ᾽
ἀρχῆς κτίσεως ἣν ἔκτισεν ὁ θεὸς
ἕως τοῦ νῦν καὶ οὐ μὴ γένηται. 20
καὶ εἰ μὴ ἐκολόβωσεν κύριος τὰς
ἡμέρας, οὐκ ἂν ἐσώθη πᾶσα σάρξ.
ἀλλὰ διὰ τοὺς ἐκλεκτοὺς οὓς
ἐξελέξατο ἐκολόβωσεν τὰς
ἡμέρας.

[E?,D?,M,C?,R][32]

Widely regarded
as the core of the
Jewish
apocalypse—often
together with
vv.21-22 (so
Bultmann, 122).
Some would argue
for independent Q
logia in vv.15-16
(cf Lk 17:31), so
Kümmel,
Lambrecht,[33] and
Beasley-Murray
(407, 417).

The analysis of unique
syntax in chapter 2 below
indicates that these verses
belong together as a unit,
rather than as a compilation
of separate sayings.
Beasley-Murray (407)
admits that the Markan
context of flight is more
appropriate for vv.15-16
than the Lukan context of
the expectation of the
parousia (Lk 17:31f), but
still insists that they "did
not originally occur in
sequence after 13:14"—yet
the string of imperative
verbs from v.14 to v.16
suggests a very cohesive
prophetic utterance leading
into the prophetic 'woe' of
v.17. The scriptural
allusions are undeniably
scattered, but the cohesion
of the prophetic rhetoric is
inescapable.

---

[32] The limitations of the classic form-critical criteria for indicating authenticity are
clearly evident in this example. Whether the sayings in vv.14-20 were an **E**mbarrassment
to—or **D**iscontinuous with—the early church or not depends on whether they are dated
before the fall of Jerusalem or after. The words *could* have contributed to the **R**ejection
and crucifixion of Jesus—but then they could equally well represent the words of a
Christian and/or Jewish prophet of the 60's (cf the prophecy against the temple by Jesus
son of Ananus, cited by Josephus, *War* 6.301). The oracle clearly can be interpreted as
Coherent with the prophecy of 13:2, and these anti-temple sentiments are attested in
general on **M**ultiple occasions in different sources if the charges against Jesus at his trial
in John and the Synoptics are considered. We suggest that the words are consistent with
the Jesus tradition (hence their location at this point), but for reasons which will become
more apparent later, that they come in this form from a (Jewish-)Christian prophet during
the Jewish war. That is, since they were spoken in the name of the Lord and were
verified by subsequent events, they were judged to be 'authentic words of the *risen*
Jesus'.

[33] Kümmel, *Promise and Fulfilment*, 98, footnote 39; Lambrecht's analysis is
summarised in *Redaktion*, 257f. This viewpoint is examined more closely in chapter 4
below.

vv.21-23: 21 καὶ τότε ἐάν τις ὑμῖν εἴπῃ, Ἴδε ὧδε ὁ Χριστός, Ἴδε ἐκεῖ, μὴ πιστεύετε· 22 ἐγερθήσονται γὰρ ψευδόχριστοι καὶ ψευδοπροφῆται καὶ δώσουσιν σημεῖα καὶ τέρατα πρὸς τὸ ἀποπλανᾶν, εἰ δυνατόν, τοὺς ἐκλεκτούς. [E,D,M,C?,R] Funk/Hoover (112) argue that the rejection of speculation by Jesus in the sayings in Lk 17:20-21 and Thom 113:2-4 are more likely to be authentic than the Markan version, though the Jesus Seminar gave v.21 a 'gray' rating.	Independent logia, joined together in the pre-Markan tradition according to Brandenburger (24), although many include these verses within the source (see Bultmann, 122, and Hahn, examined in chapter 5 below). Brandenburger argues (24) that the situation of v.22 does not correlate with that of the original source (vv.7-8,14-20,24-27), and he points out (23f), that the use of οἱ ἐκλεκτοί in v.22 could be a Markan way of integrating this parenetic insertion with the preceding verses. A close dependence on Q (Lk 17:23, supported by Lambrecht, 257, Beasley-Murray, 392f) is rejected by Brandenburger because in Mk 13:22 ὁ χριστός is compared with the ψευδόχριστος of the traditional logion in v.21, whereas both Mt 24:27 and Lk 17:24 show a contrasting christology (Son of Man vs. Messianic pretenders) to that of Mt 14:26 and Lk 17:23 respectively.	The analysis of syntax in chapter 2 below reveals that v.21 has as high a proportion of unique sequences as vv.14-20, perhaps suggesting that it comes from the same source. Otherwise the arguments of Brandenburger regarding v.22 are convincing. Note also the view of Taylor (515) that "the two sayings differ completely in character and probably in origin", though he goes on to argue that v.21 is a genuine saying of Jesus (because of the Q parallel in Lk 17:23), whereas v.22 (like vv.19f) resembles secondary apocalyptic and homiletical writings. The nature of the relationship with vv.5b-6 is a crucial consideration here. Are the same groups of false prophets and pseudo-christs the target of each warning? This question cannot be answered on form-critical grounds alone, but must await a consideration of the results of redaction and socio-political analyses. However the relevance of these verses for those caught up in the events of the Jewish War is obvious—since messianic possibilities featured strongly throughout the revolt and the fall of Masada in 74 CE, and even on into the Bar Kochba rebellion early in the next century.
23a ὑμεῖς δὲ βλέπετε· [E,Đ,M,C,Ɍ]	Parenesis (exhortation) addressed directly to the four disciples again (2nd person plural) whereas all of vv.14-22 is in the third person except for ἴδητε (v.14) and ὑμῖν (v.21).	Possible Markan insertion, given the use of βλέπετε throughout the chapter. Thus the 'elect' of vv.20,22 are "not necessarily identical with those addressed[by Mark] in v.23" (Beasley-Murray, 422, footnote 131).
23b προείρηκα ὑμῖν πάντα. [E,Đ,M,C,Ɍ]	An element of the testamentary genre, Brandenburger (13). Taylor (516) points out that προείρηκα is "regularly used of prophetic announcements" (cf Ac 1:16; Rm 9:29) and "of teaching previously given" (cf 2 Co 7:3; 8:2).	Arguably indicates the Markan *Sitz im Leben* (so Pesch, Brandenburger), because these words are used to reassure the hearer that all that has recently occurred has been within the knowledge of Jesus. Understandable as a written codicil to affirm the validity of a prophetic utterance at the conclusion of the prophetic process.

vv.24-27:

24 Ἀλλὰ ἐν
ἐκείναις ταῖς
ἡμέραις μετὰ τὴν
θλῖψιν
ἐκείνην—
ὁ ἥλιος
σκοτισθήσεται,
καὶ ἡ σελήνη οὐ
δώσει τὸ φέγγος
αὐτῆς,
25 καὶ οἱ
ἀστέρες ἔσονται
ἐκ τοῦ οὐρανοῦ
πίπτοντες,
καὶ αἱ δυνάμεις
αἱ ἐν τοῖς
οὐρανοῖς
σαλευθήσονται.
26 καὶ τότε
ὄψονται τὸν υἱὸν
τοῦ ἀνθρώπου
ἐρχόμενον ἐν
νεφέλαις μετὰ
δυνάμεως πολλῆς
καὶ δόξης. 27 καὶ
τότε ἀποστελεῖ
τοὺς ἀγγέλους
καὶ ἐπισυνάξει
τοὺς ἐκλεκτοὺς
αὐτοῦ ἐκ τῶν
τεσσάρων
ἀνέμων ἀπ'
ἄκρου γῆς ἕως
ἄκρου οὐρανοῦ.

[E,Ð,M?,Є,R (cf
14:62)]

Regarded as part of the Jewish apocalypse by many commentators (so, for example, Bultmann, 122). The verses clearly belong together as a literary unit (with the exception of the opening phrases, Ἀλλά ... ἐκείνην) and seem to be distinctly Septuagintal in content (see chapter 3 below). Together with vv.7-8,14f, these verses are often regarded as 'high apocalyptic'—but the images of vv.24,25 are common in *prophetic* writings (Is 13:10; 34:4; Jl 2:10; 3/4:15-16; Ez 32:7-8, and so on—see chapter 3 below) where they refer to theophanies or manifestations of God in history, rather than to the end of history itself. The running together of scriptural allusions in vv.24-27 is not typical of the incisive use of scripture by Jesus elsewhere in the Gospels (so also Beasley-Murray, 423), which suggests a later compiler.

Perhaps the most clearly identifiable section of the whole discourse—both because of its content and its manner of composition (see the analysis of syntax in chapter 2 below). The grouping of this section by many commentators with (typically) vv.7,8,14-20, as an apocalypse describing '*The* End' overlooks the prophetic origins of the images. As Beasley-Murray (426) states so forcefully, "[t]he darkening of the sun and moon is not remotely connected with the notion of their destruction, nor the shaking of the powers of heaven with their disappearance. The falling stars alone could tally with such notions, but not in the light of Isaiah 34." However Beasley-Murray still insists that vv.24-27 are a "description of the parousia" (422) and that they represent "the divine intervention for judgment and salvation" (425)—although *not* including the destruction of the world, not even at Mk 13:31 (451). If vv.24-27 reflect a Markan or pre-Markan situation, the exact reference of the 'they' (v.26) and the '*his* elect' (v.27) become critical in the interpretation of the discourse and its possible connections with 'The End', the 'parousia' (a word not used in Mark), or any other event or sequence of events. The arguments of R. T. France (amongst others) that this passage contains "the language of enthronement, not of parousia"[34] need to be seriously considered.

---

[34] R. T. France, *Divine Government. God's Kingship in the Gospel of Mark* (London 1990), 75. See the discussion in chapters 7 and 9 below.

vv.28-31:
28 Ἀπὸ δὲ τῆς
συκῆς μάθετε
τὴν παραβολήν·
ὅταν ἤδη ὁ
κλάδος αὐτῆς
ἀπαλὸς γένηται
καὶ ἐκφύῃ τὰ
φύλλα,
γινώσκετε ὅτι
ἐγγὺς τὸ θέρος
ἐστίν. 29 οὕτως
καὶ ὑμεῖς, ὅταν
ἴδητε ταῦτα
γινόμενα
γινώσκετε ὅτι
ἐγγύς ἐστιν ἐπὶ
θύραις.

[E?,Ð,M,C,ℝ]
Funk/Hoover
(113) argue that
the Lukan setting
might be more
original (Lk
21:31), since it
uses the budding
fig-tree as an
image of the
coming Kingdom.

Parable or similitude (with application). Bultmann regards the application as secondary (173), but has no objection to the originality of the similitude itself (123), though he finally suggests it derives from Jewish tradition (125). Although the symbol of the fig tree = Israel has traditional roots, it is consistent with the use of the fig tree in Mk 11:12f, and the 'embarrassing' (for some in the early church, at least) judgment of the temple by Jesus. It may well be a re-use of a fragment of the 'acted' parable in Mk 11:12f (cf Lk 13:6-9; 21:31).

There are strong grounds for suspecting that the parable has been taken over from another context (such as a parable of the Kingdom, as Lohmeyer with support from Taylor, 520, suggests). The introduction and setting do appear to have been truncated, and the application would be even more imprecise without the surrounding context. As it stands it is open to interpretation as to what the ταῦτα refers to, and as to whether 'he', 'she' or 'it' is near. The context suggests 'it' = 'the summer', the time of harvest for the summer fruits, but this is not the interpretation favoured by most commentators, who regard it as an allusion to the 'parousia', which follows the cosmic upheavals of vv.24-25. But a budding fig-tree and signs of summer seem "inappropriate to symbolize the fall of the stars from heaven and the failure of the sun", Funk/Hoover (113). If, however, vv.24-27 are interpreted as suggested above, the summer harvest language is entirely appropriate.

30 ἀμὴν λέγω
ὑμῖν ὅτι οὐ μὴ
παρέλθῃ ἡ γενεὰ
αὕτη μέχρις οὗ
ταῦτα πάντα
γένηται.

[E!,D?,M,C,R?]

Eschatological pronouncement with ἀμήν formula (Kee, 102). Often regarded as a variant of Mk 9:1 adapted for this context (so Bultmann, 123). Bultmann also argues that vv.30 and 32 may have originally followed v.27 and formed the conclusion to the Jewish apocalypse. But if v.30 is a re-working of a Jesuanic saying (Mk 9:1), then it is more likely that v.31 would be added by a catch-word process at that same stage to form an appropriate conclusion to a prophetic utterance.

We note here the Markan use of the ἀμήν formula to *conclude* a section of teaching with a strong emphasis—as, for example, in 3:28; 8:12; 9:1,41(?); 10:15,29; 12:43; 14:9,25,30 (but not so, in 11:23 and 14:18). Kee (102) categorises the thirteen ἀμήν sayings as follows: eschatological pronouncements (9:1; 10:29; 13:30; 14:25); 'pronouncements of sacred law' (after Käsemann—3:28f; 9:41; 10:15; 11:23); predictions and solemn pronouncements (8:12; 12:43; 14:9,18,30). In the first category the ἀμήν saying is all but final in 9:1; 10:29 and 14:25, which suggests that v.30 (together with v.31) may have served the same function originally, and formed the conclusion to a prophetic discourse or question/answer exchange.

31 ὁ οὐρανὸς καὶ
ἡ γῆ
παρελεύσονται,
οἱ δὲ λόγοι μου
οὐ μὴ
παρελεύσονται.

[E,Đ,M,Є,Ɽ]

One of the 'I'-sayings,
which because of the
specific and often
retrospective focus on the
person and importance of
Jesus, Bultmann regards as
Christian formulations
(123,151). It is unlikely to
be part of a Jewish tradition
because the speaker would
then be God (123), and the
'I'-sayings generally seem
to have come from the
Hellenistic churches anyway
(so Bultmann, 163). The
gravity of the 'my words'
affirmation would certainly
form an appropriate
conclusion to a prophecy
spoken in the name of the
Lord, and acts as a
deliberate counterfoil to
those communities where
the *Torah* takes the place of
the eternal words of Jesus
(cf Mt 5:18; Lk 16:17).

Clearly joined by key-word
association in the pre-Markan
tradition to affirm the preceding
prophetic utterance (v.30 and
whatever originally preceded it). It is
usually assumed now that the cosmic
dimensions of this verse (heaven and
earth passing away) equate with
vv.24-25 (sun and moon darkened,
stars falling, powers shaken)—a
view refuted by Beasley-Murray,
(426), or that it is merely hyperbole
emphasising the truth of the latter
half of the verse (so Beasley-
Murray, 451). But the possibility
should be considered that in the
Markan restructuring of the
discourse, the emphatic
παρελεύσονται (*'will* pass away')
of v.31 also marks the introduction
of a new dimension of events, in that
it no longer concludes the discourse.
That is, that the eternal 'my words'
of Jesus might refer at least as much
to vv.32f as to what precedes v.31.

vv.32-37:
32 Περὶ δὲ τῆς
ἡμέρας ἐκείνης ἢ
τῆς ὥρας οὐδεὶς
οἶδεν, οὐδὲ οἱ
ἄγελλοι ἐν
οὐρανῷ οὐδὲ ὁ
υἱός, εἰ μὴ ὁ
πατήρ.

[E!!,D,Ṃ,C,R]
Funk/Hoover
(114) doubt the
authenticity of
'son' and the
implied reference
to 'the End'—but
some form of the
saying *may* be
Jesuanic if it refers
to the temple.

Bultmann (123) regards this
as a Jewish saying—
perhaps even the conclusion
of the Jewish apocalypse—
without the Christian ending
οὐδὲ ὁ υἱός, εἰ μὴ ὁ πατήρ.
But it is difficult to see this
denial of absolute
knowledge to the Son as a
Christian *addition,*
especially as the textual
history of that phrase shows
that it has more often been a
Christian *deletion!* (See
Taylor, 522).

As an originally independent saying,
Taylor (523) is correct to point out
that the most obvious point of
reference for the verse is the Day of
Divine Judgment, though most
commentators take it as indicating
'those days' of the 'parousia', which
term is uncritically applied to the
events of vv.24-27. The saying in
some form may well have originated
with the historical Jesus, such has
been the embarrassment it has
caused to those interested in a high
christology—though it also contains
the absolute use of 'the Son', which
raises questions for those at the other
end of the christological spectrum.

33a βλέπετε,
ἀγρυπνεῖτε·

[E,Đ,Ṃ,C,Ɽ]

Parenesis (exhortation).
Bultmann sees all of v.33 as
a "marcan editorial
formulation" (174).

Possible Markan insertion given the
use of βλέπετε throughout the
chapter, with ἀγρυπνεῖτε used as a
transition to γρηγορεῖτε, which
occurs exclusively from this point on
in the Gospel.

33b οὐκ οἴδατε γὰρ πότε ὁ καιρός ἐστιν. [E,D,M,C,R]	An editorial exhortation repeating the sentiments of v.31 and introducing the parable which follows.	Appears to be redundant after the strong denial of knowledge in v.31, but is understandable as a redactional emphasis on the καιρός.
34 ὡς ἄνθρωπος ἀπόδημος ἀφεὶς τὴν οἰκίαν αὐτοῦ καὶ δοὺς τοῖς δούλοις αὐτοῦ τὴν ἐξουσίαν, ἑκάστῳ τὸ ἔργον αὐτοῦ, καὶ τῷ θυρωρῷ ἐνετείλατο ἵνα γρηγορῇ. [E,D,M,C,R] 35 γρηγορεῖτε οὖν, οὐκ οἴδατε γὰρ πότε ὁ κύριος τῆς οἰκίας ἔρχεται, ἢ ὀψὲ ἢ μεσονύκτιον ἢ ἀλεκτοροφωνίας ἢ πρωΐ, 36 μὴ ἐλθὼν ἐξαίφνης εὕρῃ ὑμᾶς καθεύδοντας. [E,D,M,C,R] The Jesus Seminar rate vv.34-36 as 'gray' (possibly from Jesus in some other form). Funk/Hoover (114).	Parable (containing parenesis in 35a), which appears to have elements of Lk 12:36f and Mt 24:43f mixed in it (see Bultmann, 119, and the critique in chapter 2 below of Wenham, who argues that Mark has conflated the parables in Matthew and Luke). It is thus regarded as an "unorganic composition" by Bultmann (119), with v.34 possibly "an element from the ancient tradition" (174) but perhaps the whole of v.35 a secondary formulation (see Appendix 3 for those who consider it redactional). The four Roman watches were widely known and used throughout the empire, but possibly not amongst the lower echelons of Galilean society (see further under 'Latinisms' below).	Taylor (523) argues that the change from ἄνθρωπος in v.34 to ὁ κύριος τῆς οἰκίας "reveals the standpoint of Mark's day" with the church "in daily expectation of the return of the Lord". He sees vv.34-36 together as a "homiletical echo of several parables" (Taylor, 524). However, the idea of 'daily expectancy of the Lord's return' seems to be modified somewhat by the way that the four Roman watches of the night are also used to mark the intervals of the passion story (see chapter 6 below). This seems to imply that the 'hour of the master's return' may be existentially encountered in moments of trial and testing—and not just in some kind of 'second coming'. This would fit well as a later interpretation of the emphasis on the allocation of work and responsibilities in the earliest level of the parable in v.34. That is, the master returns in the midst of the normal round of daily responsibilities.
37 ὃ δὲ ὑμῖν λέγω πᾶσιν λέγω, γρηγορεῖτε. [E,D,M,C,R]	Parenesis (exhortation). Regarded by Bultmann (130, along with 13:23,33) as being a transitional passage produced by the evangelist. As such vv.23,33 and 37 do not have the same gravity as the 'I'-saying in v.31 (151).	The final part of the redactional framework of the discourse, according to Brandenburger. Like v.23, it bears the marks of a conscious reflection on the content of the discourse and of its application to a wider audience.

Which of these smaller units were linked in pre-Markan traditions must remain an open question for the moment. It is the bracketed sections of the chapter, namely vv.7-8,14-20 and 24-27, which have most commonly been classified by source and form critics as some kind of apocalypse, largely on the grounds of the high incidence of apocalyptic elements in these verses. But it is apparent that it is no longer valid to group parts of Mk 13 together as part of an apocalyptic source merely on topical grounds, following the more positive appreciation of the diversity and repeated reinterpretation of such literature in recent times. Some more systematic means of determining the background of the various sections of the discourse and any possible pre-Markan groupings is required, such as an investigation into their linguistic origins, the occurrence of any unique vocabulary or syntax and any patterns to their use of the Old Testament traditions. All of these approaches will be undertaken in due course in the chapters which follow. But as an analysis of linguistic influences in particular might help to shed some light on which logia belonged together at different stages in the tradition, and perhaps indicate something of their possible origins, it is appropriate to undertake it here as an extension of the form critical approach.

To attempt to trace the linguistic influences on the Greek text of the Gospel of Mark—indeed even for just one chapter—is a dissertation in itself.[35] This is largely because the style of the Greek in the Gospel of Mark is so uneven. It has been common in the past to attribute this fact either to the poor Greek of the author or to the hypothesis that the Gospel was translated from Aramaic sources.[36] However recent studies making use of the evidence available from other *Koine* Greek writings of the first century, both literary and non-literary, have led to a more balanced assessment of the linguistic influences on the style of the Gospel of Mark.[37] What follows is merely an attempt to gather together the

---

[35] The most comprehensive attempt in this area is undoubtedly Maloney, *Semitic Interference*, which surveys about two-thirds of the alleged Semitisms listed by W. F. Howard in the Appendix: "Semitisms in the New Testament", in James Hope Moulton and Wilbert Francis Howard, *A Grammar of New Testament Greek, vol II, Accidence and Word Formation* (Edinburgh 1920/1956), 413-485. Maloney does not examine those alleged Semitisms listed by Howard involving the use of the verb, adverbs, prepositions, conjunctions or particles.

[36] To mix elements from different languages "was regarded as a sign of semi-education and bad style", [M. Hengel, *Studies in the Gospel of Mark* (London 1985), 137, endnote 163]. Hengel cites the scorn poured on such writings by Cicero, Horace and Lucian. Other commentators have also been less than flattering when describing Mark's style: "unpretentious, verging on the vernacular" [N. Turner, in James Hope Moulton, *A Grammar of New Testament Greek, vol IV, Style* (Edinburgh 1976), 11— betraying also Turner's underlying distaste for 'the vernacular', as if it might contaminate Holy Scripture! Cf footnote 45 below]. The theory that Mark was translated from the Aramaic gained considerable support early this century and was developed by C. C. Torrey and M. J. Lagrange amongst others.

[37] Again, Maloney, *Semitic Interference,* is a good example. The ongoing task of sifting through the evidence as it comes to hand is presented in detail in G. H. R. Horsley's series *New Documents Illustrating Early Christianity,* vols 1-4 (Macquarie University 1976-79). The term *Koine* Greek is used here rather than Hellenistic Greek, because as Horsley points out [*New Documents Illustrating Early Christianity,* vol. 5 (Macquarie University 1989), 41] the latter is a precisely defined historical period concluding at 1 BCE, whereas *Koine* Greek can be applied to the whole period from Alexander's conquests to the rise of Byzantine Greek in the 5th century of the common era.

evidence concerning these linguistic influences on Mk 13, and then to critically evaluate the relevance of such material for understanding the origins of the constituent forms of the discourse.

Similar approaches have been made in the past with the intention of detecting literary sources in the Gospel of Mark, but with inconclusive results—leading to conclusions similar to that of Nigel Turner:

> ...the attempt has never succeeded because the various stylistic features cut right across the boundaries of any literary divisions that have yet been suggested. In consequence, it seems that although there may have been literary sources to begin with a final redactor has so obliterated all traces of them that Mark is in the main a literary unity from the beginning to 16[8].[38]

To use linguistic influences as the *sole* criterion for determining the existence of literary sources or the nature of oral traditions behind the text would be as inappropriate as ignoring them altogether because they don't coincide with supposed literary divisions within the text. Certainly on one level the Gospel of Mark is a 'literary unity'—it exists as a whole text in its own right and must ultimately be interpreted that way. To claim, however, that the final redactor of the Gospel has 'obliterated all traces' of any sources is to suggest that the Gospel has a literary *uniformity* rather than unity—a stylistic homogeneity that even Turner himself goes on to implicitly deny by giving examples of different stylistic influences on the text. It is essential that the evidence of these stylistic variations be taken into account in any attempt to interpret the development of the text. Certainly not as the *only* means of differentiating between written and oral sources, or tradition and redaction, or Semitic and Hellenistic origins—but as an important corroborating factor in any such assessments.

Thus the analysis of linguistic influences on the style of Mk 13 which follows is but the first step in evaluating the evidence for any such divisions within the text. It is recognised that any one author at any stage of the composition of an eclectic text like Mk 13 may deliberately or subconsciously copy the style of another part of the text. Yet it is maintained that this process is not so entirely random or haphazard as to make the cloak of 'multitextuality' an impenetrable barrier. Rather, the patterns which may be discerned through a close examination of the linguistic influences of the text are a necessary first step in the unravelling of the processes of interpretation and reinterpretation. A specific delineation of the origin of every part of the text will not be possible of course, but some broader parameters may be established through the description of general tendencies in the text which will form an essential basis for further investigations. Such parameters may work in both a positive and a negative sense, by illuminating some possible text divisions and by eliminating others.

[38] N. Turner, *Style,* 11.

Possible Latinisms in Mk 13

Verse in Mk 13	Description and References[39]	Comments and Conclusions
2,6,9 (twice), **10,11,12** (thrice) **13,16,19,20,21** **22,24,25** (twice) **26,27**(twice), **28,34** (twice)	Parataxis—coordination of independent clauses and commencement of sentences with καί. See further details under Semitic Interference below. N. Turner argues that asyndeta (and parataxis) may be "as much a Latinism as an Aramaism, especially perhaps when it occurs in Greek books written in Rome", and gives the examples of the Acts of Pilate and the Shepherd of Hermas.[40]	Despite Turner's claim, there is *at least* as much likelihood of Semitic influence in this area of parataxis, so the question of a Roman provenance for Mark must be settled on other grounds. Maloney concludes that the extent of the use of καί in Mark indicates Hebrew and/or Aramaic influence at some stage.[41]
9 ἐπὶ ἡγεμόνων	ἡγεμών = procurator (eg Pilatus, Felix, Festus) is a translation of official Latin terminology of the chancellery. BDF §5 (3), note 6: a case of "good Greek official terminology ... used with precision for analogous Roman offices."	Correct Greek term for a Roman administrative position. Not necessarily a Latinism.
17 οὐαί	Prophetic style = Latin *vae* (cf Epictetus), but also = the LXX transcription of the Hebrew y/h, y/a BDF §4 (2)	Consistent with the cry of woe of both Hebrew and Latin prophecy. Not necessarily a Latinism.
18 ἵνα μὴ γένηται χειμῶνος	Use of ἵνα instead of the infinitive. BDF §388: "Latin has probably encouraged the use of ἵνα or ὅπως for the inf." There it is also noted that there was a tendency for this to happen with ὅπως in the Greek language from classical times. In any case, it is clearly not due to Semitic influence, since: "In the LXX ἵνα instead of the infinitive is rare because Hebr. favoured the latter."	Possible Latin influence, though also clearly a long-term trend within the evolution of the Greek language.

---

[39] The abbreviation BDF (followed by a paragraph number) refers to F. Blass and A. Debrunner, *A Greek Grammar of the New Testament and Other Early Christian Literature,* ET and ed by Robert W. Funk (Chicago 1961/1967).

[40] N. Turner, *Style,* 30.

[41] Maloney, *Semitic Interference,* 67. See further in the table listing Semitisms below.

34 ἵνα γρηγορῇ	Use of ἵνα instead of the infinitive (see v.18 above).	Possible Latin influence, though also clearly a long-term trend within the evolution of the Greek language.
35 ἢ ὀψὲ ἢ μεσονύκτιον ἢ ἀλεκτοροφωνίας ἢ πρωΐ	Four Roman watches listed (ὀψέ = 6–9pm; μεσονύκτιον = 9–12pm; ἀλεκτοροφωνίας = 12–3am; πρωΐ = 3–6am) rather than the traditional three Jewish ones (as in Jud 7:19).[42] The fourth watch (περὶ τετάρτην φυλακὴν τῆς νυκτός) is also mentioned in Mk 6:48, and the four three-hour watches seem to be an integral part of Mark's Passion account.[43] The question as to how far the Roman divisions had become part of Jewish custom by the first century is unclear.	Clearly indicative of Roman custom, though it may also have been the practice in Jewish circles in Palestine by the time of Jesus, and/or throughout the Roman Provinces by the time of the writing of the Gospel of Mark.

The presence of these possible Latinisms in Mk 13 is insufficient evidence for the demarcation of any sayings or the identification of their origins. In each instance it is apparent that there are alternative explanations for the occurrence of the terms, and in any case the Latin influence is no more than what could be expected in any Greek document written within the Roman Empire in the first century. On the basis of a linguistic analysis of this chapter alone it would be difficult to argue for any *necessary* connection with Rome as the source of any part of the discourse or as the location of its compilation. Whether this holds true as an explanation for the occurrences of Latinisms throughout the rest of the Gospel of Mark is another matter, and the arguments of Martin Hengel, amongst others, in support of Rome as its place of origin will need to be examined more closely below.[44]

A more promising area of investigation is the possible presence of Semitisms within Mk 13. Here the main problem is the over-estimation of Semitic influence by some scholars, particularly those who have argued that the New Testament was written in a distinctive Greek dialect sometimes referred to as 'Jewish-Greek'.[45] For with the benefit of com-

---

[42] So Beasley-Murray, *Commentary,* 117.

[43] See the discussion in Geddert, *Watchwords,* 94f.

[44] Hengel, *Studies,* 28f. Hengel presents the most coherent arguments of recent times for the traditional view that the Gospel of Mark originated in Rome. Part of his argument is to point to the number of latinisms throughout the Gospel (*Studies,* 29). See further the discussion of the *Sitz im Leben* of the Markan community in chapter 7 below.

[45] See for example the views of N. Turner, *Grammatical Insights into the NT* (Edinburgh 1965), 183: "Intense study of vocabulary and syntax seem to me to establish that there was a distinguishable dialect of spoken and written Jewish Greek." Also Matthew Black, "Second Thoughts IX. The Semitic Element in the New Testament", *ExpTim* 77 (1965-66), 21: "Biblical Greek is a peculiar language, the language of a peculiar people." Black supports this contention with a cross-reference to N. Turner's

parison with other *Koine* documents of the same period, many features thought previously to have been Semitisms have been found to occur elsewhere in the vernacular Greek of the day. More credence will therefore be given in the following analysis to those who evaluate the linguistic influences on the New Testament against the wider body of literature of that era. This means there will be a heavy, though not uncritical, reliance on the work of Elliott C. Maloney in particular, and on the prior work of W. F. Howard, in assessing the Semitic influences on the Greek of Mk 13.

Semitic interference in Mk 13

Verse in Mk 13	Description and References[46]	Comments and Conclusions
1 Καὶ ἐκπορευομένου	Starting a paragraph with Καί (as do 80 out of 88/89 paragraphs in Mk). Maloney (68, see also 202, & note 72): "Because Mark consistently uses καί to introduce a new paragraph, and because he does use the normal Greek particle δέ in six of the remaining eight or nine paragraphs where he does not use καί, his use of introductory καί is most likely a Hebraism, probably taken over from the style of the OG, although at some places it may represent Aramaic thinking or translation."	[G–, H4, A3, OG3: Semitism: H, A or OG].[47] Hebrew or Aramaic influence—but most probably through imitation of the Greek Old Testament.

use of the quaint phrase "Holy Ghost Language" [in James Hope Moulton, *A Grammar of New Testament Greek, vol III, Syntax* (Edinburgh 1963), 9]. Compare this with the assessment of J. H. Moulton's position by W. F. Howard: "His main concern was to support Deissmann in his contention that the New Testament was written in no Judaeo-Greek jargon but in the *lingua franca* of the first century." Moulton/Howard, *Grammar II*, 413. Howard goes on to claim, however, that Moulton showed an increasing awareness of the importance of the Semitic background to the NT, whilst maintaining that many of these constructions fell "within the range of late vernacular Greek" (*Grammar II*, 414). For a detailed evaluation of the whole debate, see Horsley, "The Fiction of 'Jewish Greek'", in *New Documents*, vol. 5, 5-40.

46 All references to Maloney are to *Semitic Interference;* to Howard, *Grammar II;* and to Taylor, *Mark* .

47 Where appropriate, Maloney's system of rating the frequency of occurrence of a particular construction is reproduced (see *Semitic Interference,* 243-252). The scale from zero (-) to 4, corresponds to the following approximate categories: unknown (-); possible but extremely rare (1); attested but infrequent (2); frequent (3); normal usage (4); and is used for each of the following areas of potential linguistic influence: Hellenistic *(= Koine)* Greek (G); Qumran and Proto-Mishnaic Hebrew (H); Middle Aramaic (A); and the Greek Old Testament (OG).

1 εἰς τῶν μαθητῶν αὐτοῦ	The numeral εἰς used as an indefinite pronoun. Black (*Aramaic Approach,* 105): argues for Semitic interference where εἰς is used as an indefinite pronoun ('a certain...', 'someone') or an indefinite article ('a', 'an'). Maloney (130), is more specific: "In 5:22; 12:28; 13:1; 14:66, where εἰς is used as an indefinite pronoun and is followed by a plural partitive genitive, such usage is incorrect in Hellenistic Greek, and due to Semitic interference (whether from Hebrew, Aramaic, or imitation of the OG)."	[G1 under Egyptian influence only, H4, A4, OG3: Semitism: H, A or OG]. Hebrew or Aramaic influence, or imitation of the Greek Old Testament.
1 Διδάσκαλε	Omission of ὦ before the vocative. BDF §146(1), "In conformity with Koine and Semitic usage vocative ὦ is frequently omitted before the vocative in the NT and always in invoking God, while it was regularly used in Attic".	Possible indication of Semitic usage, but also common in *Koine* Greek.
2,6,9 (twice), 10,11,12 (thrice),13,16, 19,20,21,22, 24,25 (twice), 26,27 (twice), 28,34 (twice)	Parataxis—coordination of independent clauses and commencement of sentences with καί. Not included here are the times καί is used to join nouns (vv.3,9,22,26,31), adjectives, adverbs, phrases (vv.1,7,8,12), infinitives or participles (v.17), nor when it is used to mean 'also' (v.29), or to introduce a question expressing incredulity or surprise at what has gone before (13:4?).[48] These uses of καί are all possible in *Koine* Greek.	The ratio of καί to δέ in the Gospel of Mark (cited by Maloney, 66, as 5.2:1) is so much higher than any other Greek writings except parts of the LXX, that Maloney (67) concludes "the likelihood of the influence of Hebrew and/or Aramaic in this matter of Mark's style is very high." [G2, H4, A4, OG3: Frequency due to H, A or OG]. Hebrew or Aramaic influence, or imitation of the Greek Old Testament.

[48] Maloney, *Semitic Interference,* 73-4, does not include the double question of 13:4 in his list of five examples of incredulous questions in Mark (4:13; 9:12; 10:26; 11:28; 12:37), yet arguably, after the statement of Jesus in 13:2, the disciples *are* showing some signs of incredulity.

2 τὰς μεγάλας οἰκοδομάς	Pre-positive attributive adjective. Maloney (54): "an unemphatic attributive adjective placed before the noun is a 'Grecism' and would eliminate the possibility of literal translation or of the author's thinking in Semitic in such a phrase."	Mk 13:2 is not listed by Maloney as one of the exceptions due to emphasis on the adjective (199, footnote 24). However, in the context there appears to be good grounds for arguing that the adjective *does* take considerable emphasis,[49] and thus the phrase τὰς μεγάλας οἰκοδομάς could reflect either a Semitic or Greek word order.
2 λίθος ἐπὶ λίθον	Repetition of the substantive. Howard (438), argues that this is an example of a Semitic idiom due to the lack in Hebrew and Aramaic of words corresponding directly to ἄλλος or ἕτερος.	Probable Semitic idiom. Hebrew or Aramaic influence.
3 Καὶ καθημένου	Starting a paragraph with Καί (as for v.1 above).	[G–, H4, A3, OG3: Semitism: H, A or OG]. Hebrew (or Aramaic) influence—but most probably through imitation of the Greek Old Testament.
5 ὁ δὲ Ἰησοῦς ἤρξατο λέγειν αὐτοῖς	Redundant auxiliary verb ἤρξατο plus infinitive. Howard (455) points out that although it occurs frequently in the LXX it has no specific Hebrew equivalent. However he cites the arguments of W. C. Allen that the 26 occurrences in Mk all occur in narrative and do not seem to imply any special emphasis,[50] and concludes with Allen that they can best be explained as translations of the use of yrIç; as an auxiliary verb in Aramaic.	Originally an Aramaism, but may have come to the Gospel of Mark via the LXX.

---

[49] Indeed, it is hard to imagine how μεγάλας could be used *without* emphasis, even if spoken ironically or sarcastically, as may be the case in 13:2.

[50] W. C. Allen, *The Gospel according to St Mark, with Introduction and Notes* (London 1915), 49f. Interestingly, Allen points out that Matthew omits all but 6 of Mark's instances, and Lk all but 2—then adds another 25! He concludes that the frequency in Mark is due to translation from the Aramaic, and Howard suggests that the occurrences in Luke are best explained as imitation of Septuagintal style.

5,6,7,8 (thrice), **9,15,23,34**

Asyndeton between sentences (where two sentences are joined without conjunction or other linking word). Black, *Aramaic Approach,* 55-61, argues that asyndeton is evidence of Aramaic interference. (In Mk it generally occurs in direct speech). BDF §458: "the unconnected (asyndetic) paratactic style…is repugnant by and large to the spirit of the Greek language, whether the parallel members joined by asyndeton are whole sentences or parts of sentences or merely words." Maloney (77,80-81) points out that this applies more to classical Greek and argues that: "Asyndeton between sentences was common in Hellenistic Greek." Though conceding that "asyndeton between sentences is not infrequent in biblical Aramaic", he goes on to say that it is "hardly an Aramaism", since it is also "quite common in the post-biblical Hebrew of Qumran" and in "later Proto-Mishnaic Hebrew".

[G3, H3, A2, OG1: both Greek and Hebrew usage]. According to the evidence of Maloney, asyndeton is possible in *Koine* Greek, post-biblical and proto-Mishnaic Hebrew (not so likely in biblical Hebrew), and biblical Aramaic. Given that the Aramaic of Daniel provides some examples of asyndeton (Maloney, 80, lists Dn 3:1, 5:2), and also provides an important context for some of the biblical allusions in Mk 13 (see chapter 3 below), then the influence of biblical Aramaic may well be more important in this context than Maloney believes.

8 ἐγερθήσεται γὰρ ἔθνος

Verb before subject in an independent clause. Maloney (53), following Zerwick (*Untersuchungen,* 97-104) and Black (*Aramaic Approach,* 51), carefully defines where the usual Semitic word order of the verb preceding the subject may have influenced the Markan word order: "in independent clauses where the subject is expressed and the word order in Mark is verb--subject and the verb is not emphatic or placed first because of one of the reasons listed above, there is a good chance of Semitic interference from Aramaic or from imitation of the OG, while less likely from contemporaneous Hebrew. It is impossible to be definite in every case…" The exceptions he lists concern imperative verbs, verbs commencing an apodosis,

Even given the skewed selection of evidence, the Semitic order verb/subject occurs in independent clauses in Mk 13:8,12 (twice) and 22. The two occurrences in v.12, apart from being sayings material, fall within Maloney's parameters (independent clauses commencing with καί), but he seems to discount those clauses (as in vv.8,22) where γάρ or δέ is post-positive (Maloney, 51-2, and footnote 8, 197). But by focusing on those clauses commencing with καί, Maloney is pre-selecting those with a more Semitic flavour and it is not surprising that the majority follow the verb/subject word order. Conversely, one would expect those sentences starting in the

(V.8 continued)	connectors in the narrative, the verb 'to be', and singular verbs with dual subjects. If the discourses are also to be considered, then clauses commencing with an emphatic denial (as in Mk 13:2 and 30) could also be excluded from consideration. Maloney (51, following Zerwick) restricts his examination of the evidence to the narrative sections of Mark where the order verb/subject is more frequent than in the discourses, due to the "emphasis upon the subject of the sentence in much of the non-narrative material of the gospel".	usual Greek manner (δέ post-positive) to follow the usual Greek word order (subject/verb).[51] In vv.8 and 22 the post-positive γάρ is combined with the Semitic word order, although it could be argued that there is special emphasis on the verb in both cases. However there would appear to be at least equal stress on the subject of these sentences, and so they should be considered as possible examples of Semitic influence. [Maloney's general conclusion (but *not* for this particular verse) G2, H4, A4, OG3: Frequency due to A, OG or (possibly) H]. Possible Semitism due to Hebrew or Aramaic influence, or imitation of the Greek Old Testament.
11 οὐ γάρ ἐστε ὑμεῖς οἱ λαλοῦντες	The initial position of the verb "also suggests translation Greek", and together with the other features of vv.11-12 "strongly suggests that an original saying spoken in Aramaic stands behind Mark's version" (Taylor, 508).	Possible Semitic influence (perhaps from the Aramaic) but concentrated in the second half of v.11.
11 τὸ πνεῦμα τὸ ἅγιον	Post-positive attributive adjective, with the article. Maloney (54): "in a pericope where all unemphatic attributive adjectives follow their substantives, that fact lends to its Semitic flavour, although Semitic interference as such would have to be proved by additional means." Note that πᾶς (vv.4,10,20 and 30), numerals (v.27), interrogatives (v.1 twice) and demonstratives (vv.11,17, 19,24 twice,30 and 32), are	[G2, H4, A4, OG3: Frequency due to H, A, or OG]. Possible Semitic interference due to Hebrew, Aramaic or the influence of the Greek Old Testament.

---

51 As Maloney, *Semitic Interference,* 52, notes, this is in fact the case in the narrative material. Only once (Mk 14:44) does the verb/subject word order occur with δέ, 90 times it is subject/verb; and the five occurrences of post-positive γάρ are with subject/verb word order. Using other criteria, J. K. Elliott, "The Position of the Verb in Mark with special reference to Chapter 13", *NovT* 38 (1996), 136-144, identifies around 60 verbs in the initial position in Mk 13, and indicates their significance for evaluating textual variants. Unfortunately it was not possible to test the full impact of Elliott's work in this study—since any adjustment to the Markan text will have profound implications for our syntactical analysis. But it is a task that needs attention.

(V.11 continued)	excluded as they can occur in similar constructions in Greek as well as in Hebrew and Aramaic.	
12 [καὶ] παραδώσει [δὲ] ἀδελφὸς ἀδελφὸν εἰς θάνατον	Verb before subject in an independent clause (see v.8 above).	[Maloney's general conclusion (but *not* for this particular verse) G2, H4, A4, OG3: Frequency due to A, OG or (possibly) H].[52] Possible Semitism due to Hebrew or Aramaic influence, or imitation of the Greek Old Testament.
12 καὶ ἐπαναστήσονται τέκνα ἐπὶ γονεῖς	Verb before subject in an independent clause (see v.8 above).	[Maloney's general conclusion (but *not* for this particular verse) G2, H4, A4, OG3: Frequency due to A, OG or (possibly) H]. Possible Semitism due to Hebrew or Aramaic influence, or imitation of the Greek Old Testament.
13 ἔσεσθε μισούμενοι	A form of εἶναι with a present participle used as a periphrases. BDF §353 (7): "Since...the Hellenistic language (even more the vernacular of the papyri) is familiar with this development only to a very limited degree...and since, on the other hand, the frequency of NT examples is highest in Lk (Gospel and first half of Acts) then Mark (less in Matthew), this idiom, which is just possible in Greek, was at least strongly supported by extensive Semitic use of such periphrases, especially in the imperfect".	Most likely a Semitic idiom.
15 τοῦ δώματος	Unusual insertion of the article— a substantive with the article which still may be translated as indefinite. Maloney (109): "Although Hebrew and Aramaic usage of the article generally coincides with that of the Gospel of Mark, nevertheless, Marcan usage of it is quite normal in Hellenistic Greek in all cases." (continued...)	

[52] The fact that post-positive δέ only occurs once with the order verb/subject in the narrative sections of the Gospel of Mark (see notes on v.8 above) tends to support the reading καὶ παραδώσει in this verse.

(V.15 continued)	However, of the 25 (or 31?) instances of unusual insertion of the article that Maloney lists (105, 109, cf 248), some 16 occur in Mk 4 (the parables chapter), which could be seen as an indication that such a use of the article may reflect an Aramaic origin, if the parables of Mk 4 are regarded as Jesuanic.[53] But it is possible to explain these articles in Mk 4 in terms of acceptable *Koine* usage also (see Maloney, 109).	[G3, H1, A3, OG3: both Greek and Semitic (A, OG and possibly H) usage]. Possible Aramaic influence, or imitation of Greek Old Testament, but also consistent with *Koine* Greek usage.
16 τὸν ἀγρὸν	Unusual insertion of the article (see v.15 above).	[G3, H1, A3, OG3: both Greek and Semitic (A, OG and possibly H) usage]. Possible Aramaic influence, or imitation of Greek Old Testament.
17 οὐαί	Prophetic style = the LXX transcription of the Hebrew y/h, y/a, but also = Latin *vae* (cf Epictetus). BDF §4 (2) (see also v.17 under Latinisms above).	Consistent with Semitic or Latin usage.
17 ἐν ἐκείναις ταῖς ἡμέραις	Adjectival use of ἐκεῖνος. Maloney (124): "the high frequency of adjectival ἐκεῖνος and a correspondingly low frequency of pronominal ἐκεῖνος in Mark must be due to the interference of Hebrew or Aramaic. Imitation of OG may also be at work here, especially in the Old Testament eschatological phrases ἐκείνη ἡ ἡμέρα (ἡ ἡμέραι ἐκείνη) in Mk 2:20 and 14:25, and ἐκεῖναι αἱ ἡμέραι (αἱ ἡμέραι ἐκεῖναι) in Mk 13:17,19,24." These references are imprecise and incomplete. See those given in chapter 5 below.	[G2, H3, A3, OG3: frequency due to H, A or OG]. Hebrew or Aramaic influence, or imitation of Greek Old Testament.
19 αἱ ἡμέραι ἐκεῖναι	Adjectival use of ἐκεῖνος (see v.17 above).	[G2, H3, A3, OG3: frequency due to H, A or OG]. Hebrew or Aramaic influence, or imitation of Greek Old Testament.

[53] Certainly this is the view of J. Jeremias, *The Parables of Jesus* (London 1963), 11 and footnote 2, though Maloney gives other reasons for the frequency of such articles in Mk 4: "Thus, the normal Hellenistic usage of the deictic article occurs in Mk 3:13; 4:3,4*(bis)*, 5,7,8,21*(quater...)*,26,38... In Mk 4:15,16,18,20 the article is simply anaphoric, referring back to the nouns in question in the parable in 4:3-8." *Semitic Interference*, 109.

19 θλῖψις οἵα οὐ γέγονεν τοιαύτη ἀπ᾽ ἀρχῆς κτίσεως	Redundant demonstrative (τοιαύτη) after a relative pronoun (οἵα). Maloney (118): "most probably due to imitation of the OG, since it is a conflation of two Old Testament texts" (Dn 12:1 Th, and Ex 9:18. See chapter 3 below)	[G–, H3, A3, OG5: Semitism: conflation of OG texts]. Secondary Semiticism (or 'Biblicism') resulting from the joining of Dn 12:1 (Th or MT) and Ex 9:18 (LXX or MT).
19 ἀπ᾽ ἀρχῆς κτίσεως ἣν ἔκτισεν ὁ θεὸς	Tautology. Howard (419), "A Semitic colouring is seen in the continual repetition of an idea by . . . a subordinate clause", and "especially when the verb seems to complete the substantive." (Taylor, 52, in support of Lagrange).	Probable Semitic influence.
20 οὐκ ἂν ἐσώθη πᾶσα σάρξ	Use of 'all flesh would not be saved' (οὐκ...πᾶσα σάρξ) instead of 'no one' (οὐδείς). Maloney (139): "although the expression οὐ ... πᾶς = οὐδείς occurs in a few non-literary Greek papyri, such usage in Mk 13:20 is probably due to Semitic interference, whether from imitation of the OG, or directly from contemporaneous Hebrew or Aramaic, since the expression πᾶσα σάρξ is obviously Semitic."	[G1, H4, A4, OG2: probable Semitism: H, A, or (possibly) OG]. The expression πᾶσα σάρξ occurs 30 times in the LXX (but only once in Dn— 4.12, Th), though not with this particular negative construction preceding it. The use of οὐ ... πᾶς = οὐδείς does occur elsewhere in the LXX (Maloney, 139), and notably in Dn 6.5 (Theodotion again). On two counts, therefore, v.20 agrees with the vocabulary and syntax of Theodotion's Daniel rather than the Daniel of the LXX. Thus the construction is probably due to imitation of the Greek Old Testament (specifically Theodotion), rather than from direct Hebrew or Aramaic influence.
20 τοὺς ἐκλεκτοὺς οὓς ἐξελέξατο	Tautology (see v.19 above).	Probable Semitic idiom.
22 ἐγερθήσονται γὰρ ψευδόχριστοι καὶ ψευδοπροφῆται	Verb before subject in an independent clause (see v.8 above).	[Maloney's general conclusion (but *not* for this particular verse) G2, H4, A4, OG3: Frequency due to A, OG or (possibly) H]. Possible Semitism due to Hebrew or Aramaic influence, or imitation of the Greek Old Testament.

24 ἐν ἐκείναις ταῖς ἡμέραις

Adjectival use of ἐκεῖνος (see vv.17 and 19 above).

[G2, H3, A3, OG3: frequency due to H, A or OG]. Hebrew or Aramaic influence, or imitation of Greek Old Testament.

25 οἱ ἀστέρες ἔσονται ἐκ τοῦ οὐρανοῦ πίπτοντες

A form of εἶναι with a present participle used as a periphrases (see v.13 above).

Most likely a Semitic idiom.

25 τοῖς οὐρανοῖς

The plural follows the occasional LXX rendering (in about 10% of uses) of the Hebrew plural of extension by the Greek plural of majesty. According to N. Turner, this is used in reference to God's abode whereas the singular in the NT usually just means 'sky' (*Grammatical Insights*, 130): "St Mark carefully distinguishes singular and plural within the limits of a single verse: 'The stars shall fall from the *sky* (singular), and the powers in *heaven* (plural) shall be shaken' (13²⁵). The evangelist was no scholar, but one always has the impression that he was systematic with what Greek he did know." But this is wishful thinking on Turner's part—no such 'careful distinction' can be maintained throughout the rest of the Gospel. The singular clearly means heaven in at least 6.41; 10.21; 11.30,31; 13.32, and 14.62.[54] Better is the explanation of Maloney (191) who follows Katz in arguing that the plural in the OG is used to translate the elevated style of Hebrew poetic texts.[55]

[G–, H4, A4, OG2: Semitism: H, A, or OG]. Maloney concludes (191-192) that the plural is the "result of Semitic interference, whether from contemporary Hebrew or Aramaic, or (especially in the case of Mk 13:25) from imitation of OG usage." Cf also BDF §4 (2) & §141 (1). In this instance the plural for 'heaven' does seem to mean 'the heavens' (with a sense of majesty/poetry) and reflects Hebrew and Aramaic usage— and occasional usage in the Greek Old Testament (but the singular means 'heaven' at least as often as it is translated 'sky' in the Gospel of Mark). This use of the plural in v.25 stems from the reference to the Greek Old Testament (Is 34.4 LXX, see chapter 3 below).

---

[54] *The New Jerusalem Bible* (London 1985), which goes so far as to translate the singular as 'sky' in 13:25,27 and 31, reverts to 'heaven' in 13:32 and in all of the verses listed above.

[55] See Maloney, *Semitic Interference,* 191 and 240, footnotes 504 and 505; and P. Katz, *Philo's Bible* (Cambridge 1950), 141-146.

26 καὶ τότε ὄψονται

Impersonal use of the third person plural active (in this case a middle deponent) in place of the passive. Howard (447, following Wellhausen) describes this as usual in Hebrew and Aramaic, and points out that it is unusual in Greek apart from λέγουσι and φασί. However Howard's caution (448) about the data (Wellhausen lists Mk 6:14; 10:13; 13:26; 15:27 as further examples of this particular usage), is well placed, as further examination shows the use of the third person plural active in each of these cases to be quite normal. If the plural is read in 6:14, it merely anticipates the 'some' and the 'others' of the following verses. In 10:13, the plural can be assumed to imply the Judean crowd of 10:1; just as in 13:26 the plural refers to the stars and powers of the preceding verse, and in 15:27 the plural is simply a continuation of those occurring in vv.22,23,24 and 25.

Raises the question as to whether ὄψονται is to be understood as an impersonal verb or not, or whether perhaps the third person plural refers to those plural entities immediately preceding the verse—the stars and powers of v.25. If these stars and powers are understood as representing earthly rulers and powers (see chapter 7 below), then the claim that they *will see* the vindication of the Son of Man parallels the saying in 14.62, where the High Priest is told the same thing, and is in keeping with the other supposed 'impersonal plurals' of Mk 13:9,11—where they can also be understood as the 'powers that be'. This expression makes best sense then, if it is understood as normal *Koine* usage.

26 τὸν υἱὸν τοῦ ἀνθρώπου

The singular arthrous form ὁ υἱὸς τοῦ ἀνθρώπου (literally 'the son of the man' or 'the man's son') does not occur in non-biblical Greek or in the OG. Maloney (176): "the phrase ὁ υἱὸς τοῦ ἀνθρώπου (fourteen times in the Gospel of Mark) and its plural οἱ υἱοὶ τῶν ἀνθρώπων (Mk 3:28) are the result of Semitic interference." Maloney goes on to point out however, that the Hebrew and Aramaic basis for the singular determinate form is very slender—one instance in Hebrew, with the article added above the line, and only the indeterminate form in Middle Aramaic. Maloney sides with Fitzmyer in discounting Vermes' evidence from Late Aramaic of a circumlocutional usage (ὁ υἱὸς τοῦ ἀνθρώπου = 'I', 'the speaker').[56]

[G–, H2, A1, OG–: Semitism: H or (possibly) A]. Ultimate origins of the term must lie either in the anarthrous Aramaic of Dn 7:13, the anarthrous Hebrew of Ezekiel and Psalms, or the circumlocutional usage (evident in later Aramaic) suggested by Vermes. Certainly the Greek form must be understood as a special designation—a title—such is its unusual construction. Thus, although there is undoubtedly some Semitic background to the term, its actual Greek form may have its origin in an attempt to combine the significance of several elements of that background.

---

[56] For further details of the debate see Geza Vermes, "The Present State of the 'Son of Man' Debate", 89-99, and Joseph A. Fitzmyer, "Another View of the 'Son of Man' Debate", *JSNT* 4 (1979), 58-68. See also footnote 16 (this chapter) above.

26 μετὰ δυνάμεως πολλῆς	Post-positive attributive adjective, without the article. Maloney (53-54), as for v.11 above, except that post-positive adjectives without the article are more common in Greek than those with the article.	[G3, H4, A4, OG3: Frequency probably due to H, A or OG]. Possible Semitic interference due to Hebrew, Aramaic or the influence of the Greek Old Testament.
33 βλέπετε ἀγρυπνεῖτε	Asyndeton between imperatives.[57] Maloney (247): "both Greek and Semitic usage."	[G3, H3, A3, OG1: both Greek and Semitic usage]. Acceptable usage in *Koine* Greek.
34 ὡς ἄνθρωπος ἀπόδημος	(i) ἄνθρωπος used in an indefinite way. Black (*Aramaic Approach,* 106): ἄνθρωπος has lost its normal meaning 'man', 'human being', and is used as a kind of indefinite pronoun due to Semitic interference. Maloney (134) clarifies this further: "While ἄνθρωπος also has an indefinite meaning in Mk 3:1; 13:34, it is modified in these verses by an attributive participle or adjective. Thus, while ἄνθρωπος could be a translation from Semitic in these verses, it is also acceptable Hellenistic Greek usage."	[G3, H4, A4, OG3: both Greek and Semitic usage]. Could be due to translation from Hebrew or Aramaic, but is also acceptable usage in *Koine* Greek.
	(ii) Post-positive attributive adjective, without the article. Maloney (53-54):[58] as for v.26 above.	[G3, H4, A4, OG3: Frequency probably due to H, A or OG]. Possible Semitic interference due to Hebrew, Aramaic or the influence of the Greek Old Testament.

These conclusions regarding Semitic interference in Mk 13 are more clearly represented in Text Sheet 1, which follows below. Because of the extreme difficulty of attributing a particular Semitic characteristic with any certainty to either Hebrew, Aramaic or to the influence of the Greek Old Testament, it would be foolish to place too much weight on the distinctions between linguistic influences made in Text Sheet 1. However if some of the broader tendencies evident are reinforced by the various analyses which follow in later chapters, then their particular contribution to the task of describing the background of the text as it now stands will need to be taken more seriously.

[57] Maloney, *Semitic Interference,* 77 and 247, lists this feature as occurring in 2:11; 4:39; 6:38; 8:15; 10:14 and 14:42 (using a hortatory subjunctive). To this list should be added 10:49 (perhaps in place of 10:14); 13:33; 15:36 (if hortatory subjunctives are included) and 16:7.

[58] Maloney, *Semitic Interference,* 199, footnote 24, seems to have overlooked Mk 13:34 in his list of post-positive adjectives.

Some of the clearest distinctions between linguistic influences on the text of Mk 13 can be made where what were previously thought to have been Semitisms have been reclassified as acceptable *Koine* Greek in the light of recent comparisons with other *Koine* literature. The following evidence is thus not intended as an exhaustive list of all the features within Mk 13 that are normal or permissible in *Koine* Greek (obviously most of the discourse would fit into this category), so much as a description of those stylistic variations—often once thought to have been of Semitic origin—which have been shown to be part of the normal vernacular Greek of the first century.

There are also some features described which are clearly of *Koine* origin because they form the corollary to a Semitic feature described above. In particular, the use of δέ rather than καί as a connecting particle (see v.1 in the 'Semitisms' table above), is an indication of normal *Koine* usage as distinct from a style influenced by Semitic languages or (un)consciously imitating the Septuagint. Thus the use of δέ rather than καί will be listed in the table below and shown on the text sheet which follows. Of course the whole text critical question regarding the hellenising tendencies of some manuscripts (which therefore show an increase in the use of δέ) is of crucial importance in this context. But the work must proceed at this stage with the available texts and then be subject to further review when the Gospels volume of the *Text und Textwert* series from the Institute for New Testament Textual Research (Münster) becomes available.

Features reclassified as normal Koine usage in Mk 13

Verse in Mk 13	Description and References	Comments and Conclusions
1 λέγει αὐτῷ εἷς τῶν μαθητῶν αὐτοῦ	The use of the historical present has been widely regarded as an indication of Semitic interference (BDF §321).[59] Maloney's careful reassessment of the evidence, however, plainly shows that the historical present was widely used by *Koine* Greek writers to mark the main action of a new story or a new turn of events.[60]	Normal *Koine* usage—may even be indicative of Markan redaction.

---

[59] Elliott C. Maloney, "The Historical Present in the Gospel of Mark", in *To Touch the Text. Biblical and Related Studies in Honor of Joseph A. Fitzmyer, S. J.,* eds Maurya P. Horgan and Paul J. Kobelski (New York 1989), 68, also cites Black, Taylor, N. Turner and Zerwick, as supporters of the view that the frequency with which the historical present occurs within the NT is indicative of Semitic interference.

[60] Maloney, "Historical Present", 78.

2,5,13,17, 27,[61] **31**	The separation of the substantive from its article occurs frequently in *Koine* Greek, but never in Hebrew or Aramaic where the article is attached to its substantive. Maloney (63) states that the article is separated from its substantive only 91 times in the Gospel of Mark (or less than 6.5% of the occurrences of the definite article). Thus, as the corollary to the closeness of article and substantive being taken as an indication of Semitic interference (see v.2 under Semitic Interference above), their separation may indicate normal *Koine* usage.	If it is accepted that there is some emphasis on μεγάλας in v.2 (see v.2, Semitisms, above), then the separation of the article from its substantive may be due to this rather than *Koine* influence. Verses 5,13 and 31, with post-positive δέ, provide clearer examples of normal *Koine* usage, as does v.17, where the article is separated by a prepositional phrase (with ἐν) [BDF §266 & 272 provide many examples of this latter construction from Classical and *Koine* Greek]. The position of the numeral before the noun in v.27 (acceptable usage in Semitic languages and *Koine* Greek; Maloney, 54), results in the separation of the article there and confirms a normal *Koine* construction overall.
5,7,9,13b,14, 15,17,18,23, 28,31,32,37	Use of post-positive δέ rather than the paratactic καί which is much more common in the Gospel of Mark (see v.2 under Semitic Interference above). The recurrence of δέ in vv.13 to 18 (5 times) is uncommon, having parallels only in 10:3-6 (4 times); 10:36-40 (6 times), and 15:4-15 (11 times, but interrupted by v.8).[62]	The sequence of five uses of post-positive δέ in vv.13 to 18 is unusually long for the Gospel of Mark and may indicate a unit of pre-Markan tradition.

Normal *Koine* usage occurs in vv.5,7,9,13b,14,15(?),17,18, 23,28,31,32,37. |
| **11** ἀλλ᾽ ὃ ἐὰν δοθῇ ὑμῖν ἐν ἐκείνῃ τῇ ὥρᾳ τοῦτο λαλεῖτε | *Casus pendens* followed by a demonstrative pronoun. Maloney (90): "normal in Greek, but unattested in Hebrew or Aramaic." | [G4, H–, A–, OG1: Grecism]. Clearly normal *Koine* usage. |
| **13** ὁ δὲ ὑπομείνας εἰς τέλος οὗτος σωθήσεται | *Casus pendens* followed by a demonstrative pronoun, as for v.11 above. | [G4, H–, A–, OG1: Grecism] Clearly normal *Koine* usage. |

---

[61] Maloney, *Semitic Interference*, 63, and 201 footnote 52, lists 13:26, but presumably means 13:27, ἐκ τῶν τεσσάρων ἀνέμων.

[62] There are lesser sequences of δέ in 2:20-21 (twice); 4:34 (twice); 5:33-36 (3 times); 6:15-16 (3 times); 7:6-7 (3 times); 8:28 (twice), and 10:24-26 (3 times).

24 ἐν ἐκείναις ταῖς ἡμέραις μετὰ τὴν θλῖψιν ἐκείνην	Pleonastic (unstressed) use of a demonstrative (...ἐκείνην), originating from a "pleonastically placed Aramaic or Hebrew demonstrative pronoun" according to J. Jeremias, *The Eucharistic Words of Jesus* (London 1976), 183-184, including footnote 3. Maloney (126): "In regard to the use of the demonstratives in Mk 4:11; 9:42; 13:24; 14:21 and 25 three statements are pertinent: (1) it is by no means certain that the demonstratives in these texts do not retain some demonstrative force; (2) there is no use of pleonastic demonstratives in biblical or contemporaneous Hebrew or Aramaic; (3) there are almost perfect parallels to Marcan usage of demonstratives in the Hellenistic author Epictetus."	[G3, H3, A3, OG3: both Greek and Semitic usage]. Perfectly acceptable *Koine* Greek, and particularly so in that there seems to be some emphasis on the whole phrase in this context.
32 οὐδεὶς οἶδεν... εἰ μὴ ὁ πατήρ	Abridged exceptive clause. Maloney (99): "normal in Hellenistic Greek, especially after the pronoun οὐδείς"—*contra* Beyer, *Semitische Syntax,* 138 and 305, who claims that εἰ μή is here used as an adversative ('but') and is thus most probably a Semitism.	[G3, H2, A1, OG1: Greek usage, attested in H and possible in A]. Normal *Koine* Greek.
33 βλέπετε ἀγρυπνεῖτε	Asyndeton between imperatives. Maloney (247): "both Greek and Semitic usage." (See v.33, Semitisms, above).	[G3, H3, A3, OG1: both Greek and Semitic usage]. Acceptable usage in *Koine* Greek.
34 ἵνα γρηγορῇ	Use of ἵνα instead of the infinitive (see vv.18,34 under Latinisms above).	Possible Latin influence, though also clearly a long-term trend within the evolution of the Greek language.

It is now possible to use these findings of Semitic influence on the text of Mk 13—as distinct from those features reclassified as normal *Koine* Greek usage—as a means of evaluating the description and origins of the proposed form critical divisions outlined previously. Not that a linguistic analysis should be the sole arbiter of such questions, but rather that if on form critical grounds it is suggested that a saying is of Palestinian origin and embedded in a Hellenistic setting, some trace of this may be evident in the language used. Thus a close analysis of linguistic influences may well corroborate—or call into question—the results of source and form analysis. In order to see the results of this linguistic analysis more clearly the conclusions are underlined in Text Sheet 1 below.

Linguistic influences in the sayings of Mk 13

This linguistic analysis of the text is by no means exhaustive, yet already the following correlations with the form critical outline above are evident:

vv.1-2:   The linguistic evidence is consistent with Bultmann's observation that the saying is probably from the Palestinian tradition whilst the framework may be of Hellenistic origin. (Thus Maloney's suggestion of some Markan redaction in v.1a may also be possible.)

vv.3-6:   There is no clear evidence of any unifying style in these verses—they may well be a redactional arrangement to 'set the scene', as is suggested by many commentators.

vv.7-8:   Some evidence of Semitic—possibly Aramaic—influence in v.8, and a remarkable similarity in wording and style to v.22.

v.9-13:   Some indication of *Koine* Greek influence in the central phrase of v.11, but quite possibly Aramaic influence elsewhere in that verse. Vv.12-13a are strongly Semitic—perhaps Aramaic—in character, and v.13b is normal *Koine* Greek.

vv.14-20: Considerable Semitic influence (especially in vv.17-20), but in clauses linked with an unusually high proportion of uses of δέ, at least until v.20.

vv. 21-23: Some Aramaic influence is possible in v.22, which may indicate that vv.14-21 is more likely to have belonged together, with v.22 being added from another tradition.

vv.24-27: A clearly identifiable unit showing very strong Semitic influence attributable to the use of Septuagintal language.

vv.28-37: Remarkably free of Semitic influence, with the exception of v.34—perhaps corroborating Bultmann's suggestion that this verse may stem from the 'ancient tradition'.

These are modest suggestions in keeping with the ambiguity of much of the evidence, but already some possibilities are emerging. No clear light is shed on many of the smaller potential units such as vv.5b,6,9a, 9b,10,23a,23b at this stage, but even such a negative result may prove meaningful in the end. On the other hand, there is some support here for a pre-Markan unit consisting of vv.14-20(21), because of the atypical use of δέ in many of these verses, combined with a strongly Semitic linguistic tendency. It appears that vv.7-8,11d-13a and v.22 show some similarities which may indicate a common Aramaic linguistic heritage. However the unit consisting of vv.24-27 is so consistently Septuagintal in style that it would appear to stem from a different tradition from that of vv.14-19 (20 or 21?) since it is separated from that section by vv.22,23 and is held together by the use of καί rather than δέ. Similarly, vv.28-37 are predominantly *Koine* Greek in style (apart from v.34), yet also contain the more typically Markan καί, and it is difficult to see them as having the same origin as vv.7-8,11d-13a,22, or 14-21.

The evidence supporting these tentative conclusions can be seen mapped out on the following text sheet:

Text Sheet 1: Linguistic influences in Mk 13

13.1 Καὶ ἐκπορευομένου αὐτοῦ ἐκ τοῦ ἱεροῦ λέγει αὐτῷ εἷς τῶν μαθητῶν αὐτοῦ, Διδάσκαλε, ἴδε ποταποὶ λίθοι καὶ ποταπαὶ οἰκοδομαί. 2 καὶ ὁ Ἰησοῦς εἶπεν αὐτῷ, Βλέπεις ταύτας τὰς μεγάλας οἰκοδομάς; οὐ μὴ ἀφεθῇ ὧδε λίθος ἐπὶ λίθον ὃς οὐ μὴ καταλυθῇ.
3 Καὶ καθημένου αὐτοῦ εἰς τὸ Ὄρος τῶν Ἐλαιῶν κατέναντι τοῦ ἱεροῦ ἐπηρώτα αὐτὸν κατ' ἰδίαν Πέτρος καὶ Ἰάκωβος καὶ Ἰωάννης καὶ Ἀνδρέας. 4 Εἰπὸν ἡμῖν πότε ταῦτα ἔσται, καὶ τί τὸ σημεῖον ὅταν μέλλῃ ταῦτα συντελεῖσθαι πάντα. 5 ὁ δὲ Ἰησοῦς ἤρξατο λέγειν αὐτοῖς, βλέπετε μή τις ὑμᾶς πλανήσῃ· 6 πολλοὶ ἐλεύσονται ἐπὶ τῷ ὀνόματί μου λέγοντες ὅτι Ἐγώ εἰμι, καὶ πολλοὺς πλανήσουσιν. 7 ὅταν δὲ ἀκούσητε πολέμους καὶ ἀκοὰς πολέμων, μὴ θροεῖσθε· δεῖ γενέσθαι, ἀλλ' οὔπω τὸ τέλος. 8 ἐγερθήσεται γὰρ ἔθνος ἐπ' ἔθνος καὶ βασιλεία ἐπὶ βασιλείαν, ἔσονται σεισμοὶ κατὰ τόπους, ἔσονται λιμοί· ἀρχὴ ὠδίνων ταῦτα. 9 βλέπετε δὲ ὑμεῖς ἑαυτούς· παραδώσουσιν ὑμᾶς εἰς συνέδρια καὶ εἰς συναγωγὰς δαρήσεσθε καὶ ἐπὶ ἡγεμόνων καὶ βασιλέων σταθήσεσθε ἕνεκεν ἐμοῦ εἰς μαρτύριον αὐτοῖς. 10 καὶ εἰς πάντα τὰ ἔθνη πρῶτον δεῖ κηρυχθῆναι τὸ εὐαγγέλιον. 11 καὶ ὅταν ἄγωσιν ὑμᾶς παραδιδόντες, μὴ προμεριμνᾶτε τί λαλήστε, ἀλλ' ὃ ἐὰν δοθῇ ὑμῖν ἐν ἐκείνῃ τῇ ὥρᾳ τοῦτο λαλεῖτε, ~~οὐ γάρ ἐστε ὑμεῖς οἱ λαλοῦντες~~ ἀλλὰ τὸ πνεῦμα τὸ ἅγιον. 12 καὶ ~~παραδώσει ἀδελφὸς~~ ἀδελφὸν εἰς θάνατον καὶ πατὴρ τέκνον, καὶ ~~ἐπαναστήσονται τέκνα~~ ἐπὶ γονεῖς καὶ θανατώσουσιν αὐτούς· 13 καὶ ἔσεσθε μισούμενοι ὑπὸ πάντων διὰ τὸ ὄνομά μου. ὁ δὲ ὑπομείνας εἰς τέλος οὗτος σωθήσεται.
14 Ὅταν δὲ ἴδητε τὸ βδέλυγμα τῆς ἐρημώσεως ἑστηκότα ὅπου οὐ δεῖ, ὁ ἀναγινώσκων νοείτω, τότε οἱ ἐν τῇ Ἰουδαίᾳ φευγέτωσαν εἰς τὰ ὄρη, 15 ὁ δὲ ἐπὶ τοῦ δώματος μὴ καταβάτω μηδὲ εἰσελθάτω ἆραί τι ἐκ τῆς οἰκίας αὐτοῦ, 16 καὶ ὁ εἰς τὸν ἀγρὸν μὴ ἐπιστρεψάτω εἰς τὰ ὀπίσω ἆραι τὸ ἱμάτιον αὐτοῦ. 17 οὐαὶ δὲ ταῖς ἐν γαστρὶ ἐχούσαις καὶ ταῖς θηλαζούσαις ἐν ἐκείναις ταῖς ἡμέραις. 18 προσεύχεσθε δὲ ἵνα μὴ γένηται χειμῶνος· 19 ἔσονται γὰρ αἱ ἡμέραι ἐκεῖναι θλῖψις οἵα οὐ γέγονεν τοιαύτη ἀπ' ἀρχῆς κτίσεως ἣν ἔκτισεν ὁ θεὸς ἕως τοῦ νῦν καὶ οὐ μὴ γένηται. 20 καὶ εἰ μὴ ἐκολόβωσεν κύριος τὰς ἡμέρας, οὐκ ἂν ἐσώθη πᾶσα σάρξ. ἀλλὰ διὰ τοὺς ἐκλεκτοὺς οὓς ἐξελέξατο ἐκολόβωσεν τὰς ἡμέρας. 21 καὶ τότε ἐάν τις ὑμῖν εἴπῃ, Ἴδε ὧδε ὁ Χριστός, Ἴδε ἐκεῖ, μὴ πιστεύετε· 22 ἐγερθήσονται γὰρ ~~ψευδόχριστοι~~ καὶ ψευδοπροφῆται καὶ δώσουσιν σημεῖα καὶ τέρατα πρὸς τὸ

ἀποπλανᾶν, εἰ δυνατόν, τοὺς ἐκλεκτούς. 23 <u>ὑμεῖς δὲ</u> βλέπετε· προείρηκα ὑμῖν πάντα.

24 Ἀλλὰ ἐν <u>ἐκείναις ταῖς ἡμέραις</u> μετὰ τὴν θλῖψιν ἐκείνην
ὁ ἥλιος σκοτισθήσεται,
<u>καὶ</u> ἡ σελήνη οὐ δώσει τὸ φέγγος αὐτῆς,
25 <u>καὶ</u> οἱ ἀστέρες <u>ἔσονται</u> ἐκ τοῦ οὐρανοῦ <u>πίπτοντες</u>,
<u>καὶ</u> αἱ δυνάμεις αἱ ἐν <u>τοῖς οὐρανοῖς</u> σαλευθήσονται.

26 <u>καὶ</u> τότε <u>ὄψονται</u> <u>τὸν υἱὸν τοῦ ἀνθρώπου</u> ἐρχόμενον ἐν νεφέλαις <u>μετὰ δυνάμεως πολλῆς</u> καὶ δόξης. 27 <u>καὶ</u> τότε ἀποστελεῖ τοὺς ἀγγέλους <u>καὶ</u> ἐπισυνάξει τοὺς ἐκλεκτοὺς αὐτοῦ ἐκ τῶν τεσσάρων ἀνέμων ἀπ᾽ ἄκρου γῆς ἕως ἄκρου οὐρανοῦ.

28 <u>Ἀπὸ δὲ</u> τῆς συκῆς μάθετε τὴν παραβολήν· ὅταν ἤδη ὁ κλάδος αὐτῆς ἁπαλὸς γένηται <u>καὶ</u> ἐκφύῃ τὰ φύλλα, γινώσκετε ὅτι ἐγγὺς τὸ θέρος ἐστίν. 29 οὕτως καὶ ὑμεῖς, ὅταν ἴδητε ταῦτα γινόμενα γινώσκετε ὅτι ἐγγύς ἐστιν ἐπὶ θύραις. 30 ~~ἀμὴν~~ λέγω ὑμῖν ὅτι οὐ μὴ παρέλθῃ ἡ γενεὰ αὕτη μέχρις οὗ ταῦτα πάντα γένηται. 31 ὁ οὐρανὸς καὶ ἡ γῆ παρελεύσονται, <u>οἱ δὲ λόγοι</u> μου οὐ μὴ παρελεύσονται. 32 <u>περὶ δὲ</u> τῆς ἡμέρας ἐκείνης ἢ τῆς ὥρας οὐδεὶς οἶδεν, <u>οὐδὲ οἱ ἄγελλοι ἐν οὐρανῷ οὐδὲ ὁ υἱός, εἰ μὴ ὁ πατήρ</u>. 33 βλέπετε ἀγρυπνεῖτε· οὐκ οἴδατε γὰρ πότε ὁ καιρός ἐστιν. 34 ὡς <u>ἄνθρωπος ἀπόδημος</u> ἀφεὶς τὴν οἰκίαν αὐτοῦ <u>καὶ</u> δοὺς τοῖς δούλοις αὐτοῦ τὴν ἐξουσίαν, ἑκάστῳ τὸ ἔργον αὐτοῦ, <u>καὶ</u> τῷ θυρωρῷ ἐνετείλατο ἵνα γρηγορῇ. 35 γρηγορεῖτε οὖν, οὐκ οἴδατε γὰρ πότε ὁ κύριος τῆς οἰκίας ἔρχεται, ἢ ὀψὲ ἢ μεσονύκτιον ἢ ἀλεκτοροφωνίας ἢ πρωΐ, 36 μὴ ἐλθὼν ἐξαίφνης εὕρῃ ὑμᾶς καθεύδοντας. 37 <u>ὃ δὲ</u> ὑμῖν λέγω, πᾶσιν λέγω, γρηγορεῖτε.

Key: Single underlining = Semitic influence (most probably Septuagintal)

~~Strike through~~
in vv.8,11,12,22 = perhaps from the Aramaic
in v.17 οὐαί and v.30 ἀμήν = from the Hebrew

Double underlining = normal usage in *Koine* Greek, and features reclassified as normal usage in *Koine* Greek.

It is at least clear that further evidence has been given here in support of the claims of many of the source and form critics that Mk 13 contains disparate elements—even perhaps including larger elements of vv.14-20(21) and vv.24-27—which have been shaped together into a discourse. However to draw definitive conclusions about the ultimate origins of these elements would be premature at this stage, and especially simply to label any larger element(s) as a Jewish apocalypse. It is within the scope of form analysis to make pronouncements on the *Sitz im Leben* and historicity of each saying or group of sayings, and some steps in this direction have been made in this chapter, such as that vv.8,11,12,22 may be of Aramaic origin, vv.24-27 Septuagintal, and that vv.2,30,32 and 34 have the highest claim to being words of the historical Jesus. However, given the potential for other types of analysis which follow below to shed light on these questions, no firm conclusions will be drawn at this stage. It should be noted, however, that any explanation of the origins of the discourse must make some sense of the patterns of linguistic homogeneity and diversity described above. In themselves they do not constitute an adequate basis for the delineation of divergent traditions within Mk 13, but corroborated by the findings of form analysis and the other approaches undertaken below, they provide helpful parameters within which the discussion can continue to be guided.

II

JESUS' ESCHATOLOGICAL DISCOURSE

Major proponents: Beasley-Murray (1954, 1957, 1982, 1986, 1990, 1993); Wenham (1984).
Basic thesis: That Mk 13 consists substantially of the words of the historical Jesus, either as a collection of early Christian eschatological catechesis (Beasley-Murray), or as part of a larger pre-synoptic eschatological discourse (Wenham).
Dominant method: Traditio-historical criticism (NT).
Critique: A re-evaluation of NT eschatological traditions and an analysis of unique vocabulary and unique syntax in Mk 13.

Almost every analysis of Mk 13 since World War II has opened with a reference to G. R. BEASLEY-MURRAY's painstaking examination of the Little Apocalypse Theory.[1] In that first major study Beasley-Murray attempted to refute the widely held view outlined in chapter 1 that Mk 13 contains a Jewish apocalypse rather than the teachings of the historical Jesus. For Beasley-Murray the issue at stake then was the 'authenticity'[2] of the discourse, and he at least succeeded in challenging the assumption that an anti- or non-apocalyptic Jesus was a methodological presupposition for the study of Mk 13. Historically, the Little Apocalypse Theory arose as an attempt to defend Jesus against being presented as a discredited apocalyptic figure,[3] but it achieved this at the expense of the historicity of the Markan text. Beasley-Murray initially endeavoured to defend both the 'integrity' of Jesus (even though he conceded that "our Lord regarded the fall of Jerusalem, and its accompanying events, as part of the judgments of the End")[4] and the 'integrity' of Mk 13 as at least substantially representing the words of Jesus. As a résumé of an era, and

---

[1] Beasley-Murray, *Jesus and the Future* (1954), now extended and reprinted in *Jesus and the Last Days* (1993). The tendency for scholars to commence their examinations of Mk 13 with a reference to Beasley-Murray's work continues into recent times. See the first sentence, for example, of Adela Yarbro Collins, "Mark 13: An Apocalyptic Discourse", in *The Beginning of the Gospel. Probings of Mark in Context* (Minneapolis 1992), 73-91.

[2] A less emotive and more accurate term would be 'historicity', since sayings attributed to Jesus after a process of interpretation and/or via the words of a Christian prophet may still have been accepted by the church as 'authentic' and authoritative.

[3] See Beasley-Murray's account (in *Jesus and the Future,* 11-21; *Jesus and the Last Days,* 18-20; and more briefly in "The Vision on the Mount", 39f) of E. Renan's *Vie de Jésus* (1863, popularising the earlier critique by D. F. Strauss, 1835-6) where Mk 13:30 is taken as evidence of the falsehood of Jesus' word; and the response by Colani, *Jésus Christ,* where to rescue the integrity and humanity of Jesus, the discourse is attributed to Jewish Christians, and the Little Apocalypse Theory is argued in its best-known form.

[4] Beasley-Murray, *A Commentary on Mark Thirteen* (London 1957), 101.

as a clear and sometimes scintillating critique of the work of scholars from Strauss to Lohmeyer, and now Drewermann—from the 'Life of Jesus' approach to the form critics, and now also to the redaction and literary critics—Beasley-Murray's work has found wide acceptance. However, his basic argument then—that "the variety of reconstructions of the hypothetical apocalypse"[5] itself disqualified the Little Apocalypse theory—has met with little support. This is despite the obvious delight with which he pointed out that at some stage in recent scholarly writings every verse in Mk 13 has been both suggested as part of the 'apocalypse' and omitted from it,[6] and every decade in the first century claimed as its time of origin![7] But such diversity of opinion in itself does not necessarily indicate untruth, it may simply be an indication of the difficulty in ascertaining the truth.

At no stage then or since has Beasley-Murray implied that Mk 13 *as it stands* represents an historical discourse of Jesus, yet he has consistently argued that the Jesuanic origins of substantial portions of the discourse should not be ruled out. His first writings were focussed on the case against the Little Apocalypse Theory to such an extent that his own positive suggestions were overshadowed, but this has been remedied in his more recent works.[8] Beasley-Murray now emphasises the composite nature of the chapter and sees "the stamp of Mark's style on every sentence of the discourse".[9] Pointing out that eschatological instruction often formed the climax of early Christian teaching discourses,[10] he

[5] Repeated in these words quite recently in Beasley-Murray, *Jesus and the Kingdom*, 414. Here he adds also the reasons: "the relation of the essential elements of the 'apocalypse' to the teaching of Jesus elsewhere attested, and the stamp of Mark's style on every sentence of the discourse".

[6] Beasley-Murray, *Jesus and the Kingdom*, note 55, 413. The reference there should be to page 15 (not 10) of *A Commentary on Mark Thirteen*.

[7] Beasley-Murray, *Jesus and the Future*, 244.

[8] First spelt out in his article "Second Thoughts", and developed more fully in *Jesus and the Kingdom*, "The Vision on the Mount" and *Jesus and the Last Days*, 350-376. Note the disclaimer in *Commentary*, 11, footnote 1: "I would take the opportunity here of disclaiming the view that *Jesus and the Future* was written to prove that Mk. 13 was spoken by Jesus precisely in the form in which it has come down to us. I had no such purpose and do not believe the proposition to be demonstrable. I wrote to show that the contents of the discourse have high claim to authenticity, which is a different matter."

[9] Beasley-Murray, "Second Thoughts", 414. Indeeed, Beasley-Murray now emphasises the Markan contribution to the discourse so much that he is quite right to question whether he should really be classified together with David Wenham in this chapter (*Jesus and the Last Days*, 321). Nevertheless, he still suggests that the Day of the Lord language and use of the prophets in Mk 13 are consistent with Jesus' teaching elsewhere (or at least that the possibility "is not to be excluded", *Jesus and the Last Days*, 361-2)—a possibility that has received significant support recently from Yarbro Collins, "An Apocalyptic Discourse", 90-91: "The possibility that much of the tradition in Mark 13 goes back to the historical Jesus, including a version of vv 14-23, and that he himself alluded to Daniel should not be ruled out unless good reasons can be articulated for doing so."

[10] He gives as examples Matthew's Sermon on the Mount and the Missionary Discourse, and the conclusion to Q (Luke 17:22f). "Second Thoughts", 415.

argues that the evangelist has shaped chapter 13 out of primitive Christian catechesis containing traditions of instructions by Jesus, to form the climax to his presentation of the teachings of Jesus.[11] Beasley-Murray detects four groups of sayings amongst the pre-Markan catechetical units:

(i)   sayings on the tribulation of Israel (vv.14 and 19, to which 15-16,17-18 and eventually 20, were added), perhaps circulating together with vv.2,3-4

(ii) sayings on the tribulation of the church (vv.9 and 11, later joined by 10,12-13a and 13b);

(iii) sayings on pseudomessiahs and the true Messiah (vv.21,24-26 and later 6,22 and 27);

(iv) and sayings on the parousia and watchfulness (vv.26 and (33),34-36).[12]

The second and fourth groups came together naturally as 'endurance through suffering' became linked with the call to 'watch' in the early church, as evident in 1 Th 5:6-8; 1 P 4:7; 5:8-9; Ro 13:11-13; Ep 6:10-18 and 2 Th 2:15.[13] The first and third groups, "encouraged, if not actually stimulated, by the Caligula episode of 39-40 A.D.,"[14] were also joined together before Mk 13 was compiled, as indicated—according to Beasley-Murray—by 2 Th 2:1-9. But a closer examination shows that these supposed connections between Mk 13 and the Thessalonian correspondence are at a topical level rather than specific links which might be demonstrated by common vocabulary or phraseology.[15] To show that

---

[11] "Second Thoughts", 415.

[12] Beasley-Murray, *Jesus and the Kingdom,* 323; "The Vision on the Mount", 42, and *Jesus and the Last Days,* 357f. V.26 occurs in both groups (iii) and (iv).

[13] Beasley-Murray initially listed 1 Th 1-3 and 4:15-5:11 as the evidence (*Jesus and the Kingdom,* 323). The former reference is very general indeed and was omitted in "The Vision on the Mount", 42, and *Last Days,* 359, but not 361. Close examination shows that there are no *specific* connections at all between these traditions. According to Beasley-Murray's own estimation of the links between Mk 13 and the Thessalonian letters (*Jesus and the Kingdom,* 323, see Table in endnote 54, 412; and *Last Days,* 361f), the only noteworthy link with the first 3 chapters of 1 Th is between Mk 13:19 (a group 1 saying) and 1 Th 2:16. Indeed, according to this table there are almost as many 'links' with the verses excluded (13:5,7,32 and 33?) from the four groups of sayings as there are with those included (13:6,14,22,24-27,13 and 19). Thus the supposed links with Thessalonians don't seem to support Beasley-Murray's fourfold groupings unless a more extended pre-synoptic eschatological discourse is assumed, a position which is analysed further below, but specifically precluded by Beasley-Murray: "Of one thing, however, we may be confident: there is neither evidence nor likelihood that the groups of sayings which we have described were brought together to form a single discourse prior to Mark." *Last Days,* 362.

[14] Beasley-Murray, *Jesus and the Kingdom,* 324; *Last Days,* 360-1.

[15] There *are some* examples of parallel vocabulary between Mk 13 and the Thessalonian letters, but not such that any necessary connection between them can be demonstrated. This is particularly evident when the differing contexts of the terminology are noted. Beasley-Murray's list of 'highly probable' links (*Jesus and the Kingdom,* 412, footnote 54; and *Last Days,* 361, footnote 24) is as follows: Mk 13:5 and 2 Th 2:3a ('deceive/lead astray' appears to be common, but is actually πλανάω in Mk and ἐξαπατάω in Th); Mk 13:6 and 2 Th 2:2,9 (the many who say Ἐγώ εἰμι in Mk

these general themes occur together elsewhere, alongside other very different material, does not necessarily help to explain their origins in the text in question unless a specific relationship can be demonstrated between Mk 13 and the Thessalonian letters. The type of doctrinal synthesis which Beasley-Murray undertakes may well be appropriate at the canonical level, but as a means of evaluating the distinctive contribution of the Gospel of Mark it assumes far too much in the area of commonality between the various New Testament writings. In this particular case, the differences between Mk 13 and Thessalonians can be shown even more clearly by the important vocabulary and themes they do *not* have in common—and it is not possible to attribute such differences to Markan redaction alone.[16]

---

compared with ἡ ἀποστασία/ὁ ἄνομος in Th); Mk 13:7 and 2 Th 2:2 (both use θροέω); Mk 13:14 and 2 Th 2:3-4 (assumes a connection between the 'abomination of desolation' and 'the lawless one/the apostasy'); Mk 13:22 and 2 Th 2:9 (σημεῖα καὶ τέρατα in Mk, and σημείοις καὶ τέρασιν ψεύδους in Th); Mk 13:24-27 and 1 Th 4:15-17 (radically different descriptions—the only common vocabulary being ἐν νεφέλαις). We could add here the use of the image of a woman in labour (Mk 13:8 and 1 Th 5:3), though the Pauline description has more in common with the vocabulary of Mk 13:17. Beasley-Murray then goes on to give even 'less certain' links, followed by 'similar viewpoints ... without apparent citation', and includes references to other Pauline letters. It would seem rather that there is no 'apparent citation' evident anywhere between Mk 13 and the Thessalonian letters, despite Beasley-Murray's comment (*Jesus and the Kingdom,* 412, repeated in *Jesus and the Last Days,* 361, footnote 24) that the "reflections of the eschatological discourse in Paul's writings have been underestimated in recent years." Again this begs the question as to whether the eschatological discourse existed in a pre-synoptic—even pre-Pauline—form, and given the dissimilarities in vocabulary just outlined it would seem that if it did then it was not known to Paul. At what stage, then, did Beasley-Murray's four groups of sayings come together? The arguments of David Wenham, "Paul and the Synoptic Apocalypse", in *Gospel Perspectives* 2, ed R. T. France and D. Wenham (Sheffield 1981), 345-375; and "'This Generation Will Not Pass...' A Study of Jesus' Future Expectation in Mark 13", in *Christ the Lord,* ed H. H. Rowdon (Leicester 1982), 127-150—are heavily qualifed: *"If these speculations are correct,* then Paul becomes an important and very early witness to our suggested interpretation of the eschatological discourse" ("'This Generation'", 146, footnote 13, italics added). It seems rather that what Paul and Mk 13 have in common is an expectation that God will act powerfully before the generation of Jesus dies out, and such a hope could stem from the common knowledge of a saying as brief as Mk 9:1.

[16] The following words and concepts from 1 Th and 2 Th *do not occur* in any specific way in the Gospel of Mark (the lists are by no means exhaustive): 1 Th—the appearance (παρουσία) of the Lord, the voice of the archangel, the trumpet of God, the dead in Christ, the meeting of the Lord in the air; 2 Th—the day of the Lord (cf 'that day' in Mk), the rebellion/apostasy, the man of lawlessness/son of perdition, condemnation/judging of the wicked. There are, therefore, profound differences between the eschatology of the Thessalonian correspondence and the Gospel of Mark. We must not read Markan eschatology through Pauline glasses. If it *is* ever demonstrated beyond question that the author of Mark had access to Paul's writings or the same sources as Paul, then these conclusions will not be invalidated so much as underlined. For then, rather than Mark merely giving a *different* expression of eschatological hope, it would have to be understood as given in *opposition* to that expressed by Paul. The description of hope in Mark would not change, but the different context (of deliberate divergence from Paul), would make it even more radical.

Despite affirming Lambrecht's discovery of Markan style and redaction throughout the chapter,[17] Beasley-Murray describes the evangelist's redactional activity as essentially organisational rather than pointing to specific words and phrases. He argues that βλέπετε (in vv.5,9,23 and 33) is Markan, as is the repetition of ταῦτα and ταῦτα πάντα in vv.28-29, but thinks that in v.10 only πρῶτον is likely to have come from Mark.[18] The ὁ ἀναγινώσκων νοείτω phrase of v.14 is "an editorial insertion"[19] presumably made by the evangelist,[20] as are μετὰ τὴν θλῖψιν ἐκείνην in v.24, the ἐν rather than μετὰ νεφέλαις in v.26, the rather incongruous ἀπόδημος of v.34 and the πᾶσιν λέγω of v.37. Apart from these specific words and phrases, Beasley-Murray uses words like 'ordering', 'conjoining' and 'including' to describe the evangelist's activities:

> It is reasonable to assume that Mark's prime function in the composition of the eschatological discourse, as in chapters 4 and 8.27-9.1, was to bring together the varied elements available to him in his tradition and to fashion them into a unitary whole in the light of the contemporary situation and needs of his church.[21]

Beasley-Murray thinks it probable that this Markan *Sitz im Leben* was during (or perhaps just after) the Jewish war (in the late 60's or early 70's of the Common Era), making the linking together of the material in chapter 13, and the connection between the fall of the temple and the end times, a subject of profound significance for the Markan church. Thus for Beasley-Murray, the evangelist has been the one largely responsible, in the light of the Jewish war, for the shaping of chapter 13 out of the words of Jesus as collected and developed in the four groups of primitive Christian catechesis. There is no doubt that this process is at least partly true, for nearly all recent commentators concede that some authentic words of Jesus remain in the chapter.[22] But many more questions need to

Of course at the canonical level Beasley-Murray is quite correct to see these differing eschatologies as expressions of the *same hope* (so "The Vision on the Mount", 51)—which is infinitely better than regarding them as expectations of separate events and thereby developing a version of one of the popular forms of 'serial eschatology'. But before reducing the diverse biblical accounts to the 'theological bottom line' it is necessary to appreciate their distinctive contributions and to savour the full implications of their differences.

17 *Jesus and the Kingdom,* 324 and endnote 59, 413.

18 *Jesus and the Kingdom,* 325. Perhaps vv.29-30 is meant for vv.28-29? As for v.10, Beasley-Murray argues that Mark inserted the verse into its new context (prompted by the closing phrase of v.9), but was only responsible for adding the πρῶτον (*Last Days,* 403).

19 *Jesus and the Kingdom,* 329; *Last Days,* 411.

20 As Beasley-Murray argued in *Commentary,* 57.

21 Beasley-Murray, "Second Thoughts", 418 = *Last Days,* 363.

22 See below for examples of the range of opinion. Interestingly, it is Lambrecht, with whose redactional analysis Beasley-Murray agrees most, who is one of the most sceptical about authentic words of Jesus in the chapter: "Little in this address... bears the marks of

be asked of the text before we can argue that substantial portions of the discourse originated with the historical Jesus.

This becomes apparent in the first place because of the acute difficulties of assigning ὁ ἀναγινώσκων νοείτω (v.14) to the words of Jesus.[23] If what appears to be attributed by the author to the historical Jesus can be shown to contain even one doubtful phrase such as this then the burden of proof shifts to those who would like to argue the historicity of each part of the discourse.[24] If it is argued that this phrase is merely an editorial aside to a wider audience, then we must also ask whether vv.37 and 23 are not more of the same, and then each of the βλέπετε sayings, and so on through the whole discourse. Now Beasley-Murray is prepared to concede this line of argument and accepts at least this much editorial interference in the chapter. But on what grounds does he divide the remainder of the discourse into four topical groups of sayings and assign them to the teachings of the historical Jesus?[25] Beasley-Murray's principal arguments are: "the relation of the essential elements of the 'apocalypse' to the teaching of Jesus elsewhere attested", mainly in the Thessalonian letters; and the failure of the Little Apocalypse Theory to explain the origins of the discourse.[26]

authenticity. Not even verses like 30 and 32 possess the characteristics of faithfully delivered words of Jesus... So much has become plain: in our modern concern for historical truth no norms can be set for the freedom in which Mark took up his task as author". *Die Redaktion der Markus-Apokalypse,* 259, translated in Beasley-Murray, "Second Thoughts", endnote 14, 420.

[23] Obviously the saying is inappropriate in the setting described in v.3, ὁ ἀκούων νοείτω would make more sense, but would still read as an aside to a larger audience. See Marxsen's discussion of this point in *Mark the Evangelist,* 163f.

[24] Contrary to Wenham's assertion: "the onus of proof must be on those who deny the teaching to Jesus, not on those who affirm it", (Wenham, *Rediscovery*, 373). A parallel to this situation is the question about the authorship of Deuteronomy. Since it contains an account of the death of Moses, it is incumbent on those who still wish to claim Mosaic authorship to demonstrate which parts were written by him, rather than assume everything was until proven otherwise. Thus the burden of proof shifts to those who make claims about the whole contrary to the evidence—even the evidence concerning just a part of the whole.

[25] The arbitrary nature of a purely topical division of the discourse is highlighted by a comparison with a similar attempt. F. Flückiger, "Die Redaktion der Zukunftsrede Mark 13", *TZ* 26 (1970), 395-409, suggests the following four-fold division: (i) words regarding The End (vv.8,12,17,19,24-27; with v.17 an insertion); (ii) mission logia (vv.5,6,21-23,7,9-11,13); (iii) a speech in the temple (vv.1-4,14-16,18,28-32); (iv) the parable about vigilance (vv.33-37). Such divisions of the text are of little use unless they can be supported by evidence other than a similarity of subject matter. Beasley-Murray claims that the fourfold grouping is "a reasonable working hypothesis" ("The Vision on the Mount", 43), and argues that it is somewhat similar in construction to that other collection of sayings, the Sermon on the Mount ("The Vision on the Mount", 39). However there is no parallel in Mk 13 to the explicit and incisive re-interpretation of Jewish scripture that so dominates the Sermon on the Mount. Nor is there any basis for the description of Mk 13 as a 'vision'.

[26] Beasley-Murray, "Second Thoughts", 414. Until "Vision on the Mount" and *Last Days,* Beasley-Murray still relied heavily on this latter argument, which at best only disqualified other viewpoints without directly supporting his own.

The first line of argument has been challenged specifically by Norman Perrin, whose response to Beasley-Murray's attempt to re-establish the historicity of the eschatological discourse was to point to the strangeness of its vocabulary compared with the rest of the teachings of Jesus in the Gospel.[27] At one level, these arguments pass each other by like ships in the night—Beasley-Murray is concerned with the similarity of 'essential elements' of teaching at a canonical level, whilst Perrin responds with an analysis of 'unique vocabulary' within the Gospel of Mark, and with some reference to Revelation. But an examination of Perrin's claims is helpful in clarifying Beasley-Murray's argument, as well as for giving an appreciation of the difficulties presented by Mk 13 and its relationship to the rest of the New Testament. Perrin argued that the percentage of words unique to vv.5-27, (21.2%), is greater than in the long ending of Mk 16:9-20, (17.2%), or Jn 7:53-8:11, (17.2%), passages widely regarded as later additions to their respective Gospels. These statistics, and the parallels that Perrin drew with the vocabulary of Revelation (15 out of the 35 words which occur *only* in chapter 13 in the Gospel of Mark are also found in Revelation), are also quoted by Eugene Boring as evidence of "the close resemblance between Mark 13 and our prime example of Christian prophecy"[28]—the Revelation of John. This forms the concluding point in Boring's argument "that the pre-redactional form of Mark 13:5b-31 is itself the product of Christian prophecy" rather than the words of the historical Jesus.[29] But there are at least three questions which arise from such assertions:

(i)   Does the concentrated occurrence of unique vocabulary necessarily indicate another source, or could it just be the result of a major change of topic?

(ii) Does the extent of the unique vocabulary in Mk 13 indicate a pre-Markan unit consisting of vv.5b-31 (so Boring), vv.5-27 (so Perrin), or some other sized unit?

(iii) What is the significance of the vocabulary common to Mk 13 and the Revelation of John?

To investigate these questions further a detailed examination of the vocabulary cited by Perrin and Boring is required. Text Sheet 2 indicates the unique vocabulary originally referred to by Perrin in vv.5-27. Those

---

[27] Norman Perrin, *The Kingdom of God in the Teaching of Jesus* (London 1963), 130-134, points to two factors which set Mk 13 apart from other examples of the teaching of Jesus, namely:

(i)   the strangeness of the vocabulary compared with the rest of the Gospel (a claim analysed in this chapter); and

(ii) the distinctive use of the LXX and Theodotion in Old Testament references, rather than the equivalent of the Hebrew as used in the words of Jesus in other places in the Gospel (a claim which is examined in chapter 3 below).

[28] Boring, *Sayings*, 195. Boring also lists another 20 parallels between Mk 13 and Revelation.

[29] Boring, *Sayings*, 195.

words occurring only once in the Gospel of Mark in the rest of chapter 13 (vv.1-5 and 28-37) are also indicated, but by using double underlining.

Text Sheet 2: Unique vocabulary in Mk 13

13.1 Καὶ ἐκπορευομένου αὐτοῦ ἐκ τοῦ ἱεροῦ λέγει αὐτῷ εἷς τῶν μαθητῶν αὐτοῦ, Διδάσκαλε, ἴδε ποταποὶ λίθοι καὶ ποταπαὶ οἰκοδομαί. 2 καὶ ὁ Ἰησοῦς εἶπεν αὐτῷ, Βλέπεις ταύτας τὰς μεγάλας οἰκοδομάς; οὐ μὴ ἀφεθῇ ὧδε λίθος ἐπὶ λίθον ὃς οὐ μὴ καταλυθῇ. 3 Καὶ καθημένου αὐτοῦ εἰς τὸ Ὄρος τῶν Ἐλαιῶν κατέναντι τοῦ ἱεροῦ ἐπηρώτα αὐτὸν κατ᾽ ἰδίαν Πέτρος καὶ Ἰάκωβος καὶ Ἰωάννης καὶ Ἀνδρέας. 4 Εἰπὸν ἡμῖν πότε ταῦτα ἔσται, καὶ τί τὸ σημεῖον ὅταν μέλλῃ ταῦτα συντελεῖσθαι πάντα. 5 ὁ δὲ Ἰησοῦς ἤρξατο λέγειν αὐτοῖς, βλέπετε μή τις ὑμᾶς πλανήσῃ· 6 πολλοὶ ἐλεύσονται ἐπὶ τῷ ὀνόματί μου λέγοντες ὅτι Ἐγώ εἰμι, καὶ πολλοὺς πλανήσουσιν. 7 ὅταν δὲ ἀκούσητε πολέμους καὶ ἀκοὰς πολέμων, μὴ θροεῖσθε· δεῖ γενέσθαι, ἀλλ᾽ οὔπω τὸ τέλος. 8 ἐγερθήσεται γὰρ ἔθνος ἐπ᾽ ἔθνος καὶ βασιλεία ἐπὶ βασιλείαν, ἔσονται σεισμοὶ κατὰ τόπους, ἔσονται λιμοί· ἀρχὴ ὠδίνων ταῦτα. 9 βλέπετε δὲ ὑμεῖς ἑαυτούς· παραδώσουσιν ὑμᾶς εἰς συνέδρια καὶ εἰς συναγωγὰς δαρήσεσθε καὶ ἐπὶ ἡγεμόνων καὶ βασιλέων σταθήσεσθε ἕνεκεν ἐμοῦ εἰς μαρτύριον αὐτοῖς. 10 καὶ εἰς πάντα τὰ ἔθνη πρῶτον δεῖ κηρυχθῆναι τὸ εὐαγγέλιον. 11 καὶ ὅταν ἄγωσιν ὑμᾶς παραδιδόντες, μὴ προμεριμνᾶτε τί λαλήστε, ἀλλ᾽ ὃ ἐὰν δοθῇ ὑμῖν ἐν ἐκείνῃ τῇ ὥρᾳ τοῦτο λαλεῖτε, οὐ γάρ ἐστε ὑμεῖς οἱ λαλοῦντες ἀλλὰ τὸ πνεῦμα τὸ ἅγιον. 12 καὶ παραδώσει ἀδελφὸς ἀδελφὸν εἰς θάνατον καὶ πατὴρ τέκνον, καὶ ἐπαναστήσονται τέκνα ἐπὶ γονεῖς καὶ θανατώσουσιν αὐτούς· 13 καὶ ἔσεσθε μισούμενοι ὑπὸ πάντων διὰ τὸ ὄνομά μου. ὁ δὲ ὑπομείνας εἰς τέλος οὗτος σωθήσεται. 14 Ὅταν δὲ ἴδητε τὸ βδέλυγμα τῆς ἐρημώσεως ἐστηκότα ὅπου οὐ δεῖ, ὁ ἀναγινώσκων νοείτω, τότε οἱ ἐν τῇ Ἰουδαίᾳ φευγέτωσαν εἰς τὰ ὄρη, 15 ὁ δὲ ἐπὶ τοῦ δώματος μὴ καταβάτω μηδὲ εἰσελθάτω ἆραί τι ἐκ τῆς οἰκίας αὐτοῦ, 16 καὶ ὁ εἰς τὸν ἀγρὸν μὴ ἐπιστρεψάτω εἰς τὰ ὀπίσω ἆραι τὸ ἱμάτιον αὐτοῦ. 17 οὐαὶ δὲ ταῖς ἐν γαστρὶ ἐχούσαις καὶ ταῖς θηλαζούσαις ἐν ἐκείναις ταῖς ἡμέραις. 18 προσεύχεσθε δὲ ἵνα μὴ γένηται χειμῶνος· 19 ἔσονται γὰρ αἱ ἡμέραι ἐκεῖναι θλῖψις οἵα οὐ γέγονεν τοιαύτη ἀπ᾽ ἀρχῆς κτίσεως ἣν ἔκτισεν ὁ θεὸς ἕως τοῦ νῦν καὶ οὐ μὴ γένηται. 20 καὶ εἰ μὴ ἐκολόβωσεν κύριος τὰς ἡμέρας, οὐκ ἂν ἐσώθη πᾶσα σάρξ. ἀλλὰ διὰ τοὺς ἐκλεκτοὺς οὓς ἐξελέξατο ἐκολόβωσεν τὰς ἡμέρας. 21 καὶ τότε ἐάν τις ὑμῖν εἴπῃ, Ἴδε ὧδε ὁ Χριστός, Ἴδε ἐκεῖ, μὴ πιστεύετε· 22 ἐγερθήσονται γὰρ ψευδόχριστοι καὶ ψευδοπροφῆται καὶ δώσουσιν σημεῖα καὶ τέρατα πρὸς τὸ ἀποπλανᾶν, εἰ δυνατόν, τοὺς ἐκλεκτούς. 23 ὑμεῖς δὲ βλέπετε· προείρηκα ὑμῖν πάντα.
24 Ἀλλὰ ἐν ἐκείναις ταῖς ἡμέραις μετὰ τὴν θλῖψιν ἐκείνην
    ὁ ἥλιος σκοτισθήσεται,
  καὶ ἡ σελήνη οὐ δώσει τὸ φέγγος αὐτῆς,
  25 καὶ οἱ ἀστέρες ἔσονται ἐκ τοῦ οὐρανοῦ πίπτοντες,
  καὶ αἱ δυνάμεις αἱ ἐν τοῖς οὐρανοῖς σαλευθήσονται.
26 καὶ τότε ὄψονται τὸν υἱὸν τοῦ ἀνθρώπου ἐρχόμενον ἐν νεφέλαις μετὰ δυνάμεως πολλῆς καὶ δόξης. 27 καὶ τότε ἀποστελεῖ τοὺς ἀγγέλους καὶ ἐπισυνάξει τοὺς ἐκλεκτοὺς αὐτοῦ ἐκ τῶν τεσσάρων ἀνέμων ἀπ᾽ ἄκρου γῆς ἕως ἄκρου οὐρανοῦ. 28 Ἀπὸ δὲ τῆς συκῆς μάθετε τὴν παραβολήν· ὅταν ἤδη ὁ κλάδος αὐτῆς ἁπαλὸς γένηται καὶ ἐκφύῃ τὰ φύλλα, γινώσκετε ὅτι ἐγγὺς τὸ θέρος ἐστίν. 29 οὕτως καὶ ὑμεῖς, ὅταν ἴδητε ταῦτα γινόμενα γινώσκετε ὅτι ἐγγύς ἐστιν ἐπὶ θύραις. 30 ἀμὴν λέγω ὑμῖν ὅτι οὐ μὴ παρέλθῃ ἡ γενεὰ αὕτη μέχρις οὗ ταῦτα πάντα γένηται. 31 ὁ οὐρανὸς καὶ ἡ γῆ παρελεύσονται, οἱ δὲ λόγοι μου οὐ μὴ παρελεύσονται. 32 περὶ δὲ τῆς ἡμέρας ἐκείνης ἢ τῆς ὥρας οὐδεὶς οἶδεν, οὐδὲ οἱ ἄγγελοι ἐν οὐρανῷ οὐδὲ ὁ

υἱός, εἰ μὴ ὁ πατήρ. 33 βλέπετε <u>ἀγρυπνεῖτε</u>· οὐκ οἴδατε γὰρ πότε ὁ καιρός ἐστιν. 34 ὡς ἄνθρωπος <u>ἀπόδημος</u> ἀφεὶς τὴν οἰκίαν αὐτοῦ καὶ δοὺς τοῖς δούλοις αὐτοῦ τὴν ἐξουσίαν, <u>ἑκάστῳ</u> τὸ ἔργον αὐτοῦ, καὶ τῷ <u>θυρωρῷ</u> ἐνετείλατο ἵνα γρηγορῇ. 35 γρηγορεῖτε οὖν, οὐκ οἴδατε γὰρ πότε ὁ κύριος τῆς οἰκίας ἔρχεται, ἢ ὀψὲ ἢ <u>μεσονύκτιον</u> ἢ <u>ἀλεκτοροφωνίας</u> ἢ πρωΐ, 36 μὴ ἐλθὼν <u>ἐξαίφνης</u> εὕρῃ ὑμᾶς καθεύδοντας. 37 ὃ δὲ ὑμῖν λέγω, πᾶσιν λέγω, γρηγορεῖτε.

Key: <u>Single underlining</u> = Perrin's 35 words (minus θλῖψις, plus recurrent uses)
<u><u>Double underlining</u></u> = Unique vocabulary outside of vv.5-27

If the words in chapter 13 (unique or otherwise) are only counted *once* regardless of how often they occur, then the proportion of unique vocabulary is as calculated by Perrin, namely: 35 out of 165 words (21.2%). But if the *total number* of words is counted rather than just the total vocabulary, the proportion of unique words drops dramatically to 41 out of 381 (or only 10.8%).[30] On this same basis, it is possible to recalculate and compare all of Perrin's figures thus:[31]

	Mk 13:5-27	Mk 13:28-37	Mk 16:9-20	Jn 7:53-8:11
Perrin's figures for unique vocabulary	35/165 = 21.2%	13/79 = 16.4%	16/92 = 17.2%	14/82 = 17.2%
Figures based on total word count	41/381 = 10.8%	14/152 = 9.2%	20/171 = 11.7%	16/169 = 9.5%

Clearly the percentages quoted by Perrin are not as impressive when calculated by the second method. Yet there would appear to be no reason why such a straight-forward counting of all words should not be as good an indicator of the 'strangeness' of the vocabulary in Mk 13 as the method adopted by Perrin. Indeed, Perrin's method was probably used simply as a matter of convenience because that is the way the vocabulary is listed

[30] The 41 includes Perrin's 35 words minus θλῖψις (which occurs in 4:17), plus the multiple counting of πλανάω (vv.5 and 6—it also occurs in 12:24 and 27, but Perrin distinguishes its apocalyptic use in Mk 13, 'deceive', 'seduce', from its more general use in Mk 12, 'mistaken', 'wrong'), πόλεμος (twice in v.7), τέλος (vv.7 and 13—used in 3:26, but not of 'The End'), κολοβόω (twice in v.20), ἐκλεκτός (vv.20,22 and 27), and ἄκρον (twice in v.27). The total number of words in vv.5-27 is 381.

[31] The unique words for all of Mk 13 are shown in Text Sheet 2. For Mk 16:9-20 [according to Robert Morgenthaler, *Statistik des Neutestamentlichen Wortschatzes* (Zürich/Frankfurt 1958), 186-7] they are πορευθεῖσα (vv.10,12 and 15), πενθοῦσι, ἐθεάθη (vv.11 and 14), ἠπίστησαν (vv.11 and 16), ἑτέρᾳ, μορφῇ, Ὕστερον, ἕνδεκα, παρακολουθήσει, ὄφεις, θανάσιμον, βλάψῃ, ἀνελήμφθη, συνεργοῦντος, βεβαιοῦντος, and ἐπακολουθούντων. For Jn 7:53-8:11 the unique words are Ἐλαιῶν, ὄρθρος, γραμματεύς, μοιχεία, αὐτοφώρῳ, μοιχεύειν, κύπτειν (v.6 only—not twice as listed by Morgenthaler, *Statistik,* 187), καταγράφειν, ἐπιμένειν, ἀνακύπτειν (vv.7 and 10), ἀναμάρτητος, κατακύπτειν, πρεσβύτερος, κατακρίνειν (vv.10 and 11).

and counted by Morgenthaler, both in his charts and his explanations.[32] But to count each word only once regardless of their actual frequency is to exaggerate the proportion of those words which really do occur only once, and thus to over-emphasise the unique vocabulary. Yet if the second and most obvious method of calculating the percentage of unique vocabulary in Mk 13 is used it does not seem to distinguish the chapter so clearly from the rest of the Gospel, nor assist in differentiating traditions within the chapter.

This becomes even more apparent when similar calculations are carried out on Mk 4, the other major discourse in the Gospel. Out of 493 words in vv.3-32, 60 are unique to that discourse, or 12.2%—an even more impressive result than for Mk 13.[33] It does not seem possible then, on the basis of the percentage of unique vocabulary alone, to suggest that a peculiar source lies behind Mk 13 unless the same is argued for Mk 4. Nor can the historicity of the discourse in chapter 13 be challenged on these grounds alone, unless the same challenge is made of chapter 4. Rather, it would appear that it is the change of topic in chapter 13 which results in a similar proportion of unusual vocabulary to that occurring in the agricultural parables of chapter 4.

Similarly, when the percentages are calculated for the larger sections within Mk 13 there is not enough variation to justify dividing one section off from another:

vv.5b-13	16/151	10.6%
vv.14-23	17/153	11.1%
vv.24-27	8/71	11.3%
vv.28-37	14/152	9.2%

On this evidence alone, there would appear to be little justification for accepting either Perrin's suggestion that vv.5-27 (41/381 = 10.8% unique vocabulary) or Boring's suggestion that vv.5b-31 (49/440 = 11.1% unique vocabulary) constitute the main concentration of unusual vocabulary—and therefore the most likely source behind the chapter.

---

[32] Morgenthaler, *Statistik,* charts 186-7, explanations 58-62.

[33] The unique vocabulary of Mk 4 is: σπείρων (vv.3,3,4,14,14,15,15,16,18,20,31 and 32! But even if this recurrent use of σπείρω in the chapter is omitted from the calculation, the proportion of unique vocabulary is still 49/493, or 9.9%, cf 10.8% in Mk 13:5-27), πετεινά (vv.4 and 32), πετρῶδης (vv.5 and 16), ἐξανέτειλεν, βάθος, ἐκαυματίσθη, ἀκάνθας (vv.7 twice, and 18), συνέπνιξαν (vv.7 and 19), αὐξανόμενα, τριάκοντα (vv.8 and 20), ἑξήκοντα (vv.8 and 20), μυστήριον, πρόσκαιροι, μέριμναι, ἀπάτη, πλούτου, ἐπιθυμίαι, ἄκαρπος, παραδέχονται, καρποφοροῦσιν (vv.20 and 28), λύχνος, μόδιον, λύχνιαν, κρυπτόν, ἀπόκρυφον, μέτρῳ, μετρεῖτε (v.24 twice), προστεθήσεται, σπόρον (vv.26 and 27), βλαστᾷ, μηκύνηται, αὐτομάτη, σῖτον, δρέπανον, θερισμός, κόκκῳ, σινάπεως, λαχάνων, κατασκηνοῦν.

It is also apparent that the parallels in vocabulary between Revelation and Mk 13 are not helpful in determining the extent of a source or its *Sitz im Leben*. The words they have in common are typical of the apocalyptic tradition,[34] and if they are indicative of any relationship more specific than a common Old Testament and apocalyptic heritage, it would be more likely that Revelation has borrowed from Mk 13. Indeed there is some evidence that the synoptic eschatological discourse does become something of a model for later Christian apocalypses.[35] However, it is still possible that both Mk 13 and Revelation may be the product of Christian prophets, as the arguments that Boring gives for such a conclusion extend further than just a common vocabulary, and will require further investigation in chapter 5 below.

Thus it is possible to conclude that attempts to demonstrate by vocabulary statistics alone that Mk 13 does not emanate from the historical Jesus but has been drawn from another distinctive source, have failed. The vocabulary of Mk 13 is no more distinctive than the other major discourse in the Gospel, Mk 4, and the parallels with the vocabulary of Revelation do not necessarily indicate a source other than Jesus. However, this does not mean that the opposite must be true—that Mk 13 is not distinctive but consistent with the teachings of Jesus attested elsewhere. As we have seen, Beasley-Murray's arguments for the historicity of the sources behind the discourse rest more on perceived links with the content of Thessalonians than with the rest of the Gospels or Revelation. But here too there are problems. There are very few specific parallels in terminology between Thessalonians and Mk 13.[36] Of course it helps if concepts like the *parousia* and the final judgment are projected anachronistically onto the text of Mk 13, but this is not permissible if we wish to examine *Markan* eschatology. Perhaps if an attempt is being made to gather unifying theological concepts—'a

---

[34] Perrin, *Kingdom,* 131, footnote 3, lists them as (number of occurrences in Revelation in brackets): ἀστήρ (14), βδέλυγμα (3), ἐκλεκτός (1), θλῖψις (5), κτίζω (2), μισέω (3), πλανάω (6), πόλεμος (9), σεισμός (7), σελήνη (4), σκοτίζομαι (4), τέλος (of The End—3), and ψευδοπροφήτης (3). To these should be added λιμός (2) and γαστήρ (1), to make the number up to the 15 words claimed by Perrin on the page above this list. The high number of occurrences of many of these words in Revelation is an indication of their 'apocalyptic' pedigree.

[35] The paradigmatic nature of the disciples' questions on the Mount of Olives (and other features of Mk 13) is evident, for example, in the Ethiopic Apocalypse of Peter: "Make known to us what are the signs of thy Parousia and of the end of the world, that we may perceive and mark the time of thy Parousia and instruct those who come after us...". See Richard Bauckham, "The Two Fig Tree Parables in the Apocalypse of Peter", *JBL* 104 (1985), 287.

[36] See the words listed in footnotes 15 and 16 above. Beasley-Murray, *Last Days,* 321, objects to my emphasis on this aspect of his argument, but it still seems to me that it is the Thessalonian correspondence that provides the crucial evidence, in his eyes, for the fourfold division of the traditions in Mk 13 and hence their origin in *early* (even Jesuanic) Christian catechesis. See, for example, the citation of evidence on this point in *Last Days,* 355-356: the Gospels/Q are referred to 6 times, Revelation 6 times, other traditions 7 times, and the Thessalonian correspondence 10 times.

canonical eschatology'—such licence is allowable, but even then it would be better to work with each distinctive tradition before attempting a synthesis. Surely we must allow the possibility that the eschatology of the Gospel of Mark is as distinctive as its christology when compared with other canonical writings? It remains to be seen how this distinctiveness can be measured and evaluated.

There has been another attempt to argue for the essential historicity of the eschatological discourse based on a close analysis of the relationship of Mk 13 to other material of a similar nature in the New Testament. DAVID WENHAM has attempted to establish that the links between the New Testament traditions relating to the content of Mk 13 indicate the existence of a pre-synoptic discourse which may be traced back to the teachings of Jesus.[37] Wenham uses a traditio-historical approach to examine the related texts in the synoptic eschatological discourses and also in the writings of Paul and the book of Revelation. Markan priority amongst the synoptic traditions is not assumed in every case, though his book basically confirms it (6).[38]

Wenham's argument commences with, and to a large degree hinges on, an analysis of the parable of the watchman in Mk 13:34-36 and parallels (15-49). He suggests that the author of Mark has commenced with the parable of the talents (in its complete form in Mt 25:14-30) and then switched to the parable of the watchman (found also in Lk 12:36-38 and a trace in Mt 24:42). From this Wenham proceeds to argue for a "pre-synoptic collection of parables including the watchman, the thief, the steward and the talents" (52) which the synoptic evangelists made use of independently, and then builds his case for the whole pre-synoptic eschatological discourse backwards from these parables, which he sees as being the original discourse conclusion. The arguments are cumulative[39] and so detailed that despite the author's plea for them to be judged on their merit rather than their implications,[40] it is impossible to avoid comment on their enormous ramifications from the very outset.

The first question that arises is whether Wenham's description of the redactional processes in Mk 13:34-36, which he attributes to the author of Mark, correspond in any way to the redactional activity evident in the rest of the Gospel. It would appear that this is not the case. There is evidence of the author of Mark inserting words and phrases into the

[37] Wenham, *Rediscovery*. Interestingly, despite the full title of the book *(The Rediscovery of Jesus' Eschatological Discourse),* the author concedes that "the findings of this book do not in themselves prove that the pre-synoptic eschatological discourse goes back to Jesus" *(Rediscovery,* 373).

[38] In order to avoid excessive footnoting, the page numbers in brackets in the main body of the text refer to D. Wenham, *The Rediscovery of Jesus' Eschatological Discourse,* until the end of this section.

[39] J. D. G. Dunn, *JTS* 38 (1987), 165, points out in his review of Wenham's book that a string of possibilities does not make a probability, but rather an even less certain possibility—mathematically demonstrated by: "$0.75^5 = 0.24$".

[40] See Wenham's concluding comments to *Rediscovery,* 374.

tradition;[41] intercalating units of tradition within another tradition;[42] collecting and arranging single sentences of tradition;[43] or framing traditions with settings and interpretations,[44] but in all cases the units of tradition themselves seem to remain relatively intact. Wenham suggests that Mk 13:34-36 has been formed by a dismembering and rejoining of two parables that were complete in the source available to the author. Thus the author of Mark is claimed to be a conflator of the material available to him, though there are many examples in Mark's Gospel illustrating that the author is averse to conflation.[45] That this process is unlikely on a small scale is supported by its improbability on a larger scale, despite those who still argue that Mark's Gospel is essentially an abbreviation of tradition.[46]

Wenham outlines a pre-synoptic eschatological discourse which contains elements from the synoptics, the Pauline corpus and Revelation. None of the authors reproduce anything like the entire discourse. Matthew, and Mark in an abbreviated way, whilst "interpreting the tradition, are seeking to preserve it and to pass it on" (373, footnote 1); Luke is much freer in his use and ordering of the material (365), and Paul and the author of Revelation even more uninhibited because "they are seeking to apply the tradition, not to transmit it" (373, footnote 1). Now this view reverses the usual process by which the handing down of

[41] The insertion of εὐθύς (1:10,12 etc.) is an obvious example, as is the phrase καὶ ἔλεγεν αὐτοῖς (2:27; 4:2,11,21,24; 6:4,10; 7:9; 8:21; 9:1,31; 11:17).

[42] Such as the dual healing stories, one within another, of 5:21-43, and other well-known 'Markan sandwiches' (cf 6:6b-32, the disciples and John the Baptist; 14:53-72, Peter and Jesus).

[43] Mk 13:9-13 will be argued as an example here.

[44] The Markan settings of 7:24,31 and 8:10, for example.

[45] Such as the extended 'aside' in 6:14-29 about John the Baptist and Herod, and the fuller treatment of miracle stories in Mark than the other synoptic parallels. Note here also the findings of the linguistic analysis in chapter 1 above that v.34 shows signs of Semitic influence—perhaps indicating its careful passing on by Mark—whereas the verses following may well be redactional.

[46] Wenham's thesis that the author of Mark conflated and drastically reduced not only the pre-synoptic eschatological parable collection but the whole discourse, attributes to the author an editorial process similar to that suggested by those who deny Markan priority. [See for example the arguments—particularly concerning Mk 13—of W. R. Farmer, *The Synoptic Problem* (London 1964), 271-283, and B. Reicke "A Test of Synoptic Relationships: Matthew 10:17-23 and 24: 9-14 with Parallels", in *New Synoptic Studies* (Macon 1983), 209-229]. An examination in any synopsis of the pericopes in Mk 1:40 through to the end of chapter 2 and their parallels, shows plainly that Mark's Gospel cannot be seen as an *abbreviation* of the tradition when compared with Matthew and Luke. To suggest that the author of Mark not only reduced the eschatological discourse (which is as far as Wenham goes), but omitted the birth narratives, the sermon on the mount and the resurrection appearances, and then deliberately scrambled Matthew's consistent use of κύριος (for example, which is what Farmer and Reicke imply), is to create insurmountable problems regarding a possible Markan *Sitz im Leben,* and raises the question as to how such a radical revision of the Gospel ever came to be accepted by enough churches to ensure its eventual inclusion in the canon. See also the pertinent comments on this matter by Howard C. Kee, *Community of the New Age: Studies in Mark's Gospel* (London 1977), 14f.

Gospel teachings and traditions is described, whereby the oral traditions of the words and actions of Jesus accumulate a number of applications and settings—perhaps are even mixed with Christian prophetic utterances and Old Testament exegesis—until they come to be written down in their various forms. In contrast, Wenham suggests a process of decay, whereby a large written (?) corpus of the teachings of the historical Jesus becomes fragmented and ultimately lost as a whole, as the New Testament writers use it selectively and apply portions of it to their church situations. Surely the words of a revered teacher grow and accumulate meaning rather than dissipate and lose meaning. A comparison here with the relatively careful way Matthew and Luke make use of the Q sayings is instructive, as it clearly illustrates the former process of a comparatively stable body of sayings accumulating different interpretations and settings as they are applied to different situations.

But even if the pre-synoptic eschatological discourse as outlined by Wenham were accepted, there are still more questions to be asked before concluding that it could be derived directly from the teachings of Jesus. Given the freedom with which each New Testament writer interprets and applies the supposed discourse, we would want to examine the possibility that other relevant material—such as Christian prophecy or Jewish apocalyptic fragments—was also included in its pre-Synoptic form. In assessing the Pauline use of the discourse we would need to examine the various references to authority made by Paul—'words of the Lord', 'traditions received' and so on[47]—and ask why so few of these are used in the relevant sections in Thessalonians. In the synoptic Gospels it would be appropriate at least to inquire into the possible use of the pseudonymous testamentary genre for the farewell discourse of Jesus, and to examine the possibility of a reading back onto the historical Jesus of words attributed by prophets to the risen Christ. Given the general lack of acceptance of Wenham's thesis,[48] it may be more profitable to direct these questions to the text of Mk 13 itself. There *is* relevance in the analysis of traditions within the New Testament, but not as the *sole* means of recovering the history of a text. Given the uncertain order of many of the writings, the doubts about the knowledge each author had of the others, the narrow time-scale encompassed, and the fact that the writers of the New Testament did not seem to consider themselves or each other to be as 'inspired' as earlier Jewish writers, it would seem that a tradition analysis of the *Old* Testament background to Mk 13 might be more productive.

---

[47] What sort of appeal to authority was Paul making, for example, by using such phrases as ἐν λόγῳ κυρίου (1 Th 4:15), ἐπιταγὴν κυρίου (1 Co 7:25), παρέλαβον ἀπὸ τοῦ κυρίου (1 Co 11:23), ὃ παρέλαβον (1 Co 15:3), and κυρίου ἐστὶν ἐντολή (1 Co 14:37)? Was he making claims about their historicity as we understand it, or verifying the appropriateness of Christian prophecy and traditions as words of the 'risen Lord'?

[48] See for example the comments of F. Burnett, *CBQ* 48 (1986), 353, in his review of Wenham's book: "the great value of W.'s reconstruction for this reviewer is that it has convinced him once again that any attempt, however brilliant it may be, to reconstruct a pre-Synoptic eschatological discourse is futile."

This is the approach taken by Lars Hartman, which is examined in chapter 3 below.

It is apparent that the results of form analysis and New Testament tradition and vocabulary analysis are less than conclusive as far as evaluating the distinctive components of Mk 13 are concerned. Possible divisions in the text are suggested by form analysis, but whether their pre-Markan development can be illuminated by thematic groupings alone, as Beasley-Murray attempts, is rather doubtful. So it is that some scholars have claimed that such lines of inquiry have reached a 'dead-end'. Yet the recent availability of grammatical codings of the New Testament texts have enabled new ways of testing the supposed distinctiveness of a passage. Given these possibilities, it may well be more profitable to undertake an analysis of syntax and style rather than vocabulary in order to evaluate whether Mk 13, or parts thereof, are in some way different to the rest of the Gospel of Mark or to the teaching of Jesus elsewhere.

Unique syntax in Mk 13

The attempt to isolate Markan redaction from pre-Markan traditions has often been approached through observations about Markan syntax made by scholars steeped in a knowledge of *Koine* Greek. Whereas vocabulary varies so much with the content of a passage, the word order and grammatical preferences of an author are much more likely to retain some consistency. Certainly it might be expected that some aspects of the verb could vary with content, such as the unusual concentration of the future tense and the imperative mood in Mk 13,[49] but an analysis of the actual ordering of words and grammatical constructions should give a more impartial insight into any distinguishing features of tradition and redaction than any examination of vocabulary alone. Recent developments in computer software have enabled far more exhaustive counts of such stylistic features in literature.[50] The most obvious result of such computer-assisted analysis is the confirmation of the extraordinary accuracy of earlier scholars who worked without the benefit of such devices and yet compiled detailed lists of distinctive vocabulary and

[49] Mk 13:3-37 contains 566 of the 11 099 words in the whole Gospel, or 5.1%, yet it has 22.6% of the verbs in the future tense (26 out of 115 in Mk), and 13.6% (20 out of 147) of the imperatives (counting γινώσκετε in v.29 as an imperative, and not including those adverbs, participles or future verbs used in an imperative sense).

[50] What follows is not an attempt to validate the developing field of analysis known as 'stylometry', valuable though endeavours in that direction may well prove to be. [See for example, Anthony Kenny, *A Stylometric Study of the New Testament* (Oxford 1986), and the works cited there, including those of A. Q. Morton, the pioneer of such methods]. Rather this analysis will merely be an extension of what scholars have always done in attempting to gain an overview of distinctive styles in the Gospels. No statistics apart from simple percentages will be used in the main body of the text, and all other details regarding data bases and software shall be relegated to Appendix 1. Computer analysis is regarded here as only a tool in the ongoing development of exegetical method, and not as a new methodology in itself.

grammatical features.[51] It is not necessary to reduplicate such efforts by mechanical means, but it is possible to attempt tasks that would be far too tedious to do manually. Such a task is the analysis of all possible three-word groupings in the Gospel,[52] as represented by their grammatical tag,[53] to see which sequences are recurrent and which unique. The results for Mk 13 are as follows:

Syntactical features unique to Mk 13
(Based on three-word groupings)

Verse	**Details** (*only* occurrence in Mark of the threefold sequence…)
1 Διδάσκαλε, ἴδε ποταποί	noun, particle, adjective
ἴδε ποταποὶ λίθοι	particle, adjective, noun
2 ἀφεθῇ ὧδε λίθος	verb subjunctive, adverb, noun
3 καὶ Ἀνδρέας, 4 Εἰπόν	conjunction, noun, verb imperative
4 Εἰπὸν ἡμῖν πότε	verb imperative, pronoun, adverb
ταῦτα συντελεῖσθαι πάντα;	adjective, verb infinite, adjective
συντελεῖσθαι πάντα; 5 ὁ	verb infinite, adjective, article
7 μὴ θροεῖσθε· δεῖ	adverb, verb imperative, verb indicative (also in vv.21/22)
θροεῖσθε· δεῖ γενέσθαι	verbs imperative, indicative and infinite
9 βλέπετε δὲ ὑμεῖς	verb imperative, conjunction, pronoun
10 πρῶτον δεῖ κηρυχθῆναι	adjective used as adverb, verb indicative, verb infinite
11 ἄγωσιν ὑμᾶς παραδιδόντες	verb subjunctive, pronoun, participle (as in v.36)

[51] The work of John C. Hawkins, *Horae Synopticae. Contributions to the Study of the Synoptic Problem* (Oxford 1899), and Morgenthaler, *Statistik,* are two outstanding examples.

[52] In fact the analysis was carried out on single, double and triple word syntactical sequences throughout the whole Gospel. The results of the triple word analysis of the Gospel are listed in Appendix 1. The single and double word sequences were only very occasionally unique, even though a full parsing scheme was used for the single words. Longer sequences proved unwieldy as almost all of them proved to be unique.

[53] Using a modified form of the grammatical analysis of Barbara and Timothy Friberg, *Analytical Greek New Testament* (Grand Rapids, 1981), such that only the broadest grammatical categories are used (noun, adjective, verb + mood, for example). See Appendix 1 for details.

παραδιδόντες, μὴ προμεριμνᾶτε	participle, adverb, verb imperative
μὴ προμεριμνᾶτε τί	adverb, verb imperative, adjective
προμεριμνᾶτε τί λαλήστε,	verb imperative, adjective, verb subjunctive
λαλήσητε, ἀλλ᾽ ὅ	verb subjunctive, conjunction, adjective
τοῦτο λαλεῖτε· οὐ	adjective, verb imperative, adverb
13 ὄνομά μου. ὁ	noun, pronoun, article used as a relative pronominal adjective
μου. ὁ δέ	pronoun, article used as a relative pronominal adjective, conjunction
ὁ δὲ ὑπομείνας	article used as a relative pronominal adjective, conjunction, participle
14 ὁ ἀναγινώσκων νοείτω	article used as a pronoun and relative, participle, verb imperative
ἀναγινώσκων νοείτω, τότε	participle, verb imperative, adverb
νοείτω τότε οἱ	verb imperative, adverb, article
Ἰουδαίᾳ φευγέτωσαν εἰς	noun, verb imperative, preposition
15 ὁ [δὲ] ἐπί	article, conjunction, preposition
μηδὲ εἰσελθάτω ἆραι	conjunction, verb imperative, verb infinite
εἰσελθάτω ἆραί τι	verb imperative, verb infinite, adjective
ἆραί τι ἐκ	verb infinite, adjective, preposition
16 μὴ ἐπιστρεψάτω εἰς	adverb, verb imperative, preposition
τὰ ὀπίσω ἆραι	article, adverb used as adjective, verb infinite
ὀπίσω ἆραι τό	adverb used as adjective, verb infinite, article
17 οὐαὶ δὲ ταῖς	particle, conjunction, article used as a pronoun and relative
ταῖς ἐν γαστρί	article used as a pronoun and relative, preposition, noun
18 γένηται χειμῶνος· 19 ἔσονται	verb subjunctive, noun, verb indicative
20 ἡμέρας, οὐκ ἄν	noun, adverb, particle

Syntactical features unique to Mk 13 (continued)

Verse	Details (*only* occurrence in Mark of the threefold sequence...)
ἂν ἐσώθη πᾶσα	particle, verb indicative, adjective
21 ὑμῖν εἴπῃ, Ἴδε	pronoun, verb subjunctive, particle
εἴπῃ, Ἴδε ὧδε	verb subjunctive, particle, adverb
Ἴδε ὧδε ὁ	particle, adverb, article
Χριστός, Ἴδε ἐκεῖ	noun, particle, adverb
Ἴδε ἐκεῖ, μή	particle, adverb, adverb
ἐκεῖ, μὴ πιστεύετε	adverb, adverb, verb imperative
μὴ πιστεύετε· 22 ἐγερθήσονται	adverb, verb imperative, verb indicative (as in v.7)
πιστεύετε· 22 ἐγερθήσονται γάρ	verb imperative, verb indicative, conjunction
22 τὸ ἀποπλανᾶν, εἰ	article, verb infinite, conjunction
23 δὲ βλέπετε· προείρηκα	conjunction, verb imperative, verb indicative
29 ἴδητε ταῦτα γινόμενα	verb subjunctive, adjective, participle
ταῦτα γινόμενα, γινώσκετε	adjective, participle, verb imperative (= indicative)
ἐπὶ θύραις. 30 ἀμήν	preposition, noun, particle
30 αὕτη μέχρις οὗ	adjective, preposition, adjective used as a demonstrative and relative
μέχρις οὗ ταῦτα	preposition, adjective used as a demonstrative and relative, adjective
οὗ ταῦτα πάντα	adjective used as a demonstrative and relative, adjective, adjective
31 παρελεύσονται. 32 Περὶ δέ	verb indicative, preposition, conjunction
32 οὐρανῷ οὐδὲ ὁ	noun, conjunction and adverb (crasis), article
οὐδὲ ὁ υἱός	conjunction and adverb, article, noun
33 βλέπετε, ἀγρυπνεῖτε· οὐκ	verb imperative, verb imperative, adverb

ἀγρυπνεῖτε· οὐκ οἴδατε	verb imperative, adverb, verb indicative
34 ἵνα γρηγορῇ. 35 γρηγορεῖτε	conjunction, verb subjunctive, verb imperative
γρηγορῇ. 35 γρηγορεῖτε οὖν,	verb subjunctive, verb imperative, conjunction
36 ἐλθὼν ἐξαίφνης εὕρῃ	participle, adverb, verb subjunctive
εὕρῃ ὑμᾶς καθεύδοντας	verb subjunctive, pronoun, participle (as in v.11)
ὑμᾶς καθεύδοντας. 37 ὃ	pronoun, participle, adjective used as a demonstrative and relative
καθεύδοντας. 37 ὃ δέ	participle, adjective used as a demonstrative and relative, conjunction
37 λέγω, γρηγορεῖτε. Then 14:1.	verbs indicative, imperative, then indicative (in 14:1)

These results are more clearly indicated by underlining them in the text of Mk 13, whereby a concentration of such underlining should indicate the likelihood of 'foreign' syntax, and the absence of any underlining the presence of 'normal' Markan syntax. It must be stressed again that each underlined phrase in the text which follows indicates a syntactical sequence that occurs nowhere else in the Gospel of Mark:

Text Sheet 3: Unique syntax in Mk 13

13.1 Καὶ ἐκπορευομένου αὐτοῦ ἐκ τοῦ ἱεροῦ λέγει αὐτῷ εἷς τῶν μαθητῶν αὐτοῦ, <u>Διδάσκαλε, ἴδε ποταποὶ λίθοι</u> καὶ ποταπαὶ οἰκοδομαί. 2 καὶ ὁ Ἰησοῦς εἶπεν αὐτῷ, Βλέπεις ταύτας τὰς μεγάλας οἰκοδομάς; οὐ μὴ <u>ἀφεθῇ ὧδε λίθος</u> ἐπὶ λίθον ὅς οὐ μὴ καταλυθῇ.
3 Καὶ καθημένου αὐτοῦ εἰς τὸ Ὄρος τῶν Ἐλαιῶν κατέναντι τοῦ ἱεροῦ ἐπηρώτα αὐτὸν κατ᾽ ἰδίαν Πέτρος καὶ Ἰάκωβος καὶ Ἰωάννης <u>καὶ Ἀνδρέας. 4 Εἰπὸν ἡμῖν πότε</u> ταῦτα ἔσται, καὶ τί τὸ σημεῖον ὅταν μέλλῃ <u>ταῦτα συντελεῖσθαι πάντα. 5</u> ὁ δὲ Ἰησοῦς ἤρξατο λέγειν αὐτοῖς, βλέπετε μή τις ὑμᾶς πλανήσῃ· 6 πολλοὶ ἐλεύσονται ἐπὶ τῷ ὀνόματί μου λέγοντες ὅτι Ἐγώ εἰμι, καὶ πολλοὺς πλανήσουσιν. 7 ὅταν δὲ ἀκούσητε πολέμους καὶ ἀκοὰς πολέμων, <u>μὴ θροεῖσθε·</u> δεῖ γενέσθαι, ἀλλ᾽ οὔπω τὸ τέλος. 8 ἐγερθήσεται γὰρ ἔθνος ἐπ᾽ ἔθνος καὶ βασιλεία ἐπὶ βασιλείαν, ἔσονται σεισμοὶ κατὰ τόπους, ἔσονται λιμοί· ἀρχὴ ὠδίνων ταῦτα. 9 <u>βλέπετε δὲ ὑμεῖς</u> ἑαυτούς· παραδώσουσιν ὑμᾶς εἰς συνέδρια καὶ εἰς συναγωγὰς δαρήσεσθε καὶ ἐπὶ ἡγεμόνων καὶ βασιλέων σταθήσεσθε ἕνεκεν ἐμοῦ εἰς μαρτύριον αὐτοῖς. 10 καὶ εἰς πάντα τὰ ἔθνη <u>πρῶτον δεῖ κηρυχθῆναι</u> τὸ εὐαγγέλιον. 11 καὶ ὅταν <u>ἄγωσιν ὑμᾶς παραδιδόντες, μὴ προμεριμνᾶτε τί λαλήστε, ἀλλ᾽ ὃ</u> ἐὰν δοθῇ ὑμῖν ἐν ἐκείνῃ τῇ ὥρᾳ <u>τοῦτο λαλεῖτε, οὐ</u> γάρ ἐστε ὑμεῖς οἱ λαλοῦντες ἀλλὰ τὸ πνεῦμα τὸ ἅγιον. 12 καὶ παραδώσει ἀδελφὸς ἀδελφὸν εἰς θάνατον καὶ πατὴρ τέκνον, καὶ ἐπαναστήσονται τέκνα ἐπὶ γονεῖς καὶ θανατώσουσιν αὐτούς· 13 καὶ ἔσεσθε μισούμενοι ὑπὸ πάντων διὰ τὸ <u>ὄνομά μου.</u> ὁ δὲ <u>ὑπομείνας</u> εἰς τέλος οὗτος σωθήσεται.
14 Ὅταν δὲ ἴδητε τὸ βδέλυγμα τῆς ἐρημώσεως ἑστηκότα ὅπου οὐ δεῖ, <u>ὁ ἀναγινώσκων νοείτω, τότε οἱ</u> ἐν τῇ Ἰουδαίᾳ <u>φευγέτωσαν εἰς τὰ ὄρη, 15 ὁ δὲ ἐπὶ</u> τοῦ δώματος μὴ καταβάτω <u>μηδὲ εἰσελθάτω ἆραί</u> τι ἐκ τῆς οἰκίας αὐτοῦ, 16 καὶ ὁ εἰς τὸν ἀγρὸν <u>μὴ ἐπιστρεψάτω εἰς τὰ ὀπίσω ἆραι τὸ</u> ἱμάτιον αὐτοῦ. 17 <u>οὐαὶ δὲ ταῖς ἐν γαστρὶ</u> ἐχούσαις καὶ ταῖς θηλαζούσαις ἐν ἐκείναις ταῖς ἡμέραις. 18 προσεύχεσθε δὲ ἵνα μὴ <u>γένηται χειμῶνος· 19 ἔσονται</u> γὰρ αἱ ἡμέραι ἐκεῖναι θλῖψις οἵα οὐ γέγονεν τοιαύτη ἀπ᾽ ἀρχῆς κτίσεως ἣν ἔκτισεν ὁ θεὸς ἕως τοῦ νῦν καὶ οὐ μὴ γένηται. 20 καὶ εἰ μὴ ἐκολόβωσεν κύριος τὰς <u>ἡμέρας, οὐκ ἂν ἐσώθη πᾶσα</u> σάρξ. ἀλλὰ διὰ τοὺς ἐκλεκτοὺς οὓς ἐξελέξατο ἐκολόβωσεν τὰς ἡμέρας. 21 καὶ τότε ἐάν τις <u>ὑμῖν εἴπῃ,</u> Ἴδε ὧδε ὁ Χριστός, Ἴδε ἐκεῖ, <u>μὴ πιστεύετε· 22 ἐγερθήσονται</u> γὰρ ψευδόχριστοι καὶ ψευδοπροφῆται καὶ δώσουσιν σημεῖα καὶ τέρατα πρὸς <u>τὸ ἀποπλανᾶν, εἰ</u> δυνατόν, τοὺς ἐκλεκτούς. 23 ὑμεῖς <u>δὲ βλέπετε· προείρηκα</u> ὑμῖν πάντα.
24 Ἀλλὰ ἐν ἐκείναις ταῖς ἡμέραις μετὰ τὴν θλῖψιν ἐκείνην
ὁ ἥλιος σκοτισθήσεται,
καὶ ἡ σελήνη οὐ δώσει τὸ φέγγος αὐτῆς,
25 καὶ οἱ ἀστέρες ἔσονται ἐκ τοῦ οὐρανοῦ πίπτοντες,
καὶ αἱ δυνάμεις αἱ ἐν τοῖς οὐρανοῖς σαλευθήσονται.
26 καὶ τότε ὄψονται τὸν υἱὸν τοῦ ἀνθρώπου ἐρχόμενον ἐν νεφέλαις μετὰ δυνάμεως πολλῆς καὶ δόξης. 27 καὶ τότε ἀποστελεῖ τοὺς ἀγγέλους καὶ ἐπισυνάξει τοὺς ἐκλεκτοὺς αὐτοῦ ἐκ τῶν τεσσάρων ἀνέμων ἀπ᾽ ἄκρου γῆς ἕως ἄκρου οὐρανοῦ.
28 Ἀπὸ δὲ τῆς συκῆς μάθετε τὴν παραβολήν· ὅταν ἤδη ὁ κλάδος αὐτῆς ἁπαλὸς γένηται καὶ ἐκφύῃ τὰ φύλλα, γινώσκετε ὅτι ἐγγὺς τὸ θέρος ἐστίν. 29 οὕτως καὶ ὑμεῖς, ὅταν <u>ἴδητε ταῦτα γινόμενα γινώσκετε</u> ὅτι ἐγγύς ἐστιν <u>ἐπὶ θύραις. 30 ἀμὴν</u> λέγω ὑμῖν ὅτι οὐ μὴ παρέλθῃ ἡ γενεὰ <u>αὕτη μέχρις οὗ</u> ταῦτα πάντα γένηται. 31 ὁ οὐρανὸς καὶ ἡ γῆ παρελεύσονται, οἱ δὲ λόγοι μου οὐ μὴ <u>παρελεύσονται. 32 περὶ δὲ</u> τῆς ἡμέρας ἐκείνης ἢ τῆς ὥρας οὐδεὶς οἶδεν, οὐδὲ οἱ ἄγγελοι ἐν <u>οὐρανῷ οὐδὲ ὁ υἱός,</u> εἰ μὴ ὁ πατήρ. 33 <u>βλέπετε ἀγρυπνεῖτε·</u> οὐκ οἴδατε γὰρ πότε ὁ καιρός ἐστιν. 34 ὡς ἄνθρωπος ἀπόδημος ἀφεὶς τὴν οἰκίαν αὐτοῦ καὶ δοὺς τοῖς δούλοις αὐτοῦ τὴν

ἐξουσίαν, ἑκάστῳ τὸ ἔργον αὐτοῦ, καὶ τῷ θυρωρῷ ἐνετείλατο <u>ἵνα γρηγορῇ</u>. 35 <u>γρηγορεῖτε οὖν</u>, οὐκ οἴδατε γὰρ πότε ὁ κύριος τῆς οἰκίας ἔρχεται, ἢ ὀψὲ ἢ μεσονύκτιον ἢ ἀλεκτοροφωνίας ἢ πρωΐ, 36 μὴ <u>ἐλθὼν ἐξαίφνης εὕρῃ ὑμᾶς καθεύδοντας</u>. 37 ὃ δὲ ὑμῖν λέγω, πᾶσιν <u>λέγω, γρηγορεῖτε</u>.

Key: <u>Triple word underlining</u> = only occurrence of this grammatical sequence in Mark
<u>Double underlining</u> = overlapping sequences of unique syntax
(Simple parsing only used, plus mood of the verb. See Appendix 1 for details).

Of course any given unique syntactical phrase could equally well be the product of tradition or redaction, but where there is a concentration of such features it is reasonable to argue that they indicate the work of someone other than the main redactor of the Gospel. Such a concentration could not merely be explained as evidence of an occasional change in style by an author, for it would indicate that the underlying structure of the text was alien to the work as a whole. To be more specific, a significant concentration of unique syntax must be seen as evidence for the use of a special source—different from any others that may have been used—in that the features it contains occur nowhere else in the Gospel.[54] However, if evidence for some kind of pre-Markan collection of traditions or other large body of traditions were being sought, it would be necessary to show that such sections contain related syntax not occurring elsewhere, rather than syntax only occurring once in the Gospel. With this in mind, the figures below showing the percentage of words involved in unique syntactical sequences in each section of the Gospel of Mark[55] include a figure in brackets indicating what the percentage would be if sequences occurring more than once but *unique to that section of the Gospel* were added.

[54] Beasley-Murray, *Last Days,* 317f, seems to misunderstand this point: "Dyer does not comment on the significance of the fact that these same three word groupings are scattered *throughout the chapter,* irrespective of the sources of these sayings." The 'same three word groupings' *are not the same—each sequence is unique—and thus they are not scattered anywhere else in Mk 13 or the rest of the Gospel*—they each only occur *once* in the whole Gospel of Mark with the exception of one sequence shared between vv.7 and 21/22, and another between vv.11 and 36. On their own, or in small concentrations such as in v.11 (which Beasley-Murray refers to), they may not signify much at all since any author may use unique syntax at times. But when there is an unusually high proportion of such unique syntax extending over several verses then we may suspect that a peculiar source is being used.

[55] The divisions of the Markan text used here are those of W. A. Gill, "Outline of Mark", unpublished paper (Melbourne 1990), which in turn were developed from those of E. Schweizer, *The Good News According to Mark,* ET D. H. Madvig (Richmond/ London 1970/71).

Percentage of unique syntax in each section of the Gospel of Mark
(Based on 3-word sequences—see Appendix 1 for details)

Chapter & verse	Percentage	Chapter & verse	Percentage
1:1-1:13	5.2 (5.2)	**10:32-10:52**	14.0
1:14-3:6	9.1	10:32-10:34	20.5 (20.5)
1:14-1:20	10.3 (10.3)	10:35-10:45	14.2 (14.2)
1:21-1:45	12.2 (13.8)	10:46-10:52	9.8 (9.8)
2:1-3:6	7.1 (9.4)	**11:1-13:37**	14.9
3:7-6:6a	10.9	11:1-11:11	12.4 (12.4)
3:7-3:35	8.6 (11.3)	11:12-11:25	16.6 (16.6)
4:1-4:34	10.5 (14.5)	11:27-11:33	0 (0)
4:35-6:6a	12.3 (15.5)	12:1-12:12	14.3 (20.9)
6:6b-8:26	10.8	12:13-13:2	12.1 (12.1)
6:6b-6:31	13.1 (13.8)	13:3-13:37	21.7 (22.8)
6:32-7:23	9.0 (10.6)	**14:1-16:8[56]**	13.9
7:24-8:21	10.9 (12.5)	14:1-14:11	13.8 (13.8)
8:22-8:26	15.0 (15.0)	14:12-14:31	16.6 (18.3)
8:27-9:29	11.3	14:32-14:72	12.1 (14.8)
8:27-9:1	6.5 (7.5)	15:1-15:47	13.9 (18.3)
9:2-9:29	14.2 (16.1)	16:1-16:8	16.2 (16.2)
9:30-10:31	13.1		
9:30-9:32	6.4 (6.4)		
9:33-9:50	10.4 (12.4)	**Short ending**	41.2 (41.2)
10:1-10:16	20.3 (21.7)		
10:17-10:31	11.7 (16.4)	**Long ending**	22.8 (22.8)

The results of this analysis show quite clearly that Mk 13:3-37 contains the most distinctive syntax in the Gospel of Mark. Mk 10:1-16 (20.3%) and Mk 10:32-34 (20.5%) also have high levels of unique syntax, but the peculiarity of chapter 13 is heightened even more if vv.14-23 are focused on, where 35.3% of the text consists of syntactical sequences found only within those verses.[57] This is a higher figure even than the long ending to

[56] If the Passion Narrative is treated as one large pre-Markan unit (as some still maintain it is) the figures in brackets are as follows: 14:1-16:8 (18.7); 14:1-14:11 (no change); 14:12-14:31 (22.8); 14:32-14:72 (17.9); 15:1-15:47 (22.5); 16:1-16:8 (20.6). This provides some evidence that 14:12-31; 15:1-47 and 16:1-8 contain significant proportions of non-Markan syntax, which may indicate some kind of pre-Markan grouping within these sections.

[57] In calculating these percentages, each word has been counted only once, even though it may have been involved in up to 3 different unique sequences (see Appendix 1 for a detailed explanation of the procedure). If the words are counted as often as they are involved the percentages are even higher, and the concentrations of unique syntax stand out even more. However, given the critique of Perrin's inflated percentages above, the more conservative figures have been used everywhere else but in the following table:

the Gospel of Mark[58] and provides stronger evidence than an analysis of vocabulary for the view long held by scholars that somewhere within these verses is a pre-Markan unit of tradition quite distinct from the other traditions that have been incorporated into the Gospel. It cannot simply be claimed that the density of Old Testament allusions in this section explains the high incidence of unusual syntax, because the verses which immediately follow (vv.24-27), consisting of almost unadulterated Old Testament language,[59] *contain absolutely no unique syntax at all.* This is clearly one of the most important results of this approach: that no matter exactly where the pre-Markan tradition is located in chapter 13, it is very difficult to see that vv.14-23 and 24-27 could have originally belonged together, such is the difference between their syntax. Yet past commentators have almost invariably included vv.24-27 along with vv.7f and 14-20 as the irreducible basis of the source behind the discourse. Vincent Taylor concluded his brief survey of the variety of opinion regarding the extent of the source with the words: "In these conjectures it will be seen that the most constant element is 7f., 14-20, 24-7. Here, if anywhere, the most primitive core is to be found."[60] Yet it is apparent from the analysis of syntax just undertaken that vv.24-27 are grammatically 'at home' in the Gospel of Mark, whereas vv.14-23 are most definitely not.

Whilst this concentration of distinctive syntax in vv.14-23, and the complete lack of it in vv.24-27, is quite significant as a means of distinguishing between traditions, it does not necessarily mean that vv.14-23 must all be traditional and vv.24-27 redactional. To say that there is no unique syntax in vv.24-27 is simply to say that it is not atypical in the context of the Gospel as a whole. It may well be representative of traditions taken over by the author of Mark and used often throughout the

	vv.5b-13	vv.14-23	vv.24-27	vv.28-37	ch.16:9-20	Short ending
Unique syntax (%)	16.6	35.3	0	23.7	22.8	41.2
Unique syntax multiple counting (%)	23.8	51.0	0	33.6	35.1	52.9

See Text Sheet 3 for the details of where the unique syntax is located within Mk 13.

[58] Compare it also with the other major discourse in the Gospel—Mk 4 (10.5%).

[59] There are references to the Septuagintal version of verses in Isaiah, Daniel and Zechariah at least. See chapter 3 for details.

[60] Taylor, *Mark,* 498. In an appendix to his commentary, Taylor then develops the suggestion that vv.24-27 do not belong to the same tradition as vv.14-20! See chapter 1, footnote 21, above. The supposed irreducibility of vv.7-8,14-20,24-27 as a pre-Markan unit is still maintained by some. See Gerd Theissen, *The Gospels in Context. Social and Political History in the Synoptic Tradition* (Minneapolis 1991), 130: "Mark's *Vorlage* would thus have included, at a minimum: the beginning of the birthpangs (13:7-8); the suffering (13:14-20); the Parousia (13:24-27). But that is only a minimum." Quite apart from their mutually exclusive syntax, the difficulties of locating vv.14-20 ('you' ... 'flee') and 24-27 ('they' ... 'see') in close proximity are often overlooked.

Gospel, for the recurrence of a feature may be an indication of an extended pre-Markan tradition or group of traditions, rather than necessarily indicating the hand of a redactor.[61] Nor can it be concluded that the concentration of peculiar syntax in vv.14-23 means that the whole section represents a pre-Markan tradition. Any given unique syntactical sequence *may* be the work of the final redactor, but the close proximity of so many of them in these verses makes this very unlikely in every case. An author's vocabulary may change dramatically with a new topic, but it is much less likely that simple word order and grammatical structures will alter to the same extent. It may be argued that the extensive use of the imperative in these verses is likely to upset the normal sequence of Markan grammar, and hence account for the unique features found there. Indeed, just over one third of such features are at least partly the result of imperative verbs,[62] but even if these are disallowed (along with any unique features associated with the other 139 imperatives in the Gospel of Mark), there is still an unusually high percentage of unique syntax in these verses.

It would be unwise to try to use the percentage of unique syntax as a basis for making even finer distinctions between verses in Mk 13. The figures become meaningless when small sections of text are considered.[63] However, if vv.14-21 are considered a unit rather than vv.14-23, the percentage of unique syntax rises slightly from 35.3 to 35.4, because of the concentration of unusual syntax in v.21. This may indicate that it is vv.14-21 which constitute the most likely unit of distinctive pre-Markan tradition in the discourse—indeed, in the whole of the Gospel of Mark— and especially so since vv.22 and 23 seem to owe their origins to other sources (see chapter 1 above and chapter 5 below).

Distinctive traditions in Mk 13

The attempts to delineate pre-Markan traditions in Mk 13 by comparison with other New Testament writings or by identifying the unique vocabulary in the discourse have been unsuccessful. However the analysis of unique syntax within the discourse clearly indicates some areas of non-Markan tradition. This syntactical approach cannot determine the

[61] This is one problem with using recurrent features as evidence of Markan redaction, and will be examined further in connection with the work of Frans Neirynck, *Duality in Mark. Contributions to the Study of the Markan Redaction* (Leuven 1988), and David Barrett Peabody, *Mark as Composer* (Macon 1987), in chapter 5 below.

[62] 11 out of the 32 unique syntactical features (or 23 out of the 54 words connected with such sequences) in vv.14-23 involve the 8 imperatives which occur in these verses. Yet even if they are excluded from the calculation, the figure is still 20.3% unique syntax in vv.14-23. See Appendix 1 for details.

[63] This would be especially true if the smallest divisions described in chapter 1 above were used. However the following figures give an idea of what the percentage of unique syntax is for the 9 larger divisions of Mk 13:
    vv.1-2 (17.5%); 3-6 (15.0%); 7-8 (12.1%); 9-13 (21.6%); 14-20 (31.0%); 21-23 (48.6% due to v.21); 24-27 (0%); 28-31 (20.0%); 32-37 (24.1%).

exact extent of this pre-Markan tradition by itself, but it does clearly confirm the likelihood of a *distinctive* tradition behind chapter 13 and the probability that it involves all or part of vv.14-23 in some sort of syntactical contrast to vv.24-27. The other concentrations of unique syntax in the chapter are more isolated and less extensive (parts of vv.11,13,29-33,36 are the next most obvious), and will require further analysis before their place in the tradition can be confirmed. It must be emphasised that these occurrences of unique syntax are not related or connected—they are *unique*. Their significance is apparent when they occur in unusually high concentrations over a few verses or within a unit of text defined by other criteria, where they are indicative of a distinctive source not used elsewhere in the Gospel. Hence our special interest in the contrast between the uniqueness of vv.14-21 and the common syntax of vv.24-27.

These conclusions are preliminary suggestions only, the theological and historical potential of which will be developed below. In the meantime, these findings (as shown in Text Sheet 3) can be correlated with the tentative conclusions of chapter 1 above, and be used as a basis on which to evaluate the results of other types of analysis in order to clarify any further distinctions which may be made within the text. Such an approach does *not* lead to a compounding of uncertainty in the final results because here each analysis is undertaken independently and not based on any of the prior conclusions.[64]

Therefore the combination of the results from the linguistic and syntactical analyses undertaken up until this stage leads to the following conclusions:

vv.14-21: This is the section with the highest proportion of non-Markan syntax in the whole Gospel, a strong Semitic influence, and yet with an unusually high proportion of uses of δέ.

vv.24-27: These verses form a distinctive unit of Septuagintal language joined together by the use of καί, and containing syntax thoroughly typical of the rest of the Gospel of Mark (and not unique in any way).

The tentative suggestion in chapter 1 that vv.7,8,12,13a,22 do not come from the same pre-Markan source as vv.14-21 is supported by the much lower proportions of unique syntax in these verses, though further evidence is required before it can be assumed that vv.7,8,12,13a,22 belong together in some way. It should also be noted that where a unique

---

[64] Therefore James Dunn's criticism of David Wenham's accumulation of possibilities in footnote 39 above does not apply in this case. Overlapping possibilities arrived at independently lead to *greater* certainty, whereas possibilities built on other possibilities lead to *diminishing* certainty. Or, to re-formulate Dunn's mathematical example, $5 \times 0.75 > (0.75)^5$.

sequence of syntax occurs *across* a major punctuation break (namely between vv.3/4,4/5,13a/13b,29/30,31/32,34/35,36/37,37/14:1), it provides some evidence that a dislocation of the text has occurred at some stage in the tradition. This would tend to support the view that vv.3-6 and vv.29-37 are a compilation of separate units of various sizes, perhaps undertaken at least partially by the author of Mark. The implications of this possibility will be examined more fully in chapters 4 and 5 below using redactional criteria. First, in order to complete the analysis of factors pointing to the use of pre-Markan traditions, it is necessary to examine any specific links between the possible units of tradition outlined above and earlier Jewish writings. This analysis of possible pre-Markan textual relationships will then be combined with the linguistic and syntactical analyses just undertaken in order to provide an overview of the most likely pre-Markan traditions and sources behind Mk 13. This will be presented in summary form at the end of chapter 3.

III

A DANIELIC 'MIDRASH'

Major proponent: Hartman (1966).
Basic thesis: That Mk 13 consists predominantly of a unitary, Danielic 'midrash'
    (which possibly goes back to Jesus).
Dominant method: Traditio-historical criticism (OT).
Critique: A re-evaluation of the possible sources for the OT allusions in Mk 13.

The approach taken by LARS HARTMAN[1] in his attempt to demonstrate the essential unity of the eschatological discourse in Mark was to analyse the use of the Old Testament in Mk 13. Hartman does not press the issue of the historicity of the speaker or setting of Mk 13, but he does claim that the interpretation of Daniel that comprises the bulk of the chapter is more likely to have originated with one teacher than a community, and that its theme is similar to the teaching of Jesus on the Kingdom of God found elsewhere in the New Testament (247-8). Hartman argues for this extended exposition of Daniel, which he somewhat hesitatingly calls a 'midrash',[2] on the basis of those texts in Mk 13 in which he finds Old Testament allusions, namely: vv.5b-8,12-16,19-22 and 24-27. The links he discovers with the Old Testament, mainly from the book of Daniel, are too numerous to cite here,[3] and are not all equally convincing.[4] However

---

[1] L. Hartman, *Prophecy Interpreted. The Formation of Some Jewish Apocalyptic Texts and of the Eschatological Discourse, Mark 13 par.* (Lund 1966). Page numbers in brackets in the main body of the text shall be used to refer to this book for the rest of this section. The use here of 'Old Testament' (rather than 'Hebrew Bible' or 'First Testament') is not intended to imply that the Jewish Scriptures are obsolete or superseded, but rather that they are ancient and venerable—the 'Old*est* Testament'. The label 'Old Testament' is in this sense more inclusive and appropriate for our purposes, since 'Hebrew Bible' excludes the Greek OT and the Aramaic Targums, and 'First Testament' excludes everything else.

[2] See J. A. Fitzmyer's rather scathing comments on Hartman's use of 'midrash' in *Int* 23 (1969), 251. "I am not sure he knows what a midrash is, especially when he speaks of a "'midrash' . . . becoming a 'mishna'" (p.174)". Beasley-Murray ("The Vision on the Mount", 42) is somewhat more gentle: "The thesis of a Danielic midrash as the basis of the discourse may be viewed as a pardonable exaggeration of an important feature of the discourse".

[3] See his summary in *Prophecy Interpreted,* 172-174.

[4] M. D. Hooker, in her review of Hartman, *JTS* 19 (1968), 263-265, pointed out the indirectness of the connections between Mk 13:8 and 2 Ch 15:6/Is 19:2, where the 'city against city' phrase linking the Old Testament texts is not used at all in Mark. So too the supposed 'certain quotation' of Gn 19:17 (Lot's flight) in Mk 13:16 (not 13:6 as Hooker says), is doubtful according to Hooker. But Hartman gives examples of this type of usage of the Old Testament within apocalyptic literature in his first four chapters. Far more vague and imprecise than Hooker's examples are the links Hartman suggests between Mk

Hartman sees these links as justifying his assessment of the discourse as "a considerably more coherent unit than has generally been assumed" (172), and that therefore, "the view of the discourse as a conglomeration of small fragments cannot be maintained."[5]

Hartman laid the basis for this assessment by analysing the patterns of thought and the use of the Old Testament in those Jewish apocalyptic texts that refer to the time of salvation. Not only did he find these apocalyptic patterns and motifs relevant to his understanding of Mk 13, but in particular he argues that the way the Old Testament is intuitively referred to and assumed as background in these apocalyptic writings explains the composition of the earliest tradition behind Mk 13. This seems a promising hypothesis, yet Hartman himself describes a *variety* of ways in which the Old Testament traditions are used in the literature. In particular, he draws attention to the differences between the Qumran texts—where a much more conscious and 'contrived' use of the Old Testament is evident—and the Jewish apocalyptic material he examines in detail (138-9). He sees the authors of this latter material as being less self-conscious in their use of the Old Testament and as following more naturally the associations between the texts stored in their minds. Thus, "the quotations and allusions do not radically alter their meanings when they are transferred to the apocalypse" (139), whereas in the Qumran texts "phrases and indeed whole sentences are adopted to serve the author's purpose and in their original context they may refer to quite different matters than those the author uses them for" (139). If only such distinctions could be made so easily. Indeed, if all the Old Testament allusions in Mk 13 could be characterized by *either* one of these descriptions,[6] and if they all made consistent use of either the Septuagint

---

13:6 (Ἐγώ εἰμι) and 'the horn magnifying itself' in Dn 7:8,11. See Lambrecht's doubts on this link in "Die 'Midrasch-Quelle' von Mk 13", *Bib* 49 (1968), 262f. Certainly Hartman's tradition analysis must be taken into account, but to make such tenuous links the sole basis for determining the origin of a text is very questionable. Clearly Mk 13:6 would be more profitably analysed, together with vv.21-22, from the standpoint of early Christian prophecy (so M. Eugene Boring, see further below), and from a redactional point of view, whereby not only the Ἐγώ εἰμι but also the ἐπὶ τῷ ὀνόματί μου might be explained, rather than saying merely that the latter phrase "may have something to do with the early history of the eschatological discourse and with its different usage and interpretation in the early church" (Hartman, *Prophecy Interpreted,* 177).

[5] *Prophecy Interpreted,* 172. This provides an interesting contrast to the views of Beasley-Murray, citing Lambrecht, (see chapter 2, footnotes 5 and 22 above). Beasley-Murray, Wenham and Hartman all argue for some kind of pre-synoptic discourse but from widely differing perspectives. For Beasley-Murray it is a four-fold collection of sayings re-worked in Mk 13; for Wenham, a large discourse abbreviated in Mk 13; and for Hartman, a unitary 'midrash' taken over by the author of Mark with minimal redaction. If we were to apply here Beasley-Murray's argument that a lack of scholarly consensus discredits an hypothesis, we should rule out the possibility of a pre-synoptic discourse.

[6] If the distinction is valid. N. Perrin, "Apocalyptic Christianity", in *Visionaries and Their Apocalypses* (Philadelphia 1983), 130-131, prefers to note the similarities between the *pesher* method of interpreting Scripture used by the Qumran community, and the

or the Hebrew text,[7] then Hartman's case for a unitary 'midrash' would be considerably strengthened. But such is clearly not the case.

The traditions suggested by Hartman to be behind certain phrases and sentences in Mk 13 should still be examined for their individual merit, but his contention that such phrases must constitute the earliest layer of the tradition merely because they allude to the Old Testament (or even to the same book) is erroneous. Such a contention not only denies the diversity of traditions and their usage in the chapter, as argued above, but it distorts any attempt to reconstruct the history of the traditions behind the eschatological discourse.[8] It means that for Hartman the 'midrashic' nucleus of vv.5b-8,12-16,19-22, and 24-27, is the earliest form of the discourse, with a *Sitz im Leben* in early Christian teaching, though probably originating mainly from the words of Jesus (236, 247). This means that such a discourse includes what Hartman calls the two poles of "the apocalyptic and eschatological field" (235):

(i)   the activity of the 'antichrist'—the 'I am', the abomination of desolation and the false prophets giving signs and wonders;

(ii)   and the Parousia of the Son of Man, described in the form of a theophany similar to the day of Yahweh in the Old Testament.

As well as this, Hartman argues (174f) that this original layer contains parenetic elements warning followers not to be led astray, as distinct from the exhortations to 'watch' which, although probably from Jesus originally (236), were added later. Hartman then contends that the πολλοί of Mk 13:6 and perhaps the plural false Christs and false prophets of v.22 were added as the early church experienced the problem of 'antichrist' in many individuals.[9]

interpretive methods of the early Christian community. It is doubtful whether either of the terms *pesher* or *midrash* are strictly appropriate to describe the mixture of Old Testament allusions in Mk 13.

[7] See T. F. Glasson, "Mark xiii. and the Greek Old Testament", *ExpTim* 69 (1957-58), 213-215, for comments on those sections of Mk 13 most clearly following the LXX against the Hebrew (namely 13:25 and 27), and the text of Daniel used by Theodotion against the Hebrew (13:7,13,14? and 19).

[8] To be fair to Hartman, he is openly sceptical of his own attempt to reconstruct the history of the eschatological discourse. See *Prophecy Interpreted*, 235.

[9] *Prophecy Interpreted*, 237-238. This view has difficulties in that it implies a 'watering down' and diversification of antichrist speculation, whereas later usage (specifically in the Johannine letters and in another form in Revelation) seems to suggest both an increased fascination for, and a more detailed particularization of, the antichrist motif. It would be better to argue that only the more general ψευδόχριστοι motif is present in Mk 13. See further the discussion below, and in particular the views of C. H. Dodd, "The Fall of Jerusalem and the 'Abomination of Desolation'", in *More New Testament Studies* (Manchester 1968), 69-83, [= *JRS* 37 (1947), 47-54] and especially the footnote on page 82: "It is not clear that the βδέλυγμα ἐρημώσεως is properly an 'antichrist' at all. If so, he comes on the scene too early, for the only proper setting for 'antichrist' in the Marcan sequence of events (so far as it conforms to apocalyptic tradition) is at xiii. 22, where his place seems to be taken by a plurality of 'pseudochrists'."

These additions were followed by the persecution logia (13:11 and 9), adapted from Jesus' prediction that his followers would be persecuted for his sake (238) and shaped in the light of the Passion of Jesus which follows immediately after the discourse. According to Hartman, the 'midrash' was then first linked with the fall of Jerusalem in the source lying behind Lk 21, because of the prophecy of Jesus regarding the city, the influence of the book of Jeremiah, and contemporary apocalyptic and eschatological expectations (239-40). Thus it was a simple step for the Markan framework, vv.1-4 and 28-32, to be added, though Hartman is doubtful whether this can be attributed to the author of Mark despite what he regards as "typical Marcan language" (222). Lastly, 13:10 was inserted because of "the Church's experience of missionary work amongst the Jews and heathens, which was of such a nature as to make it natural to insert this verse amongst logia on persecutions" (241). Hartman's only comment on vv.33-37 is that this closing parenesis was more loosely attached to the 'midrash', as the parallels to it in Matthew and Luke are scattered (175).

Such a reconstruction of the history of the eschatological discourse is problematical. Certainly it avoids attributing the points of most tension to Jesus. Verse 10 is seen as a much later addition, and v.30 is a Markan variant on a Q saying announcing judgment on the Jews (Mt 5:18; 23:26), rather than a saying expecting an imminent end (223-5). Hartman also avoids attributing anything specific to the author of Mark, except perhaps the appending of vv.33-37, and possibly the framework vv.1-4 and 28-32. This appears to side-step many of the most difficult problems in the chapter by the dubious means of assigning them to an anonymous redactor. Even the phrases not connected with the Old Testament but sitting awkwardly in the midst of the 'midrash' are attributed somewhat vaguely to the early church,[10] whilst v.23 receives no mention at all except in a list of Bultmann's 'Christian additions' (208). From a redaction critical standpoint such explanations are most unsatisfactory as there appears to be no discernible motivation behind this specific edition of the discourse compiled by the author of Mark.

On the other hand, according to Hartman, the earliest form of the tradition was a parenetic discourse on the antichrist and the Parousia which probably derived as a unit from the teaching of the historical Jesus. Yet this brief discourse was only later brought 'down to earth' when connected with other words of Jesus about the fall of Jerusalem (Lk 21) and the destruction of the Temple (Mk 13). Thus it is not surprising that the only meaningful *Sitz im Leben* that Hartman can suggest refers not to what he sees as the origin of the discourse—a 'midrash' started by Jesus—

---

[10] *Prophecy Interpreted,* 177. Namely, the πολλοί and ἐπὶ τῷ ὀνόματι μου in v.6; the ἀρχὴ ὠδίνων ταῦτα in v.8; διὰ τὸ ὄνομά μου v.13; ἐν τῇ Ἰουδαίᾳ v.14, vv.17 and 18, and the Ἴδε ὧδε ὁ Χριστός in v.21.

nor to the author of Mark, but to the adaptation of the discourse within "early Christian teaching" (236).

Indeed this encapsulates the achievements of Hartman's work. His tradition analysis does shed some light on the transmission of the discourse within the early church, yet without illuminating to any significant degree the problems surrounding the origin of the bulk of the discourse and its particular usage in Mk 13. As with Beasley-Murray and Wenham's work, Hartman's analysis must be given due consideration in any examination of specific phrases and verses, but as an explanation of the genesis and purpose of the chapter as a whole it has little to offer. The examples that Hartman has compiled from Jewish apocalyptic literature of the way in which Old Testament texts are interpreted and key-word associations made,[11] provide some insight into the growth of some sections of the tradition, but the attempt to use such features as evidence for a 'midrashic nucleus' must be regarded as unsuccessful.

Allusions to the Old Testament in Mk 13

Rather than seeing the Old Testament references as establishing the essential unity of Mk 13, it will be argued here that they are a possible means of *distinguishing* between traditions in Mk 13. The procedure will be to examine the sources of the many Old Testament references and allusions to see if they can be attributed to the text underlying the Hebrew Old Testament, the Aramaic Targums, the Septuagint (LXX) or the text of Daniel used by Theodotion. Whilst such differences between the Septuagint, the Hebrew/Aramaic text and the text of Daniel later translated by Theodotion are sometimes noted by Hartman, little systematic use is made of such distinctions. Could they be evidence of divergent traditions behind the text? T. Francis Glasson, in his brief examination focusing mainly on vv.24-27, demonstrates that those verses rely heavily on the Septuagint as distinct from the Hebrew,[12] and are therefore unlikely, he argues, to have originated from the teaching of the historical Jesus. This argument is endorsed and extended by Perrin in his critique of Beasley-Murray.[13] Perrin contends that whilst Old Testament

---

[11] Hartman correctly points to παραδιδόναι in Mk 13:9-12, and perhaps ταῦτα γενόμενα (v.29) and ταῦτα πάντα γένηται (v.30) as examples of this. *Prophecy Interpreted*, 213 and 223 respectively.

[12] T. Francis Glasson, "Mark xiii", 213-215. Hartman's response is hardly adequate—Glasson "seems to overstress the agreement with the LXX reading of Is 34:4" (*Prophecy*, 157, footnote 38)—considering that on three counts Mk 13:25 supports the LXX against the Hebrew (see details in the table below). Similarly, Dn 11:32 is preferred as the background to Mk 13:13 by Hartman (*Prophecy*, 150), whereas Dn 12:12 (Theodotion) has a much more direct connection which Hartman only notes in passing (*Prophecy*, 150, footnote 19, "also Dn 12:12f., which is stressed by T. F. Glasson"); and in connection with Mk 13:28-32, the specific differences between the LXX and Theodotion are pointed out without comment (*Prophecy*, 167, footnote 76).

[13] Perrin, *Kingdom*, 132-134.

quotations and allusions within the teaching of Jesus generally follow the Septuagint throughout the Gospel of Mark,[14] they also usually parallel the Hebrew text—with the exception of those references found in chapter 13. He goes so far as to say that: "until we come to chapter 13 we have no case of dependence upon the LXX in the recorded teaching of Jesus where that version differs from the Hebrew or does not yield the same point."[15] Whereas in Mk 13, by way of contrast, Perrin contends that:

> ... we do not have a series of quotations which could have been accommodated to the text of the LXX in the course of transmission, nor do we have a series of quotations or allusions which could equally well have been made originally from the Hebrew; we have a series of quotations and allusions woven into the text of the chapter and taken *verbatim* from the LXX or Theod., which is often quite different from the Hebrew (or Aramaic).[16]

But the evidence is not as clear-cut as Perrin has claimed.

This is apparent from the findings of R. T. France's systematic examination of the use of the Old Testament in the teaching of Jesus, undertaken with the aim of countering the arguments of scholars like Glasson and Perrin.[17] After a close scrutiny of some 64 quotations and allusions to the Old Testament in the teachings of Jesus—with special attention to Glasson's comments on Mk 13:24-27—France concludes that "whereas in no case does the evidence of the text-form demand a Greek origin for the Old Testament quotations attributed to Jesus, there are many cases where a Semitic origin seems certain."[18] It becomes apparent

---

[14] Perrin, *Kingdom,* 132-133, cites the "specific quotations from the Old Testament ... given in the LXX version" as being in Mk 12:10-11,26 and 36, but claims that "it is only to be expected that the early Church, which used the LXX, should accommodate the language of specific quotations to this version"; he lists reminiscences from the LXX where the Hebrew gives the same meaning, in 2:26; 4:29,32; 6:34; 7:6 (less clearly); 9:12; 10:4,7,8; 12:1,19 and 31; and argues that the few variations that do occur follow either the Aramaic Targum (4:12 and 8:18), require the Hebrew (7:10), or some unknown variant (12:29f). But see also Robert Horton Gundry, *The Use of the Old Testament in St. Matthew's Gospel: with Special Reference to the Messianic Hope* (Leiden 1967).

[15] Perrin, *Kingdom,* 133.

[16] Perrin, *Kingdom,* 133.

[17] R. T. France, *Jesus and the Old Testament. His Application of Old Testament Passages to Himself and His Mission* (London 1971), 255f.

[18] France, *Jesus and the OT,* 37. This is as sweeping and difficult a statement as that of Perrin's cited above. For compelling evidence against France, see Gill, "Cleansing", I/92f, where Mk 11:17 and 1:2-3 are discussed and the Septuagintal origin of part of each of the 'quotations' is demonstrated. But France's actual objective is not to analyse from which source the author may have quoted or adapted the OT in the sayings of Jesus, so much as to show that in each case it can be understood as a reasonable derivation from the Hebrew/Aramaic which he presumes Jesus originally used. Hence he argues that there is no *necessary* Greek origin for any text because he has demonstrated how they *might* possibly have been derived from the Hebrew/Aramaic in each case, under the mistaken impression that Jesus could not have cited a text in agreement with the LXX and against the MT. But rather than deal with such hypothetical reconstructions, this study will focus on textual sources and relationships based on the texts as they stand.

from these contradictory conclusions of France and Perrin that convictions about whether the text in question could or could not have come from the historical Jesus must be influencing the assessment of the evidence. But it is a simple matter to remove such a problem at the outset of this fresh investigation by stating categorically that even if Jesus knew no Greek, he may still have been aware of the textual traditions embedded in the LXX or Theodotion. This has been shown to be possible since the discovery of Hebrew texts at Qumran which seem to agree with the LXX against the MT, indicating that LXX traditions may have been 'more at home' in Palestine than has hitherto been thought.[19] Thus whether or not a text seems to come from the LXX, Hebrew or Targumic traditions is not a factor which in itself can determine if Jesus could have uttered such words. Granted this fact, it should be possible to proceed below with an investigation of the text-forms behind the OT references in Mk 13 without the added burden of the question of historicity hindering objectivity.

Given the conflicting conclusions of scholars mentioned above and evidence from other investigations which also appears to contradict the statements of Perrin,[20] it would seem appropriate to undertake a new analysis of possible sources for the Old Testament references and allusions in Mk 13. Such an analysis may help to indicate if there is any consistent pattern underlying the use of such texts which sets the chapter apart from the rest of the Gospel of Mark, or perhaps show if there are

---

[19] See William W. Combs, "The Transmission History of the Septuagint", *BSac* 146 (1989), 257f: "a number of manuscripts from Qumran have been seen to display varying degrees of affinity with the kind of Hebrew text behind the Septuagint." Combs goes on to give examples from cave four which show a Septuagintal type text in Samuel, Exodus, Jeremiah, Joshua, Judges and Kings.

[20] See, for example, Howard Clark Kee, "The Function of Scriptural Quotations and Allusions in Mark 11-16", in *Jesus und Paulus,* eds E. Ellis and E. Grässer (Göttingen 1975), 165-188. To cite two specific areas of disagreement, Perrin goes on to say of Mk 13 that: "We have no single instance of necessary dependence upon any text other than the Greek" (*Kingdom,* 133), whereas Kee lists 13:8,13,14,24,25,26 and 27 as 'quoting' the MT, and 13:12b as being based on the Targum of Mi 7:2,6—quite apart from the many allusions and influences he lists from non-LXX or non-Theodotionic sources. The verses in which he does see links with the LXX are 13:4a,5,6,22 and 30; and with 'LXX-Th': 13:7 and 19 ("Function", 168-169). Similarly the claim of Perrin above—that up until Mk 13 the use of the OT in the words of Jesus always parallels the Hebrew—is contrary to the evidence as presented by Kee ("Function", 172). In a list of 19 readings from Mark 6-11 involving OT allusions where "the force of the argument or the specifics of the statements depend on the text as preserved in the LXX", there are six instances involving words attributed to Jesus and occurring before Mk 13—11:17a (Is 56:7); 11:17b (Jr 7:11); 12:10f (Ps 118:22-23); 12:29 (Dt 6:4-5); 12:31 (Lv 19:18); 12:36 (Ps 110:1). The tantalising statistics of B. F. C. Atkinson ["The Textual Background of the Use of the Old Testament by the New", *Journal of the Transactions of the Victoria Institute* 79 (1947), 56], claiming that in the Matthean version of the 'Little Apocalypse' there are "about eleven quotations from the LXX as opposed to about seven from non-LXX sources", whereas: "In the Marcan version there are about nine or ten from the LXX and three at most (all rather doubtful) from other sources", are unfortunately not supported by any further details or references.

diverse traditions within the chapter itself. The focus of this investigation will be on specific linguistic and semantic correspondences between texts, not on any thematic allusions or imaginative exegetical links which may conceivably exist.[21]

There are obvious difficulties in attempting such a task. One is the uncertainty surrounding which actual versions of the OT may have been available for the writers of the Gospel and its sources. In the following survey, the convenient labels: MT (Masoretic Text); LXX (Septuagint); Th (Theodotion) and Targ (Aramaic Targums) shall be used, despite the fact that strictly speaking, most of them are anachronisms in the context of the Gospel of Mark.[22] Here they are used merely as indications of divergent text types without implying that they necessarily existed in their present form or as separate entities at the time of the writing of the Gospel of Mark.

Another difficulty is in the tendency for all New Testament writers, and the author of Mark is no exception, to interpret rather than quote the earlier Jewish Scriptures. Thus changes in wording quite possibly reflect an author's interpretation of a text rather than necessarily indicating the use of a different source—particularly when there is very rarely exact

---

[21] This is not to deny that such links may have had a formative influence in the discourse. Rather it is as much a reflection of the present author's lack of expertise in such areas, and an indication of a healthy suspicion of excessively creative exegesis. Hartman's *Prophecy* tends to this extreme at times (such as in the over-use of the antichrist motif), as does F. Duncan M. Derrett's attempt to locate texts from Lamentations as the background to the Gospel of Mark, including chapter 13, in *The Making of Mark, Vol II* (Shipston-on-Stour 1985), 218f. The suggestion by Geddert, *Watchwords*, 210-212, that "Ezk. 33 and 34 undergird much of his (ie the author of Mark's) theology of temple destruction" may contain some truth, although the link he suggests with Jeremiah 7 would seem to be at least equally important. However, the fact remains that there are very few, if any, *specific* textual links between the Gospel of Mark and Ezekiel—the closest being between καὶ ἐρημωθήσεται διὰ πάντα τὰ βδελύγματα αὐτῶν, ἃ ἐποίησαν (Ezk 33:29 LXX) and Mk13:14.

[22] There is at least the possibility that these later labels represent divergent traditions which may pre-date the composition of the Gospel of Mark. The debate about exactly which texts would have been available in the first century, and which phase of each language would have been most representative of the era, is far too complex to look at here. A very brief introduction to the dimensions of some of the problems may be found, together with helpful bibliographies, in Maloney, *Semitic Interference,* 36-44, (especially for the arguments of Fitzmyer and Maloney against the first century dating by M. Black and A. Díez Macho of the tradition behind the Cairo Genizah Targum fragments and Codex Neofiti I); and in Combs, "Transmission History of the Septuagint", 255-269, (for an overview of the complexities surrounding the different recensions of the early Greek translations of the Jewish scriptures). In the face of such a diversity of possible text types and linguistic influences it is indeed tempting to give up any attempt to trace possible sources behind the use of the OT in Mk 13. But to yield to such a temptation would be to lose an awareness of the *possible* range of traditions behind the text and their specific implications for the unity or otherwise of Mk 13. The increasing availability of computer-generated LXX texts will no doubt render the following overview obsolete very shortly, so no claim is made here that it is a definitive analysis, but rather just another step in an ongoing process. Such tentative conclusions that are reached will then be related to the different types of analysis undertaken in the other chapters.

verbal correspondence between any of the sources and the allusions made to them in Mk 13. Yet clearly at times there is a distinctive preference in the tradition, or by the author, for one source over against another—as in the *gathering* of the elect in v.27.[23] Such clear examples may be rare, but it is at least worth re-examining the evidence for any further instances. Whether even these allusions to specific textual traditions are indications of a conscious and deliberate choice of such texts, or of the complexities of an untraceable intertextuality, is a question that requires examination at the level of the literary structure and intentions of the Gospel. Here the attempt is made merely to list and sort through the possible textual traditions with a view to relating such findings to the results from chapter 2, and then to the other types of analysis which follow below.

Allusions to the Old Testament in Mk 13

Verse in Mk 13	Possible Background	Comments & Conclusions[24]
2 οὐ μὴ ἀφεθῇ ὧδε λίθος ἐπὶ λίθον ὃς οὐ μὴ καταλυθῇ ("there will not be left one stone upon another which shall not be cast down")	**Hag 2:15** – Hebrew has "…before stone was laid on stone in the temple of Yahweh." מִטֶּרֶם שֹּׂום־אֶבֶן אֶל־אֶבֶן בְּהֵיכַל יְהוָה: LXX has πρὸ τοῦ θεῖναι λίθον ἐπὶ λίθον ἐν τῷ ναῷ κυρίου	• *Either MT or LXX could be the source of this allusion to the reversal of the building of the temple.*
4 ὅταν μέλλῃ ταῦτα συντελεῖσθαι πάντα ("when will all these things be accomplished")	**Dn 12:6** – Hebrew has "how long before these astonishing things will be fulfilled?" (עַד־מָתַי קֵץ הַפְּלָאוֹת), LXX has Πότε οὖν συντέλεια ὧν εἴρηκάς μοι τῶν θαυμαστῶν καὶ ὁ καθαρισμὸς τούτων; Theodotion Ἕως πότε τὸ πέρας ὧν εἴρηκας τῶν θαυμασίων; **Dn 12:7** – Hebrew has "when … all these things will be completed" (תִּכְלֶינָה כָל־אֵלֶּה), LXX has συντελεσθήσεται πάντα ταῦτα, and Theodotion ἐν τῷ συντελεσθῆναι διασκορπισμὸν χειρὸς λαοῦ ἡγιασμένου γνώσονται πάντα ταῦτα.	Kee: LXX (Dn 12:7). • *Certainly seems to be a variation on "The Eschatological Question". Other than that, if any more direct link exists, it seems to be with the LXX or MT rather than Theodotion.*

[23] The *gathering* clearly follows the LXX version of Zc 2:10 (= 2:6 ET), as distinct from the *spreading abroad* of the Hebrew text (see further below in this section).

[24] Unless stated otherwise, the references to Kee (usually listing only those references found in his principal category of 'Quotation'—he also lists 'Allusions' and 'Influences') are to be found in "Function", 168-169; to Hartman, in *Prophecy,* 145-177; to Perrin, *Kingdom,* 132-134; and to the pages cited in Lambrecht, *Redaktion;* Glasson, "Mark xiii"; William L. Lane, *The Gospel of Mark* (London 1974); and France, *Jesus and the Old Testament.*

Allusions to the Old Testament in Mk 13 (continued)

Verse in Mk 13	Possible Background	Comments & Conclusions
6 Ἐγώ εἰμι ("I am")	**Is 45:18** – Hebrew has "This is what Yahweh says, who created the heavens … 'I am Yahweh and there is no other'" אָמַר־יְהֹוָה בּוֹרֵא הַשָּׁמַיִם … אֲנִי יְהֹוָה וְאֵין עוֹד LXX has Οὕτως λέγει κύριος ὁ ποιήσας τὸν οὐρανόν … Ἐγώ εἰμι, καὶ οὐκ ἔστιν ἔτι. **Is 47:8** – Hebrew has "I am God and there is no other God like me" אָנֹכִי אֵל וְאֵין עוֹד אֱלֹהִים וְאֶפֶס כָּמוֹנִי LXX has ἡ λέγουσα ἐν τῇ καρδίᾳ αὐτῆς Ἐγώ εἰμι, καὶ οὐκ ἔστιν ἑτέρα·	Kee: LXX (Is 45:18 and allusions to Dn 7:8,11, 20,25). Hartman (172): Is 14:13; 47:8 and Dn 7:8,11, 20; 8:10f,25; 11:36. •*These specific suggestions are only relevant if an unlikely connection is made between the non-eschatological use of 'I am' in Isaiah and the blasphemy of Babylon as the horn magnifying itself in Daniel. Just a general reference to the Ἐγώ εἰμι of the OT (all versions) is more likely.*
7 πολέμους καὶ ἀκοὰς πολέμων ("wars and rumours of wars")	**Dn 7:21** – Aramaic has "that horn was waging war against the saints and defeating them" וְקַרְנָא דִכֵּן עָבְדָה קְרָב עִם־קַדִּישִׁין וְיָכְלָה לְהוֹן LXX has τὸ κέρας ἐκεῖνο πόλεμον συνιστάμενον πρὸς τοὺς ἁγίους, Theodotion καὶ τὸ κέρας ἐκεῖνο ἐποίει πόλεμον μετὰ τῶν ἁγίων **Dn 11:44** – Hebrew has "but reports will alarm him" (וּשְׁמֻעוֹת יְבַהֲלֻהוּ), LXX has καὶ ἀκοὴ ταράξει αὐτόν and Theodotion has καὶ ἀκοαὶ καὶ σπουδαὶ ταράξουσιν αὐτόν	Kee: MT (allusions to Dn 11). Hartman (173): based on the sequence 'blasphemy—war' in Dn 7:21f, and on the 'anti-christ' rather than 'false-christs' connection. •*A dubious connection.* Glasson (215, footnote 1): suggests Theodotion (Dn 11:44) is better (because of the plural ἀκοαί), but the rumours of war and other horrors (earthquakes, famines &c) are common in prophetic and apocalyptic literature (cf Lane, 458). • *Only one word points to Theodotion, so it is a very weak connection. It is perhaps better to regard this verse as a variant of the widely circulating lists of apocalyptic woes.*

δεῖ γενέσθαι
("must happen")

Dn 2:28 – Aramaic of OT has simple future tense, "what will happen in days to come"
מָה דִּי לֶהֱוֵא בְּאַחֲרִית יוֹמַיָּא
LXX and Theodotion have ἃ δεῖ γενέσθαι ἐπ᾽ ἐσχάτων τῶν ἡμερῶν

Dn 2:29 – Aramaic of OT has "what will happen after this"
(מָה דִּי לֶהֱוֵא אַחֲרֵי דְנָה), LXX has ὅσα δεῖ γενέσθαι ἐπ᾽ ἐσχάτων τῶν ἡμερῶν, καὶ ὁ ἀνακαλύπτων μυστήρια ἐδήλωσέ σοι ἃ δεῖ γενέσθαι and Theodotion τί δεῖ γενέσθαι μετὰ ταῦτα, καὶ ὁ ἀποκαλύπτων μυστήρια ἐγνώρισέν σοι ἃ δεῖ γενέσθαι

Dn 2:45 – Aramaic as in v.29, LXX has τὰ ἐσόμενα and Theodotion ἃ δεῖ γενέσθαι μετὰ ταῦτα

Dn 11:36 – Hebrew has "for what has been determined must/shall take place"
(כִּי נֶחֱרָצָה נֶעֱשָׂתָה), LXX and Theodotion have εἰς αὐτὸν γὰρ συντέλεια γίνεται

Kee: LXX Th (Dn 2:29, 45). Perrin: LXX & Th (Dn 2:28). France (254): a 'hazardous reference' to LXX & Th (Dn 2:28-29). Hartman (173): suggests Dn 8:19 but all versions have the future tense: Hebrew of OT has "what will happen" (אֲשֶׁר־יִהְיֶה), LXX ἃ ἔσται, Theodotion τὰ ἐσόμενα ἐπ᾽ ἐσχάτων τῆς ὀργῆς. As the future and δεῖ are not mutually exclusive in Hebrew, the MT of both Dn 8:19 and 11:36 would be possible, as are the Dn 2 references in the LXX and Th.

• *It is best to see this phrase as a general reflection of its widespread usage in prophetic and apocalyptic literature, where it expresses the inevitability of certain recently experienced events as a prelude to the decisive intervention of God.*

Allusions to the Old Testament in Mk 13 *(continued)*

Verse in Mk 13	Possible Background	Comments & Conclusions
8 ἐγερθήσεται γὰρ ἔθνος ἐπ' ἔθνος καὶ βασιλεία ἐπὶ βασιλείαν ("for nation will rise up against nation and kingdom against kingdom")	**Is 19:2** – Hebrew has "I will stir up Egyptian against Egyptian and a man will fight against his brother, a man against his neighbour, city against city and kingdom against kingdom" וְסִכְסַכְתִּי מִצְרַיִם בְּמִצְרַיִם וְנִלְחֲמוּ אִישׁ־בְּאָחִיו וְאִישׁ בְּרֵעֵהוּ עִיר בְּעִיר מַמְלָכָה בְּמַמְלָכָה LXX has καὶ ἐπεγερθήσονται Αἰγύπτιοι ἐπ' Αἰγυπτίους, καὶ πολεμήσει ἄνθρωπος τὸν ἀδελφὸν αὐτοῦ καὶ ἄνθρωπος τὸν πλησίον αὐτοῦ, πόλις ἐπὶ πόλιν καὶ νομὸς ἐπὶ νομόν. **2 Ch 15:6** – Hebrew has "and they were crushed nation by nation and city by city because God was troubling them with every kind of distress" וְכֻתְּתוּ גוֹי־בְּגוֹי וְעִיר בְּעִיר כִּי־אֱלֹהִים הֲמָמָם בְּכָל־צָרָה LXX has Καὶ πολεμήσει ἔθνος πρὸς ἔθνος καὶ πόλις πρὸς πόλιν, ὅτι ὁ Θεὸς ἐξέστησεν αὐτοὺς ἐν πάσῃ θλίψει. The phrase ἔθνος ἐπ' ἔθνος *does* occur in the LXX of Is 2:4 and is repeated in Mi 4:3, reflecting the Hebrew in both cases. It is used in the negative ("nation will *not* take up sword against nation") as part of the famous Isaianic vision of world peace. The opposite meaning is obviously intended in this passage.	Kee: MT (Is 19:2). France (244): probable allusion to MT (or Targ) of Is 19:2. Hartman (173): Is 19:2 and 2 Chron 15:6 joined by key words (but the connecting phrase between the two verses πόλις ἐπὶ/πρὸς πόλιν is the very phrase omitted in Mk!) • *MT or Targ of Is 19:2 appears to be the closest link, with perhaps the use of the phrase ἔθνος ἐπ' ἔθνος from the MT/LXX of Is 2:4 and/or Mi 4:3.* CONTEXT: Of Is 19:2—the judgment of Egypt prior to her conversion along with Assyria. Of Is 2:4—the settling of disputes between the nations which precedes the beating of swords into ploughshares. Of Mi 4:3—the gathering of the faithful at Zion, followed by peace among the nations.
8 ἀρχὴ ὠδίνων ταῦτα ("these are the beginnings of labour")	No specific instances of this phrase occur, but the comparison of tribulation and labour pains is typical of prophetic and apocalyptic literature, as in: Is 26:17; Jr 22:23; Mi 4:9-10 (cf also 1 Th 5:3).	•*A general link with apocalyptic phraseology only.*
9 (11,12) παραδώσουσιν ὑμᾶς εἰς ... ("Deliver you up to...")	**Dn 7:25** – Aramaic of OT has "they will be given into his hand" (וְיִתְיַהֲבוּן בִּידֵהּ), LXX has παραδοθήσεται πάντα εἰς τὰς χεῖρας αὐτου, Theodotion δοθήσεται ἐν χειρὶ αὐτοῦ	Hartman (150, 173): MT or LXX (Dn 7:25). • *LXX or MT more likely than Theodotion if any link is to be made.*

10 καὶ εἰς πάντα τὰ ἔθνη πρῶτον δεῖ κηρυχθῆναι τὸ εὐαγγέλιον. ("And first the good news must be preached to all nations.")

Zc 2:15a (2:11 in the English/ET) – Hebrew has "Many nations will be joined with Yahweh in that day and will become my people"

וְנִלְווּ גוֹיִם רַבִּים אֶל־יְהוָה בַּיּוֹם הַהוּא וְהָיוּ לִי לְעָם

LXX has καὶ καταφεύξονται ἔθνη πολλὰ ἐπὶ τὸν κύριον ἐν τῇ ἡμέρᾳ ἐκείνῃ καὶ ἔσονται αὐτῷ εἰς λαὸν καὶ κατασκηνώσουσιν ἐν μέσῳ σου

Zc 14:16 – Hebrew has "then the survivors from all the nations that have attacked Jerusalem will go up year after year to worship the King"

וְהָיָה כָּל־הַנּוֹתָר מִכָּל־הַגּוֹיִם הַבָּאִים עַל־יְרוּשָׁלָם וְעָלוּ מִדֵּי שָׁנָה בְשָׁנָה לְהִשְׁתַּחֲוֹת לְמֶלֶךְ

LXX has καὶ ἔσται ὅσοι ἐὰν καταλειφθῶσιν ἐκ πάντων τῶν ἐθνῶν τῶν ἐλθόντων ἐπὶ Ιερουσαλημ, καὶ ἀναβήσονται κατ᾽ ἐνιαυτὸν τοῦ προσκυνῆσαι τῷ βασιλεῖ κυρίῳ παντοκράτορι καὶ τοῦ ἑορτάζειν τὴν ἑορτὴν τῆς σκηνοπηγίας.

Dn 11:33 – Hebrew has "Those who are wise will make many understand"

וּמַשְׂכִּילֵי עָם יָבִינוּ לָרַבִּים

LXX has καὶ ἐννοούμενοι τοῦ ἔθνους συνήσουσιν εἰς πολλούς, Theodotion καὶ οἱ συνετοὶ τοῦ λαοῦ συνήσουσιν εἰς πολλά

Dn 12:3 – Hebrew has "and those who turn many to righteousness"

(וּמַצְדִּיקֵי הָרַבִּים), LXX has καὶ οἱ κατισχύοντες τοὺς λόγους μου, Theodotion καὶ ἀπὸ τῶν δικαίων τῶν πολλῶν

Kee: MT (allusions to Zc 2:10?—meaning v.11 in the ET?—and 14:16).

Hartman (171): suggests Dn 11:33 and 12:3 as background for Mt 24:14 and Mk 13:10, making the comment, "To interpret 'the many' as 'the whole world' was not difficult for the Biblical expositor of the time".

• *But this is a very tenuous association, as Hartman tacitly acknowledges by omitting it from his list of OT verses behind Mk 13:9-13 (168).*
There would appear to be no clear OT background to this verse. Zc 2:11 is the most appropriate, as the gathering at Jerusalem in 14:16 does not fit the context of the destruction of Jerusalem in Mk 13. The phrase πάντα τὰ ἔθνη is used some 95 times in the LXX, but only 3 times preceded by εἰς (Dt 28:64; Zc 7:14 = scatter throughout or amongst all nations; and Ml 2:9 = make you vile to all nations), none of which fit the context of preaching the good news very well. Certainly the themes of Zc 2:11f (ET) fit those of Mk 13:24f, and Mk 13:10 may be seen as a necessary prelude to this.

CONTEXT: "On that day many nations will be converted to Yahweh" (Zc 2:11 ET = 2:15 LXX/MT).

Allusions to the Old Testament in Mk 13 (continued)

Verse in Mk 13	Possible Background	Comments & Conclusions
12 καὶ παραδώσει ἀδελφὸς ἀδελφὸν εἰς θάνατον καὶ πατὴρ τέκνον, καὶ ἐπαναστήσονται τέκνα ἐπὶ γονεῖς καὶ θανατώσουσιν αὐτούς· ("And brother will hand over brother to death, and father child. And children will rise up against parents and put them to death.")	**Is 19:2** – (as above for v.8) **Mi 7:2** – Hebrew has "All of them lie in wait to shed blood; each hunts his brother with a net" כֻּלָּם לְדָמִים יֶאֱרֹבוּ אִישׁ אֶת־אָחִיהוּ יָצוּדוּ חֵרֶם LXX has πάντες εἰς αἵματα δικάζονται, ἕκαστος τὸν πλησίον αὐτοῦ ἐκθλίβουσιν ἐκθλιβῇ **Mi 7:6** – Hebrew has "For a son dishonours his father, a daughter rises up against her mother, a daughter-in-law against her mother-in-law. A man's enemies are the members of his household" כִּי־בֵן מְנַבֵּל אָב בַּת קָמָה בְאִמָּהּ כַּלָּה בַּחֲמֹתָהּ אֹיְבֵי אִישׁ אַנְשֵׁי בֵיתוֹ LXX closely follows the Hebrew Διότι υἱὸς ἀτιμάζει πατέρα, θυγάτηρ ἐπαναστήσεται ἐπὶ τὴν μητέρα αὐτῆς, νύμφη ἐπὶ τὴν πενθερὰν αὐτῆς, ἐχθροὶ πάντες ἀνδρὸς οἱ ἐν τῷ οἴκῳ αὐτοῦ.	Hartman (169) & Kee favour the Targ Jon (Mi 7:2,5f) which, according to Hartman, reads: "A man delivers up his brother to destruction" and "those who *hate* a man are the men of his own house". •*v.12 (and v.13a) seem to be closest to Targ Jon.* CONTEXT: 'The day when others come to you all the way from Assyria, from Egypt, from Tyre and all the way from the Euphrates' (Mi 7:12).
13 ὁ δὲ ὑπομείνας εἰς τέλος οὗτος σωθήσεται. ("the one who endures to the end shall be saved")	**Dn 12:12-13** – Hebrew has "blessed is he who waits/endures" (אַשְׁרֵי הַמְחַכֶּה), LXX has μακάριος ὁ ἐμμένων καὶ συνάξει εἰς ἡμέρας χιλίας τριακοσίας τριάκοντα πέντε. 13 καὶ σὺ βάδισον ἀναπαύου· ἔτι γάρ εἰσιν ἡμέραι καὶ ὧραι εἰς ἀναπλήρωσιν συντελείας, καὶ ἀναπαύσῃ καὶ ἀναστήσῃ ἐπὶ τὴν δόξαν σου εἰς συντέλειαν ἡμερῶν, Theodotion has μακάριος ὁ ὑπομένων καὶ φθάσας εἰς ἡμέρας χιλίας τριακοσίας τριάκοντα πέντε. 13 καὶ σὺ δεῦρο καὶ ἀναπαύου· ἔτι γὰρ ἡμέραι εἰς ἀναπλήρωσιν συντελείας, καὶ ἀναστήσῃ εἰς τὸν κλῆρόν σου εἰς συντέλειαν ἡμερῶν	Perrin (133) and Glasson (215): Distinctively Theodotionic (Dn 12:12,13). Kee: MT (!?) of 11:32, following Hartman (173—11:32,35; 12:1!— via Mi 7:7). Hebrew of 11:32 has "but the people knowing their God will be strong and resist" וְעַם יֹדְעֵי אֱלֹהָיו יַחֲזִקוּ וְעָשׂוּ France (254) argues that the Hebrew of Dn 12:12 carries the same meaning as the Greek. Hartman's original suggestion (169) of the LXX or Targ Jon of Mi 7:7 is perhaps best.[25] (Continued next page)

[25] Links with 4 Ezra (such as those suggested by Myers, *Strong Man,* 334, between 13:12 and 4 Ezr 6:24; 13:13 and 4 Ezr 5:9) have been excluded here on the basis of the

Dn 12:1 – Hebrew has "everyone whose name is found written in the book will be delivered" יִמָּלֵט עַמְּךָ כָּל־הַנִּמְצָא כָּתוּב בַּסֵּפֶר LXX has καὶ ἐν ἐκείνῃ τῇ ἡμέρᾳ ὑψωθήσεται πᾶς ὁ λαός, ὃς ἂν εὑρεθῇ ἐγγεγραμμένος ἐν τῷ βιβλίῳ. Theodotion has καὶ ἐν τῷ καιρῷ ἐκείνῳ σωθήσεται ὁ λαός σου, πᾶς ὁ εὑρεθεὶς γεγραμμένος ἐν τῇ βίβλῳ.
Mi 7:7 – Hebrew has "I wait for God my Saviour" (אוֹחִילָה לֵאלֹהֵי יִשְׁעִי), LXX has ὑπομενῶ ἐπὶ τῷ θεῷ τῷ σωτῆρί μου

• *The specific use of* ὑπομένων *in 12:12 and* σωθήσεται *in 12:1 favour Theodotion, but other aspects of the language of the LXX are also relevant* (ἡμέραι καὶ ὧραι)*. Targ Jon or LXX of Mi 7:7 are perhaps more likely given the origins of v.12 above.*

CONTEXT: As above (Mi 7:12).

14 τὸ βδέλυγμα τῆς ἐρημώσεως ἑστηκότα ὅπου οὐ δεῖ ("the abomination of desolation standing where it should not")

Dn 9:27 – Hebrew has "the abomination which causes desolation" (שִׁקּוּצִים מְשֹׁמֵם), LXX has ἐπὶ τὸ ἱερὸν βδέλυγμα τῶν ἐρημώσεων ἔσται ἕως συντελείας and Theodotion ἐπὶ τὸ ἱερὸν βδέλυγμα τῶν ἐρημώσεων
Dn 11:31 – Hebrew has "then they will set up the abomination which causes desolation" (וְנָתְנוּ הַשִּׁקּוּץ מְשֹׁמֵם), LXX δώσουσι βδέλυγμα ἐρημώσεως, Theodotion δώσουσιν βδέλυγμα ἠφανισμένον
Dn 12:11 – Hebrew has "and the abomination which causes desolation is set up" (וְלָתֵת שִׁקּוּץ שֹׁמֵם), LXX ἑτοιμασθῇ δοθῆναι τὸ βδέλυγμα τῆς ἐρημώσεως, Theodotion τοῦ δοθῆναι βδέλυγμα ἐρημώσεως
1 M 1:54 – LXX has ᾠκοδόμησά βδέλυγμα ἐρημώσεως ἐπὶ τὸ θυσιαστήριον

Kee: MT (all references) Perrin: LXX & Th (Dn 12:11). France (254): points out that the exact phrase occurs only in Dn 12:11 (LXX and Th A, *not* Th B or Dn 11:31 LXX/Th), and that the MT of that verse can have the same meaning. He goes on to show (255) that the use of the genitive (τῆς ἐρημώσεως 'of desolation') to translate the Hebrew participle (מְשֹׁמֵם 'which makes desolate') is paralleled elsewhere in Daniel (cf 8:13).

• *The exact phrase is closest to the MT, LXX or Th A of Dn 12:11.*

dating of 4 Ezra "toward the end of the first century CE and certainly before the Bar Kochba revolt of 132-35", Robert Kirschner, "Apocalyptic and Rabbinic Responses to the Destruction of 70", *HTR* 78 (1985), 28, citing James H. Charlesworth and George W. E. Nickelsburg in support.

Allusions to the Old Testament in Mk 13 (continued)

Verse in Mk 13	Possible Background	Comments & Conclusions
14 τότε οἱ ἐν τῇ Ἰουδαίᾳ φευγέτωσαν εἰς τὰ ὄρη **15** ὁ δὲ ἐπὶ τοῦ δώματος μὴ καταβάτω μηδὲ εἰσελθάτω ἆραί τι ἐκ τῆς οἰκίας αὐτοῦ ("Then those in Judea should flee into the mountains; and those on the housetop should not go down or enter their house to take anything")	**1 M 2:28** – LXX has καὶ ἔφυγεν αὐτὸς καὶ οἱ υἱοὶ αὐτοῦ εἰς τὰ ὄρη καὶ ἐγκατέλιπον ὅσα εἶχον ἐν τῇ πόλει (said of Mattathias and sons as they fled from Modein after having killed an apostate Jew and the king's commissioner) Lane (470), points to Ez 7:14f (note especially the mountains as refuge for 'the saved' in v.16: καὶ ἔσονται ἐπὶ τῶν ὀρέων).	A specific textual link is difficult to establish. Perhaps it is better to see the Ezekiel, Maccabean and Markan texts as belonging to the wider 'flight' motif of prophetic traditions surrounding the fall of Jerusalem. • *The 'flight to the hills/mountains' seems to be a recurring theme in prophetic and apocalyptic literature—but in the context of judgement rather than epiphany/parousia.*
19 ἔσονται γὰρ αἱ ἡμέραι ἐκεῖναι θλῖψις οἵα οὐ γέγονεν τοιαύτη ἀπ᾽ ἀρχῆς κτίσεως ἣν ἔκτισεν ὁ θεὸς ἕως τοῦ νῦν καὶ οὐ μὴ γένηται. ("for in those days there will be such tribulation as has never been from the beginning of creation, which God created, until now, and never shall be.")	**Dn 12:1** – Hebrew has "there will be a time of distress such as has not happened from the beginning of nations until that time" וְהָיְתָה עֵת צָרָה אֲשֶׁר לֹא־נִהְיְתָה מִהְיוֹת גּוֹי עַד הָעֵת הַהִיא LXX has ἐκείνη ἡ ἡμέρα θλίψεως, οἵα οὐκ ἐγενήθη ἀφ᾽ οὗ ἐγενήθησαν ἕως τῆς ἡμέρας ἐκείνης· and Theodotion καὶ ἔσται καιρὸς θλίψεως, θλῖψις οἵα οὐ γέγονεν ἀφ᾽ οὗ γεγένηται ἔθνος ἐπὶ τῆς γῆς ἕως τοῦ καιροῦ ἐκείνου· **Ex 9:18** – Hebrew has "a severe hailstorm such as never was like it in Egypt from the day of its foundation until now" בָּרָד כָּבֵד מְאֹד אֲשֶׁר לֹא־הָיָה כָמֹהוּ בְּמִצְרַיִם לְמִן־הַיּוֹם הִוָּסְדָה וְעַד־עָתָּה LXX has ἥτις τοιαύτη οὐ γέγονεν ἐν Αἰγύπτῳ ἀφ᾽ ἧς ἡμέρας ἔκτισται ἕως τῆς ἡμέρας ταύτης	Kee: LXX–Th (Dn 12:1). Perrin: Th—not LXX (Dn 12:1). Maloney (118): conflation of Th (Dn 12:1) and Hebrew/LXX of Ex 9:18, resulting in the redundant τοιαύτη (see also Howard, 435). France (255) and Glasson agree that 'the Greek words represent quite fairly the meaning of the Hebrew'. • *The Theodotion Dn 12:1 and MT Ex 9:18 combination appears to be the most likely source. The addition of '... until now, and never shall be' historicises the tribulation (so Lane, 472) and disconnects it from an imminent expectation of the end.*

22 ἐγερθήσ-
ονται γὰρ
ψευδό-
χριστοι και
ψευδο-
προφῆται
και
δώσουσιν
σημεῖα και
τέρατα
πρὸς τὸ
ἀποπλανᾶν,
εἰ δυνατόν,
τοὺς
ἐκλεκτούς.
("For false
messiahs
and false
prophets
will arise
and they will
perform
signs and
wonders to
lead astray,
if possible,
the elect.")

Dt 13:1-3 – Hebrew (vv.2-3) has "If a prophet, or a dreamer of dreams, appears among you and announces to you a sign or wonder which takes place, and he says 'Let us follow other gods which you have not known, and worship them...'"

כִּי־יָקוּם בְּקִרְבְּךָ נָבִיא אוֹ חֹלֵם חֲלוֹם
וְנָתַן אֵלֶיךָ אוֹת אוֹ מוֹפֵת וּבָא הָאוֹת
וְהַמּוֹפֵת אֲשֶׁר־דִּבֶּר אֵלֶיךָ לֵאמֹר נֵלְכָה
אַחֲרֵי אֱלֹהִים אֲחֵרִים אֲשֶׁר לֹא־יְדַעְתָּם
וְנָעָבְדֵם

LXX (vv.1-2) has Ἐὰν δὲ ἀναστῇ ἐν σοὶ προφήτης ἢ ἐνυπνιαζόμενος ἐνύπνιον καὶ δῷ σοι σημεῖον ἢ τέρας καὶ ἔλθῃ τὸ σημεῖον ἢ τὸ τέρας, ὃ ἐλάλησεν πρὸς σὲ λέγων Πορευθῶμεν καὶ λατρεύσωμεν θεοῖς ἑτέροις, οὓς οὐκ οἴδατε

Dn 6:26-28 – Hebrew (v.28 = v.27 in ET) has "He (the living God) rescues and saves and performs signs and wonders in the heavens and on the earth"

מְשֵׁיזִב וּמַצִּל וְעָבֵד אָתִין וְתִמְהִין
בִּשְׁמַיָּא וּבְאַרְעָא

LXX (v. 27b-28) has αὐτὸς γάρ ἐστι θεὸς μένων καὶ ζῶν εἰς γενεὰς γενεῶν ἕως τοῦ αἰῶνος· ἐγὼ Δαρεῖος ἔσομαι αὐτῷ προσκυνῶν καὶ δουλεύων πάσας τὰς ἡμέρας μου, τὰ γὰρ εἴδωλα τὰ χειροποίητα οὐ δύνανται σῶσαι, ὡς ἐλυτρώσατο ὁ θεὸς τοῦ Δανιηλ τὸν Δανιηλ. Theodotion has ἀντιλαμβάνεται καὶ ῥύεται καὶ ποιεῖ σημεῖα καὶ τέρατα ἐν οὐρανῷ καὶ ἐπὶ τῆς γῆς, ὅστις ἐξείλατο τὸν Δανιηλ ἐκ χειρὸς τῶν λεόντων.

Dn 11:36 – Hebrew has "He will exalt and magnify himself above every god and will say unheard-of things against the God of gods"

וְיִתְרוֹמֵם וְיִתְגַּדֵּל עַל־כָּל־אֵל
וְעַל אֵל אֵלִים יְדַבֵּר נִפְלָאוֹת

LXX follows the Hebrew closely and ποιήσει κατὰ τὸ θέλημα αὐτοῦ ὁ βασιλεὺς καὶ παροργισθήσεται καὶ ὑψωθήσεται ἐπὶ πάντα θεὸν καὶ ἐπὶ τὸν θεὸν τῶν θεῶν ἔξαλλα λαλήσει καὶ εὐοδωθήσεται, Theodotion has καὶ ποιήσει κατὰ τὸ θέλημα αὐτοῦ καὶ ὑψωθήσεται ὁ βασιλεὺς καὶ μεγαλυνθήσεται ἐπὶ πάντα θεὸν καὶ λαλήσει ὑπέρογκα

Kee: LXX (Dt 13:1-3). The connection with Daniel could be argued perhaps if Mk 13:22 (or even v.6) were in the singular, but the impression given is of many false christs and false prophets, and therefore of a general connection with the false prophet tradition in Deuteronomy rather than a specific link with a particular 'anti-christ' figure as in Daniel. The use of ποιέω in Th (Dn 6), along with σημεῖα καὶ τέρατα, may underlie the variant reading of ποιήσουσιν in Mk 13:22 (or vice versa!), but it is far more likely that this was a later change to the text of Mk to bring it into line with the Dn passage, given the fascination of the Danielic prophecies. However there is a much more satisfactory context for the original allusion in the Dt text, especially as R. le Déaut[26] notes that Codex Neofiti (which contains the Pentateuch of the Palestinian Targ) has at Dt 13:1-3 the equivalent of the plural verb δώσουσιν and the plural nouns σημεῖα καὶ τέρατα, as well as specifically mentioning ψευδοπροφῆται

• *Thus the Codex Neofiti Targ of Dt 13:1-3 appears to be the most promising link.*

[26] R. le Déaut, *The Message of the New Testament and the Aramaic Bible (Targum)* (Rome 1982), 31.

24 ἐν ἐκείναις ταῖς ἡμέραις ("in those days").

The next phrase, μετὰ τὴν θλῖψιν ἐκείνην, does not appear to have any parallels in any version of the OT (nor does μετὰ τὴν θλῖψιν occur). Is it possible that the description of events *after* the great tribulation occurs here in Mk 13 for the first time? Doesn't this phrase implicitly historicise the tribulation?

Dn 10:2 – Hebrew has "at/in those days" (בַּיָּמִים הָהֵם), LXX and Theodotion have ἐν ταῖς ἡμέραις ἐκείναις

Dn 11:20 – Hebrew has "but in a few days" (וּבְיָמִים אֲחָדִים), LXX has καὶ ἐν ἡμέραις ἐσχάταις Theodotion καὶ ἐν ταῖς ἡμέραις ἐκείναις

Dn 12:1 – see also LXX (not Th!)

Jdt 8:1 – LXX has Καὶ ἤκουσεν ἐν ἐκείναις ταῖς ἡμέραις Ιουδιθ..., a reference to the days of the siege of Bethulia (in Samaria) by Holofernes and the Assyrians.

Kee (175-79): Mk 13:24-26 comprises a (redactional?) compilation of more than one OT reference (cf 1:2-3; 1:11; 11:17; 14:62)—suggesting a dialectical use of the OT texts.[27]
• *The phrase ἐν ἐκείναις ταῖς ἡμέραις (as distinct from ἐν ταῖς ἡμέραις ἐκείναις or the singular, as in v.32) occurs only at Jdt 8:1 in the whole of the LXX. By way of contrast ἐν ταῖς ἡμέραις ἐκείναις occurs 56 times (in 19 books, including Judith 1:5; 6:15). The link with Jdt is certainly appropriate and specific, but admittedly rather tenuous.* CONTEXT: Of Jdt 8:1—the involvement of a woman, a Samaritan town and Achior (the leader of the Ammonites who is converted to Judaism) in the salvation of Jerusalem.

[27] Kee calls these 'synthetic quotations'—rather than 'merged quotations' (Ellis), 'accommodated texts' (Fitzmyer), or 'compilations' (Bruce)—because "they are synthesized in such a way that a new claim is made for the fulfillment through Jesus, one that is clearly—at least for the modern reader—not anticipated in either of the component texts" (176). Kee includes 11:1-11 and 12:1-12 in his list, although in these two cases the 'quotations' are at each end of the story rather than put together in an immediate association. With the remaining examples it becomes clear that the 'dialectical' process is over-balanced in favour of the second half of the 'quotation', whose content *and* context, as Mk 1:2a makes explicit by citing Isaiah, are to override and redirect the interpretation of the initial quotation. For a detailed examination of Mk 1:2-3; 11:17, see Gill, "Cleansing", 92-97, where the redactional nature of the composite quotations is established.

Mk 1:2-3	Ml 3:1	'Look, I shall send my messenger to clear a way before me. *And suddenly the Lord whom you seek will come to his temple*'	The Isaianic wilderness tradition (and even that of Exodus) takes precedence over the temple tradition of Malachi. This is clear because attention is drawn in 1:2 to what *Isaiah* says!
	(Ex 23:20)	'Look, I am sending an angel to precede you'	
	Is 40:3	'A voice cries, Prepare in the desert a way for Yahweh. *Make a straight highway for our God across the wastelands*'	

Mk 1:11	Gn 22:2	'...your beloved son...' *(Abraham asked to take Isaac to Mt Moriah)*	2 Ch 3:1 identifies Moriah as the Jerusalem temple site, but this tradition is to be over-ridden by a wider perspective. Jesus, like Isaac, is to be taken there, but clearly with consequences for the salvation of the nations.
	Ps 2:7	'You are my son . . . ask of me and I shall give you the nations as your birthright''	
	Is 42:1	'...in whom my soul delights . . . *he will bring fair judgment to the nations*'	

ὁ ἥλιος σκοτισθήσεται, καὶ ἡ σελήνη οὐ δώσει τὸ φέγγος αὐτῆς ("the sun will be darkened and the moon will not shed its light")

Is 13:10 – Hebrew has "the stars of the heavens and their constellations will not show their light; the sun will be dark at its rising, and the moon will not shed its light"

כִּי־כוֹכְבֵי הַשָּׁמַיִם וּכְסִילֵיהֶם לֹא יָהֵלּוּ אוֹרָם חָשַׁךְ הַשֶּׁמֶשׁ בְּצֵאתוֹ וְיָרֵחַ לֹא־יַגִּיהַּ אוֹרוֹ

LXX has οἱ γὰρ ἀστέρες τοῦ οὐρανοῦ καὶ ὁ Ὠρίων καὶ πᾶς ὁ κόσμος τοῦ οὐρανοῦ τὸ φῶς οὐ δώσουσιν, καὶ σκοτισθήσεται τοῦ ἡλίου ἀνατέλλοντος, καὶ ἡ σελήνη οὐ δώσει τὸ φῶς αὐτῆς.

Ez 32:7-8 – Hebrew has "'When I snuff you out I will cover the heavens and darken their stars; I will cover the sun with a cloud and the moon will not give its light. All the shining lights in the heavens I will darken over you, and I will bring darkness over your land', declares the sovereign Yahweh"

Kee: MT (Is 13:10 and Ez 32:7-8). Hartman (156): MT/LXX? (Jl 2:10, 4:15 and Is 13:10). France (242): MT (Is 13:10), because the MT and Mk have 'the sun' as the subject of the main verb, whereas the LXX uses 'a dependent phrase in the genitive absolute'. Also Mk uses φέγγος whereas the LXX has φῶς. However, the texts from Joel may also be relevant:

Jl 2:10 – Hebrew has "the sun and moon are darkened and the stars withhold their light"

שֶׁמֶשׁ וְיָרֵחַ קָדָרוּ וְכוֹכָבִים אָסְפוּ נָגְהָם

(Continued next page)

Mk 11:17	Is 56:7	'My house shall be called a house of prayer for all nations'	Clearly the judgment of the temple rather than its rehabilitation is what the author has in mind.
	Jr 7:11	'…a brigands' hideaway'. Part of Jeremiah's anti-temple sermon, *including a threat of destruction.*	
Mk 13:24-27	Is 13:10; Ez 32:7-8; Jl 2:10; 3:4; 4:15; Is 34:4; then Dn 7:13-14.	All the texts from Isaiah, Ezekiel and Joel have 'the Day of the Lord' connections, many specifically involving judgment of the nations from Jerusalem. 'One like a Son of Man . . . and all peoples, nations and languages became his servants'	If the latter verses take precedence over the former verses again, then the non-judgmental gathering of the nations overturns the prior ethnocentric descriptions of judgment and terror for the nations.
Mk 14:62	Ps 110:1	'Seated at the right hand . . . ruling from Zion . . . judge the nations'	Again the multi-ethnic perspective overrides the more ethnocentric view.
	Dn 7:13-14	'One like a Son of Man . . . and all peoples, nations and languages became his servants'	

Allusions to the Old Testament in Mk 13 (continued)

Verse in Mk 13	Possible Background	Comments & *Conclusions*

וְכִסֵּיתִי בְכַבּוֹתְךָ שָׁמַיִם וְהִקְדַּרְתִּי
אֶת־כֹּכְבֵיהֶם שֶׁמֶשׁ בֶּעָנָן אֲכַסֶּנּוּ וְיָרֵחַ
לֹא־יָאִיר אוֹרוֹ: כָּל־מְאוֹרֵי אוֹר בַּשָּׁמַיִם
אַקְדִּירֵם עָלֶיךָ וְנָתַתִּי חֹשֶׁךְ עַל־אַרְצְךָ
נְאֻם אֲדֹנָי יְהוִה

LXX has καὶ κατακαλύψω ἐν
τῷ σβεσθῆναί σε οὐρανὸν καὶ
συσκοτάσω τὰ ἄστρα αὐτοῦ,
ἥλιον ἐν νεφέλῃ καλύψω, καὶ
σελήνη οὐ μὴ φάνῃ τὸ φῶς
αὐτῆς· πάντα τὰ φαίνοντα φῶς
ἐν τῷ οὐρανῷ συσκοτάσουσιν
ἐπὶ σέ, καὶ δώσω σκότος ἐπὶ
τὴν γῆν σου, λέγει κύριος
κύριος

LXX has ὁ ἥλιος καὶ ἡ
σελήνη συσκοτάσουσιν,
καὶ τὰ ἄστρα δύσουσιν
τὸ φέγγος αὐτῶν.

Jl 3:4 (= 2:31) –
Hebrew has "the sun will
be turned to darkness and
the moon to blood before
the coming of the great and
fearful day of Yahweh"

הַשֶּׁמֶשׁ יֵהָפֵךְ לְחֹשֶׁךְ וְהַיָּרֵחַ
לְדָם לִפְנֵי בּוֹא יוֹם יְהוָה
הַגָּדוֹל וְהַנּוֹרָא

LXX has ὁ ἥλιος
μεταστραφήσεται εἰς
σκότος καὶ ἡ σελήνη εἰς
αἷμα πρὶν ἐλθεῖν ἡμέραν
κυρίου τὴν μεγάλην καὶ
ἐπιφανῆ.

Jl 4:15 (= 3:15) –
Hebrew as in 2:10 above,
LXX has ὁ ἥλιος καὶ ἡ
σελήνη συσκοτάσουσιν,
καὶ οἱ ἀστέρες δύσουσιν
φέγγος αὐτῶν.
Glasson: MT=LXX (Is
13:10)

• *MT of Is 13:10 suffices,
but there is also substantial
agreement with the LXX of
Is 13:10 and the Joel texts.*

CONTEXT: Of Is 13:10—
Day of Yahweh (judgment
and horror). Of Ez 32:7-
8—judgment on Pharaoh
king of Egypt. Of Jl 2:10—
terrible Day of Yahweh;
3:4—Day of Yahweh
(escape to Jerusalem!);
4:15—Day of Yahweh
(Jerusalem a sanctuary).

25 οἱ ἀστέρες ἔσονται ἐκ τοῦ οὐρανοῦ πίπτοντες, καὶ αἱ δυνάμεις αἱ ἐν τοῖς οὐρανοῖς σαλευθήσονται ("the stars will fall out of heaven, and the powers in the heavens will be shaken")

Is 34:4 – Hebrew has "All the host of heaven will rot away and the skies roll up like a scroll. All their host will fall"

וְנָמַקּוּ כָּל־צְבָא הַשָּׁמַיִם וְנָגֹלּוּ כַסֵּפֶר הַשָּׁמָיִם וְכָל־צְבָאָם יִבּוֹל

LXX has καὶ τακήσονται πᾶσαι αἱ δυνάμεις τῶν οὐρανῶν καὶ ἑλιγήσεται ὁ οὐρανὸς ὡς βιβλίον, καὶ πάντα τὰ ἄστρα πεσεῖται ὡς φύλλα ἐξ ἀμπέλου, καὶ ὡς πίπτει φύλλα ἀπὸ συκῆς

Jl 2:10 – Hebrew has "Before them the earth shakes, the heavens tremble"

לְפָנָיו רָגְזָה אֶרֶץ רָעֲשׁוּ שָׁמָיִם

LXX has πρὸ προσώπου αὐτῶν συγχυθήσεται ἡ γῆ καὶ σεισθήσεται ὁ οὐρανός

Kee and Hartman: MT (Is 34:4). Glasson and Perrin: LXX (Is 34:4). France (255-6): Mk is still derivable from the MT without any necessary reference to the LXX. Glasson's 3 points of Mk-LXX agreement against the MT (αἱ δυνάμεις αἱ ἐν τοῖς οὐρανοῖς, οἱ ἀστέρες and ἔσονται .. πίπτοντες) do not agree *exactly* with the LXX and can be seen as independent translations of the MT.

• *However the coincidence in root words indicates clearly that there has been more dependence on some form of the LXX text (Is 34:4) than the MT.*

CONTEXT: Of Is 34:4— judgment and destruction of the nations (34:2). Of Jl 2:10—the terrible Day of Yahweh.

26 καὶ τότε ὄψονται τὸν υἱὸν τοῦ ἀνθρώπου ἐρχόμενον ἐν νεφέλαις ("and then you will see the son of man coming in clouds")

Dn 7:13 – Aramaic of OT has "and see! One like a son of man coming with the clouds of heaven"

וַאֲרוּ עִם־עֲנָנֵי שְׁמַיָּא כְּבַר אֱנָשׁ אָתֵה הֲוָה

LXX has καὶ ἰδοὺ ἐπὶ τῶν νεφελῶν τοῦ οὐρανοῦ ὡς υἱὸς ἀνθρώπου ἤρχετο, Theodotion καὶ ἰδοὺ μετὰ τῶν νεφελῶν τοῦ οὐρανοῦ ὡς υἱὸς ἀνθρώπου ἐρχόμενος

Kee: MT (Dn 7:13-14).

• *MT or LXX? Not as close to Th as Mk 14:62 is.*

CONTEXT: "and all peoples, nations and languages became his servants" (Dn 7:14).

μετὰ δυνάμεως πολλῆς καὶ δόξης ("with great power and glory")

Dn 7:14 – Aramaic has "He was given authority, glory and sovereign power"

וְלֵהּ יְהִיב שָׁלְטָן וִיקָר וּמַלְכוּ

LXX has ἐδόθη αὐτῷ ἐξουσία ... καὶ πᾶσα δόξα, and Theodotion αὐτῷ ἐδόθη ἡ ἀρχὴ καὶ ἡ τιμὴ καὶ ἡ βασιλεία[28]

Kee (169): MT (!?)—yet in *Community*, 44, he concedes that it is more closely linked with the LXX of 7:13!

• *Distinctively LXX or MT. Not Th.*

---

[28] The difference between this text (Mk 13:26) and Mk 14:62, which uses Ps 110:1 initially, and then follows the Theodotion text: ἰδοὺ μετὰ τῶν νεφελῶν τοῦ οὐρανοῦ ὡς υἱὸς ἀνθρώπου ἐρχόμενος ἦν, is pointed out by Barnabas Lindars, in *New Testament Apologetic: The Doctrinal Significance of the Old Testament Quotations* (London, 1961),

Allusions to the Old Testament in Mk 13 (continued)

Verse in Mk 13	Possible Background	Comments & Conclusions
27 ἐπισυνάξει τοὺς ἐκλεκτοὺς αὐτοῦ ἐκ τῶν τεσσάρων ἀνέμων ἀπ' ἄκρου γῆς ἕως ἄκρου οὐρανοῦ ("gather his elect from the four winds, from the ends of earth to the ends of heaven")	**Zc 2:10** (= 2:6 ET) – Hebrew of OT has "spread you abroad as the four winds" כְּאַרְבַּע רוּחוֹת הַשָּׁמַיִם פֵּרַשְׂתִּי אֶתְכֶם LXX has διότι ἐκ τῶν τεσσάρων ἀνέμων τοῦ οὐρανοῦ συνάξω ὑμᾶς, λέγει κύριος **Is 43:6** – Hebrew of OT has "Bring my sons from afar and my daughters from the ends of the earth" הָבִיאִי בָנַי מֵרָחוֹק וּבְנוֹתַי מִקְצֵה הָאָרֶץ LXX has ἀπ' ἄκρων τῆς γῆς **Is 11:(10-)12** – Hebrew has "He will raise a banner for the nations and gather the exiles of Israel, and he will assemble the scattered ones of Judah from the four quarters of the earth" וְנָשָׂא נֵס לַגּוֹיִם וְאָסַף נִדְחֵי יִשְׂרָאֵל וּנְפֻצוֹת יְהוּדָה יְקַבֵּץ מֵאַרְבַּע כַּנְפוֹת הָאָרֶץ LXX follows the Hebrew closely and has καὶ ἀρεῖ σημεῖον εἰς τὰ ἔθνη καὶ συνάξει τοὺς ἀπολομένους Ισραηλ καὶ τοὺς διεσπαρμένους τοῦ Ιουδα συνάξει ἐκ τῶν τεσσάρων πτερύγων τῆς γῆς	Kee: MT (Zc 2:6ET = 2:10MT; Is 27:13) Glasson and Perrin: LXX (Zc 2:10 = 2:6 ET) France (256-7): MT of Dt 30:3-4, which reads: "...he will gather you from all the nations where your God Yahweh scattered you. 4. Even if he banished you to the end of the heavens, Yahweh your God will gather you from there and bring you back". וְקִבֶּצְךָ מִכָּל־הָעַמִּים אֲשֶׁר הֱפִיצְךָ יְהוָה אֱלֹהֶיךָ שָׁמָּה׃ 4 אִם־יִהְיֶה נִדַּחֲךָ בִּקְצֵה הַשָּׁמָיִם מִשָּׁם יְקַבֶּצְךָ יְהוָה אֱלֹהֶיךָ וּמִשָּׁם יִקָּחֶךָ׃ LXX has καὶ πάλιν συνάξει σε ἐκ πάντων τῶν ἐθνῶν, εἰς οὓς διεσκόρπισέν σε κύριος ἐκεῖ. 4 ἐὰν ᾖ ἡ διασπορά σου ἀπ' ἄκρου τοῦ οὐρανοῦ ἕως ἄκρου τοῦ οὐρανοῦ, ἐκεῖθεν συνάξει σε κύριος ὁ θεός σου, καὶ ἐκεῖθεν λήμψεταί σε κύριος ὁ θεός σου· • *Definitely favours the LXX of Zc 2:10 (= 2:6ET), Is 43:6 and Dt 30:4, rather than a composite of the MT of Dt 30:4 & Zc 2:10 as France argues.* CONTEXT: Of Zc 2:6ET— "On that day many nations will be converted to Yahweh" (Zc 2:11ET = 2:15 LXX). Of Is 43:6— "Let all the nations assemble, let the peoples gather here" (Is 43:9).

49. As he concludes: "There are textual features that show that this verse in Mark 14.62 is drawn from a different version of Dan. 7.13 from that used in the Little Apocalypse (Mark 13.26)." So also Sidney Jellicoe, *The Septuagint and Modern Study* (Oxford 1968), 87. Jellicoe points out that parallels in Mt 24:30 and 26:64 cite the LXX using ἐπί "upon" rather than μετά "with" the clouds.

30 μέχρις οὗ ταῦτα
πάντα γένηται
("until all these
things happen")

Dn 12:7 – As for v.4 above.

Kee: LXX (Dn 12:7). The
only specific occurrence of
ταῦτα πάντα (as distinct
from πάντα ταῦτα) in Dn
occurs in Theodotion at
4:28, but this doesn't seem
to be a significant parallel.
It is best to see this verse as
a reflection of 'the
Eschatological Question' in
v.4 and Dn 12:7.

The results from such an analysis are often ambiguous and any conclusions must be expressed cautiously, such is the uncertainty of present scholarly opinion regarding the exact relationship between the early versions of the OT, especially those available to the Gospel writers in the first century.[29] The texts listed here are thus only a provisional assessment of the work undertaken by Hartman, Glasson, Gundry, France and Kee, amongst others, and require further adjustment as a greater understanding of the origins of the Hebrew, Septuagintal and Targumic texts develops. Nevertheless such a task as this must be attempted in order to challenge the commonly held conclusions that extensive use of the Old Testament is evidence of a unitary 'midrash' on the one hand, or that the intertextuality of Mk 13 is so complex that it defies analysis on the other. There *are* some reasonable conclusions that can be drawn regarding the differences between the textual traditions behind Mk 13, even if little can be said about the ultimate origin of such traditions. These conclusions are as follows:

(i)   General prophetic and apocalyptic usage (in all versions): Ἐγώ εἰμι (v.6); πολέμους καὶ ἀκοὰς πολέμων (v.7); δεῖ γενέσθαι (v.7); ἔσονται σεισμοὶ κατὰ τόπους, ἔσονται λιμοί (v.8); ὠδίνων (v.8); some form of τὸ βδέλυγμα τῆς ἐρημώσεως and φευγέτωσαν εἰς τὰ ὄρη (v.14).

(ii)   Phrases consistent with the Hebrew (or the Aramaic in Daniel) of the MT: λίθος ἐπὶ λίθον (v.2); ὅταν μέλλῃ ταῦτα συντελεῖσθαι πάντα. (v.4); ἐγερθήσεται γὰρ ἔθνος ἐπ' ἔθνος καὶ βασιλεία ἐπὶ βασιλείαν (v.8); παραδώσουσιν ὑμᾶς/παραδιδόντες/παραδώσει (vv.9,11,12); τὸ βδέλυγμα τῆς ἐρημώσεως ἑστηκότα

---

[29] In particular, to complete a full analysis of OT traditions would require access to all textual variations of each version of the OT. Such public access is imminent, if not already possible, through mass storage devices for computers such as optical drives. This means that the work above is already hopelessly inadequate as it will shortly be possible to consider every known textual variant of every known version of biblical and extra-biblical writings. Such a task would constitute a dissertation in itself anyway, but it serves to illustrate the claim that it is too early to give up hope of locating and describing intertextual relationships. See Walter T. Classen, "Computer Assisted Methods and the Text and Language of the Old Testament—An Overview", in *Text and Context. Old Testament and Semitic Studies for F. C. Fensham,* ed W. Classen (Sheffield 1988), and the bibliography given there.

(v.14); ἔσονται γὰρ αἱ ἡμέραι ἐκεῖναι θλῖψις οἷα οὐ γέγονεν τοιαύτη ἀπ᾽ ἀρχῆς κτίσεως ἣν ἔκτισεν ὁ θεὸς ἕως τοῦ νῦν καὶ οὐ μὴ γένηται (v.19); ὁ ἥλιος σκοτισθήσεται καὶ ἡ σελήνη οὐ δώσει τὸ φέγγος αὐτῆς (v.24); μετὰ δυνάμεως πολλῆς καὶ δόξης (v.26).

(iii) Phrases consistent with the Greek (LXX): λίθος ἐπὶ λίθον (v.2); ὅταν μέλλῃ ταῦτα συντελεῖσθαι πάντα. (v.4); παραδώσουσιν ὑμᾶς/παραδιδόντες /παραδώσει (vv.9,11,12); ὁ δὲ ὑπομείνας εἰς τέλος οὗτος σωθήσεται (v.13); τὸ βδέλυγμα τῆς ἐρημώσεως ἑστηκότα (v.14); ἐν ἐκείναις ταῖς ἡμέραις (v.24); ὁ ἥλιος σκοτισθήσεται καὶ ἡ σελήνη οὐ δώσει τὸ φέγγος αὐτῆς (v.24); καὶ οἱ ἀστέρες ἔσονται ἐκ τοῦ οὐρανοῦ πίπτοντες, καὶ αἱ δυνάμεις αἱ ἐν τοῖς οὐρανοῖς σαλευθήσονται. 26 καὶ τότε ὄψονται τὸν υἱὸν τοῦ ἀνθρώπου ἐρχόμενον ἐν νεφέλαις μετὰ δυνάμεως πολλῆς καὶ δόξης (vv.25-26); καὶ ἐπισυνάξει [[τοὺς ἐκλεκτοὺς αὐτοῦ]] ἐκ τῶν τεσσάρων ἀνέμων ἀπ᾽ ἄκρου γῆς ἕως ἄκρου οὐρανοῦ (v.27).

(iv) Phrases consistent with the Greek (Th): τὸ βδέλυγμα τῆς ἐρημώσεως ἑστηκότα (v.14); ἔσονται γὰρ αἱ ἡμέραι ἐκεῖναι θλῖψις οἷα οὐ γέγονεν τοιαύτη ἀπ᾽ ἀρχῆς κτίσεως ἣν ἔκτισεν ὁ θεὸς ἕως τοῦ νῦν καὶ οὐ μὴ γένηται (v.19).

(v) Phrases consistent with the Aramaic (Targ Jon/Neofiti): ἐγερθήσεται γὰρ ἔθνος ἐπ᾽ ἔθνος καὶ βασιλεία ἐπὶ βασιλείαν (v.8); καὶ παραδώσει ἀδελφὸς ἀδελφὸν εἰς θάνατον καὶ πατὴρ τέκνον, καὶ ἐπαναστήσονται τέκνα ἐπὶ γονεῖς καὶ θανατώσουσιν αὐτούς (v.12); ὁ δὲ ὑπομείνας εἰς τέλος οὗτος σωθήσεται (v.13); ἐγερθήσονται γὰρ [[ψευδόχριστοι καὶ]] ψευδοπροφῆται καὶ δώσουσιν σημεῖα καὶ τέρατα πρὸς τὸ ἀποπλανᾶν, [[εἰ δυνατόν, τοὺς ἐκλεκτούς]] (v.22).

Because some phrases and texts are consistent with more than one version, they are presented more clearly in Text Sheet 4 which follows.

Text Sheet 4: Allusions to the Old Testament in Mk 13

13.1 Καὶ ἐκπορευομένου αὐτοῦ ἐκ τοῦ ἱεροῦ λέγει αὐτῷ εἷς τῶν μαθητῶν αὐτοῦ, Διδάσκαλε, ἴδε ποταποὶ λίθοι καὶ ποταπαὶ οἰκοδομαί. 2 καὶ ὁ Ἰησοῦς εἶπεν αὐτῷ, Βλέπεις ταύτας τὰς μεγάλας οἰκοδομάς; οὐ μὴ ἀφεθῇ ὧδε *λίθος ἐπὶ λίθον* ὃς οὐ μὴ καταλυθῇ.
3 Καὶ καθημένου αὐτοῦ εἰς τὸ Ὄρος τῶν Ἐλαιῶν κατέναντι τοῦ ἱεροῦ ἐπηρώτα αὐτὸν κατ᾽ ἰδίαν Πέτρος καὶ Ἰάκωβος καὶ Ἰωάννης καὶ Ἀνδρέας. 4 Εἰπὸν ἡμῖν πότε ταῦτα ἔσται, καὶ τί τὸ σημεῖον *ὅταν μέλλῃ ταῦτα συντελεῖσθαι πάντα.* 5 ὁ δὲ Ἰησοῦς ἤρξατο λέγειν αὐτοῖς, βλέπετε μή τις ὑμᾶς πλανήσῃ· 6 πολλοὶ ἐλεύσονται ἐπὶ τῷ ὀνόματί μου λέγοντες ὅτι Ἐγώ εἰμι, καὶ πολλοὺς πλανήσουσιν. 7 ὅταν δὲ ἀκούσητε πολέμους καὶ ἀκοὰς πολέμων, μὴ θροεῖσθε· δεῖ γενέσθαι, ἀλλ᾽ οὔπω τὸ τέλος. 8 ~~ἐγερθήσεται γὰρ ἔθνος ἐπ᾽ ἔθνος καὶ βασιλεία ἐπὶ βασιλείαν,~~ ἔσονται σεισμοὶ κατὰ τόπους, ἔσονται λιμοί· ἀρχὴ ὠδίνων ταῦτα. 9 βλέπετε δὲ ὑμεῖς ἑαυτούς· *παραδώσουσιν ὑμᾶς* εἰς συνέδρια καὶ εἰς συναγωγὰς δαρήσεσθε καὶ ἐπὶ ἡγεμόνων καὶ βασιλέων σταθήσεσθε ἕνεκεν ἐμοῦ εἰς

μαρτύριον αὐτοῖς. 10 καὶ εἰς πάντα τὰ ἔθνη πρῶτον δεῖ κηρυχθῆναι τὸ εὐαγγέλιον. 11 καὶ ὅταν ἄγωσιν ὑμᾶς *παραδιδόντες,* μὴ προμεριμνᾶτε τί λαλήστε, ἀλλ᾽ ὃ ἐὰν δοθῇ ὑμῖν ἐν ἐκείνῃ τῇ ὥρᾳ τοῦτο λαλεῖτε, οὐ γάρ ἐστε ὑμεῖς οἱ λαλοῦντες ἀλλὰ τὸ πνεῦμα τὸ ἅγιον. 12 ~~καὶ *παραδώσει* ἀδελφὸς ἀδελφὸν εἰς θάνατον καὶ πατὴρ τέκνον, καὶ ἐπαναστήσονται τέκνα ἐπὶ γονεῖς καὶ θανατώσουσιν αὐτούς·~~ 13 καὶ ἔσεσθε μισούμενοι ὑπὸ πάντων διὰ τὸ ὄνομά μου. ~~Ο ΔΕ ΥΠΟΜΕΙΝΑΣ ΕΙΣ ΤΕΛΟΣ ΟΥΤΟΣ ΣΩΘΗΣΕΤΑΙ.~~

14 Ὅταν δὲ ἴδητε *ΤΟ ΒΔΕΛΥΓΜΑ ΤΗΣ ΕΡΗΜΩΣΕΩΣ ΕΣΤΗΚΟΤΑ* ὅπου οὐ δεῖ, ὁ ἀναγινώσκων νοείτω, τότε οἱ ἐν τῇ Ἰουδαίᾳ <u>φευγέτωσαν εἰς τὰ ὄρη</u>, 15 ὁ δὲ ἐπὶ τοῦ δώματος μὴ καταβάτω μηδὲ εἰσελθάτω ἆραί τι ἐκ τῆς οἰκίας αὐτοῦ, 16 καὶ ὁ εἰς τὸν ἀγρὸν μὴ ἐπιστρεψάτω εἰς τὰ ὀπίσω ἆραι τὸ ἱμάτιον αὐτοῦ. 17 οὐαὶ δὲ ταῖς ἐν γαστρὶ ἐχούσαις καὶ ταῖς θηλαζούσαις ἐν ἐκείναις ταῖς ἡμέραις. 18 προσεύχεσθε δὲ ἵνα μὴ γένηται χειμῶνος· 19 *ΕΣΟΝΤΑΙ ΓΑΡ ΑΙ ΗΜΕΡΑΙ ΕΚΕΙΝΑΙ ΘΛΙΨΙΣ ΟΙΑ ΟΥ ΓΕΓΟΝΕΝ ΤΟΙΑΥΤΗ ΑΠ᾽ ΑΡΧΗΣ ΚΤΙΣΕΩΣ ΗΝ ΕΚΤΙΣΕΝ Ο ΘΕΟΣ ΕΩΣ ΤΟΥ ΝΥΝ ΚΑΙ ΟΥ ΜΗ ΓΕΝΗΤΑΙ.* 20 καὶ εἰ μὴ ἐκολόβωσεν κύριος τὰς ἡμέρας, οὐκ ἂν ἐσώθη πᾶσα σάρξ. ἀλλὰ διὰ τοὺς ἐκλεκτοὺς οὓς ἐξελέξατο ἐκολόβωσεν τὰς ἡμέρας. 21 καὶ τότε ἐάν τις ὑμῖν εἴπῃ, Ἴδε ὧδε ὁ Χριστός, Ἴδε ἐκεῖ, μὴ πιστεύετε· 22 ~~ἐγερθήσονται γὰρ ψευδόχριστοι~~ καὶ ~~ψευδοπροφῆται καὶ δώσουσιν σημεῖα καὶ τέρατα πρὸς τὸ ἀποπλανᾶν,~~ εἰ δυνατόν, τοὺς ἐκλεκτούς. 23 ὑμεῖς δὲ βλέπετε· προείρηκα ὑμῖν πάντα.

24 Ἀλλὰ <u>ἐν ἐκείναις ταῖς ἡμέραις</u> μετὰ τὴν θλῖψιν ἐκείνην

<u>*ὁ ἥλιος σκοτισθήσεται,*</u>

<u>*καὶ ἡ σελήνη οὐ δώσει τὸ φέγγος αὐτῆς,*</u>

25 <u>καὶ οἱ ἀστέρες ἔσονται ἐκ τοῦ οὐρανοῦ πίπτοντες,</u>

<u>καὶ αἱ δυνάμεις αἱ ἐν τοῖς οὐρανοῖς σαλευθήσονται.</u>

26 <u>καὶ τότε ὄψονται τὸν υἱὸν τοῦ ἀνθρώπου ἐρχόμενον ἐν νεφέλαις *μετὰ δυνάμεως πολλῆς καὶ δόξης*.</u> 27 <u>καὶ τότε ἀποστελεῖ τοὺς ἀγγέλους καὶ ἐπισυνάξει τοὺς ἐκλεκτοὺς αὐτοῦ ἐκ τῶν τεσσάρων ἀνέμων ἀπ᾽ ἄκρου γῆς ἕως ἄκρου οὐρανοῦ.</u>

28 Ἀπὸ δὲ τῆς συκῆς μάθετε τὴν παραβολήν· ὅταν ἤδη ὁ κλάδος αὐτῆς ἁπαλὸς γένηται καὶ ἐκφύῃ τὰ φύλλα, γινώσκετε ὅτι ἐγγὺς τὸ θέρος ἐστίν. 29 οὕτως καὶ ὑμεῖς, ὅταν ἴδητε ταῦτα γινόμενα γινώσκετε ὅτι ἐγγύς ἐστιν ἐπὶ θύραις. 30 ἀμὴν λέγω ὑμῖν ὅτι οὐ μὴ παρέλθῃ ἡ γενεὰ αὕτη μέχρις οὗ ταῦτα πάντα γένηται. 31 ὁ οὐρανὸς καὶ ἡ γῆ παρελεύσονται, οἱ δὲ λόγοι μου οὐ μὴ παρελεύσονται. 32 περὶ δὲ τῆς ἡμέρας ἐκείνης ἢ τῆς ὥρας οὐδεὶς οἶδεν, οὐδὲ οἱ ἄγγελοι ἐν οὐρανῷ οὐδὲ ὁ υἱός, εἰ μὴ ὁ πατήρ. 33 βλέπετε ἀγρυπνεῖτε· οὐκ οἴδατε γὰρ πότε ὁ καιρός ἐστιν. 34 ὡς ἄνθρωπος ἀπόδημος ἀφεὶς τὴν οἰκίαν αὐτοῦ καὶ δοὺς τοῖς δούλοις αὐτοῦ τὴν ἐξουσίαν, ἑκάστῳ τὸ ἔργον αὐτοῦ, καὶ τῷ θυρωρῷ ἐνετείλατο ἵνα γρηγορῇ. 35 γρηγορεῖτε οὖν, οὐκ οἴδατε γὰρ πότε ὁ κύριος τῆς οἰκίας ἔρχεται, ἢ ὀψὲ ἢ μεσονύκτιον ἢ ἀλεκτοροφωνίας ἢ πρωΐ, 36 μὴ ἐλθὼν ἐξαίφνης εὕρῃ ὑμᾶς καθεύδοντας. 37 ὃ δὲ ὑμῖν λέγω, πᾶσιν λέγω, γρηγορεῖτε.

Key:	**Bold italics**	= consistent with the Hebrew/Aramaic (MT)
	Single underlining	= consistent with the Greek (LXX)
	UNCIAL SCRIPT	= consistent with the Greek (Th)
	Strike through	= consistent with the Aramaic (Targ Jon/Neofiti)
	Multiple indicators	= consistent with more than one version
	Double underlining	= general prophetic, apocalyptic and OT usage
		(occurs in all versions)

Intertextual traditions in Mk 13

It is immediately apparent from the above analysis that Glasson and Perrin's claims about the Septuagintal origin of at least vv.24-27 have some validity. But it is equally obvious that the statement by Perrin that in Mk 13 there is 'no single instance of necessary dependence upon any text other than the Greek' is not accurate. The evidence seems to support the claim that vv.12-13a and 22 at least do not originally come from Greek traditions but have existed as distinctive logia at sometime in their history, possibly having links with the Targumic traditions. It is also possible that vv.7-8 belong in this group. It could also be argued that vv.14 and 19 may have a background predominantly in the Hebrew OT tradition, also paralleling Theodotion in Daniel, as distinct from what can be seen as the purely Septuagintal origins of vv.24-27 (even though parts of v.24 and of v.26 also parallel the MT). The nature of the evidence is such that on its own it is inadequate to confirm distinctive pre-Markan traditions, so specific possibilities of this type will be cross-checked with the conclusions of the previous chapters in the table below.

It is also helpful to note the context of many of the biblical allusions in Mk 13, as presented in the table above. The verses immediately surrounding Is 19:2 (described in v.8 above); Zc 2:15LXX/11ET (vv.10,27); Mi 7:2-7f (vv.12-13); Jdt 8:1 (v.24); Is 13:10* and Jl 2:10*; 2:31ET/3:4LXX*; 3:15ET/4:15LXX* (v.24); Is 34:4* (v.25); Dn 7:13-14 (v.26); Zc 2:10 LXX and Is 43:9 (v.27) all have as a theme the Day of Yahweh and/or the fate of the nations of the world. Those verses marked with an asterisk, which lie behind the cosmic upheavals of Mk 13:24-25, contain judgment scenes and negative pictures of the fate of the nations, often contrasted directly with the glory of Jerusalem. The verses which lie behind Mk 13:26-27, contain a more positive—and arguably less ethnocentric—view of the salvation of the nations and their gathering together. If the hermeneutical principle of the latter taking precedence over the former, the last being first, holds true for the interpretation of the Old Testament 'synthetic quotations' in the Gospel of Mark,[30] then it would seem that a deliberate reinterpretation of the judgment of the nations is intended. From a range of OT scenarios, the author of Mark has given priority to those which speak of the salvation of the nations rather than the judging of them from Jerusalem. In any case, it is apparent that the fate of the nations is a major theme lurking just beneath the surface of the text of Mk 13—a theme which becomes explicit in vv.10 and 27. The examination of OT traditions behind the text thus begins to suggest ways in which parts of the discourse as a whole may have been compiled, a process which will be examined further in chapter 5 below.

---

[30] As argued in footnote 27 above, and in Dyer, "Subversive Contexts", in the *Festschrift* for Athol Gill, (Peter Lang), forthcoming.

In general terms, however, the conclusions from the analysis of OT allusions above seem to accord well with the findings of chapters 1 and 2 that the origins of vv.14-21 and vv.24-27 are dissimilar, due to the strangeness of the syntax of vv.14-21 compared with the rest of the Gospel of Mark and especially when compared with vv.24-27. More specifically, it is possible to collate the conclusions from the previous chapters regarding pre-Markan traditions in the following way:

Summary of indications of pre-Markan traditions in Mk 13

Section in Mk 13	Linguistic and Form analysis	Unique syntax	OT traditions	Conclusions
vv.1-2	*Koine* framework in v.1a introducing a saying of Palestinian origin.	Some unique syntax in v.1b,c.	λίθος ἐπὶ λίθον (v.2c) occurs in the MT and LXX of Hag 2:15.	The prophecy itself appears to come from early Palestinian tradition preceded (v.1a) by a later introduction.
vv.3-6	No clear patterns of influence.	Unique syntax across major punctuation breaks between vv.3/4 and 4/5 suggests compilation.	Only non-specific links with prophetic and apocalyptic language in vv.4b,6.	No clear pre-Markan units of tradition. May be a compilation of smaller units to set the scene for the discourse.
vv.7-8	V.8 shows Semitic (possibly Aramaic) influences (cf v.22).	Some unique syntax in v.7b only.	Non-specific links with prophetic and apocalyptic language throughout vv.7,8b,c; and more specifically with the MT or Targum of Is 19:2 in v.8a.	Possibly has connections with vv.11a,b,d,12,13a and v.22 in the Targumic tradition, but may be a compilation of scattered units.

vv.9-13	V.11 contains acceptable *Koine* Greek in central phrase (11c), but remainder of verse shows Semitic (possibly Aramaic) influences. Strong Semitic influence (possibly Aramaic) in vv.12-13a, and *Koine* Greek in v.13b.	Parts of vv.11,13 distinctive. Unique syntax across major punctuation break between v.13a/13b suggests v.13b is an addition.	The παραδιδόναι sequence (vv.9,11,12) has weak links with the MT or LXX of Dn 7:25; and v.10 with the MT or LXX of Zc 2:15a. The Targum of Mi 7:2-7 seems to provide the best connection with vv.12-13a, with the LXX of Mi 7:7 providing the link to v.13b—a later addition.	It would seem that vv.9,10,11c and 13b reflect later *Koine* style and the perspective of the Gentile mission, whereas vv.11a,b,d,12,13a may be part of an older Palestinian—even Aramaic—tradition which also includes vv.7,8,22.
vv.14-20	Fairly strong Semitic influence, but with an unusually high incidence of δέ.	Vv.14-20(21) contain the most distinctive syntax of the whole Gospel of Mark.	It is possible to see just the MT together with Th (A) in Dn providing the source for the allusions in vv.14a,19, though there is insufficient evidence to make a firm conclusion.	Vv.14-20(21) are distinguished from the rest of the discourse by their high proportion of unique syntax, their combination of Semitic influence and the use of δέ, and possibly by the MT/Th traditions behind the biblical allusions in vv.14,19.
v.21-23	V.22 shows Semitic influence (possibly Aramaic).	V.21 is syntactically unique and may therefore fit better with vv.14-20 than vv.22,23.	The Codex Neofiti targum of Dt 13:1-3 seems to provide the closest connection with v.22 (minus the later addition of the pseudochrists).	V.21 should be taken together with vv.14-20; and possibly v.22 together with vv.7,8,11a,b,d,12, 13a as part of a Targumic tradition. V.23 may well be a Markan structuring device.

vv.24-27	The whole section shows strong Semitic influence (mainly Septuagintal).	Vv.24-27 contain *no* unique syntax at all and are thus typical of the syntax of the Gospel as a whole.	The density of biblical allusions in vv.24-27 is very high, and they can all be located satisfactorily—and sometimes exclusively—in the LXX.	This section is the clearest unit of all within the discourse, being syntactically 'at home' in the Gospel of Mark and strongly Septuagintal. The phrase μετὰ τὴν θλῖψιν ἐκείνην appears to have no precedent in the literature and may well be a Markan insertion, as may be the use of τοὺς ἐκλεκτοὺς αὐτοὺς in v.27.
vv.28-31	No clear patterns of linguistic influence evident.	Some unique syntax in vv.29,30, and across the major punctuation breaks between vv.29/30 and 31/32, suggesting compilation.	No obvious links with specific OT passages.	A compilation of diverse sayings, with vv.30,31 perhaps forming a pre-Markan unit and solemn conclusion to a prophecy.
vv.32-37	V.32 is acceptable *Koine* Greek, whilst v.34 shows some Semitic influence.	Unique syntax across major punctuation breaks between vv.34/35,36/37 and 37/14:1 suggests compilation.	No obvious links with specific OT passages.	V.34 may be part of a very early parable which has been added to in vv.35,36. V.37 appears to be a Markan structuring device.

These are still relatively modest conclusions, yet they are of assistance in setting certain parameters within which a proper discussion of possible Markan literary and theological intentions may begin in the next chapter. It is still not possible to make definitive statements about the *Sitz im Leben* and historicity of each saying until after a socio-political analysis has been undertaken. However, certain trends are already apparent.

For example, the sayings most likely to have been spoken by the historical Jesus in the form in which they are recorded in Mk 13 would be (in descending order of probability): the prophecy of v.2; v.30 (perhaps the original conclusion to that prophecy); some earlier form of the saying in v. 32 (given the difficulty of such a frank admission for the

christology of the early church); and the part parable of v.34.[31]
Depending on the dating of Targumic traditions, vv.7,8,11a,b,d,12,13a
and 22 may also have a claim to be part of the Jesus traditions, or at least
early Palestinian traditions. But it would seem that these verses, together
with vv.14-21 and 24-27, display a running together of biblical allusions
which differs markedly from the specific and incisive use of the OT
evident in the teaching of Jesus elsewhere in the Gospels—the claims of
Hartman and France notwithstanding. The larger sections, vv.14-21 and
24-27, were apparently reckoned by the author of Mark as appropriate to
include with 'the words of the Lord', but as they now stand it is obvious
that they cannot both originate from the historical Jesus due to their
distinctive but mutually exclusive syntax. Of course it is not possible to
restrict all the sayings of the historical Jesus to those which show strong
Aramaic influence only, because genuine sayings may also have been
circulated in Greek from an early stage. However, the suggestions made
above do indicate those sayings *most likely* to have originated with the
historical Jesus *in their present form.*

These conclusions regarding pre-Markan traditions in Mk 13 may be
further summarised in the following way:

(i)   early Palestinian (Jesuanic) traditions: vv.2,30,31,(32 in another
        form),34;
(ii)   Palestinian (Targumic?) traditions: vv.7,8,11a,b,d,12,13a,22;
(iii)   an atypical pre-Markan source: vv.14-21;
(iv)   a distinctively Markan *pastiche* of Septuagintal references:
        vv.24-27;
(v)   editorial comments or compilations of smaller units: vv.3-6,9-
        10,13b,23,28-29,33,35-37.

In the next chapters, following a review of redaction-critical attempts to
analyse Mk 13, the extent and manner of the editorial processes required
to unite the traditions above into a coherent discourse will be investigated.
In this way the conclusions just outlined shall be tested further against the
evidence for redactional activity examined in the next two chapters.

---

[31] The general Jesuanic historicity of vv.32f is also argued by Morna D. Hooker, *A Commentary on the Gospel According to St Mark* (London 1991), 300: "it may well be this last section…that comes closest to representing Jesus' own attitude."

IV

A MARKAN ANTI-APOCALYPTIC DISCOURSE

Major proponents: Marxsen (1959); Lambrecht (1967); Pesch (1968), and many
   commentators thereafter.
Basic thesis: That in Mk 13 the evangelist is attempting to counter apocalyptic
   misunderstandings in his community, such as an 'apocalyptic timetable'
   (Marxsen), or an imminent expectation of the End (Pesch).
Dominant method: Redaction (editorial) criticism.
Critique: A re-evaluation of so-called Markan vocabulary and syntax lists.

After the difficult historical questions raised by source, form and
tradition analysis in the first half of this century, WILLI MARXSEN
attempted to grapple with an issue that seemed at the time to be more
manageable and immediate, namely: What does the author of Mark intend
to say in chapter 13?[1] Marxsen quoted with approval Busch's summary of
the situation: "the further task is apparently simple and yet sufficiently
important: to understand the evangelist by temporarily deferring every
critical question concerning authenticity and the 'historical Jesus'."[2] The
phrase 'temporarily defer' is surely significant, for questions about the
historical Jesus did not disappear with the onset of the redaction-critical
phase of Biblical studies (just as questions concerning redaction and
authorial intention linger on despite the more recent exegetical approaches
which have sought to bracket them out). The questions may be
temporarily deferred or even clarified by the newer hermeneutical phase,
but they cannot simply be dismissed whilst they still remain to be
answered. For whilst it is certainly possible to focus on the redaction—or
the final shape of the traditions—in Mk 13 as suggested by Busch and
Marxsen amongst others, some interaction between redaction analysis and
form analysis is necessary in order to distinguish between the tradition
and the evangelist's selection and shaping of it. Consequently, Marxsen
takes as his starting point the distinction between two groups of material:
   (i)   the so-called apocalyptic material, vv.7-8,12,14-22 and 24-27
         (possibly 13b, but not 21-22!?);[3]

---

[1] To avoid excessive footnoting, page numbers in brackets appearing in the main body
of the text in this section refer to Marxsen, *Mark the Evangelist* (ET 1969).

[2] Marxsen, *Mark,* 153, goes on to criticize Busch strongly for failing to live up to his
aim by rejecting "as an 'impossible undertaking' any distinction between the sayings of
Jesus and community formulations".

[3] It is unclear exactly where Marxsen intends to locate vv.21-22. He lists them here
(*Mark,* 161) as part of the apocalyptic material, but then cites Kümmel (*Promise,* 102) in
support of the conclusion that they *cannot* be part of that material. On the following page

(ii) and the "material from the synoptic tradition in the narrower sense" (161)—the so-called Christian material: vv.3,5-6,9,13a, 11,23 and 30-31.

Marxsen deliberately avoids defining these groups of sayings too narrowly, and he does not describe their exact relationship. He sidesteps the question of which sayings were 'added' to which on the grounds that this would involve "a literary judgment which is best avoided" (161). However, Marxsen has already accepted the literary judgments of Bultmann and Sundwall in the delineation of these sections. Particularly interesting is his endorsement of Sundwall's argument that on stylistic grounds, the 'Christian' material coheres and was already found connected in the order given above by the author of Mark (161).

From this starting point, Marxsen outlines the redactional activity of the author of Mark as follows (162):

(i)   to the already connected 'Christian' piece (vv.3,5-6,9,13a,11,23 and 30-31), v.4 is shaped and fitted,

(ii) to this is prefixed an individual saying (v.2) to which the geographical and temporal frame (v.1) is attached,

(iii) the whole is now mingled with the 'apocalyptic leaflet' (vv.7-8,12,14-20 and 24-27; or 'apocalyptic material'—Marxsen remains ambivalent as to whether the apocalyptic section is self-contained or not), and finally,

(iv) further individual sayings from the tradition are added (vv.10,13b,28-29,32? and 33-37).[4]

Despite the fragmentary appearance of all this, Marxsen insists that the author of Mark has unified the whole chapter by use of time references and exhortations throughout both the 'apocalyptic' and 'Christian' sections (166-7), so that the chapter is intended to be understood as a whole.

Marxsen regards the seam visible between vv.2 and 3 as an indication of the author's *Sitz im Leben,* in that a connection is made between the imminent destruction of the temple and the end times. The duplication of both motifs—temple destruction and the end—in the Markan question in v.4 confirms this viewpoint, according to Marxsen. Accordingly, he locates the writing of Mark's Gospel just prior to 70 CE, and in Galilee (168, 172), to make sense of the strongly redactional use of Galilee throughout the Gospel. Thus, vv.5-13 refer to the evangelist's own time, giving no specific answer to either of the questions in v.4, and v.14 is the beginning of the sayings on the future (178-9)—as it "not only marks a literary cæsura, but also a break in the life of the reader who is led, as it were, from present to future" (183). Or, put even more plainly: "In this verse we encounter the 'most direct' address of the entire Gospel. In no other passage are the readers spoken to so directly—'let the reader

(*Mark,* 162, footnote 40), he then seems to reject Kümmel's suggestion that vv.21-22 are part of the Christian section.

[4] Verse 32 is uncertain as Marxsen seems inclined to agree with Sundwall that 32a could well be the conclusion to the Jewish apocalypse (*Mark,* 161).

understand' ... Verse 14 is the hinge on which the sayings of chapter 13 turn" (183).

If v.14—or more particularly ὁ ἀναγινώσκων νοείτω—were regarded by Marxsen as redactional, then the weight he places on this verse would be justified. But since Marxsen agrees with the judgment of the form critics that the address to the reader in v.14 is evidence of an earlier written source, it is questionable whether the author of Mark could be placing as much emphasis on ὁ ἀναγινώσκων νοείτω as Marxsen has. There is no evidence on stylistic or vocabulary analytical grounds that the phrase is redactional.[5] Nor can the content of the rest of the Gospel sustain theologically the contention that this is the most urgent message of the author to the reader, though of course Marxsen argues otherwise. Those who do still argue that the phrase is Markan redaction should find Marxsen's conclusions all but inescapable,[6] since such a view would mean that the command to flee in v.14b must in some way be of special relevance to the Markan community, suggesting a link with the enigmatic ending in 16:8 as Marxsen speculates.

Marxsen also argues that the subject of the masculine ἑστηκότα in v.14, ostensibly the neuter τὸ βδέλυγμα followed by the feminine τῆς ἐρημώσεως, must be understood as the antichrist, and that this "suggests that the event in 14a must be divided into the threat to the temple giving rise to the flight, and the destruction resulting in the appearance of the antichrist."[7] But again, such a stress on the antichrist seems odd in the light of the further ψευδόχριστοι καὶ ψευδοπροφῆται which follow in v.22. These repeat the warnings in v.6, and seem to be rather more the concern of the Markan *Sitz* than any specific inferences in v.14. Yet Marxsen goes so far as to argue that the pseudochrists of v.22 must be the 'forerunners' to the antichrist of v.14 (185-6), which seems to be standing the discourse on its head somewhat, but perhaps explains his ambivalence over the exact location of vv.21-22 in the tradition. It also appears strange

---

[5] Both the syntax and the vocabulary of the phrase are unique to this verse in the Gospel.

[6] Such is not the case, of course, as those who attribute ὁ ἀναγινώσκων νοείτω to Mark are often arguing for the historicity of the discourse and its setting and denying any form of the Little Apocalypse theory. See for example, the way the phrase is blackened in some of the red-letter (= *Ipsissima Verba*) editions of the New Testament, but not, of course, in Matthew! One who does stand in the tradition of Marxsen and argues for the full urgency of 14b *and* its redactional nature, is Myers, *Strong Man,* 335, whose interpretation is examined in chapter 7 below.

[7] *Mark,* 186. See chapter 5, footnote 9 below for a list of scholars who argue in a similar way for a reference to the antichrist in v.14. But the clash of a masculine participle and a neuter noun is an indication only that some kind of personal being is intended by the neuter [BDF §134(3)]. This *constructio ad sensum* occurs in other units of tradition taken up by the evangelist. See 9:20,26 for example, where the neuter πνεῦμα takes masculine participles, and 6:29 (cited by Beasley-Murray, *Commentary,* 70) where John the Baptist's corpse (neuter) is referred to as 'him' in ℵ W T. It is also possible to take ἑστηκότα as a neuter plural participle, though not without diluting the motif somewhat— see chapter 7 below.

that the temple and its fate should be of such immense significance for the Markan community when the implications of the judging of the temple in 11:12-25, the prophecy of Jesus in 13:1-2, and the tearing of the temple curtain in 15:38 would seem to be that the temple is of no further relevance.

Nevertheless, Marxsen is consistent in the application of his conclusions, arguing that vv.5-13 reflect the recent history of the evangelist's own time and vv.14-23 the final act before the end. He detects some sequence of events here: vv.14-16—the beginning of troubles; vv.17-20—their duration; vv.21-23—false Christs and false prophets; and vv.24-27—the Coming of the Son of Man (186). But these events do not, for Marxsen, constitute an apocalyptic timetable:

> Mark transforms apocalyptic into eschatology. In *this* sense we can again agree with Busch that the "eschatological drama of apocalyptic with its several acts" is eliminated, and that "in the picture of the future" there is "only *one* last act". But this assertion is correct only when we realise that for Mark this act has already begun and that only the finale remains. (189)

Thus for Marxsen, the message of the author of Mark to his readers is to flee the devastation of Jerusalem and its temple, and to head for Galilee to await the coming of the Son of Man. This urgent message accords dramatically with the sudden conclusion of the Gospel in chapter 16—the Parousia replacing the resurrection for the Markan church—but the immediacy of it sits much less comfortably with Marxsen's opinion that "the period leading up to the Parousia is given an eschatological reinterpretation; it is the time of preaching to the Gentiles" (176). When Marxsen insists that the 'last act' (vv.14-23) has begun already for the author of Mark, he is in danger of relegating the missionary thrust of v.10 to the immediate past for the Markan community, since vv.5-13 "qualify the present moment as the ἀρχή of this end" (179). Nor will Marxsen allow us to conclude from v.10 "that a 'certain postponement of the Parousia' is traceable to Mark" (177, footnote 98) in order for the mission to the nations to be completed, even though he sees that they are inseparably linked and that this proclamation helps to hasten the coming of the Parousia (177). It seems that the stress Marxsen places on the imminence of the End detracts from the strong case he has made for the redactional importance of preaching the good news throughout the rest of the Gospel.

So Marxsen concludes that the author of Mark is eschatological rather than apocalyptic only in this narrowly defined sense (of replacing the apocalyptic timetable by 'one final act'), yet seems to suggest that the Gospel engenders just that type of imminent expectation that later redaction critics claim is specifically countered by the Markan editing of chapter 13. Marxsen's analysis is credited as being the first to apply a redaction critical approach to the Gospel of Mark, and his comments on the theological use of geographical settings in the Gospel and the distinctively Markan usage of εὐαγγέλιον, κηρύσσειν and Γαλιλαία in particular, remain an important contribution to Markan studies. However his particular interpretation of chapter 13 and the Gospel's abrupt end has been largely rejected by the later redaction critics as new methods for determining redaction in Mark's Gospel were developed. Most prominent among these critics have been Rudolph Pesch (1968, 1977 and 1980) and Jan Lambrecht (1967), with valuable critical contributions by Frans Neirynck (1969, 1980),[8] Ferdinand Hahn (1975) and Joachim Gnilka (1978/9).[9]

As the subtitle to JAN LAMBRECHT's dissertation suggests, a large part of his work is based on an analysis of the structure of Mk 13 itself and on its literary context in the Gospel of Mark—particularly from 10:32-14:17. Lambrecht also goes into specific detail in determining the extent of Markan redaction in the discourse, making use of vocabulary statistics and considerations of Markan style. He concludes that the author of Mark was far from being a neutral and mechanical redactor who merely collected together traditions, but rather, was a creative interpreter of traditions.[10] Consequently, the amount of redactional activity suggested by Lambrecht is extensive: besides editorially adjusting the Septuagintal references—vv.4,7,14,19 and 26 from Daniel; vv.12 and 13 from Micah (via Mt 10:35-36); vv.24 and 25 from Joel and perhaps v.27 from Zechariah—Lambrecht regards the following verses as most probably pure Markan creations: vv.1,2ab,3-4,5a,7-8,10,13,14,17,20,23 and 37.[11]

The most surprising feature of Lambrecht's analysis, however, is that he does not regard the remainder of the chapter as a unified source but as a series of logia from the sayings source Q, namely vv.2c,5b-6,9,11-13,15-16,21-22,28b?,30,31 and 32-36. Lambrecht specifically precludes the possibility that the apocalyptic descriptions that can be traced mainly from the Old Testament in vv.7-8,19-20 and 24-27 could be part of an already structured source, preferring to regard them as a Markan composition and arguing that any *Flugblatt* theories are superfluous.[12] As

---

[8] F. Neirynck, "Le discours anti-apocalyptique de Mc. XIII", in *Evangelica: Gospel Studies (Collected Essays)* (Leuven 1982), 599-608, [= *ETL* 45 (1969), 154-164], and "Marc 13: Examen critique de l'interprétation de R. Pesch", *Evangelica,* 565-597, [= *BETL* 53 (1980), 369-401].

[9] J. Gnilka, *Das Evangelium nach Markus* (EKKNT 2), vol 2, (Zürich/Einsiedeln/Köln 1978/9), 179-216.

[10] Lambrecht, *Die Redaktion,* 256: "er bearbeitete seine Quellen schöpferisch und deutete sie mehrfach um, gemäss dem Gang und den Erfordernissen der Rede, die er nach seinem eigenen Entwurf aufbauen wollte!"

[11] *Die Redaktion,* 258.

[12] *Die Redaktion,* 258. Yet later Lambrecht himself admits, in a review of Hartman's work, that he has overstated the case against any pre-Markan literary unit. Admitting a certain imbalance in his own work in this area, Lambrecht (in "Die 'Midrasch-Quelle' von Mk 13", *Bib* 49 (1968), 269 footnote, and 270) confesses that: "Einer möglichen "Midrasch"-Quelle wurde durch uns kaum Aufmerksamkeit geschenkt", and of

a result of this predominantly literary analysis, Lambrecht has little to say about the *Sitz im Leben* of the author of Mark or the various Q logia, but he does reach the conclusion that hardly anything in the speech bears the characteristics of accurately passed on logia of Jesus.[13]

Apart from Walter Schmithals,[14] and to some extent Beasley-Murray,[15] Lambrecht's arguments regarding a Q source behind Mk 13 have met with little support.[16] In those instances where Luke and Matthew might conceivably bear witness to an earlier form of a saying than appears in Mk 13, it is more profitable to look for a common link with early Christian prophecy rather than broadening the scope of Q and raising problems regarding how much of it the author of Mark was aware of, and how much he could have deliberately omitted. It would seem to be more reasonable to concede, for example, that Luke was aware of prophetic oracles concerning the fall of Jerusalem and used them in some instances in preference to Mark, than to argue that the author of Mark was aware of Q—or part thereof—and made such minimal use of it (especially given the strong discipleship theme in the Gospel of Mark). Yet Lambrecht is prepared to argue that case, mainly, it appears, because the use of fragmented logia by the evangelist leaves room for the extraordinary level of redactional activity which Lambrecht perceives as having taken place in chapter 13.

Despite the thorough method Lambrecht employs in this redaction analysis, which appears to have been more successful in his analysis of Mk 4,[17] he allows his literary and structural investigations of Mk 13 to dominate his conclusions about the composition of the chapter. Lambrecht's third chapter includes a complex analysis of the structure of Mk 13 which sets out a possible chiastic scheme (a b c b' a') in vv.5-23, and an overall inclusio (a b a') pattern, plus many other recurring features.[18] Given Lambrecht's perception of this kind of intricate structuring of the whole chapter, it is not surprising that he insists on a high level of Markan interference in the arranging of scattered sources— otherwise the structure would be purely accidental.[19] But if the author of Mark was in such complete control of the many and varied sources

Hartman's *Prophecy,* claims that: "Es zeigt die Notwendigkeit, irgendwo an der Basis der eschatologischen Rede eine "Midrasch"-Quelle zu postulieren."

[13] *Die Redaktion,* 259. See chapter 2, footnote 22 above.

[14] W. Schmithals, *Das Evangelium nach Markus* (Gütersloh 1979), 557 and 582f.

[15] See chapter 2 above.

[16] Lambrecht, however, continues to argue quite eloquently the general case for Q influence on Mark. See "Q-Influence on Mark 8,34-9,1" in *Logia. Les Paroles de Jésus—The Sayings of Jesus (BETL 59),* (Leuven 1982), 277-304.

[17] Lambrecht, "Redaction and Theology in Mk IV" in *L'Évangile selon Marc: Tradition et rédaction (BETL 34),* (Leuven 1974), 269-307.

[18] Lambrecht, *Die Redaktion,* 288-292.

[19] Interestingly, in Lars Hartman's review of Lambrecht's dissertation, he points out that Lambrecht's own writing unintentionally includes such features as inclusio and chiasm, suggesting that such patterns need not be evidence of conscious editorial work by an author. See *Bib* 49 (1968), 130-133.

suggested by Lambrecht, it is difficult to explain the obvious tensions remaining in the final form of the chapter. It is also difficult to see how the extensive redactional passages suggested by Lambrecht present a clear theological purpose that makes sense in the total context of the Gospel of Mark. Indeed it appears that the heart of Lambrecht's work is his literary and structural analysis rather than his redactional analysis, which has led to his results being curiously biased towards the literary rather than theological activity of the author of Mark.

Perhaps the most significant and influential study specifically on Mk 13 has been the one undertaken by RUDOLPH PESCH, who approached his analysis of the author's redaction from the perspective of a thorough survey of the structure of the Gospel as a whole. Interestingly, that particular part of his thesis[20] and the major conclusion resulting from it— that chapter 13 was added by the author of Mark after the basic plan of the Gospel was completed—is the section that has gained the least credibility. Pesch went to great lengths counting the verses, pericopes and lines throughout the Gospel of Mark until he derived what he thought was a balanced structure of six main parts, each of which could be sub-divided into three smaller parts:

    1:2-3:6 (1:2-34; 1:35-45; 2:1-3:6) [No. of pericopes = 6-2-6]
    3:7-6:29 (3:7-4:34; 4:35-5:20; 5:21-6:29) [= 6-2-6]
    6:30-8:26 (6:30-7:13; 7:14-23; 7:24-8:26) [= 6-2-6]
    8:27-10:52 (8:27-9:29; 9:30-50; 10:1-52) [= 6-3-7]
    11:1-12:44 (11:1-26; 11:27-12:12; 12:13-44) [= 5-2-6]
    14:1-16:8 (14:1-52; 14:53-15:5; 15:6-16:8) [= 6-3-6]

By grouping each of the six sections into a pair, Pesch demonstrated that the mathematical, and, he argued, theological centres of each of the three major sections are: 4:1-12 (the parable of mixed yields); 8:34-9:1 (the logia after Peter's misunderstanding); and 14:12-25 (the last supper).

As will be noted, apart from the extraordinary mathematical symmetry of the divisions, there is no room for chapter 13 in this structure of Mark (it is omitted from the references just given!). Pesch contends that if chapter 13 were missing from the Gospel, the reader would not notice a gap (65). But this is not to say that Pesch is arguing that chapter 13 is dispensable as far as the author of Mark is concerned. On the contrary, he contends that the very insertion of the chapter into what is otherwise a very carefully structured text means that the contents of the chapter must have particular importance for the Markan community. Where else in the Gospel is the reader directly addressed as in v.14, or is Jesus shown as repeatedly emphasizing his own words as in vv.23,31 and 37? Thus Pesch concludes that this chapter is the one most immediately relevant to the purposes of the author of Mark (66).

---

[20] Pesch, *Naherwartungen,* chapter 2. Page numbers in brackets in the main text of this section will refer to this book.

These purposes Pesch endeavours to uncover by an examination of the careful way in which the author has edited the available material in order to place it in the chosen context between chapters 12 and 14. Here Pesch revives the view that the author had at his disposal a Jewish apocalyptic pamphlet, consisting originally of vv.6,22,7b,12,13b-17,18?,19-20a and 24-27, in that order.[21] Besides this material there were persecution sayings—vv.9,11,13a; two short parables—vv.28b and 34; and two individual logia—vv.31 and 32. This leaves considerable redactional work in order to tie the whole together—all of vv.1-5,7,10,21,23,29-30,35-37—plus insertions in other verses.[22] Before investigating the purpose of this redactional activity, Pesch describes the *Sitz im Leben* of this hypothetical Jewish broadsheet. He agrees with the view of many of the form critics that the pamphlet originated in the years 38-40 CE, during the crisis provoked by Caligula's attempt to erect his statue in the temple at Jerusalem,[23] and was later used by Christians who understood it to have been spoken by Jesus. In particular it was misused apocalyptically at the time of the Jewish war (66-70 CE) by Christians who thought that the end would follow the destruction of the temple.

In this way Pesch lays the foundation for his analysis of the purpose and *Sitz im Leben* of the Markan redaction. He thinks it probable that the Gospel of Mark was written in Rome around 71 CE, and chapter 13 incorporated into it as a defence primarily against an exaggerated apocalyptic expectation which was present in the author's own community, and secondarily to continue the polemic against Jewish Christianity which features throughout the Gospel (231-35). As the detailed redaction suggested by Pesch indicates,[24] he argues that the author of Mark is concerned to combat this apocalyptic *Naherwartung* in his community, and to replace it with eschatological watchfulness. The end is 'not yet' (v.7 redactional), and will take place only 'after that tribulation'

---

[21] *Naherwartungen,* 203-215. The opinions of Hartman on this theory are interesting. Writing before Pesch (in *Prophecy Interpreted,* 207), he comments: "This broadsheet theory seems a strange one to me. If we assume that it is a matter of manifold copies of a pamphlet or a brochure, is there a single example of such a phenomenon in antiquity? Has a copy been preserved or mentioned in literature?" And reviewing Pesch's book (*Bib.* 50, 1969, 576-580), he adds: "Now Dr. Pesch will have us believe that vv.6, 7b f., 12, 13b-20a, 22, 24-27, filling satisfactorily a papyrus sheet, were written in the year 40 in Jerusalem—in Greek!—and spread *"flugblattartig"* to summon people to flight . . . Does not an hypothesis like this one presuppose the conditions of considerably later times? We know of different ways of propagandizing in Antiquity, but this one?—almost certainly no."

[22] See the redactional underlining in Appendix 3 for details.

[23] A statue was apparently erected in Alexandria in 38 CE and there was considerable disquiet in Jerusalem lest the temple should be defiled by a similar occurrence there. See Desmond Ford, *The Abomination of Desolation in Biblical Eschatology* (Washington 1979), 158-170, for a wide range of possible interpretations of τὸ βδέλυγμα τῆς ἐρημώσεως, including the Caligula episode, and chapter 7 below.

[24] Such phrases as ἀλλ᾿ οὔπω τὸ τέλος (v.7), perhaps ἀρχὴ ὠδίνων ταῦτα (v.8), the whole of v.10 and much of the parenetic material.

(v.24 μετὰ τὴν θλῖψιν ἐκείνην redactional), so the church must 'watch out' (βλέπετε redactional in vv.5,9,23 and 33). It is in this assessment of the purpose of the Markan redaction that Pesch has been most influential,[25] yet these very conclusions about the extent and nature of Markan redaction are what Pesch himself, after a reassessment of Hartman[26] and an examination of Hahn,[27] specifically rejects in his later commentary on the Gospel of Mark.

Recurrent vocabulary, phraseology and syntax in Mk 13

This about-face by Pesch over his interpretation of Mk 13 and the perceived extent of Markan redaction in general, has brought to the surface many underlying assumptions and problems concerning the determination of tradition and redaction in the Gospel of Mark. Widely divergent estimates of the nature and extent of Markan composition have called into question the validity of even attempting to divide tradition from redaction.[28] But it would be premature to give up on the task altogether because of these contradictory results, as the nature of the evidence itself is ambiguous. This does not mean that the evidence is irrelevant, inconclusive or non-existent. Since the most common methods for ascertaining redaction are based on recurrent or distinctive vocabulary, syntax and phrases in the Gospel of Mark—sometimes established by comparison with Matthew and Luke, and sometimes simply by their frequency in Mark—the evidence can be taken either as an indication of connected pre-Markan traditions or as an indication of authorial intervention. To attribute it entirely one way or the other is to over-simplify the tension between tradition received and tradition interpreted. If it is all indicative of tradition, then the date for authorship has simply been shifted and the analysis needs to proceed again at that earlier date. If it is all attributed to redaction, then Mark's story of Jesus becomes a novel, a supreme work of fiction, and a purely literary analysis of it will exhaust its meaning.

But truth seldom survives at the extremes, existing rather in the tangled relationships between. Thus it is with tradition and redaction in the Gospel

[25] See, for example, his influence on the views of Gnilka, *Markus,* 179f; and Neirynck's favourable critique of *Naherwartungen,* "Discours". The work of Kelber, *Kingdom,* also follows a similar understanding of Markan redactional purposes, though Kelber differs on the implications of this redaction for the Markan *Sitz im Leben.* See the discussion of this in chapter 7 below.

[26] Acknowledged by Pesch in "Markus 13", 356.

[27] See Pesch, *Das Markus-evangelium II,* 266-267, and "Markus 13", 358.

[28] The widely diverging estimates may be illustrated by Pesch's own opinion in *Das Markus-evangelium II,* that *no* Markan redaction is to be found in the Passion narrative (14:1-16:8), compared with Burton Mack's recent arguments in *Myth of Innocence* that the Passion narrative is a Markan composition and contains *no* pre-Markan units of tradition! Those who have called into question the validity of the whole process include C. Clifton Black, "Quest", and *The Disciples According to Mark* (Sheffield 1989), discussed briefly in the Introduction above.

of Mark. It is not always possible to separate decisively, but the evidence is there and—carefully analysed and cross-checked—it can lead to meaningful conclusions which can then be subject to the controls of the theology, structure and narrative flow of the book as a whole. The relevance of distinctive Markan vocabulary, syntax and phrases will therefore be examined closely and any results tested against the findings of form and tradition analyses from the chapters above, and then subjected to further refinement by an analysis of Markan structure and theology below.

The inadequacy of using unique vocabulary statistics as a method of isolating pre-Markan traditions has been noted already in chapter 2 above. The corollary of that method—using statistics of the *recurrent* or *distinctive* vocabulary of the Gospel of Mark as evidence of redaction—has been much more widely practised, albeit with diverse methods and results. The following is a list of words drawn from Frans Neirynck's comparative tables,[29] where the purely statistical approaches of Hawkins and Morgenthaler are compared with the lists by Gaston and Pryke drawn from supposedly redactional passages, and Friedrich's list based on those words used in Mark but avoided by Matthew and Luke.[30] It includes only those words which occur in Mk 13 and are thought by at least one commentator to be examples of distinctive Markan vocabulary, if not Markan redaction.

[29] F. Neirynck, "The Redactional Text of Mark", in *Evangelica*, 618-635; and "Words Characteristic of Mark: A New List", *ETL* 64 (1987), 367-374.

[30] Hawkins, *Horae Synopticae*, 1-53; Morgenthaler, *Statistik*, 181-185; L. Gaston, *Horae Synopticae Electronicae. Word Statistics of the Synoptic Gospels* (Missoula 1973), 18-21, 58-60; E. J. Pryke, *Redactional Style in the Marcan Gospel. A Study of Syntax and Vocabulary as Guides to Redaction in Mark* (Cambridge 1978). It was not possible to gain direct access to the following three lists, so the information on them above has been derived solely from Neirynck, "New List": Friedrich's list in J. Schreiber, *Der Kreuzigungsbericht des Markusevangeliums Mk 15,20b-41* (Berlin/New York 1986), "Exkurz V", 395-433; the lists of P. Dschulnigg, *Sprache, Redaktion und Intention des Markus-Evangeliums. Eigentümlichkeiten der Sprache des Markus-Evangeliums und ihre Bedeutung für die Redaktionskritik* (Stuttgart 1984), 84-226; and the critique of Hawkins, Morgenthaler and Gaston, and the resulting modified lists, by W. Hendriks, *Karakteristiek woordgebruik in de synoptische evangelies* (Nijmegen 1986), 118-157, 229-233. In keeping with Neirynck's usage, H[add] refers to Hawkins additions in *Horae Synopticae*, 14, H* = important, H† = less important; G refers to Gaston's longest list, G[1] to his list of Markan editorial words, and G[2] to the supplement to that list (of less certain editorial words). In column 7, (He) refers to those words listed in Hendriks's list of 100 Markan words, and He (without brackets) indicates those which are retained or added to the reduced list of 25 words indicating Markan characteristics (see Neirynck, "New List", 373-374).

Distinctive Markan vocabulary in Mk 13

Vocabulary	Hawkins	Morgenthaler	Gaston	Pryke	Dschulnigg	Hendriks	Friedrich
αἴρω	-	-	G	-	-	(He)	-
ἀκούω	-	-	G¹	-	-	-	-
ἀλλά	H^{add}	M	G	-	-	He	F
ἀμήν	-	-	-	P	-	-	-
Ἀνδρέας	-	-	G	-	-	(He)	-
ἄνεμος	-	-	G	-	-	-	-
ἄρχω	H^{add}	-	G¹	-	-	-	-
αὐτός	-	-	G²	-	-	He	-
ἀφίημι	-	-	G	-	-	He	-
βλέπω	-	-	-	P	-	-	-
γάρ	-	-	-	P	-	He	-
γινώσκω	-	-	G¹	P	-	-	-
γρηγορέω	-	-	G	-	-	-	-
δεῖ	-	-	-	P	-	-	-
διδάσκαλος	-	-	-	-	D	-	F
ἐγείρω	-	-	-	P	-	-	F
εἰ	-	-	-	-	-	He	-
εἰς	-	-	G¹	-	-	(He)	-
ἐκ	-	-	-	-	-	(He)	-
ἐκεῖνος	-	-	G²	-	-	-	-
ἐκπορεύομαι	H	M	G²	P	D	He (-πορ.)	F
ἐπερωτάω	H^{add}	M	G²	P	D	He	F
ἔρχομαι	-	-	G²	-	-	He	-
εὐαγγέλιον	H	-	G	P	D	(He)	F
ἔχω	-	-	G²	-	-	He	-
ἤδη	-	-	-	P	-	-	-
ἡμέρα ἐκείνη, (sing and plural)	-	-	-	-	-	-	F
θύρα	-	-	-	P	-	-	-
Ἰάκωβος	-	M	G	-	-	(He)	-
ἴδε	-	-	G	-	-	He	-
ἴδιος	-	-	G¹	P	-	-	-
ἱερόν	-	-	-	P	-	-	-
ἱμάτιον	-	-	G	-	-	-	F
ἵνα	H^{add}	M	G	-	-	He	F
Ἰωάννης	-	-	G	-	-	(He)	-
καθεύδω	-	-	G	-	-	-	-
κάθημαι	-	-	-	P	-	-	-
καί	H^{add}	-	G¹	-	-	He	-
καιρός	-	-	-	P	-	-	-
καταβαίνω	-	-	-	P	-	-	F
κατέναντι	-	-	-	-	D	(He)	-
κηρύσσω	-	M	G¹	P	D	(He)	F
κτίσις	-	-	-	-	-	(He)	-

Vocabulary	Hawkins	Morgenthaler	Gaston	Pryke	Dschulnigg	Hendriks	Friedrich
λαλέω	-	-	G¹	-	-	-	-
λέγω	-	-	G	-	-	He	-
λίθος	-	-	-	P	-	-	-
λόγος	-	-	G¹	-	-	He	-
μαθητής	-	-	G¹	P	-	-	-
μαρτυρία	-	-	-	-	-	(He)	-
οἶδα	-	-	G	-	-	-	-
οἰκία (no owner)	H†	-	-	P	-	-	F
ὄνομα	-	-	-	P	-	-	-
ὅπου	-	M	G²	-	-	-	F
ὄρος	-	-	G²	P	-	-	-
ὅταν	-	-	-	-	-	-	F
ὅτι (rec)	H†	-	-	-	-	He	-
οὔπω	H	-	G	-	-	(He)	-
οὕτως	-	-	-	P	-	-	-
ὀψία, ὀψέ	-	-	-	-	-	-	F
παραβολή	-	-	G¹	P	-	-	-
παραδίδωμι	-	-	G	-	-	-	-
πᾶς	-	-	G²	P	-	-	F
περί	-	-	G²	-	-	-	-
πιστεύω	-	M	-	-	-	(He)	F
πολύς (adj)	-	M	G¹	-	-	He	F
πότε	-	-	-	-	-	(He)	-
πρωΐ	H	-	G	P	D	(He)	F
πρῶτον (adv)	-	-	-	P	-	-	F
συναγωγή	-	-	-	P	-	-	-
σῴζω	-	-	-	P	-	-	-
τοιοῦτος	H†	-	G	-	-	(He)	-
Χριστός	-	-	-	P	-	-	-
ὥρα	-	-	-	P	-	-	-

It is clear from this table that there are considerable differences between the lists. Only 15 out of the 73 words are listed by three or more commentators, and only two (ἐκπορεύομαι and ἐπερωτάω) have the support of all seven! Such diversity should be expected, however, given the differing criteria used for the selection of the words. But what is perhaps even more disconcerting is that if all the words above are underlined on the text of Mk 13 they do not correlate in the way they should with any of the indicators of tradition used in the chapters above.[31]

[31] It is of course possible to demonstrate this mathematically by comparing the percentages of distinctive tradition already given in chapter 2, footnote 63 above (listed first here), with the percentages of 'Markan vocabulary' from the list above occurring in each section of the text (listed second), thus: vv.1-2 (17.5%/50.0%); 3-6 (15%/53.3%); 7-8 (12.1%/24.2%); 9-13 (21.6%/42.3%); 14-20 (31.0%/26.7%); 21-23 (48.6%/32.4%); 24-27 (0%/23.9%); 28-31 (20.0%/26.2%); 32-37 (24.1%/39.1%). It should be noted that the indicators of *distinctive* traditions do not provide evidence for *recurring* sources of tradition in Mark, and nor does a list of Markan vocabulary indicate

This situation is improved considerably, however, by the removal of those lists based on supposed redactional passages in the Gospel of Mark (Pryke's list and Gaston's longer list); and of those which seem to have been derived more from the preferences of Matthew and Luke than Mark (Friedrich's list).[32]

Clearly the practice of compiling a word list to indicate redaction from passages already assumed to be redactional is a rather dubious one.[33] Nor can the vocabulary statistics of Matthew and Luke be used without ambiguity to indicate Markan preferences. Yet such information is certainly relevant. That εὐθύς occurs 41 times in Mark, only 5 times in Matthew and once in Luke surely says something about the composition of Mark, even in the unlikely event that the author drew all the occurrences from the tradition. But it should be remembered that such statistical information, strictly speaking, reveals more about the writing of Matthew and Luke than of Mark.[34] Nevertheless, it is possible to argue that words

---

all the words used in Markan redaction, but rather it focusses on the statistically distinctive ones. Thus there cannot be perfect negative correlation between the sets of figures compared above. However it would be reasonable to expect *some* degree of negative correlation between them—the greater the amount of tradition, the less redaction, and *vice-versa*. But if all words in the list are used the correlation coefficient is *positive* 0.03 (when a negative value up to −1 would have been desirable). The figure does become negative when Pryke's list is removed, and even reaches −0.22 when only Hawkins, Morgenthaler, Gaston's lists 1 and 2, and Dschulnigg are considered.

Of course the underlying assumption in making such adjustments is that unique syntax is a better indicator of distinctive traditions than Markan word lists are of Markan redaction. Insofar as the former evidence is derived solely from the text of Mark, whereas the word lists are dependent to some extent on comparisons with later writings (Mt and Lk), this assumption is reasonable. So too is the decision to remove Pryke, Gaston's longer list and Friedrich from the calculations—*not* just to improve the result, but because their methodology for compiling the lists is clearly inappropriate in terms of determining Markan redaction.

32 Neirynck, "New List", 367, says of Friedrich: "His criterion is a synoptic one, Matthew's and/or Luke's avoidance of the Markan word". This is not established on the basis of the total number of occurrences of each word in Mt-Mk-Lk, but by a painstaking comparison of each Markan occurrence with Matthew and Luke. Thus ὅταν is included in Friedrich's list because its use in the Markan context is often avoided by Matthew and Luke, even though the total comparative occurrences of ὅταν in the synoptics [Mt 19, Mk 21, Lk 29] are statistically unremarkable. Friedrich's list is thus very useful for the study of Matthew and Luke, but it would seem to be more relevant for the study of Mark to take an approach similar to Hawkins (*Horae Synopticae*, 9), who includes: "the words and phrases which *occur at least three times* in Mark, and which either (a) *are not found at all in Matthew or Luke,* or (b) *occur in Mark more often than in Matthew and Luke together.*" The focus is thus on Markan 'over-usage' of a word, rather than Matthean and/or Lukan 'under-usage' of a word in a particular context. It was not possible to ascertain the exact basis for Hendriks's lists, but his shorter list of Markan characteristics ("New List", 373-374) did not adversely affect the correlation coefficient anywhere near as much as his longer list.

33 As Peabody, *Mark as Composer*, 7-8, argues convincingly. However, Peabody's critique, 11-14, of 'Neirynck's composite list' is based entirely on a misunderstanding of the purpose of that list. See Neirynck, "New List", 367, footnote 3.

34 Again, of course, this assumes Markan priority, which is being challenged by some in this very area of Markan style and vocabulary. See, for example, the foreword to

so obviously preferred in the Gospel of Mark must at least indicate distinctive Markan traditions if not Markan redaction, and most probably a mixture of both. That is, the words occurring in the word lists based on Markan 'over-use' in comparison with Matthew and Luke are most likely to indicate either Markan redaction or Markan selection of special material, or a mixture of both. Either way, both the actual composition of words and phrases by the author *and* the selection and insertion of distinctive material not used by later writers are essential pieces of information in the consideration of the author's preferences and intentions. Thus any of the words listed by Hawkins, Morgenthaler, Dschulnigg and/or Gaston (lists 1 and 2 only), which have been derived using an appropriate method and show some signs of negative correlation to the indicators of tradition, shall be underlined on Text Sheet 5 below as *possible* indicators of authorial composition and insertion.

Often as part of, or as a supplement to, these Markan word lists, descriptions of distinctive Markan syntax are given.[35] Such catalogues of

Peabody, *Mark as Composer,* ix-xiv, written by W. R. Farmer: "Should it be demonstrated that the tradition moved, not from Mark to Matthew and Luke, but from Matthew through Luke to Mark, then many popular notions about early Christian theological reflection will need modification and most histories of the earliest Christian communities will need to be rewritten." This is surely true, and so is his citation of C. K. Barrett to the effect that we must first patiently collect and examine the basic facts. But if Mark wrote *after* Matthew and Luke, then it would appear that the following vocabulary (all of which occurs in Mk 13) has been used with great reserve by the author of Mark [the numbers in brackets are the total occurrences in Mt-Mk-Lk, according to K. Aland, *Vollständige Konkordanz zum Griechischen Neuen Testament,* 3 vols (Berlin 1983), with corrections to the Markan figures from textual criticism—in particular a discounting of occurrences in the long ending]:

ἀγγελός [20,6,25]; ἄγειν [4,3,13]; ἅγιος [10,7,20]; ἄνθρωπος [116,56,95]; ἀπό [115,47,125]; βασιλεία [55,19,46]; γάρ [125,66,97]; γενεά [13,5,15]; δέ [495,155,548]; δόξα [7,3,13]; δοῦλος [30,5,26]; ἔθνος [15,6,13]; ἕκαστος [4,1,5]; ἐπί [122,71,161]; Ἰουδαία [8,4,10]; ἱστάναι [21,10,26]; καιρός [10,5,13]; μέλλειν [9,2,12]; μισεῖσθαι [5,1,7]; οὐαί [14,2,15]; οὖν [56,5,33]; οὐρανός [87,17,35]; προφήτης [37,5,29]; σημεῖον [13,5,11].

Apart from suggesting that Mark was 'regressing' linguistically (by consistently replacing δέ with καί *hundreds* of times), Matthean priority would also lead to the conclusion that some sort of anti-spiritual streak motivated the Markan redaction of Matthew and Luke, in that words like 'angel', 'holy', 'glory', 'heaven' and 'prophet' are heavily censored (not to mention what Mark does in the rest of his Gospel to the Christological titles, virgin birth, resurrection appearances, sermon on the mount/plain, and so on. See chapter 2, footnote 46 above). The Gospel of Mark is down-to-earth and radical enough as the *first* Gospel written. If it is the third, as Farmer suggests, then indeed we must agree with him that *all* 'histories of the earliest Christian communities will need to be rewritten'! What other historical evidence is there to support such a radical revision of the Gospel as this late in the first century—and how could it then achieve widespread (and eventually canonical) endorsement so soon afterwards?

[35] See for example the extensive notes of C. H. Turner, "Marcan Usage: Notes, Critical and Exegetical, on the Second Gospel", *JTS* 25 (1924), 377-386; 26 (1925), 12-20, 145-156, 225-240, 337-346; 27 (1926), 58-62; 28 (1927), 9-30, 349-362; 29 (1928), 275-289, 346-361, all now helpfully reprinted in one volume together with other

recurrent syntactical features analyse the text at a deeper level than the vocabulary lists, but are admittedly still ambiguous in that they may also provide evidence for recurrent syntax in related pre-Markan traditions as much as for the author's style and hence editorial interference. However it is possible to increase the probability of discovering the author's syntactical 'fingerprints' by examining the patterns of recurrence of distinctive syntax throughout the Gospel. If such features repeatedly function as links in the narrative, summary statements, and as a means of tying the plot together, they may be attributed to the hand of the author with an increased degree of probability.

It would be possible, however, to argue for multiple authors of the Gospel and therefore that some of these structuring features, evident in say the miracle stories or the Passion narrative, do not belong to the final redactor of the Gospel of Mark but to some anonymous author in the pre-Markan tradition. This is conceivable if the syntactical features are clearly localised, but it is no solution to the problem of authorship to attribute the creation of the bulk of the Gospel narrative to pre-Markan tradition.[36] By 'author' we mean the one responsible for the *major* redactional task of compiling and shaping the Gospel account, whenever that process took place. The evidence for such an 'author' (rather than a series of 'minor authors') is in the distinctive syntax which recurs *throughout* the Gospel, and functions organisationally as far as the theology and literary structure of the narrative is concerned. Thus the task of collecting together the recurrent syntax of the Gospel of Mark must be combined with the less objective but equally important task of evaluating the theological and compositional function of each item of syntax before any judgment regarding tradition or redaction can be made.[37] In this chapter, the attempt will be made to gather together the words and phrases which are most likely to be indicators of Markan redaction before subjecting them to theological and literary analysis in the next chapter.

Some lists of Markan syntax have already begun to take the literary and theological function of the features into account, whereas others are based purely on frequency of occurrence. Some lists are definitive collections of certain features within the Gospel (Turner/Elliott), whereas others are brief lists of the most striking syntax only. They are therefore of varying usefulness when it comes to determining possible Markan redaction. There is limited relevance specifically for Mk 13, for example, in the lists of Markan stylistic features given by V. Taylor and E. J. Pryke amongst

material by J. K. Elliott (ed), *The Language and Style of the Gospel of Mark. An Edition of C. H. Turner's "Notes on Marcan Usage" Together with Other Comparable Studies* (Leiden 1993); and also the considerable detail in Taylor, *Mark,* chapter V, "The Vocabulary, Syntax, and Style". Peabody, *Mark as Composer,* 14-15, footnote 16, cites some further examples.

[36] This is the extreme towards which Pesch, *Das Markus-evangelium,* tends to go when he claims there is no Markan redaction at all from Mk 14:1 onwards.

[37] The importance in this connection of the Markan 'seams', 'sandwiches', and 'structure' should be noted. See, for example, Edwards, "Markan Sandwiches".

many others, which really just note the most prominent features in the Gospel as a whole.[38] The most obvious of these distinctively Markan features—such as the use of εὐθύς, πάλιν and καὶ ἔλεγεν αὐτοῖς—do not occur in Mk 13 at all, but there are some other characteristics worth considering as possible indicators of Markan style.

From Taylor's list:

(i)   The use of εἰμί followed by a participle (of the future tense in Mk 13:13,25)

(ii)   The use of οὐ μή (double negative—in 13:2,2,19,30,31)

(iii)   The frequent use of the historic present (13:1)

(iv)   The impersonal plural (13:9,11,26)

(v)   The use of ἤρξα(ν)το as an auxiliary verb (13:5)

(vi)   Parataxis (extensive use of καί to join clauses—see chapter 1 above)

(vii)   Asyndeta (lack of connecting links—13:6,7b,8b,8c,9b,34)[39]

(viii) Anacolutha and/or parenthetical clauses (13:10,14,34)

(ix)   Pleonasms (13:19,20)

From Pryke's list—(i), (iii), (iv), (v) and (viii) as above—and also:

(i)   The genitive absolute (13:1,3)

(ii)   λέγω ὅτι (13:6b,30)

(iii)   γάρ explanatory (13:11b,19a,33,35a)

Of these features, some doubts may be expressed about the classification of the third person plural verbs as impersonal verbs for in the context of the text and of a persecuted community the 'they' fairly clearly relates to 'the powers that be' rather than simply being used as a substitute for the passive.[40] As for category (vi) Parataxis, the use of καί has already been alluded to in the word list above, but it is preferable to use Taylor's more precise category.[41] The classification of vv.10 and 34 by Taylor and

---

[38] Taylor, *Mark,* 45-52; Pryke, *Redactional Style,* 32-135. These lists are usually a summary of Turner's insights and valuable in their own right, but despite Pryke's claim to have taken into account the location of the material in the text ("Naturally it is at the beginnings and endings of pericopae . . . where redaction is mainly to be found", 30), the use of his list to convert 'source texts' to 'possible redaction on linguistic grounds' is idiosyncratic (leading, for example in Mk 13, to the suggestion of redaction in vv.9a,11a,13,19,33 and 35a, alongside an already extensive list of Markan redaction in the chapter—see Appendix 3). It would have been better to derive the list on statistical grounds and then use it to test the conclusions of the form critics and commentators regarding redaction in Mark—conclusions which Pryke assumes as a starting point (10-24).

[39] Note that v.15 is omitted from Taylor's list as the reading of post-positive δέ has been taken as the better text (see Introduction, pages 25-6, above).

[40] See also the comments under v.26 in the table in chapter 1 above, though this is equally applicable to vv.9 and 11. The 'they' would be readily identified by the community in the original context of persecution and suffering, and also with hindsight if the Markan community was situated soon after the events described.

[41] So also Maloney, as detailed in chapter 1 above in the table of Semitic influences under v.2. Thus parataxis will be considered present in this syntactical analysis only when καί is used to join independent clauses or to start sentences—and not when it joins nouns (vv.3,9,22,26,31), adjectives, adjectival or adverbial phrases (vv.1,7,8,12),

Pryke as parentheses (after C. H. Turner), is interesting, but debatable. They certainly intrude abruptly but are hardly explanatory asides in the style of the rest of the parentheses in the Gospel. It is clear that v.14 contains an explicit parenthesis, but again it is hardly typical in that 'the reader' is specifically referred to only on this occasion. These exceptions aside (the impersonal plurals and the parenthetical comments), the features listed above will be shown in Text Sheet 5 together with the other critical assessments of Markan syntax in order to indicate the most probable areas of redaction.

In contrast to these brief collections of Markan syntax there is the encyclopædic treatment of duality in the Gospel of Mark by Frans Neirynck,[42] which despite the promise of its subtitle—*Contributions to the Study of the Markan Redaction*—does not specifically answer the question as to how much of the impressive collection of dual features in the text of Mark may be attributed to the author. Rather, Neirynck avoids any "mechanical distribution between tradition and redaction"[43] and concludes in more general terms that:

> The survey of temporal and local statements, double questions, antithetic parallelism and the use of *oratio recta* and *oratio obliqua* has shown that the progressive double-step expression is a more general Markan characteristic. This does not exclude indebtedness to tradition and sources, but in each particular case the source critic has to reckon with the possibility that the composite expression reflects the author's own manner of writing.[44]

Thus whereas in the past scholars have suggested that the first part of a two-step statement may be traditional and the second part a Markan addition—or even that it is evidence of Markan conflation of two sources—Neirynck suggests that the whole double expression may be "one of Mark's most characteristic features of style."[45] This is because such features are so common throughout the Gospel and yet are very seldom purely redundant—the second statement nearly always further defining the first. Now Neirynck has done a great service to Markan scholarship by listing with characteristic detail and accuracy every conceivable dual feature occurring in the Gospel of Mark—information that has considerable significance for source critical assumptions and the 'synoptic problem'. Yet since his lists include a wide range of features— grammatical usage (8 separate categories), duplicate expressions and double statements (a further 9), correspondence within one pericope (8), and factors concerned with the structuring of the Gospel (3)—the question

---

participles (v.17), or when it means 'also' (v.29) or introduces an incredulous question (v.4).

[42] Neirynck, *Duality in Mark. Contributions to the Study of the Markan Redaction* (Leuven, 1988, revised from the 1972 edition).

[43] Neirynck, *Duality*, 49.

[44] Neirynck, *Duality*, 71-72.

[45] Neirynck, *Duality*, 49.

must be asked as to whether all are of equal value when it comes to ascertaining possible Markan redaction.[46] However the full range of dual features will be considered initially as this question will be answered in part by the correlation between Neirynck's categories of duality as applied to Mk 13, and the results of the other methods for isolating possible Markan redaction. Thus the categories of dual features drawn from Neirynck's lists which may indicate Markan redaction in Mk 13 (and in Mk 13 *only,* which explains why some numbers are omitted) are the following:[47]

Duality in Mk 13 (Neirynck)

1. Compound verb followed by the same preposition
    ἐκπορευομένου ... ἐκ (13:1); ἐπαναστήσονται ... ἐπί (13:12).

3. Verb with cognate accusative or dative

---

[46] One way of beginning to answer such a question is to compare these dual features with the unique syntax found in the Gospel of Mark as described in chapter 2 above. One would not expect that recurrent features would be associated too frequently with unique syntax, because by definition dual features must occur at least twice. However at the more subconscious syntactical level such features may reveal differences which set them apart from each other and the rest of the text of the Gospel. By comparing Neirynck's text of Mark (*Duality,* 139-191)—specially underlined to demonstrate duality—with a text underlined to indicate unique syntax it is possible to ascertain exactly how much interference occurs between the two categories. The percentage of dual features in each of Neirynck's categories that contain significant amounts (more than just one word) of unique syntax can then be calculated. It would be expected that those dual features that are the most likely indicators of Markan redaction would *not* contain a high percentage of unique syntax, since a high percentage would tend to be an indication of distinctive traditions behind the text. The results are as follows (note that the percentages become rather arbitrary when small numbers of dual features are involved, and when the features involve longer sections of text than just a few words—hence the question marks after some figures):

Neirynck's category (1) 11/64 features contain unique syntax = 17.2%; (2) 5/7 = 71.4%?, 3/7 = 42.9%?; (3) 8/30 = 26.7%; (4) 67/177 = 37.9%; (5) 25/58 = 43.1%; (6) 20/31 = 64.5%; (7) 11/104 = 10.6%; (8) 10/24 = 41.7%; (9a) 6/20 = 30.0%; (9b) 39/87 = 44.8%; (10) 20/72 = 27.8%; (11) 5/31 = 16.1%; (12) 29/64 = 45.3%; (13) 32/107 = 29.9%; (14) 5/14 = 35.7%?; (15) 5/28 = 17.9%; (16) 2/25 = 8.0%; (17) 3/23 = 13.0%; (18) 7/24 = 29.2%; (19) 8/26 = 30.8%; (20) 29/57 = 50.9%; (21) 17/28 = 60.7%; (22) 9/15 = 60.0%?; (23) 14/42 = 33.3%; (24) 6/7 = 85.7%?; (25) 16/25 = 64.0%; (26) 36/61 = 59.0%; (27) 10/35 = 28.6%; (28) no figure possible; (29a) 16/34 = 47.1%; (29b) 20/36 = 55.6%; (29c) 1/1!; (30) no figures possible.

These results suggest that categories 1, 3, 4, 7, 9a, 10, 11, 13, 14, 15, 16, 17, 18, 19, 23, and 27 would be the best indicators of Markan redaction. As far as Mk 13 is concerned, pruning down to these categories only would make little difference to the determination of possible Markan redaction, given that conclusions here will be based on more than one commentator and method. So the full list of possibilities from *Duality* will be considered above (categories 1-16 in this chapter, and 21-30 in chapter 5), which should also help to avoid the possible accusation that the evidence for redaction is being tailored to fit the evidence for tradition, especially as indicated by unique syntax.

[47] The lists of occurrences in Mk 13 are derived from Neirynck, *Duality,* 75-136; with additions from the addenda, 236-246.

ἀκούσητε ... ἀκοάς (13:7); κτίσεως ἥν ἔκτισεν (13:19); τοὺς ἐκλεκτοὺς οὓς ἐξελέξατο (13:20).

4. Multiplication of cognate verbs
βλέπετε ... (13:5,9,23,33); πλανήσῃ ... (13:5,6,22?); ἔσονται ... (13:8); παραδώσουσιν ... (13:9,11,12); λαλήσητε ... (13:11); γέγονεν ... (13:19); ἐκολόβωσεν ... (13:20); γένηται ... (13:28,29,30); παρέλθῃ ... (13:30,31); οἶδεν ... (13:32,33,35); ἀγρυπνεῖτε ...γρηγορῇ ... (13:33,34,35,37); to which could be added γινώσκετε ... (13:28,29).

5. Double participle
ἐκπορευομένου ... καὶ καθημένου (13:1,3); ταῖς ἐν γαστρὶ ἐχούσαις καὶ ταῖς θηλαζούσαις (13:17).

6. Double imperative
13:21, see category 10; βλέπετε, ἀγρυπνεῖτε (13:33).

7. Repetition of the antecedent
ὅ ... τοῦτο (13:11); ὁ δέ ... οὗτος (13:13); ἐπὶ τοῦ δώματος ... ἐκ τῆς οἰκίας αὐτοῦ (13:15); οἵα ... τοιαύτη (13:19); τὰς ἡμέρας ... τὰς ἡμέρας (13:20).

8. Double negative
οὐδεὶς οἶδεν, οὐδὲ οἱ ἄγγελοι ... οὐδὲ ὁ υἱός (13:32); also οὐ μή (13:2 twice,19,30, 31).

9. Double statement: negative/positive
Α. εἰ μὴ ἐκολόβωσεν ... οὐκ ... (13:20); οὐδεὶς οἶδεν ... εἰ μὴ ὁ πατήρ (13:32)
Β. οὔπω τὸ τέλος ... ἀρχὴ ὠδίνων ταῦτα (13:7,8); μὴ προμεριμνᾶτε ... ἀλλ᾽ ὃ ἐὰν δοθῇ ... (13:11); οὐ γάρ ... ἀλλὰ τὸ πνεῦμα ... (13:11); (13:20); παρελεύσονται ... οὐ παρελεύσονται (13:31).

10. Double statement: temporal or local
εἰς τὸ Ὄρος τῶν Ἐλαιῶν / κατέναντι τοῦ ἱεροῦ (13:3); ὅταν ... ἐν ἐκείνῃ τῇ ὥρᾳ (13:11); Ἴδε ὧδε ... Ἴδε ἐκεῖ (13:21); ἐν ἐκείναις ταῖς ἡμέραις / μετὰ τὴν θλῖψιν ἐκείνην (13:24); ἐγγύς ἐστιν / ἐπὶ θύραις (13:29); τῆς ἡμέρας ἐκείνης / ἢ τῆς ὥρας (13:32).

11. Double statement: general and special
πότε ὁ καιρός ἐστιν (13:33) / πότε ὁ κύριος τῆς οἰκίας ἔρχεται, ἢ ὀψὲ ἢ μεσονύκτιον ἢ ἀλεκτοροφωνίας ἢ πρωΐ (13:35); ὃ δὲ ὑμῖν λέγω / πᾶσιν λέγω (13:37).

13. Synonymous expression
ποταποὶ λίθοι καὶ ποταπαὶ οἰκοδομαί (13:1); οὐ μὴ ἀφεθῇ ὧδε λίθος ἐπὶ λίθον ὃς οὐ μὴ καταλυθῇ (13:2); ἐλεύσονται ἐπὶ τῷ ὀνόματί μου λέγοντες ὅτι Ἐγώ εἰμι (13:6); ἀκούσητε πολέμους καὶ ἀκοὰς πολέμων (13:7); ἕνεκεν ἐμοῦ εἰς μαρτύριον αὐτοῖς. 10 καὶ εἰς πάντα τὰ ἔθνη πρῶτον δεῖ κηρυχθῆναι τὸ εὐαγγέλιον (13:9,10); παραδώσει ἀδελφὸς ἀδελφὸν εἰς

θάνατον καὶ πατὴρ τέκνον, καὶ ἐπαναστήσονται τέκνα ἐπὶ γονεῖς καὶ θανατώσουσιν αὐτούς (13:12); μὴ καταβάτω μηδὲ εἰσελθάτω (13:15); κτίσεως ἣν ἔκτισεν (13:19); τοὺς ἐκλεκτοὺς οὓς ἐξελέξατο (13:19); δυνάμεως πολλῆς καὶ δόξης (13:26); 13:33 see category 6; ἀπόδημος ἀφεὶς τὴν οἰκίαν αὐτοῦ (13:34); δοὺς τοῖς δούλοις αὐτοῦ τὴν ἐξουσίαν, ἑκάστῳ τὸ ἔργον αὐτοῦ (13:34).

16. **Double group of persons**
    ταῖς ἐν γαστρὶ ἐχούσαις καὶ ταῖς θηλαζούσαις (13:17); ψευδόχριστοι και ψευδοπροφῆται (13:22); (Two individuals—twice: Πέτρος καὶ Ἰάκωβος καὶ Ἰωάννης καὶ Ἀνδρέας 13:3).

21. **Command and fulfilment**
    Εἰπὸν ἡμῖν πότε ... ὁ δὲ Ιησοῦς ἤρξατο λέγειν αὐτοῖς (13:4,5).

25. **Double question**
    πότε ταῦτα ἔσται, καὶ τί τὸ σημεῖον ὅταν μέλλῃ ταῦτα συντελεῖσθαι πάντα (13:4).

26. **Correspondence in discourse (question and corresponding answer)**
    <u>πότε</u> ταῦτα ἔσται, καὶ τί τὸ σημεῖον <u>ὅταν</u> μέλλῃ ταῦτα συντελεῖσθαι πάντα (13:4);
    ὅταν δὲ ἀκούσητε ... δεῖ γενέσθαι, ἀλλ᾽ οὔπω τὸ τέλος (13:7);
    ὅταν ἀγωσιν ὑμᾶς ... ὁ δὲ ὑπομείνας εἰς τέλος (13:11-13);
    Ὅταν δὲ ἴδητε ... τότε (13:14—see also τότε in vv.21,26,27)
    ὅταν ... γένηται ... γινώσκετε ὅτι ἐγγὺς ... (13:28);
    ὅταν ἴδητε ταῦτα γινόμενα γινώσκετε ὅτι ἐγγύς ... (13:29);
    μέχρις οὗ ταῦτα πάντα γένηται (13:30—see v.23 πάντα).

    Correspondence in discourse (*without* question and answer)
    ἴδε ποταποὶ λίθοι καὶ ποταπαὶ οἰκοδομαί (13:1) and Βλέπεις ταύτας τὰς μεγάλας οἰκοδομάς; οὐ μὴ ἀφεθῇ ὧδε λίθος ἐπὶ λίθον ὅς οὐ μὴ καταλυθῇ (13:2); Εἰπὸν ἡμῖν πότε...πάντα (13:4) and προείρηκα ὑμῖν πάντα (13:23) and ὃ δὲ ὑμῖν λέγω, πᾶσιν λέγω (13:37).

27. **Inclusion**
    (13:4&37; 5&22-23; 6&22; 7&14; 33&37).

29. **Parallelism in sayings**
    Antithetic (13:11,20,31);
    Synonymous (13:24,25,28-29).

30. **Doublets**
    (12:1-2 & 13:33-34; 12:41 & 13:3; 13:26 & 14:62; 13:36 & 14:37).

This collection of features adds up to an extensive list even when the categories are applied to just one chapter. It is obvious that a supplementary means of discerning Markan redaction is required to be used alongside this collection of dual features so that no one phenomenon, no matter how prevalent, becomes the sole criterion for a decision. Hence this list shall be used together with the other lists of supposed Markan features analysed in this chapter so that they may each correct the excesses of the other. All of Neirynck's categories that apply to Mk 13 have been shown above, but for the purposes of determining possible Markan redaction only categories 1 to 16 shall be entered on to Text Sheet 5 in this chapter. The remaining categories (21 to 30) shall be examined as part of the analysis of theology and structure in chapter 5 below since those categories operate more clearly as markers at the narrative level.

Thus far the use of recurrent vocabulary and syntax and the phenomenon of duality have been examined as indicators of possible Markan redaction. Another relatively recent approach to locating the redactional features of the Gospel of Mark has been the attempt by David Peabody to discover them through an analysis of recurrent phraseology.[48] There is some overlap here with the previous collections of recurrent syntax and especially Neirynck's *Duality*, but Peabody's work is distinguished by its comprehensive goal to collect "all of the combinations of two or more literary elements that recur within the Gospel of Mark two or more times."[49] Peabody argues that the longer these literary elements are, and the wider their spread of occurrences throughout the Gospel, the greater the chances are that they come from the hand of the major redactor or author. So after collecting 252 tables of such recurrent phraseology representing the *possible* redactional features of the Gospel, Peabody then analyses their compositional function, their distribution throughout the Gospel and the extent to which they accumulate or 'interlace' in close proximity with each other.

This is done to extract from the list of *possible* redactional features those which have 'the highest probability of coming from the hand of the author of Mark.' In particular, the use of πάλιν in the Gospel of Mark is seen by Peabody as meeting these criteria, in that it is often used to link together the story line by recalling previous events. By examining each such use of πάλιν and seeing which other possible redactional features are associated with them, Peabody builds a cumulative case for seeing the author's hand behind a set of verses where this 'interlacing' occurs.[50] These verses, which finish at 10:10, are seen by Peabody as being those that have the greatest probability of coming from the hand of the author of the Gospel. He does not preclude the possibility that still more redaction can be traced, however, and describes a method whereby the verses in the network of 44 tables associated with the occurrences of πάλιν can in turn be checked for 'interlacing' of possible redactional

---

[48] Peabody, *Mark as Composer*.

[49] Peabody, *Mark as Composer*, 13.

[50] Peabody, *Mark as Composer*, 162-163, lists these verses as: 1:16,21,39,45; 2:1-2,13; 3:1,7-10,20,23; 4:1-2,10,35; 5:1,21; 6:34,45,55; 7:14,17,24,31; 8:1,10,13,19-21; 9:14,28,33; 10:1,10.

features. Thereby further sets of verses with a diminishing probability of being authorial redaction can be gathered.[51]

When this method is applied with the objective of discovering any redactional features in Mk 13 the results are somewhat disappointing. No recurrent phrase from Mk 13 occurs more than once within the 44 tables held to have the highest probability of coming from the hand of the author, and only κατ' ἰδίαν in 13:3 (Table 122) and ἤρξατο λέγειν αὐτοῖς in 13:5 (Table 67) occur at all. It could also perhaps be argued that the motif of the disciples questioning Jesus privately (Table M) should include 13:3, though Peabody restricts it to those occurrences within a house. Such results from the more than 252 tables given seem to be an overly cautious assessment of the possibilities for Markan redaction in Mk 13. Indeed, the whole of the latter part of the Gospel is found to have very little redactional interference if Peabody's method is adhered to—which again leads to the question as to who the real author of Mark is if the major redactor had little to do with the last third of the narrative.

It is plain to see why Peabody's method would lead to such conclusions, however. After listing all the potential Markan redaction based on recurrent phraseology in his 252 tables, Peabody's way into a more careful assessment of the material is through those phrases associated with the retrospective use of πάλιν. Such usages of πάλιν occur only up to Mk 11:27 according to Peabody, as the remainder of usages later in the Gospel unite only verses *within* a pericope (Table 183) rather than two or more separated pericopes.[52] Thus it is not surprising that Peabody finds no strongly redactional passages after 11:27, and that even after pursuing his method further there is very little mention of the later chapters of the Gospel. But if other recurrent phrases which are widely used in the Gospel, such as καὶ ἔλεγεν αὐτοῖς or ἤρξατο + infinitive, were used alongside the πάλιν phrases then the results might be more balanced as far as the whole Gospel is concerned, rather than weighted in favour of the first half.

Nevertheless, Peabody's careful collection of recurrent phrases has at least provided a comprehensive listing of such features from the Gospel as a whole—and therefore of *possible* Markan redaction. These features alone are worth considering in any assessment of Markan redaction, and they are listed below insofar as they relate to Mk 13:

[51] Peabody, *Mark as Composer,* 165-166. The verses with the next highest probability of coming from the hand of the author are claimed to be those occurring more than once in Tables 42, 54 and 70 (but not associated with πάλιν), followed by those which occur more than once in any of the 44 tables listed on pages 163-165.

[52] Peabody, *Mark as Composer,* 146-147.

Recurrent phraseology in Mk 13 (Peabody)

Table	Description of recurrent feature (Peabody's titles)	References in Mk 13 [and in Mk]
217	καὶ ἐκπορευομένου αὐτοῦ to introduce a section	13:1 [10:17,46]
136	εἷς + partitive genitive	13:1 [5:22; 6:15; 8:28; 9:37,42; 10:37; 12:28; 14:10,20,43,47,66; 16:2; cf 9:17; 14:18]
125	διδάσκαλε as an address to Jesus	13:1 [4:38; 9:17,38; 10:17,20,35; 12:14,18,32]
88	ἴδε used to introduce an independent clause	13:1,21,21 [2:24; 3:34; 11:21; 15:4,35; 16:6]
239 (206)	καί + a participle of a verb for 'sitting' + κατέναντι	13:3 [12:41]
228	τὸ ὄρος τῶν ἐλαιῶν	13:3 [11:1; 14:26]
204	καί + genitive absolute + εἰς + name of place + 'disciples' + κατ᾽ ἰδίαν + a form of ἐπερωτάω + αὐτόν	13:3 [9:28]
122	κατ᾽ ἰδίαν/κατὰ μόνας	13:3 [4:34; 6:31,32; 7:33; 9:2,28; cf 4:10]
21,22, 23	Σίμωνος/Πέτρος καὶ Ἰάκωβος καὶ Ἰωάννης καὶ Ἀνδρέας	13:3 [1:29; 1:16-19; cf 3:16-18]
146	ὁ δὲ Ἰησοῦς	13:5 [+ 16 times cf ὁ δέ]
67	ἤρξατο/ἤρξαντο + infinitive	13:5 [+ 25 times]
121	βλέπετε, imperative, to mean 'watch' or 'beware'	13:5,9,23,33 [4:24; 8:15; 12:38; cf 4:2,12; 7:14; 8:18,21]
210	ἐπὶ τῷ ὀνόματί μου	13:6 [9:37,39; cf 9:38,41; 11:9]
(152)	(Duplication used distributively)	(cf 13:8) [6:7,39,40; cf 6:40; 14:19,49]

Table	Description of recurrent feature (Peabody's titles)	References in Mk 13 [and in Mk]
66	εἰς μαρτύριον αὐτοῖς	13:9 [1:44; 6:11]
(193)	(ἕνεκεν ἐμοῦ καὶ τοῦ εὐαγγελίου)	(cf 13:9) [8:35; 10:29; cf 10:7]
11	κηρύσσειν + εὐαγγέλιον	13:10 [1:14; 14:9]
14	τὸ εὐαγγέλιον used absolutely	13:10 [1:15; 8:35; 10:29; 14:9; cf 1:1; 1:14]
3	πνεῦμα + ἅγιον	13:11 [1:8; 3:29; 12:36; cf 1:10,12; 14:38]
4	ἐν ἐκείναις ταῖς ἡμέραις	13:17,24 [1:9; 8:1; cf 2:20; 4:35; 13:19,32]
169	noun + relative pronoun + cognate verb	13:19,20 [7:13; 10:38,38,39,39; cf 3:28; 4:24; 9:3]
216	ἀπὸ ἀρχῆς κτίσεως	13:19 [10:6]
81	ὁ υἱὸς τοῦ ἀνθρώπου	13:26 [+ 13 times]
240	καί + a form of ὄψονται + τὸν υἱὸν ἀνθρώπου + ἐρχόμενον + a form of νεφέλαι + δυνάμεως	13:26 [14:62]
109	ἀμὴν λέγω ὑμῖν (ὅτι)	13:30 [+ 12 times]
235	ἄγγελοι ἐν οὐρανοῖς/οὐρανῷ	13:32 [12:25]
12	ὁ καιρός used absolutely	13:33 [1:15]
(19)	(καί + participle of ἀφίημι + object + aorist)	(cf 13:34 - καί) [1:18,20; 8:13; 12:12; 14:50; cf 4:36; 7:8; 15:37]
(101)	(καὶ προσκαλεῖται + δώδεκα + 3rd singular of ἀποστέλλω + αὐτούς + καί + ἐξουσίαν)	(cf 13:34 partly) [3:13-16; 6:7]
241	A form of ἔρχομαι + a form of εὑρίσκω + a pronoun + καθεύδοντας	13:36 [14:37,40; cf 14:41]

These features will be added to Text Sheet 5 below and used together with the other results above to help determine the most probable areas of Markan redaction in Mk 13.

A further refinement of Peabody's approach would be to focus strictly on recurrent syntax in the Gospel, rather than a mixture of vocabulary and grammar. This can be seen as the corollary to the approach taken in chapter 2 to find the unique syntax in the Gospel of Mark. If unique syntax is accepted as an indicator of distinctive traditions, then recurrent syntax must indicate either inter-connected traditions or Markan redaction. However, rather than use three-word sequences of grammatical code as the basis for the analysis as in chapter 2, a six word sequence has been found to provide greater discrimination.[53] The results of such an analysis as applied to Mk 13—each letter representing a word in the chapter, as indicated in the adjacent key—are printed on the next page.

Obviously it would be possible to manufacture perfect negative correlation between the unique syntax of chapter 2 and the recurrent syntax above if the same phrase lengths were used in the analysis. But this would achieve nothing except to show that recurrent syntax is not unique syntax. However given that 6-word sequences have been used here, and thereby the likelihood of recurrent syntax dramatically reduced, it is particularly interesting to notice where these 'most Markan of all phrases' occur in Mk 13—especially the concentration around vv.24-27. The implications are that of all the sections in Mk 13, this one (vv.24-27) is the most in keeping with the syntax of the Gospel as a whole.[54] This fact is not picked up by any of the other approaches to locating distinctive Markan syntax or vocabulary. Apart from the phrases ἐν ἐκείναις ταῖς ἡμέραις and μετὰ τὴν θλῖψιν ἐκείνην in v.24 and some of the Son of Man language in v.26, the section vv.24-27 has not been regarded as particularly redactional or as representative of distinctive Markan sources. It has generally been located, along with vv.14-20, as part of the pre-Markan tradition. But it is now even more apparent that vv.14-20, with the highest percentage of *unique* syntax of any section in the Gospel of Mark, and vv.24-27, with an unusual concentration of *recurrent* syntax, can hardly have been part of the same source originally. Further, it can be argued that since vv.24-27 is so syntactically 'at home' in the Gospel of Mark it must at least have been added, if not *written,* by the author from those sources typical of the rest of the Gospel narrative.[55]

---

[53] Again, sequences of various lengths were tried, but anything shorter than six words led to almost everything being classed as recurrent. See Appendix 2 for the full list of recurrent six-word sequences in the Gospel of Mark.

[54] The actual percentages of recurrent syntax for the sections in Mk 13 are as follows: vv.1-2 (17.5%); 3-6 (43.3%); 7-8 (39.4%); 9-13 (52.6%); 14-20 (12.9%); 21-23 (16.2%); 24-27 (71.8%); 28-31 (56.9%); 32-37 (54.0%).

[55] In fact a combination of the two—selected *and* written—is perhaps the most likely process in this case. Clearly the vocabulary of vv.24-27 is Septuagintal (see chapter 3 above), whereas the syntax is just as plainly Markan—indicating that perhaps the passage was compiled by the author of Mark out of Septuagintal language.

These are the sorts of conclusions that an analysis of recurrent syntax may support, but only after a careful comparison with other methods of determining Markan vocabulary, syntax and phraseology. So by including a summary of this information on Text Sheet 5 below, which includes the evidence of the other indicators of Markan redaction analysed above, a clearer picture of the most probable areas of authorial intervention in the chapter emerges.

Recurrent syntax (6-word sequences) in Mk 13

13.1 C VP R P D A VI R A D N R N Q A N C A N. 13.2 C D N VI R VI A D A N B B VS B N P N A B B VS.

13.3 C VP R P D N D N P D A VI R P A N C N C N C N 13.4 VM R B A VI C A D N C VS+ A +VN A. 13.5 D C N VI VN R VM C A R VS 13.6 A VI P D N R VP C R VI C A VI. 13.7 C C VS N C N N B VM VI VN C B D N. 13.8 VI C N P N C N P N VI N P N VI N N/N N N A. 13.9 VM C R R VI R P N C P N VI C P N C N VI P R P N R. 13.10 C P A D N A@B VI VN D N. 13.11 C C VS R VP B VM A VS C A+ Q VS R P A D N A VM B C VI R D@R&A VP C D N D A. 13.12 C VI N N P N C N N C VI N P N C VI R 13.13 C VI+ +VP P A P D N R D@A+ C VP P N A VI.

13.14 C C VS D N D N VP C B VI D@R&A VP VM B D P D N VM P D N 13.15 D [C] P D N B VM C VM VN A P D N R 13.16 C D P D N B VM P D B@A VN D N R. 13.17 Q C D@R&A P N VP C D@R&A VP P A D N. 13.18 VM C C B VS N 13.19 VI C D N A N A B VI A P N N A VI D N P D B@A C B B VS. 13.20 C C B VI N D N B Q VI A N C P D A A VI VI D N. 13.21 C B C A R VS Q B D N Q B B VM 13.22 VI C N C N C VI N C N P D VN C A D A. 13.23 R C VM VI R A.

13.24 C P A D N P D N A D N VI C D N B VI D N R 13.25 C D N VI+ P D N +VP C D N D P D N VI. 13.26 C B VI D N D N VP P N P N A C N. 13.27 C B VI D N C VI D A [R] P D A N P N N P N N.

13.28 P C D N VM D N C B D N R A VS C VS D N VI C B D N VI. 13.29 B B B R C VS A VP VI/VM C B VI P N. 13.30 Q VI R C B B VS D N A P A@A&A A A VS. 13.31 D N C D N VI D C N R B B VI. 13.32 P C D N A C D N A VI B D N P N C&B D N C B D N. 13.33 VM VM B VI C B D N VI. 13.34 C N A VP D N R C VP D N R D N A D N R C D N VI C VS. 13.35 VM C B VI C B D N D N VI C B C N C N C B 13.36 C VP B VS R VP. 13.37 A@A&A C R VI A VI VM.

Key: Single underlining = part of a recurrent 6-word syntactical sequence
         Double underlining = overlapping of recurrent 6-word sequences

A = Adjective   B = Adverb   C = Conjunction   D = Determiner (article)
Q = Particle (sentential, interrogative or verbal)   R = Pronoun
V = Verb   VI = Verb, Indicative mood   VM = Verb, Imperative mood
             VN = Verb, Infinitive   VO = Verb, Optative mood
             VP = Verb, Participle   VS = Verb, Subjunctive mood
             VR = Verb, Participle (imperative sense)
@ = 'used as'
& = 'and' (that is, both analyses apply, often because crasis has occurred)
+ = connector (showing links between parts of a periphrastic verb, for example)
[ ] = brackets as used around doubtful parts of the Greek Text
(See Appendix 1 for further information).

Because recurrent syntax may indicate the recurrent use of a source as much as it indicates Markan redaction, it will only be shown on the Text Sheet below if it is supported by one (indicated by single underlining) or two (by double underlining) of the other indicators of redaction. If all four of the other indicators of redaction agree against the indications of recurrent syntax, then this will also be represented by double underlining. The result is a fairly conservative estimate of the most likely parts of Mk 13 to have been *composed* by the author of the Gospel. Some indications of possible insertions of tradition by the author will also be given by marking those places where asyndeton occurs, both at the grammatical level and at the level of the underlying syntactical sequences. But this aspect of redaction analysis—the insertion and ordering of traditions (macro-redaction or composition analysis)—will be examined more fully in the next chapter.

Text Sheet 5: Summary of the indicators of redaction in Mark 13

13.1 Καὶ ἐκπορευομένου αὐτοῦ ἐκ τοῦ ἱεροῦ λέγει αὐτῷ εἷς τῶν μαθητῶν αὐτοῦ, Διδάσκαλε, ἴδε ποταποὶ λίθοι καὶ ποταπαὶ οἰκοδομαί. 2 καὶ ὁ Ἰησοῦς εἶπεν αὐτῷ, [[Βλέπεις ταύτας τὰς μεγάλας οἰκοδομάς; οὐ μὴ ἀφεθῇ ὧδε λίθος ἐπὶ λίθον ὅς οὐ μὴ καταλυθῇ.]]
3 Καὶ καθημένου αὐτοῦ εἰς τὸ Ὄρος τῶν Ἐλαιῶν κατέναντι τοῦ ἱεροῦ ἐπηρώτα αὐτὸν κατ᾽ ἰδίαν Πέτρος καὶ Ἰάκωβος καὶ Ἰωάννης καὶ Ἀνδρέας. 4 //Εἰπὸν ἡμῖν πότε ταῦτα ἔσται, καὶ τί τὸ σημεῖον ὅταν μέλλῃ ταῦτα συντελεῖσθαι πάντα. 5 //ὁ δὲ Ἰησοῦς ἤρξατο λέγειν αὐτοῖς, βλέπετε μή τις ὑμᾶς πλανήσῃ· 6 /πολλοὶ ἐλεύσονται ἐπὶ τῷ ὀνόματί μου λέγοντες ὅτι Ἐγώ εἰμι, καὶ πολλοὺς πλανήσουσιν. 7 [[ὅταν δὲ ἀκούσητε πολέμους καὶ ἀκοὰς πολέμων, μὴ θροεῖσθε· /δεῖ γενέσθαι, ἀλλ᾽ οὔπω τὸ τέλος. 8 ἐγερθήσεται γὰρ ἔθνος ἐπ᾽ ἔθνος καὶ βασιλεία ἐπὶ βασιλείαν, /ἔσονται σεισμοὶ κατὰ τόπους, /ἔσονται λιμοί· /ἀρχὴ ὠδίνων ταῦτα.]]
9 βλέπετε δὲ ὑμεῖς ἑαυτούς· /παραδώσουσιν ὑμᾶς εἰς συνέδρια καὶ εἰς συναγωγὰς δαρήσεσθε καὶ ἐπὶ ἡγεμόνων καὶ βασιλέων σταθήσεσθε ἕνεκεν ἐμοῦ εἰς μαρτύριον αὐτοῖς. 10 καὶ εἰς πάντα τὰ ἔθνη πρῶτον δεῖ κηρυχθῆναι τὸ εὐαγγέλιον. 11 [[καὶ ὅταν ἄγωσιν ὑμᾶς παραδιδόντες, μὴ προμεριμνᾶτε τί λαλήσετε,]] ἀλλ᾽ ὃ ἐὰν δοθῇ ὑμῖν ἐν ἐκείνῃ τῇ ὥρᾳ τοῦτο λαλεῖτε, [[οὐ γάρ ἐστε ὑμεῖς οἱ λαλοῦντες ἀλλὰ τὸ πνεῦμα τὸ ἅγιον. 12 καὶ παραδώσει ἀδελφὸς ἀδελφὸν εἰς θάνατον καὶ πατὴρ τέκνον, καὶ ἐπαναστήσονται τέκνα ἐπὶ γονεῖς καὶ θανατώσουσιν αὐτούς· 13 καὶ ἔσεσθε μισούμενοι ὑπὸ πάντων διὰ τὸ ὄνομά μου.]]//[[ὁ δὲ ὑπομείνας εἰς τέλος οὗτος σωθήσεται.]]
14 [[Ὅταν δὲ ἴδητε τὸ βδέλυγμα τῆς ἐρημώσεως ἐστηκότα ὅπου οὐ δεῖ, ὁ ἀναγινώσκων νοείτω, τότε οἱ ἐν τῇ Ἰουδαίᾳ φευγέτωσαν εἰς τὰ ὄρη, 15 ὁ δὲ ἐπὶ τοῦ δώματος μὴ καταβάτω μηδὲ εἰσελθάτω ἆραί τι ἐκ τῆς οἰκίας αὐτοῦ, 16 καὶ ὁ εἰς τὸν ἀγρὸν μὴ ἐπιστρεψάτω εἰς τὰ ὀπίσω ἆραι τὸ ἱμάτιον αὐτοῦ. 17 οὐαὶ δὲ ταῖς ἐν γαστρὶ ἐχούσαις καὶ ταῖς θηλαζούσαις ἐν ἐκείναις ταῖς ἡμέραις. 18 προσεύχεσθε δὲ ἵνα μὴ γένηται χειμῶνος· 19 ἔσονται γὰρ αἱ ἡμέραι ἐκεῖναι θλῖψις οἵα οὐ γέγονεν τοιαύτη ἀπ᾽ ἀρχῆς κτίσεως ἣν ἔκτισεν ὁ θεὸς ἕως τοῦ νῦν καὶ οὐ μὴ γένηται. 20 καὶ εἰ μὴ ἐκολόβωσεν κύριος τὰς ἡμέρας, οὐκ ἂν ἐσώθη πᾶσα σάρξ. ἀλλὰ διὰ τοὺς ἐκλεκτοὺς οὓς ἐξελέξατο ἐκολόβωσεν τὰς ἡμέρας. 21

καὶ τότε ἐάν τις ὑμῖν εἴπῃ, Ἴδε ὧδε ὁ Χριστός, Ἴδε ἐκεῖ, μὴ πιστεύετε·]] 22 [[ἐγερθήσονται γὰρ <u>ψευδόχριστοι καὶ ψευδοπροφῆται</u> καὶ δώσουσιν σημεῖα καὶ τέρατα πρὸς τὸ ἀποπλανᾶν, εἰ δυνατόν, τοὺς ἐκλεκτούς.]] 23 ὑμεῖς δὲ βλέπετε· προείρηκα ὑμῖν πάντα.

24 [[ʼΑλλὰ <u>ἐν ἐκείναις ταῖς ἡμέραις μετὰ τὴν θλῖψιν ἐκείνην</u>

ὁ ἥλιος σκοτισθήσεται,

καὶ ἡ σελήνη οὐ δώσει τὸ φέγγος αὐτῆς,

25 καὶ οἱ ἀστέρες ἔσονται ἐκ τοῦ οὐρανοῦ πίπτοντες,

καὶ αἱ δυνάμεις αἱ ἐν τοῖς οὐρανοῖς σαλευθήσονται.

26 καὶ τότε ὄψονται τὸν υἱὸν τοῦ ἀνθρώπου ἐρχόμενον ἐν νεφέλαις μετὰ δυνάμεως πολλῆς καὶ δόξης. 27 καὶ τότε ἀποστελεῖ τοὺς ἀγγέλους καὶ ἐπισυνάξει <u>τοὺς ἐκλεκτοὺς αὐτοῦ</u> ἐκ τῶν τεσσάρων ἀνέμων ἀπʼ ἄκρου γῆς ἕως ἄκρου οὐρανοῦ.]]

28 Ἀπὸ δὲ τῆς συκῆς μάθετε τὴν παραβολήν· ὅταν ἤδη ὁ κλάδος αὐτῆς ἁπαλὸς γένηται καὶ ἐκφύῃ τὰ φύλλα, γινώσκετε ὅτι ἐγγὺς τὸ θέρος ἐστίν. 29 οὕτως καὶ ὑμεῖς, ὅταν ἴδητε ταῦτα γινόμενα γινώσκετε ὅτι ἐγγύς ἐστιν ἐπὶ θύραις. 30 //[[ἀμὴν λέγω ὑμῖν ὅτι οὐ μὴ παρέλθῃ ἡ γενεὰ αὕτη μέχρις οὗ ταῦτα πάντα γένηται. 31 ὁ οὐρανὸς καὶ ἡ γῆ παρελεύσονται, οἱ δὲ λόγοι μου οὐ μὴ παρελεύσονται.]] 32 //περὶ δὲ τῆς ἡμέρας ἐκείνης ἢ τῆς ὥρας οὐδεὶς οἶδεν, οὐδὲ οἱ ἄγγελοι ἐν οὐρανῷ οὐδὲ ὁ υἱός, εἰ μὴ ὁ πατήρ. 33 <u>βλέπετε ἀγρυπνεῖτε· οὐκ οἴδατε γὰρ πότε ὁ καιρός ἐστιν.</u> 34 //[[ὡς ἄνθρωπος ἀπόδημος ἀφεὶς τὴν οἰκίαν αὐτοῦ καὶ δοὺς τοῖς δούλοις αὐτοῦ τὴν ἐξουσίαν, ἑκάστῳ τὸ ἔργον αὐτοῦ, καὶ τῷ θυρωρῷ ἐνετείλατο ἵνα γρηγορῇ.]] 35 //γρηγορεῖτε οὖν, οὐκ οἴδατε γὰρ πότε ὁ κύριος τῆς οἰκίας ἔρχεται, ἢ ὀψὲ ἢ μεσονύκτιον ἢ ἀλεκτοροφωνίας ἢ πρωΐ, 36 μὴ ἐλθὼν ἐξαίφνης εὕρῃ ὑμᾶς καθεύδοντας. 37 //ὃ δὲ ὑμῖν λέγω, πᾶσιν λέγω, γρηγορεῖτε.//

Key: See Appendix 4 for the complete details regarding the indicators of redaction.

[[Square brackets]]	= Units of tradition already identified (see chapter 3)
<u>Single underlining</u>	= Possible redaction (2 or 3 indicators of redaction)
<u>Double underlining</u>	= Most likely redaction (4 indicators of redaction, or recurrent syntax plus 2 indicators)
// = Unique syntax across major punctuation break (evidence of insertion)	
/ = Asyndeta (lack of connecting links—possible insertion)	

Redaction in Mk 13

Those methods used for determining Markan redaction which are based on vocabulary and syntax point to the most likely Markan composition as occurring in vv.1a,3,(5a),6a,7c,9b,10,(11c),24a,(33), and possibly short phrases in vv.11,20,22 and 27. Of these phrases, vv.11 and 20 may be discounted in that they are firmly embedded in traditions already established in chapter 3 above, and they only stand out as possible redaction because of their Semitic syntax, which recurs throughout the Gospel due to the widespread use of the Septuagint. On the other hand, the phrase τοὺς ἐκλεκτοὺς αὐτοῦ in v.27 and at least the ψευδοχρίστοι of v.22 stand outside the tradition alluded to in each case, and it is possible to see profound reasons behind their redactional inclusion—possibilities which will be explored further in the chapters still to come.

Of course such results do not exhaust the possible extent of authorial involvement in compiling the discourse. Besides these possible examples of Markan composition, there are the wider questions of the selecting, ordering and structuring of traditions which will be examined more closely in the next chapter. But even in the evidence presented above there are indications of interruptions in the normal sequence of Markan syntax across major punctuation breaks, suggesting that traditions from diverse sources have been drawn together. It is therefore quite likely that vv.4,13b,30-31,35-36 and 37, have been added to the discourse at some stage, and the occurrence of asyndeton in vv.6,7b,8b,8c,9b and 34 may also indicate the selection and arrangement of traditions. The exploration of the theology, structure and narrative flow of the Gospel in the next chapter should help to decide just how much of this editorial activity can be attributed to the author of the Gospel and how much occurred in the pre-Markan tradition.

The exceptionally high incidence of recurrent syntax in vv.24-27, and the virtual absence of vocabulary-based indicators of redaction, confirms the suspicion that these verses were formed by a Markan arrangement of Septuagintal language. Not only is the multiple allusion to the OT similar to other key texts in the Gospel of Mark (see chapter 3 above), but its syntactical structure is entirely consistent with that of the Gospel as a whole. Similarly, the virtual absence of recurrent syntax in vv.14-21 supports the view that these verses derive from a unique pre-Markan source. It is significant that those verses displaying the next highest amount of recurrent syntax after vv.24-27 are (in descending order) vv.28-31,32-37,9-13, and 3-6. It could thus be concluded that there is also a significant amount of Markan arrangement in these verses, even though it does not show up on the Text Sheet above as likely Markan composition.

Already this evidence from vocabulary and syntax points to major authorial contributions at vv.1a,3,10 and 24. This would indicate that the double setting of the discourse (vv.1 and 3) is a Markan creation, and that two of the crucial time indicators (πρῶτον v.10, and μετά v.24) are significant references from the authorial point of view. From the standpoint of literary composition and of comparisons with other apocalyptic literature there may well be grounds for attributing further structuring devices in the discourse to the hand of the author—especially vv.23 and 37, for example—but it is important that the more objective indicators of redaction be allowed to set the parameters of the discussion first. Those redaction-critical methods which focus on the literary and theological intentions of the author can then be explored without the danger of attributing full creative control over all of the material to the major editor. Clearly the discourse is a synthesis of tradition *and* redaction—of inherited truth *and* reinterpreted truth—and an awareness of the tension between the two must be kept at all times.

V

A CHRISTIAN PROPHETIC ORACLE

Major proponents: Hahn (1975); Pesch (1977, 1980); [also Gaston (1970);
    Boring (1982); Theissen (1991)].
Basic thesis: That underlying Mk 13 is a Jewish Christian discourse dating from
    the Jewish war (so Hahn, Pesch), or Caligula's threat to erect a statue in
    the temple (Gaston, Boring, Theissen).
Dominant method: Redaction (composition) criticism.
Critique: An evaluation of the author's literary and theological preferences.

The 'new direction' that Pesch regards FERDINAND HAHN as having
given to the interpretation of Mk 13 involves Hahn's perception of the use
in the chapter of an *extended* Jewish Christian prophetic apocalypse. He
sees this as originating at the time of the Jewish war and as including
vv.9b,11-13,21-22 and 28-31, together with the commonly identified
apocalyptic sections in vv.7-8,14-20 and 24-27.[1] The related arguments
regarding the origin of this oracle are not new (and are not endorsed by
Hahn), but are developments of ancient interpretations. These are: that
part of Mk 13 comprises the oracle (χρησμός) mentioned by Eusebius as
having directed the Judean communities to flee to Pella (trans-Jordan) in
the face of the Jewish war, as argued by Pesch in his commentary; and the
arguments by Gaston, Boring and now Theissen that the oracle originates
at the time of the Caligula episode in the early 40's.[2] Rather, it is the

---

[1] Hahn, "Die Rede". Hereafter in this section page numbers for this article will be
given in brackets in the main body of the text. Others have also argued for an extended
Christian source, but less convincingly. L. Gaston, *No Stone,* suggests that Christian
prophetic sources lie behind Mk 13, but in three phases: vv.14-19 (originally relating to
Caligula); vv.20 and 24-27; and vv.5-13,21-22,28-36. Markan redaction is responsible
for vv.1-4,23,37 and 14b—making v.14 a reference to the antichrist. Thus Gaston turns
the analysis of the form critics on its head and argues that "the framework of the discourse
is provided by the parenetic, to which the apocalyptic elements have been 'added.'" (*No
Stone,* 52). These results show some insight (in the separation of vv.14-19 and 24-27,
for example) but are dependent to a certain degree on a false dichotomy between parenesis
and apocalyptic elements (see chapter 6 below), and a text critical analysis which inserts
an additional three uses of γάρ into vv.6, 7b and 9b (see Intro., pages 25-6, above).

[2] Hahn, "Die Rede", 241, cites H. J. Schoeps, "Ebionitische Apokalyptik im Neuen
Testament", *ZNW* 51 (1960), 101-111, as a developer of the Eusebian oracle thesis, and
makes reference to W. Grundmann's view that vv.14-27 originate from a Christian
prophet similar to the Agabus mentioned in Acts 11:28. See *Das Evangelium nach Markus*
(THK II), (Berlin, 2nd ed, 1959), 266. But Hahn himself cannot be held responsible for
the resurgence of the Pella thesis as some have claimed, nor counted among its adherents
(*contra* Boring, *Sayings,* 193 and footnote 34, 283-4). Neirynck, "Marc 13", 566, traces
the thesis back to the ancient commentaries (Lucas Brugensis, 394CE), and Beasley-
Murray, *Jesus and the Future,* 242-244, also gives a history of references to 'The Oracle

extended list of verses suggested by Hahn as being part of the Jewish Christian source that is unusual, and particularly the inclusion of the fig-tree parable in vv.28-29. Hahn is of the opinion that only with the allocation of vv.28-31 to the pre-Markan tradition can a satisfactory explanation of the whole eschatological discourse be gained (244). He bases this allocation on the following arguments:

    (i)   Although non-Markan in its Christology, v.32 stands in such contrast to v.30 that it clearly must have been added later to limit the expectation generated by vv.30-31 and to provide a transition to vv.33-37, which are almost universally recognised as a Markan construction.

    (ii)   Vv.28-31 are a self-contained unit carefully shaped as a conclusion—vv.28-29 with an emphasis on ἐγγύς ἐστιν, referring to the events of vv.14f immediately preceding the parousia; and vv.30-31 emphasizing ταῦτα πάντα, meaning the completion of *all* the eschatological events in vv.14-27, including the coming of the Son of Man.

    (iii)   It becomes even clearer that vv.28-31 belong with vv.7-27 when the dual use of ὅταν in vv.28-29 and in vv.7 and 14 is examined. The events *heard* in vv.7f are a preparation for the events *seen* in vv.14f, these latter visible events again being referred to by the 'growing buds' and development of leaves in v.28, and the ὅταν ἴδητε of v.29b (247).

Hahn then goes on to argue that vv.21-22 are inseparable from vv.19-20 because the seduction of the ἐκλεκτοί is at stake in each of these sections. He claims that the καὶ τότε of v.21a, just as the μετὰ τὴν θλῖψιν ἐκείνην in v.24a, plays no part in structuring the speech,[3] but that ὅταν and ταῦτα/ταῦτα πάντα fulfill that function. Thus Hahn sees no breaks in the narrative between vv.20 and 21, nor between vv.22 and 24, arguing that the events of vv.14-22 and 24-27, whilst not immediately linked, are a unit and occur in a certain sequence. However, he does concede the redactional nature of the exhortation βλέπετε and the rest of v.23, without really explaining why the evangelist felt it necessary to insert the verse into vv.14-27, interrupting what Hahn sees as a unit.[4]

---

of Eusebius' in the literature on Mk 13. As regards the Caligula theory, Theissen, *The Gospels in Context,* 137ff, and N. H. Taylor, "Palestinian Christianity and the Caligula Crisis. Part 1. Social and Historical Reconstruction", *JSNT* 61 (1996), 101-124; and "Part II. The Markan Eschatological Discourse", *JSNT* 62 (1996), 13-41, have made the most eloquent and recent defences, with Gaston (see footnote 1 above) and Boring (footnote 28 below) arguing along similar lines. These authors are significant contributors to the debate, though they each address Mk 13 in the context of other wider issues.

  [3] "Die Rede", 248. *Contra* Pesch, *Naherwartungen,* 157.

  [4] The alternative is to see v.23 as indicating the standpoint of the author of Mark reassuring the community being addressed that all they have experienced has been within the prophetic foreknowledge of Jesus, and thus the plan of God. See Pesch's views in the discussion of his commentary in this section, and Brandenburger's comments in chapter 6 below.

Hahn continues to work backwards through chapter 13, arguing on stylistic grounds that vv.5f, using ἐπὶ τῷ ὀνόματί μου and ἐγώ εἰμι rather than the more traditional apocalyptic terminology of v.21: "Ἴδε ὧδε ὁ Χριστός, Ἴδε ἐκεῖ, constitute a different level of statement which is more likely to have been formed by the evangelist in a manner analogous to vv.21f. But although vv.9-13, with their juxtaposition of short sentences, also display a style at odds with vv.7f and 14-27, Hahn points to the strong link word παραδιδόναι in vv.9b,11 and 12, and to the less foreign style of vv.10 and 12, as evidence for this section also possibly being part of the pre-Markan speech. The redactional status of v.10 is not finally resolved by Hahn, who sees that it could have been used by the evangelist to limit expectation of the coming of the Son of Man, or, if a part of the source, it could be a description of the missionary activity of the persecuted church in the period immediately prior to the final tribulation, when such mission would no longer be possible (257).

Thus far, Hahn lists the Markan redaction in the chapter as being the βλέπετε exhortations and their immediate contexts in vv.5-6,9a,23 and 33-37. But by far the most significant redactional work by the author in reinterpreting the discourse is, according to Hahn, the reworking of the setting in vv.1-4, and in particular the double question of the disciples. He argues for the traditional nature of the characteristically brief and isolated apophthegm in vv.1-2, and points out the significance of the anti-temple theme in the Gospel of Mark,[5] highlighted in this context by the location of the discourse on the Mount of Olives κατέναντι τοῦ ἱεροῦ. The temple, therefore, must still be a relevant theme for the chapter since it provides the setting and the occasion for the discourse. However, Hahn argues that the redactional two-part question of the disciples effectively

---

[5] See, for example, the judgment of the temple in 11:15-17, the temple logia in 14:58 and 15:29, and the tearing of the temple curtain in 15:38. Hahn, "Die Rede", 252. A much fuller treatment of these texts is given in Gill, "Cleansing", I/60f. That vv.1-2 are traditional and therefore part of the basis for the theme in the Gospel is disputed by Pesch, *Naherwartungen*, 87, 93f, who argues that v.2c is redactional; and by Gnilka, *Markus*, 184, who regards the prophecy as *ex eventu* since it too closely describes the condition of the temple precinct after the Jewish war. But two factors count against this view:

(i)   According to Josephus, the temple building itself was burnt to the ground, yet no mention is made of this in the prophecy [see Schweizer, *Mark*, 267; and those scholars already mentioned as having been cited by Kümmel, *Promise and Fulfilment*, 100 (see chapter 1, footnote 29 above). Schweizer also argues (*Mark*, 262) that the prophecy must have originated with Jesus because it caused the early church so much embarrassment].

(ii) Stones of the retaining wall of the temple compound, larger than those used in the pyramids, *do* remain 'one on another' to this very day and may be viewed beneath the streets of Jerusalem. Recent archæological discoveries indicate that the "Temple Mount proper continued to stand as an impressive structure; in fact its walls rose to an appreciable height for centuries thereafter." Meir Ben-Dov, *In the Shadow of the Temple. The Discovery of Ancient Jerusalem* (New York 1985), 186.

Thus the grounds for regarding 13:1-2 as prophecy *ex eventu* are weak, and when the charges laid against Jesus at his trial are considered, the case for regarding these verses as representing historical words of Jesus is quite strong.

divides and reinterprets the discourse in keeping with each part of the question:

(i) πότε ταῦτα ἔσται—concerning the destruction of the temple, prophesied in v.2 and answered in vv.7-13;[6]

(ii) τί τὸ **σημεῖον** ὅταν μέλλῃ **ταῦτα** συντελεῖσθαι **πάντα**—concerning the end times and their sign, the ταῦτα πάντα referring to vv.14-27 inclusive, (as argued previously), and the σημεῖον referring specifically to v.14.

In this way Hahn sees the author of Mark separating the destruction of the temple (vv.7-13) from the expectation of the great tribulation and the coming of the Son of Man (vv.14-27).[7] The implications of this division are that the events 'heard of' in vv.7-13 include the Jewish war of 66-70 CE *and* the destruction of the temple—events which are historical ones for the evangelist and his community,[8] whereas the events to be 'seen' in vv.14-27 remain in the future and are preceded by a sign in v.14, τὸ βδέλυγμα τῆς ἐρημώσεως, which must now refer to something other than the already destroyed temple. Pointing to the fact that the masculine accusative ἑστηκότα is used, and that this 'standing' will be ὅπου οὐ δεῖ, Hahn supports the view that the 'awful horror' must, for the evangelist, be a reference to an antichrist figure.[9] He thinks it rather doubtful that this is what the source originally intended by v.14, as vv.21-22 specifically mention ψευδόχριστοι (plural) and ψευδοπροφῆται, and Hahn has attributed these verses to the source. Indeed, if it could be shown that these verses are redactional, then it would be very difficult to sustain the view that the author of Mark intended v.14 to be a reference

---

[6] This differs from Pesch, *Naherwartungen,* 104, 179f, who distinguishes between the ταῦτα and ταῦτα πάντα (unlike Lambrecht, *Die Redaktion,* 207f, who seems to consider them interchangeable terms), but links them with vv.5-23 and 24-27 respectively, rather than the vv.5-13 and 14-27 argued by Hahn, "Die Rede", 253, and footnote 55.

[7] Hahn, "Die Rede", 253, footnote 54, and 254.

[8] There is fairly widespread agreement that the destruction of the temple had already taken place before the writing of the Gospel of Mark, although note the dissenting views of the following: K. Grayston, "The Study of Mark 13", *BJRL* 56 (1973-74), 371-387, who argues that the hostility to the temple and the priesthood in Mark is so strong that it must have been written at a time when both were still threats to Christianity. A similar argument is made by Myers, *Strong Man,* 41f. Also influential is the view of Hengel, *Studies,* 1-28, that chapter 13—particularly vv.6-13—reflect the situation between the winter of 68/69 and the winter of 69/70. There is less agreement over what part of chapter 13 shows that the temple has been destroyed: vv.7-13? [so Hahn, "Die Rede", 254, after N. Walter, "Tempelzerstörung und synoptische Apokalypse", *ZNW* 57 (1966), 41f]; v.14? [so Pesch, *Naherwartungen,* 121, 139f, 143]; or vv.17-20? [so Lambrecht, *Die Redaktion,* 172, who sees v.14 as the sign preceding the destruction in vv.17-20].

[9] Hahn, "Die Rede", 255. The following scholars are cited in support of this view: Klostermann, Lohmeyer, Schniewind, Schmid, Marxsen (see chapter 4, footnote 7 above), Walter, de Tillesse, and partly, Lambrecht, who emphasizes that a person is meant but does not say anything further about their identity. Also supporting this view are L. Gaston, *No Stone,* 61f, and Morna D. Hooker, "Trial and Tribulation in Mark XIII", *BJRL* 65 (1982), 78-99, besides Hartman, *Prophecy Interpreted,* discussed in chapter 3, footnote 9 above.

to the antichrist, as the concept of an antichrist does not fit well with the notion of many false-Christs. Even Hahn's suggestion that vv.5-6 were fashioned by the evangelist after vv.21-22 would seem to weaken the case for a redactional interest in an antichrist figure as a sign of the end.

As a consequence of this reinterpretation of the discourse by means of the double question of the disciples, Hahn concludes that ἀλλ' οὔπω τὸ τέλος in v.7, often attributed to the evangelist, must in fact be part of the source. This is because it is parallel to the use of τέλος in v.13b, which in turn accords with the delineation of the 'end' in vv.28-31 as being the events of vv.14-27 and not vv.7f. Thus the description of the events of vv.7f as 'not yet the end' fits well with Hahn's conception of the source, these events being under the influence of apocalyptic necessity and soon to occur (for the readers of the source), but decidedly not yet the τέλος and only indirectly connected with it. In contrast, the Markan community has experienced these events, according to Hahn, and the evangelist wishes to show the close proximity of the τέλος to them, hence the redactional description of them in v.8 as 'the beginning of labour'—a foretaste of the real thing, the θλῖψις such has not occurred since 'the beginning of the world'.[10]

Following this analysis of tradition and redaction, Hahn proceeds to examine specifically the *Sitz im Leben* of the pre-Markan parousia speech, and then of the Markan redaction itself. He sees the source (vv.7-8,9b,[10],11-13,14-20,21-22,24-27,28-31) as a speech written[11] within a Jewish Christian community in Judea—probably even Jerusalem itself—at the beginning of the Jewish war. In form, the speech is an extended interpretation of a genuine parable of Jesus (v.28) about the beginning of the Kingdom of God, utilizing some Jewish apocalyptic motifs, mainly from the book of Daniel, and with the interpretation placed *before* the parable.[12] In this way the parable has been transformed from one describing the beginning of the eschatological rule of God in Jesus' own life and message, to one anticipating the great tribulation preceding the fulfilment of salvation brought by the coming Son of Man. The source has already identified this Son of Man with Jesus,[13] according to Hahn, so it is Christian from the beginning, ruling out any possibility of a Jewish/Christian source dating from the threat of Caligula in 40 CE, or any other earlier incidents. Hahn reasons that the extensive but rather

[10] Hahn, "Die Rede", 254. Hahn also makes some use of vocabulary studies to establish the status of these two phrases in vv.7-8, contending that ἀρχή (also redactional in 1:1) is more distinctively Markan than τέλος (traditional in 3:26 and 13:13).

[11] Written—because of the phrase ὁ ἀναγινώσκων νοείτω, which implies the reading of the text (not Daniel!) by, or to, someone. Hahn, "Die Rede", 259, footnote 73.

[12] Hahn, "Die Rede", 258, concedes that v.29 may also be an early interpretation, or clarification, of the parable that became attached to it earlier in the tradition.

[13] Hahn, "Die Rede", 262, claims that in all the statements about the Son of Man in Mark the identification with Jesus has already been carried out in the pre-Markan tradition. He concedes that lying behind 8:38 there may be an even earlier tradition that had not yet made that equation.

selective use of Jewish apocalyptic motifs in the speech is characteristic of
the application of Jewish ideas in the proclamation of the early church.[14]

The ἐκλεκτοί of the source (vv.20,22 and 27) are therefore the
members of this Jewish Christian community, who are attempting to
understand their experience of persecution in the period between Easter
and the promised fulfilment of salvation. They expect that some sort of
desecration of the temple (v.14) will be the sign for the imminent return
of Jesus, coming as the powerful Son of Man to gather the chosen ones. In
the present they only 'hear' of 'wars and rumours of wars' (vv.7f) as the
Roman campaigns begin in Galilee round 66 CE. But when certain events,
the exact nature of which are unknown, are 'seen' in the temple area, it
will be time to flee—not specifically to Galilee (as Marxsen and, in a
different way, Pesch maintained) or Pella (as Pesch now maintains)[15]—
but simply to flee, as the coming of the Son of Man to gather the 'elect'
has been linked intimately with the outcome of the war in the source.

But for the author of Mark and the Markan community, Hahn
maintains, the expectation of the nearness of the Lord in connection with
this war has been shattered. Not that the eschatological hope of the
evangelist is waning, but the continuing experience of persecution leads to
a reinterpretation of the sign of the end times—namely, from the
destruction of the temple to the appearance of the antichrist.[16] Thus the
whole period between the death of Jesus and the destruction of the temple
is represented by vv.5-8, and summarized by the evangelist as ἀρχὴ
ὠδίνων ταῦτα. The situation of the Markan community is then
represented by vv.9-15, and is understood to be an interim period
between the events of the Jewish war and the great tribulation which is
still to come—though not in any way so developed as the Lukan idea of a
separate 'age of the church'.[17]

This does not mean that for the evangelist, as for the source, the
beginning of the Kingdom of God is connected with events that are still to
come. On the contrary, Hahn sees that in the Gospel of Mark the
Kingdom is already present in the proclamation of Jesus (1:15), and
argues that the only two extended discourses of Jesus in the Gospel

[14] Hahn, "Die Rede", 261, footnote 78, in this way, gives qualified support to the
anti-Little Apocalyptic, catechetical interpretation of Beasley-Murray, although he does not
argue for the historicity of the majority of the discourse. Nor does Hahn agree with
Beasley-Murray's claim that chapter 13 displays a relative dearth of apocalyptic
tendencies.

[15] Hahn, "Die Rede", 259, footnote 74, rejects any specific destination for the
refugees—both on the level of Markan redaction and of the source itself. Pesch,
Naherwartungen, 232, modified Marxsen's thesis by suggesting that the *Jerusalem*
church should flee from Judea, through Galilee, as a bridge to bring Christianity to the
Gentiles—underlining the central importance of v.10.

[16] Hahn, "Die Rede", 263, argues that this same process—the emergence within the
Christian church of the Jewish expectation of an antichrist as the church experiences
persecution—has also occurred in 2 Thessalonians and Revelation.

[17] Hahn, "Die Rede", 264, and footnote 85, refers here to Conzelmann's thesis about
epochs of salvation history in Luke's writings.

(chapters 4 and 13) concur in this regard (264). Thus, for the evangelist, chapter 13 can only be a continuation of events leading up to the fulfilment of salvation, and in this way, Hahn maintains, the redactional understanding of the parable in v.28 as the centre-piece of the discourse is truer to the original intent of Jesus than is the interpretation in the source (264). For the author of Mark all the events from vv.5-37 are part of the eschatological drama, begun at Easter and continuing until the parousia of the Son of Man.

Hahn concludes his article by interacting with A. Vögtle's view of the significance of the 'cosmological metaphors' of vv.24-27. In this context, Hahn emphasizes that the concern of the source to relate eschatological events to domestic historical events is even greater in the Markan redaction, and that it might be more appropriate to regard the early Christians as holding on to specific cosmological statements in spite of their tendency to present events from an historical point of view, rather than speak of them using 'cosmological figurative speech' (265). For if the fulfilment of salvation includes the whole cosmos, Hahn argues, (13:10 again shows its importance in this connection), then the reality of this world cannot remain unaffected and therefore Mk 13:24f possess real, and not only metaphorical, meaning.

Hahn's work on Mk 13 is certainly stimulating and significant, not least because it was influential in changing the views of Pesch. Before examining Pesch's about-face in his commentary on the Gospel of Mark, there are two areas of concern regarding Hahn's analysis to be noted here for further development later. Firstly, the methodology Hahn uses to determine Markan redaction appears to be uneven and perhaps inconsistent. Stylistic grounds are given for excluding vv.5-6 from the source, yet are over-ridden when vv.9-13 are considered, and perhaps not considered sufficiently for vv.21-23. The main grounds for Hahn's *tour de force*—that the parable of v.28 is the key to understanding the source and, together with the double question of v. 4, the Markan redaction— seem to be theological, together with an analysis of the literary structure of the chapter. These factors—theology and literary structure—are certainly central to any attempt to discern the intent of the author, and where Hahn has related his findings to the rest of the Gospel he has many illuminating comments to make—the reference to the anti-temple theme being one of them. However, his insistence on the antichrist as the new sign intended by the evangelist in v.14 creates a theological oddity within the Gospel which is not related meaningfully to any suggested Markan *Sitz im Leben,* nor integrated adequately into an understanding of Markan theology. With regard to literary structure, Hahn takes little account of the importance of the ἀμήν saying in v.30, nor of the one substantial piece of redaction that he concedes between v.9 and v.31—namely, v.23. Thus if theology and literary structure are to be the determinative factors for the analysis of the discourse, they must first be guided by a thorough analysis of vocabulary, style and syntax, and then applied evenly across the Gospel as a whole.

The second major question to be asked of Hahn's conclusions concerns the comprehensive reinterpretation of the source undertaken by the author of Mark. Is it possible that such a 'recycling' of the prophecy of vv.14-27, fulfilled only in part in very recent memory, could have been made by the evangelist?[18] This would seem especially doubtful, and pastorally insensitive, since such a reinterpretation involves relegating the 'great tribulation' experienced by those fleeing from Jerusalem, to the mere 'beginning of birth-pangs' (v.8). Then again, even if v.14 has been reinterpreted to refer to an antichrist figure, what possible reinterpretation can be made of the verses following it, since they still appear to relate specifically to Judea? Hahn insists that we should not interpret them metaphorically, but what possible *Sitz im Leben* of the Markan community could require the re-use of these verses involving such specific geographical terms? Finally, whilst Hahn has certainly strengthened the case for regarding the source as a Jewish Christian one, he has not adequately accounted for the genesis of such a writing. Should it be regarded as Christian prophecy, exhortation, or perhaps even the oracle spoken of by Eusebius? These are some of the very questions taken up by Pesch in his commentary.

In his generally favourable comments on RUDOLF PESCH's first analysis of Mk 13, Frans Neirynck noted the cautious assessment of Markan redaction when compared with the work of Lambrecht.[19] Pesch comments in his explanation of his change of view that such an assessment could be used again to characterize his new position,[20] for a recurring feature of his two-volumed commentary is his perception of the author of Mark as a 'conservative redactor'. Having accepted this principle for the rest of his analysis of the Gospel, Pesch was forced to re-examine his

---

[18] Of course such a reinterpretation of 'failed prophecy' is well known in Biblical traditions and in the all-too-common experience of apocalyptic cults throughout history since. This is where theories of cognitive dissonance have provided helpful analytical models. See Robert P. Carroll, "Prophecy and Dissonance. A Theoretical Approach to the Prophetic Tradition", *ZAW* 92 (1980), 108-119. Hahn's reinterpretation provides an excellent opportunity for the application of such theories to prophetic literature—whereby the tension caused by the partially 'failed' prophecy of the source (Jerusalem *was* destroyed as in Mk 13:14-23, but the Son of Man *did not* come as expected in Mk 13:24-27), is resolved in Mark by reapplying the prophecy to an event still to come. This process itself is familiar and plausible, but the critical question is whether such a radical reinterpretation could occur in the brief time span (4 or 5 years?) between the origin of the source during the Jewish War and the writing of the Gospel of Mark shortly afterwards. More problematical still, could such a desperate move as this then be attributed to the historical Jesus within a generation of his existence and in the presence, presumably, of some who were familiar with the origin of the source in the Jerusalem church? See footnote 30 below for a more likely alternative.

[19] Neirynck, "Discours", 160 (=*Evangelica*, 604), thought Pesch showed "un jugement plus réservé sur l'activité rédactionelle".

[20] Pesch, "Markus 13", 355. Hereafter in this section, page numbers in brackets in the main body of the text shall refer to this article.

earlier conclusions in *Naherwartungen* where his perception of Markan redaction, although not as extensive as Lambrecht's, was still considerable.

Although as mentioned previously, Hartman and Hahn were influential in this re-examination, Pesch had already come to the conclusion that 13:1-2 was part of the pre-Markan passion story rather than a creation of the evangelist. According to Pesch, the pre-Markan passion story stretches back at least into chapters 11 (vv.11,15,27,35) and 12 (vv.41-44), and vv.1-2 of chapter 13 also fit the style and vocabulary of these verses.[21] They also provide a conclusion for the last day of Jesus in the temple, similar to the conclusion of the first and second visits in 11:11 and 19, and give grounds for the accusations brought against Jesus by the false-witnesses in 14:58 and the scoffers at the cross in 15:29. Thus Pesch now argues that this traditional scene provided the opportunity for the evangelist to insert the eschatological discourse into the rest of the Gospel.

As well as these re-evaluations of Markan redaction, Pesch also argues now for the traditional nature of vv.32 and 34-36, and is doubtful about the redactional status of v.10 (357). These conclusions necessitated a considerable rethinking of the extent of the source within the chapter. Forced by Hahn's analysis to re-assign the origin of the source from a Jewish apocalypse dating from 40 CE to a Jewish Christian exhortation from the Jewish war, Pesch nevertheless retains a distinctive reconstruction of both the source and its *Sitz im Leben*. Pesch agrees with Hahn that vv.28-31 form a conclusion to the pre-Markan apocalypse, but for different reasons—namely:

(i)   the appropriateness of v.31 as a solemn conclusion (it can be compared with Rv 22:6);[22]

(ii)   v.30 fits the historical situation, since almost a generation has passed between the death of Jesus and the destruction of the temple;

(iii) the connection between vv.4 and 30 is paralleled by the link between vv.14 and 29 (ὅταν . . . ἴδητε);

(iv)   the word θέρος (for the Hebrew ץיק/ץק), being a technical term for the end of time and used in v.29, has through Dn 11:27 and 12:7 already influenced the shaping of the question in v.4.

Pesch considers the disciples' question in v.4 only partly redactional (πότε ταῦτα ἔσται καί), along with ὅς οὐ μὴ καταλυθῇ (v.2), κατέναντι τοῦ ἱεροῦ (v.3), οὐ μὴ γένηται (v.19), ἐπὶ θύραις (v.29) and

---

[21] "Markus 13", 362. These are just the verses relating to Jesus in the temple. In fact the pre-Markan passion story suggested by Pesch is far more extensive, and replaces the 'first draft' of the Gospel into which chapter 13 was supposedly inserted according to Pesch's original thesis in *Naherwartungen*. Neirynck, "Marc 13", 565, outlines the full extent of Pesch's pre-Markan Passion account: chapters 8:27-33; 9:2-13,30-35; 10:1,32-34,46-52; 11:1-23,27-33; 12:1-17,34c,35-37,41-44; 13:1-2; and 14:1-16: 8.

[22] Pesch, *Das Markus-evangelium II*, 309.

all of vv.6,23,33 (excluding ἀγρυπνεῖτε) and 37, besides some less significant alterations.[23] This leaves a source consisting of vv.3-5 (minus the insertions outlined above),7-9,11-22 and 24-31, and involving the themes of:

(i)   the fulfilment of the end (v.4);
(ii) the Jewish war (vv.5,7-8);
(iii) the persecution of the Christian communities in Palestine (vv.9,11-13);
(iv) the expected suffering of Judea and Jerusalem (vv.14-20) and the resultant flight of the Judean community to Pella;
(v)   the threat of eschatological seduction (vv.21-22), and finally
(vi) the reassurance of the nearness of the end (vv.28-31), which is guaranteed by the words and promises of Jesus.

Unlike Hahn, Pesch sees no radical reinterpretation of a two-part source by the evangelist whereby vv.7f are assigned to the destruction of the temple and v.14 is re-used as an antichrist prophecy, with vv.9-15 representing the situation of the Markan community. Rather, Pesch regards v.23 as the indication of the Markan *Sitz im Leben,* and argues that vv.14-20 can be left intact by the evangelist because they are events known by all to be in the recent past (360). Verse 23 is therefore a reassurance to the readers that all that they have endured thus far has been within the scope of the prophetic words of Jesus.

The implications of relegating all of vv.5-22 to the immediate past for the evangelist's view of history and eschatology are profound. The events of vv.5-22 become merely 'pre-signs', whereas *the sign* of the fulfilment of salvation—asked about by the disciples in v.4—must be the cosmic drama of vv.24f which immediately precedes the coming Son of Man (366-7). This, of course, gives a radically different view of the Markan understanding of history from that proposed above by Hahn. In Pesch's understanding, the evangelist's expectation of the eschaton transcends history—in a sense, Jesus still refuses to give a 'sign' to any generation (as in 8:12) other than the coming of the fulfilment of the Kingdom itself. This is in striking contrast to Hahn, who has the evangelist reinterpreting the 'sign' to fit the historical events of a new generation.

Perhaps the most controversial aspect of Pesch's new thesis regarding the source behind Mk 13 is his strong support for the theory that this source was the oracle, referred to by Eusebius,[24] that led to the flight of the Jerusalem church to Pella in Transjordan. This view, resting so heavily on such a brief mention in Eusebius, has met with criticism from Gnilka and especially Neirynck,[25] but Pesch insists that it must at least be

---

[23] See Appendix 3 for complete redactional details.

[24] The reference is in EusEcclHist III, 5:3—"when finally the church community in Jerusalem received an order through a revelation (τινα χρησμόν) to their leaders to leave the city before the war, and to settle down in a city of Perea, named Pella".

[25] Gnilka, *Markus,* 211f, agrees, like Hahn, that the source is a Jewish Christian one written at the time of the Jewish war, but regards the Pella reference in Eusebius as much

considered rather than rejected from the outset. He vigorously defends this possibility—that the source is the χρησμός of Eusebius—by arguing that such a specific reference as Pella must have some basis in the tradition, and that this provides a better interpretation of vv.14f than any of the other historical or non-historical attempts.[26] Certainly if such a link could be established it would be of dramatic significance for the interpretation of the chapter but, short of some new archæological or manuscript evidence, it is extremely unlikely that Pesch's case can be sustained.[27] It would be far more profitable to examine any evidence connecting Mk 13 with early Christian prophecy in general rather than any tenuous link with the oracle of Eusebius. For if a possible *Sitz im Leben* for the source can be found in early Christian prophetic circles, then that alone would be sufficient to shed light on the formation and inclusion of the discourse in the Gospel of Mark.[28] Indeed, if Christian

---

too uncertain. Neirynck, "Marc 13", 370f, gives a very useful summary of the history of the theory, and also points out the obscurity of the single reference in Eusebius, arguing that it would be more likely that Eusebius wrote the account of the escape of the Jerusalem church based on Mk 13:14-20, Mt 24:15-22 (or Lk 21:20-22), rather than there being any other credible tradition behind his account. See further footnote 27 below.

[26] Pesch, "Markus 13", 363-365. Pesch does refer to other passages in Eusebius and rejects Neirynck's suggestion that Eusebius is 'creatively interpreting' the Synoptic accounts. As for non-historical interpretations of vv.14f, E. Haenchen, *Der Weg Jesu* (Berlin 1966), 444-447, argues that Judea has a symbolic meaning for the evangelist, who is really referring to the imposition by Rome of the cult of the emperor in *every* province of the Empire.

[27] See, for example, the critique of the historicity of the Pella tradition in general, and of any Synoptic connections in particular, by Gerd Lüdemann, "The Successors of Pre-70 Jerusalem Christianity: A Critical Evaluation of the Pella-Tradition", in *Jewish and Christian Self-Definition, Vol 1: The Shaping of Christianity in the Second and Third Centuries,* ed E. P. Sanders (London, 1980), 161-173, end-notes 245-254. Lüdemann argues that the Pella tradition is evidence for a Jewish Christian community in Pella in the second century which sought to claim apostolicity through continuity with the Jerusalem church, rather than evidence for the flight of the Jerusalem church during the Jewish war—though he does not deny that this latter event may well have taken place, at least in part. Lüdemann's conclusions have been challenged by Craig Koester, "The Origin and Significance of the Flight to Pella Tradition", *CBQ* 51 (1989), 90-106. Koester reviews the evidence of Eusebius, Epiphanius and the Pseudo-Clementine *Recognitions,* before returning an open verdict on the question as to whether Luke (21:20-22) was aware of the Pella tradition. Thus attempts to establish a *direct* link between the synoptic accounts and the Pella tradition appear to have been unsuccessful thus far, but this does not exclude the possibility that Mk 13 does contain a prophetic oracle of some kind which was sent to the Judeans during the Jewish war.

[28] The most thorough attempt to describe Mk 13 in terms of early Christian prophecy appears in Boring's *Sayings,* 183-203, endnotes 281-286. Boring regards vv.5b-31 as a unit consisting substantially of Christian prophecy emanating from the time of Caligula's threat to place his image in the temple in Jerusalem in the year 39-40 CE, an argument developed recently in some detail by Theissen, *The Gospels in Context,* particularly 151f, and N. H. Taylor, "Palestinian Christianity: Part II" (see footnote 2 above). Boring lists the features of Mk 13 that indicate Christian prophecy as: use of first-person speech for the risen Lord; use of ἐγώ εἰμι as a prophetic formula; frequent parenetic second-person plural imperatives; prophetic-eschatological vocabulary such as ἡ γενεὰ αὕτη; the announcement of οὐαί (v.17); and the ἀμὴν λέγω ὑμῖν formula in v.30 (*Sayings,* 191).

prophecy regarding the temple and the Jewish war can be shown to have existed—along the lines of vv.14-20 for example—and to have been largely vindicated by the events surrounding the destruction of the temple, then it is not difficult to see how such a proven 'word of the Lord' could have been projected back onto the words of Jesus judging the temple (13:1-2).[29] This would be consistent with the prophetic process evident in many of the Jewish prophetic writings.[30]

Yet such an editorial manœuvre as this can hardly be termed 'conservative redaction', even if we accepted Pesch's latest thesis of a minimally redacted oracle inserted into a pre-existing Passion narrative.

Boring also points to the 'rhythmical formal structure' of the discourse (*Sayings*, 192, any unevenness being due to older traditions or Markan rewriting), and to the "numerous parallels between Mark 13 and Revelation" that show that Mk 13 is "more like our one clear example of Christian prophecy than anything else in early Christian literature" (*Sayings*, 193-195). Boring's analysis of the Christian prophetic tradition is very helpful, but not so his suggestion (following Pesch, *Naherwartungen*) that the author of Mark counters the 'false' prophetic activities of his opponents by quoting the very oracle causing the problems back at them to 'neutralize' its errant theology (*Sayings*, footnote 37, page 284). This is a particularly awkward line of argument given that according to Boring, *Sayings*, 197-199, the author of Mark is very suspicious of Christian prophecy—to the extent that he rejects the Q sayings. How then can he make prominent use of such prophecy? Perhaps this is why Boring, *Sayings*, 284, footnote 37, also goes on to argue that the author of Mark "probably considered it (the prophecy in Mk 13) authentic tradition from the pre-Easter Jesus." But this means that somehow a 'failed' Christian prophecy of 40 CE (Caligula's statue was *not* erected in the temple) has come to be regarded as a genuine prophecy of the historical Jesus by the late 60's. Neither Boring, Theissen, nor N. H. Taylor (who sees the Caligula crisis and failed *parousia* hopes as having even further significance, eg for early Christian mission) explain how this could have happened. Certainly the Caligula crisis must have helped keep the 'abomination' language alive in prophetic circles in Palestine and beyond, but since subsequent events did not confirm these prophecies, they could not then have been attributed to 'the Lord'.

[29] It is illuminating here to note the variations in the later descriptions of the way in which the supposed message to the Jerusalem church was communicated: "a certain oracle that was given through revelation" (τινα χρησμὸς...δι' ἀποκαλύψεως, EusEcclHist III, 5:3); "Christ had told them" (Χριστοῦ φήσαντος, Epiphanius, *Panarion* 29.7.8); and "the disciples were forewarned by an angel to migrate" (προεχρηματίσθησαν ὑπὸ ἀγγέλου, Epiphanius, *Weights and Measures* 15). (All translations and original texts cited by Koester, "Origin", 91-94). Such variations, though much later than the Gospels, may nonetheless serve to illustrate that if the ultimate source of all *proven* prophetic words is believed to be Jesus Christ, then there is every likelihood that the author of Mark would consciously assign such prophecy directly to the historical Jesus.

[30] The prophetic process referred to here is that which first qualifies the prophet as one who speaks the Word of the Lord, and whose words are therefore recorded (retrospectively) because many of them have proven to be true. Of course the process continues as those who record and interpret the words wrestle with those sayings that *did not* come true, as described in the work of Carroll, "Prophecy and Dissonance", and *When Prophecy Failed. Reactions and responses to failure in Old Testament prophetic traditions* (London 1979). Carroll also points out that the ideal picture of a prophet is "one of whom it may be said: 'Yahweh was with him and let none of his words fall to the ground'. (Cf.1 Sam 3 19)" ("Prophecy and Dissonance", 108), which corresponds with the Deuteronomic test of a true prophet. Ideal though this criterion be, is it not still the most appropriate category for understanding how a Christian prophetic oracle could have been understood as equivalent to the words of Jesus, as in Mk 13?

We may concede that the author of Mark is conservative in the treatment of units of tradition,[31] but the ordering and connecting of them to form the first Gospel was an editorial task of extraordinary creativity, and we should not allow Pesch's catch-cry of 'conservative redaction' to cloud our perception of recurrent structural patterns which might indicate such careful arrangement by the author. With this in mind for example, the recurring Markan sequence of the following features—new geographical setting; a misunderstanding by disciples; ἀμήν saying; followed by discipleship teaching—should alert us to the possibility of Markan composition in chapter 13, just as in chapters 8, 9 and 10. Thus Pesch's contention that the majority of the question in v.4 is traditional would have to be re-examined if it is understood as part of another paradigm of discipleship misunderstanding (cf 8:32f; 9:33f; 10:35f).

Such judgments require a careful examination of the structure of Mk 13 in comparison with the rest of the Gospel, and an analysis of the compositional processes of the author as revealed by any theological emphases and literary tensions evident in the text. This area of investigation is the interface between redaction analysis and literary analysis, or between redaction analysis narrowly understood and composition analysis. Therefore, rather than base conclusions regarding redaction on redactional syntax and vocabulary alone, in the analysis below the focus will be on the composition of the whole discourse and the theological intentions of the author. This will then provide a basis for an investigation into the functional structure of Mk 13 in the next chapter.

Thus Pesch's celebrated 'about-face' has at least been part of the process that has re-opened the question of tradition and redaction in Mk 13. But the continued designation by Pesch of the author of Mark as 'anti-apocalyptic', and as one who dampens the expectation of the 'parousia fanatics' in the Markan community, has provoked the most extensive critique of his work. This has been undertaken by Egon Brandenburger, who works from the perspective of a more positive appreciation of apocalyptic literature—an approach which sheds further light on the structure of the discourse. His analysis of Mk 13 shall be examined in chapter 6 below.

Markan composition and theology

A redaction-critical analysis of Mk 13 based on vocabulary and syntax was commenced in chapter 4 above. The inadequacies of using such a method *on its own* have been evident for some time in Markan

---

[31] So, for example, Ernest Best, "Mark's Preservation of the Tradition", in *Disciples and Discipleship: Studies in the Gospel According to Mark* (Edinburgh 1986), 47: "In the way in which he has placed the tradition in his total context supplying audience, place, time and sequence he has been quite obviously creative. But in the way he has preserved the material which existed before him he has been conservative. Perhaps we should not think of an author but of an artist creating a collage."

scholarship, and have been specifically highlighted in recent studies.[32] However redaction analysis correctly understood and practised moves on from a close examination of vocabulary and syntax into an appreciation of the total compositional task of the author and the situation in which it is undertaken. Thus redaction analysis leads naturally into literary and socio-political analyses.[33] Exactly where the lines are drawn between these related methodologies is less important than ensuring that they are all undertaken in such a way that the results of each inform the others. This is not to say that they cannot be undertaken independently of each other. Indeed it is a methodological requirement of some of the 'new' forms of literary analysis that the historical dimension of the text should *not* be investigated first. But in the wholistic approach to exegesis being undertaken here it is necessary that each methodology should *eventually* be related to its sister methodologies and to the ongoing hermeneutical process.

Thus although both redaction analysis and socio-political analysis may involve the description of the *Sitz im Leben* of the author and the author's community, insofar as a distinction is possible, the focus of redaction analysis here shall be on the theological dimensions of that *Sitz im Leben,* and the focus of socio-political analysis (chapter 7 below) shall be on the social and political dimensions. Similarly, although that part of redaction analysis sometimes termed 'composition' analysis shares a concern for literary structure and organisation with literary criticism, those aspects of it that are best related to the historical development of the text will be dealt with in this chapter and chapter 7 below, whilst those that focus on the whole text as it stands shall be examined in chapter 8 below. Of course the work of some scholars straddles both areas and the decision to examine them in this chapter or a later one becomes rather arbitrary.[34]

Any attempt to analyse the compositional process that has shaped Mk 13 must make sense of the many tensions apparent in the chapter. These tensions are evident at different levels. At the 'first reading' level of

[32] See the discussion in the Introduction of the comments by Black, *The Disciples,* for example.

[33] So Mary Ann Tolbert, *Sowing the Gospel. Mark's World in Literary-Historical Perspective* (Minneapolis 1989), 23. "Redaction criticism, perhaps best understood as a transitional discipline, has led directly to the beginnings of more broadly conceived literary examinations of the Gospels on the one hand and to more sophisticated sociological analyses of the Gospel's communities on the other." We only hope that by 'transitional' Tolbert does not mean 'dispensable' but rather that redaction analysis is the key methodology linking the literary approaches with the historical dimensions of the text.

[34] For example, Kelber, *Kingdom,* describes the Markan *Sitz im Leben* using many theological distinctions, yet his work is examined in chapter 7 below. Timothy J. Geddert's *Watchwords* is a literary approach which relies heavily on ascertaining authorial intention through an examination of literary structure and compositional patterns. It is dealt with substantially in chapter 8, but partly in this chapter. Similarly, the work of Hahn and particularly Lambrecht involves literary judgments and analyses of structure— yet since their dominant methodology is redaction analysis they have been included here in chapters 4 and 5.

meaning there are the tensions between the somewhat dispassionate overview of events and even reassurances ('not yet the end') of vv.5b-13, and the seeming urgency of vv.14f; between the events connected somehow with the temple and those connected with The End; and between the time signals of 'this generation'(v.30) and 'no-one knows when' (v.32). At deeper levels of meaning there is the underlying tension between historical and cosmic events and the uncertainty as to which are to be interpreted as which. Even at the linguistic level there are stylistic tensions in the use of καί and δέ, and grammatical tensions in the change from second person (vv.5b-14a,21-37) to third person (vv.14b-20). Already it can be argued that the preceding analysis of pre-Markan traditions has at least made some sense of these stylistic and grammatical tensions by suggesting that vv.14-21 have come from another source.

To say that all these tensions must be made sense of in an examination of the structure and composition of Mk 13 is not to say that the author was responsible for the *creation* of all of them or that they are all of equal significance for the reader. Rather it is merely to claim that the text as it stands when interpreted in the light of the history of its development must be intelligible as a first century document. There is an assumption here that the text meant exactly what the author wanted it to mean in the context of the recent history and present situation of the author's community, and that this meaning is at least partially recoverable and relevant to our interpretation of the text today. This is in contrast to those who would read the text as it stands without reference to its historical context—as 'mirror' *only* and not 'window'—and thus leave unresolved the 'dark apocalyptic imagery', or less satisfactory still, make disparaging remarks about the author's literary skills. But such attitudes to the text are untenable. The widespread acceptance of the Gospel of Mark leading to its eventual inclusion in the canon is guarantee enough against it being a clumsy and confusing document which has always baffled its readers.

It is intended, therefore, to utilise those units of tradition and redaction already specified in the preceding chapters as the basis for a further description of the compositional processes which have been undertaken by the author. These processes should reflect an intelligible theological framework and be locatable in a real-life situation consistent with what is known of first century history. As was shown with the interpretations of Hahn and Pesch above, it will not be possible to provide a definitive statement on these matters nor one which can be proved beyond all doubt. Rather the aim is to provide a solution to the particular set of problems surrounding Mk 13 that will leave fewer questions unanswered and make more sense for us today than any previous attempts. This in itself would be a brash claim were it not for the fact that so much of the present analysis has been built on past endeavours anyway, and that this is the recurring task of every generation of exegetes—to reinterpret the text more satisfactorily for their own situation.

Therefore this stage marks an important turning point in the analyses undertaken thus far. The argument moves beyond the use of evidence which may be more or less objectively demonstrated, and begins to examine theories of composition which are consistent with that evidence. In particular an hypothesis regarding the compilation of the discourse by the author of the Gospel will be suggested which is consistent with the evidence gathered so far, and which will then be tested and further refined by comparison with other writings of that period (chapter 6), possible socio-political scenarios (chapter 7), and various literary approaches to the text (chapter 8). The hypothesis will then be restated in chapter 9 before some of the theological implications of this interpretation of the discourse for today are briefly drawn together by way of a concluding reflection.

The raw material to be used for a re-creation of the compositional process consists of those units of tradition already described in chapter 3 above, the most likely Markan redaction specified in Text Sheet 5 above, and those guiding literary methods and theological principles of the author which are evident from a reading of the whole of the Gospel. From the point of view of literary structure, it may be noted at the outset that the creation of geographical notices in 13:1a and 13:3 to describe an appropriate setting for a teaching situation is typical of the Gospel of Mark.[35] Similarly, the layering or juxtaposing of traditions and short redactional statements evident in Text Sheet 5 is paralleled throughout the Gospel. Thus even though Mk 13 is atypical of the Gospel as a whole because it is the only long and unbroken discourse, the editorial techniques that have been used to compose it are consistent with the rest of the Gospel.

This becomes even more evident when those literary categories of duality listed by Neirynck as possible authorial constructions are examined more closely, and their possible editorial usage throughout the Gospel evaluated.[36] Because these categories are derived from the text of the whole Gospel of Mark, they lend corroborative support to the evidence cited in chapter 4 for the existence of editorial arrangement in certain verses, as well as suggesting further possible compositional processes:

---

[35] See also 7:24; 9:33; 10:32 for example.

[36] Namely Neirynck's categories 21-30, as distinct from those categories, 1-16, based more on vocabulary and syntax, which were examined in chapter 4 above.

Discourse-level duality in Mark 13 (Neirynck)

Section in Mk 13	Neirynck's category	Occurrences in the Gospel of Mark[37] and conclusions
vv.1-2	**26** Correspondence in discourse without question and answer (vv.1,2—repetition of 'the stones')	2:9,11; 3:22,*30;* 3:22,23; 3:32,35; 4:10,*13;* 4:38,40; 6:3,4; 6:22,23,24,25; 6:36,*37;* 7:27,28; 8:12; *9:9,10;* 9:22,23,24; 9:38,39; 10:2,11,12; 10:17,18; 10:17,30; 10:20,21; 10:26,27; 10:28,29; 10:35,36,38; 10:37,40; 12:19,26; 12:28,33; 13:1,2; *13:4,23,37;* 14:19,29; 14:27,29; 14:29,30; 14:30,31; 14:35,41; 14:68,71; 15:9,*12; 15:12,14;* 15:34,35,36. Clearly correspondence is at least as strong a feature in the tradition as in the redaction. Note also in this instance the likely reference in v.2 to the tradition in Hg 2:15 (see chapter 3 above).
vv.3-6	**30** Doublets (12:41 & 13:3—'sitting opposite')	1:11 & 9:7; 1:16-18,19-20 & 2:(13)-14; 1:21a,29b,33 & 2:1-*2; 1:21-22* & *6:2;* 1:23-28 & 4:35-*41*/5:1-20; *1:34c* & *3:12; 2:13* & *4:1; 3:6* & *11:18;* 3:13-*15* & 6:7; 4:3-8 & 14-20; 4:10 & *7:17;* 4:12 & *8:18;* 4:35-*41* & 6:45-52; 5:15 & 16:5; 5:27-28 & *6:56b;* 5:34 & 10:52; *5:35*,39,41-42a & 9:26b-27; *6:14-16* & 8:28; *6:29* & 15:46; 6:34-44 & 8:1-10; *6:52* & *8:17;* 7:15 & 18-23; *7:24* & *9:30;* 7:*31*-37 & 8:22-*26;* 8:31/9:31 & 10:33-34; 9:2 & *14:33; 9:6* & *14:40d;* 9:35 & 10:43-44; 9:36 & 10:16; 10:14 & 14:6; 11:1-7 & 14:12-16; 12:*1*-2 & 13:33-34; 12:29-31 & 32-33; 12:34 & *15:43;* 12:41 & *13:3; 13:26* & *14:62;* 13:36 & 14:37; *14:28* & 16:7; 14:30 & *14:72; 14:55-64* & 15:1-5; *14:58* & 15:29; 14:65 & 15:16-20; 15:23 & 36; 15:29-30 & *31-32.* There are indications that doublets, or at least one half of them, should be carefully considered as possible editorial constructions.

[37] These references are taken from Neirynck, *Duality,* 119f, but used here with the addition of:

(i) **Bold italic** type to indicate a verse that occurs in a Markan 'seam'; that functions as a summary statement; or that is used at the beginning or end of a pericope to set the scene or conclude it—suggesting that there is therefore a higher degree of probability that the verse is redactional;

(ii) *Italic* type to indicate that the verse is still possibly redactional but for other reasons—such as vocabulary, syntax and/or theology (space does not allow the presentation of evidence in each case, but see the criteria discussed in chapter 4);

(iii) Plain type to indicate that the verse is most probably part of the pre-Markan tradition.

Discourse-level duality in Mark 13 [Neirynck] (continued)

Section in Mk 13	Neirynck's category	Occurrences in the Gospel of Mark and conclusions
(vv.3-6 continued)	**21a** Command and fulfilment in direct discourse (vv.4,5)	1:*17*,18,20; 1:25,26; *1:38,39;* 1:41,42; 2:11,12; 2:14; 3:5; 5:*8*,13; *5:19,20;* 5:29,34; 5:41,42; *6:31,32; 6:37;* 7:29,30; 7:34,35; 9:*19*,20; 9:25,26; 10:21,*28;* 10:49; 10:49,50; 11:2-3,4-7; 11:29,30,33; 12:15,16; *13:4,5;* 14:13,15,16; 14:44,45,46,53; 15:13,14,15; *16:7,8* (not fulfilled). Apparently not a particularly strong redactional feature.
	25 Double question (v.4)	1:24; *1:27; 2:7; 2:8,9;* 3:4; *4:13;* 4:21; 4:30; *4:40;* 6:2; 6:3; *7:18,19; 8:17,18-19; 8:17; 8:18; 8:19,20;* 8:36,37; *9:19;* 11:28; 12:14; 12:24,26; *13:4; 14:37;* 14:60; 14:63,64. Double questions are clearly used as a structuring device throughout the Gospel and are likely to be redactional.
	26 Correspondence in discourse without question and answer (v.4,23,37)	As above (vv.1,2). Clearly correspondence is at least as strong a feature in the tradition as in the redaction. In this case, however, these verses containing πᾶς seem to play a pivotal role at the beginning, middle and end of the discourse, and may well be redactional.
	27 Inclusion (vv.4 & 37; 5 & 22,23; 6 & 22)	*1:1*,15; 1:9,*14; 1:21*,29; *1:21*,35; 1:40,*45;* 2:1,*13;* 3:1,*6;* 3:22,*30; 4:2,33-34;* 4:3,9; *8:17,21; 8:23,26;* 9:2,*9; 9:28,30; 9:30,32; 9:34,50;* 9:35-*10:1;* 9:43,48; 10:46,*52; 11:11,15,19; 12:1,12;* 12:24,*27; 12:28,34;* 12:35,37; *13:4,37; 13:5,*22-*23;* 13:6,*22;* 13:7,14; *13:33,37;* 14:6,*8;* 14:54,66-67; 15:1,15; 15:16,20; 15:17,20; 16:5,8. There is very strong evidence here to suggest that inclusion is a Markan editorial characteristic.[38]

[38] See also chapter 4, footnote 46 which suggests clearly that inclusion is one of the categories of Neirynck most likely to indicate redaction.

Section in Mk 13	Neirynck's category	Occurrences in the Gospel of Mark and conclusions
vv.7-8	26 Correspondence in discourse: question and answer (v.4 πότε/ὅταν— v.7 ὅταν)	1:40,41; 2:7,10; 2:16,17; 2:18,19; 2:19; 2:24,25,26; 3:23,24,25,26; 3:33,34; 4:10,11; 5:9; 8:23,24; 9:11,*12*,13; 9:28,29; 10:2,3,4,5; 10:38,39; 11:28,29,33; 11:30,31,32; 12:14,17; 12:23,25; 12:28,29,31; 13:*4*,7,11-13,14,28,29,30; 14:5,7; 14:12,13-15; *14:61,62;* 15:2. Very seldom a redactional feature. More typical of the tradition.
	27 Inclusion (vv.7 & 14)	As above (vv.4,5,6). There is very strong evidence to suggest that inclusion is a Markan editorial characteristic. But in this case the evidence that inclusion is present is based on the use of ὅταν which actually has a much wider use in the discourse than just these two verses (cf vv.4,11,28,29 as well). It is therefore unwise to assume that 'when you hear...' (v.7) and 'when you see...' (v.14) are closely related without also taking into account the use of 'when they lead you away...' (v.11) and 'when you see...' (v.29). Thus grounds other than inclusion would have to be found to support the existence of redaction in any of these verses.
vv.9-13	26 Correspondence in discourse: question and answer (v.4 πότε/ὅταν— vv.11-13 ὅταν)	As above (v.7). Very seldom a redactional feature. More typical of the tradition.
	29 Parallelism in sayings (antithetic v.11)	1:8; 2:19,20; 2:22; 2:27; 3:28,29; 3:33,34; 4:4-7,8; 4:11; 4:15-19,20; 4:21; 4:25; 4:31,32; 6:10,11; *7:6; 7:7; 7:8; 7:9;* 7:10; 7:10,11-12; 7:13; 7:15; 8:12; 8:35; 10:9; 10:18; *10:27;* 10:31; 10:42,43-44; *11:17; 12:44;* 13:11; 13:20; 13:31; 14:7; 14:38b; *14:58.* Parallelism seems to be a stronger feature of the tradition than the redaction.
vv.14-20	26 Correspondence in discourse: question and answer (v.4 πότε/ὅταν —v.14 ὅταν)	As above (v.7). Very seldom a redactional feature. More typical of the tradition.
	27 Inclusion (vv.7 & 14)	As above (vv.4,5,6, and especially v.7). Grounds other than inclusion would have to be found to support the existence of redaction in these verses.
	29 Parallelism in sayings (antithetic v.20)	As above (v.11). Parallelism seems to be a stronger feature of the tradition than the redaction.

Discourse-level duality in Mark 13 [Neirynck] (continued)

Section in Mk 13	Neirynck's category	Occurrences in the Gospel of Mark and conclusions
vv.21-23	**26** Correspondence in discourse without question and answer (vv.4,23,37)	As above (vv.1,2). Clearly correspondence is at least as strong a feature in the tradition as in the redaction. In this case, however, these verses containing πᾶς clearly play a pivotal role at the beginning, middle and end of the discourse, and may well be redactional.
	27 Inclusion (vv.5 & 22,23; 6 & 22)	As above (vv.4,5,6). There is very strong evidence to suggest that inclusion is a Markan editorial characteristic.
vv.24-27	**29** Parallelism in sayings (synonymous vv.24,25)	1:3; 1:7; 2:17; 2:19; 2:21,22; 2:27,28; 3:4; 3:24,25,26; 4:4,5-6,7; 4:12; *4:13;* 4:15,16-17,18-19; 4:22; 4:24; 4:30; *8:17; 8:18;* 8:36,37; 8:38; *9:19;* 9:43,45,47; 9:48; 10:11,12; 10:14; 10:38; 10:39; 10:42; 10:43,44; 10:45; 11:28; 12:17; *13:24; 13:25;* 13:28,29. Parallelism seems to be a stronger feature of the tradition than the redaction.
	30 Doublets (13:26 & 14:62)	As above (v.3). There are indications that doublets, or at least one half of them, should be carefully considered as possible editorial constructions.
vv.28-31	**26** Correspondence in discourse: question and answer (v.4 πότε/ὅταν —vv.28,29 ὅταν)	As above (v.7). Very seldom a redactional feature. More typical of the tradition.
	29 Parallelism in sayings (synonymous vv.28,29)	As above (vv.24,25). Parallelism seems to be a stronger feature of the tradition than the redaction.
	29 Parallelism in sayings (antithetic v.31)	As above (v.11). Parallelism seems to be a stronger feature of the tradition than the redaction.

Section in Mk 13	Neirynck's category	Occurrences in the Gospel of Mark and conclusions
vv.32-37	**26** Correspondence in discourse: question and answer (v.4 πότε/ὅταν —v.30?)	As above (v.7). Very seldom a redactional feature. More typical of the tradition.
	26 Correspondence without question and answer (vv.4,23,37)	As above (vv.1,2). Clearly correspondence is at least as strong a feature in the tradition as in the redaction. In this case, however, these verses containing πᾶς clearly play a pivotal role at the beginning, middle and end of the discourse, and may well be redactional.
	27 Inclusion (vv.4 & 37; 33 & 37)	As above (vv.4,5,6). There is very strong evidence to suggest that inclusion is a Markan editorial characteristic.
	30 Doublets (12:1-2 & 13:33-34; 13:36 & 14:37)	As above (v.3). There are indications that doublets, or at least one half of them, should be carefully considered as possible editorial constructions. In these cases the specific links are hardly strong enough to class the pairs of expressions as true doublets, though they obviously share common concepts. It would be consistent with this and with previous evidence (chapter 4) to argue that only 13:33 and 14:37b are redactional, rather than both halves of each pair of verses.

The most obvious conclusions from this evidence are that the redactional status of the *whole* of vv.3-6 is reaffirmed[39] and further support is given to the view that vv.23,33 and 37 are also part of the authorial shaping of the discourse. This is so because it has been shown above that the literary features of double questions (v.4), inclusion (vv.4 & 37; 5 & 22,23; 6 & 22; 33 & 37), correspondence using πᾶς (vv.4,23,37), and doublets (12:41 & 13:3; 13:26 & 14:62; 12:1-2 & 13:33) are typical of the compositional techniques of the author of Mark throughout the Gospel. This evidence can therefore be used together with the evidence of chapter 4 to help in the description of the composition of Mk 13 given in the statement below.

In additon to these literary features, there are important theological principles which have been established in the course of the Gospel narrative and which inform a reconstruction of the composition of Mk 13. Amongst the most important of these are the following:

---

[39] The evidence in chapter 4 indicated that vv.3,5a and 6a were redactional, but the compositional evidence supplied here points strongly to the whole section from vv.3-6— and especially v.4—being redactional.

(i) The anti-temple stance of Jesus in the Gospel of Mark.

The case has been well argued that both in the symbolic action of cursing the fig-tree and the direct action in the temple, the Markan Jesus judges the temple cult.[40] In fact this anti-temple stance of Jesus pervades the whole Gospel and is evident even in the opening verses (1:2,3), as has been argued in chapter 3 above. It is therefore completely consistent with this that as Jesus leaves the temple for the last time (13:1) he predicts its utter devastation (13:2), and that the further explanation of this prophecy is then situated on the Mount of Olives *over against* the temple (13:3). Jesus is then accused of anti-temple statements at the trial, and later as Jesus dies, the temple veil is ripped from top to bottom as the presence of God leaves the sanctuary (15:38).[41] It would appear that this anti-temple theme exists both in the tradition and in the Markan redaction. This much is clear and has often been pointed out, but the implications of it have not always been consistently followed through for the rest of Mk 13. For if in the traditions taken over by the author of Mark the temple has been judged as an invalid institution by the historical Jesus—13:2 having been located above in the earliest Palestinian tradition and as most probably Jesuanic—then how can the fulfilment of these predictions in the desecration of the temple in 13:14f be regarded by some interpreters as such a devastating event for the Markan community? And how then could any event associated with the temple be so significant as to constitute the 'sign' to the Markan community of the fulfilment of all things?[42] It is apparent that if 13:14f is understood as a reference to the temple, then its redactional incorporation into the discourse must be interpreted in such a way that the anti-temple thrust of the Markan Jesus is not compromised.

[40] See, for example, Gill, "Cleansing", I/101f, and William Telford, *The Barren Temple and the Withered Tree* (Sheffield 1980). Peter G. Bolt, "Mark 13: An Apocalyptic Precursor to the Passion Narrative", *RTR* 54 (1995), 10-32, makes the distinction between the temple and its ruling priests and argues that "the material in Mark 11-12 reveals that the polemic is not against the temple, but against the religious leaders of Israel" ("Mark 13", 17), and that even the prophecy in 13:1-2 is not specifically anti-temple but rather a dismissal of OT piety ("Mark 13", 20). Certainly Bolt is right to emphasise that the religious leadership are implicated in Jesus' Jerusalem teaching and actions, but it is not possible to bracket out the temple altogether, as the charges at the trial and the rending of the temple curtain in Mk 15:38 demonstrate.

[41] There *are* other interpretations of the tearing of the veil, but it is clear that for the author of Mark it *at least* signifies the departure of God. See Geddert, *Watchwords,* 140-145, for a list of 35 possible interpretations of 15:38.

[42] As Geddert, *Watchwords,* 147, concludes: "Certainly our study of Mark's temple theology has given us no warrant for associating the parousia closely with anything that happens to the temple." It could be added that a study of Markan eschatology gives no warrant for associating the parousia with anything at all in the Gospel of Mark. But Geddert's basic point about the *ultimate insignificance* of the temple in Markan eschatology still stands.

(ii) The inappropriateness of seeking 'signs'.

It is clear from Mk 8:11-13 that the request for a sign as a means of authentication or to assist in discernment is utterly rejected by the Markan Jesus.[43] The only other specific occurrences of the word σημεῖον are in Mk 13, where the disciples ask for one (13:4), and the pseudochrists and false prophets perform them (13:22), although the request for Jesus to prove his identity by coming down from the cross (Mk 15:28-32) has similar implications. It is true that the other Gospels—in particular John—use the idea of 'signs' in a positive sense, but this dimension is totally lacking in the Markan text and may even have been deliberately avoided.[44] The conclusion of Geddert therefore commends itself: "If Jesus categorically refuses to give any sign at all to 'this generation' (8.12), should we not seriously consider the possibility that the ταῦτα πάντα ('these things') which 'this generation' (13.30) will live to see does not include signs?"[45] Strictly speaking, it would be more accurate to say that though this generation will continue to ask for signs (13:4), the only ones they will receive are those of the pseudochrists and false prophets (13:22). Those who follow the example of the Pharisees (8:11-13) and persist in asking for signs will receive the only signs and wonders they deserve (13:22), and stand in danger of being led even further from the truth.

(iii) The ambiguity of time references.

There is an interesting interplay between the use of eschatological and historical time references in the Gospel of Mark, and in particular the use of 'this generation', 'in those days', 'that day' and 'the hour', and 'the

---

[43] See the full discussion of this issue in Geddert, *Watchwords,* chapter 2, "A Markan Perspective on Signs", 29-58. Geddert's arguments are not weakened in any way by the views of Jeffrey Gibson, "Jesus' Refusal to Produce a 'Sign' (Mk 8.11-13)", *JSNT* 38 (1990), 37-66, who argues that the Markan Jesus is not opposed to 'signs' as such, but only to those 'signs from heaven for this generation' which are associated with Messianic claims to liberate Israel from its oppressors. Gibson makes a good case for all the Markan instances of σημεῖον (8:11-13; 13:22—no mention of 13:4!; and by inference in 15:28-32) being used in this way anyway—so it is puzzling that he should then wish to argue that 2:1-12 constitutes a σημεῖον that the Markan Jesus *does* approve of, even though the word is not used in that context and Gibson has to derive another definition of 'signs' from the OT to support his case. But the fact that σημεῖον may be understood positively in the OT (or in the Gospel of John, or in the use of 'the sign of Jonah' in Q) does not alter the fact that the *Markan* Jesus clearly refuses to have anything to do with 'signs' *as they are understood in the context of the Gospel of Mark.* This has important implications for the framing of the disciples' question in 13:4.

[44] Geddert, *Watchwords,* 34-39, lists six instances where the word σημεῖον *may* have been present in Markan sources (and occurs in synoptic parallels), but where it has been 'deleted' in the text of the Gospel of Mark. They are: (i) Mt 12:39; 16:4; Lk 11:29; (ii) Mt 24:30; (iii) Mk 13:14! (after Beasley-Murray, *Commentary,* 70); (iv) Lk 21:25; (v) Lk 21:11; (vi) Mt 26:48.

[45] Geddert, *Watchwords,* 57.

καιρός'. It appears that eschatological time references dominate the Gospel almost to the exclusion of historical and chronological time markers up until the mention of the Passover in 14:1, and the hours of the crucifixion day in Mk 15, though these latter references have eschatological implications anyway.[46] It also becomes apparent that the very phrases that have often been interpreted eschatologically earlier in the Gospel—particularly in the context of Mk 13, 'the hour' (13:32) and the four watches of the night (13:35)—are used again in the passion narrative in a way that either heightens the eschatological implications of the betrayal and death of Jesus, or points to the historical relevance of eschatological language in the Gospel. 'The hour' of Jesus (14:41) recalls 'the hour' of those handed over for trial (13:11) as well as the unknown hour of 13:32. The four watches of the betrayal night (ὀψία—last supper, 14:17; μεσονύκτιον—Gethsemane, 14:37; ἀλεκτοροφωνία—Peter's denial, 14:72; πρωΐ—trial before Pilate, 15:1), seem specifically to 'live out' the four watches of the eschatological night in 13:35.[47] Such parallels in language underscore the existential dimension of the final 'day and hour', in that the hour of discipleship testing and martyrdom is described in exactly the same terms as the eschaton (13:32f).[48] It is therefore not possible to conclude that any one of these references is unequivocally one-dimensional, referring *only* to 'historical events' or *only* to 'eschatological events'. Such clear-cut distinctions do not appear to be part of the understanding of the author of the Gospel of Mark.

Equally significant is the use of καιρός to indicate:

(a)   the time for the rule of God to break into history (1:15)
(b)   the present time for the life of the new community (10:30)
(c)   *not the time* for the 'fig tree' to bear fruit (11:13)
(d)   the time of assessment for 'the vineyard' (12:2)
(e)   the unknown time of The End (13:33)[49]

Again it can be seen in these references that there is no easy distinction possible between future and present, nor between 'normal time' and 'eschatological time'. Rather the use of καιρός seems to indicate that 'significant time'—be it of new beginnings (1:15; 10:30; 13:33?) or of

---

[46] The mention of 'after six days' (9:2), which seems to hang unconnected in the narrative, is hardly an exception to this observation, nor are the 'on the third day' sayings in the passion predictions.

[47] 'Midnight' is the only watch not specifically mentioned, though as Geddert, *Watchwords,* 100, points out, the three hours of that watch are represented by the three one-hour prayers of Jesus.

[48] It is difficult at this point not to project a twentieth century perspective on to a first century text! But even if an existentialist perspective is possible, we should at least refrain from reading an individualistic interpretation into the text. Jesus is the only one who dies alone in the Gospel of Mark and whose death can truly be equated with 'that day and hour', whereas the sufferings of vv.9-11f are in the context of the faithful *community* of followers.

[49] So also Myers, *Strong Man,* 339-340.

implied endings (11:13; 12:2f; 13:33?)—impinges on, and is inseparable from, present reality.

The distinction between 'in those days' and 'in that day' also seems to be made deliberately. The former phrase is used of a significant period or process, as in:

(a) the baptism and testing of Jesus (1:9);
(b) the feeding of the Gentiles (8:1);
(c) the great tribulation (13:17, and with a different word order, 13:19); and
(d) the vindication of the Son of Man and the gathering of the elect (13:24-27).

The singular equivalent, 'in that day', is used of a specific event:

(a) the day the bridegroom is taken away (2:20);
(b) the day/evening of discipleship testing (4:35);
(c) that day (= ὁ τέλος? 13:32); and
(d) the day of the eschatological banquet (14:25).

Whilst the obvious overlap between 'historical' and 'eschatological' events has been preserved in the use of these phrases, it is apparent that a distinction ought to be made between 'those days' and 'that day'—between 'process' and 'event'. This is of particular significance for the interpretation of the relationship between vv.24-27 and 32, where the former clearly refers to a process (ἐν ἐκείναις ταῖς ἡμέραις . . . καὶ τότε . . . καὶ τότε), and the latter to an event—the most likely in the immediate context being ὁ τέλος of v.31, a possibility which shall be explored further below. This also points to the likelihood that ὁ τέλος (vv.7c,13b) includes 'The End' alluded to in the final stages of the discourse as well as 'the ends' faced by those faithful followers who endure through the persecutions of vv.9-13, even to their martyrdom.

The time reference in Mk 13 that has caused the most debate is undoubtedly ἡ γενεὰ αὕτη in v.30, yet this is the most unambiguous reference of all. Despite many ingenious attempts to find alternative meanings,[50] it is clear from its usage elsewhere in the Gospel of Mark and

---

[50] See, for example, Lövestam, "The ἡ γενεὰ αὕτη Eschatology"; and Wenham, "'This Generation Will Not Pass…'". Lövestam reviews the possibilities: ἡ γενεὰ αὕτη = Jesus' contemporaries/the Jewish people/humanity in general/the faithful/the unbelievers; and rejects them all. After examining the OT usage, he then argues that in contrast to the survival of Noah and Joshua after the demise of their respective generations, 13:30 means simply that the disciples should *not* expect to live on after the death of the evil generation around them. The parousia is thus an 'end' qualitatively different to the flood and the wilderness, and 'this generation' is a 'type' expressing the evil nature of humanity at the time of the end, rather than an indication of the time within which the end will occur. Yet in the end Lövestam fails to convince. The generation of Noah and of Joshua, though evil, were still their contemporaries and were literal generations, which is just what 'generation' seems to mean in the rest of the Gospel of Mark (8:12,38; 9:19). It is doubtful, given the disciples' request for a sign (v.4), whether the author of Mark would distinguish between them and the generation of 8:11-12 who also seek a sign anyway. Wenham presents the more common argument that the saying in v.30 refers to the fall of Jerusalem rather than The End or the parousia. Such arguments

in Hebrew literature that its primary meaning is a literal 40 year generation.[51] It is equally apparent that its location in the discourse implies that 'all these things' must include everything up to v.30. This is the most obvious sense of the statement and there are no compelling reasons to interpret it in any other way.[52] The analysis of redaction summarised in Text Sheet 5 has already shown clearly that vv.30-31,32 are deliberate editorial insertions, and therefore they must not be assumed at the Markan level to have been 'misplaced' or to refer to anything other than their immediate context, regardless of their original meaning. This means that the process described up to and including v.29 must have been observable—if not complete—at the time the Gospel was being written, and raises the possibility that v.32 should be understood as referring to v.31f rather than the same events that v.30 refers to.

(iv) The inappropriateness of the disciples' questions and comments.

It follows naturally from (i), (ii) and (iii) that the question the disciples ask in v.4 is totally inappropriate. Not only do they link the temple with the 'fulfilment of all things', but they ask for the 'signs and times' that would indicate when such an event would occur. This follows the pattern in the Gospel of Mark where the disciples display a lack of perception in their questions and comments which then provides the basis on which the teaching of Jesus proceeds (see 4:38; 5:31; 6:37; 8:4,16,32; 9:11,28,32, 34,38; 10:13,26,37; 14:32f; for example, not to mention the comments in

---

rely on making ταῦτα πάντα in v.30 refer to anything but its immediate context, and are ultimately unsustainable—even if it is argued that v.30 has been 'misplaced' by the evangelist.

[51] This is made explicit in the parallel reference to Mk 13:24-30 occurring in Mk 8:38-9:1. Both refer to seeing the vindication of the Son of Man in power (9:1; 13:26) and glory (8:38; 13:26), and both are followed by a redactional insertion emphasising that not all will die before this event occurs (9:1; 13:30). On *this* point we certainly do have the agreement of Paul in 1 Th 4:15, and later, after more of the first generation have died, he re-affirms it in 1 Co 15:51-52. Given the Kingdom language of 9:1, it could be argued that this is the earliest tradition—an expectation by Jesus that God would act powerfully amongst his contemporaries—which is then interpreted in various ways by Paul, the Jerusalem community, the Markan community and the other NT traditions. This interpretation sees 9:1 as redactionally linked primarily to 8:38, whilst conceding that the transfiguration (9:2f) may be seen as a foretaste of the later vindication of the Son of Man. See Enrique Nardoni, "A Redactional Interpretation of Mark 9:1", *CBQ* 43 (1981), 365-384, for a review of the literature.

[52] Of course for some there may be compelling *theological* reasons if the text is approached with a certain theological agenda already in mind. For example, Geddert, *Watchwords,* 242, is one of the more lucid supporters of the argument that the text in Mk 13 "'doubles back' temporally", citing as examples of this phenomenon at least vv.28,33 and 37, and therefore suggests that it might also 'double back' at v.30, so that "13.29 brings the End into view and then 13.30 reverts back to the events preceding the End." But such an approach randomises the whole structure of the discourse into a collection of eschatological symbols that may be re-arranged at will. One might as well go even further with this 'doubling back', as does Myers, *Strong Man,* 343f, who sees vv.24-27 as referring to the crucifixion, thus making v.30 true! (See chapter 7 below).

13:1!). Obviously the questions and comments of the disciples are used as a literary device to structure the responses of Jesus—even when they provide a negative paradigm—and to draw attention to those parts of the teaching of Jesus which are of particular relevance to the Markan community. But in the context of Mk 13:4 this points to the probability that the rest of the chapter may not provide a direct answer to the 'signs and times' question at all, but rather a correction of that sort of inadequate perception of the fulfilment of all things. Thus we should not force a division on the text between an answer to the 'time question' and an answer to the 'sign question' (usually suggested in the reverse order), but be open to the possibility that the whole discourse transcends and renders inadequate the double question of the disciples. Similarly, whilst the disciples seem to assume in their question that the destruction of the temple must figure prominently in the events of the end times, it would be more consistent with the rest of the Gospel if the author of Mark argues the opposite case and denies its eschatological significance altogether.

(v) The nexus between judgment of the temple State and mission to the Gentiles (a nascent Markan 'new temple' ecclesiology).

On the three occasions when the judgment of the temple is referred to in the Gospel of Mark (11:12-25; 13:1-2; 15:38) there is a corresponding reference to the Gentile mission (11:17; 13:10; 15:39). This is consistent with the Markan understanding that the priority of the Jews in salvation history has been satisfied by the ministry of Jesus up until Mk 7:23, and from then on it is the time for the Gentiles.[53] It also helps to explain the lack of a judgment motif in the descriptions of the vindication of the Son of Man in the Gospel of Mark. The judgment on those who rejected the boundary-breaking revelation of God in Jesus has already been pronounced (Mk 11-13) and has been fulfilled in the destruction of Jerusalem and the temple. All that remains then, is to gather together the re-defined elect from all quarters (vv.24-27), including those Judeans who heed the warning of 13:14f.[54] This of course assumes that the Gospel

---

[53] So Gill, "Beyond the Boundaries", 39: The key word 'first' (7:27) "indicates not only the 'priority' of the Jews in salvation history, but a priority which, according to Mark, belongs in the past. They have already been fed (6.32-44). Now is the time for the Gentiles to be fed, says Mark. Their time has come (8.1-9)."

[54] The judgment is *not* understood as falling on all Jews regardless, since the whole point of 13:14f is to save (if possible) some of 'the elect'. But this category of 'the elect' is obviously widened in v.27 beyond the Judeans (τοὺς ἐκλεκτοὺς αὐτοῦ is most likely Markan redaction as it stands outside the allusions to Zc 2:10LXX (= 2:6ET); Is 43:6; Dt 30:4—see chapters 3 and 4 above) to include the elect of the Son of Man from all directions. Also see Geddert, *Watchwords*, 125f, and 136f, who makes a good case for the judgment of Jesus falling specifically on the religious leaders rather than the ordinary Jew.

was written after the fall of Jerusalem in 70 CE, an assumption which will be more thoroughly examined in chapter 7 below.

The linking of temple destruction with Gentile mission has even more profound implications, however, which are hinted at by that enigmatic charge brought against Jesus at the trial: "We heard him say, 'I am going to destroy this temple made by human hands, and in three days build another, not made by human hands.'" (Mk 14:58). These implications are that the author of Mark displays an implicit understanding that the 'body' of Jesus—the community of the faithful—is the new temple 'not made by human hands' that replaces the old 'hand-made' (= idolatrous, Ps 115:4; Is 46:6) temple of Jerusalem. Gill concludes that the theology evident in the cleansing of the temple (Mk 11:15-17), the parable of the wicked husbandmen (Mk 12:1-12), the narrative of clean-unclean and the Syrophoenecian woman (Mk 7:1-30) "suggests that by the temple 'made without hands' the Evangelist intends the eschatological community, the predominantly Gentile church, for in each instance the positive correlative to judgment on Israel is salvation of the Gentiles".[55] The veracity of this insight and its relevance to the discourse is confirmed by the framing of Mk 13 by the two women who give all they have—the poor widow, unfortunately, to the Jerusalem temple and the authorities who 'devour her living' (12:41-44), and the comparatively wealthy woman who gives her all to anoint the condemned body of Jesus, the new Temple (14:1-9). The significance of this for interpreting Mk 13 has been admirably stated by Geddert:

> If the old temple was a centre to which all nations would come (Mark 11.17) and if the new temple would expand to fill the whole world (Cf. Dan. 2.35; Mark 14.9) then perhaps Mark 13 is fundamentally concerned with the issue of breaking free from Jerusalem-centredness into worldwide mission. Perhaps Mark sees the faithful scattered from the old temple at 13.14 and regathered fully and finally into the new temple at 13.27.[56]

It is unfortunate that Geddert does not pursue all the implications of this statement for the situation of the Markan community (see chapters 6 and 7 below), but at least it does help to underline the importance of the mission theme for understanding Mk 13. This underlying agenda of the discourse has already been noted in the analysis of the Old Testament allusions in chapter 3 above, but in the context of this chapter it confirms the likely redactional nature of the most explicit reference to mission in Mk 13—v.10. Thus this statement about the necessity of mission (13:10) must be interpreted in terms of its deliberate placement into a context of being 'handed over' (vv.9,11).

---

[55] Gill, "Cleansing", I/122. A similar conclusion has been arrived at through different arguments by Geddert, *Watchwords,* 113-147.

[56] Geddert, *Watchwords,* 138.

(vi) The vindication of the Son of Man.

The three descriptions of 'the coming of the Son of Man' in the Gospel of Mark (8:38; 13:26; 14:62) are clearly related to Dn 7:13,14 in some way. Yet in Daniel it is *'one like a* Son of Man' who comes to the Ancient of Days in heaven, rather than one who returns again to earth. This raises questions regarding the whole Son of Man debate which are far too complex to discuss fully here.[57] But since Daniel's usage is the closest known precedent to the usage in the Gospel of Mark, it seems preferable to examine links in that direction rather than impose the Pauline or Matthean concept of the *parousia* on the Markan texts in question.[58] This is especially so because each of the three Markan texts can be understood in the light of the Danielic vision:

(a) In 8:38 the Son of Man will be ashamed before his Father of any who are ashamed of him on earth;

(b) In 13:26 the Son of Man will be seen by the powers that are shaken as he approaches God in heaven. He then sends out his 'messengers' on earth to gather his elect;

(c) In 14:62 the High Priest and Sanhedrin will see the Son of Man seated (on a chariot?) at the right hand of power and coming with the clouds of heaven to the Father.

Since in each of these statements it is the *opponents* of the Son of Man who are made aware of his exaltation and authority, it is surely more appropriate to speak of the *vindication* of the Son of Man than the *parousia* of the Son of Man in the context of the Gospel of Mark. It is also worth noting that the corporate nature of the Son of Man in Daniel—as the embodiment of the faithful community—may lie behind the Markan usage of the term. These possibilities will be examined more thoroughly below, but they must be referred to here because of their significance for understanding the motivation behind the editorial compilation and use of vv.24-27.

---

[57] See chapter 1, footnote 16 above for details of the general debate. In terms of the Markan use of 'the Son of Man', we note the possibility of a significant Markan contribution to the development of the 'title'. See, for example, Norman Perrin, "The Creative Use of the Son of Man Traditions by Mark", *USQR* 23 (1968), 357-365; and Barnabas Lindars, *Jesus Son of Man: A Fresh Examination of the Son of Man Sayings in the Gospels* (Grand Rapids/London 1983), 24-28. Lindars argues here that the translation of the five authentic Son of Man sayings (Mk 2:10; 8:38 and the passion sayings) into Greek led to the development of the 'titular' Son of Man through the precedent found in Dn 7:13. Thus as Donahue, "Recent Studies", 493, summarises: "The picture of Jesus as the authoritative agent of God is developed by Mark in two directions: Jesus as the one who must suffer and as the one who will be vindicated at the parousia."

[58] A further possibility might be to examine the links with the *merkabah* imagery of an ascent to God on a chariot. See Jane Schaberg, "Mark 14.62: Early Christian Merkabah Imagery?" in *Apocalyptic and the New Testament, Essays in Honor of J. Louis Martyn,* eds Joel Marcus and Marion L. Soards (Sheffield 1989), 69-94. This approach makes some sense of the description of the Son of Man in 14:62 as 'seated' *and* 'coming' at the same time.

These theological emphases of the author of Mark, together with the literary features described above, must now be taken into account in an attempt to describe the way in which the discourse was compiled. There is much of theological significance yet to be examined, but these key issues seem to have been particularly crucial in the selecting and ordering of the material that comprise Mk 13.

The composition of Mk 13

It is helpful at this point to recall the findings of earlier chapters. The analyses of chapters 1, 2 and 3 led to the following conclusions regarding the pre-Markan traditions:
(i)   Most probable Jesuanic traditions: vv.2,30,32 in another form),34
(ii)   Palestinian (Targumic?) traditions: vv.7,8,11a,b,d,12,13a,22
(iii) Distinctive pre-Markan source (Christian prophetic oracle): vv.14-21
(iv)   Markan *pastiche* of Septuagintal references: vv.24-27
(iv)   Editorial comments or compilations of smaller units: vv.3-6,9-10,13b,23,28-29,33,35-37

The analysis based on vocabulary and syntax in chapter 4 pointed to the most likely Markan redaction as occurring in vv.1a,3,(5a),6a,7c, 9b,10,(11c),24a,(33), and possibly short phrases in vv.22 and 27. It was also shown that vv.4,13b,30-31,35-36 and 37 may have been inserted into the discourse at some stage because of the disruption of normal Markan syntax caused immediately before and after each of these verses. Similarly, it was suggested that the occurrence of asyndeton in vv.6,7b,8b,8c,9b and 34 may also indicate the selection and arrangement of traditions, though less certainly than the evidence of unique syntax across a major punctuation break. It was noted that the dominance of *recurrent* syntax in vv.24-27 strongly suggests that these verses are a Markan compilation of Septuagintal allusions, just as the dominance of *unique* syntax in vv.14-21 suggests an atypical pre-Markan source.

In the analysis of Markan literary and theological preferences just completed, indications of editorial activity were confirmed in vv.3-6 (and especially v.4), and in vv.10,23,33 and 37. It was also suggested that the double question in v.4 is another case of that Markan literary device of using the disciples to ask the wrong question in order to emphasise the right answer from Jesus. Thus just as in 8:12, it is still inappropriate for this generation to ask for a sign (13:4) and the only ones they will receive are false (13:22). It was already obvious to the reader, but not to the disciples, that the temple could not have provided the sign for the fulfilment of all things anyway, for it has been judged as far as the Gospel of Mark is concerned long before its eventual destruction. It was also noted that any discussion of the composition of the discourse would have to take into account the eschatological and historical ambiguity of the time references ('that day', 'hour', 'time', 'the watches of the night') and their links with the Passion Narrative. So also the apparent distinction between 'that day and hour' (v.32) and 'those days' (vv.17,19,24), and the deliberate placement of vv.10 and 30-31 into seemingly 'awkward' contexts.

Bearing these factors in mind, the following is an attempt to describe the compositional process undertaken by the author of the Gospel in compiling Mk 13:

(i)   To the genuine prophecy of Jesus and its traditional temple setting, the author has added v.1a, the final departure of Jesus from the temple. What may have been the original ending to the prophecy against the temple (v.30) has been deliberately placed in a later context, consistent with the expectation generated by Mk 9:1.

(ii) The second scene of the discourse (opposite and 'against' the temple, v.3), the second inappropriate comment from the disciples (the double question of v.4 based on Dn 12:6, following on from the comment in v.1), and the beginnings of Jesus' answer (vv.5,6), have been created by the author. They summarise the intent of the discourse—that though the temple is doomed it will not figure in 'the fulfilment of all things', despite many deceptive claims by messianic pretenders to the contrary. The addition of 'not yet the end' (7c) by the author defers expectation until later in the discourse, and reassures the hearers/readers that 'the eschatological event' has not occurred elsewhere and nor will news of it be spread abroad along with other rumours.

(iv) Early Palestinian sayings (vv.7a,b,c,8,11a,b,d,12,13a) reflecting Aramaic (possibly Targumic) influences and the experiences of the Judean Jewish Christians are then fused with mission sayings (vv.9,11c) more representative of a Gentile mission perspective (vv.9a,11c *Koine* not Semitic). The Markan redactional insertion of v.10 then underscores the necessity of worldwide mission despite persecution from both Jews and Gentiles. The addition of v.13b *(Koine),* possibly redactional, reassures those undergoing persecution that their endurance to 'the end' (the martyrdom hinted at in vv.9,12,13—or 'The End' of vv.31f later in the discourse?) will result in salvation.

(v)   A Christian prophetic oracle (vv.14-21) addressed to the Jewish Christians of Judea[59] and warning of great tribulations is inserted

---

[59] The distinction between Jews and Christians in Judea (and even further afield) at this stage is in all probability anachronistic—the fall of Jerusalem being the key event that ultimately forced the distinction to be made. Thus it would be quite proper to describe the oracle as a Jewish one directed to other Jews in Judea—provided that it was understood that it involved the followers of Jesus of Nazareth and their sympathisers as well. Certainly the 'Christians' weren't the only ones forced out of Jerusalem by the revolutionary and 'nationalistic' movements which took over the city. Just as no doubt

at this stage. Clearly there is some reference to the temple and Jerusalem intended in vv.14f, yet no mention is made that its desecration is reversed and its destroyers punished, indicating that it is understood by the author of Mark as one event in the historical process rather than part of The End itself. Indeed the '...until now, and never will be' added (by Mark?) effectively historicises the events and tribulations of vv.14-19.

(vi)   The warning about messianic pretenders is repeated, both in the concluding words of the oracle (v.21) and in a further addition from Palestinian (Targumic?) tradition (v.22). The author adds the reassuring statement that all these events occur with the foreknowledge of Jesus (v.23).

(vii)   There follows a Markan compilation of Septuagintal allusions (vv.24-27) describing the shaking of the powers, the vindication of the Son of Man and the gathering of the elect (including those who flee in vv.14f) from the ends of earth to the ends of heaven. Again, the Markan phrase '...after that tribulation' of v.24 puts the previous events into recent historical context.

(viii) The author then inserts a parable and its application (vv.28,29), which alludes to all that precedes it, and then the saying solemnly vowing that all these things will happen within a generation (v.30—possibly originally referring only to the destruction of Jerusalem, but here deliberately applied to 'all these things' by the evangelist). The second half of this statement (v.31), linked in the pre-Markan tradition by the key word 'pass away', is usually interpreted merely as an authentication of the preceding verses, but it should also be considered to refer to those which follow—and therefore the gap which many texts show between v.31 and v.32 should be removed.

(ix)   The radical denial of knowledge of the time of 'that day or hour' (13:32) is followed by a Markan repetition of the theme (v.33), which serves as the motivating factor to keep on the alert.

(x)   This in turn is followed by an allegory of the need for alertness and discernment (vv.34-36; v.34 possibly being part of a very early parable), and by the author's own conclusion (v.37) which makes public the secret revelation to the four disciples.

This brief summary of the author's compositional processes hardly begins to spell out all the theological implications of the text, but serves to indicate some of the parameters within which it may have been compiled. A comparison in the next chapter with similar texts from the same period will further illuminate the composition and structure of the text, and then an examination of the historical situations surrounding the text will be undertaken in chapter 7.

there were some 'Christians' who remained in Jerusalem in the hope that it would be Jesus who would return as messiah to restore Israel.

VI

A MARKAN APOCALYPSE

Major proponent: Brandenburger (1984).
Basic thesis: That in Mk 13 the evangelist makes use of apocalyptic traditions
    and patterns of thought to reinterpret a Jewish Christian apocalypse and
    oral tradition.
Dominant method: Religio-literary criticism.
Critique: A re-evaluation of the influence of apocalyptic thought forms on the
    structure of the discourse.

The analysis of Mk 13 by EGON BRANDENBURGER comes from such a
different direction that it was some time before it began to provoke a
detailed response.[1] After publishing work on the apocalyptic writings 4
Ezra and The Assumption of Moses, Brandenburger has taken umbrage at
the commonly held view that Mk 13 is in some way anti-apocalyptic. He
seeks to show that not only apocalyptic imagery, but also apocalyptic
thought forms and concepts, dominate both the source *and* the Markan
redaction, and that Mk 13 must be interpreted in terms of these
apocalyptic structures and patterns of thinking. Brandenburger does not
deny that the full spectrum of the apocalyptic imagination evident in some
Jewish texts has been starkly reduced in chapter 13, but he insists in the
strongest possible language that this does not mean that the source or the
author of Mark are anti-apocalyptic (10). Similarly he rejects as invalid
the pejorative distinctions many exegetes have made when studying Mk 13
between eschatological revelation and apocalyptic teaching, and between
parenesis and esoteric instruction.[2] Such antitheses are based on a

---

[1] See the reviews of Brandenburger, *Markus 13 und die Apokalyptik* by Barnabas
Lindars, *JTS* 37 (1986), 177-180; Jan Lambrecht, *TLZ* 111 (1986), 746-748; John M.
McDermott, *TS* 48 (1987), 348-350; and Adela Yarbro Collins, *JBL* 106 (1987), 142-
143. For the rest of this section, references to *Markus 13* shall be by way of page
numbers in brackets in the main body of the text.

[2] *Markus 13,* 11, footnote 5, tackles head-on one of the few areas of consensus in the
interpretation of Mk 13—the distinction between 'apocalypticism' and eschatological
parenesis within the chapter. He summarises some of the various antitheses of previous
interpretations as follows, accusing them all of failing to take serious and unbiased
account of the proper theological solutions attempted in apocalyptic literature. Mk 13, is
supposed to show, according to these exegetes:
   —not only apocalyptic teaching, but also eschatologically motivated parenesis [J.
    Schmid, *Das Evangelium nach Markus* (Regensburg 1963), 237];
   —eschatological promise, not apocalyptic instruction (Kümmel, *Promise and
    Fulfilment,* title of chapter 2, argued as specifically relating to Mk 13 in pages 95f);
   —that for the redactor Mark the parenesis was more relevant and important than any of
    the apocalyptic instruction (Lambrecht, *Redaktion,* 287);

misinterpretation of apocalyptic theology, Brandenburger contends, and bring historical-critical exegesis into disrepute because of the theologically motivated pre-suppositions and biases they contain (9). Indeed, he claims that nowhere in previous studies on Mk 13 is the word 'apocalyptic' used in a positive sense (9)!

By referring constantly to examples drawn from 4 Ezra and The Assumption of Moses, Brandenburger demonstrates that many of the so-called 'anti-apocalyptic' features of Mk 13—such as the recurring parenesis and the denial of knowledge of the time of the end (v.32)—are in fact features of other apocalyptic literature.[3] Then he proceeds to argue in detail how the whole structuring of the chapter reflects an apocalyptic world view. This approach is undoubtedly helpful and necessary, but surprisingly the actual results of Brandenburger's analysis, in terms of tradition and redaction and implications for the Markan *Sitz im Leben,* are not all that dissimilar to the scholars who have preceded him.

This is not to downplay the significance of Brandenburger's work—the new perspective he gives on Mk 13 cannot be disregarded, arising as it does out of a formidable knowledge and appreciation of the apocalyptic world view and literature. But a considerable portion of the stinging criticism Brandenburger directs at his predecessors can be attributed not so much to their misinterpretation of Mk 13 as to their narrow definitions—or even caricatures—of apocalyptic writings, which have led to their assessment of Mk 13 as 'anti-apocalyptic. Granted their assumed definitions of apocalyptic literature are somewhat biased: involving an over-emphasis on apocalyptic timetables, intense speculation, and the

---

—admonition is relevant, not apocalyptic. The intention is not to pass on esoteric information, but to encourage faith and obedience [C. E. B. Cranfield, *The Gospel According to Saint Mark* (Cambridge 1974), 388].

Brandenburger also refers to Hahn, Lohmeyer, Pesch and Schnackenburg as making similar false distinctions and value judgments against apocalyptic literature, climaxed by the more general statement of Schmithals: 'Apocalypticists, like Gnostics, do not acknowledge any ethic', which typifies 'their abandonment of historical responsibility.' [*Die Apokalyptik. Einführung und Deutung* (Göttingen 1973), 82. Quoted by Brandenburger, *Markus 13,* 11. In the English Translation of Schmithals' book by John E. Steely, *The Apocalyptic Movement. Introduction and Interpretation* (Nashville, 1975), see page 108]. Interestingly, Brandenburger shows no awareness of the prior work of Kelber or Kee, both of whom have a positive appreciation of the apocalyptic background to the Gospel of Mark (see chapter 7 below).

3 This is not to say that such features in Mk 13 have been *taken* from the parallel literature, but rather that they are consistent with 'an apocalyptic mind-set'. Indeed, whilst AssMos is commonly dated well before the fall of Jerusalem, 4 Ezra is usually dated towards the end of the first century CE, some 20 years later than the Gospel of Mark. The date is established by identifying the three heads of the eagle in chapter 13 with the Flavian emperors. So Michael E. Stone (ed), *Jewish Writings of the Second Temple Period. Apocrypha, Pseudepigrapha, Qumran Sectarian Writings, Philo, Josephus* (Assen/ Philadelphia 1984), 412f. Similarly, James Hamilton Charlesworth, *The Old Testament Pseudepigrapha and the New Testament. Prolegomena for the Study of Christian Origins* (Cambridge 1985), 41-42; and George W. E. Nickelsburg, *Jewish Literature: Between the Bible and the Mishnah* (London 1981), 287-288.

reduction of all revelation to the present age—features *not* characteristic of all apocalyptic literature; their description of Mk 13 as 'anti-apocalyptic' is understandable and even meaningful.[4] But of course such terminology distorts any understanding of what might be meant by 'apocalyptic'. With the new and positive appreciation of the world of apocalyptic literature gained by the religio-literary approach of writers such as Brandenburger, the term 'anti-apocalyptic' must now be abandoned as an inappropriate description of the characteristics of chapter 13, and a re-examination of all assumptions and conclusions regarding the interpretation of the discourse carried out. This is the task that Brandenburger sets himself.

He commences with discussions of the form and structure of Mk 13 and the problem of a source behind the chapter, followed by an examination of the situation and theology of the source. The final lengthy chapter is then devoted to the theological perspective of the Markan redaction. This seems to be a well-worn methodological path, but where Brandenburger differs from his predecessors in this type of analysis is in the greater emphasis he places in his reconstruction of the tradition on a religio-historical awareness of the problem situations addressed by other apocalypses. Thus he relies much less in his determination of tradition and redaction on questions of editorial style or the structure of the Gospel as a whole. This is a refreshing approach, validated somewhat ironically as much by certain key areas of agreement with his major discussion partner—Rudolf Pesch—as by any new findings. Indeed, Brandenburger finds himself agreeing with Pesch in some important conclusions but for totally different reasons.[5] It is the conviction that Brandenburger's work

---

[4] Clearly Brandenburger has the benefit of a more comprehensive understanding of apocalyptic literature than many of his predecessors, but before castigating them for using the term 'anti-apocalyptic' he should take into account what their understanding of 'apocalyptic' is. It then becomes apparent that they are using the term 'apocalyptic' in different ways. For example, for Marxsen (see chapter 4 above), the understanding is that an apocalypse provides a timetable for the End, and thus Marxsen concludes that the evangelist is eschatological rather than apocalyptic in that he sees that the evangelist is claiming that the 'final act' has *already* begun. For Pesch *(Naherwartungen),* the understanding is almost the opposite to this. He argues that the Markan redaction is *countering* a fervent apocalyptic expectation that the End is imminent because of the demise of the temple.

Obviously there is a major problem here over the definition and use of the word 'apocalyptic', for which Brandenburger does not make any sympathetic allowances. Yet just as clearly, if Brandenburger's functional definition of an 'apocalypse' were the common basis of the discussion, then many other scholars would perhaps agree that even the Markan redaction was 'apocalyptic'. Brandenburger's 'definition' is something like: 'an apocalypse clarifies a crisis situation by means of a revelation of eschatological secrets which mediate guidelines of behaviour', *Markus 13,* 13, (see also *Markus 13,* 45-46, referred to below). In her generally favourable review of *Markus 13,* A. Y. Collins, *JBL* 106 (1987), 142, notes that "the applicability of this definition of function to all apocalypses is yet to be tested."

[5] See for example the discussion of their agreement that the evangelist writes from the standpoint of v.23 and wishes to differentiate between the fall of the temple and the sign of the end. *Markus 13,* 29.

in turn needs to be related more directly to the intent of the author of Mark in the Gospel as a whole—as discovered by further analysis of structure, style and theology—that is a major motivation for the writing of the present thesis.

The clarity of Brandenburger's form critical analysis is quite outstanding, and a good example of how his religio-historical-literary perspective has paid handsome dividends. Drawing on his familiarity with the *Schulgespräch* genre found in 4 Ezra, he sees Mk 13 as consisting of two scenes which provide the settings for two scholastic dialogues:

Scene 1: an apophthegm in vv.1-2, whilst leaving the temple, between the teacher and a pupil;

Scene 2: an esoteric apocalyptic dialogue in vv.3-37, occurring opposite the temple, between the teacher and four disciples (κατ᾽ ἰδίαν).

The first scene, based on Jesus tradition (v.1a redactional), simply provides the occasion for the main dialogue, which Brandenburger divides into two parts with further sub-sections.[6]

Part A:	vv.5-27, an historical review of the whole eschaton, answering the questions 'when' (referring to the temple destruction) and 'what' (referring to the sign),[7] and comprising three stages separated by parenetic insertions:
vv.5b-6:	*First parenetic insertion;* key word—βλέπετε (v.5b); theme—warning about seduction by false prophets.
vv.7-8:	**First stage:** the beginning of the birth pangs (ὅταν δὲ ἀκούσητε...).
vv.9-13:	*Second parenetic insertion;* key word—βλέπετε (v.9); theme—perseverance during times of persecution.
vv.14-20:	**Second stage:** the climax of the end-time tribulation (ὅταν δὲ ἴδητε...).
vv.21-23:	*Third parenetic insertion,* with a testamentary conclusion; key word—ὑμεῖς δὲ βλέπετε (v.23); theme—elaboration on first parenetic insertion.
vv.24-27:	**Third stage:** the turning point of the age—judgment and salvation.

---

[6] *Markus 13,* 13-20, and in particular the outline of the structure given on pages 164-165.

[7] Brandenburger takes the question of the disciples as being determinative for the answer of Jesus, and sees the request for a sign from the positive perspective of apocalyptic literature rather than from the negative perspective of the Gospel of Mark. Yet on the question of timing he does see that Jesus' answer rectifies the 'fixation of the question regarding the moment of salvation' (*Markus 13,* 113).

Part B: vv.28-36, a **teaching reflection** (vv.28-32); key word—μάθετε(v.28); with **parenetic consequences** (vv.33-36); key word—βλέπετε (v.33); and followed by the concluding framework of the apocalypse, v.37, where ὑμεῖς and πάντες are contrasted.

Already it is plain that Brandenburger sees that the structuring of the whole chapter by the author of Mark is far from being anti-apocalyptic but actually follows the pattern of an esoteric apocalyptic dialogue which contains part of a three stage apocalypse. This apocalypse consists of vv.7-8,14-20 and 24-27,[8] plus a beginning and end now lost, and is a written document. As for the *Sitz im Leben* of this source, Brandenburger argues that it is of Christian origin and from the period between the start of the Jewish war and the destruction of the temple. He sees that the purpose of such an apocalypse is to bring to a community in the midst of a crisis situation some clarification and assurance through the revelation of secret heavenly wisdom and insight into the final events of the world (45-6). Thus the writer of the source looks back on the events of vv.7-8 (the beginning of the war in the north) and expects the impending desecration of the temple to be followed by the coming of the Son of Man, modelled on the Old Testament idea of a theophany. These prophetic writings originated in, and were directed at, the Christian community in Jerusalem (69), for whom the temple was still important. But rather than join the battle against the Romans or await God's intervention in Jerusalem, they were urged to flee from the tribulation surrounding the fall of the temple . There is a problem here in that if the source so closely links the appearance of the Son of Man with the fall of the temple (that is, if vv.24-27 follow directly on from vv.14-20 with no apparent change in location), then the call to flee such a *denouement* is hard to understand. In such a context, if the prophecy were believed, then the action of those 'Zealots' who danced on the roof of the burning temple portico awaiting the Messiah would have been more appropriate.[9] Thus it would seem that there are other grounds for suspecting that vv.24-27 should not be regarded as part of the source—quite apart from the results of the analyses of syntax in chapters 2 and 4 above.

Brandenburger argues that as the source is a Christian composition containing prophecy vindicated by recent events (except for the non-appearance of the Son of Man!), the author of Mark has no hesitation in attributing it to the historical Jesus and reworking the apocalypse together with other Jesuanic oral traditions. This updating of apocalypses for each new crisis is a feature of such writings, so Brandenburger sees the

---

[8] Only the μετὰ τὴν θλῖψιν of v.24 is considered redactional in this section. *Markus 13,* 41.

[9] See the excursus of Gnilka, *Markus,* vol 2, 184-185, on the destruction of the temple and the Jewish war, for a graphic description of the final hours of the temple derived from the accounts of Josephus.

process as occurring within the stream of apocalyptic consciousness, rather than from outside—or against—such a world view. Thus he argues that Markan redaction is found in the parenetic insertions (vv.5b-6,9a,23 and 33); the framework (vv.1a,3-4 and 37); vv.29 and 33, and parts of vv.24,28 and 35.[10] These insertions, including the parenesis, are common features of apocalypses and are not to be understood as anti- or even non-apocalyptic. This leaves vv.1c-2,9b-13 (10?),21-22b and most of 33-36 as oral tradition based on the sayings of Jesus. Despite protestations by Lambrecht,[11] the net effect of such analysis does appear similar to the sandwiching and intercalating of traditions within traditions typical of Markan redaction elsewhere in the Gospel. Throughout the Gospel it can be consistently shown that the units of tradition are left relatively untouched but are freely arranged and often joined together by short redactional insertions.

Brandenburger maintains that the Markan community, like the source, expected the fulfilment of the Kingdom to occur in connection with the Jewish war. After the non-appearance of the Son of Man, the solution to their cognitive dissonance was to modify rather than reject apocalyptic expectation. The *Sitz im Leben* of the Markan community is represented by v.23, so the sign of the end becomes the cosmic events of v.24 rather than any reinterpretation of v.14, the sign in the source. The prophecy concerning the desecration of the temple is understood by the evangelist as having been fulfilled in its destruction. In this Brandenburger follows Pesch *(Das Markus-evangelium)* rather than Hahn, although his analysis of tradition and redaction is closer to Pesch *(Naherwartungen)* in that he argues for a brief source and considerable Markan redaction. Thus Brandenburger, like Pesch *(Das Markus-evangelium),* argues for a Markan eschatology dissociated from earthly, historical events, and focussed ultimately on a Christological event—the theophany of the Son of Man.

Yet Brandenburger does not agree with Pesch that the evangelist is in any way attempting to counter 'parousia enthusiasts' or delay expectation of the day of salvation. Indeed, a large proportion of Brandenburger's final chapter is given to the analysis of vv.28-33, illustrating that these often over-looked verses are in fact the climax to the secret revelation, where the Markan community is instructed in the appropriate way to act in their situation—to be vigilant. This is made clear by the final piece of Markan framework which breaks open 'the secret': "But what I am saying to you, I am saying to everyone: 'Be on the alert!'" (v.37).

[10] See Appendix 3 for full details. Verse 10 and most of 28 are left unresolved by Brandenburger, though he is inclined to regard v.10 as a pre-Markan insertion into vv.9-13.

[11] Lambrecht, Review, 748: "Es scheint mir noch immer, daß die markinische Redaktion an vielen Stellen unterschätzt wird".

Mk 13 in its religio-literary context

The text of Mk 13 has been read against the background of four broad groups of literature:

(i)   The Old Testament, which it alludes to extensively (in many versions—see chapter 3). We have included Daniel in this category.

(ii) Other apocalyptic writings (examined briefly in this chapter— hence the classification of the method as 'religio-literary', to distinguish it from analysis of Biblical traditions on the one hand, and from comparisons with the broader spectrum of first century literature on the other).

(iii) The rest of the New Testament, for which it becomes something of a paradigm (with the exception of the earlier writings of Paul). This was partly examined in chapter 2 above and is explored further in chapter 8 below.

(iv) The world of Greco-Roman (or Hellenistic) literature, which is investigated in chapter 8 below.

The analysis of the intertextuality in Mk 13 has often been approached almost entirely through *one* of these four broad groups to the exclusion of the others, and in particular the exclusion of the apocalyptic writings. It has been correctly pointed out that there are many aspects of the apocalyptic imagination that are not represented in Mk 13, but then wrongly concluded that Mk 13 is non- or even anti-apocalyptic. The many parallels to Mk 13 found in the apocalyptic literature by Brandenburger, and to a lesser extent Howard Clark Kee,[12] have helped to provide a balance to the perception of the relationship between Mk 13 and apocalyptic thinking. That this balance has been established by a corresponding over-emphasis on the connections between the Gospel of Mark and apocalyptic literature was perhaps inevitable, even to the point where Mk 13 is interpreted by Brandenburger more in the context of The Assumption of Moses and 4 Ezra than the Gospel of Mark itself. Nevertheless, a brief examination of these parallels is essential for a final assessment of the compositional processes of the author, and hence the structure of the discourse.

Brandenburger defines the final shape of the discourse as a small apocalypse in the form of a testamentary scholarly dialogue (15). This statement could equally well be reversed since 'apocalypses' take so many forms—visions, testaments, letters, discourses—that it is open to question whether or not they should be seen as a genre in their own right. It may be more helpful to use the adjective 'apocalyptic' to describe an all-pervasive socio-literary influence on other genres—analogous to the use of the terms 'gnostic' and 'new age'—rather than as a separate genre of

---

[12] Kee, *Community,* especially 65f. Kee focuses mainly on the Qumran literature.

its own.[13] Yet the following *structural* similarities between Mk 13 and other apocalyptic literature which are pointed out by Brandenburger (15-18) clearly demonstrate his case that the discourse is conceived by the author 'under the influence' of apocalyptic thought-forms:

(i)   The esoteric scene commencing the discourse (vv.3-5a, κατ' ἰδίαν).

(ii)   The key apocalyptic question asked by the students [v.4, cf the 'double leading question' in 4 Ezr 4:33 (110)].

(iii)   The answer by the teacher in the style of a revelation of eternal secrets—aiming to instill confidence in difficult times and convey appropriate behaviour for the final events.

(iv)   The use of apocalyptic parenesis up to and including the final phase of tribulation—including a connection with the idea of salvation [vv.13,23, cf their usage in the last stage of the present time through the period of increasing catastrophe in AsMos 9; 4 Ezr 9:7f; 13:23 (18)].

(v)   The meaning and function of 'signs' in apocalyptic literature [vv.28f and the first three visions of 4 Ezra (110-112)] and especially the 'when...then...' scheme of v.29 [cf 4 Ezr 8:63f (117)].

(vi)   The use of parables as part of the answer to 'the eschatological question' [vv.28f,34f, cf 4 Ezr 4:44-50; 5:50-55, which include the parenesis 'consider yourself', similar to βλέπετε (116)].[14]

(vii)   The problem of communicating traditional secret teachings (the contrast of ὑμεῖς and πάντες in v.37).

The strength of Brandenburger's analysis is that these parallels are evidence of apocalyptic thought patterns which lie behind the very structure of the discourse. Others have conceded that apocalyptic imagery, symbols and language occur in the chapter, but they have usually used this as a basis for isolating a non-Markan apocalyptic source *against* which the Markan parenesis and redaction is directed. Brandenburger also sees much of the parenesis as Markan redaction, but argues that it is part of the overall apocalyptic structuring of the discourse rather than in tension with the apocalyptic source used in the discourse. This then allows Brandenburger to give a more positive and even-handed assessment of both the source itself and the Markan updating of it, since he is not concerned to show a fundamental difference of perspective between them. It becomes apparent, however, that the motive he describes for that updating is not as clear as he assumes. For since he

---

[13] See, for example, Lars Hartman, "Survey of the Problem of Apocalyptic Genre", in *Apocalypticism in the Mediterranean World and the Near East,* ed D. Hellholm (Tübingen 1983), 329-343; and also Brandenburger's own comments, *Markus 13,* 14, footnote 9.

[14] See also Priscilla Patten, "The Form and Function of Parables in Select Apocalyptic Literature and their Significance for Parables in the Gospel of Mark", *NTS* 29 (1983), 246-258. Unfortunately, however, Patten makes no reference to the parables in Mk 13.

regards vv.24-27 as part of the source he concludes that the Markan revision was necessitated by the non-return of the Son of Man at the fall of Jerusalem. This results in some difficulties for Brandenburger's interpretation. How is it possible for a recently 'failed' prophecy to be fixed up and then attributed to the historical Jesus by the author of Mark? And why is it that in the updated version of the source the only changes made to the actual chronology of events are the addition of vv.9-13 *before* the fall, and vv.21-23 and the μετὰ τὴν θλῖψιν ἐκείνην of v.24 afterwards? Surely a greater motivation than this relatively minor shift in timing is required in order to justify bringing out a new edition of the apocalypse? Wouldn't the devastation of Jerusalem and the non-appearance of the Son of Man have required a change in *perspective* rather than just a brief postponement of the expected event?

In any case, the analyses in chapters 1 to 5 above have demonstrated that vv.24-27 are not part of the source but are a Markan compilation of Septuagintal phrases. Similarly, vv.7-8 do not appear to have belonged originally to the source, but rather to a group of sayings displaying Aramaic influence which includes vv.11a,b,d,12,13a, and 22. This forces adjustments to Brandenburger's conclusions in at least two directions—a re-examination of his conclusion that vv.24-27 contain a description of a theophany and an assurance of salvation (57f), and a re-evaluation of the structural outline he gives for the discourse.

Brandenburger points out that parenesis is present in apocalyptic literature up until the end of what is perceived as the present age (v.23 in Mk 13), and therefore concludes that vv.24-27 represent the final event— the turning point of the ages—where the theophany of the Son of Man brings righteous judgment for the nations and salvation for the elect. The occurrence of parenesis in vv.5b-23 and its total absence in vv.24-32 (18, 106) is basic to his argument, as is the presence of an underlying concern over the question of salvation (vv.13,20) which finds its answer, according to Brandenburger, in vv.24-27. Yet it is open to challenge whether Brandenburger's neat divisions between parenesis and other material are valid. He concedes himself that parenesis returns in vv.33f, but argues that this is part of a teaching reflection on the first section of the chapter rather than an indication that parenesis pervades the whole discourse and therefore may not be so easy to separate from it. His conclusion that all of vv.9-13 constitute a parenetic insertion could also be questioned, since v.12 at least could be seen as a continuation of the apocalyptic woes of vv.7-8. Clearly parenesis *does* occur at vv.5b,9a,13b,23,33,35-37; and arguably in a number of other places, such as vv.7b,11,14-16,18,21,28-29, though this is dependent on the definition of 'parenesis' and whether it includes *both* exhortation (such as in vv.5b,9a,21,33,35,37) *and* reassurance (such as in vv.7b,11,13b,23). Ultimately, such definitional problems do not in themselves cloud the issue, as it is at least clear that it is not possible simply to claim that vv.5b-6,9-13, and 21-23 are 'the parenetic insertions' made by the evangelist (164). It follows that in terms of using the presence or absence of parenesis to locate the last stage of the present time, the question must remain open as to whether v.23 represents the *end* of the Markan present or its *beginning,* and thus also whether vv.24-27 are an 'end' in themselves or part of the present process.

Similarly, it is possible to challenge Brandenburger's assumption that the idea of salvation is the underlying theological question of the discourse which finds its answer in vv.24-27. This seems to be a case where the parallels found in 4 Ezra and The Assumption of Moses have dictated the agenda in Mk 13 rather than its context in the Gospel of Mark. Of course it depends on how 'salvation' is understood—whether in purely 'spiritual' terms, or as healing, as political deliverance, as the path of discipleship, or just simply as surviving. Throughout the Gospel of Mark σῴζω is used of healing (3:4; 5:23,28; 6:56); as part of the taunting of Jesus on the cross where it has an ambiguous sense (15:30,31,31); as survival (13:20: 'no human being would have survived', *NJB*); and in an ultimate or spiritual sense ('losing life to save it' 8:35,35; 10:26). The usage in 13:13b is clearly at this latter level, assuring those who endure to 'the end' that they shall be saved. But the 'end' referred to must surely be understood in the first place as being that described in vv.9-13a—the 'hour' of being 'handed over'. Given the Markan sequence of the 'handing over' of John the Baptist (1:14), Jesus of Nazareth (9:31; 10:33; 14:41,42) and true followers (13:9-13)—even into martyrdom—the promise of salvation and the reference to 'the end' in 13:13b are clearly not dependent only on the later events of vv.14-21 or 24-27 for their meaning. Indeed, the Judeans are not exhorted to *endure* the events of vv.14-21, but to flee!

Given these understandings of 'salvation' in the Gospel of Mark, it would appear that the events of vv.24-27 do not offer a Markan picture of 'salvation' (as used by Brandenburger) as such, but rather one of a gathering together—a new community. Certainly vv.9-13 and the theme of losing life in faithful witness provide the best context for the primary interpretation of v.13b. The other occurrence of σῴζω (v.20), is unrelated to this theme and concerned with the question of surviving the tribulation. It is difficult then to argue that 'salvation' as such is a key concern underlying the discourse. There *are* clear indications that a re-phrasing of Christian hope and purpose is being undertaken, and that encouragement and assurance is being directed at those suffering— including the assurance of salvation for the faithful (v.13b). But the overriding concern of the discourse appears to be a call to mission and alertness—to be found on active duty when 'The End' comes—rather than a preoccupation with the end itself.

Thus if neither the presence or absence of parenesis nor the theme of salvation point directly to vv.24-27 as 'The End' as Brandenburger has argued, then what do vv.24-27 describe and is there any other 'End' in view in Mk 13? The imagery of vv.24-27 clearly overlaps with that used in theophanies, descriptions of the Day of Yahweh, and the language used by later writers to describe the parousia. These concepts themselves are not mutually exclusive in the tradition anyway, so it not necessary to decide on just one of these three categories but rather to describe what it actually means in Markan terms. Brandenburger does this from the perspective of other apocalyptic literature by identifying the stages and symbolism of a theophany, and by stating that it is of salvific significance for the Markan community. We have used Hartman as the example of those who examine the problem from the perspective of the Old Testament and identify the 'Day of the Lord' in vv.24-27, complete with the judgment of the nations. Beasley-Murray has also explored the Old Testament imagery of 'that Day' extensively,[15] but ultimately connects the Danielic coming of the Son of Man with New Testament traditions, and identifies the event in vv.24-27 as the parousia. These links with other traditions must certainly be explored, but they should not be permitted to obscure what the author of Mark might be intending to communicate through such imagery. Ultimately it is the Markan context which must determine the interpretation of vv.24-27, yet it is that very context which many commentators seek to relocate or avoid.[16]

At the risk of repetition, we suggest that it is manifestly obvious that Mk 13:24-27 and its context indicates:

(i)   that the events of vv.24-27 occur soon after the tribulation of vv.14-21 and within a generation of the historical Jesus (v.30; indicating that the beginning of these events must have *already* been apparent to the evangelist and to the Markan community);

(ii) that it is a sequence of events—a process—rather than one climactic event ['... in those days ...', *plural*, '... and then' (v.26) '... and then' (v.27)];

(iii) that the one clear precedent to v.26 (Dn 7:13) has a Son of Man *coming to* the Ancient of Days on the clouds, not returning to earth;

(iv) that as in Mk 14:62, it is the powers *opposing* Jesus (13:26 'when *they* see ...') who will see his vindication, *not* the elect;

(v)   that given the apocalyptic and prophetic symbolism of heavenly bodies representing earthly rulers, and the ambiguous use of ἄγγελος in the Gospel of Mark (cf 1:2), it is not at all certain that vv.24-27 are to be understood as purely celestial events;

---

[15] See especially Beasley-Murray, *Jesus and the Kingdom of God*. Note also his comment in "The Vision on the Mount", 46: ""'Day of the Lord'" it may be, but not every "day" of the Lord signifies the last day."

[16] Certainly Brandenburger cannot be accused of avoiding the context, but he does cite a classic example of this (*Markus 13*, 105). He quotes E. Gräßer, *Das Problem der Parusieverzögerung in den synoptischen Evangelien und in der Apostelgeschichte* (Berlin 1960), 164f, as concluding: "We do not know how the compiler (!) has intended the transition from v.27 to 28 to be. In any case, the parable in this position is misplaced and secondary."

(vi)   that although vv.24-25 contain Old Testament allusions whose context includes the judgment of the nations from Jerusalem, the final and overriding allusions behind vv.26-27 are of the positive images of the gathering of the nations to worship Yahweh (Dn 7:13; Zc 2:10 LXX);

(vii)   that therefore these things occur without any specific reference to a judgment of the nations (apart from the judgment on the Jerusalem temple State itself), and without any hint that the 'abomination causing desolation' has been defeated or is not still 'standing where he ought not' even as the gathering takes place— which questions their status as events of the eschaton;

(viii) that the parable in vv.28f *includes* vv.24-27 amongst those things that indicate that *it* (= the summer, the time of fruiting and harvest) is near (v.29); and

(ix)   that the most significant change in parenesis occurs in the transition from βλέπετε through ἀγρυπνεῖτε to γρηγορεῖτε, commencing in v.33, not in the absence of parenesis between vv.24-32.

We are compelled then to accept what was once a more common interpretation of these verses, namely that up until v.30 the discourse refers to discernible historic events surrounding the fall of Jerusalem.[17] The implications of this for the *Sitz im Leben* of the source and the writing of the Gospel shall be explored further in chapter 7 below, but it remains to ask if Mk 13 has any other 'end' in view if vv.14-27 are not understood as such, and to examine the impact of these conclusions on the structure of the discourse as a whole.

It has been shown in chapter 5 above that the references to 'that day and hour' and 'the end' are used in such a way as to include both the 'eschatological' in the 'historical' and the 'personal' in the 'corporate'— that is, they are deliberately ambiguous. It has also already been argued in this chapter that 'the end' spoken of in v.13b should be understood in terms of the persecution of faithful missionaries in vv.9-13a, which raises the question as to whether there is a corresponding allusion to an ultimate 'End' within the discourse. Clearly the parable of v.34f speaks of an 'event' that comes as unexpectedly as the returning master of a household, whilst v.32 denies any knowledge of the timing of such an event. There also appears to be a shift in the nature of the parenesis from v.33 onwards—there being one last βλέπετε to sum up the need to *discern* historical events, before changing to the call for *vigilance* and *alertness* in

---

[17] This position (with the exception that most make v.32 the start of the reference to the 'parousia') has been argued most recently by France, *Jesus and the OT,* Appendix A: "The Reference of Mark 13:24-27", 227-239, which includes a list of earlier and recent scholars who support this interpretation; and *Divine Government. God's Kingship in the Gospel of Mark* (London 1990). France seems to remain largely unaware of the radical implications of his basic position, and strives to preserve vv.32f as a reference to the parousia so that the integrity of Jesus *and* Mark *and* also a unified (monolithic?) interpretation of NT eschatology can all be maintained.

preparation for the ultimate event. Is it possible that v.31 acts as the transition between the 'historical' and the 'eschatological' and is therefore understood by the evangelist as referring to the ultimate 'End'—the passing away of the heavens and the earth?[18]

Most have taken this verse to be a solemn affirmation of the verses that precede it, and certainly it seems to be linked in the pre-Markan tradition with v.30. In this view, the stress is placed on the second half of the verse, ' . . . but my words will never pass away', and the assumption is that it is the words preceding v.31 that are referred to. Indeed, if vv.30-31 originally provided the climax to a prophecy then this is exactly how they should have been understood. But the question is whether the author of Mark interpreted the verse that way when he followed it with the strong denial of knowledge of the time or details of 'That Day': 'But concerning *that day* no-one knows...' (13:32). Why is 'That Day' usually interpreted by ignoring the immediate context (v.31) and by referring back to the process occurring in 'Those Days' (vv.24-27)? Might it not be possible to read the *first* half of v.31 just as emphatically as the second: "Heaven and earth *will pass away*...", and see it as interpreted by the evangelist as affirming that there will be an ultimate End? A cosmic End about which we know nothing, but which—by analogy—might also come unexpectedly and existentially in the form of 'that day' or 'that hour' of our own test of discipleship (13:11; 14:41)?

At the level of tradition history it is not possible to split v.31 away from v.30 so easily, but in the re-evaluation of the structure of the discourse which follows, the possibility that v.32 has been deliberately placed after v.31 to reinterpret it has been taken seriously. At the very least, we would suggest that v.32 should follow straight on from v.31, rather than, as in most texts, there being a break between them.

In general terms then, the perspective of the 'when' and 'what sign of fulfilment' question of the disciples has been corrected in the discourse to indicate that for the Markan Jesus:

(i)   The demise of the temple is just a small part of the tumultuous events that will soon overtake Judea and surrounding areas (vv.5b-23), and discernment must be used to avoid being deceived into overestimating its significance—it is, after all, a human idol, a 'temple made with human hands' which falls far short of its intended use as 'a house of prayer for all nations';

(ii) Rather than provide a 'sign' of 'The End', the gathering of the new multi-ethnic community after the fall of the temple will

---

[18] The modern categories 'eschatological' and 'historical' are retained in inverted commas because, as has been pointed out, the text of the Gospel of Mark shows scant regard for such distinctions. Even this 'ultimate end' of vv.31f is spoken of in terms that are used again in the passion narrative (and 13:11) of profoundly significant but thoroughly 'historical' events (see chapter 5 above). Yet it can be argued that the 'passing away of heaven and earth' (as *distinct* from the cosmic activity of vv.24-27) represents an 'End' of an ultimate nature that is the prerogative of God alone—only the Creator may de-create the cosmos.

indicate the authority given to the vindicated Son of Man (vv.24-30), and provide evidence that the harvest is about to begin and the kingdom come with power within a generation of Jesus (Mk 9:1; 13:30);

(iii) The ultimate 'End'—the passing away of heaven and earth (v.31)—is totally in the hands of the Father (v.32), but there are also other 'ends' that must be faced in the course of faithful mission (13:32 and its links with 13:11 and 14:41; 13:35 echoed in the Passion night). The community must be alert and vigilant so as not to be caught sleeping.

It is possible now to show the implications of such interpretations for the perceived structure of the discourse as a whole.

The structure of Mk 13

At this stage we are able to present a compositional structure of Mk 13 which attempts to indicate the organisational motivations of the author rather than the specifically theological (see chapters 5 and 9) or literary (see chapter 8) intentions. The synthesis of all of these approaches is shown in chapter 9. Here we are taking Brandenburger's divisions of the text, based on his religio-literary comparison with other apocalyptic literature, and modifying them and their headings on the basis of what we perceive as the distinctive Markan agenda.

The compositional structure of Mk 13

Scene 1: *vv.1-2—The completion of the temple narrative: final departure and judgment.*

Scene 2: *vv.3-4—Opposite the temple: the teacher and four disciples— 'the eschatological question': 'when and what sign?'*

vv.5-23—a correction of the perspective of the question by means of an historical review and reinterpretation of recent events, which forms the basis for continued hope and direction for the Markan community.

vv.5b-6:   **Warning** of seduction by false prophets; key word— βλέπετε (v.5b).

vv.7-8:   **Description:** the beginning of the birth pains (ὅταν δὲ ἀκούσητε...).

Reassurance (v.7b): Don't be afraid—these things must happen!

v.9a: **Warning** about being handed over; key word—βλέπετε (v.9a).

vv.9b-13:   **Description:** perseverance and persecution during mission (ὅταν ἄγωσιν ὑμᾶς παραδιδόντες...).
Reassurance (v.11): Don't worry beforehand what to say—the Holy Spirit will give you the words—and the one who endures to the end will be saved.

vv.14-18:   **Warning** about the 'sacrilegious destroyer'; key word—φευγέτωσαν (v.14c).

vv.19-20:   **Description:** the great tribulation (αἱ ἡμέραι ἐκεῖναι...).
Reassurance (v.20): God will shorten the days of tribulation.

vv.21-23a: **Warning** about seduction by pseudochrists and false prophets; key word—μὴ πιστεύετε (v.21) ... ὑμεῖς δὲ βλέπετε (v.23a).

v.22:   **Description:** falsechrists, falseprophets, false signs (σημεῖα καὶ τέρατα...)
Reassurance (v.23b): Everything happens with the prophetic foreknowledge of Jesus.

vv.24-30—the new order: the re-arrangement of the powers, the vindication of the Son of Man and the gathering of the elect. Key word—μάθετε ... ὅταν ἴδητε ... γινώσκετε (v.28).
Reassurance (v.30): These things are beginning to happen now!

vv.31-37—the unknown nature of The End; key word—βλέπετε (v.33), replaced by γρηγορεῖτε—be ready at any time!; and followed by the concluding framework of the apocalypse, v.37, where ὑμεῖς and πάντες are contrasted.

This is not suggested as the final structure of the discourse but rather an insight into the patterns of the language and symbols used. The overlapping sequences of *Warning—Description—Reassurance* are clearly established throughout vv.5-23 in four cycles: the beginnings of troubles (vv.5b-8); mission and persecution (vv.9-13); the awful tribulation (vv.14-20); the false signs and wonder-workers (vv.21-23). Then follows a description of the new community (vv.24-30) and the unknown nature of The End (vv.31-37). But how does such a structuring of the discourse reflect the Markan *Sitz im Leben?* Is there any further way to ensure that such a structure owes more to first century thought patterns than our own? In order to answer these questions, it is necessary to locate the source, the whole discourse, and ultimately the Gospel of Mark, in a meaningful and historically plausible socio-political framework, which is our task in the following chapter.

VII

A PARENESIS FOR THE MARKAN COMMUNITY

Major Proponents: Kelber (1974), Kee (1977), Belo (1981), Myers (1988), Waetjen (1989).
Basic Thesis: That the urgent appeals in Mk 13 indicate events of immediate social, political and theological significance for the Markan community.
Dominant Methods: Socio-political and socio-literary analyses.
Critique: A reappraisal of the situation of the Judean church and the Markan community.

In many respects Willie Marxsen's *Mark the Evangelist* was the forerunner to the sociologically influenced approaches to the Gospel listed above. Yet whilst Marxsen's application of redaction analysis to the Gospel of Mark contained some stunning socio-political implications for the Markan *Sitz im Leben,* it led initially to a series of studies on the *theological* significance of the Markan redaction.[1] The 'crossroad' that the 'main street' of redaction analysis led to seems to have been used primarily for right-hand turns into theology and literature in the decade following Marxsen's work.[2] However, with the development of sociology and related disciplines and their increasing use in the field of Biblical studies, there have been a number of studies since that have 'turned left' and used the text of the Gospel of Mark as evidence primarily for the setting of the Markan community. Not that the theology of the Markan community and its socio-political setting are mutually exclusive areas of inquiry. On the contrary, for redaction analysis leads in both directions at once—illuminating the theological intentions of the author as well as suggesting the social and cultural context for which—and in which—the writing takes place. The exact nature and value for exegesis of this relationship between the meaning of texts and their social contexts—between literary and sociological approaches—is a critical issue in current Biblical interpretation that will surface again in the next chapter. Here we focus on those investigations into the Markan *Sitz im Leben* resulting from the application of redaction analysis which move in the direction of sociological analysis, where sociological models derived and tested elsewhere are applied to the Biblical text.

These first descriptions of the socio-political context of the Gospel of Mark entered into the social world of the Gospel in an attempt to describe

---

[1] See chapters 4 and 5 above.

[2] We refer here again to the phrases coined by Perrin, "The *Wredestrasse* Becomes the Haupstrasse", and developed by Donahue, "Redaction Criticism", 48, who asks whether the main street has become a dead-end or a cross-road.

further the christological opponents it was assumed the author was writing against. For Theodore Weeden this was an errant divine-man christology, whereas for WERNER KELBER, who makes more use of Mk 13 in his analysis, it was an errant eschatology—that of the pro-Jerusalem parousia prophets.[3] After a perceptive treatment of the Kingdom theme in Mark as far as chapter 12, Kelber argues that Mk 13 describes "the very crisis which gave rise to the gospel composition, the destruction of Jerusalem and its temple" (110). The prophecy of Jesus against the temple in 13:2c "functions as a 'peg' on which the apocalypse hangs" (112), and it is presented in this way because the destruction of Jerusalem was a recent event for the Markan community. The four disciples in 13:3, whom Kelber sees as being portrayed by the author as the opponents of Jesus and therefore also of the Markan community, reveal by their question that they expect the arrival of the Kingdom to be centred on Jerusalem and linked with the destruction of the temple (113). But this is an ethnocentric eschatology that the author of Mark specifically counters by reinterpreting the events of recent history.

Kelber argues that this is done by framing these recent events (vv.5b-23) with the warnings against false prophets "who have arrogated to themselves the authority and identity of the Messiah Jesus" (115). These parousia prophets claim that the fulfilment of the eschaton has come by "enacting the parousia of Jesus", and it is the main objective of the Markan apocalypse to correct this "erroneously conceived realized eschatology" (115). Thus these pseudo-prophets and christs of vv.5b,6 and vv.21,22 are one and the same group as far as Kelber is concerned, and the author of Mark is opposed to them "both because they miscalculated the time and because they chose the wrong place" (116) for the fulfilment of the Kingdom. The parousia will not occur in Jerusalem at the fall of the temple as the Jerusalem Christians expected, but in Galilee before the present generation in the Markan community passes away.

This reconstruction of recent history is in three sections: the war years (vv.5b-8), persecution and the Gentile mission (vv.9-13), and the abominable destruction of Jerusalem (vv.14-23). The situation of the Markan community is clearly indicated by the 'now' of v.19b and by the aside in v.23, whereby the author reassures the community that "nothing has digressed from Jesus' eschatological masterplan" (122). That this section is a "retrospective contemplation of history" (117) is also indicated by the use of δεῖ (v.7), which is used in this same way of 'events that had to happen' elsewhere in the Gospel (8:31; 9:11). The descriptions of the war years in vv.5b-8 and the persecution of the Christians in vv.9-13 are best explained by events in Israel, not Rome, because at "a time when the people of Israel were divided on the issue of how to deal with the Roman

---

[3] Theodore J. Weeden, *Mark—Traditions in Conflict* (Philadelphia 1971); Kelber, *Kingdom*. The page numbers in brackets in the main body of the text refer to this latter book. It is significant that these two students of Norman Perrin would be among the first in NT studies to explore the exegetical frontiers beyond the limits of redaction analysis.

threat, the exclusively apocalyptic appropriation of Jesus was suited to set Christian against Christian, Christian against Jew, and Christian against Gentile" (118). But these persecutions are not to be understood as the eschaton either, which is why, Kelber argues, the author inserts v.10 to show that the suffering and dispersion of the Christians leads to mission: "As the death of John the Baptist had coincided with the apostolic commission, foreshadowing the death of Jesus which was to usher in the Gentile mission, so does the death of Christians pave the road to the Gentiles" (118).

The reason why the devastation of 13:14 is conceived "in terms of a personal power" (119) is because the "city and its temple have been visited with evil in such unparalleled, concentrated form that it compels the definition of the personification of evil in the end time" (120). Kelber tells us that the destruction of the temple is "*the* apocalyptic disaster" when "Satan has taken possession of the holy temple" (120). This presents difficulties for Kelber's interpretation of vv.14f in at least three areas:

(i) Kelber has very persuasively argued that for Jesus (and therefore for the author of Mark) the temple had already been judged in the ministry and death of Jesus, and that in fact Mk 13 forms "the carefully redacted climax of Jesus' anti-temple mission" (111). How then can it be portrayed as such an evil event for the Markan community when forty years later it is finally destroyed in fulfilment of Jesus' prophecy? Kelber claims that the author "avails himself of apocalyptic symbols, not because he has no real event in mind, but because the event he is reflecting upon is of such horrendous magnitude that it is adequately conveyed only through the medium of apocalypticism" (120). But why would the author reserve such dark and mysterious symbols (if indeed that is what they are) for the destruction of an institution which was already symbolically judged by Jesus in 11:12-25 and deserted by God in 15:38?

(ii) Another difficulty is to understand how it is possible for the Judeans (or the even wider audience suggested by the second person plural 'you') to *see* this abominable event? This "invitation to see, when taken literally, is nonsensical" (120), Kelber admits, and proceeds to argue that *seeing* in the Gospel of Mark is used primarily in an eschatological sense, meaning to perceive truly, to "break through the veil of secrecy" and have "a vision of eschatological glory" (120). Thus in the context of v.14 it is possible for Christians wherever they live to *see* the disaster "if they perceive its eschatological significance. What they 'see' is an epiphanic event, the epiphany *ad malam partem:* the parousia of the Evil One" (120). This perhaps makes some sense of the general 'when *you* see' of v.14a, except that now not only is the event itself mysterious, according to Kelber, but so too is its perception.

(iii) Even if all this were so, would it not already be too late to flee from such an abomination? If the event is linked closely with the desecration of the temple and the fall of Jerusalem, what is the point of *Judeans* fleeing once it is all over? The army of Titus must have been a heavy burden on the surrounding Judeans as it lay siege to Jerusalem for some five months before the final sacking—shouldn't the exhortation to flee have been issued *before* the army even arrived in Judea?

These questions will be examined further in the analysis below, but it should be noted here that if it is maintained that the Gospel of Mark dates from after the fall of Jerusalem then the prophetic integrity of Jesus depends on a *detailed* fulfilment of Mk 13, and especially vv.14f. That is, if the author of Mark portrays vv.14f as coming from the lips of Jesus and writes after the events it foretells, *then it must have recently been fulfilled in every respect!*

Regarding the problem of exhorting people already dwelling in the mountains of Judea to flee *into the mountains,* Kelber is inclined to agree with those who affirm the redactional nature of ἐν τῇ Ἰουδαίᾳ, arguing that "the evangelist updates the text to make it respond to Christians who live disoriented in Judea" (121). From Kelber's perspective the whole of the Gospel narrative points away from Judea to Galilee (1:5; 3:7), so the flight of the Judeans into the mountains is to be understood "in the broader system of Mark's geographical coordinates" as ultimately pointing to Galilee. Thus it becomes "an eschatological exodus out of the land of Satan into the promised land of the Kingdom" (121), reinforced by the call to Galilee which concludes the Gospel (16:7). 'Those days' (v.17) which follow the flight are the present time of great tribulation (v.19a) for the Markan community, which for Kelber is the period "between the parousia of Satan on the one hand and the parousia of the Son of Man on the other" (122). Like Pesch and Brandenburger, Kelber recognises that v.23 clearly indicates the *Sitz im Leben* of the Markan community, but he seems to locate it more between the 'now' of v.19b and v.23. It is not clear how Kelber justifies historically the description of this time *after* the fall of Jerusalem as the worst tribulation in history (v.19) when most accounts of the period, including those of Josephus, would seem to indicate that such a description might be more appropriate for the time of the siege of Jerusalem itself.

The central section of the discourse, vv.24-27, is also in three parts according to Kelber—the cosmic drama (vv.24-25); the coming of the Son of Man (v.26); and the ingathering of the elect (v.27). These events, to which Kelber uncritically applies the non-Markan term *parousia,* are to occur 'in those days' of the Markan community but 'after that tribulation' (v.24). This rather "cumbersome dating" is "indicative of Mark's effort to keep the parousia as near as possible to his own present, while at the same time preserving a necessary distance" (122-123). This coming of the Son of Man is not in order to execute judgment, however, for that has already been experienced because "the judgment which Jesus executed over the temple has come to pass in Mark's time" (124). Nor is the Son of Man linked with judgment anywhere in the Gospel of Mark, 8:38 being a "word of warning, not a true judgment saying" (124) according to Kelber. Rather, the purpose of his coming is to gather the dispersed 'elect ones' and to inaugurate life in the Kingdom.

The final section of the discourse, vv.28-37, is also divided into three parts by Kelber: the parable of the fig tree (vv.28-29); three sayings on the nearness of the end (vv.30-32); and the parable of the doorkeeper (vv.33-37). It aims to re-awaken enthusiasm for the parousia and to establish its rightful relationship to the events in Jerusalem. Whereas the first use of the "eschatological fig tree symbolism" in 11:12-14,20-21 "served to illustrate how the Kingdom had come to grief in the temple" (124), the second (vv.28-29) announces the hope of the fulfilment of the Kingdom. The reference in v.29 is to the first half of the disciples' question in v.4, and shows that the destruction of the temple indicates the nearness of the parousia. Thus Kelber concludes that: "If a *sēmeion* is given at all, the Satanic usurpation of the temple is the negative sign presaging the beginning of the end" (125). The ταὗτα πάντα of v.30 refers to the second half of the disciples' question, concerning the fulfilment of *all things,* and shows clearly that the author of Mark "intends to preserve the parousia hope for his own generation" (127). The only sure grounds for this hope are the words of Jesus (v.31), and though the parousia will certainly occur after "the destruction and during this generation" (125), no more exact timetabling is possible (v.32) as the day and hour are unknown even to the angels and the Son. Therefore the parenetic conclusion to the speech enjoins watchfulness on all because "Jesus may well come suddenly and without further advance sign" (126).

It is both the strength and weakness of Kelber's interpretation that he attempts to describe a Markan situation which explains the genesis of the Gospel as a whole.[4] The strength lies in the appeal of a model which appears to explain many of the various puzzles and themes of the Gospel narrative. From the emphasis on Galilee, the negative picture of the disciples and family of Jesus, to the final mysterious ending, Kelber claims to have found a unifying key—a Gospel written in northern Palestine after the devastation of those Jewish Christians in the south who expected the parousia of the Son of Man at the fall of the temple. So varied and often incidental is the evidence Kelber marshals for this interpretation that a Roman provenance for the Gospel of Mark can never be taken for granted again.[5] However the weakness of Kelber's

---

[4] In fact, *Kingdom* focuses on the first 13 chapters of the Gospel of Mark only, but Kelber's contribution to Kelber, W. H. (ed.) *The Passion in Mark. Studies on Mark 14-16,* (Philadelphia 1976), completes his analysis of the Gospel and develops further his view of the literary control of the author over the content of the whole Gospel.

[5] See, for example, Kelber's pertinent comments on the occurrence of Latinisms throughout the Gospel. After listing 10 specific instances, *Kingdom,* 129, footnote 1, he

interpretation is evident when it becomes clear that *everything* in the Gospel is to be used as evidence to support his model. As a result, very little is said about pre-Markan traditions and their effect on the shaping of the narrative.[6] Instead all levels of the tradition are bent, and sometimes twisted, to fit the *Sitz im Leben* of the Markan community. Even the sense of time in the narrative is overridden by Kelber's interpretation of the καιρός of the Kingdom, such that the 'now' (v.19b) and 'this generation' spoken of by Jesus in the narrative become the 'now' and 'this generation' of the Markan community. Kelber is correct to see in v.23 an indirect indication of the Markan present, but it is not then appropriate to re-set the narrative clock and violate specific time references within the text in order to fit this insight. Could the first hearers of the Gospel be so naïve as to understand the 'this generation' of Jesus, set in a narrative context, as restarting with their own generation some forty years later?

A further example of the problems caused by a failure to take full account of possible traditions behind the text is the incongruity of the heavy emphasis Kelber places on the Satanic nature of the temple destruction. As argued above, this detracts somewhat from the strong case Kelber had already made regarding Jesus' anti-temple mission. Why would the destruction of the temple be such a disaster for the Markan community? If they see the rise of the evil one as judgment on the misguided Jews and Christians of Jerusalem, which seems to be Kelber's interpretation at times (124), why should they regard the actual event with such horror? These questions would have some hope of resolution if Kelber were to take seriously the possibility of a separate *Sitz im Leben* for the source behind vv.14f, but he mentions that possibility only in passing (135). Already in these examples the later tendency of Kelber to emphasise the novelty of the written Gospel can be seen, with the corresponding down-playing of the significance of pre-Markan oral and written traditions.[7]

points out that: "Upon analysis, the Latin loan-words in Mark fall exclusively into the category of military and economic terms. This reflects the situation not of Rome, but of an occupied country, because it is there that the imperial power imposes its military might and economic structure most tangibly upon the people. Roman origin of the gospel would have resulted in a penetration of Latinisms into the domestic, social and religious language of the gospel." It is in this type of comment that Kelber begins to move from composition analysis towards the direction of socio-political analysis.

[6] Indeed, in the preamble to the interpretation of Mk 13 Kelber, *Kingdom,* 110, says more about the possibility of post-Markan redactors than of pre-Markan tradition. He does eventually give some space to the interpretation of Lars Hartman in his final chapter, but there to make the dubious equation between Hartman's proposed 'Danielic midrash', Colani's 'Little Apocalypse' and the errant theology of the Markan opponents (135)! This must have been an 'off the top of the head' suggestion without an examination of the contradictions involved.

[7] See W. H. Kelber, *The Oral and Written Gospel: The Hermeneutics of Speaking and Writing in the Synoptic Tradition, Mark, Paul and Q* (Philadelphia 1983); and the interesting assessment of Kelber's "over-strict distinction between 'orality' and 'textuality'" by L. W. Hurtado, "The Gospel of Mark: Evolutionary or Revolutionary Document?", *JSNT* 40 (1990), 15-32.

But the most serious problem of all in Kelber's interpretation of Mk 13 is in the reasons he suggests for the disagreement between the parousia prophets and the author of Mark, and the resulting reinterpretation of the parousia hope for the Markan community. The real bone of contention, according to Kelber, is the place and time of the parousia and the fulfilment of the Kingdom—not Jerusalem before the fall of the temple, but in Galilee within a generation of the fall. Yet on closer examination, the parousia hope is not to be diminished at all. The present experience of the Markan community is the 'crack' between v.23 and v.24, a precarious position, which is perhaps why Kelber sometimes seems to push it back into the tribulations of v.19. Kelber himself declares that it is "a tenuous borderline which separates the Markan present from the parousia" (123), which means that there is not much difference as far as timing goes between the Markan position and that of the opponents. This makes Kelber's claim that: "Out of the ruins of misconstrued time he reconstructs new time" (128) seem a little extravagant. Is not that 'new time' also misconstrued? Just what was it that happened back in Galilee that constituted a more valid fulfilment of the parousia hope than what occurred in Jerusalem?

It is also apparent that there isn't any clear distinction—such as Kelber makes—between Jerusalem and Galilee in Mk 13. The exhortation for the Judeans to flee further into the mountains is more naturally understood as a call to keep clear of the war, rather than a call to flee to Galilee. Undoubtedly the Gospel concludes with a call to return to Galilee (16:7), but this can be better understood as a call to return to the beginning of the Gospel again—to the place of discipleship, call and mission—in order to walk again 'on the way' with the knowledge of the true identity of the suffering Son of Man. If Kelber were to argue that this is what is meant by the 'parousia' in the Gospel of Mark, as opposed perhaps to those expecting a returning Son of Man who rules and judges from Jerusalem, then there might be better grounds for his position. But he insists that the "Markan apocalypse is exclusively concerned with the parousia despite its recent bankruptcy. All its energies are devoted to the preservation and reinstatement of the parousia as imminent hope" (128). Just what this 'parousia' means for Kelber (let alone the author of Mark, who never uses the term) is not clear, but he insists that for the Markan community this event will occur within a generation and in Galilee.

Here then is the nub of the matter as far as Kelber's interpretation is concerned. Does the author of Mark simply relocate the parousia a few miles further north in Palestine and a few years later than the fall of Jerusalem, so that Mk 13 becomes the first example of that favourite obsession of some Christians in every generation since—the recalculation of The End, or the 'rapture', or 'the second coming'? Or does Kelber have something else in mind for the Markan community when he summarises the theological intentions of the author: "Having purged the parousia hope of its unfortunate involvement in history, he can once again offer it as the unbroken promise of a true future" (127)? Did the promise remain unbroken for only one generation of Galilean Christians? Or was there some event fitting the description of vv.24-27 which at least *began* to satisfy that hope and realise that true future? In other words, is there not a case for suspecting that the author of Mark does not merely rehabilitate the parousia hope of the Jerusalem opponents, but radically reinterprets and transforms it altogether? Otherwise the Gospel of Mark merely succeeds in relocating the fulfilment of the Kingdom from one misconstrued time and place to the next.

The collection of studies on the Gospel of Mark by HOWARD C. KEE focuses even more deliberately on the community situation and ethos out of which the Gospel arose, and takes a tentative step towards using sociological models to sharpen the analysis.[8] The book itself is a curious collection of approaches to interpreting the Gospel, representing, by the author's own confession, a "social-cultural-historical method in New Testament study" (ix), but 'religio-historical' and 'religio-literary' could easily have been added to the description. Kee commences with an examination of the possible literary antecedents of the Gospel of Mark, but concludes that the Gospel is a wholly new genre whose closest links are with the Jewish apocalyptic narratives. A survey of Markan style, syntax and structure follows, which leads to the conclusion that attempts to provide a theological outline of the Gospel are fruitless and even misleading. Rather, Kee contends, the narrative must be understood as a complex thematic development of the central motif of God's rule, with the "one architectural feature that stands out" being the "eschatological vision of Jesus' exaltation at God's right hand" (75) seen on the mount of transfiguration (9:2f). The biographical style of the Gospel, Kee argues, is consistent with other apocalyptic writings which focus on a special agent of God who addresses the critical needs of his community, and it is an examination of the community behind the Gospel of Mark that occupies the rest of Kee's book.

It is in this attempt to describe the social and cultural setting of the Markan community that Kee comes closest to a true socio-political approach. He makes some use of Weber's analysis of 'break-away' movements, arguing that such a category must surely include apocalyptic groups (78). The point of this sociological analysis is Weber's concept of the importance of a prophet figure, and in particular the 'ethical prophet', who provides a new framework of understanding for a community afflicted by social and political impotence. Such a re-shaping of a community's symbolic universe leads to a "hope of transformation and meaning" (78) amidst overwhelming hostile forces. Kee believes that this task of re-shaping and conveying a new reality to the community is

[8] Kee, *Community*. From now on, page numbers in brackets in the main body of the text refer to this book. It is interesting to note that Kee, like Kelber, dedicates his book to Norman Perrin—further evidence of the profound influence of Perrin on post-war Markan scholarship.

achieved through the Markan portrayal of Jesus and his disciples. The disciples in the Gospel of Mark are regarded by Kee as the models for the Markan community, and thus despite their many failings are not interpreted like Kelber in a totally negative way. The "disciples of the ethical prophet are an alienated people" but rather than retreat and deny the world, like some of the other Jewish sects of the day, "they claim the world for God, and by means of a 'messianic eschatology', they await the ultimate political and social transformation of the world" (78). Kee then briefly links this model with the work of the social anthropologist K. O. L. Burridge, who has "traced the stages by which movements arise which expect radical transformation in the future, knowledge of which has been given to the members of the community through a divinely endowed prophet" (78).

These sociological models may have been important in shaping the initial direction of Kee's work, but he does not go on to make any systematic use of them in his later chapters. Rather he turns to a religio-historical comparison of Jewish sectarian groups, including Hasidism and other alienated religious communities, in order to illuminate the background of the Markan situation. It is perhaps in this section of the book with the parallels adduced from apocalyptic literature, and in the final section on the ethics of the Markan community, that Kee makes his most enduring contribution to Markan scholarship.

Thus this final half of Kee's work comprises a description of the disciples as models for the Markan community, the provenance of the Gospel itself, and a description of the Markan community—its christology, eschatology and ethics. In presenting the essential characteristics of the disciples Kee draws attention to the links with the Cynic-Stoic style of itinerant charismatic preaching;[9] the radical break with all ordinary human ties and obligations; the "avoidance of political involvement" (93); and the esoteric and inclusive aspects of the community of followers. These features are then interpreted as being normative for the Markan community, thus:

An essential element of the role of his (ie Jesus') followers in Mark is the prophetic-apocalyptic figure whose coming heralds and even precipitates the breakdown of the family and other basic social structures. The end is at hand; there is no time to lose: all human obligations and ties must give way before the urgent demands of preparing God's elect people for the last days. (87)

---

[9] Thereby anticipating the direction later taken by some prominent members of the Jesus Seminar. See Marcus J. Borg, *Jesus in Contemporary Scholarship* (Valley Forge 1994), for a helpful overview of the recent tendency for many North American scholars to interpret Jesus and the earliest Jesus traditions as reflecting a Cynic-Stoic, and therefore non-eschatological, sapiential origin. Kee in turn is very critical of such 'flights from apocalyptic'. See his comments in: "A Century of Quests for the Culturally Compatible Jesus", *TheolToday* 52 (1995), 17-28.

Yet despite the urgency of the times and a tendency towards some esoteric traditions in some parts of the Gospel (κατ' ἰδίαν, and the 12, 4 and 3 of the inner circles), Kee sees the community as remaining radically open—to women, children, Gentiles from all the surrounding districts—in short "open across social, economic, sexual, and ethnic barriers." (97) The community was not to retreat into itself nor develop a theology of judgment on the world around it, but rather to "carry forward the work of preaching, healing, and exorcisms that Jesus had begun" (96-97).

This fact highlights a major tension in Kee's interpretation. How is it possible for the community to remain so open and for there to be such an extended emphasis on discipleship, ethics and mission in the Gospel of Mark, when according to Kee the time is so short and the end will occur within the current generation? In other words, if the end is so imminent why does the author of Mark write a Gospel and community handbook when just an apocalyptic pamphlet (= Mk 13) would seem to be more appropriate? It is difficult to see how the discipleship teaching of a community so dominated by imminent disaster could be understood as anything but 'interim ethics', yet to his credit Kee avoids such a conclusion, for it is not possible to write off the ethical teaching in the Gospel so simply. Kee is somewhat hesitant about his pre-fall dating of the Gospel, stating that: "The lack of precision in the prophetic description of the fate of Jerusalem in Mark 13, while not conclusive evidence, points to its having been written prior to the events which it predicts" (100-101). This of course may well be true, but the Gospel itself (as distinct from that part of Mk 13) could still date from after the fall, at which time, contrary to Kee's assertion (101), the whole issue of the Temple and The End and appropriate models of discipleship and mission would still be very relevant for the Markan community.

The evidence Kee gathers in support of a rural, southern Syrian provenance is more convincing than his pre-fall dating of the Gospel. On linguistic grounds, Kee argues for a bilingual community (Aramaic and Greek), who use the LXX version of the Bible (101). On cultural grounds, and in particular the mention in the Gospel of "practices having to do with agriculture, housing, employment, and land-ownership and taxation" (102), Kee argues that the area of Syria-Palestine is the most likely place of origin. On the grounds that the author appears to have an aversion to the city and locates nearly all the positive action of the narrative specifically in the rural areas, Kee argues that the Gospel must have originated outside of major centres (103). Then because parts of the narrative seem to display an ignorance of Galilean geography, Kee rules Galilee out as a possible location for the Markan community. In summarising the nature of that community, Kee concludes that:

> Mark speaks to and from a community which is influenced both by the Jewish-
> Hasidic-Essene-apocalyptic tradition, with its belief in cosmic conflict about to
> be resolved by divine intervention and the vindication of the faithful elect, and

the Cynic-Stoic style of gaining adherents by itinerant preaching, healing and exorcisms (105).

Unlike the Cynics who urged a withdrawal from worldly pretensions to the simple life, the Markan community held a hope that God would soon reward his covenant people—the elect. This was not to be an exclusive group, but like "the Stoic vision of universal human brotherhood, their membership would transcend all national, religious, and ethnic barriers" (105). Kee gives some examples of similar mixtures of influences amongst religious groups around the borders of Palestine, and concludes that the rural areas of southern Syria meet all the criteria listed above and therefore provide the most likely setting for the Markan community.

In building all these arguments Kee makes full use of the Gospel text as a primary source for developing an understanding of the Markan community. In many instances his case is the stronger because of the incidental nature of the evidence he collects, such as the all-pervasive rural emphasis throughout the Gospel. This is a valid approach, but it may be questioned as to whether Kee has differentiated sufficiently between tradition and redaction in the evidence he has used, and as to whether he has been fully aware of the constraints of the narrative as whole. Because he contends that there is no valid outline for the Gospel, Kee plunders the text everywhere for isolated pieces of evidence, regarding each piece as an equally appropriate indication of the Markan situation. But it is certainly possible that some of the distinctive Palestinian terminology Kee identifies in the Gospel is a reflection of the language and situation of the historical Jesus rather than an indication of the Markan *Sitz im Leben*. Kee's approach also means that he has very little to say about the implications of the overall narrative or about extended passages in the Gospel, such as Mk 13, because each piece of text is used as evidence in its own right rather than as part of a continuous narrative. But it is the text as a *whole* which provides the most balanced evidence for the nature of the Markan community.

Thus the specific contribution of Kee's interpretation towards the understanding of Mk 13 is limited. Aspects of the background of the Markan community described by Kee, and the possible parallels to it both within and outside Judaism, are helpful for an appreciation of the world behind the text, and of particular value is his positive view of the apocalyptic elements in that world. However his review of the issues in Mk 13 is cursory,[10] and at no stage does he treat the discourse as a whole. He concludes in favour of both the importance of the Danielic background

---

[10] Kee, *Community,* 44f, only mentions the work of Lamprecht (= Lambrecht) and Hartman in any detail, and makes the puzzling statement that Hartman's work (arguing for a unitary Danielic 'midrash' with minor Markan editing) is "confirmatory of Lamprecht's conclusions on the whole", the latter's conclusions being that Mk 13 consists of small units of tradition (including Q sayings) held together by major Markan redaction. The work of Pesch and Beasley-Murray is not mentioned, but there are brief references to Bultmann, Haenchen, Lohmeyer, Vielhauer and Gaston.

to the discourse (44-47), and of Markan responsibility for the final form (101), without making specific comments on the extent of any pre-Markan source. Kee's more recent contribution to the discussion about the Old Testament allusions in the discourse *is* significant (46-47), and has been referred to extensively in chapter 3 above. However Kee fails to consider seriously the possibility that part of Mk 13 might represent a socio-political situation different to that of the rest of the Gospel. There is therefore no clear indication as to how the urgent address to the Judeans (vv.14f) relates directly to those in southern Syria, though Kee does point out that Jews and presumably Christians (insofar as any distinction could be made at that time) also suffered persecution in these areas at the time of the Jewish war. Yet clearly the most urgent appeals and the worst of the suffering in Mk 13 are focussed on Judea rather than further afield, which is a factor not adequately accounted for by Kee. It is uncertain therefore as to exactly how the great tribulation suffered in Judea is associated with the imminent expectation of the "cosmic rectifier" (133) by the community in southern Syria. Nor does the complete absence of judgment and victory over evil (the abomination appears to *remain* standing where it oughtn't) in Mk 13 help Kee's case that the Markan community had traditional apocalyptic expectations about the decisive intervention of God.[11]

So whilst Kee's approach provides helpful insights into a possible profile of the theology and ethics of the Markan community and gives many illuminating parallels and contrasts from other contemporary communities, his attempt to describe the community as a pre-fall apocalyptic group must be judged a failure. Ultimately the issue is whether the extreme urgency of Mk 13:14f can be reconciled with the emphasis on discipleship teaching elsewhere in the Gospel in such a way that it too can be seen as indicative of the Markan situation. Kee argues that "the sense of urgency pervades the whole gospel" (101), and support may be found for this position in the recurrent use of εὐθύς and in the dramatic ending at 16:8. However the situation described in 13:14f is clearly of another order of magnitude altogether and requires the most drastic of responses—immediate flight! Yet because the author of Mark conceives of a time 'after that tribulation' (v.24), there are indications that already the worst of the troubles are past as far as the Markan community is concerned, and this is re-affirmed by the assurance of Jesus in v.23. Such reasoning supports a post-fall dating, which would free the Gospel

---

[11] Kee, *Community,* 133f, manages to overlook the fact that the judgmental aspect of the coming Son of Man is absent in Mk 13, but makes a good case for its presence in Mk 8:38. Kee's understanding of the Son of Man in the Gospel of Mark as a corporate figure whose destiny and fate the community share (131) is helpful, as is his brief mention of the 'eschatological vision of ultimate vindication' (132-133) and its possible links with 'Merkabah mysticism'. Yet in the final analysis, Kee's understanding of Mk 13:24-27 reverts to a full-blown apocalyptic conception including all the features *not even referred to in the passage:* "the role of judge, both as punisher of the wicked and as vindicator of the faithful"; "the battle with demonic powers"; and "defeating the hostile powers" (133).

from the intolerable tension between imminent expectation and responsible ethics, and would enable a balanced assessment of the life of the Markan community to be undertaken. Kee's analysis has much to offer in this area once the apocalyptic dimension has been put into its proper perspective.

Socio-political models have been applied far more systematically to the Gospel of Mark in the years since Kelber and Kee. In that they approach the text from the perspective of a pre-determined theory—of society, of politics, or of language itself—they show some similarity to the 'readings' of the more recent literary interpretations. This is exactly the case in the work of FERNANDO BELO, who titles his book *A Materialist Reading of the Gospel of Mark.*[12] The particular socio-anthropological paradigm—a curious mixture of Marxist and structuralist thought—through which Belo interprets the text involves a distinction between the 'system of pollution' and the 'system of debt'. These categories are developed out of Palestinian Judaism, the former being the dominant mode of operation of the conservative religious authorities centred in Jerusalem, and the latter that of the peasant culture of reciprocity—the seed-bed of many prophetic reform movements, including for Belo, the Jesus of the Gospel of Mark. The 'system of pollution' with its ritual purity and cleanliness regulations is seen as the means of maintaining the religious hierarchy and social elite, whereas the 'system of debt'—mutual giving and indebtedness—operates at the level of social praxis in order to bring about equality. Belo then interprets the whole of Jesus' ministry in terms of this praxis of releasing debts and opposing elitist ideas of purity through his unceasing action involving the poor, the outcasts, the women and the Gentiles. For Belo this is the earliest layer of the Jesus tradition which has been clouded and largely ignored by later theological readings of the Gospel—even before the text was written down (238)—and by bourgeois exegesis.

It may be argued that by interpreting the Gospel through such a pre-determined Marxist grid Belo is guilty of one-dimensional exegesis, and to some extent this is undoubtedly true. Belo *has* reduced the Gospel message to a limited set of truths as revealed by one particular methodology. However this is not to deny the validity of the features that have been thrown into sharp relief through this particular approach. Kelber and Kee both mentioned the radical openness of the Markan community and its concern for Gentiles and the fringe-dwellers of Jewish society, but nowhere have they outlined the political and social implications so graphically as Belo: "The oppositions child-youth/adult, servant/master, first/last, rich/poor, define this messianic-ecclesial practice as an *inversion* of the codes that are dominant in the SOC (= social code): *power is the inverse of authority*" (203). Kee also speaks of the Danielic collective Son of Man, but nowhere does he spell out the

---

[12] Fernando Belo, *A Materialist Reading of the Gospel of Mark* (Maryknoll 1981). Page numbers in brackets from here onwards refer to this book.

practical—as distinct from ethical—implications of this concept to the same extent as Belo. The Jesus of the Gospel of Mark, according to Belo, proclaims the collective Son of Man which is a "political strategy aimed at a worldwide table at which the poor are filled" (249). Thus Belo's insight into the social polarisation of the world of first century Palestine demands serious consideration, though it is something of a puzzle to see that Belo then goes on to locate the writing of the Gospel of Mark in Rome.

In his interpretation of Mk 13, Belo locates the Markan community in the time between the fall of the temple and the coming of the Son of Man (200). Therefore the only prediction in the Gospel that stands as a genuine one, according to Belo, is the eschatological event promised in Mk 13:30, since it concerns the only event not to have taken place at the time of writing. "It is therefore a prediction by Mark himself, in response to a problem raised by the *ekklesiai* of Rome" (200). The first part of the discourse is seen as being divided into the 'pains' (vv.5-23) and the liberation of birth (vv.24-27), which are related as sign and fulfilment (197). Belo regards v.14 as referring "undoubtedly to the capture of Jerusalem in 70 by the legions of Titus (this is the desolation) and the burning of the temple (this is the abomination)" (198, brackets are Belo's). Yet ultimately he maintains that:

> Since the text is markedly apocalyptic in character, we must not be overzealous in seeking a strict correspondence with narratives attested by history. Apocalyptic writing, a literature that has to do with the mysterious, is deliberately obscure in its allusions to contemporary events that its readers were reading elsewhere with full clarity. (197)

This is a strange statement from an economic rationalist who has managed to interpret all the rest of the Gospel in terms of historical and social realities. It also displays a lack of understanding of the need for apocalyptic literature to employ symbolic language when attacking the present power structures, a lack that is particularly hard to fathom given the author's involvement with liberation struggles in South America. Perhaps it is another example of how early liberation theology has tended to read apocalyptic imagery as purely 'other-worldly' and 'a-political'. Clearly vv.14f are not meant to remain mysterious symbols for the reader—rather, they have a specific and very urgent message. As if to compensate for this misreading, Belo then goes on to provide a very perceptive remythologisation of vv.14f:

> Judea, Jerusalem and the temple are the center of the world for a Jew; their desolation is the worst of catastrophes according to the Jewish codes. Once the Jewish symbolic field has been destroyed, people must abandon it and flee from it, for it no longer guarantees blessing (that is why to be pregnant or to be nursing becomes a misfortune). In short, this desolation represents the disorganization of the current codes, their upheaval, and the collapse of the symbolic field and the codes that inscribe it. (198)

Such a description seems particularly apt for the post-fall calamity facing Jews and Jewish Christians in Palestine, but exactly how it affects the Markan community in Rome where Belo locates it, is less clear.

In the cosmic events of vv.24-27, Belo sees that "the Jewish *heaven* now collapses along with the Jewish symbolic field" (199), since if "the temple falls, the heaven has no support and will collapse in turn...This is the logic at work in the writing of Mark, which is situated in the 'now' between the two" (199)—and indeed, according to Belo, "We are still in the 'now' between the two events" (200). Yet this assertion creates considerable tension in the interpretation of the text, for Belo clearly states that 'this generation' is to be taken at its face value and that therefore "the end of the delay in the eschatological closure is thus quite precisely determined: it is the lifetime of a generation now growing old (forty years have passed) and of which many in fact are no longer alive" (201). The actual expectation of the Markan community is that "the messianic practice of J(esus) and the ecclesial practice of the disciples will lead, in the eschatological ascent of the Son of man, to the definitive blessing, and this last is drawing near, 'Mark' predicts" (204). Thus Belo's specific conclusions regarding Mk 13 are somewhat confusing—suspended somewhere between Palestine and Rome, between the first generation and the eschaton. But the basic thrust of his attempt to apply a sociological model to the whole text cannot be overlooked, and indeed has set the pattern for many of the following interpretations.

The most substantial socio-political reading of the Gospel of Mark is undoubtedly CHED MYERS, *Binding the Strong Man*,[13] which the author describes as a political reading using a socio-literary methodology. The overarching model which unifies Myers' exegesis, interpretation and application is the use of the Gandhian concepts of nonviolence, liberation and truthforce (xxvii, 47) to illuminate the political stance of Jesus in the Gospel of Mark. The results of this analysis are then used to inform and encourage the involvement of the radical discipleship movement in nonviolent action and symbolic protest against oppressive military and political structures around the world today. Thus the whole book— beginning from its stated presuppositions, its exegetical methods and right through to its application—is unashamedly political in emphasis. It is as if a strong light has been shone from a new direction across a familiar landscape—new perspectives and appreciations of the text are bound to result, as well as new shadows across once familiar ground. No-one in future will ever be able to pretend to be reading Mark a-politically.

In the tradition of Lohmeyer, Marxsen and Kee, Myers argues for a pre-fall northern Palestinian provenance for the Gospel of Mark (41, 417). This he sees as crucial for his interpretation of the Markan anti-Temple polemic and of the political pressures surrounding the Markan

---

[13] Ched Myers, *Binding the Strong Man. A Political Reading of Mark's Story of Jesus* (Maryknoll, NY 1988). Page numbers in brackets in this section refer to this book.

community. Indeed it would be fair to say that Myers has provided the most detailed application of the implications of an immediate pre-fall dating for the interpretation of the Gospel. Arguing that the author of Mark writes for a community in Galilee during the Jewish war, Myers finds evidence of socio-political tension between Roman and Zealot ideologies both within and beneath the text of the whole Gospel. At times this requires considerable exegetical ingenuity, but at other times it is presented with simple force: "Mark knows that his 'non-aligned radicalism,' having rejected the scribal establishment, the Zealot opposition, and the Hellenistic collaborators, places him virtually alone in the historical moment: 'you will be hated by all for the sake of my name' (13:13)" (353). In taking this stance the author of Mark follows truly the "most revolutionary insight" of Jesus "that the powers could only be defeated by the power of what we today call 'non-violence'" (446), an insight which is also related to—and interpreted in the light of—the Gandhian concept of *satyagraha* (47,454). Obviously such an interpretation of the Gospel of Mark is going to range over unfamiliar territory, making it impossible to critique the whole of Myers' work in this context—nor is it all relevant to an understanding of Mk 13. But whatever its weaknesses, the scope of the author's endeavour and his passionate commitment to showing the relevance of the text for today are impressive.

Myers' work does help to bring into sharper focus the problems associated with a pre-fall dating of the Gospel of Mark, and his interpretation of Mk 13 is a critical part of this issue. In many respects the *Sitz im Leben* described by Myers sheds valuable light on some portions of Mk 13, particularly vv.5-13. The deceivers of v.6 are messianic pretenders, according to Myers, who are trying to win support for their fight against Rome and other rival factions. He regards the apocalyptic woes of v.7f as having historical referents in the wars (Rome/Parthia, Rome/Palestine, 66-70), famines (Palestine, early 50's), and earthquakes (Laodicea and Pompei, 61-62) of the Mediterranean world in the two decades preceding the fall of Jerusalem. Indeed so have many other commentators, but Myers goes on to argue that the arrangement of vv.5-13 shows that the Markan interpretation of these events is in opposition to those Jewish rebels who "identified these cataclysmic political and natural events with the 'end time'", thereby using them "as a means to recruit support for their 'messianic' war" against Rome (332). In the Markan scheme of things, these events are not yet the end (v.7b), but only the beginning (v.8b). They do not therefore oblige "the faithful Jew to join the revolt; indeed 'it is necessary that they happen'" (δεῖ, v.7). Since the Markan community incurs the wrath of both sides in the conflict because of their stance (v.13) they will be 'handed over' to both Jewish and Roman authorities (vv.9,11), and this *must* result in mission 'to all nations' (δεῖ, v.10).

These two uses of the 'apocalyptic δεῖ' (vv.7,10) represent the logical outcomes of the two sides in the debate: "The armed struggle of the rebels make the war (i.e., the siege of Jerusalem) *inevitable;* similarly, the nonviolent resistance of the disciples leads to mission 'to all nations'" (333). Thus the insertion of v.10 does *not* indicate that some in the Markan community will survive the persecutions to carry on the mission to the nations, but rather, according to Myers, it completes the cycle of παραδιδόναι sayings and illustrates the necessity of suffering.

> The importance (indeed, the *necessity*) of John/Elijah's mission did not prevent him from being "delivered up," nor will the Messiah's mission save him: thus *the disciples' mission will not "save" them.* This is the discursive function of Mark's placement of the affirmation of the *necessity* of the evangelistic mission between two statements on the *inevitability* of the disciples' being delivered up." (*sic*, 334)

In support of this, Myers points out that Mk 9:11, the question about Elijah coming first, and 13:10 are the only places where πρῶτον δεῖ occur in the Gospel. The depth of this suffering by the community is underscored by the references to internal betrayal (v.12) and the hatred incurred from all quarters (v.13a). Even the reassurance that those enduring to the end will be saved (v.13b) "can be understood only in the context of Jesus' courtroom/cross discourse: to save life was to lose it 'for my sake and the gospel's'" (334).

The unity that this perspective of Myers' brings to the disparate traditions in vv.5b-13 is a strong argument in favour of the particular *Sitz im Leben* he suggests—but does it best describe the recent past of the community or its current situation? Problems arise when this interpretation is extended to include vv.14f and is assumed to apply to the situation of the Markan community in general. Myers interprets v.14 as referring to "the devastation of the entire city by invading soldiers" (335), rather than just an act of desecration in the temple. Why the Judeans should flee *after* this event is not explained,[14] but instead Myers takes refuge both in the mystery of apocalyptic language and symbols and in the imprecision and inaccuracy of genuine prophecy. Because vv.14f do not reflect known events surrounding the fall of Jerusalem with any accuracy, Myers supports J. A. T. Robinson's conclusion that the discourse must have been written pre-fall (335).[15] At the same time he also argues that

---

[14] In fact later on the same page (335), Myers suggests that "when the siege begins Mark instructs Judeans to '*then* flee to the hills'." But neither the beginning of the siege nor the aftermath of devastation would seem to have been very appropriate times to flee—for Judeans or Jerusalemites.

[15] This is becoming an increasingly popular position to take. See for example the comment of Robert A. Guelich, *Mark 1-8:26* (Dallas 1989), xxxi, "a detailed analysis of Mark 13:14 set against the historical background of the war in 67-70 . . . shows that the events associated in much of the current scholarship with the fall of Jerusalem and the destruction of the Temple simply do not fit with this verse that contains both a reference to

apocalyptic language should not be historicised: "The temptation to identify a simple correlation between narrative world and historical events in apocalyptic has been the occasion for most of the abuse of the literature" (327). But to confuse the issue further, not only has Myers given a detailed historical interpretation of vv.5b-13, as outlined above, but his own example of apocalyptic 'updating' from the Assumption of Moses shows specifically how "'historical review' is inserted right into the apocalypse" (326). Thus it appears that for Myers specific historical interpretations of apocalyptic language are made selectively, which would perhaps make sense if he did this consistently when they are written in retrospect (vv.5b-13), but not if the language describes events still in the future for the writer (vv.14f). But as if to prove this wrong, Myers then goes on to suggest that vv.24,25 refer to the moment of Jesus' execution (343) and vv.26-27 to the implied gathering in Galilee at the end of the Gospel (344). In other words, it appears that everything in Mk 13:5b-30 has a specific historical explanation for Myers except for vv.14-19.

It would be more consistent to argue that the whole of vv.5b-30 represents the recent history of the Markan community and look for a more satisfactory historical parallel for the language of vv.14f. As Myers illustrates from his own examples (325-326, 341), this is the normal pattern in apocalyptic literature. It is written to make sense of the present in the light of the recent past. Oral traditions, acts of martyrs, prophetic fragments of exhortation and prediction—and apocalyptic symbols—may all no doubt have circulated in the community whilst suffering tribulation, but it is only from a position after the events that some sense can be made of them and a new hope generated by the reinterpretation of this recent history. That is not to say that the community may not still be suffering as the text is written or updated. Nor does it imply that there are no genuine prophetic elements in the text—indeed, those which have proved to be true 'words of the Lord' may form the very basis of the text. But it does suggest that apocalyptic and prophetic language referring to all events up to the time of writing the text should have a reasonable historical explanation. Typically this point in the text is indicated in apocalyptic literature by the last stage before the final events—which in Mk 13 corresponds to either v.13 (so Hahn, Myers, Kee), v.23 (so Pesch, Brandenburger, Kelber), or v.27 (France). What makes Myers' interpretation unusual then, is not that he sees vv.5b-13 as representing the Markan *Sitz im Leben,* but that vv.24-27 are *not* seen as representing the final events.

It is clear that for Myers the "'advent' of the Human One" (in Mk 8:38; 13:26 and 14:62) *does not* refer to the tradition of the parousia (248). Instead he sees the time when 'the kingdom comes in power' (9:1) as being fulfilled in the event of the cross, which is also when the 'powers'

the 'abomination of desolation' and the note about 'fleeing into the hills'", therefore "13:14 fits more appropriately a setting preceding the destruction of the Temple in A.D. 67-69, when the evangelist could see the impending doom of Jerusalem and the Temple."

(both Roman and Jewish, 13:26; 14:62) *see* the vindication of the Human One. That this should be described in Mk 13 *after* the devastation of Jerusalem does not seem to worry Myers because he argues that it is a "mistake to look for *chronological* meaning in the apocalyptic discourse of temporality" (339). However, it appears that it is at just this very point that the author of Mark *does* have chronological order in mind: "In those days, *after* that tribulation…" (13:24). How then is it possible for the cross to *follow* the period of tribulation?[16]

There are problems for Myers' interpretation in these two areas of chronology and dating. We have mentioned his support for those who argue for a pre-fall dating of the Gospel on the grounds of 'imprecise prophecy', but there is an even more fundamental reason why Myers dates the Gospel before the fall of Jerusalem. He argues that the "vigorous criticism of the temple state and its political economy would obviously have been superfluous once the temple had been destroyed", and that therefore the "coherency of the political and economic ideology of Mark's narrative" (41) is dependent on a dating between 66 and 70 CE. Indeed, he charges those who date the Gospel after 70 CE with a "(docetic) tendency to suppress the economic and political aspects of the text in favour of the theological" (41). This may be a valid criticism of some exegesis, but it is not valid for Myers to apply it purely on the basis of a post 70 CE dating of the Gospel of Mark for the following reasons:

(i)   Political and economic turmoil did not cease in the eastern Mediterranean with the fall of Jerusalem. Indeed, there was arguably a *greater* need for a 'politically and economically coherent Gospel' *after* the collapse of the temple state than before or during the crisis, when there would be little time or interest in writing one amongst those involved in the events.

(ii) Myers initially assumes that the anti-temple invective of the Gospel is Markan rather than Jesuanic, in order to date the Gospel, but then later seems to equate the political and theological positions of Jesus and the author of Mark. It would surely still be 'coherent'— and perhaps even more politically meaningful—to argue that a 'post-fall' author has endorsed the 'pre-fall' words and actions of the historical Jesus against the temple, and that these words were supplemented by a Christian prophetic utterance.

---

[16] This problem is solved more rigorously—but also becomes more acute—in the interpretation of Bolt, "Mark 13", who tries from a literary perspective to interpret the passion narrative as the *fulfilment* of all the prophecies of Mk 13. Thus the 'awful horror' is the crucifixion of the Messiah by Israel's leaders, the fleeing is the rout of the disciples, the great stress the cry of dereliction, the exalted Son of Man the resurrection, and the gathering of the elect the promised outcome of the return to Galilee (Mk 16:7) and the launch of the Gentile mission ("Mark 13", 24-25). This is a brave attempt, and in many smaller details agrees with much of what France and Geddert argue and my own position in chapter 9 below, but it raises enormous difficulties for interpreting Matthew and Luke's versions of the discourse—even if we could accept such a radical reinterpretation of Mk 13:14-27. See further comments in chapter 8, footnote 30, below.

(iii) *If* the Gospel was written amidst the horrors of the Jewish wars, why is the 'awful horror which causes devastation' left standing where he ought not? Why is there no explicit hope of retribution and judgment? And why is the Mt 24 so similar in overall perspective if it was written on the other side of such momentous events?

Despite such problems, Myers' analysis of the Gospel of Mark thoroughly deserves its reputation as one of the most creative and relevant exegetical forays of our time. The call to active non-violence and the general thrust of Myers' conclusions regarding the attitude of the author of Mark to history are powerfully expressed: "Mark advocates neither fatalism nor escapism, but a revolutionary commitment to the transformation of history, which always demands political vigilance and discernment." But it is just this sort of focus on discerning discipleship which would be even more relevant to a new community gathering together after the collapse of the Jewish restorationist cause and the failure of those eschatological hopes that might have been shared by Judean-based followers of Jesus.

HERMAN WAETJEN approaches his reading of the Gospel of Mark through a sociology of power.[17] It is a less ambitious and less complicated book than either Belo's or Myers', being written quite literally as a 'reading' through of the Gospel from the perspective of power, with a minimum of methodological discussion and footnoting. Yet it is plain that there is a deep awareness of scholarly debate behind the relatively straightforward approach. The use of recent sociological studies to profile first century society adds great depth to Waetjen's claim that the thrust of Jesus' mission in Mark is to empower the powerless. Like Kee, Waetjen locates the Markan community in southern Syria (14-15), but unlike Kee and Myers, he argues for a post-fall dating.

Waetjen's conclusions regarding Mk 13 are similar to Hahn's in that he argues that though the abomination of desolation prophecy of 13:14 applied to the desecration of the temple originally, in the post-fall Markan community it is understood to point to a new event. Thus in v.14b, "the narrator is calling the reader disciple to reflect on this great tragedy and the circumstances that accompanied it and to understand them paradigmatically" (199). It follows then that the 'now' of v.19b refers to the time of the Markan community after the destruction of Jerusalem, and that therefore an "even greater affliction lies in the future" (200) for them, once the new abomination has revealed itself. Waetjen arrives at this conclusion through a literary method similar to Myers, assuming that *all* the dramatic moments of the text *must* reflect the situation of the Markan community directly. Because Waetjen locates this community on the other side of the fall of Jerusalem to Myers, he then insists on imbuing the whole text with a new future meaning for the Markan reader. The

---

[17] Herman C. Waetjen, *A Reordering of Power: A Socio-Political Reading of Mark's Gospel* (Minneapolis 1989). From now on, the page numbers in brackets refer to this book.

possibility that a reinterpretation of recent events rather than a recycling of prophecy might also have significance for the reader does not seem to be entertained.

Waetjen's interpretation of vv.24-27 is undertaken in a 'down to earth' manner similar to Myers, and makes use of the work of Walter Wink.[18] Rather than seeing the language of cosmic turmoil in vv.24-27 as indicating primarily a Theophany or the Day of the Lord, Waetjen interprets it against the background of Jewish apocalypticism, which "considers stars to be angels or heavenly beings who are representative of the empires, kingdoms, and polities of the divine council" (200). Thus the falling of the stars indicates the "passing away of the institutional structures they had erected for the exploitation of the masses of humankind" (200-201). This leads to the following magnificent piece of remythologizing:

> All those realities which transcended individual human life, the so-called powers and principalities, established by the forces of imperialism that by oppression and dispossession have diminished human existence, will be transformed. Only after the powers in heaven have been shaken, only after hierarchical structures have been horizontalized, can and will the New Humanity be born as a corporate, social reality. (201)

Waetjen then reverts to less enlightened exegesis when he argues that 'this generation' which 'will by no means pass away until all these things happen' (v.30), refers to the generation of humankind rather than Jesus' contemporaries (202). He then concludes his interpretation of the rest of Mk 13 in traditional terms, stating that "nothing, not even the passing away of heaven and earth, can prevent the fulfilment of Jesus' words" (202); that the precise time is incalculable (v.32); and that therefore everyone must be on the alert.

Mk 13 in its socio-political context

The socio-political models of Belo, Myers and Waetjen show convincingly that the Gospel of Mark was written to empower the powerless and create hope for the hopeless.[19] The particular evidence of

---

[18] Walter Wink, *Naming the Powers: The Language of Power in the New Testament*, (Philadelphia 1984).

[19] These oppositions are stated most vividly by Joong Suk Suh, "Discipleship and Community in the Gospel of Mark", unpublished PhD thesis, Boston University, 1986, 223f, where the Gospel of Mark is seen as an expression of the 'rumored story' of 'the crowd' as opposed to the 'official kerygma' of the apostles. But Suh's insight into the sociology of the crowd is overwhelmed by the emphasis on the opposition to Jerusalem, which given the *implied* meeting of the apostles and Jesus in Galilee (16:7) cannot be understood as absolute and unremitting. A more convincing analysis is provided by Dorothy A. Lee-Pollard, "Powerlessness as Power: A Key Emphasis in the Gospel of Mark", *SJT* 40 (1987), 173-188.

this in Mk 13 is that the discourse provides the struggling Christian community with a world-view—a symbolic universe—that opposes that of *both* the Jewish restorationist and Roman imperial authorities.[20] The Judeans are urged to flee *both* powers as their armies battle for Jerusalem. Yet clearly the author of Mark envisages that these powerless refugees, together with the Gentile Christians, will be the foundation of a new community which will provide evidence to all that the kingdom of God *has* come in power (9:1)—albeit the 'power' of the powerless. Yet whilst it may be claimed that these recent publications are beginning to reach some sort of consensus on a sociological description of the Gospel of Mark as being directed at and for 'the little ones', interpretations of the exact historical situation of the Gospel are as diverse as ever.

The problem with describing the specific socio-political context of the evangelist lies in the wide range of historically plausible solutions which have been suggested that fit the approximate time of the Gospel's origin, many of which are based substantially on a creative interpretation of Mk 13. As the reviews of scholarly studies above and in previous chapters have indicated, the discourse has been used to suggest a date of composition anywhere between the attempt of Caligula to place his statue in the temple (38-40 CE) and the erection of a statue of Capitalone Jupiter by Hadrian on the temple site (c 120 CE).[21] Such diversity of opinion—extending as it does from the very earliest of commentators[22]—is rather daunting. However it is still the interpretation of Mk 13:14f which holds the greatest promise for providing an externally verifiable dating and *Sitz im Leben* for the Gospel of Mark, even though we have argued that these verses are part of a pre-Markan source. This is so because the dating of such a source would shed valuable light on the provenance of the Gospel as a whole. Yet care must be taken to distinguish between those historic occasions on which the use of the phrase τὸ βδέλυγμα τῆς ἐρημώσεως *may* have been appropriate, and those which fit the phrase and its immediate context as it stands in Mk 13:14f. Clearly an awareness of the

[20] In such a situation of community transition and uncertainty, we note here the application of Victor Turner's concepts of *liminality* and *communitas* to the Markan text by William R. Herzog, "Apocalypse Then and Now: Apocalyptic and the Historical Jesus Reconsidered", *PTR* 18 (1984), 17-25; and Mark McVann, "The Passion in Mark: Transformation Ritual", *BTB* 18 (1988), 96-101. The categories they discuss give a helpful sociological perspective to a community in transition struggling to re-shape a meaningful world.

[21] See Beasley-Murray, *Commentary,* 59-72, and Ford, *Abomination,* 158-175. In support of the Caligula theory they cite: Spitta, Pfleiderer, Holtzmann, Schmiedel, Menzies, J. Weiss, C. C. Torrey (partially) and Bacon—to which we can now add Boring, Theissen and N. H. Taylor. In support of Hadrian, and thus a very late dating of the Gospels, Baur. The attempt of Pilate (c 26-36 CE) to keep the standard(s) of his cohort in the temple precincts provides an even earlier, if somewhat uncertain, dating.

[22] Beasley-Murray, *Commentary,* 59, comments that: "It is striking to observe how the interpretations of the βδέλυγμα prevailing at the present time were all suggested in the earliest stages of the critical discussion." By 'earliest stages' Beasley-Murray means to include such interpretations as those of Irenaeus, Jerome and Victorinus.

history of the traditions behind the phrase is important background, but ultimately the task is to interpret the specific form the phrase takes in Mk 13:14f.

When examining the historical background to the phrase it should be noted that βδέλυγμα for the Hebrew ץקּוּשׁ is used primarily of idols and 'graven images', leading to the later specific association with the profaning of the altar in the temple in Jerusalem by Antiochus Epiphanes referred to in Dn 9:27; 11:31; 12:11 and 1 M 1:54.[23] Given the actions of Pilate and intentions of Caligula, it is likely that the immediate pre-Markan historical context reinforced this view of the βδέλυγμα as a 'graven image' or a person representing Roman authority threatening the temple. However it is difficult to maintain that the genitive ἐρημώσεως for the Hebrew שֹׁמֵם simply underlines the desecration implied in the abomination. Beasley-Murray refers to Dn 8:13 and the use of ἐρημώσεως there to describe 'the appalling sin' before concluding that τὸ βδέλυγμα τῆς ἐρημώσεως "has by itself no thought of the temple's destruction but purely of its desecration. The Abomination horrifies."[24] But the arguments of Pesch and Ford, amongst others, are more persuasive.[25] They point out that the Old Testament usage usually implies devastation of the land and the destruction of Jerusalem, its temple or the Royal palace. This is especially so in Dn 11:31 and 12:11 which both refer back to 9:26f where the devastation of the city is described together with the profanation of the temple. Thus the translation best fitting the phrase is not the tautological 'Awful Horror', but rather 'the sacrilege of devastation' or 'the abomination which causes desecration'. The use of the genitive and the masculine singular participle which follow immediately show that it is not possible to split this phrase into a two-part event, such as: the 'sacrilege' perpetrated by the Jewish Zealots in the temple which then *causes* the 'devastation' carried out by the Romans.[26] Rather, the

---

[23] See the discussion in Beasley-Murray, *Commentary*, 54f, and Ford, *Abomination*, 158f. Support is given here for Beasley-Murray's view that the βδέλυγμα refers primarily to a 'graven image' of some kind rather than the more general interpretation of Ford; but also to Ford's interpretation of ἐρημώσεως as indicating a desolation more devastating than the 'wave of horror passing over the people' suggested by Beasley-Murray, *Commentary*, 55. Beasley-Murray himself seems to conclude later that the βδέλυγμα "connotes both profanation and destruction" and "the notion of horror by reason of blasphemy and the devastation of city, temple and land" (*Jesus and the Last Days*, 357-8 and 411).

[24] Beasley-Murray, *Commentary*, 54-55.

[25] Pesch, *Naherwartungen*, 143; Ford, *Abomination*, 168-169.

[26] Marxsen, *Mark*, 186, (see ch. 4, footnote 7 above), is one who suggests a two-part fulfilment of the prophecy: a threat to the temple necessitating flight, and the destruction accompanied by the rise of the antichrist—but this is very difficult to support from the text. The argument of Geddert, *Watchwords*, 308, footnote 21, is more plausible. He draws on Ez 33:29 and argues that it is the Jewish leaders who abominate the temple (consistent with Markan understanding) and bring it to the brink of destruction by the Romans. This agrees with the general anti-temple stance of the Markan Jesus but still does not make sense of the specific saying in 13:14f—in particular the phrase 'standing

whole phrase complex of 'person/graven image/sacrilege/devastation' is inseparably linked.

The Markan context for this phrase, however, is even more specific: "When *you see* the abomination which causes devastation *standing where he ought not* (let the reader discern) *then* those in Judea should flee to the mountains." The sequence here is problematical. If a desecration of the temple by a Roman idol of some kind is envisaged together with a devastation of Jerusalem, why are Judeans exhorted to flee *after* they (= you?) see the event? Clearly this is because an even worse devastation is envisaged by Mk 13:15f—one such as has never been experienced before. But if v.14 refers to the final destruction of the temple and Jerusalem in 70 CE—which occurred *after* horrific suffering by its inhabitants—then to what does this post-flight tribulation of vv.15f refer? And if v.14 is therefore argued to refer only to a *desecration* of the temple and vv.15f to the actual destruction of Jerusalem, what historical events could possibly fit the sequence desecration/flight/devastation in such a way that the exhortation remains possible to heed?[27] And then why should those *in Judea* (*not* specifically those in Jerusalem!) be told to wait so late until they *see* the 'abomination standing where it ought not' before fleeing? How is it possible for Judeans (or the 'you' of v.14) to *see* the abomination in the temple unless they are in Jerusalem? Why then isn't the exhortation addressed directly to those in Jerusalem, as some have claimed it originally must have been?[28] But then how could such witnesses of the 'abomination standing where he ought not', if they were in Jerusalem, flee through the surrounding Roman armies which laid siege to Jerusalem for five months before destroying both city and temple?[29]

where *he* ought not' *followed* by the flight. If the exhortation to flee occurred *between* the Jewish abomination and the Roman destruction, Geddert's case would be much stronger.

[27] Perhaps the actions of the Zealots in the temple prior to its destruction could be argued as constituting an abomination (so Pfleiderer), though such an interpretation would not be consistent with the traditional usage of the term βδέλυγμα as outlined above. There is also the problem of identifying exactly which event constituted an abomination. Was it the spilling of Zealot blood in the temple or perhaps the improper appointment of a High Priest? And how could such events be *seen*—wouldn't it be better to say: 'When you hear of the abomination...' given that the oracle appears to be addressed to Judeans in general rather than Jerusalemites in particular. See Beasley-Murray, *Commentary,* 61-62, and Ford, *Abomination,* 159-160.

[28] Marxsen, *Mark,* 182; Pesch, *Naherwartungen,* 147 and 232. Pesch has been strongly criticised for suggesting that the source originally said 'then let those in *Jerusalem* flee to the mountains', but many commentators assume that 'Judeans' really means 'Jerusalemites', and that the discourse was addressed mainly to the Jerusalem church (eg Brandenburger, *Markus 13,* 69; Geddert, *Watchwords,* 146, "Flee the *City*").

[29] This was the final siege of Jerusalem by Titus in 70 CE, which appears to have been a particularly determined and sometimes brutal one. This is not really surprising given the abortive sieges of Cestius Gallus in 66 CE (who withdrew in disarray), and Vespasian in 68 CE (who withdrew to return to Rome via Egypt to become Emperor). The descriptions of the siege by Josephus are quite horrific, and it is clear that deserters from Jerusalem who managed to avoid being killed by the revolutionary parties were not always well received by the surrounding armies—particularly when it was found that some had tried to smuggle out gold by swallowing it! *The Jewish War,* V, §550f.

Given these unanswered questions there would seem to be compelling reasons for seeing the prophecy either as a reference to an earlier event (such as those surrounding the actions of Pilate or Caligula) which has been re-interpreted by the author of Mark in the light of the impending Jewish war, or as a prophetic 'near-miss' of the historical Jesus.[30] If the Gospel of Mark is assumed to have been written *before* 70 CE, then any inaccuracies are simply given as evidence that the prophecies of vv.14f are in fact not *ex eventu*. But whilst such interpretations may account for the 'imperfect fit' of the prediction with the events as we know them, they create still further difficulties. For if the prophecy came from an early Christian prophet speaking of the Caligula episode, why was it attributed to Jesus 'second time around' when it had already been shown to be an overstatement in its first application? Or if it is argued that 13:14f is a genuine prophecy of Jesus which, like 13:1-2, has been preserved in the Gospel of Mark despite its imperfect later fulfilment, the question still remains as to what on earth it meant—both for Jesus and for the author of Mark. At least vv.1-2 were fulfilled in substance if not in every detail by the destruction of the temple by the Romans, but it is difficult to see how vv.14-20 can be understood in the same light—either in substance or in detail. The desecration and destruction of the temple itself will *not* suffice as an approximate fulfilment of v.14. For if the exhortation to flee is to have any integrity at all it must be possible for it to be obeyed, rather than merely occurring as an afterthought. Or in the terms of the text, it must

---

[30] For an example of the first line of argument—an earlier Christian prophecy re-used by the author of Mark—see the interpretations of Gaston, Boring and Theissen (chapter 5, footnotes 2,3 and 28 above). The older literature abounds with examples of the second option, arguing that Jesus gave a composite prophecy—partly of the fall of Jerusalem, and partly of the end-times and an anti-christ figure, which explains why the prophecy has not been completely fulfilled yet. This is given as an example of so-called 'prophetic foreshortening'—Jesus saw clearly the 'peaks of future history' without full awareness of the 'valleys which lay between'. But such arguments are merely picturesque ways of admitting that no-one, not even Jesus or Mark, knows the exact meaning of the prophecy.

More respectable, but hardly any more illuminating, are those 'explanations' that exaggerate the nature of apocalyptic secrecy and actually affirm the unintelligibility of the language, turning the parenthetical invitation to the reader to understand/take note (v.14) into a means of obscuring the urgent message still further. See, for example, the comments of Taylor, *Mark,* 512, regarding v.14b: It functions "More like a dark hint, a clue to Christian eyes but an enigma to others...More precise language was politically dangerous"; and of Myers, *Strong Man,* 335: "Here Mark comes closest to the secretive, "underground" political discourse so characteristic of classic apocalyptic literature written at a time of persecution, such as Daniel or Revelation. He simply cannot speak directly about Roman military operations, for to do so would be to betray his resistance community. Thus, when the siege begins Mark instructs Judeans to '*then* flee to the hills'." Now Taylor and Myers are correct insofar as the words of v.14 as they stand now are concerned—they require more than the usual amount of interpreting—but not insofar as the meaning or intention of the author is concerned, which they both remain vague about as if the cryptic language used were intended to confuse *all* readers and hearers of the Gospel. Clearly there is a very specific and urgent message being communicated which with the help of the reader will be made *very* clear to the earliest hearers of the message. The challenge is to interpret that message with the benefit of hindsight so that its idiosyncratic details can be interpreted within a plausible historical framework.

be possible for those in *Judea* to actually *see* (or to hear from those who see) the 'abomination which causes devastation standing where he ought not' in time for them to escape the tribulation which followed.

Those who claim that the Gospel was written before these prophesied events took place, thereby excusing rather than explaining the seemingly non-specific fulfilment of them, often go on to argue that Luke presents a 'corrected' version from a later perspective. But this leaves us with the problem as to why Matthew follows Mark so closely—suggesting that Matthew was written pre-fall also. If the Gospel of Mark was written after the tumultuous events of 70 CE however, then a recognizable fulfilment of the prophecy (be it genuine or *ex eventu*) must have taken place. For only if the sequence of events in vv.14-21 made sense historically to the readers of the Gospel would such a prophecy be endorsed and handed on in the tradition as a 'word of the Lord', and perhaps even read back into the words of the historical Jesus. This is not to say that the prophecy must therefore be a *vaticinium ex eventu,* for it has already been demonstrated that 13:14-21 is not of Markan origin, and it is difficult to suggest that a non-Markan post-fall tradition could have become established as a 'word of the Lord' or saying of the historical Jesus in time for it to be used in the Gospel as such.[31] However it is conceivable that if the words of a Christian prophet genuinely predicting the fall of Jerusalem were fulfilled in detail, they could then be incorporated into the Gospel narrative after the event as a *bona fide* 'word of the Lord'.[32] The only problem with such a view is to show that the prophecies of vv.14f could reasonably have been made by a pre-fall prophet and then that they were specifically fulfilled in the events of the Jewish war.

It is not necessary here to outline a definitive solution, and short of some amazing new manuscript discovery, one is never likely. What is required is an historically plausible set of possibilities which attempts to account for all of the questions raised thus far and make some historical sense of each specific detail in v.14f. One hypothesis which appeals is to argue that the 'abomination which causes devastation standing where he ought not' is a reference to the image of Vespasian as emperor-elect appearing on coins minted during the year 69 CE. Vespasian's 'graven

---

[31] Unless of course the Gospel of Mark is dated much later than the fall of Jerusalem—but this presents too many other problems for synoptic and New Testament interpretation.

[32] This was the normal pattern for the verification of a prophet: "When the thing takes place—and it is beginning to happen now—they will know that there has been a prophet among them" (Ez 33:33, *NJB,* cf Dt 18:21-22). To suggest that the author of Mark could then have no qualms about attributing such a recent prophecy to the historical Jesus is not such a preposterous idea. Mk 13 itself tells us that prophets spoke in the name of Christ. That is not the problem for the Markan community—the problem is to discern the *true* prophets—those that really do speak 'the word of the Lord'. Ultimately, as throughout the Old Testament tradition, this can only be determined retrospectively, when events themselves demonstrate that it was really the Lord speaking through the prophet.

image' is legitimately termed the 'abomination which causes devastation' because of his crushing military campaign throughout Galilee, Perea and Judea to the walls of Jerusalem in 68 CE. But at that stage, just as he prepared for the final siege and assault on Jerusalem and its temple, he seized instead the opportunity to return to Rome via Egypt to settle the growing civil war and be endorsed as emperor. Support for Vespasian was (shrewdly) proclaimed earlier in the Eastern provinces from the 1st July 69 CE, and coins were minted from then on as evidence of that support in Antioch (Syria), Illyricum (modern Yugoslavia), Tyre and Ephesus, and later during the same year in Rome and Lugdunum.[33] These coins commonly bore portraits of Vespasian, and sometimes even his sons Titus and Domitian. One of the first coins minted for Vespasian in Rome, a *denarius,* includes a full length portrait of Vespasian standing in military dress on the obverse side—the would be destroyer of Jerusalem standing where he should not as the emperor of Rome![34]

Now if similar coins to this, perhaps minted in Antioch, Tyre or Alexandria—or even that very *denarius* from Rome—circulated as far as Judea in advance of Titus' army of 70 CE, might they not provide the precise detail required for the exhortation in Mk 13:14? 'When you *see* the abomination which causes devastation standing where *he* ought not be...'. It would certainly be within the realms of possiblity that Christians to the north or south of Judea, upon seeing such coins, would send a prophetic word to the Judean Christians (= the 'you' of v.14?) warning them that their recent near-destroyer would certainly ensure that the task was finished now that he was about to become emperor of Rome.[35] Indeed, a coin may well have been sent with 'the reader' of the prophetic message to make his task of 'interpreting' the cryptic words that much easier (v.14b, 'reader note well!'). Alternatively, the address to the

---

[33] See, for example, the accounts in James Mackay, *Greek and Roman Coins* (London 1971), 105-107; R. A. G. Carson, *Coins: Ancient, Medieval and Modern, vol 1. Coins of Greece and Rome* (London 1971), 137-139; and R. A. G. Carson, *Principal Coins of the Romans, vol 2* (London 1980), 35-39.

[34] Carson, *Principal Coins*, 35. This coin may even date from 69 CE since it bears no imperial title (Vespasian was acknowledged as emperor by the Senate on 22 Dec 69 CE). The perfect coin to match the prophecy would be one dating from 69 CE but *anticipating* Vespasian's victory by showing him standing in the temple of Jerusalem. There *are* in existence the famous Judaea Capta coins of 70-71 CE showing a Jewess seated under a palm tree with a bound Jew in the background, and a coin from 72 CE bearing the inscription IMP CAES VESP AUG P M COS IIII, which, when added up in its Hebrew equivalents totals 666! (See W. G. Baines, "The Number of the Beast in Revelation", *Heythrop Journal* 16 (1975), 195-196). But there is no complete listing of all the coin variations as it seems that those from Antioch are only known about through Tacitus, and coins from some of the other regional centres are very rare (Carson, *Coins: Anc.,* 137).

[35] In that the news of Vitellius' defeat in Rome (December 69 CE) reached Vespasian whilst he was arriving in Alexandria with Titus (*Jewish War,* IV, §656)—whom he then sent back overland to complete the siege of Jerusalem—the possibility of the prophetic oracle (Mk 13:14-21) originating in Egypt should at least be considered. It appears, however, that the Egyptian currency may not have enjoyed the wider circulation of the official Roman coinage, or even that of the coins from Antioch.

'reader' could be directed to all who see and 'read' the coins and their symbols of power and inscriptions. This hypothesis, improbable as it may seem at first sight, meets each of the questions raised above about the specific Markan context for the 'abomination which causes desolation'. It enables the Judeans to 'see' and flee in time, it fits the traditional interpretations of the 'abomination' as both a foreign ruler and a graven image who threaten the temple, and it explains why the 'abomination' remains standing in the Markan text—the house of Flavian ruled for the rest of the first century.

It must also be pointed out that such a use of coinage as a means of political pronouncement and propaganda amongst the illiterate masses is entirely consistent with practices at the time, and much more plausible than the *Flugblatt* (= pamphlet) hypothesis which has received undue coverage in the literature. One of the first acts of the Jewish rebels themselves was to mint 'silver shekels of the revolt' to proclaim their independence and to rid themselves of the idolatrous Roman coinage.[36] Richard Oster's seminal article on the value of coinage for understanding the social world of early Christianity answers the skepticism of historians who have regarded coins as providing only a sidelight on a given period of history.[37] He cites literature pointing out that in an age when news could not be disseminated by radio or newspaper, it was the coinage which announced to the public the aspirations and recent achievements of the ruling classes and gave 'currency' to their symbols of self-aggrandisement.

Thus the Jewish Christians of Judea, even if they had been forced out of Jerusalem from 66 CE and had suffered under Vespasian in 68 CE, would have been given a real opportunity to see with their own eyes the sign of their impending fate and flee before the final devastation occurred.[38] If the warning reached them during the summer or autumn of 69 CE, then the words "Pray that it might not be in winter" (Mk 13:18) would be most appropriate. Yet even a coin struck soon after Vespasian was endorsed as

[36] A 'Shekel of Israel', Year 3 (of the revolt), is shown as the cover of David M. Rhoads, *Israel in Revolution, 6-74 C.E.* (Philadelphia 1976).

[37] Richard Oster, "Numismatic Windows into the Social World of Early Christianity: A Methodological Inquiry", *JBL* 101 (1982), 195-223. See also the articles illustrating different aspects of the same theme by Larry J. Kreitzer, "A Numismatic Clue to Acts 19.23-41: The Ephesian Cistophori of Claudius and Agrippina", *JSNT* 30 (1987), 59-70; "Hadrian and the Nero Redivivus Myth", *ZNW* 79 (1988), 92-115; "The Personification of Judaea: Illustrations of the Hadrian Travel Sestertii", *ZNW* 80 (1989), 278-279; "Nero's Rome: Images of the City on Imperial Coinage", *EvQ* 61 (1989), 301-309; and "Apotheosis of the Roman Emperor", *BibArch* 53 (1990), 211-217.

[38] Certainly Vespasian's march south in 67-68 CE would have already devastated much of Judea, to the extent that Josephus (*Jewish War,* IV, §555) states that only Jerusalem and the three fortresses of Herodion, Masada and Machaerus remained to be conquered. Yet even though Vespasian left troops at Jericho, Gophna, Caesarea and other strategic places before he left for Alexandria in the summer of 69 CE, it would seem that on Titus' return to Caesarea in the spring of 70 CE there was still a need to subjugate the Judean countryside ("As Titus advanced into enemy territory...", *Jewish War,* V, §47).

emperor in December 69 CE might reach Judea in the spring just ahead of Titus and his armies and provide a warning that what restorationist hopes remained amongst Judeans were doomed. They were *not* to retreat into Jerusalem and be seduced by the rampant Jewish nationalism and pseudo-messiahs (13:21) of those extraordinary final months, but were exhorted to flee the collapse of their own culture and to recognise that God's purposes were wider than those of the feuding Jewish power groups.

Such would be a possible *Sitz im Leben* for a prophetic oracle (written or spoken) consisting of vv.14-21. Because of its substantial accuracy in predicting the events of 69-70 CE,[39] it could have been legitimately incorporated into the Gospel of Mark after the fall as a genuine 'word of the Lord' and a fitting post-script to the anti-temple action and prophecy of the historical Jesus. The implications for the provenance of the Gospel of Mark of such a possibility are that it must have been written soon after the fall of Jerusalem in a predominantly Gentile area close enough to Palestine to make these events, and the persecutions preceding them, of immediate significance. The simplest way to understand the Markan use of the oracle is to suggest that refugees from the crisis (if not Mark himself) brought it with them to the Markan community.[40] The inclusion of vv.14-

[39] It might be argued that the oracle is inaccurate in that the warning of v.21 about pseudochrists (v.22 added later) would fit the sequence of events better if it could be applied to the entry of Simon ben Giora into Jerusalem in April-May 69 CE, when it would have been unlikely that any Vespasian coins had been minted. But this is to read a text which is in the plural as if it were in the singular—clearly the pseudochrists and false-prophets in Mk 13 could be applied to *all* the rebel leaders and to those prophets Josephus claims were deluding the people even as the temple was burning (*Jewish War,* VI, §285f). Indeed the description would fit from a Markan perspective until the last of the rebel causes was ended at Masada, some four years later. It also appears that the Romans continued to take possible messianic claims seriously immediately following the fall of Jerusalem—to the extent that they rounded up and eliminated all the members of the family of David they could find [see E. Mary Smallwood, *The Jews Under Roman Rule* (Leiden 1981), 351, who cites EusEcclHist III, 12, citing Hegesippus—but concludes that "the tradition is entirely credible"].

[40] This would mean that the location of the Markan community would most probably be in northern Palestine or Southern Syria, although Egypt should not be ruled out altogether. Lyle Dale Vander Broek, "The Markan 'Sitz im Leben': A Critical Investigation into the Possibility of a Palestinian Setting for the Gospel", unpublished PhD thesis, Drew University, 1983; and Myers, *Strong Man,* 40f, 414f, have both shown that the objections to the Palestinian location (the supposedly poor Galilean geography of the evangelist, and so on) can all be resolved satisfactorily. However, a little further north in southern Syria is perhaps an even more likely location, since it would permit a perspective on the war to be written down a little earlier than in Galilee, yet would be close enough to experience the persecution of Jews and Christians that occurred in the area in those times. Interestingly, two recent studies of the Markan *Sitz* have both reached the conclusion that Mark himself is a Judean who then moves to join a Gentile-oriented community in the north. For Joel Marcus, "The Jewish War and the *Sitz im Leben* of Mark", *JBL* 111 (1992), 441-462, Mark may even have fled with the Jerusalem church to Pella, where he retrospectively reinterpreted the calamitous events of the War for his new community. Whereas for Dean W. Chapman, "Locating the Gospel of Mark. A Model of Agrarian Biography", *BThB* 25 (1995), 24-36, Mark is a member

21 then becomes part of the process of including the refugees into the Markan community, and of affirming their flight from Judea as part of the will of God. Ultimately, with the Markan addition of vv.24-27 to the prophetic words of vv.14-21, the Christian communities, Jewish and Gentile, were called to recognise that the gathering of God's elect would not take place in Jerusalem or Judea—but would involve people from the four corners of the earth and occur in another place and at another time.[41] This is the implication of the re-use of τοὺς ἐκλεκτούς, and especially the addition of αὐτοῦ, in v.27—the author is re-defining the ethnically defined, chosen ones of Judea (vv.20,22) as the elect of the vindicated Son of Man from all nations.

If vv.26-27 are to be interpreted 'historically' in this way, it may be asked what the cosmic events of vv.24-25 refer to. If we understand the apocalyptic imagery to be a representation of earthly powers by corresponding heavenly bodies,[42] then vv.24-25 could well be a reference to the power-shifts and re-alignments which took place in Judea and on the eastern frontier once Vespasian became emperor. Of particular interest in this connection are the reported disturbances in Syria during the fourth year of Vespasian's reign, involving King Antiochus and his sons,[43] although there were a number of other incidents in the first years of the Flavian dynasty that would qualify as 'falling stars' in the area of the eastern provinces. In support of such a reading of vv.24-25, Jonathan Price describes the *milieu* of those revolutionary times in the following way:

> ... sustained political tension ... helped fashion, as in a crucible, diverse visionary ideologies predicting a violent, cosmic overthrow and reordering. ... It

of the Jerusalem church who moves to live in community with Galilean peasants—a combination which explains the geography of the Gospel.

[41] "A new place and a new time", to quote Kelber's famous phrase. But contrary to Kelber's location of this place in Galilee, it must be pointed out that Mk 13 is as uncommunicative about a specific place as it is about the sign and the time. To view vv.26-27 as referring in the first place to an historical gathering is the most obvious option for the exegete. As Beasley-Murray, *Commentary,* 90, points out, it has *none* of the usual themes associated with The End (judgment of the living and dead, banishment of the faithless, Satan's fall) but "simply speaks of the gathering of the new Israel to the Son of Man." Beasley-Murray then goes on to claim that it "presumes the others", which is to assume that Mk 13 is really Mt 24.

[42] As is argued by France, *Jesus and the OT,* 253: "The phrases which make up these verses are part of the stock-in-trade of Old Testament prophecy, and they are used to describe especially political disasters, and the destruction of cities and nations, particularly those which played a leading role." See also Myers, *Strong Man,* 343; and Waetjen, *Reordering,* 200; both citing Walter Wink, *Naming the Powers,* 162. In any case, these cosmic portents are in the same vein as those described by Josephus as accompanying events in Judea from 66-70 CE (see, for example, those described in *Jewish War,* VI, §288-300, which include a comet and a strange light at midnight). They must therefore be distinguished from the cosmic events of a different scale in 13:31.

[43] See, for example, G. A. Williamson, *Josephus. The Jewish War* (Harmondsworth 1959), 355.

might fairly be said that the expectation of a new order was common to all the eschatologically inspired revolutionary movements, which viewed the political struggle on a cosmic scale: this is the proper background for rebellion in first-century Judæa.[44]

The Markan compilation of vv.24-27 speaks to such a situation, and suggests that out of the political upheavals and chaos of those years, the messengers of the Human One will gather together a new multi-ethnic community that will itself be evidence to all who oppose them of the vindication of the crucified one and of the coming of God's rule with power. Just where this gathering took place—in its Markan form—is not possible to say with any degree of certainty, but a location in northern Palestine or southern Syria would fit the criteria outlined above.

The Sitz im Leben of Mk 13

We have described vv.14-21 as a prophetic oracle directed to the Judean Christians somewhere between the summer of 69 CE and the spring of 70 CE. This oracle exhorts them to flee from the returning Roman armies certain to be sent by the emperor-elect Vespasian, whose appearance on coins in the eastern empire is the signal to the Judeans to depart. The general who had devastated the Galilee and Samaria would show no mercy to Judea and Jerusalem as Emperor. The oracle could have been passed on orally and reference made to such coins for the Judeans to 'read' of their impending fate, bearing in mind that if the illiterate of the day could be said to 'read' anything, it would have been the propaganda in the form of images and inscriptions placed on coins for that purpose by their overlords. Alternatively, it is still possible that the oracle may have been a written tract, if any precedent for such a thing exists in antiquity. This hypothesis, improbable as it may sound at first, accords precisely with the specific Markan sequence of events: 'seeing/abomination/flight/tribulation/pseudoprophets and christs'. It also satisfies the traditional understandings of what constitutes an abomination (graven image, foreign ruler, threat to the temple), and the specific Markan context of 'standing where *he* ought not'. Nevertheless, the substance of our interpretation does not stand or fall with this hypothesis—it may be that there are other historically plausible ways of understanding the text.

Such a scenario as this enables the whole of Mk 13 (and the Gospel itself) to be interpreted as an immediate post-war reflection on the nature

[44] Jonathan J. Price, *Jerusalem Under Siege. The Collapse of the Jewish State 66-70CE* (Leiden 1992), 7. In the course of this section, Price quotes G. Scholem, *The Messianic Idea in Judaism and Other Essays on Jewish Spirituality* (New York 1971), 6: "A wider cosmic background is superadded to the national content of eschatology and it is here that the final struggle between Israel and the heathens takes place." This combination of national identity, cosmic language and the fate of the heathens provides the precise hermeneutical background for Mk 13:24-27.

of Christian hope and on the emergence of a new multi-ethnic Christian community—in contrast with (and possibly some opposition to) the failed ethnocentric eschatological hopes of at least some in the Jerusalem church. This is evident because of the addition of vv.24-27, *'after* that tribulation' (13:24), which immediately historicises what some must have thought was the tribulation preceding The End. Vv.25-26 then describe the alternative vision of the Markan community—not an ethnically pure 'elect' ruled by a Jerusalem Messiah, nor an undifferentiated populace under the Roman authorities—but a truly multi-ethnic community gathered in the name of the suffering and vindicated Human One. This Markan community was actively engaged in—and the product of—the Gentile mission, and was probably situated close enough to Palestine to receive some of the Judean 'elect' as refugees in the aftermath of the war.

We find the arguments of Kee and Waetjen[45] for a southern Syrian location of the Gospel the most persuasive because they are based on a linguistic and sociological analysis of the text of the Gospel itself, rather than on presuppositions drawn from early church traditions or creative interpolations from a literary reading of the Gospel. Similarly, Waetjen's description of the community is supported by a careful evaluation of the vocabulary and content of the text, leading him to conclude that the authorial audience comprised mainly agricultural peasants. These "rural gentile Christians belonged to the lower-class strata of Roman occupied Syria".[46] Thus they were empowered by the Markan emphasis on 'the little ones' and on the re-ordering of power that occurs in the kingdom of God when communities dare to live by an alternative symbolic universe not dominated by national or imperial interests. As such, they identify themselves with the Human One (the corporate Son of Man) who was also 'handed over' to the authorities—but has now been vindicated by God in the presence of those authorities. The evidence of this vindication is the re-alignment of human authorities and their cosmic counterparts that occurs with the collapse of the Jerusalem Temple State and other petty tyrants post 70CE, and ultimately the gathering of the new community itself.

---

[45] Now further strengthened in many respects by the detailed work of Theissen, *The Gospels in Context,* and Marcus, "The Jewish War".

[46] Waetjen, *Reordering,* 14-15. Now further supported by the creative analysis of the world views of Galilean peasants by Chapman, "Locating the Gospel of Mark".

VIII

THE TEACHER'S FAREWELL DISCOURSE

Major proponents: Petersen (1978, 1980, 1984); Robbins (1984); Vorster (1987); Mack (1988); Tolbert (1989); Geddert (1989); Fowler (1991).
Basic thesis: It is not possible to summarise the range of methods and their results in one statement, but the approaches reviewed here are united by their common aim to interpret the Gospel of Mark as a whole, and Mk 13 within that context.
Dominant method: Contemporary literary analyses of various types.
Critique: An examination of the literary contexts of the Gospel of Mark.

In recent times, the range of literary approaches to the Gospel of Mark has become almost as great as the range of historical-critical methods that preceded them. By their nature, these literary approaches have focussed on the Gospel of Mark as a whole and on its wider literary context(s), rather than examining chapter 13 specifically. At this wider level they have been profoundly significant in challenging the frameworks within which the Gospel has been read and interpreted.[1] At the level of interpreting the particular issues raised by chapter 13 the results have been rather less impressive. It seems almost as if Rudolph Pesch's original intuition may have been correct—the Gospel of Mark really does 'read better' (to the modern mind at least) with chapter 13 omitted.[2] Even the obvious appeal of 13:14b 'let the reader understand' to those interested in reader-response approaches and to those mapping the narrative levels of the Gospel has not encouraged the rigorous evaluation of the discourse *itself* in recent literary interpretations. The phrase *has* been used to 'break open' the more subtle asides of the narrator to the reader that exist throughout the rest of the Gospel,[3] but the reasons for 'the reader' to be addressed specifically at this point in the narrative—and *only* at this point—have not been advanced beyond those suggested by historical-

---

[1] We note here the extraordinary influence of David Rhoads and Donald Michie's *Mark as Story. An Introduction to the Narrative of a Gospel* (Philadelphia 1982). Although not the earliest of the literary approaches to the Gospel of Mark, it mapped out some of the methods and possibilities of such readings with remarkable clarity and insight.

[2] See the outline of Pesch's original thesis in chapter 4 above. Actually, the links between chapter 13 and the rest of the Gospel suggested by literary methods demonstrate the unlikely nature of Pesch's theory, yet this confirmation of its Markan literary setting has seldom been accompanied by an investigation into the implications of such a setting for the interpretation of the discourse.

[3] Robert M. Fowler's *Let the Reader Understand. Reader-Response Criticism and the Gospel of Mark* (Minneapolis 1991) carries out this task thoroughly. See especially pages 82f.

critical methods. It seems that either the chapter has been relegated to a motivational speech given by the departing teacher and subservient to the (admittedly) dominant themes of the Gospel: discipleship, christology and mission; or the distinctive language of 13:14f has encouraged some to read the whole Gospel in a stereotypically apocalyptic light—so that Mark is seen as having such a negative view of history that he hopes only for the intervention of the eschaton. The aim of this chapter is to strike a balance between such extremes: between interpreting all of the Gospel through the lens of chapter 13, and interpreting the whole Gospel so as to avoid chapter 13. In this way the detailed investigation of chapter 13 undertaken so far will be balanced by an appreciation of its literary context within the Gospel as a whole, within the New Testament canon, and within the wider world of first century literature.

It is in their focus on the whole text as it stands and as it is interpreted within a stated literary context that these newer literary approaches can be said to cohere, if they do at all. Yet they may also be distinguished from each other by the place they give, if any, in the hermeneutical process to the role of the author, the reader (implied, ancient, contemporary, ideal, and so on) and the wider literary context (Markan, canonical, first century Greco-Roman, or wider). The context for the investigation of Mk 13 assumed by each of the scholars listed above is clearly evident in their work, and often specifically stated. The nature of the 'reader'—and the role of the author—is much more difficult to comprehend, even when it *is* specifically stated.[4] Here it will suffice to classify together those who actually write of the author's aims and intentions (whether or not the author is called 'Mark'), those who use historical together with literary methods to describe the response of first century 'readers', and those who distinguish other 'readers' using various literary models and theories. We shall use the labels 'Ancient reader response' and 'Contemporary reader response' respectively for these latter two categories, even though they are manifestly unsatisfactory. Clearly ancient 'readers' were mostly 'hearers' of the Gospel for a start, and all the readers we are examining are strictly contemporaries, whether they try to read from a first century perspective or not. Clearly also, we are avoiding the question of the status of an 'implied' or 'encoded' reader. Is it a contemporary construct or inherent in every text from when they were written? It seems that usage of the term varies, as we shall see below, so we will persist in making our distinction between 'ancient' and 'contemporary' on the basis of the scholars' own references to historical or literary criteria for describing the 'reader'.

It is possible therefore to use these categories to map the literary approaches to the Gospel of Mark (and Mk 13) into six overlapping

---

[4] I am indebted to Fowler's *Let the Reader Understand,* 1-58, for demonstrating just how varied the different reader-oriented approaches are in their understandings of the 'reader'—whether it be the real reader, or the implied, the informed, intended, original, authorial, optimal, super, composite, the encoded reader, and so on (26).

groups depending on their primary understanding of the author/'reader' and of the context of the text:

(i) The text used primarily to examine authorial intention (Mack, Geddert).

(ii) The text used primarily to examine ancient reader response (Petersen, Robbins, Tolbert).

(iii) The text used primarily to examine contemporary reader response (Vorster, Fowler).

(iv) The text examined in its wider first century literary context (Robbins, Mack, Tolbert).

(v) The text examined in its full Markan literary context (Geddert, Mack, Tolbert, Fowler).

(vi) The text examined as text only (Mk 13) (Vorster, and some of the earlier historical-critical studies).

This may be simplified and represented in tabular form for greater clarity:

Mapping some literary interpretations of Mk 13

	Authorial intention	Ancient reader response	Contemporary reader response
Focus on the text of Mk 13 only	[Typical of some earlier historical-critical studies]	[Typical of some earlier historical-critical studies]	Vorster
Focus on Mk 13 in its Markan context	Geddert (Petersen)	Petersen (Tolbert)	Fowler
Mk (and Mk 13) in first century literary context	Mack	Robbins Tolbert	(Fowler)

This diagram does not do justice to the many subtleties in the methods employed by the scholars named, but it attempts to classify the *primary* thrust of their analyses in relation to each other. So whilst Petersen (1984) claims to focus on the 'implied reader' and suggests that "a study of 'Mark' the implied author might be equally revealing",[5] he incurs the criticism of Vorster for allowing his implied reader a historical existence (see further below). Therefore, although they both use the same terminology, they appear in different columns above. Similarly, Tolbert consciously considers the *whole* of the Markan literary context as well as

---

[5] Norman R. Petersen, "The Reader in the Gospel", *Neot* 18 (1984), 50.

the wider Greco-Roman literary context in her work.[6] Yet it is this latter perspective, together with an analysis of the likely response of the earliest audience, which distinguishes Tolbert's interpretation and results in the primary classification above. Her own assessment of her method is: "We have tried to read the Gospel of Mark in the light of its own Hellenistic milieu, to enter imaginatively the ranks of its authorial audience."[7] Tolbert also attempts, like many of the recent literary and socio-political interpreters, to state briefly what the implications of her analysis might be for an understanding of the text today. This conscious involvement of the contemporary reader and context is perhaps the most exciting and significant trend of all in recent hermeneutical developments. However, in the classification above the category 'contemporary reader' has been used of those approaches which interpret the text *primarily* from that perspective—whether uncritically, or by making deliberate use of recent literary theories. It is intended therefore that there should be some degree of latitude in the schematic presentation given above, since although the *basic* position of each interpreter is represented clearly, it is not meant to exclude the possibility of them touching on some other area as well.

Such a classification of literary approaches helps to clarify the position taken—or at least assumed—by an interpreter on the role of the author/reader and on the nature of the text and its context, and this is necessary for open and honest interpretation. Even a structuralist approach to the text, eschewing any interest in the author and reader, assumes someone who is able to uncover the deep structure of the text, and this reader must be named.[8] If in any method the 'reader' is merely

[6] Mary Ann Tolbert, *Sowing the Gospel* (Minneapolis 1989).

[7] Tolbert, *Sowing,* 309.

[8] We do not actually examine a *pure* structuralist interpretation here (it seems that the method is already *passé*), though structuralist influences can be seen in the work of Vorster, Petersen and Tolbert in particular. Proponents of the extreme position claim that the author has no privileged insight into their own work ('the *death* of the author') because genre and deep structure are more significant than individual intention. It is apparent that there are 'deep structures' underlying Mk 13, and some that are typical of the genre 'apocalypse':—the 'eschatological question' ('when and what sign?'); binary oppositions such as ethnocentricity/universalism, process/crisis, insider/outsider, fleeing/gathering, heaven/earth—but the locus of our interpretation is in the distinctive use the author of Mark makes of such structures. Structural analysis is thus seen here as more an exercise in pre-interpretation than an exegetical method in itself. To use an analogy: there is only limited value in classifying all buildings together because they each have a roof, floor, windows and doors (an identical 'deep structure')—the task is then to describe what is distinctive about each building which might then indicate its *intended* usage. So it is with the 'building' and 'intended purposes' of texts. We cannot agree with those who would argue that the author's intentions are either inaccessible or irrelevant. Rather we would concur with Watson, "Authorial Intention", 9, that "In matters of meaning the author himself should be given the first word." Watson refers to E. D. Hirsch, "Three Dimensions of Hermeneutics", in *On Literary Intention,* ed David Newton-De Molina (Edinburgh 1976), 196f, and supports his contention that though there may not be a *logical* necessity to take the author's intentions seriously, there is an *ethical* obligation not to disregard authorial intention. This does not imply that to describe authorial intention is to exhaust the meaning and significance of a text, for Hirsch also

taken for granted or left undifferentiated or claimed to be universal, then it may be concluded that the text is really being interpreted through the eyes of an uncritical contemporary reader since no conscious effort is being made to balance that perspective with that of the earliest readers, or of the author, or of a community of critical readers. Whether such efforts to shift perspective are convincing or not is another question, but at least the possibility of reading the text 'through other eyes' is being consciously addressed by such methods.

Similarly, it is necessary to declare a position on whether the text (Mk 13) is to be interpreted as it stands, or in the context of the Gospel of Mark as a whole, or in a wider literary context.[9] Admittedly in some cases the focus on Mk 13 by some interpreters is more because of the limitations of space than because of a specific methodological position. Nevertheless, the context in which the text is examined as literature remains a valid criterion for differentiating between literary interpreters, especially since each of the main possibilities (the text itself; the Gospel context; the canonical context and the wider literary world) is often specifically mentioned in the various approaches reviewed here. In reviewing and critiquing the following studies we are seeking to broaden our understanding both of the literary context and of the author/reader(s) implicit in our own interpretation, consistent with our conviction that the obvious tensions between hermeneutical paradigms and between communities of interpretation are productive ones which should be continued through ongoing dialogue.

NORMAN R. PETERSEN was amongst the first to apply the newer literary perspectives to the Gospel of Mark and his work has provided an interesting blend of literary and historical concerns.[10] His early work led the way in applying some of the basic distinctions of narrative criticism, such as between 'story time' and 'plotted time', and between 'implied author' and 'implied reader'.[11] In later articles he established that the viewpoints of Jesus and the narrator of Mark are identical,[12] and then pointed out that in terms of the narrative as a whole Jesus has been portrayed as a reliable and trustworthy character, while the disciples are presented as being unreliable and unable to comprehend. According to

distinguishes between 'meaning' and 'significance'. 'Meaning' is to be related to the author's intention, 'significance' to the application that readers draw on the basis of their own background and interests, and accordingly *should* vary between interpreters— though not to the extent that the 'meaning' is lost.

[9] In this case the literary context of the first century, though comparisons with literature from other eras can also be most illuminating. See Northrop Frye, *The Great Code. The Bible and Literature* (San Diego 1983).

[10] See Norman R. Petersen, "'Point of View' in Mark's Narrative", *Semeia* 12 (1978), 97-121; "When is the End not the End? Literary Reflections on the Ending of Mark's Narrative", *Int* 34 (1980), 151-166; "The Reader".

[11] Petersen's method is outlined in his *Literary Criticism for New Testament Critics* (Philadelphia 1978), especially "Story Time and Plotted Time", 49-80.

[12] This is the conclusion reached by Petersen in "'Point of View'".

Petersen, this creates a tension between the expectations of the narrator, principal character and many of the minor characters, and the contrasting lack of understanding and inconsistency of the disciples. He therefore maintains that for "the plot to be resolved and this theme to be closed, something closural must either happen or be firmly implied."[13] Petersen argues that the foreshadowed meeting of Jesus and the disciples in Galilee (Mk 16:7) provides this closure, and that the implied readers of the narrative would have understood that a reversal of the disciples' attitude had occurred at that meeting. This already suggests that Petersen understands that these implied 'reader(s)' existed historically between the end of the plotted time of the narrative and the writing of the Gospel.

Thus it can be seen that, in contrast to many literary critics, Petersen is prepared to become entangled in the possible historical implications of his findings. Using a more clearly defined reader-response methodology than in his earlier articles, he focuses on the role of Mk 13 in confirming what he sees as the reversal of the disciples' errant eschatology.[14] At the level of the actors in the story in chapters 1-12 and 14-16, there is presented an erroneous messianic expectation—typified by the attitude of the disciples but opposed at the level of the author and implied readers—which is then specifically countered by Jesus in Mk 13. Petersen argues that Mk 13 shows that the four disciples named *do,* in the implied future of the narrative, gain a new and correct understanding from Jesus in Galilee because they are the ones who take the Gospel to all nations (13:10) and suffer faithfully on behalf of it (13:9-13). He contends that the authorial readers would have been well aware of this, and also of the fate of the other seven disciples, since most of the events in Mk 13 would have already taken place for them. He then goes so far as to hint that the other seven may have remained in Jerusalem, captive to political messianism and an erroneous eschatology.[15]

Petersen distinguishes even further between the false messianism of the disciples in chapters 1-12 and 14-16 (= the false messianism of the opponents in chapter 13) and the correct christological and eschatological position of the implied author and main character. The former he

---

[13] Petersen, "When is the End", 161. Contrast the views of Fowler, *Let the Reader Understand,* 79, at this point: "readers commonly argue that the last scene of the Gospel holds forth hope for some kind of future reconciliation or restoration (16:7; cf, 14:28). I am convinced, however, that to read the ending of Mark in this fashion is to read it through the overlays of Matthew, Luke, and John."

[14] Petersen, "The Reader", 48f. Petersen claims that he is undertaking "a more exhaustive search *within* the text for information about its own historical context", and thus he is "only calling for a more rigorous adherence to the first principle of historical criticism, namely that a text is first and foremost evidence for the time in which it is written" (38). This is certainly a foundational principle, but whilst Petersen adheres to this 'first principle' he seems to ignore other historical practices as he bases his historical interpretation purely on a *literary* approach. Surely it would be preferable to use such suggestions from a literary inquiry to test earlier historical research, rather than using them as the sole basis for describing the situation addressed by the Gospel.

[15] "The Reader", 49f.

describes as 'the ideas of messiah and kingdom', and the latter as the concepts of 'the Son of Man and his *parousia*'.[16] He notes that the kingdom/messiah sayings are those usually regarded as part of the earlier synoptic traditions by form critics, and wonders at the implications of the overruling of this eschatology by the Markan Son of Man/parousia formulations. More specifically, he suggests that the author of the Gospel of Mark acts as a mediator between the traditional authority of the four disciples and 'the elect' of Mk 13, in direct opposition to those false messianists who claim another authority.[17]

Such suggestions show a remarkable similarity to the conclusions of those redaction critical studies which found an anti-Jerusalem church polemic in the Gospel of Mark.[18] Since Petersen's analysis is not based on an examination of the historical and theological possibilities underlying the formation of the whole text, but rather proceeds from a literary perspective back to a historical and theological hypothesis, it requires adjustments in at least two areas:

(i)   It is the words of Jesus that speak of the future in Mk 13 and hold hope of a 'reversal', not the attitude of the disciples. As their inappropriate double-question of v.4 reveals, they are still lacking in comprehension in chapter 13 just as in every other chapter of the Gospel. Petersen is correct to suggest that a future reversal of the disciples' intransigence is assumed by the narrative (13:9-13; 14:28; 16:7)—or at least the possibility of such a reversal is left open—but it is left open to *all* who would be followers and not just restricted to the four (13:37).

(ii) The division between kingdom/messiah language and Son of Man/parousia language that Petersen suggests is not tenable. It certainly could be argued that the evangelist is wary of messianic claims and titles,[19] but the kingdom language lies at the very heart of the Gospel and constitutes the basic proclamation and teaching of Jesus (1:15 cf chapter 4). Thus the expectation that the powerful Kingdom of God will be seen shortly (9:1) is not *opposed* by the expected vindication of the Son of Man (13:24-27), but the one is interpreted by the other. It is not possible, therefore, to agree with Petersen that for the messianic pretenders "messiah and kingdom have a human, even political quality" whereas for "Jesus and Mark messiah and kingdom have a trans-human, even heavenly quality, because these notions refer to the *parousia* from heaven of the Son

---

[16] "The Reader", 49.

[17] "The Reader", 50.

[18] Such as Kelber (see chapter 7 above), and Joseph B. Tyson, "The Blindness of the Disciples in Mark", *JBL* 80 (1961), 261-268.

[19] For example, the use of χριστός is always qualified by another title occurring nearby in the Gospel of Mark, except at 9:41, where it is textually suspect.

of Man, who is Jesus".[20] Such 'heaven-earth' and 'political-spiritual' polarities are impossible to maintain in the Gospel of Mark (cf Mk 10:30—"...now, in *this life*..."), and yet again we must underline that the term 'parousia' is an anachronism, since it does not occur in this Gospel.

Despite these problems it is at least refreshing to see a literary critic prepared to interact with historical issues—if not historical methods—though such a venture has not necessarily been endorsed by others in the same field.

W. S. VORSTER is one who takes Petersen to task for allowing his implied reader to become "a real flesh and blood reader implied by the text" rather than just "a textual construct, a reader encoded in the text".[21] Apparently from Vorster's literary perspective, to actually consider that the authorial readers of the text might be real people "is misleading and nothing less that the construction of a possible reader" (221). In our classification of Vorster's approach above we have taken the liberty of assuming that the 'abstract reader' he has in mind must be a recent concept and therefore an indication of his intention to interpret the text from the perspective of the contemporary reader. This would be helpful in itself if it did not exclude other possible readers. Vorster himself quotes with approval the principle that to "enjoy and understand a narrative the reader has to suspend his own feelings and beliefs and accept those of the text" (209)—and this is especially so, he argues, for New Testament critics who have been educated to read the text as layers of tradition rather than narrative. He is surely right to stress the importance of reading the narrative as it is, but just how he thinks it is possible to accept the 'feelings and beliefs' of the text without positing a 'flesh and blood' context is not clear.

By using this more narrowly defined literary approach, Vorster reaches the conclusion that Mk 13 is a narrated speech "told from the perspective of a reliable character who is trusted to talk about the future, even though he himself does not know everything (13:32)" (222). It might be suggested that such self-evident conclusions are not an adequate reward for the effort taken to understand the literary terminology used in the analysis, although with a few exceptions Vorster does at least present his case clearly.[22] He builds this case by endorsing the findings of Petersen

---

[20] "The Reader", 46. How this 'earth-heaven' distinction could be argued throughout the Gospel as a whole is very difficult to see. We have already noted Mark's miserly use of words like 'angel', 'holy', 'heaven', 'glory' (see chapter 4, footnote 34 above).

[21] W. S. Vorster, "Literary reflections on Mark 13:5-37: A narrated speech of Jesus", *Neot* 21 (1987), 221. Until the next major author, page numbers in brackets shall refer to this article.

[22] The letters and numbers used to trace the chronological order of the plot ("Literary reflections", 210-211) remain a mystery despite the author's claim that "the order of Mark's emplotted narrative is most remarkable". Is number 4 (= the prediction of the fall/parousia, or the event itself?) *meant* to be missing from the second set of numbers? The distinction between "events which will come about (beginning)" in the near, but

that "the closure of Mark's gospel is strongly implied in the Galilee episode and that the reader is invited to read Mark 13 in view of the reliability of the narrator, Jesus" (215). But Vorster insists that Petersen has erred in historicising the closure of the Gospel, preferring himself to see both Mk 13 and the ending of the Gospel as an 'open-ended story'. Hence the reader "is left with the gap of the fulfilment of the Galilean episode, but also with the gap of the fulfilment of the predictions in Mark 13" (222). Certainly from the perspective of the contemporary reader these gaps appear to remain, but it is a reasonable assumption that the authorial audience would have been able to fill at least some of the gaps from their knowledge of what for them may have been recent events, and yet this is the specific area that Vorster's method has declared 'off-limits'.

Indeed Vorster states plainly that Mk 13 should *not* be interpreted primarily in either its Markan context or its historical context—hence his classification in the diagram above ('text only', 'contemporary reader'). He concedes that chapters 1-12 "undoubtedly generate certain expectations about the future by previews and hints through which the reader is educated on how to read Mark 13", but insists that ultimately Mk 13:5-37 "refers to a narrative world which is different from that in previous chapters and the reader is expected to have a different frame of reference from the previous sections in Mark's story in order to understand the codes of the text" (217). Similarly, Vorster concedes that apocalyptic texts do reflect to some extent the real world out of which they arise, but insists that "their primary function should not be looked for in terms of extratextual reference" (219). Now if these two positions are stressed—that Mk 13 should be approached differently to all the other chapters in the Gospel and any historical references should be left in the background—and if it is also maintained that the 'possible flesh and blood' authorial audience should be excluded from consideration, is it any wonder that the chapter remains cloaked in mystery if analysed from a purely literary (as defined by Vorster) point of view? What then is the value of this kind of contemporary reading of the text when such potentially vital information is specifically excluded? Surely such readings should be permitted to interact with other 'flesh and blood' ways of reading the text in order to avoid the incipient literary docetism that threatens Vorster's analysis.

Such a tendency—to replace the 'Word become flesh' by the 'written Word'—develops even further in BURTON L. MACK's *A Myth of Innocence*. Mack consciously sets out to explore the origins of Christianity in the creation of the Gospel account, which he sees as being a deliberate fusing of the Palestinian Jesus traditions and the Hellenistic Christ cult by the author of the Gospel of Mark. Or in the words of Tillich referred to earlier, Mack is arguing that "the New Testament picture of Jesus is

uncertain future (13:32), and the (end) being imminent (13:30) is also not at all clear ("Literary reflections", 216).

essentially a creation of Mark", which literary masterpiece then becomes "the bearer of the Spirit through whom God has created the church".[23] Mack is quite explicit when it comes to describing how this process took place, and it is worth quoting at length:

> Mark's Gospel was not the product of divine revelation. It was not a pious transmission of revered tradition. It was composed at a desk in a scholar's study lined with texts and open to discourse with other intellectuals. In Mark's study were chains of miracle stories, collections of pronouncement stories in various states of elaboration, some form of Q, memos on parables and proof texts, the scriptures, including the prophets, written materials from the Christ cult, and other literature representative of Hellenistic Judaism. . . . One "text" he did not have was a copy of the passion narrative because there was none until he wrote it. One might imagine Mark's study as a workshop where a lively traffic in ideas and literary experimentation was the rule for an extended period of time. Colleagues may well have contributed ideas and experimental drafts for many of the little story units used throughout the gospel in a common effort to think things through on the new storyline. The passion narrative is simply the climax of the new storyline. The story was a new myth of origins.[24]

This is the inevitable outcome of a one-dimensional (in this case, a purely literary) approach to interpreting the New Testament. Just as the 'Jesus of history (alone)' biographies led to the creation of Jesus in the image of the biographer, so this 'Gospel as literature (alone)' approach has led to a description of the creation of the Gospel as if it occurred in the book-lined study of a Professor at a West Coast American University. Nevertheless Mack insists that this process of creating the foundational myths of biblical Christianity occurred in southern Syria after the fall of Jerusalem, and that it was triggered by that disaster and by the failure of the synagogue reform movement. The resultant 'post-separation crisis' in the Markan community was resolved by the creation of an apocalyptic vision of divine intervention by the evangelist. Indeed for Mack, "Apocalyptic means the imagination of divine intervention in history" which unfolds "under the signs of crisis, conflict, judgment, and transformation" (326). This divine intervention does not *follow* the woes and final judgment according to the normal apocalyptic pattern, but because of the joint role of Jesus as 'seer' *and* 'king of the new kingdom' it is seen by the evangelist as overlapping with the period of judgment.

Thus the "announcement of judgment and the announcement of the new kingdom coincided in the appearance of Jesus in Galilee", meaning that for Mack it is not a question of resolving whether Markan eschatology is "a 'realized' eschatology" or "an imminent future apocalyptic eventuality", but rather a "both/and approach" is a more accurate

---

[23] P. Tillich, "Rejoinder", referred to in the Introduction, footnotes 24 and 36 above.

[24] Mack, *Myth,* 322-333. Until the next major author, page numbers in brackets shall refer to this book.

description.[25] This is because Mack maintains that the evangelist has "superimposed an apocalyptic script, starting with the appearance of Jesus in Galilee, on top of a myth of origins according to which Jesus was the inaugurator of the new group to whom the secret of the kingdom was given" (328). There is a threefold vindication which indicates that this 'double connotation' regarding the significance of Jesus is endorsed by God:

> Jesus' own vindication was assured in the resurrection that follows. The destruction of the temple in 70 C.E. answered the establishment's destruction of Jesus. And the yet-to-occur manifestation of the kingdom in power would vindicate the kingdom announced and represented by Jesus at his appearance in Galilee, temporarily postponed by the forces still lodged for a time in Jerusalem. (328)

These three vindications occurring in 'story time' but *beyond* the actual 'plotted time' of the Gospel account are matched by the endorsement of Jesus *within* 'plotted time' at the baptism, transfiguration and crucifixion. Mack's diagrammatic presentation of this overall 'apocalyptic' schema is most helpful—an excellent example of the positive results of a literary approach to the whole text—and will be reproduced and modified in the analysis which follows. But his corresponding portrayal of the Markan community as an apocalyptic sect awaiting the judgment of all those 'outside' does not do justice to the evangelist's intentions.[26] We have already noted above the absence and even inversion of the judgment theme in Mk 13, and the radical openness of the Markan community to the elect from the ends of the earth—and even from Judea. Thus it is not possible to accept Mack's description of that community as "cut off from the social orders of human history, isolated from social reality, without even a history of its own, waiting between appearances of Godot" (331). Nor can it be maintained that hostility in the Gospel is 'focused on Judaism' as such when the elect of Judea are clearly to be welcomed into the new community (13:20,22,27). Rather the source of the hostility to Jesus is shown throughout the Gospel specifically to be the rulers of Jerusalem and its temple. Certainly it can be seen that such judgment as is implied by

---

[25] *Myth,* 328. This is supported by the contention of Dan O. Via, *The Ethics of Mark's Gospel—in the Middle of Time* (Philadelphia 1985), 31 cf 37,60, that "the eschatological kingdom—the end—is both projected into the future and seen as realized in the present". Apart from making this one point very well, Via's work does not contribute much more of specific significance to the interpretation of Mk 13.

[26] See for example *Myth,* 330: "From within the sect privileged to read this gospel, the world beyond the borders came under the judgment of God. While the fixation of hostility was focused on Judaism, that which Judaism represented, history, tradition, law, and structured society, all fell under the sign of the inadequate if not depraved. Encounter with those outside was conceived as confrontation. One had to be careful, for the possibility of conflict was inherent in the world. Beware was the watchword with regard to those outside." For a similar negative interpretation of the Markan perspective on history and the world, see the summary and critique of Tolbert's work below.

Mk 11-15 is directed towards the temple and the Sanhedrin rather than Judaism in general, and even then there is the hope of salvation for at least one of the members of the Sanhedrin (15:43).

Thus we reject Mack's characterization of the Markan community as an isolated apocalyptic sect, and also his description of the deliberate intellectual processes that he argues went into the creation of the Gospel. But his plotting of narrative levels and his location of the Markan community in southern Syria after the fall of Jerusalem means that his diagrammatic presentation of the 'apocalyptic structure' of the whole Gospel (329) is much more useful, however, and it shall be explored further in the analysis below. Mack has made a bold attempt to relocate the origins of Christianity by attributing full creative control over the structure and content of the Gospel to the evangelist, but in the process he has lost sight of the importance of the traditions received by the Markan community, and of the assumed but not uncritical continuity with the Judean church which is left open by the Markan narrative.

The basic task that VERNON K. ROBBINS sets himself is to interpret the Gospel of Mark in terms of its Jewish and Greco-Roman literary antecedents.[27] He sees Mk 13 as a particularly good example of the overlapping of these two spheres of influence to the extent that he describes it as "material in the tradition of farewell discourses and apocalyptic visions in Israelite and Jewish literature ... placed in the framework of the Greco-Roman tradition of the temple dialogue" (171). According to Robbins, the use of this literary device of the temple dialogue "links the giving of one's livelihood to the temple with the giving of one's life for the gospel", connecting the sacrificial acts recorded in Mk 12:41f; 13:11f; and 14:3f. Thus "Giving to the temple treasury is replaced by preaching the gospel to all nations" (179).

Robbins analyses the features of farewell speeches and Jewish apocalypses closely, and concludes that "Mark 13 combines a marginal farewell speech with a marginal apocalypse" (177), which is then shaped as a temple dialogue. The outcome is somewhat confusing as he cites parallels from Greco-Roman temple dialogues *and* farewell speeches (Socrates in Xenophon's *Memorabilia*), as well as Jewish testaments *and* apocalypses. So often commentators have explored *either* the parallel forms of Mk 13 in the Jewish literature *or* in the Greco-Roman literature, but seldom both at once as Robbins attempts. The implications of this "merging of Jewish concepts with Greco-Roman concepts and traditions" are that according to Robbins it "provides an opportunity to advance from the system of blessings and curses in the covenant system toward a system of thought and action that accepts suffering and rejection as a natural part of fulfilling the 'new' system which is called gospel." Exactly how this transpires is not explained further, but Robbins' work has at least

---

[27] Vernon, K. Robbins, *Jesus the Teacher* (Philadelphia 1984). Page numbers in brackets now refer to this book until the next major commentator.

underlined the cross-cultural nature of the intertextual traditions behind the discourse.

These traditions, and particularly those from the Greco-Roman world, are explored more thoroughly by MARY ANN TOLBERT, who aims to interpret the whole Gospel in the context of Hellenistic literature and from the perspective of its authorial audience.[28] Tolbert's work is undoubtedly the most thorough of the newer literary studies of the Gospel of Mark, and contains the most highly developed methodological rationale for approaching the text in a literary-critical way.[29] She is aware on the one hand of the need to preserve "the desiderata of historical criticism" whilst undertaking a literary analysis, and on the other hand of the danger of dishonest literary approaches being used to avoid historical problems and thereby bolster neo-fundamentalism (25). Therefore Tolbert states categorically that "Literary criticism understands the text as *fiction,* the result of literary imagination, not of photographic recall" (25). This does not necessarily imply that the events described in a text have no connection with history, but rather it stresses that the story, plot, characters and style *could have been presented differently,* and therefore that the author has exercised 'choice and construction' in compiling the narrative (26). The Gospel narrative is therefore interpreted as a "consciously manipulated and conventionally formulated story" (26), which can be read in a variety of equally valid ways subject only to the literary imaginations of the readers. Tolbert then goes on to spell out the implications of this potential fecundity by describing the "impressive political agenda" implied by literary approaches which can challenge those authorized versions "cherished by the power structure—to evaluation, testing, and debate" (26).

Such a positive assessment of the promise of literary analysis rests on two key assumptions:

(i)   The accessibility of literary analysis to the average reader ["all literate people possess some rudimentary knowledge of literary concepts" (26)]; and

(ii) The ability of literary approaches to engage older historical approaches *on their own terms* [again Tolbert asserts that a literary approach "does not sacrifice the desiderata of historical research" (26)].

From Tolbert's perspective these are reasonable assumptions which she demonstrates to an impressive extent in her own analysis. However it is apparent that many literary interpretations do not share her clarity and are far from accessible to professional exegetes of another methodological persuasion, let alone to the general reader. It is also clear that many

---

[28] Tolbert, *Sowing.* Until the next major commentator, page numbers in brackets refer to this book.

[29] Tolbert, *Sowing,* especially 21-34. The work of Geddert, *Watchwords* (see below), also bids high as belonging in this category, although it is more of an 'older literary study' making use of what some would call 'composition criticism'.

literary interpreters *intentionally* sacrifice the benefits of an historical perspective, even though some are then lured back into making historical judgments on the basis of their purely literary analysis. Yet even if Tolbert's optimism may be misplaced from the perspective of literary criticism in general—though we may hope that she represents a turning back towards the best insights of earlier historical approaches—her own work must be credited as a serious attempt to adopt a literary perspective without losing sight of the historical context.

Having said this, we should also note that it is a very specific historical context in which Tolbert locates the Gospel of Mark—it is indeed as her sub-title suggests, a *literary-historical* context. Arguing that all we can know of the Gospel's production is that it came from an "anonymous author writing in *Koine* Greek to a Greek-speaking, predominantly Gentile audience during the second half of the first century C.E." (36), Tolbert proceeds to interpret the Gospel almost entirely from a Hellenistic perspective. She points to the universality of the Greek education system and its dependence on classical writers—particularly Homer (36-37)—and also to the essential aurality of written texts (41f) as two key factors for an understanding of the Gospel narrative. It was written to be read aloud, and therefore the author's use of "parataxis, asyndeta, ordinary diction, and brevity of narration, allowing the hearer/reader to fill in the 'gaps,' all find a home in Greek rhetorical theory" (43). Tolbert presents these two foundational principles most convincingly, however it could not be claimed that the question as to how applicable these understandings of literature and education would be to a landless peasant culture in northern Palestine or southern Syria, for example, has been finally settled. But having established these foundational principles to *her* satisfaction, Tolbert proceeds to analyse the particular type of literature that the Gospel represents.

After defining genre in sociological terms as the "common ground or shared expectations of authors and audiences" (78), Tolbert describes the Gospel of Mark as stylistically similar to the genre of the ancient erotic novel (especially the writings of Chariton and Xenophon of Ephesus), arguing that such popular literature was even more dependent on conventions and formulas than elite literature (65,78). Thus the perspective of the authorial audience in this type of literature must be carefully discerned if readers today are "to have any hope of following the story" (79). By adopting such a reader-response approach, Tolbert hopes to penetrate the "opacity, confusion, and muddle" that is the "prevailing judgment of modern readers of Mark" and to "interpret the Gospel in all its parts integrally and consistently" (80). This is a commendable aim, but her suggestion that interpretations like this of the *whole* Gospel of Mark have been lacking (29) is somewhat inaccurate given the recent spate of such readings of the Gospel.[30]

Tolbert gives a very clear and helpful presentation of the literary basis for her overview of the Gospel (90f). She takes Petersen's identification of the viewpoint of Jesus and the narrator even further by pointing out that the first degree narrative (of the implied author/narrator, and with which the implied reader/narratee identifies) and the second degree narrative involving Jesus have an identical point of view. Thus any other characters that are introduced are assessed according to this uniform position, and if they respond positively to Jesus then the implied reader identifies with them too. Thus the "reader's view of the disciples, and all other characters in the Gospel, depends entirely on their affiliation with Jesus" (97, footnote 13). Also, by allowing Jesus as a second degree character to "function with abilities normally reserved for public narrators alone, the story portrays Jesus' divine/human status in form as well as in content" (125).

This emphasis on Jesus heightens the significance of the only examples of third degree narrative in the Gospels—namely the parables—where a second degree character, Jesus, tells a story "with independent agents and actions" (103). In particular, Tolbert focuses on the parable of the sower (Mk 4:3-8,14-20) and the parable of the Tenants (Mk 12:1-11) as functioning as synopses of the plot of the Gospel as a whole, after the fashion of an oracle at the beginning of Xenophon's *An Ephesian Tale* (105f, 125). Tolbert then bases the whole structure of the Gospel and her interpretation of it on this supposed paradigmatic function of these two parables, thus:

(i)   Jesus the Sower of the Word (1:16-5:43)
(ii) The Good Earth (Miracles and Faith, 6:35-11:25) and the Rocky Ground (Failure and Fear, 14:17-72)
(iii) Jesus, the Heir of the Vineyard (11:27-13:37)

---

[30] See the socio-political approaches of Belo, Myers and Waetjen discussed in chapter 7 above, for example, and the specific claim of Geddert to have interpreted Mk 13 in the light of the Gospel as a whole, in the next section below. It should be added that earlier scholars such as Lambrecht and Pesch have also taken considerable pains to explore the wider context of the Gospel in their studies on Mk 13, although the most thorough attempt to interpret Mk 13 (solely!) within the parameters of the Gospel itself must be the brief study proffered by Bolt, "Mark 13" (see chapter 5, footnote 40, and chapter 7 footnote 16, above). We are sympathetic to Bolt's general intention to historicise much of the discourse and in particular would affirm his contention that the whole of the Gospel expects the imminent harvest—the coming Kingdom/gathering of the elect—within a generation of Jesus ("Mark 13", 15), his emphasis on the process of fulfilment implied in vv.24f ("Mark 13", 30), and on the foolishness of the disciples' question about signs in 13:4 ("Mark 13", 26-27). However there remain grave difficulties with trying to see *all* of Mk 13 fulfilled within the Gospel itself—in effect, collapsing story time into plotted time, and leaving no extra-textual references within which the Markan audience can locate itself. How can 13:15,17 and 18 be related to the crucifixion, even if we accept Bolt's arguments for 13:14 (against all OT traditions) and 13:16,19? Why should the disciples be *told* to flee the crucifixion (13:14)?

(iv) The Death of the Heir (14:32-15:5; 15:16-39; Suffering and Alienation, 15:40-16:8)

The basis for using these two parables as the hermeneutical key to the whole Gospel is very slender, however, as Tolbert virtually concedes. Of the dreams, visions and oracles which make up the "small amounts of third degree narrative" (104) in Xenophon and Chariton, *one* oracle at the beginning of Xenophon's *An Ephesian Tale* is cited as setting out "in concise form the outline of the entire plot of the novel" (105), yet Tolbert concedes it is "not technically third degree narrative" (104).[31] On this basis it is then suggested that two of the parables in the Gospel of Mark also set out the plot of the entire narrative. Surely it would be just as valid to choose the announcement of the Kingdom (1:15-16) and the eschatological discourse (Mk 13, containing an oracle in vv.14-21 which arguably qualifies as third degree narrative) as paradigms for the structure and interpretation of the Gospel as a whole?

Tolbert would probably concede as much, since she makes no claim to having written a "final or authoritative word" (89), but the whole question of the validity of such a basis for the reading of the Gospel is raised. It may have been better to have argued on other grounds that the parable of the sower "performs a special function for the Gospel" (127) as many have done before, and as Tolbert herself points out. But she is convinced that it is *both* the parable of the Sower and of the Tenants which "provide the audience of the Gospel with summaries or synopses of the main action of surrounding material" (128). Clearly they *are* important parables in the Markan narrative, but so too, for example, are the two 'parables' of the fig tree (11:12-14; 20-25; and 13:28-29), and the 'parable' showing how difficult it is to truly perceive (8:22-26). A balanced appraisal of all the parables would have produced a surer basis for an understanding of the Gospel as a whole, for the particular stress Tolbert places on the parable of the Tenants in particular leads to at least one major problem in her interpretation of Mk 13.

The problem lies not in the identification of 12:9 ("What will the owner of the vineyard do? He will come and destroy the tenants and give the vineyard to others") as a reference to the fall of Jerusalem. Rather it is in the collapsing of Markan eschatology into this one allegory. For Tolbert the parable is not just directed against the Jewish leadership in Jerusalem,

---

[31] Tolbert, *Sower,* 104, footnote 27, rather lamely argues that "the point of using such a narrative model at all is the insight it provides into narrative dynamics, not its ability to label everything definitively." But after the clarity and precision of her earlier analysis it is something of a disappointment to find such a major link in her interpretation unsupported by the evidence. We are still left wondering if there is any other precedent in the popular literature for a third degree parable/story/oracle/dream providing a plot synopsis for the rest of the narrative. It is not surprising that Tolbert's summary of her position is appropriately hesitant: "*if* the parables of the Sower and the Tenants also function as plot synopses and *if* the rhetorical structure of two major divisions ... is generally correct— that is, *if* we have actually uncovered and properly understood several basic conventions as guides ... " (125, italics mine).

but conveys a picture of The End itself, so that the whole of Mk 13 is interpreted through it. Thus she refers to the "frightful nature of this final assault by the tenants on all existence" (264) in her description of the tribulation in 13:14-22, and 'this generation' in 13:30 is taken as a reference not to the disciples or contemporaries of Jesus, but to "the present evil tenants who control the vineyard and harrow the faithful" (268).[32] This leads to an interpretation of Mk 13 in terms of classic apocalyptic dualism—"this present evil, oppressive, and suffering-filled existence" (265) is but "a passing interlude before the coming of the Son of man on the clouds and eternal life for the faithful" (264-265). And even more colourfully, the "world in which Jesus and his followers live is a bleak, ugly, and painful place filled with wars, persecutions, trials, betrayals, death, and a yet to be experienced last bloodbath of cosmic dimensions" (264), but the "winter of suffering, persecutions, and terrible tribulations will soon make way for a new summer of eternal life" (267).

This is an unfortunate distortion of Markan eschatology, the implications of which Tolbert herself begins to realise in her conclusion:

> The difficulty Mark furnishes for modern appropriation is not its negative assessment of the human situation but its solution to the problem. Mark argues that only direct divine intervention can preserve the elect from the mess this generation is making of the cosmos. While some even now may wish to continue affirming Mark's view, such acquiescence has unfortunately permitted this generation to keep increasing the mess for almost two thousand years. (310)

We would suggest that in fact the supposed 'negative assessment of the human situation' in the Gospel of Mark is one side of the problem of Tolbert's interpretation, leading to a corresponding over-emphasis on the significance of 'eternal life' and a purely 'other-worldly' solution to the evils of this age.[33] It is not possible to impose such a polarised scheme onto the Markan narrative. Certainly the Gospel is realistic in its portrayal of suffering and evil, but there is also the joy of the healed sick and the welcomed outcasts, and the fellowship of the road and the table which pervades the narrative and generates hope for *this* life as well as the next (10:30). In Mk 13 itself, great tribulation notwithstanding, there is the hope of the gathering of the elect which, as we have shown, should not

---

[32] This leads to considerable difficulties in interpreting 13:30, for if 'this generation' (= the 'tenants' of Jerusalem and Judea) shall *not* pass away until *all* these things have happened (which includes what Tolbert sees as the 'granting of eternal life', 13:24-27), then how can it fit the parable where the tenants are destroyed at the owner's return prior to the vineyard being handed over to others? Clearly the parable of the Tenants is best interpreted at the historical level (12:9 = the destruction of Jerusalem) rather than used as a template for interpreting all of the events in Mk 13.

[33] 'Eternal life' can hardly be posited as a major theme in the Gospel of Mark when it occurs only at 10:17 and 30. Tolbert's repeated references to it (264, 267, 294 at least) as if it were the key underlying reassurance of the whole Gospel read like 'Johannine thunderbolts from a Markan sky'.

be interpreted solely in other-worldly language, but can be seen as the new community—the rule of God come in power—which provides a positive purpose for mission, discipleship and community in human history.

By way of contrast, mission in the Gospel of Mark from Tolbert's perspective is merely a means of hastening the end: "sowing the gospel abroad becomes the one human act that can expedite the demise of this present evil, oppressive, and suffering-filled existence" (265), since the Gospel must first be preached to all nations before the end can occur (13:10).[34] At other times Tolbert shows evidence of a more enlightened interpretation when she correctly notes that "the Gospel of Mark does *not* portray the coming as a judgment on the nations" (266), and that "the elect of the kingdom are defined solely by doing the will of God and not by national, racial, social or sexual categories" (267). She also perceives that the vocabulary of the parable of the Lord of the House (13:34-36) is repeated in the Gethsemane account, implying a "more personal and individual meaning of the coming hour" (269), just as the arrests and trials of vv.9-13 are enacted in the fate of Jesus, the one who endures faithfully to the end in the Passion narrative. But perhaps the insight that benefits most from Tolbert's comparisons with Greco-Roman literature is her interpretation of the Markan ending.

She points out that in ancient literature what the text 'does' or 'achieves' is more important than the meaning itself (288-289), and that the ending of the Gospel can therefore be seen as a deliberate motivational ploy to inspire its authorial audience to get involved in mission. The sudden disappointment in 16:8 after expectations had been raised that at last someone might fulfill the requirements of Jesus, indicates that ultimately the women were 'rocky ground' also, and raises the question in the mind of the hearer/reader: "What type of earth am I? Will *I* go and tell?" (299). Thus the Gospel account forces a response of commitment or rejection from each reader/hearer.

That Tolbert's interpretation of the Gospel leads to many valid insights is beyond question, but on the basic issues of Markan structure and Markan eschatology her work has been found wanting. Her 'literary agnosticism' over the date and place of the formation of the Gospel account also extends into her interpretation of Mk 13, leading her to state that: "For modern readers ... entering the ranks of the authorial audience of Mark 13:14 becomes an impossibility. We do not know and probably

---

[34] The similarity of this position and of the motivation for the 'saving of souls' by some fundamentalist and pentecostal mission groups today is striking. Such a utilitarian view of mission justifies the avoidance of any meaningful action leading to social justice (because The End is coming soon anyway) and focuses on the mass evangelization (actual conversion is not even necessary to fulfill the mandate) of as many people as possible in as short a time as possible in order to satisfy the technical requirement that 'first the Gospel must be preached in all nations' before 'the Second Coming' can occur! Such a position is as sub-Christian as it is non-Markan, and Tolbert is at least somewhat embarrassed by it in her conclusion (309-310).

cannot know for sure what 'the desolating sacrilege' was supposed to represent" (264). Such frankness is commendable, but if Tolbert is to live up to her claim of not ignoring the benefits of historical analysis, then some outline of the historical parameters within which such a text might be interpreted would have been helpful. For it is apparent that despite her best intentions, Tolbert's literary approach does lead to an undermining of the historical context of the Gospel, and even worse, to a negative interpretation of the Markan understanding of history.

A similar charge, though not as severe, could be laid against the analysis of TIMOTHY J. GEDDERT, who deliberately seeks to interpret Mk 13 in the context of a literary appreciation of the Gospel as a whole.[35] Geddert's findings have already been commented on above to some extent (see chapter 5), because of the overlap of his literary approach with that part of redaction analysis often termed composition analysis. His own assessment of his aim and method is to "uncover the intentions of the author of Mark's Gospel as they can be known by studying Mark 13 in its Gospel context" (19). Geddert dismisses any problems with 'the intentional fallacy' by insisting that "(a)uthors are still basically in control of the communication process" (20). He concedes that they may use "implied narrators and literary characters to help them make their points, but they do not create autonomous communicators and stand by helplessly as the readers are told things the author never intended them to hear" (20). Thus with disarming frankness Geddert proceeds to make his case. If Tolbert has been described as the literary critic who explains her methodology most clearly, then Geddert is the one who knows and explains the Gospel of Mark most clearly. We have already had reason to affirm Geddert's conclusions in the following areas:[36]

(i) *The Markan perspective on signs.* The Markan Jesus will have nothing to do with signs and therefore the disciples' question in 13:4 is misguided (57f). [Though we have not gone so far as to agree that "Mark is concerned to explicate a Christian epistemology" (52), and all the implications that this holds for Geddert].

(ii) *The four night watches in Mk 13 and in the Passion narrative.* The call to faithful discipleship and alertness (γρηγορεῖτε from 13:33 onwards) has an existential as well as an eschatological dimension, and Jesus is the supreme example of 'the one who endures to the end'. [Though we have not gone so far as Geddert in identifying Jesus as both the Doorkeeper *and* the Master (105f)].

---

[35] Timothy J. Geddert, *Watchwords. Mark 13 in Markan Eschatology.* See chapter 5 above for further comments on Geddert's work. Page numbers in brackets will refer to this book until the end of this section.

[36] Not all the conclusions are *distinctively* Geddert's—(i) and (ii) are most clearly, but for (iii) we have referred to Gill and Telford, and for (iv) to Myers, though the same point was made earlier by Perrin and Schweizer at least.

(iii) *Mark's temple theology.* The Markan Jesus judges the temple and there is an incipient temple-replacement theme present, whereby the new temple, "Jesus and his community" (138), replaces the old temple. [Though we maintain that this judgment is *more clearly* seen in the 'cleansing' and the 'rending of the veil' incidents than Geddert seems to think—they are *not* "subtle points" and "veiled in secrecy"(145)—but plainly evident to the authorial audience].

(iv) *Mark's theology of suffering and persecution.* Mark takes "the 'passion paradigm' which fits the transition from John to Jesus" and reapplies it "for the transition from Jesus to the disciples" (173). [Though we do not agree with all of Geddert's suggestions about the 'journey theme' (151f)].

Clearly there is much that this present analysis affirms in Geddert's interpretation of the Gospel, including many smaller points that cannot be documented here. It should be repeated that even though Geddert specifically eschews a redaction critical methodology (19),[37] his familiarity with the Gospel as a whole and his willingness to examine authorial intention means that of all the more recent literary approaches, his is the one that builds on the prior foundations of historical critical investigations most constructively. Yet Geddert does not make the links specific and tries too hard to solve all of the 'exegetical problems' of the Gospel at the literary and epistemological level. Possible historical and tradition-critical solutions to tensions in the text are not even considered, because it is assumed that the whole text and each part of the text represent the intentions of the author equally. Of course in practice Geddert has carefully selected those themes which are particularly representative of the mind of the author, and this is what makes his analysis so similar in places to a redaction or composition critical approach. But in that he looks for ultimate explanations and solutions at a literary level only, Geddert along with many other literary analysts, tends to remove the Gospel of Mark from a meaningful historical context.

This becomes evident at the outset when Geddert states that "the issue of the date of Mark's Gospel is not very important in determining what Mark intended to say in Mark 13" and that his interpretation "is compatible with any date prior to the fall of the temple and also with a date *immediately* after it" (27). The second statement is true of a strictly literary interpretation (if the word 'immediately' is removed), but it is not

---

[37] To be more specific, Geddert states that 'redaction' analysis is variously defined (19). If it is understood teleologically as 'listening to the author's perspective' then it is what Geddert is attempting to do, but he rejects that definition. If it is understood methodologically as 'analysing the changes an author makes to their sources', then it is an inadequate methodology to achieve its goal. It is interesting to note, however, that Geddert himself makes use of this very method when analysing the Markan attitude towards 'signs' (31f), in that he considers the possibility that the author omits the use of σημεῖον from his sources and examines the synoptic parallels very closely to support this possibility. Similarly, his distinction between the Markan uses of βλέπω and γρηγορέω assume a redaction critical methodology (109f).

then legitimate to make the historical judgment that the author of Mark was unconcerned with history purely on the basis of a literary methodology. The first statement therefore requires close *historical* scrutiny before it can be justified.

Similarly, Geddert should remain strictly agnostic over the issues of the provenance and authorship of the Gospel, but like so many literary analysts he cannot resist a passing comment: "Though our interpretation does not lean heavily on any assumptions concerning authorship, there are no adequate reasons for denying the oldest view, that John Mark, companion of both Paul and Peter, wrote the Gospel in Rome" (27). Again it must be insisted that literary critics should not make gratuitous comments about the historical origins of texts unless they are prepared to enter into historical debate. Otherwise, as Tolbert warned above, the 'newer literary' approaches become an illegitimate way of bolstering neo-conservative positions. Once historical debate is entered into it becomes plain that the text itself is the primary evidence for authorship and not other traditions however old they are. If Geddert wishes to make comment on the historical issues of authorship on the basis of his literary analysis of the whole text, then he simply needs to consciously *interact* with such issues—for we are not suggesting that literature and history are mutually exclusive realms. Nor are we suggesting that 'a solution' of the problems of authorship and dating is essential for a meaningful interpretation of the Gospel, but rather that if they *are* to be tackled as issues then it must be done properly. We would, however, affirm that such historical issues cannot be totally ignored—and should never be deliberately ignored—or the Gospel may once again be understood as 'fiction' only and not history, as 'written word' only and not 'word become flesh'.

It may seem unnecessary to focus on a passing comment of Geddert's in this way, but it serves to illustrate what we maintain is the basic flaw in his interpretation of Mk 13 and its context—namely the assertion that everything can be explained in literary terms. Geddert adopts this strategy by attributing every difficult reading in the text to the deliberate subtlety of the author. Repeatedly Geddert tells us "that Mark's Gospel features very intricate and subtle ways of telling a story and alluding to its deeper significance" (54). Even more, we are informed that in writing in this way the author is merely adopting the ambiguous teaching style of Jesus (55) and preserving the secret of the coming Kingdom of God until it is revealed at the parousia of the Son of Man. This perspective is maintained throughout his analysis of the Gospel by suggesting that the dominant theme, widely recognised as being that of 'discipleship', is in fact matched by another—of 'discernment'. Thus for Geddert the unifying Markan concern in the Gospel becomes one of epistemology (or 'discipleship discernment') rather than ecclesiology, christology or eschatology.[38] This he proceeds to demonstrate by arguing that the central point at issue in the dialogue in the boat and the warning about the leaven of the Pharisees and Herod (8:14-21) is epistemological. How is it possible to apprehend and evaluate the claims of Jesus? By the 'sign-seeking' of the Pharisees and Herod (= 'the leaven'), or by the 'meaning-discernment' model through which Jesus endeavours to get the disciples to 'see' and 'hear' (68)? Similarly, the parables chapter (Mk 4) is held to provide a parallel (4:1-20 cf 8:1-21) which is also concerned with teaching the disciples *how* they are to understand, rather than simply giving an explanation of what the parables mean: "Both 8.14-21 and 4.13-20 are designed to instruct the disciples on the *means by which* true understanding is made possible" (72).

This preoccupation with discernment is carried forward into Mk 13 by the recurrent use of βλέπετε (= 'discern' for Geddert), being an exhortation to the disciples to perceive truly the events around them and to understand the hidden nature of the Kingdom. From 13:33 onwards the exhortation switches to γρηγορεῖτε, which Geddert translates as 'remain faithful', in the sense of following the example of Jesus as he faces the events of the Passion night, so that 'next time round' the true disciples might also emulate their Lord as they follow in his way (13:9-13). Geddert argues that these two 'watchwords'—βλέπετε and γρηγορεῖτε—demonstrate that the major concern of the author in Mk 13 is not "to teach readers how they can determine the timing of the End by the signs that precede it", but rather to "teach them how to live as faithful disciples without knowing when the End will come" (109). It is therefore appropriate that the Gospel "uses the first term in the twelve and a half chapters where the disciples are taught about the kingdom's secrecy and the need for divine illumination", and then switches to the second term "in the final chapters where we see on the one hand Jesus, working out of what has been taught, and on the other, the disciples failing to do what they should have learned" (109-110).

Geddert is on firm ground when he speaks of the significance for discipleship teaching of the exhortations in Mk 13. However, when he attempts to 'explain' the many tensions and difficulties remaining in the text of Mk 13 purely in terms of the deliberate ambiguity of the author of Mark, his argument begins to wear thin. We are asked to believe that the author of Mark was being *deliberately* obscure and ambiguous about:

(i)   the nature of 'prophetic perspective' (231f);
(ii)   whether the fall of the temple is connected to The End (228);
(iii)   the time interval between vv.23 and 24 (229f);
(iv)   when the time of mission and discipleship is to occur (225f);
(v)   whether vv.24f indicate judgment as well as blessing (226f);

---

[38] "Mark is much more concerned to commend an implicit epistemology than to describe an explicit eschatology." *Watchwords*, 72.

(vi)   whether v.7 is part of The End (235);

(vii) whether the 'birth pains' (v.8) are a sign of imminence or not (236);

(viii) what the 'abomination of desolation' refers to (237);

(ix)   who it is who will see the Son of Man (243);

(x)   what is meant by γενεά in 13:30 (244); and therefore

(xi)   the implications of 13:30 (239f).

In short, Geddert contends that the readers of the Gospel "are left with an uncertainty which was deliberately cultivated by the author of the text" (254).

The effect of Geddert's special pleading in support of this deliberate Markan ambiguity is to reduce the whole discourse to a loose collection of meaningless conundrums and multi-purpose symbols. At times Geddert justifies this because of the *ignorance* of the author: "If Mark did not know whether the tribulation would be brought to an end *so that* history and mission could continue, or whether it would be brought to an end by the returning Son of Man, would he not have done just what he has in fact done?" (237). At other times he seems to suggest it is because of the *omniscience* of the author—who purposely leaves open the options for a multiple fulfilment of prophecy. Thus to take just one example, he argues that 13:14 is deliberately ambiguous because the author may have wanted to "indicate that the prophecy would be fulfilled at least once in the Jerusalem temple, and *perhaps* also thereafter in subsequent crises wherever Satan would exert influence" (237). But such an interpretation is unsatisfactory on several grounds:

(i)   It confuses the (post)modern reader's interpretation and possible application of the text to other situations, with the author's specific intentions. *We may* validly apply the 'abomination of desolation' imagery to other historical situations, but it is quite another matter to suggest that this is what the author intended from the outset.

(ii) It disconnects the text from any *specific* historical situation and turns it into a general description of many possible future outcomes. Thus the text becomes a loose-fitting multi-purpose myth rather than something which—because of its specific applicability to one historical moment—has been found to be true in the author's judgment, and may therefore be re-applied and re-interpreted as truth in other situations.

(iii) It misunderstands the nature of the prophetic process, since it leads to the position where the discourse is regarded as an assortment of loosely arranged prophecies which the author intended to be applied in haphazard fashion to any number of subsequent events.[39] This does not accord well with the careful procedure

---

[39] Geddert would say they were 'carefully arranged to be ambiguous' rather than 'loosely arranged', but in practice there may be little difference. If the discourse had no detailed and accurate applicability to specific events in the memory of the original 'readers', what is to prevent it from being regarded as a smorgasbord of prophetic

whereby prophecy was retrospectively tested and endorsed as a 'word of the Lord' in Jewish and early Christian circles.[40]

(iv) It makes light of the urgent and specific appeal in 13:14f to flee, and of the horrific suffering of 13:17f. *If* this is an event within recent memory for some of the authorial audience, as we have argued, then how could the prophecy be generalised and re-cycled for still further fulfilment so soon afterwards? *If* on the other hand it represents an event still anticipated by the authorial audience, on what basis and for what purpose would the author *deliberately* suggest a multiple fulfilment of the prophecy? From a pastoral perspective alone there are compelling reasons to interpret 13:14-23 as a retrospective affirmation of those of the 'elect' who were not deceived and who were able to flee at some stage during the awful tribulation of those days.

(v) If the text were made deliberately ambiguous by the author to the extent suggested by Geddert, whereby not only the timing but also the order and meaning of each event is uncertain for the authorial audience, then how can later readers hope to understand and apply the text? It *cannot* be interpreted any further. It is not then discernment that is required for the reader to understand, but a new revelation!

After agreeing with so much of Geddert's analysis of the Gospel of Mark as a whole, it is something of a disappointment to find so little to affirm in his comments specifically on Mk 13. This may be attributed to his determination to avoid the historical questions raised by the discourse in favour of leaving them as intentional literary puzzles. But his passing suggestion that the "mission question, especially as it relates to the Gentiles, might prove to be more significant in Mark 13 than is usually noted" is one that shall be affirmed and examined further in chapter 9 below.

The work of ROBERT FOWLER, *Let the Reader Understand,* is the most consistently applied reader-response analysis of the Gospel of Mark yet undertaken. As well as this, the first few chapters provide a very helpful mapping of the rather confusing terrain of 'reader-oriented' approaches

---

imagery to be plundered for use in all sorts of bizarre apocalyptic scenarios? If critical scholarship cannot demonstrate the historical relevance and truth of the discourse for the Markan reader, how can it hope to guide and inform (and limit!) the apocalyptic imagination of the modern reader?

[40] As well as the work of Boring, *Sayings,* cited above, on early Christian prophets and 'the sayings of the risen Jesus', see D. E. Aune, *Prophecy in Early Christianity and the Ancient Mediterranean World* (Grand Rapids 1983); Gerald F. Hawthorne, "The Role of Christian Prophets in the Gospel Tradition", in *Tradition and Interpretation in the New Testament. Essays in Honor of E. Earle Ellis,* ed Gerald F. Hawthorne with Otto Betz (Grand Rapids/Tübingen 1987), 119-133; and Robert J. Miller, "The Rejection of the Prophets in Q", *JBL* 107 (1988), 225-240.

to texts.[41] As a 'critical reader' with three persona—individual, communal and textual (40)—Fowler is uncompromising in his insistence that Mark must be read as Mark, and not through the lens of Matthew or other later traditions. This in itself makes his book profoundly significant, as we have had cause to note many times already how difficult it has been for everyone to read the Gospel of Mark on its own terms. Unfortunately, despite championing this cause and persisting with it fearlessly in such areas as the Gospel's treatment of the disciples, for instance, Fowler himself lapses into Matthean language when he comes to Mk 13 and speaks of "the *parousia* of the Son of Man on the clouds of heaven" (131, italics mine). Indeed, despite a very helpful analysis of the dramatic nature of the discourse (82-87)—where Fowler shows clearly how the words of Jesus are directed above the disciples' heads directly at *all* the audience of the Gospel—his discussion of the impact of Mk 13 on the critical reader is probably the least satisfactory part of Fowler's book. With reference to Mk 13:14 he admits that "(c)omplications here suggest that we shall never fully understand who 'the reader' of 13:14 is, or for that matter exactly what the reader is to understand" (83). This is commendably modest and refreshingly honest, but ultimately disappointing in a book which stresses so heavily that the Gospel of Mark's chief concern is "the fate of the reader outside the story" (80). Just what, then, is the reader to make of Mk 13? Only that it is "full of the veiled, figurative language of apocalyptic" (85)?

It should be underlined that Fowler's approach *does* result in some stunning reconstructions of the Gospel's distinctive impact in other parts of the narrative, but his method seems particularly inadequate on its own to penetrate the mysteries of Mk 13. We may gain some satisfaction from his admission that Mk 13 must refer in some way to the events of the Jewish War: "I see no reason to dispute this supposition about the referential meaning of the cryptic allusions in Mark 13" (87). This is so especially since he has earlier emphatically stated of Mark that "this narrative does not claim to be history. It is not even referentially oriented" (80). This is stated even more categorically when Fowler distinguishes between the mimetic (referential) focus of previous Markan scholarship, and the rhetorical (communicative) focus of his own reader-oriented approach (55f). We applaud Fowler's aim to explore the *effect* of hearing the Gospel rather than to attend only to what it *refers* to, but ultimately even he admits—and this especially with regard to Mk 13—that some account of first century events is necessary to make sense of this particular part of the narrative. It is ironic indeed that reader-oriented criticism is shown to be inadequate on its own precisely at that one point in the text where the reader is directly addressed.

---

[41] Robert M. Fowler, *Let the Reader Understand. Reader-Response Criticism and the Gospel of Mark* (Minneapolis 1991). Page numbers in brackets in the main text refer to this book from now until further notice.

Mk 13 in the context of the Gospel of Mark

One of the positive outcomes of the literary approaches to Mk 13 is that it is no longer questioned that the discourse belongs in its present location in the Gospel.[42] Indeed the links between Mk 13 and the Passion narrative were pointed out by R. H. Lightfoot in an earlier era of exegetical methodology,[43] but the recent growth in awareness of the evangelist's authorial activity—both in Mk 13 and in the Passion narrative—has emphasised the likelihood of the intentionality of such links, and suggested many others as well. We have already commented above that Mack's diagrammatic presentation of the structure of the Gospel of Mark is most helpful in visualising these links and the wider context of Mk 13 in general. We offer it on the following page with some substantial additions and modifications.

The diagram clarifies the situation of the discourse in relation to the events still to follow within the Gospel, the events foretold beyond the plotted time of the Gospel, and the situation of the Markan community itself. Thus although the whole discourse is set in the future tense, from the perspective of the authorial audience some of those future events are already past, some are more recent, some still occurring, and some still in the future. Indeed, in terms of the exhortation to stay awake for 'the hour of being handed over', the Markan audience would have been familiar with both the faithfulness of Jesus within the Gospel account itself, and the faithfulness of those of their own number who were 'handed over' in the events described in 13:9-13. It is this sequence—John the Baptist/Jesus/the followers, or the 'Passion paradigm' as Geddert terms it—which demonstrates most clearly the role Mk 13 plays in locating the authorial audience (the Markan community) within the promise-fulfilment scheme of the narrative. Therefore we have made the sequence more prominent on Mack's diagram. As well as the continuity the Markan community have with John the Baptist and Jesus as expressed by the 'Passion paradigm', they are obviously also included within the scope of the prophetic words of Jesus and the Jewish scriptures. This is shown clearly on the diagram, but is made specific in the text at 13:23, where they are reassured that their recent experiences have all been within the foreknowledge of Jesus, and therefore there is a solid basis for their continuing hope.

[42] *Contra* Pesch's suggestion that it was a last minute addition by the author. See chapter 4 above. Of course it is a *presupposition* of recent literary approaches that Mk 13 is part of the whole text of the Gospel—but the results of these methods also seem to have confirmed that assumption in the eyes of those who might operate from other presuppositions—at least I am unaware of any who still argue that Mk 13 was a late, or later, inclusion in the Gospel from another source.

[43] R. H. Lightfoot, *The Gospel Message of St. Mark* (London 1950), 48-59, 106-116.

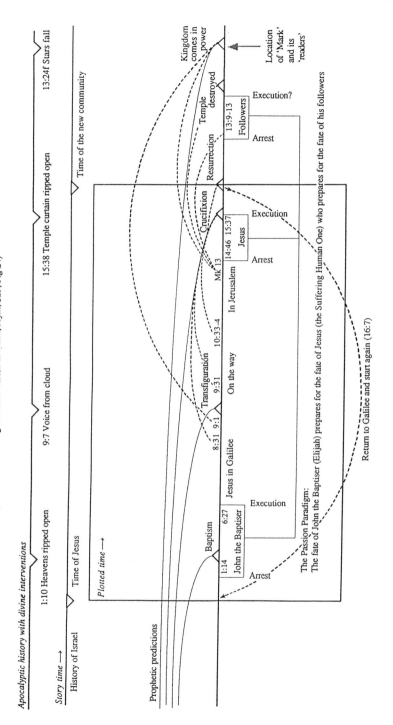

A Map of the Gospel of Mark
(with due acknowledgements to Burton L. Mack, *Myth*, 329, Fig 24)

Thus although the narrative appears to us to end abruptly with a call to discipleship renewal at 16:8,[44] the authorial audience have already been able to locate themselves in a context projected by the text which affirms them as being in direct continuity with the teachings and promises of Jesus. *They* are the ones who will witness the kingdom coming in power and be part of the gathering of the elect. *They* are the product of—and participants in—faithful mission to the nations,[45] and *they* now also embrace the elect who fled from Judea at the appropriate time, to form the elect of the vindicated Son of Man.

Mk 13 in the context of the NT Canon

As has been evident from our refusal to use non-Markan terminology such as 'parousia', and non-biblical terminology such as 'the second coming', we have chosen to approach Mk 13 initially through the Gospel of Mark alone. Such an approach leaves unanswered many doctrinal questions regarding the nature of Christian hope and eschatology, but we are convinced that ultimately an understanding of the *distinctive Markan contribution* in these areas will be of more assistance than forever interpreting Markan eschatology through Matthean or Pauline eyes. Therefore after briefly examining the possibility of direct links with Pauline eschatology (in chapter 4 above), which we rejected, and after noting some parallels with later Christian prophecies in Revelation, we have focussed almost exclusively on the Markan text. As Tolbert comments, the Gospel of Mark "must be read as much as possible on its own terms rather than on terms set out by manifestations of its *Nachleben,* especially the Gospels of Matthew and Luke."[46]

This is not the place for a detailed investigation into the synoptic parallels of Mk 13, but when a brief comparison of Mk 13 *is* made with the other synoptic Gospels the following points become apparent:

(i)   The differences between the synoptic eschatological discourses are insufficient to justify dating one pre-fall and the others post-fall. Pre-fall and post-fall datings could only be maintained if it was also held that the destruction of the mother church in Jerusalem had little impact on any of the Gospels, which is difficult to believe. Lk 21 shows some signs of a later perspective on events (Lk 21:20,24), but the lack of change in perspective between

---

[44] Here again we are in agreement with Geddert, *Watchwords,* 166f, and a growing number of other exegetes who see the command to return to Galilee (16:7) as an invitation to discipleship renewal—to go back to the beginning and start on The Way again.

[45] We are not suggesting that it was the fall of Jerusalem itself that precipitated a "great time of mission" (as does France, *Divine Government,* 78-80; see also Bolt's critique of France, "Mark 13", 11)—rather, that the inclusive mission of Paul and others was embraced and continued by the Markan community (and then vindicated by the events of 70CE).

[46] Tolbert, *Sowing,* 29. This is insisted on even more strongly by Fowler, *Let the Reader Understand,* "Matthew as a Reading Grid", 237f, for example.

eschatological discourses is especially noticeable when comparing the Gospels of Matthew and Mark. Therefore either the Gospels of Matthew and Mark must both be located pre-fall or—more probably—all three synoptic Gospels must be dated post-fall.

(ii) There are no convincing grounds for suggesting that the Gospel of Matthew was written before that of Mark. The occurrence in the Gospel of Matthew of phrases like, "Pray that your flight may not be in winter *or on a sabbath'* (Mt 24:20//Mk 13:18), and of the judgment theme, are consistent with the additions to the Markan text made elsewhere in the Gospel of Matthew, and do not therefore indicate an earlier text.[47] It is apparent that the Matthean redaction surrounding the parousia of the coming Son of Man leads to a very different interpretation to that of the Markan text,[48] as do the descriptions of the 'abomination of desolation' "standing in the holy place" (Mt 24:15) and of the pseudochrists "in the inner rooms" (Mt 24:26). It seems that Matthean redaction connects the 'abomination' and the warning to flee with the Zealot occupation of the temple rather than Roman threats to the temple. To place the blame for the destruction of the temple on certain groups within Judaism is again consistent with Matthean emphases evident in the passion narrative (Mt 27:25) and elsewhere (Mt 23).

(iii) The parallel text in the Gospel of Luke may well contain primitive material not available to the author of Mark,[49] but the discourse as a whole clearly reflects Lukan redaction that is consistent with that seen in the rest of the Gospel. Thus, for example, the discourse itself takes place *in the temple,* consistent with the Lukan focus on the Jerusalem temple throughout Luke/Acts and much more in keeping with the Greco-Roman temple discourse genre described by Robbins above. Two further Lukan modifications indicate that our suggested interpretation of Mk 13 may not have been unfamiliar to Luke. The well-known Lukan substitution for the 'abomination of desolation'—"When you see Jerusalem surrounded by armies" (Lk 21:20)—locates the signal to flee as being the arrival of Vespasian's troops near Jerusalem (spring/summer 68

---

[47] *Contra* Bo Reicke, "A Test of Synoptic Relationships: Matthew 10: 17-23 and 24: 9-14 with Parallels", in *New Synoptic Studies,* ed William R. Farmer (Macon 1983), 209-229. See rather: Graham N. Stanton, "'Pray that your flight may not be in winter or on a sabbath' (Matthew 24.20)", *JSNT* 37 (1989), 17-30, where it is argued convincingly that flight on a Sabbath is to be avoided because it would provoke further persecution of the Matthean community, and is thus best seen as Matthean redaction.

[48] Perhaps the returning and judging Son of Man in the Gospel of Matthew arises through the influence of Q? See Adela Yarbro Collins, "The Son of Man Sayings in the Sayings Source", in *To Touch the Text. Biblical and Related Studies in Honor of Joseph A. Fitzmyer, S. J.,* eds Maurya P. Horgan and Paul J. Kobelski (New York 1989), 369-389, for an analysis of the coming Son of Man sayings in Q.

[49] As argued for example by C. H. Dodd, "The Fall of Jerusalem and the 'Abomination of Desolation'", in *More New Testament Studies,* (Manchester 1968) [= *JRS* 37 (1947), 47-54].

CE) or Titus's troops (spring 70 CE), which accords well with the time span we have suggested from the summer of 69 CE to the spring of 70 CE. Then again, the reading "when you see these things taking place, know that *the kingdom of God* is near" (Lk 21:31) supports our equation of Mk 9:1 and 13:30 as two expressions of hope that the kingdom would come in power within a generation of Jesus—and also that it may be described in terms of the vindication of the Son of Man and the gathering of the elect. The writing of Acts may be said to be an extended exposition of the Markan theme that the kingdom *has come with power* within a generation of Jesus—in the form of the new multi-ethnic community. In many respects, Luke is Mark's best interpreter.

It is apparent, therefore, that the Markan eschatological discourse provides the basis and pattern for the other synoptic writers, and that any editorial changes that they make can be understood in terms of their own theological agenda. We would suggest that although in most places the amount of redaction of the Markan account is minimal, there are profound differences underlying the envisioning of the role of the Son of Man in each synoptic account—*but differences such as should be expected given the equally profound differences in christology and ecclesiology.* We use the word 'profound' (= of deep insight, meaningful) advisedly, because the differences are not necessarily contradictory or inexplicable.

The extent to which Mk 13 has been reinterpreted is even more evident in non-canonical writings. For example, in the Mount of Olives scene in the Apocalypse of Peter we read the disciples' question to Jesus:

> Make known to us what are the signs of thy Parousia and of the end of the world, that we may perceive and mark the time of thy Parousia and instruct those who come after us, to whom we preach the word of thy Gospel and whom we install in thy Church, in order that they, when they hear it, may take heed to themselves that they mark the time of thy coming. (Apoc Pet E1)[50] (cf Mk 13:4)

Clearly the 'eschatological question' and the fascination for the 'signs' and the 'time' have long been a problem for the church. But at least this text serves to illustrate the problem of the *Nachleben* of the Gospel and the need to let Mk 13 be interpreted in its own context. Despite this, the tendency throughout much of the church's history has been towards a greater particularisation of the 'eschatological question', and a more parochial understanding of the answers given.

Mk 13 in its Greco-Roman literary context

We have seen that both Robbins and Tolbert have attempted to take serious account of the Greco-Roman literary background to the Gospel of

---

[50] See Richard Bauckham, "The Two Fig Tree Parables in the Apocalypse of Peter", *JBL* 104 (1985), 287. He locates the writing of the document in Palestine, 132-5 CE.

Mark in general, and Mk 13 in particular.[51] For Robbins, this means that as well as the strong links between Mk 13 and Jewish apocalyptic writings and testaments, Mk 13 shows some similarity to the Greco-Roman temple dialogues and the teacher-disciple farewell discourses. In this latter connection Robbins cites the *Memorabilia* of Xenophon of Athens (where Socrates gathers his disciples together before dying), and argues that such a parallel explains the parenetic element in Mk 13. This is because in this "final phase of the teacher/disciple cycle":

> Preparation for independence from the teacher brings exhortation to remember the mandates laid upon them by the system of thought and action transmitted to them during their time with the teacher. Before the teacher goes to his death, he talks with them about the situation they will face when he is no longer with them.[52]

But because of the setting of this discourse, Robbins also argues that it has been influenced by the Greco-Roman temple dialogue tradition, where after a 'stroll with the teacher' in the temple, a disciple asks a question about the temple which provides an opportunity for a speech by the teacher. Contrary to Robbins statement, however, the temple does *not* provide the setting for the dialogue in the Gospel of Mark and the speech itself would be better termed an 'anti-temple dialogue'.[53]

As mentioned above, Tolbert sees the whole Gospel of Mark as stylistically similar to the ancient erotic novels, and draws parallels especially from Xenophon of Ephesus (c 50 CE–253 CE) and Chariton (c 100 BCE–50 CE). She points out that Robbins' use of Xenophon of Athens' *Memorabilia,* with its linguistic and literary superiority, is inappropriate for the Gospel of Mark where the language used is at the popular level. Thus the "simplicity of Greek style, the unpolished rhetorical development, the lack of philosophical or literary pretension, and the typological, conventional narration which characterize the Gospel of Mark"[54] place it on a different plane to the elite Greek literature— perhaps at the level of *"popular culture and popular literature"*.[55]

---

[51] Mention should also be made of C. Clifton Black's recent detailed analysis of Greco-Roman rhetorical patterns in Mk 13: "An Oration at Olivet: Some Rhetorical Dimensions of Mark 13", in *Persuasive Artistry. Studies in New Testament Rhetoric in Honor of George A. Kennedy,* ed Duane F. Watson, (Sheffield 1991), 66-92; see footnote 55 below.

[52] Robbins, *Jesus the Teacher,* 172.

[53] Robbins, *Jesus the Teacher,* 178. Robbins description would fit Luke's account much better (Lk 21). Robbins does not comment on whether Greco-Roman temple dialogues were ever directed *against* the temple.

[54] Tolbert, *Sowing,* 59.

[55] Tolbert, *Sowing,* 60. This same critique that Tolbert makes of Robbins' use of inappropriate classical literature might also be applied to Black's rhetorical analysis of Mk 13 ("An Oration at Olivet") which is undertaken in comparison with classical rhetorical patterns. Black shows he is aware of the distance between the Gospel of Mark and classical literature when he comments that aspects of Mk 13 "would have jarred most

Amongst the specific parallels between the Gospel of Mark and the popular novel, Tolbert points out that Xenophon of Ephesus also uses καί parataxis and day/night plot sequences.

Yet despite these parallels from the Greco-Roman world there are no *specific links* with the Markan text. Indeed, after surveying these genres and more besides—aretalogy, Greek tragedy, 'origin myths', Hellenistic romance, tragi-comedy, martyrologies, and Hellenistic *chria*—Kee came to the following conclusion:

> The result of our survey is to show that Hellenistic models which have been appealed to as having served Mark as a paradigm for his representation of Jesus are either too formless to have functioned as a genre model or are merely modern constructs, lacking either precise definitions or ancient exemplars. The features that Mark does share with Hellenistic rhetorical forms serve only to make the general and obvious point that Mark was influenced by the predominant Hellenistic culture of his time.[56]

Kee goes on to argue that the most important background to the Gospel of Mark lies in the literature of Jewish apocalyptic groups, but arguably he overstates the case as much in that direction as do those who focus on the Hellenistic background.

We conclude, however, that once the Old Testament allusions are taken into account, it is the Jewish background that is of prime importance for interpreting Mk 13 and the Gospel as a whole. Nevertheless, Tolbert's insistence that the Gospel of Mark is written at the 'popular novel' level

classical rhetoricians" and yet he goes on to claim that "Although Mark is no Cicero, one wonders if, in every respect, Quintillian would have disapproved." ("An Oration at Olivet", 90-91). There is much in Black's analysis that is helpful, but again it must be stressed that if a classical literary background is allowed to determine the interpretive context of Mk 13 to the exclusion of socio-historical possibilities, then there is the danger of lapsing into 'literary docetism'. Black himself concedes that "the current reclamation of classical rhetoric requires correction by, and coordination with, other appropriate interpretive perspectives" ("An Oration at Olivet", 92), and this is nowhere more evident than when he suggests that Mk 13:14 is deliberately intended by the author as a teasing puzzle—something "provocative and pleasurable for his audience" ("An Oration at Olivet", 90). Such an interpretation reduces the most urgent appeal in the Gospel to an amusing literary puzzle rather than allowing the possibility that at some level it represents a prophetic summons before calamitous events actually overtake the hearers.

Black claims that the Markan audience would have interpreted the discourse at this literary level "by appropriating the material in the rhetorical manner in which it is patently presented" rather than "by means of discriminating its antecedent tradition(s) from its later redaction(s)" ("An Oration at Olivet", 91). But surely the hearers of Mk 13 (both of the source and of the Markan redaction of it) *would* have been aware of some of the traditions behind 'the abomination which causes desolation' and *would* have been able to discern the new context it was placed in—'standing where *he* ought not'? Is not this a more likely assumption than that the earliest audiences were fully aware of the rhetorical subtleties of the classical writers? To put it more plainly, surely the redactional nature of prophetic and apocalyptic literature is a more appropriate starting point for interpreting Mk 13 than the rhetorical features of epideictic addresses in classical literature.

[56] Kee, *Community*, 30.

and the examples she gives as to what that means, and Robbins' description of the teacher's farewell discourse, are helpful perspectives. They must at least indicate how the Gospel of Mark and Mk 13 would have been *received* within Greco-Roman culture, if not provide the models by which they were constructed.

The literary context of Mk 13

The reviews and analyses above have demonstrated that Mk 13 is an integral part of the Gospel of Mark. Moreover, provided it is interpreted within that context and its apocalyptic language not permitted to dominate the Gospel as a whole, it makes sense as a discourse which brings to a climax the teaching of Jesus on discipleship and mission and which it then applies to the particular context of the Markan community. Although Mk 13 undoubtedly contains elements of apocalyptic language and symbolism and subsequently becomes a paradigm for apocalyptic writings, it is best understood in its context in the Gospel as a scholarly discourse containing elements of a testament or farewell discourse, fashioned together in accordance with the prophetic processes long established within Judaism. In its content and shape it draws mainly on Jewish texts, though its language and style may be said, along with the rest of the Gospel, to be pitched at the level of a Greco-Roman popular novel. Its *literary* antecedents *(Vorleben)* and successors *(Nachleben)* may be summarised as in the diagram over the page.

Omitted from the diagram are any reference to the words of Jesus and to early Christian prophetic oracles, since these were most probably still in oral form when incorporated into the Gospel. Yet we have argued that these oral sources were *the* formative factors in the construction of the discourse, which was modelled according to the normal processes by which prophecy ('words of the Lord') were remembered and reconstructed when subsequently verified by the course of events. The genuine prophecy of Jesus regarding the Temple and its rulers provided the foundation on which the later oracle regarding the imminent destruction of Jerusalem was laid, and the events confirming these prophecies provided the occasion for their transformation into written words of the Lord. To place these written words into a wider literary context of texts and genres is necessary for understanding their later significance and interpretation as literature (their effect on readers), but to grapple with their pre-literary forms and the prophetic processes which shaped them is necessary for understanding their earliest context (and their effect on the producers of the text). Both contexts—literary and historical—are essential for our (re)reading and (re)producing of the text today, so the following diagram should be interpreted together with the literary structures of chapters 5 and 6, and the socio-historical context of chapter 7.

Mk 13 in its wider literary context

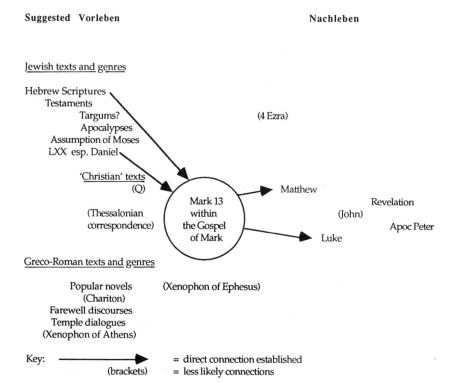

Suggested Vorleben

Nachleben

Jewish texts and genres

Hebrew Scriptures
Testaments
Targums?
Apocalypses
Assumption of Moses
LXX esp. Daniel

(4 Ezra)

'Christian' texts
(Q)

Matthew

(Thessalonian
correspondence)

Mark 13
within
the Gospel
of Mark

Revelation

(John)

Apoc Peter

Luke

Greco-Roman texts and genres

Popular novels
(Chariton)
Farewell discourses
Temple dialogues
(Xenophon of Athens)

(Xenophon of Ephesus)

Key: ⟶   = direct connection established
(brackets)   = less likely connections

It is apparent that the specific literary antecedents (texts and genres) of Mk 13 are the Jewish scriptures in their various first century versions. It may be possible to argue for non-specific influence from Greco-Roman literature and genres and early Christian writings (Q and Thessalonians), but they should not be made the controlling factor in any interpretation of the discourse. It is also patently clear from the diagram above that the text must not be interpreted backwards through its *Nachleben*. The influence of the Markan eschatological discourse in the world of early Christian literature is considerable, but the recurring tendency to take the disciples' part and ask for signs and times has meant that many interpretations must be set aside if the text is to be allowed to speak for itself.

IX

A MARKAN DISCOURSE ON DISCIPLESHIP AND MISSION

The sum of the analyses

There is no need to review here in detail all the findings of the previous chapters but it is helpful to recall briefly the methods used and the major conclusions reached. A form critical approach was used to break the discourse into its smallest components, which were then analysed for evidence of Latin, Semitic and *Koine* Greek linguistic influences. This approach uncovered textual patterns which confirmed the presence of disparate traditions behind the discourse, and began to build up a profile of some of the larger units in the text. Most important of these were the Aramaic influence present in vv.8,12-13a,22; Semitic (most probably Septuagintal) influence in vv.24-27; Semitic influence together with the use of δέ in vv.14-21; and the lack of any clear patterns evident in vv.1-6 and 28-37, although there was a marked absence of Semitic influence in the latter section.

The text was analysed, unsuccessfully, for any specific links with earlier New Testament traditions. The uniqueness of its vocabulary and its syntax was then explored to determine just how different the chapter is from the rest of the Gospel of Mark. It was shown that vv.14-21 are syntactically the most unique section of the whole Gospel, whereas by way of total contrast, vv.24-27 contain no unique syntax at all. This result has had a profound effect on the shaping of our interpretation, for it clearly showed that the vindication of the Son of Man and the oracle concerning the abomination and tribulation did not originally belong together.

The analysis of the Old Testament traditions behind the text confirmed the Septuagintal origins of vv.24-27, and the Aramaic roots of vv.7,8,11a,b,d,12,13a,22. However it was when the findings of each of the different methods was combined that a clearer picture of the pre-Markan traditions emerged. We have summarised them as:

(i)   The Jesuanic traditions: vv.2,30,32 (in another form),34;

(ii)   Palestinian (possibly Targumic?) traditions: vv.7,8,11a,b,d,12,13a, 22;

(iii) A pre-Markan Christian prophetic oracle: vv.14-21;

(iv)   A Markan pastiche of Septuagintal allusions: vv.24-27.

The redaction analysis based on vocabulary and syntax in chapter 4 pointed to the most likely Markan redaction as occurring in vv.1a,3,(5a),6a,7c, 9b,10,(11c),24a,(33), and possibly short phrases in vv.22 and 27. It was also indicated that vv.4,13b,30-31,35-36 and 37 may have been inserted into the discourse at some stage because of the occurrence of unique syntax across major punctuation breaks at these points. It was noted that the dominance of recurrent syntax (syntax common to the rest of the Gospel) in vv.24-27, and the absence of Markan vocabulary, indicates that these verses are a Markan pastiche of Septuagintal allusions, whereas there was almost a total absence of recurrent syntax in vv.14-21, again suggesting an atypical pre-Markan source.

From these more or less objectively demonstrated parameters, we proceeded to questions of evaluation and interpretation. The analysis of Markan literary and theological preferences in chapter 5 indicated editorial activity was also present in vv.3-6 (and especially v.4), and in vv.10,23,33 and 37. It was suggested that the double question in v.4 was another case of that Markan literary device of using the disciples as a foil in order to emphasise the subsequent teaching of Jesus. It was also noted that any discussion of the composition of the discourse would have to take into account the eschatological and historical ambiguity of the time references and the deliberate placement of vv.10 and 30-31 into seemingly 'awkward' contexts.

The comparison with other apocalyptic writings in chapter 6 uncovered a fourfold 'warning-description-reassurance' sequence in the text and suggested sub-divisions at vv.1-2,3-5a,5b-8,9-13,14-20,21-23; vv.24-30; vv.31-37. The socio-political analysis of chapter 7 led to the working hypothesis that the oracle in vv.14-21 was delivered to the Judean church within the twelve months prior to the final siege of Jerusalem, and that the Gospel of Mark itself was written after the fall of Jerusalem. As a consequence, it was suggested that Mk 13 (as part of the Gospel of Mark) was not written so much in anticipation of an imminent apocalyptic crisis, as out of an awareness of the continuing eschatological process. That is, it was not written just before the fall of Jerusalem—in order to dissociate that event from an otherwise imminent parousia—but after that tumultuous event, in order to reassure the authorial audience that God's kingdom was still being formed and that the new community (= *his* elect, the summer harvest, the 'kingdom coming with power', cf Mk 9:1) was still being gathered Thus the Markan *Sitz im Leben* was seen to be represented by vv.24-29.

The literary analyses of chapter 8 set the discourse in its Markan context—as a scholarly discourse and farewell speech—and briefly in its wider first-century literary context. It was found that the specific literary and pre-literary links of the chapter were with the Jewish Scriptures (Hebrew, Aramaic and Greek) and with early Christian prophecy, and that other less specific influences might be traced to Greco-Roman literature. More significantly, the place of the discourse within the plotted narrative of the Gospel was illustrated, such that the means by which the Markan community—the authorial audience—identified with and felt included in the projections of the narrative was revealed. It was argued that the hearers of the Gospel would see themselves as included within the prophetic words of Jesus, and as the successors to the discipleship teaching and missionary mandate (13:9-13) given through the four disciples to everyone (v.37).

A reinterpretation of Mk 13

There can be no doubt that the final author of Mk 13 regarded it in total as a 'word of the Lord'—just as there can be no doubt that the same author must have been aware that parts of it came via Christian prophets and Christian teachers who reinterpreted the Jewish Scriptures through their experience of the Christ event. To put such an amalgam of sources into a discourse purporting to be a speech of the historical Jesus is no more unlikely or dishonest than has been the practice of evangelists and teachers ever since. Consider the modern-day preacher who states: "Jesus says, 'Come to me all you people suffering stresses and heartaches, and I will give you rest.'" It is of the nature of exhortation and evangelism that words of current relevance are projected back onto the one who is the source of the Good News. This is legitimate as long as there are criteria by which the new words may be tested against The Word. In the example of the preacher just given, the hearers could evaluate the preaching in the light of other known words of Jesus and also in the light of its relevance to their situation. They might judge that the new words bear a close enough resemblance to the English translation of Mt 11:28, which, because of its striking divergence from the piety of the day, stands a good chance of having originated with the historical Jesus. They might also then ponder the relevance of the words for their own life situation. In a similar way, the hearers of the many diverging prophecies around the time of the fall of Jerusalem would evaluate them in the light of the known sayings of Jesus about the temple, and for relevance and truth in the light of their own current situation. Those sayings incorporated into Mk 13 were judged to be consistent both with the known anti-temple stance of the historical Jesus and with the events that had subsequently occurred.

Thus vv.14-21 cannot have been an apocalyptic tract used by the evangelist's opponents and against which he writes (otherwise, how could it have been attributed to Jesus?), but rather they comprise a true word of prophetic warning—similar to that of Agabus in Acts 11:28—proven by recent events and affirmed by the author of Mark as a true 'word of the Lord'. The oracle contains no imminent expectation of a messianic appearance (or second appearance) because vv.24-27 (however they are interpreted) are a later addition from another (probably Markan) context. Indeed, the intent of the oracle would have been in opposition to those in Jerusalem who expected a theophany or messianic appearance before the fall of the temple and who even danced on the burning temple portico in expectation of it. *They* expected the messiah, the oracle warned them of false messiahs. *They* waited in Jerusalem for the event, the oracle exhorted them to flee. Why would a prophetic word exhort people to flee if it also included an expectation that the messiah/son of man/God were about to intervene? In other words, how could it be possible for the oracle to contain vv.24-27 also? But in any case, the objective analysis of syntax undertaken above has shown that vv.14-21 and 24-27 cannot be from the same source. So it is those ones who fled—perhaps even as far as the Markan community and taking the oracle with them—who were the ones who heard and obeyed the true word of the Lord. This the author of Mark affirms by the inclusion of their story in the προείρηκα . . . πάντα of v.23, and by the inclusion of the Judean elect in the gathering of the elect from all the nations (v.27). If the prophetic oracle had proven itself a true word of the Lord, then those who heeded its warning deserved to be accepted as true members of the elect, just as the oracle itself deserved to be included in the story of the community of faith. This is no more than the continuation of the ancient prophetic process—where verified prophecy is recorded retrospectively and incorporated into the salvation history of the faith community.

Again we point out that it is inappropriate, therefore, to speak of Mk 13 as inauthentic—its authenticity has been assured from its antecedents to its final authoring and on into its acceptance by the other Synoptics and ultimately its inclusion in the canon. However, we should be careful to distinguish this notion of authenticity from the non-historicity of the discourse and its setting. It is a composite creation of the author of Mark (a Prophecy on the Mount analogous to Matthew's Sermon on the Mount), deliberately placed in its context between two acts of devotion—one to the old temple (12:41-44), one to the new (14:3-9)—and most significantly of all, subordinated to the climactic passion account.

This subordination is evident not just in the placement of the discourse prior to the climax of the Markan narrative, but also in the way it prepares the reader/hearer to interpret the faithfulness of Jesus and the failure of the disciples in Mk 14-16. Jesus remains vigilant throughout the four watches of the Passion night, but the disciples are found sleeping at their post. In terms of plotted time, the passion narrative is foreshadowed by a description of the passion of the church (13:9-13)—also made specific by the four watches of 13:35 and the repeated call to 'be alert' (γρηγορεῖτε), as used again by Jesus in the Gesthemane scene. But from the perspective of the earliest authorial audience it is the Passion of Jesus which precedes the suffering of the church. These overlapping links indicate that the Markan concern evident throughout the Gospel to spell out the conditions of true discipleship and mission is in no way diminished in Mk 13. On the contrary, as the analysis above of the context of the Old Testament allusions underlying the discourse has shown, the Markan discipleship theme of mission to the Gentiles is a key to the organisation of the chapter. The sayings in vv.9-13 are best understood as reflecting the cost of the Gentile mission—the sowing of the Gospel seed—whilst those of vv.24-29 indicate the promised gathering of the eschatological community—the summer harvest of international dimensions.

This is not the negative view of history of some apocalyptic cult— where the only hope in an evil world is to await the returning Lord and the promise of eternal life. Such interpretations can only be made if all the exhortations to 'watch out' and 'be alert' are understood to mean that the disciple should be passively looking and waiting for the Son of Man on the clouds. Rather, the call to 'watch out' that occurs up until v.33 is an exhortation to discern carefully so as not to be led astray by competing claims to truth (vv.5b,23). From v.33 onwards the image of the returning Lord *is* used, but here the call is to 'be on the alert', to be found—like the doorkeeper—'on the job' and at one's post. It is thus a positive call to faithful discipleship and mission that dominates the discourse from beginning to end, not despair over the evils of the world and a longing to escape from them. Seen in this light, v.30 becomes an encouragement to further action—*this* generation will see all these things happen, culminating in the gathering of the new community.

It is tempting to speculate on the eschatology and christology of the Judean church prior to the fall of Jerusalem, and on how the author of Mark might have been retrospectively correcting a totally discredited perspective within that branch of the church.[1] But interpretations which suggest a total break between the Markan and Jerusalem communities have failed to take account of the open invitation to the Judean elect in Mk 13 to join the 'non-Jerusalem' community—the diverse international elect of v.27—and of the hope of reconciliation for Peter expressed in Mk 16:7. Radical openness to *all* people and radical grace are hallmarks of the Markan community, so it is not possible to compromise these features by positing an absolute break with the Jerusalem church. It is better to see the Markan portrayal of the disciples as a lesson to all in the church on the dangers inherent in religious leadership.

It is true that temple based Judaism is judged unequivocally in the Gospel, but it is not an anti-Jewish tract. The elect who flee to the hills— who endure to the end—*will* be saved. There is no absolute break with Jerusalem such that the elect from Judea are disinherited by the Markan community. Rather, the 'elect' has been re-defined to include those from Judea and those from the ends of the earth. It was not the time or place for fruit in Judea—but the summer has now come and the harvest has already begun elsewhere. This should not be understood as incipient Christian universalism and imperialism destroying the ethnic particularity of the Jewish followers of Jesus—although sadly, that is what eventually happened in the later history of the church. Rather, it should be seen for what it was, a courageous open community of diverse origins daring to

---

[1] In particular, it is tempting to suggest that the Markan vindicated Son of Man sayings (8:38; 13:26; 14:62) were developed in response to the failed messianic expectations of the Jerusalem/Judean church. But the relationship of these sayings to the more judgmental Son of Man in Q remains a difficult question.

defy both the hyper-nationalism and ethnocentricity of Jerusalem and the universalism and imperialism of Rome. In that respect it should be noted that the Markan community was not unique—there were other Jewish and Greek groups with similar agendas.

The key to our analysis has been the initial specification of the intertextual relationships behind the text, to the extent to which they could be determined.[2] To see clearly that vv.14-21 are a pre-Markan source and to be able to locate it in a meaningful *Sitz im Leben* enables the discourse to be seen in a perspective consistent with the rest of the Gospel narrative. It is not possible to recognise the dominant theme of discipleship and mission in the Gospel and suggest that it was written in the heat of the Jewish wars without creating severe tensions in the interpretation of the text. Attempts to locate the Gospel in Rome or to suggest that Mk 13 was added after the rest of the Gospel was completed are intended to circumvent those tensions, but they must be judged unsuccessful. The specific Judean context of Mk 13:14-22 remains, and cannot be allegorised or passed off as a commentary from a distance on events in Judea without sacrificing the meaning and immediacy of the discourse. Nor is it possible to analyse the chapter meaningfully at a literary level only and without reference to the historical situation which is so apparent in the text and which this interpretation has emphasised.

What then happens to the 'parousia' hope within the Gospel of Mark? That question shall remain for the final reflection below because it is a question of systematic theology and is not strictly part of an exegesis of the Gospel of Mark.[3] But it should be noted here that our interpretation does not reduce Christian hope to mere historical events. On the contrary! By arguing that The (ultimate) End in Mk 13 is described only by vv.31f, the non-chronological and non-historical dimensions of the eschaton are heightened. But at the same time, our interpretation has 'made space' in Mk 13 (in vv.24-29) for a meaningful *Sitz im Leben* for the Markan community, where the discipleship and missionary concerns of the Gospel as a whole can find a valid expression and not be overwhelmed by imminent apocalyptic expectation on the one hand, or despair at the evil of the world on the other.

An interpretive outline of Mk 13

It is possible now to provide a new interpretive outline of Mk 13 which takes into account the situation of the Markan community in relation to

---

[2] We note again the need for a full analysis of the Old Testament allusions behind Mk 13 using all the known Hebrew and Greek texts. This investigation was restricted to the texts available at the time, and can only be regarded as continuing a little further the task already begun by others.

[3] It may be argued that this is a valid question for canonical criticism to handle, and so it is. But it is a question to be asked when exegesis of the text(s) is finished, and not a distraction to be introduced into the exegetical process at the beginning.

the discourse, and which allows for the different perspective of the Judean elect. Mk 13:1-2 provides the closing scene of the (anti-)temple stories and the setting over and against which the scene commencing in v.3 is written.

vv.3-4: The temple and The End—the eschatological question: 'When and what sign?'

vv.5b-13: *The future which is past (and still present for the Markan community!)—The faithful planting of the seed.*
Despite false alarms (13:5b-8) the seed of the kingdom has been planted in all nations (13:10) and at great cost to those sowing it (13:9-13). Yet the Spirit has been with them in their trials (13:11) and the salvation of the faithful ones is assured (13:13).

vv.14-23: *The future which is recent (and still present for the Judean refugees)—The awful tribulation.*
The elect in Judea are exhorted to flee both restoration Judaism centred in Jerusalem and its Roman destroyers (13:14-20) and to ignore messianic pretenders (13:21-22 cf 13:5b-6). They are encouraged to be watchful and reassured that all these events have been within the scope of Jesus' prophecy (13:23).

vv.24-30: *The future which is present (and still coming)—The harvest is imminent!*
The opposing powers shall witness the vindication of the Son of Man (13:24-26), and his elect from all directions including Judea will be gathered together into a new community by the messengers (13:27). These events are the sign that the summer harvest is breaking in—and the kingdom coming with power (9:1)—even as the evangelist writes (13:28-30).

vv.31-37: *The future which is to come (and may occur at any time)*
There *is* an ultimate End when heaven and earth will pass away (13:31) but it remains the prerogative of the Father alone (13:32). Yet it may be encountered existentially at any time (13:33-37; cf 13:11; 14:41) and therefore alertness ('readiness on-the-job') is essential (13:33,35-37).

The discourse is thus interpreted here as a Markan compilation from diverse sources, the most significant of which have been confirmed as true prophecy by recent events. Although it functions as a farewell discourse in the Gospel of Mark, it has been deliberately placed before the Passion narrative to conclude the temple sequence, and to ensure that nothing detracts from the overriding theme of the Gospel—faithful discipleship and mission through suffering. The projection of this theme into the future beyond the plotted story of the Gospel ensures that the authorial audience understand themselves as invited to be the successors of that tradition. This privilege they have not as an automatic right or because of special links with Jerusalem, but because of the faithful mission of 'the little ones' who spread the Good News abroad despite the failure of some of those closer to Jesus to understand the full nature of his mission. Therefore the discourse acts as both an affirmation of the pre-fall Gentile mission which led to the founding of the Markan community, and as a call to continue in mission as the new community—the elect of the vindicated Son of Man gathered from all nations—even including the refugees from Judea.

CONCLUSION

BACK TO THE FUTURE—HOPEFULLY

What are the implications of the interpretation of Mk 13 we have suggested for explaining the nature of Christian hope today? Jürgen Moltmann makes the perceptive comment that: "Renunciation of hope for the messiah was the price the Jews paid for emancipation in modern society; and similarly, very early on, renunciation of hope for the parousia was the price paid for Christianity's integration into the Roman empire."[1] Moltmann goes on to analyse how this renunciation has been made acceptable to the faithful over the years in many subtle and even well-meaning ways. The realists have spoken of the 'delay of the parousia' as if it were an event in time and in the name of 'consistent eschatology', but "if Christ's parousia takes place in time, then it is transient, like every other temporal future; it cannot be thought of together with 'the end of time'"(316-317). The mystics went to the other extreme and argued that God's grace can be experienced in every moment and so therefore every moment is the 'End Time'. But "if Christ's parousia is equated with God's eternity, then there is no moment at which it can enter time", which puts an end "to all the real and futurist expectation of the parousia which echoes in the early Christian 'maranatha—come soon!'" (318). Neither is it possible to argue for multiple parousias: "Christ came in the flesh— Christ comes in the Spirit—Christ will come in glory" for this is "simply adapting Christ's eternity into the three modes of time: past-present-future" (318). Moltmann argues that the best approach lies in recognising that the eschatological *process* was commenced with the cross, and that the eschatological *event* involves the end of time: "the parousia of Christ and the end of this world-time belong together" (321).

Our overview of the literature on Mk 13 has revealed similar types of responses as these to the problem of the prophecies in the chapter. We make use of the functions of a video-cassette player to typify (at the risk of trivialising) each approach, and include the name of an eloquent representative of each position:

(i)   The author of Mark has passed on the prophecies of Jesus, most of which applied to that time, but some of which (the parousia) have yet to be fulfilled ('prophetic foreshortening'). [Beasley-Murray] *Result:* history is in 'freeze-frame' (or slow motion) until the eschatological event occurs.

---

[1] Jürgen Moltmann, *The Way of Jesus Christ. Christology in Messianic Dimensions* (London 1990), 313. For convenience, this book shall be referred to by page numbers in brackets in the main body of the text.

(ii) The author of Mark completely re-interpreted early fulfilled prophecies about the fall of Jerusalem to apply to a later anti-christ figure who would precede the End. [Hahn]
    Result: history is 'replayed' and there are many eschatological events (indeed, each 'generation' interprets its own).

(iii) The author of Mark wrote before the fall of Jerusalem and expected the End to follow soon after that event. [Myers]
    Result: history is on 'fast forward', rushing to an End which still hasn't occurred.

(iv) The author of Mark subjected all prophecies and apocalyptic expectations of his day to the refusal of the historical Jesus to give either a sign or a time, or to entertain an ethnocentric hope of fulfilment.
    Result: all history is part of the ongoing eschatological process, and open at any time to the eschatological event.

We have argued that it is the fourth of these interpretations that does justice to the Markan text and its view of history. By insisting that The End is the prerogative of God the Father alone (13:32) and that it is useless to speculate on the signs or times of such an event, the author of Mark refocusses the energies of the church on the ongoing processes of mission and discipleship that have dominated the rest of the Gospel narrative. If the sayings of Mk 9:1 and 13:24-30 can be understood as the kingdom coming in 'power' in the form of the new post-Jerusalem community, as we have argued, then indeed all of human history has a potentially meaningful purpose as part of the eschatological process of gathering the elect from the four corners.

What then of the 'parousia'? If it is understood as the ultimate epiphany, it is clear that it belongs together with the end of time (Mk 13:31f)—which is the context in which the evangelist first speaks of the returning Lord, and where Moltmann has argued it belongs. As such it should not be confused with vv.24-27 as a temporal event expected within a generation, nor as something which is re-scheduled for each generation, nor linked with signs and times. It should be understood as the fulfilling of the creator's prerogative to conclude (or re-create) the creation (Mk 13:31), to end time, and to vindicate finally the faithful Human One who has represented us all in our suffering. This event can interrupt human history at any moment—both at the existential level[2]—and at the global

---

[2] Here we disagree with Gary Dean Smith, "Mark 13:9-13: Mission in Apocalyptic, with Special Reference to Jesus' Gentile Mission in Mark", unpublished PhD thesis, Southern Baptist Theological Seminary, 1981, 251, that τέλος in the Gospel of Mark "never clearly refers to the end of a personal life". The context of 13:13b is surely that of 'persons' suffering for their faith. We would agree that *individualism* is not intended by the text, but the overlapping of references between The End of everything and of Jesus on the cross, and 'the ends' of those who faithfully follow surely justifies our interpretation. See also Beasley-Murray's summation ("The Vision on the Mount", 50) of the 'double polarity' of H. D. Wendland's concept of the consummation: "it has to do with final salvation and final judgment on the one hand, and it is *personal and cosmic-*

and cosmic level. The life of discerning discipleship is to be lived in prophetic awareness of that ultimate End, and not in the stupor of thinking that our present personal and national existence will continue forever. Perhaps the most significant function of the prophetic process we have described is that once the prophet speaks truly and fearlessly of those Ends which confront our worlds, it provides the foundation for a reconstruction of a new world out of the ashes of the old. The words of the prophets are the seeds of renewal and reconstruction—which is precisely how the prophetic oracle of Mk 13:14-21 has functioned for the Markan community, we have argued.

We have interpreted the task of the author of Mark as one of renewing and re-defining Christian origins and expectations in response to the collapse of the Mother Church of Jerusalem and the crushing of any messianic hopes centred on Jerusalem. This was achieved by affirming that the oracle urging the Judeans to flee both the Jewish restorationist cause and the Roman imperium was indeed a true 'word of the Lord', and worthy to provide the postscript to the genuine prophecy of Jesus against the Jerusalem temple. Indeed, the whole ministry of Jesus in the Gospel of Mark is cast in the light of this opposition to the Jerusalem Temple State, in contrast to the overwhelmingly positive treatment of 'the crowd'—the people of the land. Thus whilst the Jewish and particularly Galilean origins of the Jesus movement are affirmed by the evangelist, any ethnocentric hopes and vestiges of an exclusive nationalistic and militaristic Davidic messianism have been explicitly rejected in the Gospel narrative (Mk 12:35-37). In its place the refugees from the south and true followers from every direction are invited by the messengers of the Son of Man to be part of the new multi-ethnic gathering of the elect (13:27).

The powers that be, both the Jewish and Roman opponents of Jesus and his followers, witness this vindication of the Son of Man—his exaltation to heavenly power and the corresponding gathering of his followers. This gathering is the event which is already beginning as the evangelist writes, such that it can be said that when these things are observed, then the summer—the time of fruiting and harvesting—is near (13:29), and that all these things will happen within the generation of Jesus (13:30). But of the ultimate End (13:31-32), and of the lesser ends—'the hour' faced by each true follower (13:11; 14:41)—the only word is to keep alert for 'the time' is unknown by all but the Father (13:32).

Thus have we attempted to sketch a 'consistent Markan eschatology'. 'Consistent' not only because it does not militate against the significant emphasis on mission and discipleship throughout the Gospel, but because it accords with the Jesuanic parameters of Markan eschatology. These include the refusal to speak of 'signs' of any kind and in particular the rejection of the already condemned temple as a sign of The End. More

universal on the other" (*italics* added). Beasley-Murray contends that the author of Mark maintains a balance between these polarities.

positively, Markan eschatology is shaped by the dual expectations of Jesus that the Kingdom would come with power within a generation (Mk 9:1), but that the ultimate 'Day of the Lord' would be like a master returning at an unknown time (13:34). Between these 'two poles of eschatological thought'—the meaningfulness of a history already invaded by God's rule (the eschatological process), and the prerogative of God over all 'ends', personal, community, national and cosmic (the eschatological crisis)—lies scope for all the developments of Christian hope expressed in the New Testament writings, and more besides. Unfortunately it has been the tendency of so much Christian eschatology to lean too heavily towards one pole or the other. For if we focus in an unbalanced way on the 'historical process' to the exclusion of the 'eschatological event', we will be caught sleeping in the hour of discipleship testing when our Lord returns. Conversely, to the extent that we focus on the event and not the process, we will be found with those who seek signs and times, and ultimately perish with them in the flames of our own nationalistic and ethnocentric temples.

SELECT BIBLIOGRAPHY

1. Primary Sources and Reference Works

Aland, K. *Vollständige Konkordanz zum Griechischen Neuen Testament,* 3 vols, Berlin: Walter de Gruyter, 1983.

Aland, Barbara and Kurt; Karavidopoulos, Johannes; Martini, Carlo M.; Metzger, Bruce M. (eds) *Novum Testamentum Graece,* Stuttgart: Deutsche Bibelgesellschaft, 27th edition, 1993.

Aland, Kurt; Black, Matthew; Martini, Carlo M.; Metzger, Bruce M.; Wikgren, Allen (eds) *The Greek New Testament,* Stuttgart: United Bible Societies, 4th ed, 1993.

Bauer, Walter *A Greek-English Lexicon of the New Testament and Other Early Christian Literature,* ET and eds William F. Arndt, F. Wilbur Gingrich, Frederick W. Danker, Chicago: University of Chicago Press, 1979.

Blass, F. and Debrunner, A. *A Greek Grammar of the New Testament and Other Early Christian Literature,* ET and ed Robert W. Funk, Chicago: The University of Chicago Press, 1961/1967.

Eusebius, *The Ecclesiastical History,* ET Kirsopp Lake, vols 1 & 11 (Loeb Classical Library), London/Cambridge, Massachusetts: William Heinemann/ Harvard University Press, 1959.

Legg, S. C. E. *Nouum Testamentum Graece,* Oxford: Clarendon Press, 1935.

Metzger, Bruce M. *A Textual Commentary on the Greek New Testament,* London: United Bible Societies, 1975.

Moulton, James Hope and Howard, Wilbert Francis *A Grammar of New Testament Greek, vol II, Accidence and Word Formation,* Edinburgh: T. & T. Clark, 1920/1956.

Moulton, James Hope *A Grammar of New Testament Greek,* vol III, *Syntax,* Edinburgh: T. & T. Clark, 1963.

Rahlfs, Alfred (ed) *Septuaginta id est Vetus Testamentum Graece iuxta LXX Interpretes,* Stuttgart: Privilegierte Württembergische Bibelanstalt, 1935; used here in the form of *The Super-Greek Old Testament,* P. B. Payne (ed), S. Hamilton: Linguists' Software, 1986; (The UBS Greek Old Testament data base was derived, in part, from the machine-readable text created by the Thesaurus Linguae Graecae Project, University of California, Irvine).

Thackeray, H. St. J. *et al* (ed and ET) *Josephus with an English Translation by H. St. J. Thackeray,* vols 2-3 (Loeb Classical Library), London/Cambridge, Massachusetts: William Heinemann/ Harvard University Press, 1926-1967.

Wansbrough, Henry (ed) *The New Jerusalem Bible,* London: Darton, Longman & Todd, 2nd ed, 1985.

2. Commentaries

Anderson, Hugh *The Gospel of Mark* (New Century Bible), London: Marshall, Morgan & Scott, 1976; Grand Rapids: Eerdmans, 1981.

Allen, W. C. *The Gospel According to St Mark, with Introduction and Notes* (CCBC),London, 1915.

Beasley-Murray, G. R. *A Commentary on Mark Thirteen,* London: Macmillan, 1957.

Bowman, John *The Gospel of Mark. The New Christian Jewish Passover Haggadah,* Leiden: E. J. Brill, 1965.

Cranfield, C. E. B. *The Gospel According to Saint Mark* (Cambridge Greek Testament Commentary), Cambridge: University Press, 1959.

Davies, W. D. and Allison, Dale C. *The Gospel according to St. Matthew,* vol 1, Edinburgh: T. & T. Clark, 1988.

Derrett, F. Duncan M. *The Making of Mark,* 2 vols, Shipston-on-Stour: P. Drinkwater, 1985.

Gnilka, Joachim   *Das Evangelium nach Markus* (EKKNT 2), 2 vols, Zürich/Einsiedeln/Köln: Benziger Verlag/Neukirchener Verlag, 1978/9.

Grundmann, W. *Das Evangelium nach Markus* (ThHdKomm II), Berlin: Evangelische Verlagsanstalt, 2nd ed, 1959.

Guelich, Robert A. *Mark 1-8:26* (Word Biblical Commentary, 34A), vol 1, Dallas: Word Books, 1989.

Haenchen, E. *Der Weg Jesu,* Berlin: Alfred Töpelmann, 1966.

Hooker, Morna D. *A Commentary on the Gospel According to St Mark* (BNTC), London: A. & C. Black, 1991.

Lane, W. L. *The Gospel of Mark* (The New London Commentary on the New Testament), London: Marshall, Morgan and Scott, 1974.

Lührmann, Dieter *Das Markusevangelium* (HNT 3), Tübingen: Mohr-Siebeck, 1987.

Mann, C. S. *Mark* (The Anchor Bible), Garden City NY: Doubleday & Company, 1986.

Nineham, D. E. *The Gospel of St. Mark* (Pelican Gospel Commentaries), London/New York: A. & C. Black, 2nd ed, 1968.

Patte, Daniel *The Gospel According to Matthew: A Structural Commentary on Matthew's Faith,* Philadelphia: Fortress Press, 1987.

Pesch, Rudolf *Das Markus-evangelium,* 2 vols, Freiburg: Herder, 1977.

Schmid, J. *Das Evangelium nach Markus* (Regensburger Neues Testament, 2), Regensburg: Friedrich Pustet, 1963.

Schmithals, Walter *Das Evangelium nach Markus,* 2 vols, Gütersloh: Mohr, 1979.

Schweizer, E. *The Good News According to Mark,* ET D. H. Madvig, Richmond: John Knox Press, 1970; London: SPCK, 1971.

Taylor, V. *The Gospel According to St. Mark,* London: Macmillan, 2nd ed, 1966.

3. Books and Monographs

Achtemeier, Paul J. *The Inspiration of Scripture: Problems and Proposals,* Philadelphia: Fortress Press, 1980.

Adam, A. K. M. *What is Postmodern Biblical Criticism?* Minneapolis: Fortress Press, 1995.

Allison, Dale C. *The End of the Ages Has Come. An Early Interpretation of the Passion and Resurrection of Jesus,* Philadelphia: Fortress Press, 1985.

Anderson, Janice Capel and Moore, Stephen D. (eds) *Mark and Method: New Approaches in Biblical Studies,* Minneapolis: Augsburg Fortress, 1992.

Aune, D. E. *The Cultic Setting of Realized Eschatology in Early Christianity* (Supplement to *Novum Testamentum* XXVIII), Leiden: E. J. Brill, 1972.

——, *Prophecy in Early Christianity and the Ancient Mediterreanean World,* Grand Rapids: Eerdmans, 1983.

Beale, G. K. *The Use of Daniel in Jewish Apocalyptic Literature and in the Revelation of St. John,* Lanham: University Press of America, 1984.

Beasley-Murray, G. R. *Jesus and the Future. An Examination of the Criticism of The Eschatalogical Discourse, Mark 13, with Special Reference to the Little Apocalypse Theory,* London: Macmillan, 1954.

——, *Jesus and the Kingdom of God,* Grand Rapids: Eerdmans; Exeter: Paternoster, 1986.

——, *Jesus and the Last Days. The Interpretation of the Olivet Discourse,* Peabody: Hendrickson Publishers, 1993.

Belo, Fernando *A Materialist Reading of the Gospel of Mark,* ET Matthew J. O'Connell, Maryknoll: Orbis, 1981.

Ben-Dov, Meir *In the Shadow of the Temple: The Discovery of Ancient Jerusalem,* New York: Harper & Row, 1985.

Bilde, Per *Flavius Josephus between Jerusalem and Rome: His Life, his Works, and their Importance,* (JSP SS 2), Sheffield: JSOT Press, 1988.

Black, C. Clifton *The Disciples According to Mark. Markan Redaction in Current Debate* (JSNTS SS 27), Sheffield: JSOT Press, 1989.

Black, Matthew *The Book of Enoch or I Enoch,* Leiden: E. J. Brill, 1985.

Borg, Marcus J. *Jesus in Contemporary Scholarship,* Valley Forge: Trinity Press International, 1994.

Boring, M. Eugene *Sayings of the Risen Jesus. Christian Prophecy in the Synoptic Tradition* (SNTS MS 46), Cambridge: Cambridge University Press, 1982; updated as *The Continuing Voice of Jesus: Christian Prophecy and the Gospel Tradition,* Westminster: John Knox Press, 1991

Brandenburger, Egon *Markus 13 und die Apokalyptik,* Göttingen: Vandenhoeck & Ruprecht, 1984.

Brandon, S. G. F. *The Fall of Jerusalem and the Christian Church,* London: SPCK, 1951.

Bultmann, R. *The History of the Synoptic Tradition,* ET J. Marsh from the 2nd German edition, 1931; 2nd English edition with corrections and additions to the 1962 Supplement, Oxford: Basil Blackwell, 1963.

Carroll, Robert P. *When Prophecy Failed. Reactions and responses to failure in Old Testament prophetic traditions,* London: SCM Press, 1979.

Carson, R. A. G. *Coins: Ancient, Medieval and Modern, vol 1. Coins of Greece and Rome,* London: Hutchinson, 1971.

——, *Principal Coins of the Romans, vol 2,* London: British Museum Publications, 1980.

Charlesworth, James Hamilton *The Old Testament Pseudepigrapha and the New Testament. Prolegomena for the Study of Christian Origins,* Cambridge: Cambridge University Press, 1985.

Colani, T. *Jésus Christ et les croyances messianiques de son Temps,* Strasbourg, 1864.

Collins, John J. *Daniel: with an Introduction to Apocalyptic Literature* (The Forms of the Old Testament Literature, vol. XX), Grand Rapids: Eerdmans, 1984.

Collins, Adela Yarbro *The Beginning of the Gospel. Probings of Mark in Context,* Minneapolis: Fortress Press, 1992.

Déaut, R. le *The Message of the New Testament and the Aramaic Bible (Targum),* ET Stephen F. Miletic, a revised edition of *Liturgie juive et Nouveau Testament,* 1965; Rome: Biblical Institute Press, 1982.

Donahue, John R. *The Gospel in Parable. Metaphor, Narrative, and Theology in the Synoptic Gospels,* Philadelphia: Fortress Press, 1988.

Dunn, James D. G. *Unity and Diversity in the New Testament. An Inquiry into the Character of Earliest Christianity,* London: SCM Press, 1977.

Dupont, Jacques *Les trois apocalypses synoptiques. Marc 13; Matthieu 24-25; Luc 21* (Lectio Divina 121), Paris: Cerf, 1985.

Elliott, J. K. *The Language and Style of the Gospel of Mark. An Edition of C. H. Turner's "Notes on Marcan Usage" Together with Other Comparable Studies,* Leiden: E. J. Brill, 1993.

Evans, Craig A. and W. Richard Stegner *The Gospels and the Scriptures of Israel* (JSNTSS 104/SSEJC 3), Sheffiled: Sheffield Academic Press, 1994.

Farmer, W. R. *The Synoptic Problem,* London: Collier/Macmillan, 1964.

Ford, Desmond *The Abomination of Desolation in Biblical Eschatology,* Washington: University Press of America, 1979.

France, R. T. *Jesus and the Old Testament. His Application of Old Testament Passages to Himself and His Mission,* London: The Tyndale Press, 1971.

——, *Divine Government. God's Kingship in the Gospel of Mark,* London: SPCK, 1990.

Friberg, Barbara and Timothy *Analytical Greek New Testament* (Baker's Greek New Testament Library 1), Grand Rapids: Baker Book House, 1981.

Frye, Northrop *The Great Code. The Bible and Literature,* San Diego: Harcourt Brace Jovanovich, 1983.

Fujita, Neil S. *A Crack in the Jar,* New York/Mahwah: Paulist Press, 1986.

Gager, John *Kingdom and Community: The Social World of Early Christianity,* Englewood Cliffs N. J.: Prentice Hall, 1975.

Gaston, L. *No Stone on Another,* Leiden: E. J. Brill, 1970.

282 The Prophecy on the Mount

——, *Horae Synopticae Electronicae. Word Statistics of the Synoptic Gospels,* Missoula: Society of Biblical Literature, 1973.

Geddert, Timothy J. *Watchwords: Mark 13 in Markan Eschatology* (JSNT SS 26), Sheffield: JSOT Press, 1989.

Gill, W. A. *Life on the Road,* Homebush West: Lancer, 1989.

——, *Fringes of Freedom,* Homebush West: Lancer, 1990.

Gräßer, Erich *Das Problem der Parusieverzögerung in den synoptischen Evangelien und in der Apostel geschichte,* Berlin: Alfred Töpelmann, 1960.

Gundry, Robert Horton *The Use of the Old Testament in St. Matthew's Gospel: with Special Reference to the Messianic Hope* (Suplements to *Novum Testamentum,* vol. XVIII), Leiden: E. J. Brill, 1967.

Hahn, Ferdinand *Mission in the New Testament,* London: SCM Press, 1965.

Hanson, Paul D. (ed.) *Visionaries and Their Apocalypses* (Issues in Religion and Theology 2), Philadelphia/London: Fortress Press/SPCK, 1983.

Hartman, Lars *Prophecy Interpreted: The Formation of some Jewish Apocalyptic Texts and of the Eschatalogical Discourse Mark 13 Par* (Coniectanea Biblica: New Testament series), ET by N. Tomkinson and Jean Gray. Lund: Gleerup, 1966.

Hawkins, John C. *Horae Synopticae. Contributions to the Study of the Synoptic Problem,* Oxford: Clarendon Press, 1899.

Hay, David M. *Glory at the Right Hand: Psalm 110 in Early Christianity* (SBL MS 18), Nashville: Abingdon Press, 1973.

Hengel, Martin *Studies in the Gospel of Mark,* London: SCM Press, 1985.

——, *The Zealots. Investigations into the Jewish Freedom Movement in the Period from Herod I until 70 AD,* ET David Smith, Edinburgh: T. & T. Clark, 1989.

Horsley, G. H. R. *New Documents Illustrating Early Christianity,* vols 1-5, Sydney: Macquarie University Press, 1976-1979, 1989.

Horsley, Richard A. *Jesus and the Spiral of Violence. Popular Jewish Resistance in Roman Palestine,* San Francisco: Harper & Row, 1987.

Jeansome, Sharon Pace *The Old Greek Translation of Daiel 7-12* (CBQ MS 19), Washington: The Catholic Biblical Association of America, 1988.

Jellicoe, Sidney *The Septuagint and Modern Study,* Oxford: University Press, 1968.

Jeremias, J. *Jerusalem in the Time of Jesus,* London: SCM Press, 1969.

——, *New Testament Theology* (vol 1), ET J. Bowden, London: SCM Press, 1971.

——, *The Parables of Jesus* (New Testament Library), London: SCM Press, 1963.

——, *The Eucharistic Words of Jesus,* London: SCM Press, 1976.

Juel, Donald *Messianic Exegesis. Christological Interpretation of the Old Testament in Earliest Christianity,* Philadelphia: Fortress Press, 1988.

Käsemann, Ernst *New Testament Questions of Today,* ET W. J. Montague, London: SCM Press, 1969.

Kee, Howard C. *Community of the New Age,* London: SCM Press, 1977.

Kelber, W. H. *The Kingdom in Mark. A New Place and a New Time,* Philadelphia: Fortress Press, 1974.

——, (ed.) *The Passion in Mark. Studies on Mark 14-16,* Philadelphia: Fortress Press, 1976.

——, *The Oral and Written Gospel: The Hermeneutics of Speaking and Writing in the Synoptic Tradition, Mark, Paul and Q,* Philadelphia: Fortress Press, 1983.

Kenny, Anthony *A Stylometric Study of the New Testament,* Oxford: Clarendon Press, 1986.

Kuhn, Thomas S. *The Structure of Scientific Revolutions,* Chicago: The University of Chicago Press, 2nd ed, 1970.

Kümmel, W. G. *Promise and Fulfilment,* ET D. M. Barton from the 3rd German edition, 1956, London: SCM Press, 1957.

Lambrecht, J. *Die Redaktion der Markus-Apokalypse. Literarische Analyse und Strukturuntersuchung,* Rome: Pontifical Biblical Institute, 1967.

Lightfoot, R. H. *The Gospel Message of St. Mark,* London: Oxford University Press, 1950.

Lindars, Barnabas *New Testament Apologetic: The Doctrinal Significance of the Old Testament Quotations,* London: SCM Press, 1961.

——, *Jesus Son of Man: A Fresh Examination of the Son of Man Sayings in the Gospels,* Grand Rapids/London: Eerdmans/SPCK, 1983.

Lohse, Eduard *The New Testament Environment,* ET: J. E. Steely. London: SCM Press, 1976.

Mack, Burton L. *A Myth of Innocence. Mark and Christian Origins,* Philadelphia: Fortress Press, 1988.

Mackay, James *Greek and Roman Coins,* London: Arthur Barker, 1971.

Malbon, Elizabeth Struthers and McKnight, Edgar V. (eds), *The New Literary Criticism and the New Testament,* Sheffield: JSOT Press, 1994.

Maloney, Elliott C. *Semitic Interference in Markan Syntax* (SBLDS 51), Chico: Scholars Press, 1981.

Marxsen, W. *Mark the Evangelist,* ET: R. A. Harrisville from the German edition, 1959; Nashville: Abingdon Press, 1969.

McNamara, Martin *Targum and Testament. Aramaic Paraphrases of the Hebrew Bible: A Light on the New Testament,* Shannon: Irish University Press, 1972.

Meier, John P. *A Marginal Jew. Rethinking the Historical Jesus,* New York: Doubleday, 1991.

Moltmann, Jürgen *The Way of Jesus Christ. Christology in Messianic Dimensions,* London: SCM Press, 1990.

Moore, Stephen D. *Literary Criticism and the Gospels: The Theoretical Challenge,* New Haven: Yale University Press, 1989.

Morgenthaler, Robert *Statistik des Neutestamentlichen Wortschatzes,* Zürich: Gotthelf-Verlag, 1958.

Myers, Ched *Binding the Strong Man. A Political Reading of Mark's Story of Jesus,* Maryknoll: Orbis, 1988.

Neirynck, Frans *Duality in Mark. Contributions to the Study of the Markan Redaction* (BEThL XXXI), Leuven: Leuven University Press, revised from the 1972 edition, 1988.

Nickelsburg, George W. E. *Jewish Literature: Between the Bible and the Mishnah,* London: SCM Press, 1981.

Patte, Daniel *What is Structural Exegesis?* (Guides to Biblical Scholarship, New Testament Series), Philadelphia: Fortress Press, 1976.

Peabody, David Barrett *Mark as Composer* (New Gospel Studies 1), Macon: Peeters/Mercer University Press, 1987.

Perrin, Norman *The Kingdom of God in the Teaching of Jesus* (NTL), London: SCM Press, 1963.

——, *Jesus and the Language of the Kingdom. Symbol and Metaphor in New Testament Interpretation,* London: SCM Press, 1976.

Pesch, Rudolf *Naherwartungen. Tradition und Redaktion in Mk13,* Düsseldorf: Patmos-Verlag, 1968.

Petersen, Norman R. *Literary Criticism for New Testament Critics,* Philadelphia: Fortress Press, 1978.

Price, Jonathan J. *Jerusalem Under Siege. The Collapse of the Jewish State 66-70CE,* Leiden: E. J. Brill, 1992.

Pryke, E. J. *Redactional Style in the Marcan Gospel* (SNTS MS 33), Cambridge, Cambridge University Press, 1978.

Rhoads, David M. *Israel in Revolution 6-74 CE,* Philadelphia: Fortress Press, 1976.

Rhoads, David and Michie, Donald *Mark as Story. An Introduction to the Narrative of a Gospel,* Philadelphia: Fortress Press, 1982.

Rist, John M. *On the independence of Matthew and Mark,* Cambridge: Cambridge University Press, 1978.

Robbins, V. K. *Jesus the Teacher,* Philadelphia: Fortress Press, 1984.

Rowland, Christopher *The Open Heaven. A Study of Apocalyptic in Judaism and Early Christianity,* London: SPCK, 1982.

Sanders, E. P. *The Tendencies of the Synoptic Tradition* (SNTS MS 9), Cambridge: Cambridge University Press, 1969.

Schmithals, W. *The Apocalyptic Movement. Introduction and Interpretation,* ET John E. Steely, Nashville: Abingdon Press, 1975, from the German: *Die Apokalyptik. Einführung und Deutung,* Göttingen: Vandenhoeck & Ruprecht, 1973.

Schürer, Emil *The History of the Jewish People in the Age of Jesus Christ (175 BC—AD 135),* vol III, part 1, eds Geza Vermes, Fergus Millar, Martin Goodman, Edinburgh: T. & T. Clark, revised ed, 1986.

Senior, D. *The Passion of Jesus in the Gospel of Mark,* Wilmington: Michael Glazier, 1984.

Shires, Henry M. *Finding the Old Testament in the New,* Philadelphia: The Westminster Press, 1974.

Smallwood, E. Mary *The Jews Under Roman Rule: From Pompey to Diocletian,* Leiden: E. J. Brill, 1981.

Stone, Michael E. (ed) *Jewish Writings of the Second Temple Period. Apocrypha, Pseudepigrapha, Qumran Sectarian Writings, Philo, Josephus* (Compendia Rerum Iudaicarum as Novum Testamentum, section 2), Assen/Philadelphia: Van Gorcum/Fortress Press, 1984.

Telford, William *The Interpretation of Mark* (Issues in Religion and Theology 7), Philadelphia: Fortress Press: London: SPCK, 1985.

——, *The Barren Temple and the Withered Tree* (JSNT Supplement Series 1), Sheffield: JSOT Press, 1980.

Theissen, Gerd *The Sociology of Early Palestinian Christianity,* Philadelphia: Fortress Press, 1978.

——, *The Gospels in Context. Social and Political History in the Synoptic Tradition,* ET Linda M. Maloney from the 1989 German edition (*Lokalkolorit und Zeitgeschichte in den Evangelien*), Minneapolis: Fortress Press, 1991.

Thiselton, Anthony C. *New Horizons in Hermeneutics. The Theory and Practice of Transforming Biblical Reading,* Grand Rapids: Zondervan Publishing House, 1992.

Tolbert, Mary Ann *Sowing the Gospel. Mark's World in Literary-Historical Perspective,* Minneapolis: Fortress Press, 1989.

Turner, N. *Grammatical Insights into the NT,* Edinburgh: T. & T. Clark, 1965.

Vermes, Geza *Jesus and the World of Judaism,* Philadelphia: Fortress Press, 1984.

Via, Dan O. *The Ethics of Mark's Gospel—in the Middle of Time,* Philadelphia: Fortress Press, 1985.

Waetjen, Herman C. *A Reordering of Power: A Socio-Political Reading of Mark's Gospel,* Minneapolis: Fortress Press, 1989.

Weeden, Theodore J. *Mark—Traditions in Conflict,* Philadelphia: Fortress Press, 1971.

Wenham, David *The Rediscovery of Jesus' Eschatalogical Discourse* (Gospel Perspectives 4), Sheffield: JSOT, 1984.

Wilcox, Max *The Semitisms of Acts,* Oxford: Clarendon Press, 1965.

Williamson, G. A. *Josephus. The Jewish War,* Harmondsworth: Penguin, 1959.

Wink, Walter *Naming the Powers: The Language of Power in the New Testament,* Philadelphia: Fortress Press, 1984.

Zerwick, Maximilian *Untersuchungen zum Markusstil,* Rome: Biblical Institute, 1937.

4. Articles

Allen, Leslie C. "Some Prophetic Antecedents of Apocalyptic Eschatology and their Hermeneutical Value", *Ex Auditu* 6 (1990), 15-28.

Anderson, Hugh "The Old Testament in Mark's Gospel", in *The Use of the Old Testament in the New and Other Essays. Studies in Honor of William Franklin Stinespring,* ed James M. Efird, Durham, N. C.: Duke University Press, 1972, 280-306.

Atkinson, B. F. C. "The Textual Background of the Use of the Old Testament by the New", *Journal of the Transactions of the Victoria Institute* 79 (1947), 39-69.

Baines, W. G. "The Number of the Beast in Revelation", *Heythrop Journal* 16 (1975), 195-196

Barr, James "Jewish Apocalyptic in Recent Scholarly Study", *BJRL* 58 (1975-6), 9-35.

Barrett, C. K. "The Gentile Mission as an Eschatological Phenomenon", in *Eschatology and the New Testament. Essays in Honor of George Raymond Beasley-Murray,* ed W. Hulitt Gloer, Peabody: Hendrickson Publishers, 1988, 65-75.

Bauckham, Richard "The Apocalypses in the New Pseudepigrapha", *JSNT* 26 (1986), 97-117.

——, "The Two Fig Tree Parables in the Apocalypse of Peter", *JBL* 104 (1985), 269-287.

——, "The Son of Man: 'A Man in My Position' or 'Someone'?", *JSNT* 23 (1985), 23-33.

Beale, G. K. "The Use of Daniel in the Synoptic Eschatological Discourse and in the Book of Revelation", in *The Jesus Tradition Outside the Gospels* (Gospel Perspectives 5), ed David Wenham, Sheffield: JSOT Press, 1985, 129-153.

Beardslee, William A. "New Testament Apocalyptic in Recent Interpretation", *Interp.* 25 (1971), 419-435.

Beasley-Murray, G. R. "A Century of Eschatological Discussion", *ExpTim* 64 (Oct. 1952-Sept. 1953), 312-316.

——, "The Rise and Fall of the Little Apocalypse Theory", *ExpTim* 64 (Oct. 1952-Sept. 1953), 346-349.

——, "The Parousia in Mark", *RevExp* 75 (1978), 565-581.

——, "Jesus and Apocalyptic: With Special Reference to Mark 14, 62", in *l'Apocalypse johannique et l'Apocalyptique dans le Nouveau Testament,* ed Jan Lambrecht, Leuven: University Press, 1980, 415-429.

——, "Second Thoughts on the Composition of Mark 13", *NTS* 29 (1982), 414-420.

——, "The Vision on the Mount: The Eschatological Discourse of Mark 13", *Ex Auditu* 6 (1990), 39-52.

——, "The Kingdom of God in the Teaching of Jesus", and an exchange of responses with Craig L. Blomberg, *JETS* 35 (1992), 19-38.

Beck, N. A. "Reclaiming a Biblical Text: The Mark 8: 14-21 Discussion about Bread in the Boat",*CBQ* 43 (1981), 49-56.

Berkey, Robert F. "Εγγιζειν, Φθανειν, and realized Eschatology", *JBL* 82 (1963), 177-187.

Best, Ernest "Mark's Preservation of the Tradition", in *Disciples and Discipleship: Studies in the Gospel According to Mark,* Edinburgh: T. & T. Clark, 1986.

——, "The Gospel of Mark: Who was the Reader?", *IrBibStuds* 11 (1989), 124-132.

Black, C. Clifton "The Quest of Mark the Redactor: Why has it been pursued, and what has it taught us?", *JSNT* 33 (1988), 19-39.

——, "An Oration at Olivet: Some Rhetorical Dimensions of Mark 13", in *Persuasive Artistry. Studies in New Testament Rhetoric in Honor of George A. Kennedy* (JSNT SS 50), ed Duane F. Watson, Sheffield: JSOT Press, 1991, 66-92.

Black, Matthew "The Theological Appropriation of the Old Testament by the New Testament", *SJTh* 39 (1986), 1-17.

——, "Second Thoughts IX. The Semitic Element in the New Testament", *ExpTim* 77 (1965-66), 20-23.

——, "The Problem of the Aramaic Element in the Gospels", *ExpTim* 59 (1947-48), 171-176.

Bolt, Peter G. "Mark 13: An Apocalyptic Precursor to the Passion Narrative", *RTR* 54 (1995), 10-32.

Boring, M. Eugene "The Influence of Christian Prophecy on the Johannine Portrayal of the Paraclete and Jesus", *NTS* 25 (1978), 113-123.

Botha, Pieter J. J. "The Historical Setting of Mark's Gospel: Problems and Possibilities", *JSNT* 51 (1993), 27-55.

Braaten, Carl E. "The Significance of Apocalypticism for Systematic Theology", *Interp.* 25 (1971), 480-499.

Broadhead, Edwin K. "Mk 1,44: The Witness of the Leper", *ZNW* 83 (1992), 257-265.

Brown, Raymond E. "Not Jewish Christianity and Gentile Christianity but Types of Jewish/Gentile Christianity", *CBQ* 45 (1983), 74-79.

Bruce, F. F. "The Book of Daniel and the Qumran Community", In *Neotestamentica et Semitica*, eds E. Earle Ellis and Max Wilcox, Edinburgh: T. & T. Clark, 1969, 221-235.

Burkett, Delbert "The Nontitular Son of Man: A History and Critique", *NTS* 40 (1994), 504-521.

Carroll, Robert P. "Prophecy and Dissonance. A Theoretical Approach to the Prophetic Tradition", *ZAW* 92 (1980), 108-119.

Chapman, Dean W. "Locating the Gospel of Mark. A Model of Agrarian Biogrpahy", *BThB* 25 (1995), 24-36.

Classen, Walter T. "Computer Assisted Methods and the Text and Language of the Old Testament—An Overview", in *Text and Context. Old Testament and Semitic Studies for F. C. Fensham* (JSOT SS 48), ed W. Classen, Sheffield: JSOT Press, 1988.

Collins, A. Y. "The Early Christian Apocalypses", *Semeia* 14 (1979) 61-121.

——, "The Origin of the Designation of Jesus as 'Son of Man'", *HTR* 80 (1987), 391-407.

——, "The Son of Man Sayings in the Sayings Source", in *To Touch the Text. Biblical and Related Studies in Honor of Joseph A. Fitzmyer, S. J.*, eds Maurya P. Horgan and Paul J. Kobelski, New York: Crossroad, 1989, 369-389.

Collins, J. J. "The Jewish Apocalypses", *Semeia* 14 (1979) 21-59.

——, "Inspiration or Illusion: Biblical Theology and the Book of Daniel", *Ex Auditu* 6 (1990), 15-28.

Combs, William W "The Transmission History of the Septuagint", *Bibliotheca Sacra* 146 (1989), 255-269.

Cousar, Charles B. "Eschatology and Mark's *Theologia Crucis* : A Critical Analysis of Mark 13", *Interp.* 24 (1970) 321-335.

Cranfield, C. E. B. "Thoughts on New Testament Eschatology", *SJTh* 35 (1982), 497-512.

Crawford, Barry S. "Near Expectation in the Sayings of Jesus", *JBL* 101 (1982), 225-244.

Crotty, R. B. "Changing Fashions in Biblical Interpretation", *ABR* 33 (1985), 15-30.

Cullmann, O. "Eschatology and Missions in the New Testament", in *The Background of the New Testament and its Eschatology: Studies in honour of C. H. Dodd*, eds W. D. Davies and D. Daube, Cambridge: Cambridge University Press, 1956.

Davies, Philip R. "Eschatology at Qumran", *JBL* 104 (1985), 39-55.

Dodd, C. H. "The Fall of Jerusalem and the 'Abomination of Desolation'", in *More New Testament Studies,* Manchester: University Press, 1968 [= *JRS* 37 (1947), 47-54].

Donahue, John R. "Recent Studies on the Origin of 'Son of Man' in the Gospels", *CBQ* 48 (1986), 484-498.

Edwards, James R. "Markan Sandwiches: The Significance of Interpolations in Markan Narratives", *NovT* 31 (1989), 193-216.

Elliott, J. K. "An Eclectic Textual Commentary on the Greek Text of Mark's Gospel", in *New Testament Textual Criticism—Its Significance for Exegesis. Essays in Honour of Bruce M. Metzger,* eds Eldon Jay Epp, Gordon D. Fee, Oxford: Clarendon Press, 1981, 47-60.

——, "The Position of the Verb in Mark with special reference to Chapter 13", *NovT* 38 (1996), 136-144.

Evans, Craig A. "Jesus' Action in the Temple: Cleansing or Portent of Destruction?", *CBQ* 51 (1989), 237-270.

Fiorenza, Elisabeth Schüssler "The Phenomenon of Early Christian Apocalyptic. Some Reflections on Method", in *Apocalypticism in the Mediterranean World and the Near East,* ed D. Hellholm, Tübingen: J. C. B. Mohr/Paul Siebeck, 1983, 295-316.

Fitzmyer, Joseph A. "Another View of the 'Son of Man' Debate", *JSNT* 4 (1979), 58-68.

Flückiger, F. "Die Redaktion der Zukunftsrede Mark 13", *ThZ* 26 (1970), 395-409.

Gibson, Jeffrey "Jesus' Refusal to Produce a 'Sign' (Mk 8.11-13)", *JSNT* 38 (1990), 37-66.

Gill, W. A. "Women Ministers in the Gospel of Mark", *ABR* 35 (1987), 14-21.

———, "Beyond the Boundaries. Marcan Mission Perspectives for Today's Church", in *Mission to the World. Essays to celebrate the 50th anniversary of the ordination of George Raymond Beasley-Murray to the Christian Ministry,* ed Paul Beasley-Murray, Supplement to the *Baptist Quarterly,* 1991, 35-41.

Glasson, T. Francis "Mark xiii. and the Greek Old Testament", *ExpTim* 69 (1957-8), 213-215.

———, "Theophany and Parousia", *NTS* 34 (1988), 259-270.

Glasswell, M. E. "St. Mark's Attitude to the Relationship between History and the Gospel", in *Studia Biblica 1978: JSNT SS 2,* Sheffield: University Press, 1980, 115-127.

Graham, Helen R. "A Passion Prediction for Mark's Community: Mark 13:9-13", *BThB* 16 (1986), 18-22.

Grayston, K. "The Study of Mark XIII", *BJRL* 56 (1973-4), 371-387.

Gundry, Robert H. "The Hellenization of Dominical Tradition and Christianization of Jewish Tradition in the Eschatology of 1-2 Thessalonians", *NTS* 33 (1987), 161-178.

Hahn, F. "Die Rede von der Parusie des Menschensohnes Markus 13", in *Jesus und der Menschensohn,* FS for A. Vögtle, eds R. Pesch and R. Schnackenburg, Freiburg: Herder & Herder, 1975, 240-266.

Hamerton-Kelly, R. G. "The Temple and the Origins of Jewish Apocalyptic", *VT* 20 (1970), 1-15.

Hartman, Lars "Survey of the Problem of Apocalyptic Genre", in *Apocalypticism in the Mediterranean World and the Near East,* ed D. Hellholm, Tübingen: J. C. B. Mohr/Paul Siebeck, 1983, 329-343.

———, "The Functions of some so-called Apocalyptic Timetables", *NTS* 22 (1976), 1-14.

Hawthorne, Gerald F. "The Role of Christian Prophets in the Gospel Tradition", in *Tradition and Interpretation in the New Testament. Essays in Honor of E. Earle Ellis,* ed Gerald F. Hawthorne with Otto Betz, Grand Rapids/Tübingen: William B. Eerdmans/J. C. B. Mohr (Paul Siebeck), 1987, 119-133.

Herzog, William R. "Apocalypse Then and Now: Apocalyptic and the Historical Jesus Reconsidered", *PacThR* 18 (1984), 17-25.

———, "The Quest for the Historical Jesus and the Discovery of the Apocalyptic Jesus", *PacThR* 19 (1985), 25-39.

Hirsch, E. D. "Three Dimensions of Hermeneutics", *New Literary History* 3 (1972), 245-261; reprinted in *On Literary Intention,* ed David Newton-De Molina, Edinburgh: Edinburgh University Press, 1976.

Hooker, Morna D. "Trial and Tribulation in Mark XIII", *BJRL* 65 (1982), 78-99.

———, "Mark", in *It is Written: Scripture Citing Scripture. Essays in Honor of Barnabas Lindars,* ed D. A. Carson and H. G. M. Williamson, Cambridge: Cambridge University Press, 1988, 220-230.

———, "Traditions About the Temple in the Sayings of Jesus", *BJRL* 70 (1988), 7-19.

Hudson, James T. "The Aramaic Basis of St. Mark", *ExpTim* 53 (1941-42), 264-270.

Hurtado, L. W. "The Gospel of Mark: Evolutionary or Revolutionary Document?" *JSNT* 40 (1990), 15-32.

Kalimi, Isaac "The Land of Moriah, Mount Moriah, and the Site of Solomon's Temple in Biblical Historiography", *HTR* 83 (1990), 345-362.

Kee, Howard Clark "The Function of Scriptural Quotations and Allusions in Mark 11-16", in *Jesus und Paulus,* eds E. Ellis and E. Grässer (Göttingen 1975), 165-188.

———, "A Century of Quests for the Culturally Compatible Jesus", *TheolToday* 52 (1995), 17-28.

Kelber, Werner H. "Mark and Oral Tradition", *Semeia* 16 (1980), 7-55.

———, "Gospel Narrative and Critical Theory", *BThB* 18 (1988), 130-136.

Kilpatrick, G. D. "The Gentile Mission in Mark and Mark 13: 9-11", in *Studies in the Gospels: Essays in Memory of R. H. Lightfoot,* ed D. E. Nineham, Oxford: Basil Blackwell, 1957, 145-158.

———, "Mark XIII.9-10", *JThS* 9 (1958), 81-86.

Kingsbury, Jack Dean "The Religious Authorities in the Gospel of Mark", *NTS* 36 (1990), 42-65.

Kirschner, Robert "Apocalyptic and Rabbinic Responses to the Destruction of 70", *HThR* 78 (1985), 27-46.

Koester, Craig "The Origin and Significance of the Flight to Pella Tradition", *CBQ* 51 (1989), 90-106.

Kreitzer, Larry J. "A Numismatic Clue to Acts 19.23-41: The Ephesian Cistophori of Claudius and Agrippina", *JSNT* 30 (1987), 59-70.

——, "Hadrian and the Nero Redivivus Myth", *ZNW* 79 (1988), 92-115.

——, "The Personification of Judaea: Illustrations of the Hadrian Travel Sestertii", *ZNW* 80 (1989), 278-279.

——, "Nero's Rome: Images of the City on Imperial Coinage", *EvQ* 61 (1989), 301-309.

——, "Apotheosis of the Roman Emperor", *BibArch* 53 (1990), 211-217.

Kümmel, Werner Georg "Eschatological Expectation in the Proclamation of Jesus", in *The Future of Our Religious Past: Essays in Honour of Rudolf Bultmann*, ed James M. Robinson, ET Charles E. Carlston and Robert P. Scharlemann, London: SCM Press, 1971, 29-48.

Lambrecht, Jan "Die Logia-Quellen von Markus 13", *Bib.* 47 (1966), 321-360.

——, "Die 'Midrasch-Quelle' von Mk 13", *Bib.* 49 (1968), 254-270.

——, "Q-Influence on Mark 8,34-9,1", in *Logia. Les Paroles de Jésus - The Sayings of Jesus. Mémorial Joseph Coppens (BEThL 59)*, Leuven: University Press and Peeters, 1982, 277-304.

——, "Redaction and Theology in Mk , IV", in *L'Évangile selon Marc: Tradition et rédaction (BEThL 34)*, ed M. Sabbe, Leuven: University Press, 1974, 269-307.

Laws, Sophie "Can Apocalyptic be Relevant?", in *What About the New Testament? Essays in Honour of Christopher Evans,* eds Morna Hooker and Colin Hickling, London: SCM Press, 1975.

Lee-Pollard, Dorothy A. "Powerlessness as Power: A Key Emphasis in the Gospel of Mark", *SJT* 40 (1987), 173-188.

Lincoln, Andrew T. "The Promise and the Failure: Mark 16:7,8", *JBL* 108 (1989), 283-300.

Lövestam, E. "The ἡ γενεὰ αὕτη Eschatology in Mk 13,30 parr.", in *l'Apocalypse johannique et l'Apocalyptique dans le Nouveau Testament,* ed Jan Lambrecht, Leuven: University Press, 1980, 403-413.

Lührmann, Dieter "The Gospel of Mark and the Sayings Collection Q", *JBL* 108 (1989), 51-71.

Lüdemann, Gerd "The Successors of Pre-70 Jerusalem Christianity: A Critical Evaluation of the Pella-Tradition", in *Jewish and Christian Self Definition, Vol 1: The Shaping of Christianity in the Second and Third Centuries,* ed E. P. Sanders, London: SCM Press, 1980, 161-173; end-notes 245-254.

Mack, Burton L. "The Kingdom Sayings in Mark", *Forum* 3 (1987), 3-47.

Malbon, Elizabeth Struthers "Mark: Myth and Parable", *BThB* 16 (1986), 8-17.

——, "Fallible Followers: Women and Men in the Gospel of Mark", *Semeia* 28 (1983), 29-48.

——, "The Jewish Leaders in the Gospel of Mark. A Literary Study of Marcan Characterization", *JBL* 108 (1989), 259-281.

Maloney, Elliott C. "The Historical Present in the Gospel of Mark", in *To Touch the Text. Biblical and Related Studies in Honor of Joseph A. Fitzmyer, S. J.,* eds Maurya P. Horgan and Paul J. Kobelski, New York: Crossroad, 1989, 67-78.

Manson, T. W. "Realized Eschatology and the Messianic Secret", in *Studies in the Gospels. Essays in Memory of R. H. Lightfoot,* ed D. E. Nineham, Oxford: Basil Blackwell, 1957, 209-222.

Marcus, Joel "Mark 9,11-13: 'As It Has Been Written'", *ZNW* 80 (1989), 42-63.

——, "'The Time Has Been Fulfilled!' (Mark 1.15)", in *Apocalyptic and the New Testament. Essays in Honor of J Louis Martyn (JSNT SS 24)*, eds. Joel Marcus and Marion L Soards, Sheffield: JSOT Press, 1989, 49-68.

——, "The Jewish War and the *Sitz im Leben* of Mark", *JBL* 111 (1992), 441-462.

Marshall, I. Howard "Is Apocalyptic the Mother of Christian Theology?", in *Traditon and Interpretation in the New Testament. Essays in Honor of E. Earle Ellis,* ed

Gerald F. Hawthorne with Otto Betz, Grand Rapids/Tübingen: William B. Eerdmans/J. C. B. Mohr (Paul Siebeck), 1987, 33-42.
Martin, James P. "Towards a Post-Critical Paradigm", *NTS* 33 (1987), 370-385.
Masuda, S. "The Good News of the Miracle of the Bread. The Tradition and its Markan Redaction", *NTS* 28 (1982), 191-219.
McVann, Mark "The Passion in Mark: Transformation Ritual", *BThB* 18 (1988), 96-101.
Mealand, David "Computers in New Testament Research: An Interim Report", *JSNT* 33 (1988), 97-115.
Miller, Robert J. "The Rejection of the Prophets in Q", *JBL* 107 (1988), 225-240.
Moloney, F. J. "The End of the Son of Man?" *DRev* 94 (1980), 280-290.
——, "The Reinterpretation of Psalm 8 and the Son of Man Debate [a discussion of the Regia Targum]", *NTS* 27 (1981), 656-672.
Mowery, Robert L. "Pharisees and Scribes, Galilee and Jerusalem", *ZNW* 80 (1989), 266-268.
Murphy, Frederick J. "The Temple in the Syriac *Apocalypse of Baruch"*, *JBL* 106 (1987), 671-683.
Nardoni, Enrique "A Redactional Interpretation of Mark 9:1", *CBQ* 43 (1981), 365-384.
Neirynck, Frans "Le discours anti-apocalyptique de Mc., XIII", in *Evangelica: Gospel Studies (Collected Essays),* ed F. van Segbroeck, Leuven: University Press, 1982, 599-608. [=*EThL* 45 (1969), 154-164].
——, "Duplicate Expressions in the Gospel of Mark", in *Evangelica: Gospel Studies (Collected Essays),* ed F. van Segbroeck, Leuven: University Press, 1982, 83-142. [= *EThL* 48 (1972), 150-209].
——, "The Redactional Text of Mark", in *Evangelica: Gospel Studies (Collected Essays),* ed F. van Segbroeck, Leuven: University Press, 1982, 618-635. [= *EThL* 57 (1981), 144-162].
——, "Words Characteristic of Mark: A New List", *EThL* 64 (1987), 367-374.
Oster, R. "Numismatic Windows into the Social World of Early Christianity: A Methodological Inquiry", *JBL* 101 (1982), 195-223.
Patten, Priscilla "The Form and Function of Parables in Select Apocalyptic Literature and their Significance for Parables in the Gospel of Mark", *NTS* 29 (1983), 246-258.
Perrin, Norman "Eschatology and Hermeneutics: Reflections on Method in the Interpretation of the New Testament", *JBL* 93 (1974), 3-14.
——, "The *Wredestrasse* Becomes the *Hauptstrasse:* Reflections on the Reprinting of the Dodd Festschrift", *JR* 46 (1966), 296-300.
——, "The Creative Use of the Son of Man Traditions by Mark", *USQR* 23 (1968), 357-365.
——, "Apocalyptic Christianity", in *Visionaries and Their Apocalypses* (Issues in Religion and Theology 2), ed Paul D. Hanson, Philadelphia/London: Fortress Press/SPCK, 1983, 121-145.
Pesch, Rudolf "Markus 13", in *l'Apocalypse johannique et l'Apocalyptique dans le Nouveau Testament,* Jan Lambrecht, Leuven: University Press, 1980, 355-368.
Petersen, Norman R. "'Point of View' in Mark's Narrative", *Semeia* 12 (1978), 97-121.
——, "When is the End not the End? Literary Reflections on the Ending of Mark's Narrative", *Int* 34 (1980), 151-166.
——, "The Reader in the Gospel", *Neotestamentica* 18 (1984), 38-51.
Reicke, Bo "Synoptic Prophecies on the Destruction of Jerusalem", in *Studies in New Testament and Early Christian Literature. Essays in Honour of Allen P. Wikgren,* ed David E. Aune, Leiden: E. J. Brill, 1972, 121-134.
——, "A Test of Synoptic Relationships: Matthew 10: 17-23 and 24: 9-14 with Parallels", in *New Synoptic Studies,* ed William R. Farmer, Macon: Mercer University Press, 1983, 209-229.
Roark, Dallas M. "The Great Eschatalogical Discourse", *NT* 7 (1964-5) 123-127.
Rousseau, François "La structure de Marc 13", *Bib.* 56 (1975), 157-172.
Schaberg, Jane, "Daniel 7,12 and the New Testament Passion-Resurrection Predictions", *NTS* 31 (1985), 208-222.

———, "Mark 14.62: Early Christian Merkabah Imagery?" in *Apocalyptic and the New Testament, Essays in Honor of J Louis Martyn* (JSNT SS 24), eds. Joel Marcus and Marion L Soards, Sheffield: JSOT Press, 1989, 69-94.

Schneidau, Herbert N. "'Let the Reader Understand'", *Semeia* 30 (1987), 135-145.

Schlosser, Jacques "La Parole de Jésus sur la fin du Temple", *NTS* 36 (1990), 398-414.

Schoeps, H. J. "Ebionitische Apokalyptik im Neuen Testament", *ZNW* 51 (1960), 101-111.

Schottroff, Luise "Die Gegenwart in der Apokalyptik der synoptischen Evangelien", in *Apocalypticism in the Mediterranean World and the Near East,* ed D. Hellholm, Tübingen: J. C. B. Mohr/Paul Siebeck, 1983, 707-728.

Schweizer, Eduard "Eschatology in Mark's Gospel", in *Neotestamentica et Semitica. Studies in Honour of Matthew Black,* eds E. Earle Ellis and Max Wilcox, Edinburgh: T. & T. Clark, 1969, 114-118.

———, "The Significance of Eschatology in the Teaching of Jesus", in *Eschatology and the New Testament. Essays in Honor of George Raymond Beasley-Murray,* ed W. Hulitt Gloer, Peabody: Hendrickson Publishers, 1988, 1-13.

Senior, Donald "'With Swords and Clubs...' The Setting of Mark's Community and His Critique of Abusive Power", *BThB* 17 (1987), 10-20.

Smith, D. Moody "The Use of the Old Testament in the New", in *The Use of the Old Testament in the New and Other Essays. Studies in Honor of William Franklin Stinespring,* ed James M. Efird, Durham, N. C.: Duke University Press, 1972, 3-65.

Smith, Stephen H. "The Role of Jesus' Opponents in the Markan Drama", *NTS* 35 (1989), 161-182.

———, "The Literary Structure of Mark 11:1-12:40", *NovT* 31 (1989), 104-124.

Stanton, Graham N. "'Pray that your flight may not be in winter or on a sabbath' (Matthew 24.20)", *JSNT* 37 (1989), 17-30.

Stein, Robert H. "What is Redaktionsgeschichte?", *JBL* 88 (1969), 45-56.

Taylor, N. H. "Palestinian Christianity and the Caligula Crisis. Part 1. Social and Historical Reconstruction", *JSNT* 61 (1996), 101-124; and "Part II. The Markan Eschatological Discourse", *JSNT* 62 (1996), 13-41.

Taylor, Vincent "The 'Son of Man' Sayings relating to the Parousia", in *New Testament Essays,* London: Epworth Press, 1970, 119-126.

Tillich, P. "Rejoinder", *JR* 46 (1966), 192.

Tyson, Joseph B. "The Blindness of the Disciples in Mark", *JBL* 80 (1961), 261-268.

Vassiliadis, Petros "Behind Mark: Towards a Written Source", *NTS* 20 (1974), 155-160.

Villegas, Beltran "Peter, Philip and James of Alphaeus", *NTS* 33 (1987), 292-294.

Vorster, W. S. "Literary reflections on Mark 13:5-37: A narrated speech of Jesus", *Neotestamentica* 21 (1987), 203-224.

———, "Intertextuality and Redaktionsgeschichte", in *Intertextuality in Biblical Writings,* ed Sipke Draisma, Kampen: Uitgeversmaatschappij J. H. Kok, 1989, 9-26.

Waetjen, Herman "The Ending of Mark and the Gospel's Shift in Eschatology", *AS* 14 (1965), 114-131.

Walter, N. "Tempelzerstörung und synoptische Apokalypse", *ZNW* 57 (1966), 38-49.

Watson, Nigel "Authorial Intention—Suspect Concept for Biblical Scholars?", *ABR* 35 (1987), 6-13.

Weeden, Theodore J. "The Conflict between Mark and his Opponents over Kingdom Theology", *Society of Biblical Literature Seminar Papers,* vol 2, 1973, 203-241.

Wenham, David "Recent Study of Mark 13: Parts 1 and 2", *TSFBull* LXXI (1975), 6-15; LXXII (1975), 1-9.

———, "'This Generation Will Not Pass...' A Study of Jesus' Future Expectation in Mark 13", in *Christ the Lord. Studies in Christology presented to Donald Guthrie,* ed II. H. Rowdon, Leicester: IVP, 1982, 127-150.

Wilson, Robert R. "From Prophecy to Apocalyptic: Reflections on the Shape of Israelite Religion", *Semeia* 21 (1981), 79-95.

Wright, Addison G. "The Widow's Mites: Praise or Lament?—A Matter of Context", *CBQ* 44 (1982), 256-265.

5. Book Reviews and Critiques

EGON BRANDENBURGER, *Markus 13 und die Apokalyptik,* Göttingen: Vandenhoek und Ruprecht, 1984.
> Reviewed by Barnabas Lindars in *JThS* 37 (1986), 177-180; by Jan Lambrecht in *ThLit* 111 (1986), 746-748; by John M. McDermott in *TS* 48 (1987), 348-350; by Adela Yarbro Collins in *JBL* 106 (1987), 142-143.

W. D. DAVIES & DALE C. ALLISON, *Critical and Exegetical Commentary on the Gospel According to Saint Matthew,* vol 1, Edinburgh: T. & T. Clark, 1988.
> Reviewed by J. D. Kingsbury in *JBL*110 (1991), 344-346.

LARS HARTMAN, *Prophecy Interpreted: The Formation of some Jewish Apocalyptic Texts and of the Eschatalogical Discourse Mark 13 Par.* (Coniectanea Biblica: New Testament series), ET by N. Tomkinson and Jean Gray, Lund: Gleerup, 1966.
> Reviewed by M. D. Hooker in *JThS* 19 (1968), 263-265; by Jan Lambrecht in *Bib.* 49 (1968), 254-270; by Joseph A. Fitzmyer in *Interp.* 23 (1969), 249-251.

G. D. KILPATRICK, "The Gentile Mission in Mark and Mark 13: 9-11", in *Studies in the Gospels: Essays in Memory of R. H. Lightfoot,* ed D. E. Nineham, Oxford: Basil Blackwell, 1957, 145-158.
> Reviewed by C. F. D. Moule in *JThS* 7 (1956), 280-282; by A. Farrer, "An Examination of Mark XIII.10", *JThS* 7 (1956), 75-79.

JAN LAMBRECHT, *Die Redaktion der Markus-Apokalypse. Literarische Analyse und Strukturuntersuchung* (Analecta Biblica 28), Rome: Pontifical Biblical Institute, 1967.
> Reviewed by Lars Hartman in *Bib.* 49 (1968), 130-133.

DANIEL PATTE, *The Gospel According to Matthew: A Structural Commentary on Matthew's Faith,* Philadelphia: Fortress Press, 1987.
> Reviewed by Graham Stanton, "A Structuralist Approach to Matthew", *Int* 43 (1989), 184-186.

RUDOLF PESCH, *Naherwartungen. Tradition und Redaktion in Mk 13* (Kommentare und Beiträge zum Alten und Neuen Testament), Düsseldorf: Patmos-Verlag, 1968.
> Reviewed by Lars Hartman in *Bib.* 50 (1969), 576-580; by Jan Lambrecht in *ThRv* 65-6 (1969), 457-459. See also under Neirynck, "Le discours anti-apocalyptique", above.

RUDOLF PESCH, *Das Markusevangelium. 2. Teil: Kommentar zu Kap. 8,27-16,20* (Herders Theologischer Kommentar zum Neuen Testament, Band II/2), Freiburg: Herder, 1977.
> Reviewed by Frans Neirynck in two articles in *Evangelica: Gospel Studies (Collected Essays),* ed F. van Segbroeck, Leuven: University Press, 1982. "L'évangile de Marc (II)", 520-564 [=*EThL* 55 (1979) 1-42] and "Marc 13: Examen critique de l'interprétation de R. Pesch", 565-597 [= *BEThL* 53 (1980) 369-401].

DAVID WENHAM, *The Rediscovery of Jesus' Eschatalogical Discourse* (Gospel Perspectives 4), Sheffield: JSOT, 1984.
> Reviewed by Fred W. Burnett in *CBQ* 48 (1986), 351-353; by James D. G. Dunn in *JThS* 38 (1987), 163-166; by Frans Neirynck in *EThL* 61 (1985), 192-193; by James Swetnam in *Biblica* 66 (1985), 424-426; by J. Ramsey Michaels in *JBL* 106 (1987), 133-134.

6. Dissertations

Geddert, Timothy J. "Mark 13 in its Markan Interpretive Context", unpublished dissertation, Aberdeen University, 1986.

Gill, W. A. "The Cleansing of the Temple", unpublished Dr. theol. thesis, Zürich University, 1971.

Peabody, David Barrett "The Redactional Features of the Author of Mark: A Method Focussing on Recurrent Phraseology and its Application", unpublished Ph.D. thesis, Southern Methodist University, 1983. (Since published as *Mark as Composer,* 1987).

Smith, Gary Dean "Mark 13:9-13: Mission in Apocalyptic, with Special Reference to Jesus' Gentile Mission in Mark", unpublished Ph.D. thesis, Southern Baptist Theological Seminary, 1981.

Suh, Joong Suk "Discipleship and Community in the Gospel of Mark", unpublished Ph.D. thesis, Boston University, 1986.

Vander Broek, Lyle Dale "The Markan 'Sitz im Leben': A Critical Investigation into the Possibility of a Palestinian Setting for the Gospel", unpublished Ph.D. thesis, Drew University, 1983.

The following grammatical codes representing three word sequences (regardless of punctuation), have been adapted from the code developed by Barbara and Timothy Friberg in *The Analytical Greek New Testament* (Grand Rapids, 1981, used with permission). Each letter stands for a part of speech (A = Adjective, N = Noun and so on), with the exception of the verbs, where a two-letter code is used so that the mood of each verb might be included in the analysis (hence VI = Verb Indicative, VM = Verb Imperative, VP = Participle, and so on).

The reason for abbreviating the more complex code of the Fribergs is that the focus of this analysis is syntactical word order, rather than a complete analysis of grammar. Listed here are those syntactical sequences of three words which occur only once in Mark, or, if they recur, do so only in close proximity—within the small literary units listed in chapter 2 above. Such an analysis of grammatical features is not claimed to be an infallible guide to each non-Markan phrase, but a concentration of unique syntax must surely be an indication of material belonging to traditions behind the Gospel of Mark, rather than the hand of the redactor. (See the statistical summary given in chapter 2).

The percentages calculated as a summary of these findings (in chapter 2, p.88) have been calculated by counting the number of words involved in sequences unique in the Gospel of Mark (counting each word only *once*—even though the sequences may overlap and each word could be involved up to three times), and expressing that figure as a percentage of the total number of words in each section. It is worth noting in this connection that the total number of words for the Gospel of Mark found by adding together these sections is 11 099, not 11 304 as suggested by Kenny (*A Stylometric Study*, 14) because he has included *both* the short (34 words) and the longer (171 words) endings of Mark in his total! These later endings are shown here as separate sections.

Explanation of symbols: (see the Fribergs' book for complete explanations)

A = Adjective
C = Conjunction
Q = Particle (sentential, interrogative or verbal)
V = Verb
VM = Verb, Imperative mood
VO = Verb, Optative mood
VR = Verb, Participle (imperative sense)

B = Adverb
D = Determiner (article)
R = Pronoun
VI = Verb, Indicative mood
VN = Verb, Infinitive
VP = Verb, Participle
VS = Verb, Subjunctive mood

» = function, 'used as...'
/ = 'or' (two analyses are possible—the one in **bold type** is used in this study)
† = 'or' (two analyses are possible if different accenting is given from that appearing in the Greek Text, but the first analysis is the one based on the text as it stands, and the one used in this study)
& = 'and' (that is, both analyses apply, often because crasis has occurred)
+ = connector (showing links between parts of a periphrastic verb, for example)
[ ] = brackets as used around doubtful parts of the Greek Text
{ } = this sequence has *not* been included as a unique feature after considering the possible analyses and the reasons for them (such as when a word may be legitimately analysed in two ways, but neither of which form a unique sequence)

Example: A complex code like A»A&A (for ὅν in 13:30), stands for a relative pronoun (classified functionally by the Fribergs as a pronominal adjective, hence the 'A'), used as ('»') a demonstrative adjective in the antecedent (whether the antecedent actually occurs or not) and as a relative in its own clause (hence the 'A&A'). More detailed explanations are given in the *Analytical Greek New Testament*, 799f.

Sequence	Occurrences	Sequence	Occurrences
VI N D»A	1.4	C R P	4.1
A VP VN	1.7	R VM Q	4.2
R A B	1.7	Q VI D»R&A	4.3
VI A VP	1.7	VM Q VI	4.3
B»VM P R	1.17	A»A C VI	4.4
N B»VM P	1.17	D VN A»A	4.4
R VN N	1.17	VN A»A C	4.4
R P C	1.13	A C A»B	4.5
A»B VI N	1.19	D B VN	4.5, 4.6
VP A R	1.24	P D B	4.5, 4.6
A»B B P	1.28	VN N VI	4.6
R A»B B	1.28	R R D	4.11
R A D»A	1.32	{A VI C/C	4.11, 4.41}
A N C&B	1.35	{VI C/C VP	4.11}
A»B B VP	1.35	VP VS C	4.12, 4.12
B A»B B	1.35	{C/C VP VS	4.12}
C&B VI C	1.35	C VS A»B	4.15
N C&B VI	1.35	VI D»R&A P	4.16, 4.18, 4.20
B P D»A+	1.38	VI D»R&A D	4.18
P D»A+ VP	1.38	N VS B	4.21
VS B P	1.38	Q C P	4.21
{VP R A»B	1.43}	VS C P	4.21
A A VS»VM	1.44	VI B A»A&A	4.25
A VS»VM C	1.44	A»A/A N P	4.28
N R A»A&A	1.44	A»B N B	4.28
N R D»R	1.44	B A»A/A N	4.28
VM A A	1.44	N VI A»B	4.28
VM R VM	1.44	A R N	4.30
VS»VM C VM	1.44	R N VS	4.30
B R VN	1.45	VI B VS	4.30
VN B P	1.45	VN P C	4.33
VP VI VN	1.45	A VP VS	4.35
B VN B	2.2	B»A C VP	4.35
VN B D	2.2	VP VS P	4.35
VP VN R	2.4	B VN D	4.37
C VN VM	2.9	{B/C D N	4.41}
C VN A	2.12	{C/C B/C D	4.41}
C D»R&A B	2.17	{VI C/C B/C	4.41}
N P A»A&A	2.19	B»A D N	5.1
P A»A&A D	2.19	D B»A D	5.1
VI VN VI	2.19	B N C	5.4
A»A&A B VI	2.24	D R B	5.4
N A»A&A B	2.24	P D R	5.4
Q A»B VI	2.24	C N VN	5.4, 14.48
R Q A»B	2.24	B R VS»VM	5.7
B D»R&A P	2.26	R VS»VM VI	5.7
VI B D»R&A	2.26	VS»VM VI C	5.7
R Q D	3.2, 3.32	C R VM	5.8
D»A D A	3.3	R A»B C	5.10, 5.43
N D»A D	3.3	A»B C B	5.10
VP VM P	3.3	R VS P	5.10
C VN D»R	3.4	C VP D»A	5.15
VN N VN	3.4, 3.15	VP VP VP	5.15
A VP A»A&A	3.8	VP C P	5.16, 5.18
R VS A»A&A	3.10	VN R VN	5.17, 5.43
{N/N N A	3.17}	R A»A&A D	5.19
{R N/N N	3.17}	N A»A&A VI	5.20
D»A P N	3.22	B»A VI N	5.21
N D»A P	3.22	D B»A VI	5.21
VN C C	3.23, 3.25	A»B VP C	5.23
A»B D A	3.27	R A»B VP	5.23
B A»B D	3.27	VP VS D	5.23
D A VS	3.27	VP VP P	5.26, 5.30
N A Q	3.28	C C C	5.28
Q VS A»A&A	3.28	C VS B&Q	5.28
C VP D»R&A	3.34	VS B&Q D	5.28
VI Q D	3.34	D»R&A A VP	5.32
VP D»R&A P	3.34	VN D»R&A A	5.32

VP D C	5.32		VS N A	6.37
VP VP A»A&A	5.33		C VI D»A+	6.44
N»N D N	5.34		D VN VI	6.48
R N»N D	5.34		D»R C A»B	6.50
VM A P	5.34		VM R VI	6.50
VM P N	5.34		N D»R&A B	6.55
A»B B VI	5.35		A»A&A Q VI	6.56
A»B VM C	5.36		C B&Q D	6.56
B VM A»B	5.36		R C B&Q	6.56
VM A»B VM	5.36		B N VS	7.3
A»B C VP	5.38		VI VM D	7.10
VP A»B C	5.38		A»A&A Q P	7.11
N VM A	5.41		N A»A&A Q	7.11
R N VM	5.41		Q P R	7.11
[A»B] N A	5.42		VI N A»A&A	7.11
A VS A	5.43		A»A VI C	7.13
A»B C A	5.43		N R A»A	7.13
VS A C	5.43		R A»A VI	7.13
R VP Q	6.2		VP VI D»R&A	7.15
VP Q A	6.2		A VI B/Q	7.18
VP VI VP	6.2		C A D»A	7.18
B A A	6.2, 6.5		B VP P	7.18, 7.31
D»A+ VP A	6.2, 6.31		C C D»A+	7.20
B VN A	6.5		C D»A+ P	7.20
VN A A	6.7		D»A+ P D	7.20
B N A»B	6.8		VN C A»B	7.24
N A»B B	6.8		A»B VP N	7.25
B VS»VM A	6.9		A»B VN D	7.27
VS»VM A N	6.9		R VM A»B	7.27
Q VS B	6.10		VM A»B VN	7.27
VM C Q	6.10		N VM VI	7.29
A Q N	6.11		VM VI P	7.29
B VM D	6.11		A VS A»A&A	7.36
Q N B	6.11		{B A/A»B VI	7.36}
R VR B	6.11		{R B A/A»B	7.36}
VR B VM	6.11		VN C [D]	7.37
VS R VR	6.11		{A VI B/C	7.37}
C N D»A	6.14		{B/C D A	7.37}
R VN D	6.18		{VI B/C D	7.37}
{R D C/C	6.18}		A VS VP	8.1
{C/C N VI	6.19}		VP A VS	8.1
{D C/C N	6.19}		VS VP D	8.1
{R A/A»B VI	6.20}		R P B»A	8.3
{VP R A/A»B	6.20}		A B VN	8.4
Q VS C	6.22		B A VN	8.7
A»A&A†C+ A†+C Q†C	6.23		VN R VP	8.11
[A»B] A»A&A†C+ A†+C	6.23		A/A»B D N	8.12
A†+C Q†C R	6.23		VI A/A»B D	8.12
R [A»B] A»A&A†C+	6.23		VI N Q	8.12
{A/A D N	6.23}		{R VI A/A»B	8.12}
{P A/A D	6.23}		B»A C VI	8.13
{Q†C R VS	6.23}		VP R B	8.13
{R P A/A	6.23}		VM VM P	8.15
N N D»A	6.24		VP VM VM	8.15
VP A»B P	6.25		VI C B/Q	8.18
B VN VI	6.31		N VP B/Q	8.18, 8.18
B»VM R R	6.31		VP B/Q VI	8.18, 8.18
R B»VM R	6.31		{C B/Q VI	8.18}
R R P	6.31		R Q A	8.23
VI C D»A+	6.31		VP B B	8.24
VI R B»VM	6.31		VP VI VI	8.24
VP VI A	6.34, 6.38		D N VS»VM	8.26
B»A N C	6.36		N VS»VM C	8.26
D B»A N	6.36		VS»VM C VI	8.26
R R VN	6.37		VP R A	8.27
R VN D»R	6.37		VI D D	8.33
R VP VS	6.37		R VN VM	8.34
VM R R	6.37		VN VM R	8.34
VP VS N	6.37		R VN VI	8.35

VS N N	8.37
VP A B	9.1, 9.3
A B A	9.3
VN C VS	9.5
VS A N	9.5
A A»A&A VI	9.9
A»A&A VI VS	9.9
C A A»A&A	9.9
VI VS C	9.9
D P A	9.10
P A VN	9.10
A»B D»R C	9.11
VI VN A»B	9.11
VN A»B D»R	9.11
N Q VP	9.12
Q VP A»B	9.12
A»B A D	9.15
C A»B A	9.15
B VI D»R	9.18
C Q R	9.18
{Q R VS (in 6.23 also)	9.18, 9.37}
VI P B»A	9.19, 9.21
B»A P R	9.19
Q N A	9.19
P B»A C	9.21
VR P R	9.22
{B B/C P	9.22}
{B/C P N	9.22}
{C B B/C	9.22}
A A D»R&A	9.23
D C VI	9.23
D»R&A VP A»B	9.23
VI VI VM	9.24
B VS»VM P	9.25
VS»VM P R	9.25
A»B VP VI	9.26
N C&B VP	9.29
C&B VP VI	9.30
N VI D»R	9.31, 9.33
A VN VI»VM	9.35
VI»VM A A	9.35
VN VI»VM A	9.35
A»A&A Q A	9.37
A»A&A Q R	9.37
Q A D	9.37
VS B R	9.37
{R VI/VI R	9.37}
A»B VN R	9.39
VI A»B VN	9.39
VN R A»A&A	9.39
A»A&A C B	9.40
R VI A»A&A	9.40
VI A»A&A C	9.40
VS R N	9.41
VS A D	9.42
VS R VM	9.45, 9.47
VP R D»R	10.2
VN VP R	10.2, 10.26
VI VI N	10.4
VN D C	10.4
A P C	10.5
A VI»VM N	10.7
[C VI»VM P	10.7
N [C VI»VM	10.7
P A VI»VM	10.7
R] C VI»VM	10.7
VI»VM P D	10.7
A N A»A&A	10.8
C VI»VM D	10.8

N A»A&A C	10.8
A»A&A C D	10.9
VM C P	10.9
C C R	10.12
C R VP	10.12
R VS D	10.13
A»A&A Q B	10.15
Q B VS	10.15
{R VI†VI VP	10.16}
{VI†VI VP D	10.16}
B VS»VM VM	10.19
VI B VS»VM	10.19
VS»VM VM D	10.19
B VS»VM B	10.19, 10.19, 10.19, 10.19
VS»VM B VS»VM	10.19, 10.19, 10.19, 10.19
A»A&A VI VM	10.21
B»VM VM R	10.21
C B»VM VM	10.21
N C B»VM	10.21
VI VM A»A&A	10.21
VM A»A&A VI	10.21
VM [D] A	10.21
VM R D»R	10.21
B B D»R&A	10.23
B D»R&A D	10.23
N VN A	10.24
Q R VI	10.28
R Q R	10.28
{R VI/VI D	10.28}
{VI R VI/VI	10.28}
{VI/VI D N	10.29}
A B P	10.30
VS A B	10.30
D»R&A C VP	10.32
R VN D»R&A	10.32
VI D»R&A C	10.32
VI+ +VP R	10.32
+VN B Q	10.32
VP+ R +VN	10.32
VS R VS	10.35
VI VN D»R	10.38
D C VN	10.40
VN C A»A&A	10.40
N C A»A&A	10.43
P R VI»VM	10.43
R C A»A&A	10.43
R VI»VM R	10.43
VI»VM R N	10.43
A VI»VM A	10.44
VI»VM A N	10.44
VN A VI»VM	10.44
D»R C A	10.48
R VM VM	10.49
VM VM VI	10.49
VP R VM	10.49
R VI VS	10.51
VI VS D	10.51
C A»B R	11.3
R VS A»B	11.3
VI A VM	11.3
A D»R&A B	11.5
N VP D»A+	11.9
Q VP D»R&A	11.9
VI Q VP	11.9
VP D»R&A VP	11.9
Q P D	11.10
B»A VP R	11.12

D B»A VP	11.12	Q A N	13.1
B»A VP N	11.13	VS B N	13.2
Q Q A	11.13	C N VM	13.3
VI Q Q	11.13	A +VN A	13.4
A N VO	11.14	VM R B	13.4
N VO C	11.14	+VN A D	13.4
VO C VI	11.14	B VM VI	13.7, 13.21
N D»R&A VP	11.15	VM VI VN	13.7
A VS N	11.16	{N VI N/N	13.8}
VS N P	11.16	{N/N N N	13.8}
N N VI»VM	11.17	{VI N/N N	13.8}
N VI»VM A	11.17	VM C R	13.9
Q VI C	11.17	A»B VI VN	13.10
VI»VM A D	11.17	A VM B	13.11
N Q D	11.21	B VM A	13.11
N N Q	11.22	VM A VS	13.11
R VM N	11.22	VP B VM	13.11
VI VP VM	11.25	VS C A+	13.11
A N C&A	12.4	VS R VP	13.11, 13.36
N C&A VI	12.4	D»A+ C VP	13.13
A A A»A	12.5	N R D»A+	13.13
A A»A C	12.5	R D»A+ C	13.13
A VI C&A	12.5	D»R&A VP VM	13.14
C VP A»A	12.5	N VM P	13.14
VI C&A VI	12.5	VM B D	13.14
VP A»A C	12.5	VP VM B	13.14
C&A VI C	12.4, 12.5	C VM VN	13.15
A»A C VP	12.5, 12.5	D [C] P	13.15
A/A»B P R	12.6	VM VN A	13.15
R A/A»B P	12.6	VN A P	13.15
{VI R A/A»B	12.6}	B VM P	13.16
B»VM VS R	12.7	B»A VN D	13.16
N B»VM VS	12.7	D B»A VN	13.16
A B/Q D	12.9	D»R&A P N	13.17
{N A B/Q	12.9}	Q C D»R&A	13.17
B VS D»R	12.14	VS N VI	13.18
VM R N	12.15	N B Q	13.20
N VM N	12.17	Q VI A	13.20
VM N C	12.17	B B VM	13.21
N B VN	12.18	N Q B	13.21
N A»B A	12.22	Q B B	13.21
VI N A»B	12.22	Q B D	13.21
R N VI/VI	12.23	R VS Q	13.21
VS] A R	12.23	VS Q B	13.21
Q P A	12.24	VM VI C	13.21, 13.37
C VI B/Q	12.26	D VN C	13.22
{B/Q VI P	12.26}	C VM VI	13.23
R VP VP	12.28	A VP VI/VM	13.29
VI C VI»VM	12.29	P N Q	13.29
VI VM N	12.29	VS A VP	13.29
C VI»VM N	12.30	{VI/VM C B	13.29}
A A VI»VM	12.31	{VP VI/VM C	13.29}
A VI»VM D	12.31	A P A»A&A	13.30
B»A R C	12.31	A»A&A A A	13.30
D B»A R	12.31	P A»A&A A	13.30
VI»VM D B»A	12.31	VI P C	13.31
B»A C R	12.33	C&B D N	13.32
VN D B»A	12.33	N C&B D	13.32
R B A»B	12.34	VM B VI	13.33
{B A»B VI	12.34}	VM VM B	13.33
R R N	12.36	C VS VM	13.34
VM P A	12.36	VS VM C	13.34
VS D A	12.36	R VP A»A&A	13.36
A»B VP A	12.40	VP A»A&A C	13.36
C N A»B	12.40	VP B VS	13.36
A VI D»A	12.43	VI VM VI	13.37
C P D»R»A	12.44	N VP VS	14.1
P D»R»A VP	12.44	VP VS VI	14.1
N Q A	13.1	A»B R N	14.6

VM R A»B	14.6
B VI A»A&A	14.7
A»A&A VI A	14.9
Q C VI	14.9
R B VS	14.11
R N VN	14.11
VI VP VS	14.12
Q VS VM	14.14
R B D	14.14
VS C R	14.14
VS VM D	14.14
C B VM	14.15
R D»A VP	14.18
VI R D»A	14.18
A P A»A	14.19
A»A Q R	14.19
P A»A Q	14.19
Q R D»R	14.19
D A D»A	14.20, 16.6
C D C	14.21
P R Q	14.21
Q C D	14.21
VI VM A	14.22
VP N VP	14.22, 14.23, 15.46
A Q VI	14.24
P A Q	14.24
B B B	14.25
VS A P	14.25
A B R	14.25, 15.43
{C N VI/VI	14.29}
{VI/VI R C	14.29}
B C B	14.30
C R B	14.30
N VN B	14.30, 14.72
VN B R	14.30
R VI D»R	14.30, 14.60, 14.69
B C/C B	14.31
R VN R	14.31
{C/C B A	14.31}
{VI B C/C	14.31}
R VM B	14.32
B C VM	14.34
N VM B	14.34, 15.32
A VI VS	14.35
VI VS P	14.35
A R VM	14.36
B A R	14.36
D N»N A	14.36
N D N»N	14.36
N»N A A	14.36
A A R	14.36, 14.60
{C VM C/C	14.38}
{C/C B VS	14.38}
{VM C/C B	14.38}
A VS R	14.40
C R D	14.40
A VM VS	14.41
{A C VI†VM	14.41}
{C VI†VM VI	14.41}
{R VI†VM D	14.41}
{VI R VI†VM	14.41}
{VI†VM VI VI	14.41}
VS Q D»R&A	14.42
Q D»R&A VP	14.42, 15.29
VM VS Q	14.42, 15.36
C A»B B	14.43, 15.1
A»B B R	14.43
C VM B	14.44
VP A+Q	14.44
VS R VI	14.44
N VN R	14.48, 15.36
P B P	14.54
R P B	14.54
B B A	14.59
N VP B	14.60
P A VP	14.62
A VN N	14.64
A VN R	14.65
VN R D	14.65, 15.36
VM C D	14.65
R C VN	14.65, 14.65
B VN D»R&A	14.69
VP C A	14.69, 15.36
A VI D»R	14.70
A»B P A	14.72
B/C B»C N	14.72
B»C N VN	14.72
N B/C B»C	14.72
VN B B	14.72
{D N B/C	14.72, 14.72}
{B/C VI R	14.72}
{N B/C VI	14.72}
A D»R C	15.2, 15.12, 15.14
D A D»R	15.2, 15.12
A Q A	15.4
Q A R	15.4
VI A Q	15.4
+VP A P	15.7
VI VS R	15.9
VP VI VS	15.9
[A»A&A VI] D	15.12
C [VI] VS	15.12
[VI] VS [A»A&A	15.12
B VI VM	15.13, 15.14
VI A D»R	15.14
A VN VI	15.15
R VM»Q N	15.18
VM»Q N D	15.18
VN R VM»Q	15.18
VI+ +VP N	15.22
A N VM	15.29
C VP Q	15.29
VP Q D»R&A	15.29
VR P D	15.30
B B D	15.31, 16.2
VM B P	15.32
VS C D»R&A	15.32
N»N R D	15.34
N»N R P	15.34
R D N»N	15.34
+VP D N»N	15.34
D N»N R	15.34, 15.34
Q N VI	15.35
VP VP VI	15.35
VP VM VS	15.36
VS Q VI	15.36
B»A P B»A	15.38
B»A VP C	15.38
VI VI B	15.39
B»A +VP P	15.40
D»A VP R	15.41
B A VP	15.42
[D] P N	15.43
R Q B	15.44
VI Q B	15.44
Q B VI	15.44, 15.44
VP VS R	16.1
A VP N	16.5

B Q D	16.6
B VM N	16.6
VI B Q	16.6
VM N VI	16.6
VP VI B	16.6
C VM VM	16.7
C (ending with γάρ!)	16.8
VI C (as above)	16.8

In the 'short ending' to Mark are found: A C D»A, C D»A VP, D»A VP D, P C A, B R D, A N Q.

The 'long ending' contains the following unique sequences (largely due to crasis): 16.10 C VP C&A, VP C&A VP, 16.11 C&A VP C, 16.12 P C A, A A P, P N C&A, N C&A VP, 16.13 C&A VP VI, D A C&B, A C&B A, C&B A VI, 16.15 VI R VR, 16.18 N VI C&C, VI C&C A, C&C A A, A VS B, VS B B, 16.19 D C C, 16.20 VP P D»A+, D»A+ VP N.

The abbreviated code used here to express the six-word syntactical sequences is identical to that used for Appendix 1. This list includes all such sequences in the Gospel of Mark that occur more than once. A passage which contains a high number of such sequences (such as Mk 13:24-27) must therefore be considered consistent with the overall style of the Gospel.

Sequences	Occurrences	References
A A C A A C	4	4.8,4.20, 4.8,4.20
A A VP D N VI		26.5,14.3
A C A A C A	2	4.8,4.20
A C A A C VI	2	4.8,4.20
A C A C VI R	2	6.20,7.32
A C B A D N	2	10.18,4.13
A C C B VI D	2	2.22,2.21
A C D A N VI	2	4.34,15.33
A C D N C D	2	8.31,14.53
A C VI C VI N	2	6.42,9.6
A C VI P D N	3	5.13,6.55, 15.41
A C VI P R C	2	14.56,9.2
A C VI R C A	3	9.35,4.4,6.7
A C VI R P A	2	4.34,11.27
A C VI R P D	2	4.2,2.22
A C VI R Q VI	2	4.20,8.38
A D N C D N	2	12.13,1.39
A D N C P A	2	12.33,12.33
A D N C VI R	3	1.24,15.16, 4.10
A D N D N VI	2	14.21,10.18
A D N N C VI	2	14.32,7.31
A D N P D N	2	13.24,4.1
A D N R C P	3	12.30,12.30, 12.30
A D N R C VI	3	11.17,14.13, 11.1
A D N VI P D	3	5.3,14.55, 16.2
A D@R C B VI VM	2	15.12,15.14
A N B VI C VI	2	12.31,2.18
A N C D N VI	2	4.37,13.1
A N C N C N	2	10.30,13.3
A N C VI R VN	2	6.38,6.37
A N VI A C VI	2	6.41,4.34
A N VP C B VP	2	8.1,14.39
A N +VP P D N	2	1.13,6.41
A N VP VN P D	3	9.47,9.45, 9.43
A P D N D N	2	14.25,10.25
A P D N N VI	2	15.7,9.17
A P D N R C	3	13.15,9.42, 1.6
A P D N R VP	2	9.38,6.2
A VI C VI D N	2	14.52,3.30
A VI C VP D N	3	2.4,5.20, 2.16
A VI D N D N	6	9.2,5.40, 3.28, 6.3, 11.29,10.14
A VI D N R C	3	3.33,14.59, 14.22
A VI D N R D	2	9.7,14.24
A VI D N R N	2	7.25,1.2
A VI D N R P	2	7.33,14.34

Sequences	Occurrences	References
A VI D@R&A P D N	2	4.20,4.18
A VI N P [D] N	2	10.25,9.39
A VI P D N C	4	14.10,14.35, 4.7,5.13
A VI P D N D	2	4.8,10.24
A VI P D N R	2	2.8,13.6
A VI P R C C	2	10.11,14.7
A VI P R C VI	3	1.26,1.20, 9.16
A VI R C VI R	2	10.10,1.37
A VI R D N C	2	4.33,2.9
A VI R VN P D	2	9.45,5.3
A VS D C N VI	2	10.17,11.28
A@A&A VI VI P R C	2	4.25,3.8
A@B VI D N C VI	3	4.29,4.15, 5.42
A@B VP D N D N	2	2.8,9.24
B C D N D N	2	10.45,9.9
B C VI P D N	2	6.52,6.1
B D N C VI B	2	2.26,2.28
B D N D N VI	2	13.35,8.38
B D N P D N	3	2.27,14.14, 7.28
B D N VI C N	2	13.33,13.7
B P D N C A	2	2.13,2.16
B P D N C VI	3	3.1,14.2, 11.4
B VI C B D N	2	13.35,13.33
B VI C VI R D	2	12.31,2.18
B VI C VP D N	2	15.47,15.44
B VI D N A C	2	4.13,14.21
B VI D N D N	4	7.9,2.22, 4.26,13.26
B VI VM R D C	2	15.13,15.14
B VS D N D N	2	10.15,4.30
B VS@VM B VS@VM B VS@VM	3	10.19,10.19, 10.19
C A A C A A	2	4.8,4.20
C A C VI R C	3	2.15,6.20, 7.32
C A D N VI P	2	14.55,2.13
C A VI C B VI	2	12.32,12.14
C A VI C VI R	2	5.9,6.30
C A VI C VP D	2	5.20,2.16
C A VI D N C	2	6.35,2.15
C A VI D N D	2	3.28,10.14
C A VI D@R&A P D	3	4.16,4.20, 4.18
C A VI P D N	2	4.7,4.8
C A@B D N VP P	2	1.21,5.30
C A@B VP P D N	2	2.12,1.18
C A@B VP P D N	2	8.10,1.10
C B B VS D N	2	13.30,9.41
C B D N VI C	2	13.33,13.7
C B VI A P R	2	12.32,5.37
C B VI C A VS	2	11.16,9.30

Syntax	No.	References
CB VID N A	2	14.71,14.21
CB VIDND	2	2.22,13.26
CB VI VMRD	2	15.13,15.14
CCB VIDN	2	2.22,2.21
CCDNR VS	2	9.47,9.45
CCNPR VS	2	3.25,3.24
CC VIPNP	2	7.17,11.1
CDANVIA	2	6.41,4.34
CDANVPVN	2	9.45,9.43
CDNAR VI	2	10.39,10.38
CDNCDA	4	11.27,6.21, 14.1,14.43
CDNCDN	4	9.2,8.31, 14.53,14.33
CDNCVIR	3	10.33,16.7, 9.2
CDNDAC	2	3.11,13.11
CDNDNC	5	6.18,12.24, 4.19,11.15, 4.19
CDNDN VI	5	2.26,2.18, 10.33,15.38, 9.31
CDNRB VI	2	5.23,3.32
CDNR VS R	2	9.47,9.45
CDN VIPD	3	4.37,11.18, 13.25
CDN VIPR	2	3.26,9.10
CDN+VPC VI	2	2.18,1.39
CDPRC VI	3	5.40,2.25, 1.36
CNB VP VIR	2	15.12,10.24
CNCADN	3	14.55,6.15, 15.1
CNCNCN	14	3.18,10.29, 3.18,10.30, 10.29,3.18, 10.30,10.29, 6.3,7.4,3.18, 10.30,10.29, 13.3
CNCNC VI	2	13.22,7.4
CNCNDN	2	3.18,5.37
CNC VIRD	2	1.16,7.4
CNDDNC	3	3.18,3.17, 16.1
CNDNCN	3	15.40,15.47, 3.18
CNDNN VP	2	1.16,10.35
CNDN VIC	2	14.21,8.32
CNPDNC	4	14.43,12.38, 12.39,5.5
CNPNCN	2	1.29,13.8
CNPR VS B	2	3.25,3.24
CN VIC B VI	2	3.26,3.35
CN VIDND	2	2.28,2.10
CN VIPDN	2	10.24,1.11
CN VIRDN	2	10.39,12.17
CN VIRPD	2	15.16,10.5
CN VPDNR	2	14.63,9.27
CN VPPRC	2	9.14,1.10
CPADNC	2	12.33,12.33
CPADNR	3	12.30,12.30, 12.30
CPDNCP	4	3.8,7.19,3.8, 3.7
[C]PDNC VI	4	10.1,6.43, 5.14,5.16
CPDNDN	2	7.21,3.22
CPDN VI VP	2	7.19,5.5
CQ VIDNR	2	6.3,8.35
[C]Q VS DND	2	3.35,9.1
CR VIDNC	2	6.45,12.7
C VIAACA	2	4.8,4.20
C VIADNC	2	14.53,15.16
C VIBPDN	3	2.13,14.68, 3.1
C VIC VIC VI	3	8.25,12.25, 8.8
C VIC VIDN	5	9.18,5.40, 6.13,9.18, 3.5
C VIC VIN VP	2	11.4,9.6
C VIC VIRA	2	12.16,14.68
C VIC VIRC	2	11.24,14.16
C VIC VPRP	3	6.53,9.27, 3.4
[C VIDA]C VI	4	3.16,4.4, 14.41,6.7
C VIDNBC	2	11.32,7.23
C VIDNCD	4	14.1,14.33, 11.18,8.27
C VIDNC VI	13	4.29,9.18, 12.9,1.15, 6.41,4.39, 8.6,5.29, 14.16,4.7, 11.6,9.32, 8.11
C VIDNDN	8	8.31,14.72, 15.43,14.62, 7.35,15.26, 12.9,1.15
C VIDNPD	4	14.53,6.30, 11.7,5.13
C VIDNRA	2	12.6,9.21
C VIDNRC	10	3.31,3.9, 9.18,6.14, 11.14,14.46, 6.29,3.5, 8.6,6.41
C VIDN VIC	3	16.4,12.12, 4.6
C VINAC VI	2	4.41,4.39
C VINC VIN	2	12.1,12.1
C VINC VIR	2	15.1,12.1
C VINPDN	2	9.7,15.46
C VINPNC	2	10.21,13.12
C VIPDNC	12	4.36,5.29, 9.42,1.13, 5.13,5.14, 5.21,3.13, 14.16,4.4, 5.15,6.52
C VIPDND	4	5.38,12.2, 2.26,1.2
C VIPDNP	2	6.32,1.9
C VIPDNR	3	6.6,6.1,1.22
C VIPNC VI	2	3.20,8.22
C VIPNC VP	2	11.15,10.46
C VIPNPD	2	11.11,7.17
C VIPRAC	2	4.41,14.23
C VIPRAD	2	1.5,12.13
C VIPRCA	2	14.56,11.7
C VIPRC VI	6	3.13,6.34, 12.17,9.34, 6.3,5.24
C VIPRPD	2	6.51,1.5

C VIR A C A	2	7.32,14.46
C VI[R] A C VI	3	8.20,8.22, 4.24
C VIR A D N	3	12.16,5.33, 9.29
C VIR A VI D	2	14.24,14.34
C VIR B VI D	2	4.13,7.9
C VIR C A VI	3	9.35,4.4, 1.37
C VIR C A VS	3	7.36,6.8, 8.30
C VIR C D N	3	9.31,2.15, 7.26
C VIR C Q VS	2	14.9,6.10
C VIR C VI C	2	10.34,5.19
C VIR C VI D	6	14.16,11.6, 15.25,11.6, 1.27,15.24
C VIR C VI R	6	5.33,6.22, 1.37,10.34, 10.34,4.38
C VIR C VP D	2	5.13,15.19
C VIR C VP VI	3	6.33,2.13, 16.7
C VIR C VS R	2	15.20,7.32
C VIR D C N	2	15.8,14.5
C VIR D N C	8	14.27,6.4, 7.5,6.28, 1.31,10.33, 2.2,14.47
C VIR D N Q	2	2.19,14.30
C VIR D N R	6	8.4,11.7, 15.20,6.1, 15.2,5.31
C VI+ R D N +VP	3	6.52,12.26, 1.25
C VIR N C VI	3	12.1,10.33, 15.17
C VIR P A D	3	4.35,2.18, 7.29
C VIR P A N	2	11.28,11.29
C VIR P D N	6	12.8,16.7, 10.52,15.22, 4.2,2.23
C VIR P N A	4	1.8,4.2,9.2, 15.46
C VIR Q D N	2	3.32,3.2
C VIR VM A VI	2	4.24,7.34
C VIR VM P D	3	14.13,11.2, 5.19
C VIR VM R C	2	10.37,2.14
C VIR VN C VI	2	12.12,9.32
C VIR VP C VI	2	6.33,14.37
C VIR VP N N	2	7.7,12.18
C VI VN C VN C	2	14.71,14.33
C VI++VP P D N	2	14.54,1.39
C VM D N R C	2	2.9,8.34
C VM P D N C	2	11.23,1.15
C VM P D N R	2	1.44,2.11
C VP B VI D N	2	1.32,11.20
C VP D N D A	2	5.13,8.23
C VP D N D N	2	2.5,5.41
C VP D N [P D	2	5.21,8.34
C VP D N R N	2	6.22,1.20
C VP D N R VI	5	8.12,6.29, 8.33,12.43, 8.32
C VP D N VI D	2	9.5,10.23
C VP D N VI R	7	2.17,15.19, 14.48,4.36, 11.21,15.44, 11.22
C +VP P D N D	3	14.54,14.62, 1.16
C +VP P D N R	3	2.6,7.30, 8.23
C VP P D N VI	8	12.41,7.34, 15.45,9.14, 16.5,6.53, 9.20,10.22
C VP P N A VI	2	13.13,7.24
C VP R D N VI	3	10.51,12.15, 10.42
C VP R P D N	7	5.2,6.54, 13.3,7.33, 9.9,5.18, 6.49
C VP R P N VP	2	10.17,3.5
C VP R VI C VI	2	12.3,12.12
C VP R VI P D	2	5.22,6.46
C VP VI D N C	2	6.22,4.39
C VP VI D N R	2	6.24,7.33
C VP VI P D N	3	14.26,7.24, 16.8
C VP VI R A@B VI	2	8.17,5.39
C VP VI R C VI	3	9.15,12.8, 2.14
C VS C VI D N	2	14.32,8.6
D A C A N VI	2	2.21,7.5
D A C D N C	2	8.31,14.53
D A C VI R C	3	9.35,4.4,6.7
D A C VI R D	2	14.5,15.18
D A D N C VI	2	1.24,4.10
D A N VI A C	2	6.41,4.34
D A N VP VN P	2	9.45,9.43
D A VI P D N	2	14.10,5.13
D A VI P R C	2	14.7,1.20
D A VI R D N	2	5.7,2.9
D C A VI R N	2	10.51,12.23
D C N B VP VI	2	15.12,10.24
D C N C A D	2	7.3,14.55
D C N VI D N	2	15.11,6.20
D C N VI R D	3	9.23,10.39, 12.17
D C N VI R P	2	15.16,10.5
D C N VI R VI	2	14.62,11.29
D C N VI R VP	2	10.13,15.9
D C N VP D N	4	15.15,14.63, 9.27,5.36
D D N C N D	2	3.17,1.19
D N A C D N	2	13.32,12.16
D N A C VI D	2	11.32,12.8
D N A C VI P	2	6.55,1.5
D N A D A C	2	8.38,14.58
D N A D N VI	2	13.24,14.4
D N A P R C	2	14.36,9.8
D N A R VI VI	2	10.39,10.39
D N A VN C VN	2	3.4,8.31
D N B VI D N	3	4.15,13.24, 5.27
D N C A D N	3	4.1,2.13,7.1
D N C A VI C	4	4.19,14.27, 5.20,2.16
D N C A VP VI	2	14.16,6.2
D N C A@B VI R	2	3.11,1.19
D N C B D N	3	13.28,13.32, 15.11

Syntax	N	References
DNCBNA	2	8.2,6.35
DNCCDN	2	9.50,9.45
DNCCVIP	2	7.15,10.52
DNCCVSR	2	9.42,13.10
DNCDAC	2	14.53,11.27
DNCDNC	11	11.27,14.43, 9.2,14.33, 5.40,1.10, 12.13,11.18, 10.33,9.2, 8.31
DNCDND	2	12.24,4.19
DNCDNN	3	7.11,8.15, 12.35
DNCDNP	3	7.5,14.53, 14.33
DNCDNR	3	8.27,2.15, 7.9
DNCDNVI	8	14.14,2.22, 14.27,13.31, 4.41,6.28, 1.13,2.23
DNCDNVN	2	5.4,7.27
DNCDNVP	3	7.30,1.39, 7.12
DNCNCN	2	3.18,5.37
DNCNDN	4	15.40,3.17, 1.19,15.47
DNCNPD	2	12.38,12.39
DNCPAD	2	12.33,12.33
DNCPDN	8	7.19,3.8, 10.1,5.14, 8.27,7.19, 5.5,4.21
DNCPNC	2	3.8,3.7
DNCVIAD	3	14.53,5.21, 14.12
DNCVIBN	2	10.1,3.1
DNCVICVI	5	4.20,9.18, 3.5,14.16, 5.15
DN[CVIDA]	3	3.15,4.4, 13.27
DNCVIDN	13	12.9,6.51, 4.29,4.7, 15.43,7.35, 1.15,4.15, 5.13,6.41, 6.27,4.39, 15.15
DNCVINA	3	4.39,4.32, 8.6
DNCVIND	2	14.2,14.35
DNCVIPD	4	5.29,1.13, 14.16,1.9
DNCVIPR	3	16.2,12.17, 4.1
DNCVIRA	3	6.30,1.31, 5.8
DNCVIRB	2	7.17,7.8
DNCVIRC	7	11.4,8.29, 1.34,7.26, 4.7,11.6, 10.33
DNCVIRD	10	14.26,1.31, 2.2,14.47, 11.7,15.20, 5.30,6.52, 12.26,1.24
DNCVIRN	3	10.33,15.16, 14.13
DNCVIRP	5	7.28,16.7, 9.2,15.46, 6.17
DNCVIVNR	3	6.48,5.16, 8.11
DNCVI++VPP	2	14.54,2.2
DNCVPDN	6	5.40,8.33, 6.21,9.4, 14.47,14.66
DNC+VPPD	5	14.54,14.62, 1.15,7.29, 8.23
DNCVPRP	3	7.32,14.2, 3.22
DNCVPRVI	3	14.49,12.2, 6.45
DNCVSCVS	2	15.32,4.26
DNDACN	2	12.40,15.40
DNDACP	2	7.3,15.26
DNDACVI	4	13.11,4.8, 6.7,8.38
DNDACVP	2	1.26,5.1
DNDAD@RC	2	15.12,15.2
DNDAVIC	2	15.9,1.27
DNDAVIN	2	12.36,7.21
DNDAVIR	2	5.7,8.23
DNDCNC	2	7.2,14.54
DNDCNVI	2	15.10,15.43
DNDCNVP	2	14.62,5.35
DNDNCA	3	12.34,9.47, 9.12
DNDNCD	10	3.28,9.2, 5.40,4.19, 11.15,8.15, 7.9,2.22, 7.27,4.19
DNDNCN	3	10.15,6.3, 4.26
DNDNCP	2	4.30,10.1
DNDNCVI	8	5.38,12.17, 7.8,14.26, 14.47,3.17, 7.28,14.54
DNDNCVP	6	1.14,14.66, 15.45,12.2, 16.3,14.25
DNDNDA	2	14.61,7.21
DNDNDC	3	15.46,15.43, 14.62
DNDNDN	4	3.28,6.3, 7.21,7.13
DNDNPA	3	7.31,14.62, 9.9
DNDNPD	3	13.3,14.25, 14.41
DNDNPN	2	2.26,11.30
DNDNQVI	2	1.2,10.14
DNDNRC	3	2.8,7.35, 5.29
DNDNRVI	3	2.5,7.6,3.5
DNDNVIA	3	2.26,11.1, 14.21
DNDNVIC	2	13.35,12.9
DNDNVID	5	2.18,10.23, 10.33,3.22, 7.8
DNDNVIP	2	15.38,9.31

DNDNVIR	2	8.38,5.41
DNDNVIVI	2	9.24,12.14
DNDNVPC	2	13.14,2.16
DNDNVPP	2	9.1,13.26
DNDPDN	3	4.31,6.11, 13.25
DND@AVPPA	2	14.24,15.39
DND@RCVIR	4	7.5,11.5, 12.16,5.33
DNNCDN	4	2.18,12.26, 12.26,2.18
DNNCVID	2	8.10,14.32
DNNCVIP	2	5.37,8.15
DNNCVIR	2	7.31,15.19
DNNDNC	3	6.25,16.1, 8.27
DNNDNR	1	6.17
DNPADN	3	14.9,6.47. 7.31
DNPAVID	2	7.33,14.60
DNPDAVI	2	1.20,13.3
DNPDNA	2	14.25,13.24
DNPDNB	2	5.13,5.21
DNPDNC	6	6.26,2.27, 14.53,6.30, 11.7,4.26
DNPDND	4	9.43,5.1, 14.41,16.3
DNPDNP	2	5.13,4.1
DNPDNR	5	8.25,3.7, 8.10,8.34, 14.14
DNPDNVI	3	2.27,4.1, 7.28
DNPDN+VP	2	4.38,1.14
DNQVIDN	3	2.19,14.41, 1.2
DNRA+[C]Q	2	3.34,8.37
DNRANVI	2	9.21,12.19
DNRBVIC	2	9.48,5.23
DNRCAN	2	7.2,2.15
DNRCBVI	2	6.4,2.8
DNRCDN	12	6.21,16.7, 10.7,10.19, 3.34,3.32, 3.31,3.32, 7.10,3.33, 13.34,13.24
DNRCPA	3	12.30,12.30, 12.30
DNRCVIB	2	7.35,11.25
DNRCVIC	3	2.11,6.14, 8.25
DNRCVID	3	6.6,5.29,1.5
DNRCVIP	3	9.42,11.14, 11.7
DNRCVIR	11	14.46,5.22, 9.31,15.20, 6.1,11.17, 15.21,6.29, 7.26,14.13, 11.1
DNRCVPD	4	3.5,14.59, 13.34,6.28
DNRC+VPN	3	1.6,6.1, 14.22
DNRCVPR	2	12.44,5.17
DNRCVPVI	3	6.23,7.33, 6.27
DNRCVSC	3	11.23,8.6, 5.23
DNRDCN	3	10.24,7.25, 10.37
DNRDNC	3	7.17,7.29, 12.19
DNRPAD	2	1.39,12.30
DNRPDN	5	7.5,8.38, 8.27,14.8, 7.33
DNRPNR	2	1.2,6.11
DNRVIA@BB	2	14.63,5.35
DNRVICA	2	2.15,6.35
DNRVICVI	3	6.29,5.19, 1.41
DNRVIDN	5	15.2,1.11, 3.5,7.30, 5.31
DNRVIPD	4	1.12,11.8, 3.7,8.10
DNRVIRC	3	8.34,10.52, 9.27
DNRVIRQ	2	8.23,12.43
DNR+VPDN	2	15.26,8.23
DNRVSRVM	2	9.47,9.45
DNVIADN	2	14.66,11.1
DNVIARVI	3	5.30,6.16, 10.51
DNVIBVIC	2	11.33,15.47
DNVICBD	2	2.27,13.28
DNVICBVI	2	11.15,13.25
DNVICDN	2	13.24,2.22
DNVICPD	3	4.6,3.7, 14.27
DNVICVID	2	12.9,6.41
DNVICVIP	3	6.5,1.21, 14.21
DNVICVIR	3	4.1,7.34, 10.14
DNVIDCN	2	13.31,10.23
DNVIDNC	2	10.33,3.22
DNVIDND	4	4.11,7.8, 14.47,15.45
DNVIDNR	2	10.23,8.27
DNVIPDN	8	12.22,5.3, 4.37,7.28, 14.55,11.18, 13.25,16.2
DNVIPRC	2	3.26,2.13
DNVIPRVP	2	9.10,6.48
DNVIRCVI	4	4.41,4.36, 15.41,14.61
DNVIRCVS	2	8.38,3.2
DNVIRDN	3	6.28,7.17, 14.3
DNVIVPVIC	2	6.25,10.22
DNVMDNC	2	13.28,3.5
DNVND@RCVI	2	7.27,8.27
DN+VPCBVI	2	14.40,13.14
DNVPCDN	5	9.24,4.18, 13.25,5.35, 6.15
DNVPCVIP	2	2.16,1.39
DNVPDNC	2	1.19,16.2
DNVPDND	2	1.14,7.12
DNVPPDN	6	5.27,7.30, 1.33,2.14, 10.23,1.21

Code	Freq	References
DN VP PNC	4	9.1,10.32, 7.1,11.20
DN VP VIDN	2	5.36,6.17
DN VP VIPD	2	15.43,1.29
DN VS PDN	2	12.2,7.26
D@R CB VI VM R	2	15.13,15.14
D@R C VIC VIR	2	12.16,7.28
N ACCB VI	2	2.22,2.21
N AC DAN	2	15.33,9.45
N AC VIDN	3	11.32,12.8, 6.14
N AC VIPD	2	6.55,15.40
N AC VIPR	2	4.41,1.5
N AC VIR A@B	2	4.39,5.42
N AC VIR C	2	5.24,15.25
N AC VIR P	2	4.2,2.22
N ADACP	2	14.58,14.43
N APDNR	3	9.42,1.6,6.2
N APNAC	2	2.22,2.22
N A VIC VID	2	14.52,3.30
N A VIDND	2	9.2,11.29
N B VIC VIR	2	12.31,2.18
N B VIC VP VI	2	2.4,8.16
N B VIDNR	2	13.24,5.27
N CADN VI	2	14.55,2.13
N CADN VP	3	6.15,15.1, 7.1
N CA VIC VP	2	5.20,2.16
N CA@B DN VP	2	1.21,5.29
N CA@B VIR C	2	3.11,1.19
N CA@B VP DN	2	2.7,1.17
N CC VIPN	2	7.15,10.52
N CDAN VP	2	6.41,9.43
N CDNCD	5	11.27,14.43, 9.2,14.33, 5.40
N CDNC VI	3	11.18,10.33, 9.2
N CDNDN	5	12.24,4.19, 2.26,2.18, 10.33
N C[D]NNC	2	12.26,8.15
N CDN VIC	2	2.22,14.27
N CDN VIR	5	4.41,6.28, 1.13,2.23, 13.1
N CDN VPC	3	7.30,2.18, 1.39
N CDPRC	2	5.40,1.36
N CNAC VI	2	15.40,1.6
N CNCDN	2	12.33,4.27
N CNCNC	16	3.17,10.29, 3.18,10.30, 10.29,3.18, 10.30,10.29, 6.3,7.4,3.18, 10.30,10.29, 13.3,6.3,7.4
N CNCND	3	3.18,3.18, 5.37
N CNCNP	2	10.30,10.29
N CNDDN	3	3.18,3.16, 16.1
N CNDND	2	15.40,3.17
N CNDNN	3	5.37,1.16, 10.35
N CNPDN	6	4.17,14.43, 12.38,5.5, 11.1,12.39
N CNPNC	2	1.29,10.30
N CPADN	2	12.33,12.33
N CPDNC	6	3.8,7.19,3.8, 10.1,6.43, 5.14
N CPDN VI	3	8.27,7.19, 5.5
N CPDN VS	2	4.21,12.2
N CPNCP	2	3.7,6.56
N C VIADN	4	14.53,15.16, 5.21,14.12
N C VIC VID	2	9.18,3.5
N C VIC VIR	2	14.16,5.15
N C VIC VPR	2	1.42,6.53
N [C VIDA] C	2	3.15,4.4
N C VIDNC	6	6.51,14.1, 11.17,4.29, 4.7,8.10
N C VIDND	3	15.43,7.35, 1.15
N C VIDNP	2	6.29,5.13
N C VIDN [R]	3	6.41,6.27, 14.32
N C VINAC	4	4.40,4.39, 4.32,8.6
N C VINC VI	2	12.1,12.1
N C VIPDN	6	5.29,1.13, 14.16,5.37, 1.1,1.9
N C VIPRA	2	1.4,16.2
N C VIPRC	3	8.15,6.34, 12.17
N C VIRAC	3	7.31,8.22, 1.31
N C VIRCA	2	11.4,8.29
N C VIRCB	2	1.34,9.38
N C VIRC VI	3	11.6,10.33, 13.12
N C VIRC VP	2	15.19,9.31
N C VIRDN	15	1.16,14.26, 7.4,6.28, 1.31,10.33, 2.2,14.47, 11.7,15.20, 15.1,5.30, 6.52,12.26, 1.24
N C VIRNC	3	12.1,10.33, 15.16
N C VIRPN	3	9.2,15.46, 6.17
N C VIRQD	2	3.32,3.1
N C VPDNP	2	5.5,8.33
N C VPDNR	2	6.21,12.42
N C VPDN VI	3	9.4,14.47, 11.20
N C+VP PDN	6	14.54,14.62, 1.15,7.29, 8.23,12.40
N C VPRDN	2	10.50,10.41
N C VPRPN	3	10.46,14.2, 3.22
N C VPR VIP	2	5.22,6.45
N C VSDNR	2	15.21,12.19
N DAC VIN	2	13.11,4.8
N DAC VIR	3	6.7,15.18, 8.38
N DCNCA	2	7.2,14.54
N DCN VPD	2	14.62,5.35

Code	No.	References	Code	No.	References
NDDNCN	4	3.18,3.17, 1.19,16.1	NPNCVIR	2	8.4,13.12
NDNCAN	2	8.28,9.47	NPNVICP	2	2.1,11.30
NDNCDN	10	3.28,9.2, 5.40,4.19, 11.15,7.11, 8.15,7.9, 2.22,7.27	NPRVSBVI	2	3.25,3.24
			NQVIDND	2	2.19,14.41
			NQVIRCVI	2	4.38,8.12
			NRA+[C]QVS	2	3.34,8.37
NDNCND	3	16.1,15.40, 15.47	NRCDNC	3	6.21,16.7, 10.7
NDNCNN	2	3.18,6.3	NRCDNR	6	3.34,3.32, 3.31,3.32, 7.10,3.33
NDN[C]PD	2	10.1,8.27			
NDNCVIP	2	1.9,12.17	NRCDNVI	2	13.34,13.24
NDNCVIR	6	7.8,7.26, 14.26,14.47, 3.17,7.28	NRCPAD	4	13.9,12.30, 12.30,12.30
			NRCVIDN	3	6.6,5.29,1.5
			NRCVIRC	2	9.31,15.20
NDNCVPR	2	14.2,12.2	NRCVIRN	2	11.17,5.9
NDNCVPVI	2	16.3,14.25	NRCVIRP	3	15.21,1.8, 6.29
NDNDAC	2	15.40,6.7			
NDNDAVI	2	7.21,5.7	NRCVIRVM	3	7.26,14.13, 11.1
NDNDCN	3	15.46,15.43, 14.62	NRCVPDN	4	3.5,14.59, 13.34,6.28
NDNDNC	3	3.28,6.3, 3.17			
			NRCVPRP	2	12.44,5.17
NDNNCN	2	15.21,3.16	NRCVPVID	2	6.23,7.33
NDNNDN	2	6.25,6.17	NRDCNVI	2	7.25,10.37
NDNPDN	2	14.25,14.41	NRPADN	2	1.39,12.30
NDNRCVI	2	7.35,5.29	NRPDND	2	7.5,8.38
NDNRPA	2	12.30,9.28	NRVICVIR	2	5.19,1.41
NDNRVID	3	2.5,7.6,3.5	NRVIDNVP	2	7.30,5.31
NDNVICVI	2	12.9,14.21	NRVIPDN	4	11.8,3.7,8.3, 8.10
NDNVIDC	2	2.18,10.23			
NDNVIDN	3	10.33,3.22, 7.8	NRVIRVMP	2	5.34,9.25
			NRVSRVMR	2	9.47,9.45
NDNVPPN	2	9.1,13.26	NVIACVIA	2	6.41,12.11
NNCDND	2	2.26,2.18	NVICAVIC	2	12.32,12.14
NNC[D]NN	2	12.26,12.26	NVICBDN	2	2.27,13.28
NNCNCN	3	3.17,6.3,7.4	NVICVIAC	2	2.1,6.49
NNCPDN	2	6.43,12.2	NVICVIDN	3	12.9,6.41, 14.72
NNCVIDN	3	11.17,8.10, 14.32			
			NVICVINC	2	12.1,15.1
NNCVIPD	2	5.37,1.1	NVICVIPD	2	6.5,1.21
NNCVIPR	2	1.4,8.15	NVICVIPR	2	1.45,14.21
NNCVIRC	2	15.19,9.31	NVICVIRVM	2	7.34,10.14
NNNNNN	4	7.22,7.21, 7.21,7.21	NVICVPDN	3	8.32,11.32, 15.7
NNPNCN	2	13.12,9.41	NVIDNDN	6	4.11,2.28, 7.8,14.47, 15.45,2.10
NNVMRCVI	2	7.10,10.47			
NPACVIR	2	14.51,6.32			
NPAVIDN	2	7.33,14.60	NVIDNNA	2	15.34,9.5
NPDNAD	2	8.38,13.24	NVIDNRB	2	10.23,2.16
NPDNCA	2	12.41,3.29	NVIPDNC	3	5.3,4.37, 10.46
NPDNCN	3	12.38,12.39, 2.27			
			NVIPDND	2	12.36,7.28
NPDNCVI	4	14.53,6.30, 11.7,12.26	NVIPDNR	3	11.18,10.24, 1.11
NPDNDA	3	9.43,5.1, 14.41	NVI+PDN+VP	2	13.25,16.2
			NVIPNPD	2	11.11,7.31
NPDNDN	5	16.3,15.46, 7.31,11.1, 10.25	NVIPRCVI	3	3.26,4.36, 2.13
			NVIQVIRC	2	14.18,9.41
NPDNPD	3	1.20,5.13, 4.1	NVIRACVI	2	15.14,8.35
			NVIRA@BRVI	2	10.18,12.15
NPDNRC	2	9.39,8.25	NVIRCVIP	2	4.41,4.36
NPDNRVI	3	3.7,8.10, 8.34	NVIRCVIR	3	15.41,14.61, 6.19
NPDNVIC	3	2.27,3.7,4.1	NVIRDNR	2	6.28,7.17
NPNCNP	3	14.43,11.1, 13.8	NVIRDNVI+	2	2.5,14.3
			NVIRPDN	2	15.16,10.5

Syntax	Count	References
N VI VN D N R	2	6.27,10.27
N VP C D N D	2	4.18,13.25
N VP D N D N	3	1.14,7.12, 7.7
N VP D N R VI	2	14.63,9.27
N VP P D N C	5	7.30,11.8, 1.33,1.13, 2.14
N VP P D N D	2	3.5,10.23
N VP P D N VI	3	1.16,6.41, 1.21
N VP P N C VP	2	7.1,11.20
N VP VI C N VI	2	3.22,6.49
N VP VI D N C	2	4.19,6.17
N VP VI P D N	2	15.43,1.29
N VP VN P D N	4	9.47,4.1, 9.45,9.43
N VS P D N R	2	7.26,9.37
P A C A P A	2	15.27,10.37
P A D N C D	2	1.39,12.33
P A D N C P	2	12.33,12.33
P A D N N C	2	2.18,7.31
P A D N R C	3	12.30,12.30, 12.30
P A N A VI C	2	11.28,11.33
P A N VI C VI	3	14.72,1.45, 10.34
P B@A VI C VI R	2	5.6,8.3
P D A A N N	2	8.19,8.20
P D A C D N	3	8.31,11.15, 2.23
P D A C VI+ P	2	1.12,11.10
P D N B D N	2	10.10,9.47
P D N B VI D	2	4.15,5.27
P D N C A D	2	4.1,2.13
P D N C A N	2	3.7,4.36
P D N C A VI	2	3.29,2.16
P D N C B N	2	8.2,5.3
P D N C B VS	3	10.29,11.23, 3.9
P D N C C VS	3	4.28,9.42, 4.31
P D N C D N	3	14.43,1.13, 7.30
P D N C D@R&A VP	3	6.26,11.8, 5.13
P D N C N P	2	12.38,12.39
P D N [C N VI]	2	14.68,2.27
P D N C P D	5	7.19,3.8, 5.14,7.19, 5.5
P D N C P N	2	3.8,3.7
P D N C VI A	3	1.33,14.53, 5.21
P D N C VI B	2	10.1,3.1
P D N C VI C	2	14.35,14.16
P D N C VI D	6	4.4,6.51,4.7, 15.43,5.13, 6.27
P D N C VI P	2	1.13,4.1
P D N C VI R	10	6.30,5.8, 11.4,2.2, 11.7,6.52, 12.26,14.13, 2.14,8.14
P D N C VI VN	3	5.14,6.48, 5.16
P D N C +VP P	3	14.54,1.15, 8.23
P D N C VP R	2	10.50,6.47
P D N C VS C	2	15.32,4.26
P D N D A C	5	7.5,9.43,4.8, 8.38,5.1
P D N D A VP	2	4.20,3.27
P D N D C N	2	14.54,14.28
P D N D N C	12	12.34,9.47, 9.12,8.15, 10.1,5.38, 14.26,7.28, 14.54,12.2, 16.3,14.25
P D N D N D	3	15.46,14.62, 7.21
P D N D N P	4	7.31,13.3, 14.25,2.26
P D N D N R	2	8.38,3.5
P D N D N VI	4	11.1,10.23, 3.22,1.16
P D N D N VN	3	10.24,10.25, 10.25
P D N N C VP	2	6.8,7.24
P D N N P D	2	12.26,14.55
P D N N VI P	2	7.31,3.6
P D N P D N	5	5.13,9.43, 8.10,4.1, 4.38
P D N R C VI	8	9.39,2.11, 8.25,6.6, 9.42,5.22, 6.1,7.26
P D N R C +VP	3	1.6,5.17, 7.33
P D N R D C	3	10.24,7.25, 10.37
P D N R VI D	2	1.11,7.30
P D N R VI P	2	3.7,8.10
P D N R VI R	2	8.34,10.5
P D N VI C B	3	2.27,5.10, 13.25
P D N VI C VI	4	6.41,1.21, 4.1,7.34
P D N VI D N	3	2.4,15.45, 8.27
P D N VI R C	2	9.9,15.41
P D N VI VP C	2	9.20,5.5
P D N VI VP VI	2	6.25,10.22
P D N VP A VI	2	7.20,4.18
P D N +VP C D	2	13.25,5.35
P D N VP D N	3	1.19,16.2, 1.14
P D N VP P D	1	5.27
P D N VP P R	1	7.15
P N A C C B	2	2.22,2.21
P N A C VI R	2	4.2,2.22
P N C N P D	2	14.43,11.1
P N C P D N	3	3.8,10.30, 9.33
P N C VI R A	2	8.22,8.4
P N D N N D	2	6.25,6.17
P N P D A C	2	11.11,11.11
P N P D N VI	3	6.56,7.17, 6.25
P N VI C P N	3	13.9,2.1, 11.30
P R C A D N	2	14.56,11.7
P R C VI B VI	2	4.25,3.26
P R C VI P D	3	9.34,5.21, 2.25

Code		References	Code		References
PRCVIRC	2	1.36,2.13	RDNCVI[C]	2	7.6,1.42
PRCVPRD	2	9.20,1.25	RDNCVID	2	7.35,15.15
PRCVPRP	2	9.8,10.16	RDNCVIR	4	1.31,7.17,
PRDNCD	2	11.27,5.4			10.33,15.20
PRDNCVI	3	7.6,1.42,	RDNPDN	2	16.3,2.27
		14.35	RDNRCVI	3	11.25,11.7,
PRPDNC	3	14.20,6.51,			15.20
		8.14	RDNRCVP	2	6.28,6.1
QDNRCD	2	3.34,3.32	RDNRVID	2	15.2,5.31
QVIDNDN	2	2.19,14.41	RDNVI+CA	2	2.5,14.3
QVIDNRP	2	1.2,8.35	RD@RCVIRA	2	14.19,10.35
QVIRCBB	3	14.25,13.30,	RD@RCVPDN	2	14.51,10.49
		9.41	RPADNA	3	14.4,13.11,
QVSDNDN	2	3.35,9.1			4.35
RAVIDNR	4	14.24,7.25,	RPADNC	2	1.39,12.33
		1.2,14.34	RPANAVI	3	11.28,11.33,
RCBVPVIP	2	9.50,3.31			11.29
RCCVSVIR	2	14.7,1.40	RPDNCP	2	7.19,5.12
RCDNDN	2	9.31,2.15	RPDNCVI	3	6.51,6.27,
RCDNRC	4	3.31,3.32,			8.14
		7.10,3.33	RPDNDA	2	7.5,8.38
RCNBVIC	2	4.7,8.16	RPDNRC	2	2.15,7.33
RCPADN	4	13.9,12.30,	RPDNVIR	2	9.9,5.18
		12.30,12.30	RPNACVI	2	1.8,4.2
RCVICVID	2	9.18,5.40	RVICAVID	2	12.7,6.35
RCVIDNC	4	14.16,5.29,	RVICVIDN	2	14.62,6.29
		14.15,11.6	RVICVIPR	2	12.12,6.56
RCVIDND	2	8.31,15.25	RVICVIRC	3	5.19,5.33,
RCVIDNR	3	1.27,3.8,			16.7
		15.24	RVIDNCVI	3	8.29,5.30,
RCVIPDN	5	9.34,4.36,			15.46
		9.42,5.21,	RVIDNCVP	2	6.45,12.7
		2.25	RVIDNDN	2	3.11,14.61
RCVIPNC	3	1.20,3.19,	RVID@RCBVI	2	14.69,14.30
		11.14	RVIPDNC	3	3.7,8.3,8.1
RCVIPRC	3	11.7,3.13,	RVIVICDN	2	10.39,6.17
		6.3	RVIVMCA@BVI	2	5.41,1.41
RCVIRAC	3	14.46,4.24,	RVMRAVIR	2	9.43,9.45
		10.47	RVPCVIDN	2	14.37,12.6
RCVIRAD	2	5.33,9.28	RVPVIPDN	2	10.50,5.35
RCVIRCA	2	15.41,1.37	RVSRD@RCVI	2	10.35,10.36
RCVIRCVI	3	10.34,1.36,	RVSRVMRA	2	9.47,9.45
		10.34	VIAACAA	2	4.8,4.20
RCVIRDN	3	6.3,14.29,	VIACBVIP	2	9.12,12.3
		6.1	VIACVICVI	2	6.42,9.6
RCVIRNN	2	11.17,5.9	VIADNRC	3	14.13,11.1,
RCVIRPD	2	12.8,15.21			12.44
RCVIRPN	2	1.8,6.29	VIAVINCN	2	10.29,2.25
RCVIRVMP	3	14.13,11.1,	VIBCVIPD	2	6.51,6.1
		5.19	VIBCVIRC	2	7.35,6.33
RCVIRVNC	2	6.19,12.11	VIBPDNC	3	2.13,14.68,
RCVPDNR	4	13.34,1.20,			3.1
		8.11,6.28	VICAVICB	2	12.32,12.14
RCVPDNVI	3	14.18,15.19,	VICAVIDN	2	12.7,6.35
		10.48	VICAVID@R&AP	2	4.19,4.17
RCVPPDN	3	7.33,9.13,	VICAVIPD	2	4.6,4.7
		9.20	VICBDNVI	2	13.28,13.33
RCVPRDN	2	9.20,1.25	VICBPDN	2	14.2,5.11
RCVPRPD	3	12.44,9.8,	VICBVIAP	2	3.26,12.32
		5.17	VICDNAR	3	6.48,10.39,
RCVPVIDN	2	6.23,7.33			10.38
RCVSRCVI	2	3.2,15.20	VICDNBVI	2	9.48,13.24
RDCNBVP	2	15.11,10.24	VICDNDN	2	6.18,15.37
RDCNVIR	4	15.13,10.37,	VICNACVI	2	5.42,15.25
		9.22,15.8	VICVIACB	2	12.3,2.1
RDNCAVI	2	14.27,5.20	VICVIBPD	2	2.12,14.68
RDNCBVI	2	6.4,2.20	VICVIDNB	2	7.23,5.39
RDNCDN	4	11.27,7.5,	VICVIDNC	4	9.18,12.9,
		6.28,5.4			6.41,5.40

VIC VI DND	2	14.72,14.62	VI DNRC VS	2	8.6,6.41
VIC VI DNR	5	3.30,9.18,	VI DNRDA	2	1.11,9.7
		6.29,3.5,8.6	VI DNRN VP	2	8.17,1.2
VIC VINC VI	2	12.1,15.1	VI DNRPD	2	7.5,7.33
VIC VI PDN	5	5.14,12.1,	VI DNRPN	3	6.28,1.2,
		6.31,6.5,			14.34
		1.21	VI DNRPR	2	8.35,9.17
VIC VIRC VI	6	5.19,14.16,	VI D@RCB VIC	2	14.69,14.30
		1.27,15.23,	VI NAPRC	2	9.14,5.21
		5.33,14.22	VIN C VINC	2	12.1,12.1
VIC VIRC VP	2	5.6,16.7	VI NPDNC	2	12.41,3.29
VIC VIRDN	4	15.2,12.31,	VI NPDND	2	15.46,10.25
		2.18,8.3	VI PDAAN	2	8.19,1.13
VIC VIRNC	3	1.35,10.34,	VI PDNCA	3	3.7,4.36,8.3
		10.12	VI PDNCB	4	8.2,5.3,9.30,
VIC VIRPN	2	4.1,11.33			4.37
VIC VPDN VI	5	11.32,2.16,	VI PDNC VI	10	5.21,3.13,
		15.44,11.21,			14.35,14.16,
		15.7			4.4,4.7,
VIC VPRPN	2	9.27,3.4			15.43,5.13,
VIC VP VIDN	2	2.4,4.38			5.15,6.52
VID AC VIR	4	9.35,4.4,	VI PDNC VP	3	11.19,10.46,
		14.41,6.7			10.50
VID CNRB	2	13.31,7.6	VI PDNDA	2	4.8,12.36
VID NA VNC	2	3.25,3.4	VI PDNDN	10	12.34,9.12,
VID NB VIC	2	5.39,2.4			10.1,5.38,
VID NCA VI	2	4.19,12.29			14.26,7.28,
VID NCDN	8	14.1,14.33,			12.2,2.26,
		11.18,10.33,			1.2,10.24
		12.35,8.27,	VI PDNNC	3	1.29,8.10,
		2.15,14.27			7.24
VID NC VIC	2	4.20,9.18	VI PDNNP	2	12.26,14.55
VID NC VID	7	13.27,12.9,	VI PDNRC	4	11.18,6.6,
		4.29,1.15,			5.22,6.1
		4.15,6.41,	VI PDNRD	3	10.24,7.25,
		4.39			7.29
VID NC VIN	2	4.39,8.6	VI PDNR VI+	2	1.22,1.11
VID NC VIP	2	5.29,14.16	VI+ PDN+VP C	2	13.25,5.35
VID NC VIR	7	8.29,4.7,	VI PNPDA	2	11.11,11.11
		11.6,5.30,	VI PNPDN	2	7.31,7.17
		15.46,6.17,	VI PRCAD	2	14.56,11.7
		9.32	VI PRC VIA	2	3.13,1.26
VID NC VPR	2	3.22,6.45	VI PRC VIB	2	4.25,3.26
VI]DNDAD@R	2	15.12,15.2	VI PRC VIN	2	4.36,12.17
VID NDCN	2	7.2,5.35	VI PRC VIP	2	9.34,1.20
VID NDNA	2	4.11,8.31	VI PRC VIR	5	9.16,2.13,
VID NDNC	9	3.11,9.2,			6.3,5.24,
		5.40,7.9,			6.50
		2.22,4.26,	VI PRC VPP	2	9.13,11.13
		7.8,14.47,	VI PRDNC	3	7.1,11.27,
		15.45			1.42
VID NDND	4	14.61,15.43,	VI PRPDN	3	6.51,8.14,
		3.28,6.3			1.5
VID NDNP	4	14.62,2.19,	VIQ VIRCA	2	14.18,3.27
		14.41,11.29	VIR AA VIC	2	6.30,11.24
VID NDNR	3	7.35,5.29,	VI[R]AC VIR	2	8.20,8.22
		15.26	VIR APDN	2	9.17,9.33
VID NDN VM	2	1.15,6.22	VIR A VIDN	2	14.24,14.34
VID ND@RC VI	2	7.5,14.67	VIR B VIA VI	2	2.25,10.38
VID NPDN	6	14.53,6.30,	VIR B VIDN	2	4.13,7.9
		11.7,5.13,	VIR CA VIP	2	4.4,8.34
		8.25,1.14	VIR CA VSP	2	6.8,8.30
VID NRBP	2	2.16,6.3	VIR CBB VS	2	13.30,9.41
VID NRCD	4	6.21,3.31,	VIR CBN VI	2	9.13,2.17
		3.33,13.24	VIR CDND	2	9.31,2.15
VID NRC VI	4	6.14,11.14,	VIR C VIC VI	2	9.18,5.19
		14.46,6.29	VIR C VIC VP	2	9.27,4.38
VID NRC VP	4	3.5,14.59,	VIR C VIDN	7	8.12,14.16,
		14.22,7.33			11.6,15.25,

Entry		References
		11.6,1.27, 15.24
VIRCVIPD	2	4.41,4.36
VIRCVIPR	2	14.23,3.13
VIRCVIRA+	4	4.24,5.33, 10.21,9.15
VIRCVIRC	4	15.41,1.37, 10.34,10.34
VIRCVIRVM	2	1.43,5.19
VIRCVPDN	3	5.13,1.20, 15.19
VIRCVPNA	2	15.32,5.6
VIRCVSRC	2	3.2,15.20
VIRDCNVI	3	9.38,15.8, 14.5
VIRDNCA	2	14.27,5.20
VIRDNCD	2	7.5,6.28
VIRDNCVI	7	7.35,15.15, 1.31,10.33, 15.20,4.33, 2.2
VIRDNPD	2	16.3,2.27
VIRDNQVI	2	2.19,14.30
VIRDNRC	5	8.4,11.7, 15.20,6.28, 6.1
VIRDNRVI	2	15.2,5.31
VIRDNVI+C	2	2.5,14.3
VIRD@RCVPD	2	14.51,10.49
VIRNCVIR	2	10.33,15.17
VIRPADN	3	4.35,2.18, 7.29
VIRPANA	3	11.28,11.33, 11.29
VIRPDNA	2	12.8,15.16
VIRPDNC	4	10.52,7.19, 6.27,8.23
VIRPDNN	2	15.22,5.2
VIRPDNR	2	10.5,4.2
VIRPNAC	2	1.8,4.2
VIRPRCVP	2	9.20,1.30
VIRQVIRC	2	12.43,9.1
VIRRVIDN	2	8.29,14.61
VIRVICVIR	2	5.33,15.2
VIRVMPDN	3	14.13,11.2, 5.19
VIRVNCBVI	2	6.19,7.18
VIVIPRCVI	2	4.25,3.8
VIVMPRNC	2	8.33,9.50
VIVMRDCN	2	15.13,15.14
VIVNCBDN	2	2.26,13.7
VIVNPDNC	2	6.2,4.1
VIVNRD@RCVP	2	8.32,6.48
VMCVMPDN	2	11.23,1.15
VMDNRCD	3	16.7,10.19, 7.10
VMDNRCVM	3	2.9,2.11, 8.34
VMVMDNRC	2	16.7,2.11
VNACVNDN	2	1.45,2.12
VNCBDNC	2	5.37,2.26
VNCVICVIC	2	6.55,8.7
VNDNDNR	2	6.18,1.7
VNPDACD	2	8.31,2.23
VNPDNCA	2	4.1,6.2
VPCRVIDN	2	14.58,3.11
VPCVICVIR	2	14.68,2.18
VPCVIDNR	2	12.6,9.20
+VPC+VPPDN	2	2.6,6.52
VPDNCDN	3	1.10,12.24, 2.23
VPDNCVIR	2	1.31,3.1
VPDNCVPP	2	15.29,14.62
VPDNDAC	3	12.40,7.3, 15.26
VPDNDAVI	2	5.13,8.23
VPDNDNR	2	2.8,2.5
VPDNDNVI	3	7.8,5.41, 9.24
VPDN[PDN]	3	5.21,6.26, 8.34
VPDNRCVP	2	13.34,15.29
VPDNRVIC	2	6.29,1.41
VPDNRVIR	3	9.27,8.23, 12.43
VPDNVICVI	2	15.1,6.5
VPDNVIDN	3	14.47,9.5, 10.23
VPDNVIR[C]	5	2.17,15.19, 14.48,4.36, 1.18
VPPDNBVI	2	5.27,7.18
+VPPDNCVI	4	1.33,1.13, 2.14,6.48
VPPDNDN	4	14.62,3.5, 10.23,1.16
VPPDNVIC	4	1.16,6.41, 1.21,7.34
VPPDNVIN	2	9.14,16.5
VPPDNVIVP	3	9.20,1.10, 10.22
VPPRCAVI	2	4.15,10.26
VPPRPDN	2	14.20,15.31
VPRCVPDN	2	8.11,14.18
VPRDNVIR	2	12.15,10.42
VPRPDNA@B	2	5.2,6.54
VPRPDNVI	2	9.9,5.18
VPRVICVIP	2	5.14,12.12
VPRVIPDN	2	5.22,6.46
VPVICNVIC	2	3.22,6.49
VPVICVIDN	2	8.6,16.4
VPVIDNCVI	2	4.39,6.17
VPVIPDNC	3	9.30,15.43, 10.50
VPVIPDND	2	10.1,14.26
VPVIPDNN	2	1.29,7.24
VPVIRA@BVIC	2	8.17,5.39
VPVIRCVIR	2	9.15,12.8
VPVIRVPDN	2	1.31,15.29
VPVNPDNC	2	4.1,9.45
VPVSCBVSC	2	4.12,4.12
VSCVIDNC	2	14.32,8.6
VSDCNVIR	4	10.17,15.15, 11.28,10.13
VSDNDNC	2	10.15,4.30
VSDNDNVP	2	13.14,9.1
VSDNRCVS	2	10.11,5.23
VSPDNDN	3	12.2,14.25, 8.38
VSPDNRC	2	7.26,11.23
VSPRDNC	2	2.20,14.35
VSRCDAN	2	8.38,6.41
VSRD@RCVIR	2	10.35,10.36
VS@VMBVS@VM BVS@VMB	2	10.19,10.19

Key: Single underlining = considered redactional
        Broken underlining = possibly redactional
        // = unique syntax across major punctuation break

13.1 Καὶ ἐκπορευομένου αὐτοῦ ἐκ τοῦ ἱεροῦ λέγει αὐτῷ εἷς τῶν μαθητῶν αὐτοῦ,

Anderson
Brandenburger
Gill
Gnilka
Lambrecht
Pesch (1)
Pesch (2)
Pryke
Schweizer

Διδάσκαλε, ἴδε ποταποὶ λίθοι καὶ ποταπαὶ οἰκοδομαί. 2 καὶ ὁ Ἰησοῦς εἶπεν αὐτῷ,

An.
Br.
Gi.
Gn.
La.
P(1)
P(2)
Pr.
Sc.

Βλέπεις ταύτας τὰς μεγάλας οἰκοδομάς; οὐ μὴ ἀφεθῇ ὧδε λίθος ἐπὶ λίθον ὃς οὐ μὴ

An.
Br.
Gi.
Gn.
La.
P(1)
P(2)
Pr.
Sc.

καταλυθῇ. 3 Καὶ καθημένου αὐτοῦ εἰς τὸ Ὄρος τῶν Ἐλαιῶν κατέναντι τοῦ ἱεροῦ ἐπηρώτα

An.
Br.
Gi.
Gn.
La.
P(1)
P(2)
Pr.
Sc.

αὐτὸν κατ' ἰδίαν Πέτρος καὶ Ἰάκωβος καὶ Ἰωάννης καὶ Ἀνδρέας. 4 //Εἰπὸν ἡμῖν πότε

An.
Br.
Gi.
Gn.
La.
P(1)
P(2)
Pr.
Sc.

ταῦτα ἔσται, καὶ τί τὸ σημεῖον ὅταν μέλλῃ ταῦτα συντελεῖσθαι πάντα. 5 //ὁ δὲ Ἰησοῦς

An.
Br.
Gi.
Gn.
La.
P(1)
P(2)
Pr.
Sc.

ἤρξατο λέγειν αὐτοῖς, βλέπετε μή τις ὑμᾶς πλανήσῃ· 6 πολλοὶ ἐλεύσονται ἐπὶ τῷ ὀνόματί

An.
Br.
Gi.
Gn.
La.
P(1)
P(2)
Pryke
Sc.

μου λέγοντες ὅτι Ἐγώ εἰμι, καὶ πολλοὺς πλανήσουσιν. 7 ὅταν δὲ ἀκούσητε πολέμους καὶ

Anderson..
Brandenburger..
Gill...
Gnilka...
Lambrecht...
Pesch (1)..
Pesch (2)..
Pryke..
Schweizer...

ἀκοὰς πολέμων, μὴ θροεῖσθε· δεῖ γενέσθαι, ἀλλ' οὔπω τὸ τέλος. 8 ἐγερθήσεται γὰρ ἔθνος

An..
Br..
Gi..
Gn..
La..
P(1)..
P(2)..
Pr..
Sc..

ἐπ' ἔθνος καὶ βασιλεία ἐπὶ βασιλείαν, ἔσονται σεισμοὶ κατὰ τόπους, ἔσονται λιμοί·

An..
Br..
Gi..
Gn..
La..
P(1)..
P(2)..
Pr..
Sc..

ἀρχὴ ὠδίνων ταῦτα. 9 βλέπετε δὲ ὑμεῖς ἑαυτούς· παραδώσουσιν ὑμᾶς εἰς συνέδρια καὶ

An..
Br..
Gi..
Gn..
La..
P(1)..
P(2)..
Pr..
Sc..

εἰς συναγωγὰς δαρήσεσθε καὶ ἐπὶ ἡγεμόνων καὶ βασιλέων σταθήσεσθε ἕνεκεν ἐμοῦ εἰς

An..
Br..
Gi..
Gn..
La..
P(1)..
P(2)..
Pr..
Sc..

μαρτύριον αὐτοῖς. 10 καὶ εἰς πάντα τὰ ἔθνη πρῶτον δεῖ κηρυχθῆναι τὸ εὐαγγέλιον. 11 καὶ

An..
Br..
Gi..
Gn..
La..
P(1)..
P(2)..
Pr..
Sc..

ὅταν ἄγωσιν ὑμᾶς παραδιδόντες, μὴ προμεριμνᾶτε τί λαλήστε, ἀλλ' ὃ ἐὰν δοθῇ ὑμῖν ἐν

An..
Br..
Gi..
Gn..
La..
P(1)..
P(2)..
Pr..
Sc..

ἐκείνῃ τῇ ὥρᾳ τοῦτο λαλεῖτε, οὐ γάρ ἐστε ὑμεῖς οἱ λαλοῦντες ἀλλὰ τὸ πνεῦμα τὸ ἅγιον.

An..
Br..
Gi..
Gn..
La..
P(1)..
P(2)..
Pr..
Sc..

12 καὶ παραδώσει ἀδελφὸς ἀδελφὸν εἰς θάνατον καὶ πατὴρ τέκνον, καὶ ἐπαναστήσονται

Anderson..
Brandenburger..
Gill...
Gnilka..
Lambrecht...
Pesch (1)..
Pesch (2)..
Pryke..
Schweizer...

τέκνα ἐπὶ γονεῖς καὶ θανατώσουσιν αὐτούς· 13 καὶ ἔσεσθε μισούμενοι ὑπὸ πάντων διὰ τὸ

An...
Br..
Gi..
Gn...
La..
P(1)..
P(2)..
Pr..
Sc..

ὄνομά μου. // ὁ δὲ ὑπομείνας εἰς τέλος οὗτος σωθήσεται. 14 Ὅταν δὲ ἴδητε τὸ βδέλυγμα

An...
Br..
Gi..
Gn...
La..
P(1)..
P(2)..
Pr..
Sc..

τῆς ἐρημώσεως ἑστηκότα ὅπου οὐ δεῖ, ὁ ἀναγινώσκων νοείτω, τότε οἱ ἐν τῇ Ἰουδαίᾳ

An...
Br..
Gi..
Gn...
La..
P(1)..
P(2)..
Pr..
Sc..

φευγέτωσαν εἰς τὰ ὄρη, 15 ὁ δὲ ἐπὶ τοῦ δώματος μὴ καταβάτω μηδὲ εἰσελθάτω ἆραί τι ἐκ

An...
Br..
Gi..
Gn...
La..
P(1)..
P(2)..
Pr..
Sc..

τῆς οἰκίας αὐτοῦ, 16 καὶ ὁ εἰς τὸν ἀγρὸν μὴ ἐπιστρεψάτω εἰς τὰ ὀπίσω ἆραι τὸ ἱμάτιον

An...
Br..
Gi..
Gn...
La..
P(1)..
P(2)..
Pr..
Sc..

αὐτοῦ. 17 οὐαὶ δὲ ταῖς ἐν γαστρὶ ἐχούσαις καὶ ταῖς θηλαζούσαις ἐν ἐκείναις ταῖς

An...
Br..
Gi..
Gn...
La..
P(1)..
P(2)..
Pr..
Sc..

ἡμέραις. 18 προσεύχεσθε δὲ ἵνα μὴ γένηται χειμῶνος· 19 ἔσονται γὰρ αἱ ἡμέραι ἐκεῖναι

An...
Br..
Gi..
Gn...
La..
P(1)..
P(2)..
Pr..
Sc..

θλῖψις οἵα οὐ γέγονεν τοιαύτη ἀπ' ἀρχῆς κτίσεως ἣν ἔκτισεν ὁ θεὸς ἕως τοῦ νῦν καὶ οὐ

Anderson..
Brandenburger..
Gill..
Gnilka...
Lambrecht...
Pesch (1)...
Pesch (2)...
Pryke..
Schweizer..

μὴ γένηται. 20 καὶ εἰ μὴ ἐκολόβωσεν κύριος τὰς ἡμέρας, οὐκ ἂν ἐσώθη πᾶσα σάρξ. ἀλλὰ

An..
Br...
Gil..
Gn..
La...
P(1)..
P(2)..
Pr...
Sc...

διὰ τοὺς ἐκλεκτοὺς οὓς ἐξελέξατο ἐκολόβωσεν τὰς ἡμέρας. 21 καὶ τότε ἐάν τις ὑμῖν εἴπῃ,

An..
Br...
Gi...
Gn..
La...
P(1)..
P(2)..
Pr...
Sc...

Ἴδε ὧδε ὁ Χριστός, Ἴδε ἐκεῖ, μὴ πιστεύετε· 22 ἐγερθήσονται γὰρ ψευδόχριστοι καὶ

An..
Br...
Gi...
Gn..
La...
P(1)..
P(2)..
Pr...
Sc...

ψευδοπροφῆται καὶ δώσουσιν σημεῖα καὶ τέρατα πρὸς τὸ ἀποπλανᾶν, εἰ δυνατόν, τοὺς

An..
Br...
Gi...
Gn..
La...
P(1)..
P(2)..
Pr...
Sc...

ἐκλεκτούς. 23 ὑμεῖς δὲ βλέπετε προείρηκα ὑμῖν πάντα. 24 Ἀλλὰ ἐν ἐκείναις ταῖς ἡμέραις

An..
Br...
Gi...
Gn..
La...
P(1)..
P(2)..
Pr...
Sc...

μετὰ τὴν θλῖψιν ἐκείνην ὁ ἥλιος σκοτισθήσεται, καὶ ἡ σελήνη οὐ δώσει τὸ φέγγος αὐτῆς,

An..
Br...
Gi...
Gn..
La...
P(1)..
P(2)..
Pr...
Sc...

25 καὶ οἱ ἀστέρες ἔσονται ἐκ τοῦ οὐρανοῦ πίπτοντες, καὶ αἱ δυνάμεις αἱ ἐν τοῖς

An..
Br...
Gi...
Gn..
La...
P(1)..
P(2)..
Pr...
Sc...

οὐρανοῖς σαλευθήσονται. 26 καὶ τότε ὄψονται τὸν υἱὸν τοῦ ἀνθρώπου ἐρχόμενον ἐν

Anderson..
Brandenburger...
Gill...
Gnilka..
Lambrecht..
Pesch (1)...
Pesch (2)...
Pryke...
Schweizer...

νεφέλαις μετὰ δυνάμεως πολλῆς καὶ δόξης. 27 καὶ τότε ἀποστελεῖ τοὺς ἀγγέλους καὶ

An..
Br...
Gi...
Gn..
La...
P(1)..
P(2)..
Pr...
Sc...

ἐπισυνάξει τοὺς ἐκλεκτοὺς [αὐτοῦ] ἐκ τῶν τεσσάρων ἀνέμων ἀπ᾽ ἄκρου γῆς ἕως ἄκρου

An..
Br...
Gi...
Gn..
La...
P(1)..
P(2)..
Pr...
Sc...

οὐρανοῦ. 28 Ἀπὸ δὲ τῆς συκῆς μάθετε τὴν παραβολήν· ὅταν ἤδη ὁ κλάδος αὐτῆς ἁπαλὸς

An..
Br...
Gi...
Gn..
La...
P(1)..
P(2)..
Pr...
Sc...

γένηται καὶ ἐκφύῃ τὰ φύλλα, γινώσκετε ὅτι ἐγγὺς τὸ θέρος ἐστίν. 29 οὕτως καὶ ὑμεῖς,

An..
Br...
Gi...
Gn..
La...
P(1)..
P(2)..
Pr...
Sc...

ὅταν ἴδητε ταῦτα γινόμενα γινώσκετε ὅτι ἐγγύς ἐστιν ἐπὶ θύραις. 30 //ἀμὴν λέγω ὑμῖν

An..
Br...
Gi...
Gn..
La...
P(1)..
P(2)..
Pr...
Sc...

ὅτι οὐ μὴ παρέλθῃ ἡ γενεὰ αὕτη μέχρις οὗ ταῦτα πάντα γένηται. 31 ὁ οὐρανὸς καὶ ἡ γῆ

An..
Br...
Gi...
Gn..
La...
P(1)..
P(2)..
Pr...
Sc...

παρελεύσονται, οἱ δὲ λόγοι μου οὐ μὴ παρελεύσονται. 32 //Περὶ δὲ τῆς ἡμέρας ἐκείνης ἢ

An..
Br...
Gi...
Gn..
La...
P(1)..
P(2)..
Pr...
Sc...

316   *The Prophecy on the Mount*

τῆς ὥρας οὐδεὶς οἶδεν, οὐδὲ οἱ ἄγγελλοι ἐν οὐρανῷ οὐδὲ ὁ υἱός, εἰ μὴ ὁ πατήρ. 33 βλέπετε

Anderson
Brandenburger
Gill
Gnilka
Lambrecht
Pesch (1)
Pesch (2)
Pryke
Schweizer

ἀγρυπνεῖτε· οὐκ οἴδατε γὰρ πότε ὁ καιρός ἐστιν. 34 ὡς ἄνθρωπος ἀπόδημος ἀφεὶς τὴν

An.
Br.
Gi.
Gn.
La.
P(1).
P(2).
Pr.
Sc.

οἰκίαν αὐτοῦ καὶ δοὺς τοῖς δούλοις αὐτοῦ τὴν ἐξουσίαν, ἑκάστῳ τὸ ἔργον αὐτοῦ, καὶ τῷ

An.
Br.
Gi.
Gn.
La.
P(1).
P(2).
Pr.
Sc.

θυρωρῷ ἐνετείλατο ἵνα γρηγορῇ. 35 //γρηγορεῖτε οὖν, οὐκ οἴδατε γὰρ πότε ὁ κύριος τῆς

An.
Br.
Gil.
Gn.
La.
P(1).
P(2).
Pr.
Sc.

οἰκίας ἔρχεται, ἢ ὀψὲ ἢ μεσονύκτιον ἢ ἀλεκτοροφωνίας ἢ πρωῒ, 36 μὴ ἐλθὼν ἐξαίφνης

An.
Br.
Gi.
Gn.
La.
P(1).
P(2).
Pr.
Sc.

εὕρῃ ὑμᾶς καθεύδοντας. 37 //ὃ δὲ ὑμῖν λέγω, πᾶσιν λέγω, γρηγορεῖτε.//

An.
Br.
Gi.
Gn.
La.
P(1).
P(2).
Pr.
Sc.

Key: Single underlining = considered redactional
        Broken underlining = possibly redactional
        // = Unique syntax across major punctuation break

Appendix 4: Indicators of Redaction in Mk 13

Key: <u><u>Double underlining</u></u> = three or four indicators of redaction agree
         // = Unique syntax occurs across a major punctuation break (possible insertion)
         V = from Markan vocabulary lists; S = Markan syntax lists; N = Neirynck's *Duality;*
         P = Peabody's recurrent phraseology; R = Recurrent syntax (6-word sequences) [See chapter 5]

13.1 <u>Καὶ ἐκπορευομένου αὐτοῦ</u> ἐκ τοῦ ἱεροῦ λέγει αὐτῷ εἷς τῶν μαθητῶν αὐτοῦ,

Vocab...............
Syntax...............
Neirynck...............
Peabody...............
Rec. Syn...............

Διδάσκαλε, ἴδε ποταποὶ λίθοι καὶ ποταπαὶ οἰκοδομαί. 2 καὶ ὁ Ἰησοῦς εἶπεν αὐτῷ,

V...............
S...............
N...............
P...............
R...............

Βλέπεις ταύτας τὰς μεγάλας οἰκοδομάς; οὐ μὴ ἀφεθῇ ὧδε λίθος ἐπὶ λίθον ὃς οὐ μὴ

S...............
N...............
P...............
R...............

καταλυθῇ. 3 <u>Καὶ καθημένου αὐτοῦ εἰς τὸ Ὄρος τῶν Ἐλαιῶν κατέναντι τοῦ ἱεροῦ</u> ἐπηρώτα

V...............
S...............
N...............
P...............
R...............

<u>αὐτὸν κατ' ἰδίαν Πέτρος καὶ Ἰάκωβος καὶ Ἰωάννης καὶ Ἀνδρέας.</u> 4 //Εἰπὸν ἡμῖν πότε

V...............
S...............
N...............
P...............
R...............

ταῦτα ἔσται, καὶ τί τὸ σημεῖον ὅταν μέλλῃ ταῦτα συντελεῖσθαι πάντα. 5 //ὁ δὲ Ἰησοῦς

V...............
S...............
N...............
P...............
R...............

ἤρξατο λέγειν αὐτοῖς, βλέπετε μή τις ὑμᾶς πλανήσῃ· 6 <u>πολλοὶ ἐλεύσονται ἐπὶ τῷ ὀνόματί</u>

V...............
S...............
N...............
P...............
R...............

<u>μου</u> λέγοντες ὅτι Ἐγώ εἰμι, καὶ πολλοὺς πλανήσουσιν. 7 ὅταν δὲ ἀκούσητε πολέμους καὶ

V...............
S...............
N...............
P...............
R...............

ἀκοὰς πολέμων, μὴ θροεῖσθε· δεῖ γενέσθαι, <u>ἀλλ' οὔπω τὸ τέλος.</u> 8 ἐγερθήσεται γὰρ ἔθνος

V...............
S...............
N...............
P...............
R...............

ἐπ' ἔθνος καὶ βασιλεία ἐπὶ βασιλείαν, ἔσονται σεισμοὶ κατὰ τόπους, ἔσονται λιμοί·

S...............
N...............
P...............
R...............

ἀρχὴ ὠδίνων ταῦτα. 9 βλέπετε δὲ ὑμεῖς ἑαυτούς· παραδώσουσιν ὑμᾶς εἰς συνέδρια καὶ

V...............
S...............
N...............
P...............
R...............

εἰς συναγωγὰς δαρήσεσθε καὶ ἐπὶ ἡγεμόνων καὶ βασιλέων σταθήσεσθε ἕνεκεν ἐμοῦ εἰς

Vocab.......

Syntax.......

Neirynck.......

Peabody.......

Rec. Syn.......

μαρτύριον αὐτοῖς.10 καὶ εἰς πάντα τὰ ἔθνη πρῶτον δεῖ κηρυχθῆναι τὸ εὐαγγέλιον. 11 καὶ

V.......

S.......

N.......

P.......

R.......

ὅταν ἄγωσιν ὑμᾶς παραδιδόντες, μὴ προμεριμνᾶτε τί λαλήστε, ἀλλ' ὃ ἐὰν δοθῇ ὑμῖν ἐν

V.......

S.......

N.......

P.......

R.......

ἐκείνῃ τῇ ὥρᾳ τοῦτο λαλεῖτε, οὐ γάρ ἐστε ὑμεῖς οἱ λαλοῦντες ἀλλὰ τὸ πνεῦμα τὸ ἅγιον.

V.......

S.......

N.......

P.......

R.......

12 καὶ παραδώσει ἀδελφὸς ἀδελφὸν εἰς θάνατον καὶ πατὴρ τέκνον, καὶ ἐπαναστήσονται

V.......

S.......

N.......

P.......

R.......

τέκνα ἐπὶ γονεῖς καὶ θανατώσουσιν αὐτούς· 13 καὶ ἔσεσθε μισούμενοι ὑπὸ πάντων διὰ τὸ

V.......

S.......

N.......

P.......

R.......

ὄνομά μου. //ὁ δὲ ὑπομείνας εἰς τέλος οὗτος σωθήσεται.14 Ὅταν δὲ ἴδητε τὸ βδέλυγμα

V.......

S.......

N.......

P.......

R.......

τῆς ἐρημώσεως ἐστηκότα ὅπου οὐ δεῖ, ὁ ἀναγινώσκων νοείτω, τότε οἱ ἐν τῇ Ἰουδαίᾳ

V.......

S.......

N.......

P.......

R.......

φευγέτωσαν εἰς τὰ ὄρη, 15 ὁ δὲ ἐπὶ τοῦ δώματος μὴ καταβάτω μηδὲ εἰσελθάτω ἆραί τι ἐκ

V.......

S.......

N.......

P.......

R.......

τῆς οἰκίας αὐτοῦ, 16 καὶ ὁ εἰς τὸν ἀγρὸν μὴ ἐπιστρεψάτω εἰς τὰ ὀπίσω ἆραι τὸ ἱμάτιον

V.......

S.......

N.......

P.......

R.......

αὐτοῦ. 17 οὐαὶ δὲ ταῖς ἐν γαστρὶ ἐχούσαις καὶ ταῖς θηλαζούσαις ἐν ἐκείναις ταῖς

V.......

S.......

N.......

P.......

R.......

ἡμέραις. 18 προσεύχεσθε δὲ ἵνα μὴ γένηται χειμῶνος· 19 ἔσονται γὰρ αἱ ἡμέραι ἐκεῖναι

V.......

S.......

N.......

P.......

R.......

θλῖψις οἵα οὐ γέγονεν τοιαύτη ἀπ' ἀρχῆς κτίσεως ἣν ἔκτισεν ὁ θεὸς ἕως τοῦ νῦν καὶ οὐ

V.......

S.......

N.......

P.......

R.......

μὴ γένηται. 20 καὶ εἰ μὴ ἐκολόβωσεν κύριος τὰς ἡμέρας, οὐκ ἂν ἐσώθη πᾶσα σάρξ. ἀλλὰ
Vocab.......................
Syn.......................
Neir.......................
Peabody.......................
Rec. Syn.......................

διὰ <u>τοὺς ἐκλεκτοὺς οὓς ἐξελέξατο</u> ἐκολόβωσεν τὰς ἡμέρας. 21 καὶ τότε ἐάν τις ὑμῖν εἴπῃ,
V.......................
S.......................
N.......................
P.......................
R.......................

Ἴδε ὧδε ὁ Χριστός, Ἴδε ἐκεῖ, μὴ πιστεύετε· 22 ἐγερθήσονται γὰρ ψευδόχριστοι καὶ
V.......................
S.......................
N.......................
P.......................
R.......................

ψευδοπροφῆται καὶ δώσουσιν σημεῖα καὶ τέρατα πρὸς τὸ ἀποπλανᾶν, εἰ δυνατόν, τοὺς
V.......................
S.......................
N.......................
P.......................
R.......................

ἐκλεκτούς. 23 ὑμεῖς δὲ βλέπετε προείρηκα ὑμῖν πάντα.24 Ἀλλὰ <u>ἐν ἐκείναις ταῖς ἡμέραις</u>
V.......................
S.......................
N.......................
P.......................
R.......................

<u>μετὰ τὴν θλῖψιν ἐκείνην</u> ὁ ἥλιος σκοτισθήσεται, καὶ ἡ σελήνη οὐ δώσει τὸ φέγγος αὐτῆς,
V.......................
S.......................
N.......................
P.......................
R.......................

25 καὶ οἱ ἀστέρες ἔσονται ἐκ τοῦ οὐρανοῦ πίπτοντες, καὶ αἱ δυνάμεις αἱ ἐν τοῖς
V.......................
S.......................
N.......................
P.......................
R.......................

οὐρανοῖς σαλευθήσονται.26 καὶ τότε ὄψονται τὸν υἱὸν τοῦ ἀνθρώπου ἐρχόμενον ἐν
V.......................
S.......................
N.......................
P.......................
R.......................

νεφέλαις μετὰ δυνάμεως πολλῆς καὶ δόξης. 27 καὶ τότε ἀποστελεῖ τοὺς ἀγγέλους καὶ
V.......................
S.......................
N.......................
P.......................
R.......................

ἐπισυνάξει τοὺς ἐκλεκτοὺς [αὐτοῦ] ἐκ τῶν τεσσάρων ἀνέμων ἀπ᾿ ἄκρου γῆς ἕως ἄκρου
V.......................
S.......................
N.......................
P.......................
R.......................

οὐρανοῦ.28 Ἀπὸ δὲ τῆς συκῆς μάθετε τὴν παραβολήν· ὅταν ἤδη ὁ κλάδος αὐτῆς ἁπαλὸς
V.......................
S.......................
N.......................
P.......................
R.......................

γένηται καὶ ἐκφύῃ τὰ φύλλα, γινώσκετε ὅτι ἐγγὺς τὸ θέρος ἐστίν. 29 οὕτως καὶ ὑμεῖς,
V.......................
S.......................
N.......................
P.......................
R.......................

ὅταν ἴδητε ταῦτα γινόμενα γινώσκετε ὅτι ἐγγύς ἐστιν ἐπὶ θύραις. 30 //ἀμὴν λέγω ὑμῖν
V.......................
S.......................
N.......................
P.......................
R.......................

ὅτι οὐ μὴ παρέλθῃ ἡ γενεὰ αὕτη μέχρις οὗ ταῦτα πάντα γένηται. 31 ὁ οὐρανὸς καὶ ἡ γῆ
V..
S..
N..
P..
R..

παρελεύσονται, οἱ δὲ λόγοι μου οὐ μὴ παρελεύσονται. 32 //Περὶ δὲ τῆς ἡμέρας ἐκείνης ἢ
V..
S..
N..
P..
R..

τῆς ὥρας οὐδεὶς οἶδεν, οὐδὲ οἱ ἄγγελλοι ἐν οὐρανῷ οὐδὲ ὁ υἱός, εἰ μὴ ὁ πατήρ. 33 βλέπετε
V..
S..
N..
P..
R..

ἀγρυπνεῖτε· οὐκ οἴδατε γὰρ πότε ὁ καιρός ἐστιν. 34 ὡς ἄνθρωπος ἀπόδημος ἀφεὶς τὴν
V..
S..
N..
P..
R..

οἰκίαν αὐτοῦ καὶ δοὺς τοῖς δούλοις αὐτοῦ τὴν ἐξουσίαν, ἑκάστῳ τὸ ἔργον αὐτοῦ, καὶ τῷ
V..
S..
N..
P..
R..

θυρωρῷ ἐνετείλατο ἵνα γρηγορῇ. 35 //γρηγορεῖτε οὖν, οὐκ οἴδατε γὰρ πότε ὁ κύριος τῆς
V..
S..
N..
P..
R..

οἰκίας ἔρχεται, ἢ ὀψὲ ἢ μεσονύκτιον ἢ ἀλεκτοροφωνίας ἢ πρωΐ, 36 μὴ ἐλθὼν ἐξαίφνης
V..
S..
N..
P..
R..

εὕρῃ ὑμᾶς καθεύδοντας. 37 //ὃ δὲ ὑμῖν λέγω, πᾶσιν λέγω, γρηγορεῖτε.//
V..
S..
N..
P..
R..

Key: Double underlining = three or four indicators of redaction agree

// = Unique syntax occurs across a major punctuation break (possible insertion)
V = from Markan vocabulary lists; S = Markan syntax lists; N = Neirynck's *Duality;*
P = Peabody's recurrent phraseology; R = Recurrent syntax (6-word sequences)

INDEX OF AUTHORS

Contemporary and ancient authors are listed here, with **bold text** indicating more substantial discussions of an author. See the Scripture Index for Biblical authors.

Achtemeier, Paul J., 11n9
Adam, A. K. M., 11n7
Aland, Barbara, 25n41
Aland, Kurt, 25, 25n41, 34n26, 136n34
Allen, W. C., 51, 51n50
Allison, Dale C., 17n23
Anderson, Janice Capel, 10n6, 10n7, 11n8, 18n26, 27n2
Atkinson, B. F. C., 99n20
Aune, D. E., 256n40
Bacon, B. W., 222n21
Barrett, C. K., 136n34
Bauckham, Richard, 77n35,262n50
Baur, F. C., 222n21
Beasley-Murray, G. R., 9n1, 19n28, 24, 24n38, 24n40, 25, 25n44, 27n1, 29n7, 30n15, 31n16, 31n18, 32n21, 35n28, 39, 40, 41, 43, 48n42, **67-78**, 81, 87n54, 93n2, 94n5, 97, 125n7, 128, 153-4n2, 158n14, 175n44, 195, 195n15, 211n10, 222n21-22, 223, 223n23-24, 224n27, 230n41, 275, 276-7n2
Belo, Fernando, **213-215**, 220, 221, 247n30
Ben-Dov, Meir, 155n5
Best, Ernest, 29n8, 165n31
Betz, Otto, 256n40
Beyer, K., 62
Black, C. Clifton, 13n11, 13n13, 131n28, 166n32, 263n51, 263-4n55
Black, Matthew, 48n45, 50, 52, 59, 60n59, 100n22
Blass, F., 47, 47n39, 50, 52, 54, 55, 57, 60, 61
Bolt, Peter G., 174n40, 219n16, 247n30, 260n45
Borg, Marcus J., 209n9
Boring, M. Eugene, 29n8, 31n15, 32n23, 73, 73n28-29, 76, 77, 94n4, 153, 153-4n2, 163-4n28, 225n30, 256n40
Bornkamm, G., 13n13
Brandenburger, Egon, 19n27, 20-1, 20n30, 24, 30n12, 30n13, 31n16, 32, 32n20, 35n28, 36, 37, 38, 40, 44, 154n4, 165, **185-200**, 204, 218, 224n28
Broadhead, Edwin K., 37n31
Bruce, F. F., 110n27

Brugensis, Lucas, 153n2
Bultmann, R., 27n2, 29, 30, 30n9, 30n10, 30n14, 31, 35, 35n28, 36, 37, 38, 39, 40, 41, 42, 43, 44, 63, 96, 124, 211n10
Burkett, Delbert, 31n16
Burnett, Fred W., 80n48
Burridge, K. O. L., 209
Busch, F., 123, 123n2, 126
Carroll, Robert P., 160n18, 164n30
Carson, R. A. G., 227n33-34
Chapman, Dean W., 229n40, 232n46
Chariton, 246, 248, 263, 266
Charlesworth, James Hamilton, 107n25, 186n3
Cicero, 45n36, 264n55
Classen, Walter T., 115n29
Colani, T., 19n27, 27, 28, 28n4, 30, 30n11, 32n22, 67n3, 206n6
Collins, Adela Yarbro, 30n12, 30n13, 31n16, 67n1, 68n9, 185n1, 187n4, 261n48
Collins, John J., 30n12, 30n13
Combs, William W, 99n19, 100n22
Conzelmann, Hans, 13n13, 158n17
Cranfield, C. E. B., 186n2
Crossan, John Dominic, 28n3
Crotty, R. B., 18n25
Cullmann, O., 34n27
Davies, W. D., 17n23
Déaut, R. le, 109, 109n26
Debrunner, A., 47, 47n39, 50, 52, 54, 55, 57, 60, 61
Deissmann, A., 49n45
Derrett, F. Duncan M., 100n21
de Tillesse, G. M., 156n9
Dibelius, M., 31n18
Dodd, C. H., 12n10, 95n9, 261n49
Donahue, John R., 12n10, 13n13, 15n19, 16n20, 31n16, 181n57, 201n2
Drewermann, E., 68
Dschulnigg, P., 132-136
Dunn, James D. G., 78n39, 91n64
Dyer, Keith D., 87n54, 118n30
Edwards, James R., 137n37
Elliott, J. K., 53n51, 137, 137n35
Ellis, E., 99n20, 110n27
Epictetus, 47, 55
Epiphanius, 163n27, 164n29

Eusebius, 32, 153, 153n2, 160, 162, 162-163n24-27, 163, 164n29, 229n39
Farmer, W. R., 79n46, 136n34, 261n47
Fensham, F. C., 115n29
Fiorenza, Elisabeth Schüssler, 30n12
Fitzmyer, Joseph A., 58, 58n56, 60n59, 93n2, 100n22, 110n27
Flückiger, F., 72n25
Ford, Desmond, 130n23, 222n21, 223, 223n23, 223n25, 224n27
Fowler, Robert M., 19n27, 233, 233n3, 234n4, 235, 238n13, **256-257**, 260n46
France, R. T., 41, 41n34, 70n15, 98, 98n17-18, 99, 101n24, 103, 104, 106, 107, 108, 111, 113, 114, 122, 196n17, 218, 230n42, 260n45
Friberg, Barbara and Timothy, 82n53, Appendix 1
Friedrich, G., 132-135
Frye, Northrop, 237n9
Fuller, R. H., 30n15
Funk, Robert W., 28n3, 34n27, 35, 35n28, 40, 42, 43, 47n39, 50, 52, 54, 55, 57, 60, 61
Gager, John, 34n27
Gaston, L., 25, 25n43, 132-136, 153, 153n1, 154n2, 156n9, 211n10, 225n30
Geddert, Timothy J., 16n21, 19n27, 24, 24n38, 48n43, 100n21, 166n34, 174n41-42, 175, 175n43-45, 176n47, 178n52, 179n54, 180, 180n56, 223n26, 224n28, 233, 235, 245n29, 247n30, **251-256**, 260n44
Ghandi, Mahatma, 215, 216
Gibson, Jeffrey, 175n43
Gill, W. A., 7, 35, 35n28, 87n55, 98n18, 110n27, 155n5, 174n40, 179n53, 180, 180n55, 251n36
Glasson, T. Francis, 95n7, 97, 97n12, 98, 101n24, 102, 106, 108, 112, 113, 114, 115, 118
Gnilka, Joachim, 127, 127n9, 131n25, 155n5, 162, 162n25
Gräßer, Erich, 99n20, 195n16
Grayston, K., 24n38, 156n8
Grundmann, W., 153n2
Guelich, Robert A., 217-218n15
Gundry, Robert Horton, 98n14, 115
Haenchen, E., 163n26, 211n10
Hahn, Ferdinand, 24, 24n39, 32n22, 40, 127, 131, **153-162**, 166n34, 167, 186n2, 190, 218, 220, 276
Hartman, Lars, 29n7, 81, **93-97**, 100n21, 101n24, 102-115, 122, 127-8n12,

128n19, 130n21, 131, 156n9, 161, 192n13, 195, 206n6, 211n10
Hawkins, John C., 82n51, 132-136
Hawthorne, Gerald F., 256n40
Hegesippus, 229n39
Hellholm, D., 30n12, 192n13
Hendriks, W., 132-136
Hengel, Martin, 45n36, 48n44, 156n8
Herzog, William R., 28n3, 222n20
Hirsch, E. D., 236n8
Holtzmann, O., 222n21
Homer, 246
Hooker, Morna D., 93n4, 122n31, 156n9
Hoover, Roy W., 28n3, 34n27, 35, 35n28, 40, 42, 43
Horace, 45n36
Horgan, Maurya P., 60n59, 261n48
Horsley, G. H. R., 45n37, 49n45
Howard, Wilbert Francis, 45n35, 49, 49n45, 49n46, 51, 51n50, 56, 58, 108
Hurtado, L. W., 206n7
Irenaeus, 222n22
Jellicoe, Sidney, 114n28
Jeremias, J., 55n53, 62
Jerome, 222n22
Josephus, 39n32, 204, 224n29, 227n35, 228n38, 229n39, 230n42
Karavidopoulos, Johannes, 25n41
Käsemann, Ernst, 42
Katz, P., 57, 57n55
Kee, Howard C., 21n31, 42, 79n46, 99n20, 101n24, 102-115, 186n2, 191, 191n12, 201, **208-213**, 215, 218, 220, 232, 264
Kelber, W. H., 13-14, 13n14, 16n20, 21n31, 35n28, 38, 131n25, 166n34, 186n2, **202-208**, 209, 213, 218, 230n41, 239n18
Kenny, Anthony, 81n50, Appendix 1
Kilpatrick, G. D., 25, 25n42
Kingsbury, Jack Dean, 17n23
Kirschner, Robert, 107n25
Klostermann, E., 35n29, 156n9
Kobelski, Paul J., 60n59, 261n48
Koester, Craig, 163n27, 164n29
Kreitzer, Larry J., 228n37
Kuhn, Thomas S., 10n3, 15n18
Kümmel, Werner Georg, 31, 31n18, 32, 32n19-20, 32n22, 35n29, 39, 39n33, 123-4n3, 155n5, 185n2
Lagrange, M. J., 45n36, 56
Lambrecht, J., 19n27, 31n18, 39, 39n33, 40, 71, 71-2n22, 94n4, 94n5, 101n24, 123, **127-129**, 156n6, 156n8-9, 160, 161, 166n34, 185n1-2, 190, 190n11, 211n10, 247n30
Lane, W. L. 101n24, 108

Lee-Pollard, Dorothy A., 221n19
Legg, S. C. E., 25, 25n41
Lightfoot, R. H., 258, 258n43
Lindars, Barnabas, 31n16, 113-4n28,
    181n57, 185n1
Lohmeyer, E., 30n15, 31n18, 32n21,
    35n29, 37, 42, 68, 156n9, 186n2,
    211n10, 215
Lövestam, E., 177n50
Lucian, 45n36
Lüdemann, Gerd, 163n27
Macho, A. Díez, 100n22
Mack, Burton L., 23n36, 28n3, 131n28,
    233, 235, **241-244**, 258, 259
Mackay, James, 227n33
Malbon, Elizabeth Struthers, 10n7, 11n8
Maloney, Elliott C., 45n35, 45n37, 47,
    47n41, 49, 49n46, 49n47, 50,
    50n48, 51, 52, 53, 53n51, 54, 55,
    55n53, 56, 57, 57n55, 58, 59,
    59n57, 59n58, 60, 60n59, 60n60,
    61, 61n61, 62, 63, 100n22, 108,
    138n41
Marcus, Joel, 181n58, 229n40, 232n45
Martin, James P., 9n2, 10n3, 10n4, 21n32
Martini, Carlo M., 25n41
Martyn, J. Lous, 181n58
Marxsen, W., 19n27, 21n31, 22n35,
    29n8, 35n28, 37, 72n23, **123-127**,
    156n9, 158, 158n15, 187n4, 201,
    215, 223n26, 224n28
McDermott, John M., 187n1
McKnight, Edgar V., 10n7, 11n8
McVann, Mark, 222n20
Mealand, David, 13n12
Meier, John P., 34n27
Menzies, A., 222n21
Meyer, E., 32n22
Metzger, Bruce M., 25n41
Michie, Donald, 233n1
Miller, Robert J., 256n40
Moloney, F. J., 31n16
Moltmann, Jürgen, 275, 275n1, 276
Moore, Stephen D., 10n6, 10n7, 11n8,
    18n26, 27n2
Morgenthaler, Robert, 75n31, 76, 76n32,
    82n51, 132-136
Morton, A. Q., 81n50
Moulton, James Hope, 45n35, 49n45,
Myers, Ched, 23n37, 38, 106n25, 125n6,
    156n8, 176n49, 178n52, **215-220**,
    221, 225n30, 229n40, 230n42,
    247n30, 251n36, 276
Nardoni, Enrique, 178n51
Neirynck, Frans, 22n34, 90n61, 127,
    127n8, 131n25, 132, 132n29-30,
    135n32-33, **139-143**, 153n2, 160,

160n19, 161n21, 162, 162-163n25-
    26, 168, 168n36, **169-173**
Nestle, E., 34n26
Newton-De Molina, David, 236n8
Nickelsburg, George W. E., 107n25,
    186n3
Oster, R., 228, 228n37
Patte, Daniel, 9n2, 10n5, 14, 17n23
Patten, Priscilla, 192n14
Peabody, David Barrett, 22n34, 90n61,
    135-6n33-34, 137n35, **143-147**
Perrin, Norman, 12n10, 15, 16n20, **73-
    78**, 88n57, 94-5n6, 97, 97n13, 98,
    98n14-16, 99, 99n20, 101n24, 103,
    106, 107, 108, 113, 114, 118,
    181n57, 201n2, 202n3, 208n8
Pesch, Rudolf, 19n27, 19n28, 24, 24n39,
    27, 29n5, 29n8, 32, 32n24, 35n28,
    40, 125, 129, **129-131**, 137n36,
    153, 154n3-4, 155n5, 156n6,
    156n8, 158, 158n15, 159, **160-
    165**, 167, 186n2, 187n4, 190, 204,
    211n10, 218, 223, 223n25,
    224n28, 233, 233n2, 247n30,
    258n42
Petersen, Norman R., 233, 235, 235n5,
    236n8, **237-240**, 241, 247
Pfleiderer, J., 222n21, 224n27
Price, Jonathan J., 230, 231n44
Pryke, E. J., 38, 132-136, 137, 138n38,
    139, 140n38, 141
Pseudo-Clementine, 163n27
Quintillian, 264n55
Reicke, Bo, 79n46, 261n47
Renans, E., 67n3
Rhoads, David M., 228n36, 233n1
Robbins, V. K., 233, 235, **244-245**,
    263, 263n53, 263n55
Robinson, J. A. T., 219
Rousseau, François, 19n27
Rowdon, H. H., 70n15
Rowland, Christopher, 30n12
Sanders, E. P., 163n27
Schaberg, Jane, 181n58
Schmid, J., 156n9, 185n2
Schmiedel, P. W., 222n21
Schmithals, Walter, 128, 128n14, 186n2
Schnackenburg, R., 24n39, 186n2
Schneidau, Herbert N., 9n2
Schniewind, J., 156n9
Schoeps, H. J., 153n2
Scholem, G., 231n44
Schweitzer, A, 28, 28n3
Schweizer, E., 87n55, 155n5
Smallwood, E. Mary, 229n39
Smith, Gary Dean, 24n38, 276n2
Soards, Marion L, 181n58
Socrates, 244, 263

Spitta, F., 222n21
Stanton, Graham N., 17n23, 261n47
Streeter, B. H., 37
Stone, Michael E., 186n3
Strauss, D. F., 67n3, 68
Suh, Joong Suk, 221n19
Sundwall, J., 124, 124n4
Tacitus, 227n34
Taylor, N. H., 154n2, 163-4n28, 222n21
Taylor, Vincent, 32, 32n21, 35, 35n28,
        35n29, 36, 37, 38, 39, 40, 42, 43,
        44, 49n46, 53, 56, 60n59, 89,
        89n60, 137, 137n35, 138, 138n38-
        9, 225n30
Telford, William, 174n40, 251n36
Theissen, Gerd, 89n60, 153, 154n2, 163-
        164n28, 225n30, 232n45
Thiselton, Anthony C., 10n7
Tillich, P., 17-18n24, 23n36, 241-2,
        242n23
Tolbert, Mary Ann, 19n27, 166n33, 233,
        235, 236, 236n8, 243n26, **245-
        251**, 253, 260, 263, 263n55, 264
Torrey, C. C., 45n36, 222n21
Turner, C. H., 37, 38, 136n35, 137, 139
Turner, N., 45n36, 46, 46n38, 47, 47n40,
        48n45, 57, 60n59
Tyson, Joseph B., 239n18
Vander Broek, Lyle Dale, 229n40
Vermes, Geza, 31n16, 58, 58n56
Via, Dan O., 243n25
Victorinus, 222n22
Vielhauer, P., 211n10
Vögtle, A., 159
Vorster, W. S., 21n33, 233, 235, 236n8,
        240-241
Waetjen, Herman C., **220-221**, 230n42,
        232, 232n46, 247n30
Walter, N., 156n8, 156n9
Watson, Duane F., 263n51
Watson, Nigel, 20n29, 236n8
Weber, M., 208
Weeden, Theodore J., 202, 202n3
Weiss, J., 222n21
Wellhausen, J., 37, 58
Wendland, H. D., 276n2
Wenham, David, 24, 24n38, 24n39,
        24n40, 29n7, 44, 67, 68n9, 70n15,
        72n24, **78-80**, 91n64, 94n5, 97,
        177n50
Williamson, G. A., 230n43
Wink, Walter, 221, 221n18, 230n42
Xenophon of Athens, 244, 263, 266
Xenopnon of Ephesus, 246, 247, 248,
        263, 266
Zerwick, Maximilian, 52, 53, 60n59

INDEX OF BIBLICAL AND ANCIENT TEXTS

Hebrew Bible and Septuagint

Genesis
19:17   93n4
22:2   110n27

Exodus
9:18   56,108
23:20   110n27

Leviticus
19:18   99n20

Numbers

Deuteronomy 164n30
6:4-5   99n20
13:1-3   109,120
28:64   105
30:3-4   114
30:4   114,179n54

Joshua

Judges
7:19   48

Ruth

1 Samuel
3:19   164n30

2 Samuel

1 Kings

2 Kings

1 Chronicles

2 Chronicles
3:1   110n27
15:6   93n4,104

Ezra

Nehemiah

Esther

Job

Psalms   58
2:7   110n27
110:1   99n20,111n27,113n28

115:4   180
118:22-23   99n20

Proverbs

Ecclesiastes

Song of Solomon (Canticles)

Isaiah   89n59
2:4   104
11:10-12   114
13:10   41,111,111n27,112,118
14:13   102
19:2   93n4,104,106,118,119
26:17   104
27:13   114
34:2   113
34:4   41,57,97n12,
            111n27,113,118
40:3   110n27
42:1   110n27
43:6   114,179n54
43:9   114,118
45:18   102
46:6   180
47:8   102
56:7   99n20,111n27

Jeremiah
7   100n21
7:11   99n20,111n27
22:23   104

Lamentations 100n21

Ezekiel   58
7:14-23   108
32:7-8   41,111,111n27,112
33:29   100n21,223n26
33-34   100n21

Daniel   89n59,93,97,127
2:28   103
2:29   103
2:35   180
2:45   103
3:1   52
4:12   56
4:28   115
5:2   52

6	109
6:5	56
6:26-28	109
7:8	94n4,102
7:11	94n4,102
7:13	31n16,58,113, 114n28,181,181n57, 195,196
7:13-14	111n27,113,118
7:14	113,181
7:20	102
7:21	102
7:25	102,104,120
8:10f	102
8:13	107,223
8:19	103
8:25	102
9:26f	223
9:27	107,223
10:2	110
11	102
11:20	110
11:27	161
11:31	107,223
11:32	97n12,106
11:33	105
11:35	106
11:36	102,103,109
11:44	102
12:1	56,106,107,108,110
12:3	105
12:6	101,183
12:7	101,115,161
12:11	107,223
12:12	97n12,106,107
12:12-13	106

Hosea

Joel	127
2:10	41,111,111n27, 112,113,118
2:31ET (= 3:4LXX/MT)	111n27,112,118
3:15-16ET (= 4:15-16LXX/MT)	41,111,111n27, 112,118

Amos

Obadiah

Jonah

Micah	127
4:3	104
4:9-10	104
7:2	99n20,106
7:2-7	118,120
7:5f	106

7:6	99n20,106
7:7	106,107,120
7:12	106,107

Nahum

Habakkuk

Zephaniah

Haggai	
2:15	101,119,169

Zechariah	89n59,127
2:6ET (= 2:10 LXX/MT)	101n23,105,114,118, 179n54,196
2:11ET (= 2:15 LXX/MT)	105,114,118,120
7:14	105
14:16	105

Malachi	
2:9	105
3:1	110n27

New Testament

Q	31n18,77n36,80,127, 128
Matthew	79,80,136n34,226,260
5:18	43,96
5-7	68n10
10	68n10
10:17-23	79n46
10:35-36	127
11:28	269
12:39	175n44
16:4	175n44
23	261
23:26	96
24	220,230n41
24:9-14	79n46
24:14	105
24:15	30,261
24:15-22	163n25
24:20	261
24:26	40,261
24:27	40
24:30	114n28,175n44
24:42	78
24:43f	44
25:14-30	78
26:48	175n44
26:64	114n28
27:25	261

Mark
1
1:1   146,157n10,170
1:1-13   88
1:1-12:44   238,241
1:2a   110n27
1:2   174,195
1:2-3   98n18,110,110n27
1:2-34   129
1:2-3:6   129
1:3   172,174
1:5   204
1:7   172
1:8   146,171
1:9   146,170,177
1:10   79n41,146
1:11   110,110n27,169
1:12   79n42,146
1:14   146,170,194
1:14-20   88
1:14-3:6   88
1:15   146,158,170,176,239
1:15-16   248
1:16   143n50
1:16-18   169
1:16-19   145
1:16-5:43   247
1:17   170
1:18   146,170
1:19-20   169
1:20   146,170
1:21a   169
1:21   143n50
1:21-22   169
1:21-45   88
1:23-28   169
1:24   170
1:25   170
1:26   170
1:27   170
1:29   36n30,145,170
1:29b   169
1:33   169
1:34c   169
1:35   170
1:35-45   129
1:39   143n50,170
1:40   170,171
1:40f   79n46
1:41   170,171
1:42   170
1:44   37,146
1:45   143n50,170
Mark 2
2:1   170
2:1-2   143n50,169
2:1-12   175n43
2:1-3:6   88,129

2:7   170,171
2:8   170
2:9   169,170
2:10   171,181n57
2:11   59n57,169,170
2:12   170
2:13   143n50,169,170
2:13-14   169
2:14   170
2:16   171
2:17   171,172
2:18   171
2:19   171,172
2:20   55,146,171,177
2:20-21   61n62
2:21   172
2:22   171,172
2:24   145,171
2:25   171
2:26   98n14,171
2:27   79n41,171,172
2:28   172
Mark 3
3:1   59,143n50,170
3:4   170,172,194
3:5   170
3:6   169,170
3:7   204
3:7-10   143n50
3:7-35   88
3:7-4:34   129
3:7-6:6a   88
3:7-6:29   129
3:12   169
3:13   55n53
3:13-15   169
3:13-16   146
3:16-18   36n30,145
3:20   143n50
3:22   169,170
3:23   143n50,169,171
3:24   171,172
3:25   171,172
3:26   75n30,157n10,171,172
3:28   42,58,146,171
3:29   146,171
3:30   169,170
3:32   169
3:33   171
3:34   145,171
3:35   169
Mark 4   55,71,76,76n33,
                77,89n58,128,239,254
4:1   169
4:1-2   143n50
4:1-12   129
4:1-20   254
4:1-34   88

4:2	79n41,145,170	5:23	194
4:3	55n53,170	5:27-28	169
4:3-8	55n53,169,247	5:28	194
4:3-32	76	5:29	170
4:4	55n53,172	5:31	178
4:4-7	171	5:33-36	61n62
4:5	55n53	5:34	169,170
4:5-6	172	5:35	169
4:7	55n53,172	5:39	169
4:8	55n53,171	5:41	170
4:9	170	5:41-42a	169
4:10	143n50,145,169,171	5:42	170
4:10-13	36	*Mark* 6	
4:11	62,79n41,171	6:2	169,170
4:12	98n14,145,169,172	6:3	169,170
4:13	50n48,169,170,172	6-11	99n20
4:13-20	254	6:4	79n41,169
4:14-20	169,247	6:6b-31	88
4:15	55n53,172	6:6b-32	79n42
4:15-19	171	6:6b-8:26	88
4:16	55n53	6:7	145,146,169
4:16-17	172	6:10	79n41,171
4:17	75n30	6:11	37,146,171
4:18	55n53	6:14	58
4:18-19	172	6:14-16	169
4:20	55n53,171	6:14-29	79n45
4:21	55n53,79n41,170,171	6:15	145
4:22	172	6:15-16	61n62
4:24	79n41,145,146,172	6:22	169
4:25	171	6:23	169
4:26	55n53	6:24	169
4:29	98n14	6:25	169
4:30	170,172	6:29	125n7,169
4:31	171	6:30-7:13	129
4:32	98n14,171	6:30-8:26	129
4:33-34	170	6:31	145,170
4:34	61n62,145	6:32	145,170
4:35	143n50,146,177	6:32-44	179n53
4:35-41	169	6:32-7:23	88
4:35-5:20	129	6:34	98n14,143n50
4:35-6:6a	88	6:34-44	169
4:36	146	6:35-11:25	247
4:38	55n53,145,169,178	6:36	169
4:39	59n57	6:37	169,170,178
4:40	169,170	6:38	59n57
Mark 5		6:39	145
5:1	143n50	6:40	145
5:1-20	169	6:41	57
5:8	170	6:45	143n50
5:9	171	6:45-52	169
5:13	170	6:48	48
5:15	169	6:52	169
5:19	170	6:55	143n50
5:20	170	6:56	194
5:21	143n50	6:56b	169
5:21-43	79n42	*Mark* 7	
5:21-6:29	129	7:1-30	180
5:22	50,145	7:6	98n14,171

7:6-7	61n62
7:7	171
7:8	146,171
7:9	79n41,171
7:10	98n14,171
7:11-12	171
7:13	146,171
7:14	143n50,145
7:14-23	129
7:15	169,171
7:17	143n50,169
7:17-23	36
7:18	170
7:18-23	169
7:19	170
7:23	179
7:24	79n44,143n50,
	168n35,169
7:24-8:21	88
7:24-8:26	129
7:27	169,179n53
7:28	169
7:29	170
7:30	170
7:31	79n44,143n50
7:31-37	169
7:33	145
7:34	170
7:35	170
Mark 8	165
8:1	143n50,146,177
8:1-9	179n53
8:1-10	169
8:1-21	254
8:4	178
8:10	79n44,143n50
8:11-12	177n50
8:11-13	175,175n43
8:12	32,42,162,169,
	171,175,177n50,182
8:13	143n50,146
8:14-21	254
8:15	59n57,145
8:16	178
8:17	169,170,172
8:18	98n14,145,169,170,172
8:18-19	170
8:19	170
8:19-21	143n50
8:20	170
8:21	79n41,145,170
8:22-26	88,169,248
8:23	170,171
8:24	171
8:26	170
8:27-33	161n21
8:27-9:1	71,88
8:27-9:29	88,129

8:27-10:52	129
8:28	61n62,145,169
8:31	169,202
8:32	178
8:32f	165
8:34-9:1	129
8:35	146,171,194
8:36	170,172
8:37	170,172
8:38	157n13,172,177n50,
	178n51,181,181n57,
	205,212n11,218,271n1
8:38-9:1	178n51
Mark 9	165
9:1	42,70n15,79n41,
	178n51,183,198,218,
	222,239,262,268,273,
	276,278
9:2	145,169,170,176n46
9:2f	178n51
9:2-13	161n21
9:2-29	88
8:3	146
9:6	169
9:7	169
9:9	169,170
9:10	169
9:11	171,178,202,217
9:11-13	36
9:12	50n48,98n14,171
9:13	171
9:14	143n50
9:17	145
9:19	170,172,177n50
9:20	170,125n7
9:22	169
9:23	169
9:24	169
9:25	170
9:26	125n7,170
9:26b-27	169
9:28	143n50,145,170,171,
	178
9:29	171
9:28f	36
9:30	169,170
9:30-32	88
9:30-35	161n21
9:30-50	129
9:30-10:31	88
9:31	79n41,169,194
9:32	170,178
9:33	143n50,168n35
9:33f	165
9:33-9:50	88
9:34	170,178
9:35	169
9:35-10:1	170

9:36	169	10:39	146,171,172
9:37	145	10:40	169
9:38	145,169,178	10:42	171,172
9:39	145,169	10:43	172
9:41	42,145,239n19	10:43-44	169,171
9:42	62,145	10:44	172
9:43	170,172	10:45	172
9:45	172	10:46	145,170
9:47	172	10:46-52	88,161n21
9:48	170,172	10:49	59n57,170
9:50	170	10:50	170
Mark 10	165	10:52	169,170
10:1	58,143n50,161n21	*Mark* 11	161
10:1-16	88	11:1	35,145
10:1-52	129	11:1-7	169
10:2	169,171	11:1-11	88,110n27
10:3	171	11:1-23	161n21
10:3-6	61	11:1-26	129
10:4	98n14,171	11:1-12:44	129
10:5	171	11-12	174n40
10:6	146	11:1-13:2	35
10:7	98n14,146	11:1-13:37	88,179
10:8	98n14	11:1-15:47	244
10:9	171	11:2-3	170
10:10	143,143n50	11:4-7	170
10:10-12	36	11:9	145
10:11	169,172	11:11	161,170
10:12	169,172	11:12f	42
10:13	58,178	11:12-14	205,248
10:14	59n57,169,172	11:12-25	88,126,179,203
10:15	42	11:13	176,177
10:16	169	11:15	161,170
10:17	145,169,249n33	11:15-17	155n5,180
10:17-31	88	11:17a	99n20
10:18	169,171	11:17	79n41,98n18,110,
10:20	145,169		110n27,111n27,171,
10:21	57,169,170		179,180
10:24-26	61n62	11:17b	99n20
10:26	50n48,169,178,194	11:18	169
10:27	169,171	11:19	161,170
10:28	169,170	11:20-21	205
10:29	42,146,169	11:20-25	248
10:30	169,176,240,249,	11:21	145
	249n33	11:23	42
10:31	171	11:27	144,161
10:32	168n35	11:27-33	88,161n21
10:32-34	88,161n21	11:27-12:12	129
10:32-52	88	11:27-13:37	247
10:32-14:17	127	11:28	50n48,170,171,172
10:33	194	11:29	170,171
10:33-34	169	11:30	57,170,171
10:35	145,169	11:31	57,171
10:35f	165	11:32	171
10:35-45	88	11:33	170,171
10:36	169	11:35	161
10:36-40	61	*Mark* 12	130,161,202
10:37	145,169,178	12:1	98n14,170
10:38	146,169,171,172	12:1-2	142,173

12:1-11	247
12:1-12	88,110n27,180
12:1-17	161n21
12:2	176
12:2f	177
12:9	248,249n32
12:10	99n20
12:10-11	98n14
12:12	146,170
12:13-44	129
12:13-13:2	88
12:14	145,170,171
12:15	170
12:16	170
12:17	171,172
12:18	145
12:19	98n14,169
12:23	171
12:24	75n30,170
12:25	146,171
12:26	98n14,169,170
12:27	75n30,170
12:28	50,145,169,170,171
12:29	98n14,99n20,171
12:29-31	169
12:31	98n14,99n20,171
12:32	145
12:32-33	169
12:33	169
12:34	169,170
12:34c	161n21
12:35	170
12:35-37	161n21,277
12:36	98n14,99n20,146
12:37	50n48,170
12:38	145
12:41	142,145,169,173
12:41f	244
12:41-44	161,161n21,180,270
12:43	42
12:44	171
Mark 13	See the text sheets and tables on pages 64-65,74-75,86-87, 116-117,119-121,148,149-150,198-199
13:1a	119,150,151,168,182,183,188,190,267
13:1	49,50,53,60,82,124,127,138,138n41,140,141,142,145,151,169,172,173,174,179,183
13:1b,c	119
13:1-2	28,34n26,35,63,90n63,119,126,134n31,147n54,155,155n5,161,161n21,164,169,
13:1c-2	174n40,179,188,198,225,268,273
13:1-4	190
13:1-5	72n25,96,153n1,155
13:1-6	74,130
13:2a,b	267
13:2	127
13:2	34n27,35n29,39n32,47,50,50n48,51,51n49,53,61,65,69,82,101,115,116,121,122,124,138,138n41,141,142,156,161,169,172,173,174,182,267
13:2c	119,127,155n5,202
13:3	35,50,51,82,124,138,138n41,141,142,144,145,150,151,161,168,169,172,173,173n39,174,182,183,202,267,273
13:3/4	119
13:3-4	69,91,127,190,198,273
13:3-5a	192,268
13:3-5	33,162
13:3-6	34n26,36,63,90n63,92,119,122,134n31,147n54,151,169,170,173,173n39,182,268
13:3-37	35,81n49,88,188
13:4a	99n20
13:4	50,50n48,53,82,91,101,115,116,124,127,139n41,142,151,159,161,162,165,169,170,171,172,173,173n36,175,175n43,177n50,178,179,182,183,192,205,239,247n30,251,262,268
13:4b	119
13:4/5	119
13:5a	127,150,173n39,182,267
13:5	36,51,52,61,63,69n13,69n15,71,72n25,75n30,91,99n20,131,138,141,142,144,145,162,170,171,172,173,183,
13:5b	188,193,198,202,271
13:5f	155
13:5-6	124,155,157,159
13:5b-6	36,40,127,188,190,193,198,273
13:5-8	32n21,158
13:5b-8	93,95,199,202,268,273

Mark 13:5-13   124,126,153n1,156n6,
                 216
13:5b-13   76,89n57,167,217,218,
                 273
13:5b-14a   167
13:5-22   162
13:5-23   128,156n6,198,199,214
13:5b-23   193,197,202
13:5-27   29,73,75,75n30,76,188
13:5b-30   218
13:5-31   28,30,73,76
13:5b-31   163n28
13:5-37   36,159,241
13:6a   150,173n39,182,267
13:6   25,36,47,50,52,63,69,
                 69n13,69n15,72n25,
                 75n30,93n4,94n4,95,
                 96n10,99n20,102,109,
                 115,119,125,130,130n2
                 1,138,141,142,145,151,
                 153n1,162,170,171,
                 172,173,182,183,202,
                 216
13:6b   138
13:6-13   156n8
13:7a   183
13:7   25,30,37,41,50,52,61,
                 69n13,70n15,72n25,
                 75n30,82,87,91,95n7,
                 99n20,102,103,115,
                 119,120,121,122,127,
                 130,130n24,138n41,
                 141,142,154,157,170,
                 171,172,173,182,202,
                 216, 217,255,267
13:7b   119,130,138,151,
                 153n1,182,183,193,
                 199,216
13:7c   150,177,182,183,267
13:7f   89,154,155,158,162,
                 216
13:7bf   130n21,157
13:7-8   29,30,32,34n26,37,40,
                 41,44,63,64,89n60,
                 90n63,118,119,123,
                 124,127,134n31,
                 147n54,153,157,
                 157n10,162,171,188,
                 189,193,198
13:7-9   162
13:7-13   156,156n8
13:7-27   154
13:8a   119
13:8   30,37,41,50,52-53,63,
                 65,70n15,72n25,91,
                 93n4,96n10,99n20,104,
                 115,116,118,119,120,
                 121,122,130n24,

                 138n41,141,145,157,
                 160,182,183,255,267
13:8b   138,151,182,216
13:8b,c   119
13:8c   138,151,182
13:9a   138n38,155,183,190,
                 193,199
13:9   25,37,38,47,50,52,58,
                 61,63,69,71,71n18,82,
                 96,104,115,116,120,
                 124,127,130,131,138,
                 138n40,138n41,141,
                 145,146,159,162,180,
                 183,188,216
13:9b   138,150,151,153,
                 153n1,155,157,182,267
13:9-10   122,182
13:9-11   25,25n42,37,38,72n25
13:9-11f   176n48
13:9-12   97n11
13:9-13a   194,196
13:9-13   32n21,34n26,37-39,63,
                 79n43,90n63,105,120,
                 134n31,147n54,151,
                 155,159,171,177,188,
                 190n10,193,194,199,
                 202,238,239,250,254,
                 258,268,269,270,273
13:9b-13   190,199
13:9-15   158,162
13:10   38,47,50,53,63,69,71,
                 71n18,82,96,105,118,
                 120,124,126,127,130,
                 130n24,138,141,146,
                 150,151,155,157,
                 158n15,159,161,179,
                 180,182,183,190,
                 190n10,203,216,217,
                 267,268,273
13:11a   138n38
13:11a,b,d   119,120,121,122,182,
                 183,193,267
13:11   38,47,50,53,58,61,63,
                 65,69,82,87,91,96,104,
                 115,116,120,124,130,
                 138,138n40,141,142,
                 146,150,155,171,172,
                 176,180,193,197,
                 197n18,198,199,216,
                 273,277
13:11b   138
13:11c   120,150,182,183,267
13:11f   244
13:11-13   127,142,153,157,162,
                 171
13:11d-13a   64
13:11-22   162

Mark 13:12   29,30,32,38,47,50,52,
53,54,65,72n25,91,104,
106,106n25,115,116,
119,120,121,122,123,
124,127,130,130n21,
138n41,140,141,142,
155,182,183,193,217,
267
13:12b   99n20
13:12-13a   118,120,267
13:12-13   37,38,63,69,118
13:12-16   93,95
13:13a   120,121,122,124,130,
182,183,193,217,267
13:13a/b   120
13:13   30,37,38-39,47,50,
54,61,63,69,69n13,
72n25,75n30,83,91,
95n7,96n10,97n12,
99n20,106,106n25,116,
120,127,138,138n38,
141,157n10,183,192,
193,216,218,273
13:13b   106-107,120,122,123,
124,151,157,177,182,
183,193,194,196,217,
268,276n2
13:13b-17   130
13:13-18   61
13:13b-20a   130n21
13:14a   125,203
13:14   16,16n22,29,29n8,30,
32,37,39,40,41,61,69,
69n13,70n15,71,72,83,
95n7,96n10,99n20,
100n21,107,108,115,
116,118,120,124,125,
125n7,127,129,138,
142,153n1,154,156,
158,159,160,161,162,
170,171,175n44,180,
190,203, 214,217,217-
218n15,220,224,
225n30,227,247n30,
250,255,257, 264n55
13:14b   125,125n6,153n1,220,
225n30,227,233
13:14c   199
13:14f   154,163,167,174,179,
179n54,184,203,204,
206,212,214,217,218,
222,223,223n26,225,
226,234,256
13:14-16   39,72n25,126,193
13:14-18   199
13:14-19   64,153n1,184,218
13:14-20   29,32,34n26,36,39,
39n32,40,41,44,63,64,

65,89,89n60,90n63,91,
120,124,134n31,147,
147n54,153,157,162,
163n25,164,171,188,
189,199,225,268,273
13:14b-20   167
13:14-21   63,64,65,90,91,119,
121,122,151,167,182,
183,194,195,226,
227n35,229,230,231,
248,267,268,269,270,
272,277
13:14-22   30,40,91,123,154,249,
272
13:14-23   32n21,68n9,76,88,89,
89n57,90,90n62,91,
126,160n18,202,256,
273
13:14-27   153n2,154,155,156,
156n6,157,160,196,
219n16
13:15   26,32,52,54-55,
61,83,108,138n39,141,
142,247n30
13:15f   224
13:15-16   39,69,127
13:16   47,50,55,83,93n4,
247n30
13:17   39,47,50,53,55,61,
70n15,72n25,83,96n10,
127,139n41,141,142,
146,163n28,177,183,
204,247n30
13:17f   256
13:17-18   69
13:17-20   63,126,156n8
13:18   47,61,72n25,83,96n10,
130,193,228,247n30,
261
13:19a   138,204
13:19   30,37,40,47,50,53,55,
56,69,69n13,72n25,83,
95n7,99n20,108,116,
118,120,127,138,
138n38,141,142,146,
161,177,183,204,207,
247n30
13:19b   202,204,206,220
13:19-20a   130
13:19-20   127,154,199
13:19-22   93,95
13:20   40,47,50,53,56,63,69,
75n30,83,127,138,141,
142,146,150,153n1,
154,158,171,193,194,
199, 243
13:21a   154

Mark 13:21   34n27,40,47,50,69,84,
              90,96n10,120,130,141,
              142,145,154,155,184,
              193,199,202,229,
              229n39
13:21-22   39,82,87,94n4,123,123-
              124n3,125,127,153,
              153n1,154,156,157,
              162,273
13:21-22b   190
13:21-23a   199
13:21-23   34n26,40,63,72n25,
              90n63,120,126,134n31,
              147n54,159,172,188,
              193,199,268
13:21-37   167
13:22   36,37,40,47,50,52,53,
              56,63,64,65,69,69n13,
              70n15,75n30,84,95,
              95n9,99n20,109,116,
              118,119,120,121,122,
              125,130,130n21,
              138n41,141,142,150,
              154,156n8,158,170,
              172,173,175,175n43,
              182,184,193,199,202,
              229n39,243,267,268
13:22-23   142,170
13:23a   199
13:23   40,44,52,61,63,64,71,
              72,84,96,120,122,124,
              127,129,130,131,141,
              142,145,151,153n1,
              154,154n4,155,159,
              162,169,170,172,173,
              182,184,187n5,188,
              190,192,193,194,202,
              204,206,207,212,218,
              254,258,268,270,271,
              273
13:23b   199
13:24a   150,154,182,267
13:24   41,47,50,53,55,57,62,
              71,99n20,110,111,112,
              116,118,127,131,141,
              142,146,147,151,154,
              172,183,184,189n8,
              190,193,207,212,218,
              219,232,254
13:24f   105,159,162,247n30
13:24-25   42,43,118,196,204,230
13:24-26   69,110,273
13:24-27   28,29,30,31n16,32,
              32n21,33,34n26,37,40,
              41,42,43,44,63,64,65,
              69n13,70n15,72n25,76,
              89,89n57,89n60,90n63,
              91,93,95,97,98,111n27,

              118,119,120,121,122,
              123,124,126,127,130,
              130n21,134n31,147,147
              n54,147n55,151,153,
              153n1,154,156n6,157,
              159,160n18,172,177,
              178n52,179,181,182,
              184,188,189,193,194,
              195,196,197,197n18,
              204,208,212n11,214,
              215,218,221,230,231,
              231n44,232,239,
              249n32,267,268,269,
              270,276
13:24-30   178n51,198,199,268,
              273,276
13:24-29   268,271,272
13:24-31   162
13:24-32   193,196
13:25   41,47,50,57,57n54,58,
              95n7,97n12,99n20,113,
              116,118,127,138,142,
              172,218
13:25-26   232
13:26   41,47,50,58,59,61n61,
              69,69n12,71,99n20,
              113,113-114n28,116,
              118, 127,138,138n40,
              138n41,142,146,147,
              169,172,173,178n51,
              181,195,204,218,219,
              271n1
13:26-27   118,196,218,230,
              230n41
13:27   26,30,41,42,47,50,53,
              57n54,61,61n61,69,
              75n30,95n7,99n20,101,
              114,116,118,121,127,
              142,150,158,179n54,
              180,182,195,195n16,
              204,218,230,243,268,
              270,271,273,277
13:28   42,47,50,61,141,142,
              154,157,159,171,172,
              178n52,189,190,
              190n10,195n16,199
13:28b   127,130
13:28f   192,196
13:28-29   34n27,71,71n18,122,
              124,142,154,182,184,
              193
13:28-31   34n26,42,90n63,121,
              134n31,147n54,151,
              153,154,157,161,162,
              172
13:28-32   72n25,96,97n12,189
13:28-33   190
13:28-36   153n1,189

Mark 13:28-37   32n21,63,64,74,75,76,
              89n57,205,267
13:28-29   205,248
13:28-30   273
13:29   50,81n49,84,91,
              97n11,121,139n41,141,
              142,157n12,161,171,
              172,178,178n52,190,
              192,196,205,277
13:29b   154
13:29/30   121
13:29-30   71n18,130
13:29-33   91
13:29-37   92
13:30   28,30,42,43,53,62,
              72n22,84,91,96,
              97n11,99n20,115,
              121,122,127,138,
              141,142,146,154,159,
              161,163n28,167,171,
              173, 175,177,177-
              178n50,178,178n51,
              178n52,182,183,184,
              195,196,197,198,199,
              205,214,241n22,249,
              249n32,255,262,267,
              271,277
13:30-31   124,151,154,178,182,
              183,197,268,273
13:30-32   205
13:31   41,42,43,44,50,57n54,
              61,84,91,121,122,127,
              129,130,138,138n41,
              141,142,159,161,171,
              172,177,184,197,198,
              205,230n42,276
13:31/32   121
13:31f   178,183,197n18,272,
              276
13:31-32   277
13:31-37   199,200,268,273
13:32   26,28,30,34n27,38,42,
              43,53,57,61,62,65,
              69n13,72n22,84,91,
              121,122,124,124n4,
              130,141,146,154,161,
              167,176,177,178,182,
              183,184,186,196,
              196n17,197,198,205,
              240,241n22,267,273,
              276,277
13:32f   122n31,176,196
13:32-36   127
13:32-37   34n26,43,90n63,121,
              134n31,147n54,151,
              173
13:33   36,43-44,59,59n57,
              62,69,69n13,71,84,122,

              131,138,138n38,141,
              142,145,146,150,162,
              170,173,176,177,
              178n51,182,184,189,
              190,193,196,199,251,
              254,267,268,271,273
13:33f   193
13:33-34   142,169,173
13:33-36   189,190
13:33-37   72n25,96,124,154,155,
              205,273
13:34   44,47,48,50,52,59,
              59n58,62,63,64,65,71,
              79n45,84,91,121,122,
              130,138,141,142,146,
              151,182,184,267,278
13:34/35   121
13:34f   192,196
13:34-36   34n27,44,69,78,79,161,
              184,250
13:35a   138,138n38
13:35   44,47,84,85,91,121,
              141,176,190,193,198,
              270
13:35-36   151,182,268
13:35-37   122,130,182,193,273
13:36   44,85,87,91,121,142,
              146,169,173
13:36/37   121
13:37   44,61,71,72,85,91,121,
              127,129,141,142,151,
              153n1,162,169,170,
              172,173,178n52,182,
              184,189,190,192,193,
              199, 239,268,269
13:37/14:1 121
Mark 14   38,130
14:1   85,91,176
14:1f   137n36
14:1-9   180
14:1-11   88,88n56
14:1-52   129
14:1-16:8   88,88n56,129,131n28,
              161n21,238,270,
              244
14:3f   270
14:3-9   270
14:5   171
14:6   169,170
14:7   171
14:8   170
14:9   42,146,180
14:10   145
14:12   171
14:12-16   169
14:12-25   129
14:12-31   88,88n56
14:13   170
14:13-15   171

14:15	170
14:16	170
14:17	176
14:17-72	247
14:18	42,145
14:19	145,169
14:20	145
14:21	62
14:25	42,55,62,177
14:26	145
14:27	169
14:28	169,238n13,239
14:29	169
14:30	42,169
14:31	169
14:32f	178
14:32-72	88,88n56
14:32-15:5	248
14:33	169
14:35	169
14:37	142,146,169,170,173, 176
14:37b	173
14:38	146
14:38b	171
14:40	146
14:40d	169
14:41	38,146,169,176,194, 197,198,273,277
14:42	59n57,194
14:43	145
14:44	53n51,170
14:45	170
14:46	170
14:47	145
14:49	145
14:50	146
14:53	170
14:53-72	79n42
14:53-15:5	129
14:54	170
14:55-64	169
14:58	155n5,161,169,171,180
14:60	170
14:61	171
14:62	41,57,58,110,111n27, 113,113-4n28,142,146, 169,171,172,173,181, 181n58,195,218,219, 271n1
14:63	170
14:64	170
14:65	169
14:66	50,145,170
14:67	170
14:68	169
14:71	169
14:72	169,176

Mark 15	38,176
15:1	170,176
15:1-5	169
15:1-47	88,88n56
15:2	171
15:4	145
15:4-15	61
15:6-16:8	129
15:8	61
15:9	169
15:12	169
15:13	170
15:14	169,170
15:15	170
15:16	170
15:16-20	169
15:16-39	248
15:17	170
15:20	170
15:22	58
15:23	58,169
15:24	58
15:25	58
15:27	58
15:28-32	175,175n43
15:29	155n5,161,169
15:29-30	169
15:30	194
15:31	194
15:31-32	169
15:34	169
15:35	145,169
15:36	59n57,169
15:37	146
15:38	126,155n5,174,174n40, 174n41,179,203
15:39	179
15:40-16:8	248
15:43	169,244
15:46	169
Mark 16	
16:1-8	88,88n56
16:2	145
16:5	169,170
16:6	145
16:7	59n57,169,170,204, 207,221n19,238, 238n13, 239,271
16:8	125,170,212,250,260

Short ending of Mark

88,89n57

Long ending of Mark
16:9-20	73,75,75n31,88,89n57
16:10	75n31
16:11	75n31
16:12	75n31

16:14	75n31
16:15	75n31
16:16	75n31
Luke	79,80,136n34,226,260
11:29	175n44
12:36-38	78
12:36f	44
13:6-9	42
16:17	43
17:22	68n10
17:23	40
17:24	40
17:31	39
21	96,260
21:11	175n44
21:19	39
21:20	35,260,261
21:20-22	163n25,163n27
21:24	260
21:25	175n44
21:31	42,262
John	
7:53-8:11	73,75,75n31
8:6	75n31
8:7	75n31
8:10	75n31
8:11	75n31
Acts	
1:16	40
11:28	153n2,269
Romans	
9:29	40
13:11-13	69
1 Corinthians	
7:25	80n47
11:23	80n47
13:12	12
14:37	80n47
15:3	80n47
15:51-52	178n51
2 Corinthians	
7:3	40
8:2	40
Galatians	
Ephesians	
6:10-18	69
Philippians	
Colossians	

1 Thessalonians	70n16,77,77n36, 80
1:1-3	69n13
1:15ff	31n16
2:16	69n13
4:15	80n47,178n51
4:15-17	70n15
4:15-5:11	69n13
5:3	70n15,104
5:6-8	69
2 Thessalonians	70n16,77,77n36,80, 158n17
2:1-9	69
2:2	69n15,70n15
2:3a	69n15
2:3-4	70n15
2:9	69n15,70n15
2:15	69
1 Timothy	
2 Timothy	
Titus	
Philemon	
Hebrews	
James	
1 Peter	
4:7	69
5:8-9	69
2 Peter	
1 John	
2 John	
3 John	
Jude	
Revelation	30n13,73,73n29,76-77, 77n34,77n36,78,79, 158n17,164n28
1:3	29n8
22:6	161

Extra-Biblical Literature

4 Ezra (= 2 Esdras)	30n13,106-107n25,185,186,186n3, 188,191,192,194
4:33	192
4:44-50	192

5:9   106
5:50-55   192
6:24   106
6:25   39
8:63f   192
9:7f   192
13:23   192

Hermas   30n13

Test Lord
1:1-14   30n13

Quest Bart   30n13

Assumption of Moses 185,186,
                186n3,191,194
9:4   192
13   186n3

Ethiopic Apocalypse of Peter 77n35
E1   262

Targumic Material
        Targum of Isaiah   104
        Targum Neofiti (Dt 13:1-3)
                        109,120
        Targum Pseudo-Jonathan (Micah)
                        106,107

1 Maccabees
1:54   107,223
2:28   108

Judith
1:5   110
6:15   110
8:1   110,118

Qumran Literature   191n12

References to the following authors and their works will be found classified in the Author Index:

Chariton
Cicero
Epictetus
Epiphanius
Eusebius
Hegesippus
Horace
Irenaeus
Jerome
Josephus
Lucian
Pseudo-Clementine
Quintillian
Socrates
Tacitus
Victorinus
Xenophon of Athens
Xenophon of Ephesus

This book was written and typeset on an Apple Macintosh Plus computer using MS Word 4, finally edited on a Macintosh LC630 running MS Word 5, and printed on an Apple Laserwriter II. It is set in Times 14, 12 and 10, SymbolGreek and SuperHebrew fonts.